*For Dr. Katie, Dr. Melinda, and Dr. Megan,
who must practice the healing arts
amidst a swirling sea of politics*

MEDIA POWER IN POLITICS

Fifth Edition

Edited by
Doris A. Graber
University of Illinois at Chicago

CQ PRESS

A Division of Congressional Quarterly Inc.
Washington, D.C.

CQ Press
1255 22nd Street, NW, Suite 400
Washington, DC 20037

Phone: 202-729-1900; toll-free, 1-866-427-7737 (1-866-4CQ-PRESS)

Web: www.cqpress.com

Cover design: Nancy Bratton Design (www.NancyBrattonDesign.com)

♾ The paper used in this publication exceeds the requirements of the American National Standard for Information Sciences—Permanence of Paper for Printed Library Materials, ANSI Z39.48-1992.

Printed and bound in the United States of America

10 09 08 07 06   1 2 3 4 5

Library of Congress Cataloging-in-Publication Data

Media power in politics / edited by Doris A. Graber. — 5th ed
    p. cm.
 Includes bibliographical references and index.
  ISBN 1-933116-77-3 (pbk. : alk. paper)
  1. Mass media—Political aspects—United States. 2. Mass media—Social aspects—United States. I. Graber, Doris A. (Doris Appel). II. Title.

HN90.M3M43 2006
302.23—dc22

2006047540

CONTENTS

PREFACE

The "fourth branch of government," "a political institution," "an integral part of the American political system," "a tool for governing." All of these labels have been used to characterize the power of U.S. media. Are news media really an essential, albeit unelected and self-appointed, part of government whose influence rivals that of the other branches? Is their power waning in the twenty-first century, or is it merely shifting from old media to new media? The authors whose writings are featured in this book present impressive evidence pertaining to these questions, but it is quite contradictory. *Media Power in Politics* guides readers through the maze of recent literature and older landmark studies that explore seminal ideas and major controversies about the influence of news media. That the book is now in its fifth edition is testimony to the need for such a wide-ranging collection of essays and to its success in familiarizing political communication students with policy-relevant, cutting-edge research.

Media Power in Politics is designed as primary reading for courses on mass media and politics, public opinion, political communication, and mass media and society. It can also serve as supplementary reading in American government courses that highlight the impact of news media and in courses that focus on public policy formation. The selections in the book span several social science disciplines, enabling students to view problems from interdisciplinary perspectives. Contributors include social scientists representing diverse areas of expertise and media professionals familiar with a variety of print and electronic venues. Many of the academic authors have also worked for media organizations; their theories, analyses, and recommendations are therefore tempered by the realism that comes from practical experience.

Media Power in Politics is divided into six parts, each prefaced by an introduction that outlines a particular sphere of media impact. Brief editorial notes introduce every selection, identifying its author or authors and highlighting its principal contributions to understanding news media influence. The articles reproduce the original texts except for clearly marked deletions and editorial inserts. Notes have been renumbered when necessary to maintain unbroken sequences, but note styles have been retained. Factual errors in dates and misspelled names have been corrected.

The thirty-six selections reprinted in this book represent the work of fifty-four authors. Many of them are nationally and internationally recognized scholars; others have just embarked on promising careers. I thank all of them for the contributions they have made to understanding media power in politics and for the authors' and copyright holders' willingness to allow me to include their work in this collection. For guidance in choosing essays that accomplish the goals set for this book, I am deeply indebted to the many colleagues who suggested what to include and what to leave out. Had I followed all of their recommendations, this book would have tripled in length. If your favorite study seems to be missing, take heart! You will most likely find it cited in the many references sprinkled throughout the selections, indicating that its findings are part of the knowledge contained in these pages.

Preparation of a book of readings entails many tasks beyond selecting and editing the contents and writing introductory comments. I am grateful to the staff at CQ Press for handling these tasks ably and expeditiously. Special thanks are due to Charisse Kiino for overseeing the editorial process, and to production editor Gwenda Larsen for encouragement and extraordinary care in shepherding the manuscript through its final stages. Project editor Lorna Notsch took charge of polishing the various editorial notes. Dwain Smith provided survey data that guided the essay selection process, and Hans Manzke took care of permissions. Kevin Navratil, my research assistant at the University of Illinois at Chicago, contributed in major ways to the successful completion of the book, and James M. Smith did yeoman service when it came to checking page proofs. I would also like to thank the following people, who gave me detailed feedback on the book to help me effectively plan and revise for this new edition: Bruce Altschuler (State University of New York at Oswego), Joan Conners (Randolph-Macon College), Robert Dion (University of Evansville), Lois Duke-Whitaker (Georgia Southern University), Alison Howard (Dominican University of California), Robert Klotz (University of Southern Maine), Richard Powell (University of Maine), Staci Rhine (Wittenberg University), Brian Smith (St. Edward's University), and Jacqueline Vaughn (Northern Arizona University). Last, but not least, I owe a heap of thanks to my family for their unfailing support for all I do.

Doris A. Graber

INTRODUCTION

How powerful are American mass media in shaping politics? No definitive answers are in sight, despite a great deal of research and informed speculation. The full scope of media power and the many factors and circumstances that make it wax and wane remain elusive. However, research continues to shed light on many factors that explain various aspects of media power in ever-changing political and technological environments. Research provides clues to the intriguing questions about when, where, and why media power peaks or plunges. The literature exploring media power continues to expand rapidly, making it difficult for newcomers to the field to gain an overview of what is currently known and what is happening on the research frontiers. This book of readings simplifies the task. In this fifth edition, the new selections introduce readers to cutting edge research targets and methods.

Media Power in Politics analyzes mass media effects on the political system in general, and on its formal and informal components, such as Congress, the executive branch, public opinion and pressure groups, in particular. The interactions of the mass media with political institutions have influenced the conduct of American politics and shaped political outcomes. The magnitude of these media effects raises profound questions about the roles that privately controlled businesses—the mass media enterprises—do play and should play in the government and politics of a democratic society.

Each of the six parts into which the essays have been grouped illustrates the influence of mass media on an important facet of U.S. politics. Part I deals with mass media effects in general. The selections in Parts II through V explore the influence of mass media on political opinions and preferences, on presidential and congressional elections, on participants within and outside the political power structure, and on the formation and implementation of domestic and foreign public policies. Part VI examines private and public efforts in the United States and abroad to control the impact of the mass media and to shape media offerings.

1

The essays assembled in this book were chosen primarily because they represent high quality research designed to shed light on diverse aspects of media power. Several studies provide information about the media's role in foreign countries. The contrasts between practices abroad and U.S. practices bring media effects into sharper focus. To introduce readers to the intellectual origins and contemporary milestones in the field of media research, a few classics were also included. Clarity of presentation and ease of reading were other selection criteria.

While this new edition again features well-known media scholars from different social science disciplines, newcomers to the field and practitioners continue to receive space. Sixteen essays from the fourth edition have been retained in the current volume. The sixteen new selections reflect the most recent and thought-provoking scholarship about traditional and new media. This thoroughly revised edition therefore alerts readers to the latest developments in a rapidly growing, interdisciplinary area of study. It presents the work of political scientists, sociologists, communication researchers, and media practitioners, including many authors whose training spans several disciplinary fields and who have worked for a variety of media.

Readers should keep in mind that the excerpts were chosen with a specific purpose in mind: to illustrate and assess the dimensions and scope of media power in politics in a variety of contemporary arenas. This was not necessarily the primary purpose of each of the authors. Therefore, the precise thrust of the unabridged work cannot always be judged from the thrust of the excerpts presented here. The extent of editing varies greatly, with some essays edited only lightly and others cut substantially. Many tables, footnotes, and endnotes had to be eliminated. Interesting methodological and factual details and arguments were shortened or fell by the wayside. That is the price that must be paid when selections are condensed to hone the argument and accelerate its pace. The reward is a more succinct presentation of relevant information that allows the main arguments to emerge with greater force and clarity. Readers who want the full account should go to the original sources, which are fully identified for each selection. In fact, scholars should always use the original versions of each edited selection when quoting it in their own work.

Instead of the six broad categories into which these essays have been divided, other groupings are possible. Guided by the index entries, readers may wish to focus on essays that illustrate research methods, such as quantitative and qualitative content analysis or small- and large-scale surveys that use cross-sectional or panel approaches. Other research techniques described in the book are intensive interviews and experimental studies. In addition, the footnotes and bibliographies in most selections provide ample leads to methodological explanations and communication theories.

The essays can also be used to examine various aspects of the news-making process. All selections are relevant, but several address the topic explicitly. The study of news-making raises questions about the effects of the television age on American democracy, since public opinion, elections, and pressure groups have all been influenced by audio-visual media. Readers may wish to cluster the essays around that topic. The media's role in crises is explored repeatedly, suggesting interesting comparisons. Finally, several essays compare media uses in different countries or by different groups. These essays allow readers to move beyond the confines of the United States and assess comparable phenomena in other democratic nations.

The boundaries between the six parts of the book are porous. For example, essays in Part I, which addresses how media effects are studied, can be supplemented by relevant illustrations in selections in several other parts. The concept of agenda-setting surfaces throughout the book, either explicitly or implicitly. Insights into mass media campaigning are enriched by comparing the essays about election campaigns in Part III with the lobbying campaigns featured in Part V. Similarly, discussion of media impact on public policy is not limited to Part V. Articles in other parts raise policy issues concerning the stigmatizing of criminals, the regulation of the Internet, and issues of censorship in times of crisis. Part VI, which discusses efforts to control media output, also sheds light on the reciprocal influence of the media and the executive branch, Congress, and pressure groups covered in Part IV. All of these selections broaden the picture sketched out in other parts of the book.

The flexibility of *Media Power in Politics* springs from its rich content and from the variety of disciplinary viewpoints that are represented. The importance of the issues raised by the media's role in contemporary politics and the fascination of exploring these new areas in the study of politics have attracted many brilliant scholars. You are invited to sample their works in whatever order best suits your purposes.

Part I

PUTTING MASS MEDIA
EFFECTS IN PERSPECTIVE

This section puts research on mass media effects into historical and contextual perspective. Where have we been? Where are we going? In the
first selection, Bruce Bimber discusses how the nature of information transmission technologies shapes political institutions in democratic societies.
When technologies change, societies undergo major transformations. The
United States has experienced four major media revolutions in its history.
It has now entered the age of abundance. Access to information is universal and cheap, the suppliers of news for the mass public are mushrooming,
and government control over news is ebbing.

Denis McQuail's essay follows, presenting a broad overview of major
theories, research, and knowledge about mass media influence on politics.
He explains why and how the myth of the 1960s—that mass media have
minimal effects—has been exploded, and describes the new phase that
media research has entered. Thanks to new approaches and new research
tools that take a broad view of the scope and variety of possible media effects, scholars now know that media can be powerful. They realize that it
is necessary to identify and analyze a variety of effects occurring in diverse situations in addition to paying attention to the contexts in which
effects occur.

The next essay, by sociologist Michael Schudson, offers a surprising
twist on the foremost criticisms heaped on the performance of the news
media. Schudson provides a full account of media misbehaviors that rile
the critics most. He concedes that the criticisms are well taken, but then,
like a medieval alchemist, he ventures to turn lead into gold. The features
of American journalism that are damned most frequently—subservience to
official sources; shallow, often cynical, accounts of daily happenings; an
emphasis on conflicts, scandals, and crimes; a rigid application of journalism norms—are really blessings in disguise that serve democratic ideals. An
unlovable press is an independent press, beholden to no one, free to praise
and criticize at will.

In the next selection, Walter Lippmann comments on the role presumably and actually played by the media in informing citizens. He notes the wide discrepancy between the role assigned to the media by democratic theory and the capabilities of the media in the real world. News is not truth. It is merely a tiny slice of reality removed from the context that gives it meaning. No study of the effects of news on public thinking would be complete without including at least a minute portion of the wisdom of this modern political philosopher. His trenchant writings about public affairs spanned more than fifty years. They continue to provide important insights into public opinion and the impact of the news media on politics.

Sean Aday sheds further light on the problem of conveying truth. In addition to all of the difficulties that journalists face in identifying important events, getting all the facts right, and condensing them into appealing stories, they must also weigh the likely consequences of news. Particularly in times of crisis, an exposé can harm the actors in the story, the people who hear and watch it, and the government policies designed to cope with the impact of crisis events. Aday uses the display on television of the bodies of dead and wounded soldiers in wartime as an example of stories that are extraordinarily difficult to report. He concludes that journalists have been conditioned by their training, their sensibilities, and their sense of patriotism to conceal the ugly "truth" of battlefront carnage from impressionable audiences.

In the final selection, Linda L. Putnam points to yet another problem that journalists routinely face in their efforts to inform the public about important issues in the public realm. From what perspectives should the story be told? Whose viewpoints should be featured? Which aspects of the story should be stressed? She describes the battles over allocation of water resources in Texas, fought among many different stakeholders eager to win the public's approval of their particular claim. The stakeholders included farmers and ranchers; business and industry leaders; environmentalists; a bevy of government agencies, ranging from local to national; and official mediators charged with resolving the disputes. Putnam praises the media for telling this story as calmly and fairly as possible, avoiding framing that might help or hinder any of the parties to the dispute.

The Putnam essay, like many others in this volume, describes the use of content analysis as a research technique to identify media stimuli that produce or fail to produce a particular effect. The technique can be employed informally, through reading or watching mass media stories and gleaning general impressions, or it can be employed formally, through rigorous research procedures. In formal content analysis, researchers specify the features of the story that relate to their particular concerns and record ("code" is the technical term) their presence or absence. Content analysis still is most commonly done by human coders because categorizations often require complex judgments, but numerous sophisticated computer programs have also become available to count words and concepts and analyze their verbal context.

1

HOW INFORMATION SHAPES POLITICAL INSTITUTIONS

Bruce Bimber

Editor's Note

Bruce Bimber's essay highlights the crucial role that information transmission plays in structuring politics in democratic societies. He points out how changes in the structure, costs, and accessibility of information alter the political system. The United States has moved through four major communications revolutions in its history, mostly fueled by technological developments. Currently, the Internet and other new media have created an era of information abundance, fracturing the communication monopoly of old-style organizations and allowing many resource-poor new voices to be heard. These developments are changing the political landscape in ways that remain as yet unpredictable.

Bimber is director of the Center for Information Technology and Society and professor of political science and communication at the University of California, Santa Barbara. He is the coauthor with Richard Davis of *Campaigning Online: The Internet in U.S. Elections* (2003), which won the McGannon Communication Policy Award for social and ethical relevance in communication policy research. He has also written numerous articles dealing with technology and politics. The following selection is from *Information and American Democracy: Technology in the Evolution of Political Power* (2003), which won the Don K. Price Award for best book on science, technology, and politics.

Defining "Information" and "Communication"

Knowledge about facts, subjects, or events is inextricably bound to virtually every aspect of democracy. Such knowledge may concern the interests, concerns, preferences, or intentions of citizens as individuals or collectives. It may also concern the economic or social state of communities or society, or the actions and intentions of government officials and candidates for office. In what follows, political information constitutes any knowledge relevant to the working of democratic processes.

In his classic *The Nature and Origins of Mass Opinion,* John Zaller observes that the content of elite discourse, such as claims about the state of the world from party leaders and editorial positions of newspapers, contains information, but it is not "just information."[1] Because political discourse is the product of values and selectivity as much as verifiably "objective" observations, it comprises a mix of information and other factors. For my purposes this definition too narrowly constrains the concept of information by associating it with "truth" and "objectivity." I assume that when a political actor communicates a personal statement about the world containing a mix of facts and values, that actor is simply communicating a package of information, some of it dealing with "facts" and some of it with his or her values and predispositions. Some "facts" may even be wrong, but they can be communicated nonetheless and they constitute information.[2]

"Information" need not stand in opposition to opinions, stories, rhetoric, or signals about value structures. Information might be a "fact" about the rate of inflation published by the Bureau of Economic Analysis just as well as a political official's statement about the need to control inflation. A candidate's promise on a web site or broadcast advertisement "to protect Social Security" conveys certain political information, just as a Congressional Budget Office report on Social Security fund solvency conveys other information of a different and perhaps more satisfyingly "objective" sort. Information is simply something that can be known or communicated.

. . . [I]t is useful not to bind the definition of information too tightly to the human acts of perception and knowing. I assume that information can exist independently of its perception and understanding by any particular political actor. It is important, however, to observe the intimacy of the connection between "communication" and "information" . . . I use "communication" to mean simply the transfer or exchange of information. Certainly, different forms of communication may convey different quantities of information in different ways, but I do not attempt to isolate the two concepts.

My definition of information therefore extends well beyond facts, and my definition of communication well beyond a quantitative transmission model. My conception of information is consistent with Inguun Hagen's interpretation of the process of television news-watching by citizens, which may involve not only becoming informed in a narrow sense, but also diversion, habit or ritual, and fulfillment of a sense of duty or obligation.[3] Information defined this way permeates human activity, and in principle the complete range of human meaning can be conveyed by communication.

[Defined 'this broadly, information becomes vital to democracy in myriad ways: in the processes by which citizen preferences are formed and aggregated, in the behaviors of citizens and elites, in formal procedures of representation, in acts of governmental decision making, in the administration of laws and regulations, and in the mechanisms of accountability that freshen democracy and sustain its legitimacy. None of these elements of the democratic process can operate apart from the exchange and flow of information among citizens and their associations and organizations, among citizens and government, and within government itself.

More to the point, the *structure* of information in America at the outset of the twenty-first century is very different from that at the outset of the twentieth century, just as its structure then differed from that in the age of Jefferson. Not only the volume of political information available in society, but also its distribution and cost, have varied from one age to another. . . . How do historically changing properties of political information affect the evolution of democracy? What patterns might exist in the evolving nature of information and its relationship to politics? To what extent can the character of democracy be traced to causes rooted in the informational characteristics of a particular age? To pose these questions is to situate modern technology and applied questions about the contemporary information revolution in the larger sweep of American political development.

Overview of the Theory

. . . How can the relationship between information and political change be approached theoretically? My perspective is based on the observation that many features of social and economic structure were derived from the characteristics of information during the period in which they arose. Throughout most of the twentieth century, for example, the information necessary for economic transactions, education, social interaction, and many other facets of modernity had certain properties. It was hierarchically organized, costly to obtain and difficult to manage, and in most settings asymmetrically distributed. French social theorist Pierre Levy refers to these properties as a "communications ecology," the basic features of information and communication to which human institutions and organizations are adapted.[4] Vertically integrated firms, retail stores, administrative organizations, and even universities are in part adaptations to a communications ecology in which information is costly and asymmetric.

From this perspective, the contemporary information revolution involves deep changes in the communications ecology, with potential consequences for institutions and processes whose structures are in substantial ways adapted to older communications arrangements. This revolution is not simply an increase in the volume of information. . . . It is also qualitative, as information of all kinds becomes cheaper, its structure ever more complex and nonlinear, and its distribution far more symmetric than at any time in the past.

In principle, such developments could have structural consequences that are far-reaching. Indeed, it is already apparent that economic structure is sensitive to such changes, as economic transactions are transformed on a large scale, new methods of retailing visibly overtake the commercial world, and old business relationships and structures give way to new, information-intensive arrangements. Perhaps less abruptly but no less profoundly, other institutions sensitive to features of information and communication may change as well. Education may be altered for better or worse (or both) as printed matter grows less central to the transmission of knowledge, meaningful engagement with others at a distance becomes more readily possible, and the kinds of skills relevant to economic and personal well-being change. The fabrics of social association, cultures, even private lives may be rewoven, insofar as these depend upon the nature and accessibility of information. And so it may be for democracy, to the extent that its structures represent adaptations to particular informational circumstances.

. . . I believe that there are good but underappreciated reasons that scholars have noticed the relevance of information technology at what are arguably the two most important historical turning points in American political development: the rise of party-based majoritarian politics and the evolution of group-based political pluralism. My aim is to explore what integration might be possible between those two developmental milestones and the present, using information as the nexus. I should add that in so doing, it is not my primary aim to predict the *future* of the information revolution and American politics, a risky temptation to which a number of writers have succumbed. I restrict myself instead to analyzing the nature and causes of changes under way in American democracy *at present*. I intend this . . . to be an argument for conceptualizing the evolution of information as an important contributor to political change at the largest scale—not information defined narrowly as the quantifiable messages exchanged by rational agents in signaling games and the like, but as a universally important ingredient in political processes.

Much of my thesis is based on the observation that elites exercise a powerful influence on the organization of democracy, through their capacity to influence public opinion, set agendas, mobilize citizens into collective action, make decisions, and implement policies. The identity and structure of elites is neither fixed across time nor random in its changes. Many factors affect the identity and structure of elites, and the state of information is one of them. Exogenous changes in the accessibility or structure of information cause changes in the structure of elite organizations that dominate political activity, and these in turn affect the broad character of democracy.

Information Regimes and Revolutions

I develop this theoretical claim in two steps, one historical and one contemporary. First, I reinterpret parts of American political history in informational terms. I argue that information regimes exist in American political history as periods of stable relationships among information, organizations, and democratic structure. The features of an information regime are: (1) a set of dominant properties of political information, such as high cost; (2) a set of opportunities and constraints on the management of political information that these properties create; and (3) the appearance of characteristic political organizations and structures adapted to those opportunities and constraints. Information regimes in the United States have been interrupted by information revolutions, which involve changes in the structure or accessibility of information. These revolutions may be initiated by technological developments, institutional change, or economic outcomes. An information revolution disrupts a prior information regime by creating new opportunities for political communication and the organization of collective action. These changes create advantages for some forms of organization and structure and disadvantages for others, leading to adaptations and change in the world of political organizations and intermediaries. This is to say that democratic power tends to be biased toward those with the best command of political information at any particular stage in history.

The first information regime in the United States emerged from an information revolution during the Jacksonian democratization. It was facilitated by the creation of the first national-scale system for communicating political information, namely, the remarkable U.S. Postal Service and the equally remarkable American newspaper industry. . . . National flow of political information was largely impossible in the decades after the founding. Its absence had blocked the development of new parties prior to the 1830s. Those parties that arose in the mid-nineteenth century were the final component of this information regime, an adaptation in part to the opportunities and constraints for the flow of information created by the postal service and newspaper systems. Beneath America's majoritarian politics of the nineteenth century was a distinguishing set of arrangements for the distribution of political information. These arrangements would eventually be superceded by others; but for a half to three-quarters of a century, they defined the majority of possibilities for large-scale political communication and civic engagement in the United States.

The second American information revolution led to an information regime that lasted into the middle of the twentieth century. That revolution was a product of the industrial revolution and the growing American state, which transformed the landscape of political information requisite to politics. Information became enormously complex and highly differentiated between about 1880 and 1920 because the number of policy issues on the national agenda multiplied, as did the number of private and public actors engaged in the exchange of information. Such complexity favored a new form of organization adapted to the management and flow of specialized and increasingly costly information: the organized interest group. Though this new form of organization would eventually rise to prominence after the New Deal, interest-group politics of the twentieth century reflected and rested upon the new set of informational characteristics that emerged at the turn of the century. Interest groups can be understood as information specialists that prevailed over generalists (the parties) in some of the central communication functions in politics.

The pluralism connected with the second information regime persisted throughout the twentieth century, but was affected by a third, transitional revolution during the period of the 1950s–1970s involving broadcasting. The broadcast information revolution had two distinct phases. In the first, the mass audience for communication tended to weaken party organizations as central players in campaigning and at the same time create new possibilities for mass politics—a trend counter to the group-based politics of the second information regime. However, in the later stage of this information revolution, the rise of cable television and the multiplication of channels began a process of fragmentation and division of communication and information. These developments set the stage for the contemporary information revolution involving the Internet and associated technologies.

It should be clear that an information revolution is not simply an abrupt change in the technology of communication. A set of technological changes becomes revolutionary when new opportunities or constraints associated with political intermediation make possible altered distributions of power. These new capacities and possibilities are a function of the political and social context in which technology evolves. Moreover, an information revolution need not necessarily be driven by communication technology at all. My approach to analyzing political history has not been to draw up a list of technologies—telegraph, steamboat, railroad, telephone, radio, television, and so on—and ask how each affected politics. I have approached the problem orthogonally, by asking when, if ever, the properties of information and communication have changed abruptly, and then inquiring how such changes influenced politics. This approach implicates some technological innovations in abrupt information revolutions but not others. It identifies sources of informational change that would not make most lists of interesting technologies, such as the postal service. It also includes socioeconomic developments involving technologies but which are not, strictly speaking, technologies at all, such as the industrial revolution.

The Current Information Regime

. . . The second large step in my theory of information and democracy deals with contemporary political change, and involves applying lessons from the history of information in American politics to the present situation. The information-regime model of American politics and insights from the study of interest groups and political participation provide the means to investigate how contemporary information technology affects democracy. In the current period, as in the Jacksonian age and era of industrialization, the properties of information are again changing. Technology is increasing the complexity and specialization of information while at the same time decreasing its cost, thereby making abundant political information and communication available to anyone with the motivation to acquire it, provided they have access to information technology. In a general sense, the information regime model predicts that such a large-scale change in the cost of information should lead to political change, through its effects on the identity and structure of political intermediaries.

. . . [A]mong the most important trends predicted from theory are a decreasing association between the distribution of traditional political resources and the capacity to organize political action, . . . This phenomenon involves the substitution of information infrastructure for organizational infrastructure. It suggests the rise of new ad hoc political associations and groups, as well as altered strategies and commitments of resources on the part of traditional organizations. It entails increasing attention in the policy process toward "outside" lobbying and public opinion, as well as increasing orientation toward issues and events, rather than more stable interests and long-term political agendas.

My main thesis about contemporary political developments is that *technological change in the contemporary period should contribute toward information abundance, which in turn contributes toward postbureaucratic forms of politics.* This process involves chiefly private political institutions and organizations such as civic associations, as well as interest groups, rather than formal governmental institutions rooted in law or the Constitution. To the extent that the central functions of these private institutions involve the collection, management, or distribution of information under circumstances where information has been costly and asymmetrically distributed, the contemporary information revolution has the capacity to alter organizational structures. The result is a diminished role on many fronts for traditional organizations in politics. The pluralism of the 1950s and 1960s was a politics of bargaining among institutionalized interests. That changed in the 1970s and 1980s to a pluralism of more atomistic issue groups, less inclined and able at elite bargaining and more tightly focused on so-called single issues. The accelerated pluralism of the 1990s and 2000s increasingly involves situations in which the structure of group politics is organized around not interests or issues, but rather events and the intensive flow of information surrounding them.

This progression from interest groups to issue groups to event groups does not imply that the former organizational form is displaced entirely. It should involve, rather, the loosening of certain organizational boundaries and structures and an increasing heterogeneity of forms working alongside one another, . . . As in previous information regimes, political influence in the fourth regime should remain biased toward those with the best command of political information. The contemporary information revolution should make traditional, bureaucratically structured organizations of all kinds less able to dominate political information—this is the central motor of political change.

In this way, it is possible to array contemporary developments with historical ones. The first information revolution made national-scale political information available for the first time, which contributed to centralized, hierarchical organizations serving as the basis for collective action in politics. In the second information revolution, national-scale political information grew complex and costly, which led to the rise of decentralized, specialized, and bureaucratized organizations as the basis for collective action. The third information revolution created a modern tension between mass politics and pluralism, but left major, highly institutionalized organizational forms in a position of dominance. In the contemporary revolution, national-scale information is growing abundant, but no less complex than ever. The result should be a weakening of the organizational structures of the previous regimes. This sequence is summarized in Figure 1-1.

One of the major problems facing social scientists concerned with American democracy is the sttate of citizenship and levels of civic engagement. By many traditional measures, these are in decline, as the literatures on social capital, public opinion, voting participation, and the public sphere indicate. On the other hand, critics of declinist arguments have posited alternative interpretations of the data, based on new forms of engagement and changes in the meaning of citizenship. Many have suggested that participation in affinity groups, youth soccer leagues, support groups, interest organizations, and other novel associations may be replacing memberships in venerable but outdated groups such as Elks Clubs, Rotaries, and Boy Scouts. If so, the research indicating a decline in social capital may be due to a combination of inadequate conceptualization and measurement of the wrong activities.[5] Likewise, in influencing explicitly political engagement, new forms of "lifestyle" politics, political consumerism, and other novel ways of being "political" may be displacing the traditional political actions that scholars have measured.[6] Therefore, to the extent that political and civic identity and modes of action are changing, civic engagement may also simply be changing shape rather than decaying.

This debate will benefit substantially from the passage of time, as historical perspective sharpens assessments of stability and change and as new survey evidence differentiates long-term from short-term trends. The debate is

Figure 1-1 Summary of the Four Political Information Revolutions
in the United States

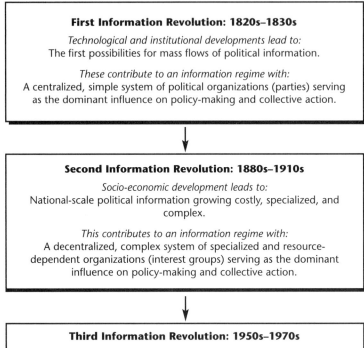

First Information Revolution: 1820s–1830s

Technological and institutional developments lead to:
The first possibilities for mass flows of political information.

These contribute to an information regime with:
A centralized, simple system of political organizations (parties) serving
as the dominant influence on policy-making and collective action.

Second Information Revolution: 1880s–1910s

Socio-economic development leads to:
National-scale political information growing costly, specialized, and
complex.

This contributes to an information regime with:
A decentralized, complex system of specialized and resource-
dependent organizations (interest groups) serving as the dominant
influence on policy-making and collective action.

Third Information Revolution: 1950s–1970s

Technological development leads to:
Possibilities for commanding the attention of a
national-scale mass audience.

This contributes to an information regime with:
A centralized, extremely resource-dependent system of market-
driven organizations capable of influencing policy-making and some
forms of collective action, along with the specialized political
organizations of the previous information regime.

Fourth Information Revolution: 1990s–present

Technological development leads to:
A condition of information abundance.

This contributes to possibilities for an information regime with:
Post-bureaucratic political organizations as the basis for policy-
making and collective action.

relevant here, nonetheless, because of the possible role of information technology in it. One of the most persistent speculations about "the Internet and politics" has been that cheap, ubiquitous information and communication will expand possibilities for engagement and fuel a rise in overall levels of citizen involvement with their communities and political system. It is clear that the contemporary information revolution is making the individual's political *environment* far more information-rich. It is also clear from research on political behavior and public opinion that political knowledge—information that has been assimilated by individuals—is connected with political action. In other words, more knowledgeable citizens are indeed more engaged. But the link between changes in citizens' informational environment and changes in their internal political knowledge is far less clear. It seems intuitive that exposure to more information should lead to the internalization of more information and to changes in behavior. Some rational theories of political behavior formalize that link, interpreting the cost of information as an important regulator of its "consumption" and of the action that follows. Decrease the cost of a desired good, such as information, and more will be acquired by citizens, up until the point where marginal costs match marginal value. Empirical verification of this apparently straightforward model has been highly problematic, however, especially when it is framed in terms of longitudinal variation in citizens' information environments.

It is important that a theoretical account of information and political change take up this problem as a counterpart to organizational-level matters. My approach involves a psychological perspective on political information that stands in contrast to instrumental conceptions of information as a rationally consumed good. Following work in political psychology, I posit that the informed citizen in the age of the Internet is not a rational actor, nor necessarily even one who pursues short-cuts and satisficing strategies in lieu of exhaustive and thorough information-gathering. Instead, informed citizenship involves the information-rich growing even richer as the cost of information falls, while those poor in information remain so. In practice, people should acquire information in so-called biased ways that support existing beliefs rather than reducing uncertainty. Most important, their consumption of information should occur in ways that are highly contingent on context and the stimulus provided by elites and organizations.

This view leads to the hypothesis that in the cycle of information revolutions and regimes, including contemporary developments, changes in the nature of political information should typically exert little direct influence on levels of citizen engagement. As a force in democracy, therefore, information should work somewhat differently at the level of organizations and the level of individuals. Information revolutions, including the present one, should have profound and direct consequences for organizations and political structure, but only indirect, less tangible consequences for politics at the level of individual political engagement. The effects of changes in information, I argue, are concentrated on *political form* through an increasing independence of political structure from traditional economic and social structures.

Notes

1. John Zaller, *The Nature and Origins of Mass Opinion* (Cambridge, Eng.: Cambridge University Press, 1991), p. 13.
2. That a recipient of communication may have difficulty distinguishing the facts and values in a message or may be unable to verify truth claims does not change the fact that information in a broad sense has been transmitted, perhaps with a high level of uncertainty associated with it. How much "true" information recipients extract from a message is a function of their own sophistication and their knowledge of the person communicating. Imagine, for instance, a situation where a candidate for office broadcasts a factually false message that his opponent is a communist, or an opponent of civil rights, or an adulterer. If a voter, believing the message, abandons her support for the accused candidate and votes instead for the accuser, there can be no doubt that communication has occurred and that information—albeit containing a false claim—has been transmitted. Whether the information in a message is "true" or "objective," and whether in this case the accuser sincerely believes his propaganda, is a separate question from the existence of information and communication.
3. Inguun Hagen, "Communicating to an Ideal Audience: News and the Notion of an 'Informed Citizen,' " *Political Communication* 14, no. 4 (1997): 405–419.
4. Pierre Levy, *Collective Intelligence: Mankind's Emerging World in Cyberspace* (Cambridge, Mass.: Perseus, 1997).
5. Theda Skocpol, "Unravelling from Above," in Robert Kuttner, ed., *Ticking Time Bombs: The New Conservative Assault on Democracy* (New York: New Press, 1996), pp. 292–301; Michael Schudson, "What If Civic Life Didn't Die?" in Kuttner, ed., *Ticking Time Bombs*, pp. 286–291; Nicholas Lemann, "Kicking in Groups," *The Atlantic Monthly* 277, no. 4 (1996): 22–26.
6. For a discussion, see W. Lance Bennett, "The UnCivic Culture: Communication, Identity, and the Rise of Lifestyle Politics," *PS: Political Science and Politics* 31, no. 4 (1998): 741–761.

2

THE INFLUENCE AND EFFECTS OF MASS MEDIA

Denis McQuail

Editor's Note

Questions about the effects of the mass media cannot be answered in broad generalities. Scholars have learned to ask how various types of effects impact various types of people and institutions, at various levels of society, under various conditions. Denis McQuail provides an overview of these contingencies in a diverse array of important media situations. In addition to discussing the general nature of mass media effects, McQuail traces the history of research findings produced by several kinds of investigations. His bibliography is an excellent starting point for review of the English language literature on media effects through 1976. Readers will find reviews of more recent research and literature in a massive volume edited by Raymond W. Preiss, Barbara Mae Gayle, Nancy Burrell, Mike Allen, and Jennings Bryant entitled *Mass Media Effects Research: Advances Through Meta-Analysis* (Mahwah, N.J.: Erlbaum, 2006).

When this essay was written, McQuail was a professor of sociology and mass communication. He has taught at two British universities—the University of Southampton and the University of Leeds—and at the University of Amsterdam in the Netherlands. His books on the sociology of mass communication and on mass communication theory have become staples in mass communication courses in the United States and Europe. He is also one of the founding editors of the *European Journal of Communication.*

The questions most insistently asked of social research on mass communication, and perhaps least clearly answered, have to do with the effects and social influence of the different mass media. The reasons for asking are understandable enough, given the amount of time spent attending to the mass

---

media in many countries and the amount of resources invested in mass media production and distribution. Although much has been written by way of answer and a good deal of research carried out, it has to be admitted that the issue remains a disputed one—both in general about the significance of mass media and in particular about the likely effect of given instances of mass communications. Inevitably, this discussion has to begin with some clarification of terms, since one of the perennial difficulties in the case has been the lack of communication between those who have investigated the question of media influence on the one hand and, on the other, the public, media producers and those concerned with public policy for the media.

Perhaps it should first be claimed that the question of effects is a somewhat unfair one, one rarely asked of comparable institutions like religion, education or the law which all in their way communicate to the public or to particular publics and where questions about effects as well as aims could well be asked. The mass media are highly diverse in content and in forms of organization and include a very wide range of activities which could have effects on society. To make the question not only more fair, but also more meaningful, we need to introduce a number of qualifications and specifications.

First, we can distinguish between effects and effectiveness, the former referring to any of the consequences of mass media operation, whether intended or not, the latter to the capacity to achieve given objectives, whether this be attracting large audiences or influencing opinions and behaviour. Both matters are important, but a different set of considerations relates to each. A second, though perhaps minor, point on which to be clear concerns the reference in time. Are we concerned with the past, or with predictions about the future? If the former, we need to be precise. If the latter, and often it is a prediction about what is going on now and its results which is a main concern, then some uncertainty is inevitable.

Third, we need to be clear about the level on which effects occur, whether this is at the level of the individual, the group, the institution, the whole society or the culture. Each or all may be affected in some way by mass communication. To specify the level meaningfully also requires us to name the kinds of phenomena on which influence may be exerted. We can investigate some phenomena at several levels—especially opinion and belief which can be a matter of individual opinion as well as the collective expression of institutions and societies. On the other hand to study the effect of the media on the way institutions operate requires us to look at the relationships between people occupying different roles and at the structure and content of these roles. Politics provides a good example, where the mass media have probably affected not only individual political opinions but also the way politics is conducted and its main activities organized. Political roles may have been changed, as well as our expectations of politicians, the relationships of followers to leaders, and even perhaps some of the values of political life. All this is a matter of historical change, much slower and less reversible than any influence on opinion, attitude or voting behaviour. Again it is clear that difference of level of effect is also related to different time spans. Changes in culture and in society are slowest to occur, least easy to know of with certainty, least easy to trace to their origins, most likely to persist. Changes affecting individuals are quick to occur, relatively easy to demonstrate and to attribute to a source, less easy to assess in terms of significance and performance. Hence we tend to find a situation in which the larger and more significant questions of media effect are most subject to conflicting interpretation and the most certain knowledge we have is most open to the charge of triviality and least useful as a basis for generalization. Perhaps one could usefully add a further set of distinctions which have to be made early on, whatever the level of analysis. This relates to the direction of effect. Are the media changing something, preventing something, facilitating something or reinforcing and reaffirming something? The importance of the question is obvious, but it is worth stressing early in the discussion that a 'no change' effect can be as significant as its reverse and there is little doubt that in some respects the media do inhibit as well as promote change.

The History of Research Into the Effects of Mass Communication

. . . [W]e can characterize the 50 years or more of interest in media effects in terms of three main stages. In the first phase, which lasts from the turn of the century to the late nineteen thirties the media, where they were developed in Europe and North America, were attributed considerable power to shape opinion and belief, change habits of life, actively mould behaviour and impose political systems even against resistance. Such views were not based on scientific investigation but were based on empirical observation of the sudden extension of the audience to large majorities and on the great attraction of the popular press, cinema and radio. The assumption of media power was also acted upon, as it were, by advertisers, government propagandists in the First World War, newspaper proprietors, the rulers of totalitarian states, and accepted defensively by nearly all as the best guess in the circumstances. It is not irrelevant that this stage of thinking coincided with a very early stage of social science when the methods and concepts for investigating these phenomena were only developing.

The second stage extends from about 1940 to the early 1960s and it is strongly shaped by growth of mass communications research in the United States and the application of empirical method to specific questions about the effects and effectiveness of mass communication. The influence of this phase of research is surprisingly great, given the rather narrow range of the questions tackled and relatively small quantity of substantial studies. Most influential, perhaps, were the studies of Presidential elections in 1940 and

1948 by Lazarsfeld [*et al.*] (1944), Berelson [*et al.*] (1954) and the pro-
gramme of research into the use of films for training and indoctrination of
American servicemen undertaken by Hovland *et al.* (1950). An earlier and
longer tradition of social-psychological inquiry into the effects of film and
other media on crime, aggression and racial and other attitudes should also
be mentioned (e.g. Blumler, 1933). In practice, a small number of much cited
studies provided the substance for the general view of media effects and effectiveness which was generally being disseminated in social and political science by the end of the 1960s. Where there was research outside the United
States (e.g. Trenaman and McQuail, 1961), it was in the same mould and
tended to confirm rather than challenge the agreed version of media effects.
Basically, this version affirmed the ineffectiveness and impotency of mass
media and their subservience to other more fundamental components in any
potential situation of influence. The mass media—primarily radio, film, or
print at the time most research was conducted—emerged as unlikely to be
major contributors to direct change of individual opinions, attitudes or behaviour or to be a direct cause of crime, aggression, or other disapproved social phenomena. Too many separate investigations reached similar negative
conclusions for this to be doubted. The comment by Klapper (1960) in an influential view of research, that 'mass communication does not ordinarily
serve as a necessary and sufficient cause of audience effects, but rather functions through a nexus of mediating factors' well sums up the outcome of the
second phase. Of course, research had not shown the different media to be
without effects, but it had established the primacy of other social facts and
showed the power of the media to be located within the existing structures
of social relationships and systems of culture and belief. The reversal of a
prior assumption by scientific investigation was striking and seemed the more
complete because the myth of media power was so strong and occasionally
uncritical and naive. At the same time, it should be admitted that neither
public anxiety about the new medium of television nor professional opinion
in the field of advertising and mass communication was much changed by the
verdict of science. In fact, hardly had the 'no effect' conclusion become generally accepted than it became subject to re-examination by social scientists
who doubted that the whole story had yet been written.

The third phase, which still persists, is one where new thinking and new
evidence is accumulating on the influence of mass communication, especially
television, and the long neglected newspaper press. As early signs of doubts
we could cite Lang and Lang (1959) or Key (1961) or Blumler (1964) or Halloran (1964). The case for re-opening the question of mass media effects rests
on several bases. First of all, the lesson of 'no-effects' has been learned and
accepted and more modest expectations have taken the place of early belief.
Where small effects are expected, methods have to be more precise. In addi-

tion, the intervening variables of social position and prior audience disposition, once identified as important, could now be more adequately measured. A second basis for revision, however, rested on a critique of the methods and research models which had been used. These were mainly experiments or surveys designed to measure short-term changes occurring in individuals, and concentrating especially on the key concept of attitude. Alternative research approaches might take a longer time span, pay more attention to people in their social context, look at what people know (in the widest sense) rather than at their attitudes and opinions, take account of the uses and motives of the audience member as mediating any effect, look at structures of belief and opinion and social behaviour rather than individual cases, take more notice of the *content* whose effects are being studied. In brief, it can be argued that we are only at the start of the task and have as yet examined very few of the questions about the effects of mass media, especially those which reveal themselves in *collective* phenomena. Some of these matters are returned to later, and at this point it is sufficient to conclude that we are now in a phase where the social power of the media is once more at the centre of attention for some social scientists, a circumstance which is not the result of a mere change of fashion but of a genuine advance of knowledge based on secure foundations. This advance has been uneven and buffered by external pressure, but it is real enough. . . .

The Evidence of Effects

In order to discuss the results of research into mass media effects in a meaningful way, it may be helpful to divide up the problem under a set of headings which in a composite way reflects the various distinctions which have already been mentioned: of level; of kind of effect and of process; of research strategy and method. Although the headings which follow do not divide up the field in a mutually exclusive way, they do separate out the main topics which have been discussed, and provide a basis for evaluating research evidence. Basically what is being indicated is a set of media situations or processes which have distinctive features and require separate evaluation. The most important media situations are: (1) the campaign; (2) the definition of social reality and social norms; (3) the immediate response or reaction; (4) institutional change; (5) changes in culture and society.

The Campaign

Much of what has been written about the effects or effectiveness of the media either derives from research on campaigns or involves predictions about hypothetical campaign situations. . . . The kinds of media provision which might fall under this heading include: political and election campaigns, attempts at public information; commercial and public service advertising, some forms of education; the use of mass media in developing countries or generally for the diffusion of innovations. We recognize the similarity of these different activities. The campaign shares, in varying degrees, the following characteristics: it has specific aims and is planned to achieve these; it has a definite time-span, usually short; it is intensive and aims at wide coverage; its effectiveness is, in principle, open to assessment; it usually has authoritative sponsorship; it is not necessarily popular with its audience and has to be 'sold' to them; it is usually based on a framework of shared values. The campaign generally works to achieve objectives which in themselves are not controversial—voting, giving to charity, buying goods, education, health, safety, and so on. . . .

. . . Rather than discuss evidence in detail, which space would not allow, a brief assertion of a general condition of effect is made, with some reference to a source or summarizing work which justifies the assertion. One set of relevant factors has to do with the audience, another with the message and a third with the source or the system of distribution. Amongst audience factors, an obvious primary condition is that a large audience should be reached. Second, the appropriate members of the audience should be reached, since size alone does not guarantee the inclusion of those for whom the campaign is relevant. . . . Third, the dispositions of the audience should at least be not antipathetic or resistant. Political campaigning is most subject to this constraint and there is evidence that the lack of strong disposition either way and a condition of casual attention may be most favourable to the success of mass propaganda. (Blumler and McQuail, 1968.) A part of this condition relates to the need for consistency with the norms of locality and sub-culture as well as the presence of broad societal consensus. Fourth, success is likely to be greater when, within the audience, the flow of personal communication and structure of relevant interpersonal status is supportive of the mass media campaign and its aims. (Lazarsfeld [et al.] 1944; Katz and Lazarsfeld, 1956; Rogers and Shoemaker, 1971.) Fifth, it is important that the audience understands or perceives the message as intended by its originators (Cooper and Jahoda, 1947; Belson, 1967) and does not selectively distort it.

Factors to do with the message or content are also important. First, the message should be unambiguous and relevant to its audience. The factor of relevance and a parallel self-selection by the audience makes it likely that campaigns are most successful at reinforcing existing tendencies or channelling them into only slightly different pathways. Second, the informative campaign seems more likely to be successful than the campaign to change attitudes or opinions. (Hovland et al., 195[0]; Trenaman and McQuail, 1961.) Third, in general, subject matter which is more distant and more novel, least subject to prior definitions and outside immediate experience responds best to treatment by the campaign. The essential point is that the receiver has no competing sources of information and no personal stake in resisting an appeal or disbelieving information. It is easier to form opinions and attitudes about events abroad than events at home, about unfamiliar than about familiar matters. Fourth, the campaign which allows some immediate response in action is most likely to be effective, since behaviour generally confirms intention and attitude, whether in voting or buying, or donating to a charity. Fifth, repetition can be mentioned as a probable contributor to effect, although this is a common-sense assumption rather than well demonstrated. As far as the source is concerned, we should mention first the condition of monopoly. The more channels carrying the same campaign messages, the greater the probability of acceptance. This is not easy to demonstrate and there are circumstances where an imposed monopoly invites distrust and disbelief (e.g. Inkeles and Bauer, 1959). But, in general, this condition is presupposed in several of the conditions already stated. Second, there is evidence that the status or authority of the source contributes to successful campaigning and the principle is applied in most campaigns whether commercial or not. The source of attributed status can of course vary, including the strongly institutionalized prestige of the political or legal system or the personal attractiveness of a star or other 'hero' of society or the claim to expert knowledge. Endorsement by an individual or institution embodying strong claims to trust and attachment can be crucial in a campaign. Third, there is a variable condition of affective attachment to a media source. There is evidence that loyalty and affective ties exist in relations to some media rather than others which may affect their ability to influence. (Butler and Stokes, 1969; Blumler *et al.* 1975.)

These factors are all important in the process of intentional influence. . . . If we accept the validity of these points we are already very far from thinking the mass media to be ineffective, [n]or can it be said that we have no certain knowledge of the effects of mass media.

The Definition of Social Reality and the Formation of Social Norms

The topics we should look at under this heading are diverse and the processes involved equally so. Here we mainly consider the process of learning through the media, a process which is often incidental, unplanned and unconscious for the receiver and almost always unintentional on the part of the sender. Hence the concept of 'effectiveness' is usually inappropriate, except in societies where the media take a planned and deliberate role in social development. This may be true of some aspects of socialist media (see Hopkins, 1970) or of some media applications in developing countries. (Pye, 1963; Frey, 1973.) There are two main aspects to what occurs. On the one hand, there is the provision of a consistent picture of the social world which may lead the audience to adopt this version of reality, a reality of 'facts' and of norms, values and expectations. On the other hand, there is a continuing and selective interaction between self and the media which plays a part in shaping the individual's own behaviour and self-concept. We learn what our social environment is and respond to the knowledge that we acquire. In more detail, we can expect the mass media to tell us about different kinds of social roles and the accompanying expectations, in the sphere of work, family life, political behaviour and so on. We can expect certain values to be selectively reinforced in these and other areas of social experience. We can expect a form of dialogue between persons and fictional characters or real media personalities and also in some cases an identification with the values and perspectives of these 'significant others.' We can also expect the mass media to give an order of importance and structure to the world they portray, whether fictionally or as actuality. There are several reasons for these expectations. One is the fact that there is a good deal of patterning and consistency in the media version of the world. Another is the wide range of experience which is open to view and to vicarious involvement compared to the narrow range of real experience available to most people at most points in their lives. Third, there is the trust with which media are often held as a source of impressions about the world outside direct experience. Inevitably, the evidence for this process of learning from the media is thin and what there is does little more than reaffirm the plausibility of these theoretical propositions. The shortage of evidence stems in part from a failure to look for it, until quite recently, and in part from the long-term nature of the processes which make them less amenable to investigations by conventional techniques of social research than are the effects of campaigns. . . .

A long list of studies can be cited showing the media to have certain inbuilt tendencies to present a limited and recurring range of images and ideas which form rather special versions of reality. In some areas, as with news reporting, the pattern is fairly inescapable; in others the diversity of media allows some choice and some healthy contradiction. What we lack is much evidence of the impact of these selective versions of the world. In many cases discount by the audience or the availability of alternative information must make acceptance of media portrayals at face value extremely unlikely or unusual. We should certainly not take evidence of content as evidence of effect. There is no close correspondence between the two and some studies show this. For example Roshier (1973) found public views about crime to be closer to the 'true' statistical picture than the somewhat distorted version one might extract from the content of local newspapers. Similarly Halloran's study of audience reaction to television reports of the 1968 demonstration shows this to have been rather little affected by the 'one-sided' version presented on the screen. Even so, there is enough evidence as well as good theory for taking the proposition as a whole quite seriously. The case of the portrayal of an immigrant, especially coloured, minority provides a good test, since we may expect the media to be a prominent source of impressions for those in Britain who have little or very limited personal contact with 'immigrants.' . . .

[T]he media are associated with a view of immigrants as likely to be a cause of trouble or be associated with conflict. It also seems that impressions attributed to the media as source show a rather higher degree of internal similarity and to be in general less evaluative than those derived from personal contact. The main contribution of the mass media is not, according to this study, to encourage prejudice (often the reverse) but in defining the presence of immigrants as an 'objective' problem for the society.

. . . [T]he terms 'amplification' and 'sensitization' and 'polarization' have been used to describe the tendency of the media to exaggerate the incidence of a phenomenon, to increase the likelihood of it being noticed and to mobilize society against a supposed threat. In recent times, it has been argued that this treatment has been allotted to drug-taking (by Young, 1973), to mugging and to left-wing militants. It is notable that the groups receiving this form of polarizing treatment tend to be small, rather powerless and already subject to broad social disapproval. They are relatively 'safe' targets, but the process of hitting them tends to reaffirm the boundaries around what is acceptable in a free society.

When the question of media effects on violence is discussed, a rather opposite conclusion is often drawn. It seems as if general public opinion still holds the media responsible for a good deal of the increasing lawlessness in society (Halloran, 1970), a view based probably on the frequency with which crime and violence is portrayed, even if it rarely seems to be 're-warded.' It is relevant to this section of the discussion to explore this view. American evidence obtained for the Kerner Commission on Violence and reported by Baker and Ball (1969) shows there certainly to be much violence portrayed on the most used medium, television. It also shows that most people have rather little contact with real violence in personal experience. The authors chart the public expression of norms in relation to violence and also television norms as they appear in content and find a gap between the two. Thus, while public norms cannot yet have been much affected directly, the gap suggests that the direction of effects is to extend the boundaries of acceptable violence beyond current norms. In brief then, the authors of this study lend support to one of the more plausible hypotheses connecting crime and violence with the media—that the tolerance of aggression is increased by its frequent portrayal and it becomes a more acceptable means of solving problems whether for the 'goodies' or the criminals. It should not be lost sight of, even so, that most dependable research so far available has not supported the thesis of a general association between any form of media use and crime, delinquency or violence. (Halloran, 1970.) The discussion linking social norms with violence takes place on the level of belief systems, opinions, social myths. It would require a long-term historical and cultural analysis to establish the propositions which are involved. Nor should we forget that there are counter-propositions, pointing for instance to the selectivity of public norms about violence and aggression. It is not disapproved of in general in many societies, only in its uncontrolled and non-institutionalized forms. . . .

. . . It has already been suggested that the media help to establish an order of priorities in a society about its problems and objectives. They do this, not by initiating or determining, but by publicizing according to an agreed scale of values what is determined elsewhere, usually in the political system. Political scientists have been most alert to the process and the term 'agenda-setting' has been given to it by McCombs and Shaw (1972). They found the mass media to present a very uniform set of issues before the American public in the 1968 presidential election and found public opinion to accord in content and order rather closely to this pattern. The phenomenon had been noted earlier in election campaign studies, where order of space given to issues in media content was found to be predictive of changes in order of importance attributed to issues over the course of the campaign. (Trenaman and McQuail, 1961; Blumler and McQuail, 1968.) In one sense the media only record the past and reflect a version of the present but, in doing so, they can affect the future, hence the significance of the 'agenda' analogy. . . .

Given the sparseness of evidence, it is not surprising that we cannot so adequately state the conditions for the occurrence or otherwise of effects from the media in the sphere of forming impressions of reality and defining social norms. In particular, we are dealing with society-wide and historically located phenomena which are subject to forces not captured by normal data-collecting techniques in the social sciences. However, if we re-inspect the list of conditions associated with media campaign success or failure, a number will again seem relevant. In particular, we should look first at the monopoly condition. Here what matters is less the monopoly of ownership and control than the monopoly of attention and the homogeneity of content. Uniformity and repetition establish the important result of monopoly without the necessity for the structural causes to be present. The more consistent the picture presented and the more exclusively this picture gains wide attention then the more likely is the predicted effect to occur. (cf. Noelle-Neumann, 1974.) We can suppose, too, that matters outside immediate experience and on which there are not strongly formed, alternative views will also be most susceptible to the level of influence spoken of. Further, we can think that here, as with media campaigns, a trust in the source and an attribution of authority will be an important factor in the greater extension of media-derived opinions and values. Other conditions of social organization must also be taken into account. It is arguable, but untestable, that circumstances of greater individuation and lower ties of attachment to intermediary groups and associations will favour an influence from the media. Finally, we might hypothesize that conditions of social crisis or danger might also be associated with strong short-term effects from the media on the definition of problems and solutions.

Immediate Response and Reaction Effects

To discuss this, we return to questions relating largely to individuals and to direct and immediate effects. We are concerned exclusively with unintended, generally 'undesirable,' effects which fall into two main categories. One relates again to the problem of crime and violence, another to cases of panic response to news or information, where collective responses develop out of individual reception of the media. . . .

. . . One school of thought is now convinced that media portrayals of aggression can provoke aggression in child audiences (e.g. Berkowitz, 1964). Another favours the view that the effect of fictional evidence is more likely to be a cathartic or aggression-releasing tendency. (Feshbach [and Singer], 1971.) Many experiments have been inconclusive and majority opinion seems inclined to the cautious conclusion that direct effects involving disapproved behaviour are rare or likely to occur only where there is a strong disposition in that direction amongst a small minority of the already disturbed. . . .

The possibility that information received from the mass media will 'trigger' widespread and collective panic responses has often been canvassed, but rarely demonstrated. The 1938 radio broadcast of Wells' *War of the Worlds* which involved simulated news bulletins reporting an invasion from Mars is the case most often cited in this connection mainly because of [research by Cantril *et al.* (1940)] after the event. An event with some similarities in Sweden in 1973 was investigated by Rosengren (1976) and the results cast doubt on the thesis as a whole. It seems that in neither case was there much behavioural response, and what there was was later exaggerated by other media. Investigations of news transmission in times of crisis, for instance the studies by Greenberg of the dissemination of news of the assassination of Kennedy (Greenberg [and Parker], 1965) tells us a good deal more of the processes which begin to operate in such circumstances. Essentially, what happens is that people take over as transmitters of information and those who receive news seek independent confirmation from other media or trusted personal sources. The circumstance of solitary, unmediated, reception and response is unusual and short-lived. Shibutani (1966) reminds us that rumour and panic response are the outcome of situations of ambiguity and lack of information and, on the whole the mass media operate to modify rather than magnify these conditions.

In dealing with this aspect of potential media effects, more attention should perhaps be paid to various kinds of 'contagion' or spontaneous diffusion of activities. The situations most often mentioned relate to the spreading of un-rest or violence. For instance at times during the late 1960s when urban vi-olence and rioting was not uncommon in American cities it was suggested that television coverage of one event might lead to occurrences elsewhere. Research into the possibility (e.g. Pal[e]tz and Dunn, 1967) does not settle the matter and it remains a reasonable expectation that given the right pre-conditions, media coverage could spread collective disturbance by publicity alone. Political authorities which have the power to do so certainly act on the supposition that unrest can be transmitted in this way and seek to delay or conceal news which might encourage imitators. The imitation of acts of terrorism or criminality, such as hijacking, seems also likely to have oc-curred, although the proof is lacking and the phenomenon is different be-cause of its individual rather than collective character. In many areas where there is no institutionalized prohibition there is little doubt that spontaneous imitation and transmission do occur on a large scale by way of the mass media. In the sphere of music, dress, and other stylistic forms, the phenom-enon is occurring all the time. It is this which has led to the expectation that the media on their own are a powerful force for change in developing coun-tries (Lerner, 1958), through their stimulation of the desire first to consume and then to change the ways of life which stand in the way of earning and buying. Research evidence (e.g. Rogers and Shoemaker, 1971) and more considered thought (e.g. Golding, 1974) have led to the realization, however, that facts of social structure and of social institutions intervene powerfully in the process of imitation and diffusion. Even so, we should beware of dis-missing the process as a misconception or, where it occurs, always as trivial. It is at least plausible that the movement for greater female emancipation owes a good deal to widely disseminated publicity by way of mass media.

Consequences for Other Social Institutions

It was emphasized at the outset that the 'effects' of mass media have to be considered at a level beyond that of the individual audience member and the aggregate of individual behaviours. The path by which collective effects are produced is, in general, simple enough to grasp, but the extent to which ef-fects have occurred resists simple or certain assessment and has rarely been the subject of sustained investigation or thought. As the mass media have de-veloped they have, incontrovertibly, achieved two things. They have, be-tween them, diverted time and attention from other activities and they have become a channel for reaching more people with more information than was available under 'pre-mass media' conditions. These facts have implications for any other institution which requires allocation of time, attention and the communication of information, especially to large numbers and in large quantities. The media compete with other institutions and they offer ways of reaching continuing institutional objectives. It is this which underlies the process of institutional effect. Other social institutions are under pressure to adapt or respond in some way, or to make their own use of the mass media. In doing so, they are likely to alter. Because this is a slow process, occurring along with other kinds of social change, the specific contribution of the media cannot be accounted for with any certainty.

If this argument is accepted, it seems unlikely that any institution will be unaffected, but most open to change will be those concerned with 'knowledge' in the broadest sense and which are most universal and unselective in their reach. In most societies, this will suggest politics and education as the most likely candidates, religion in some cases and to a lesser degree, legal institution[s]. In general we would expect work, social services, science, [and] the military to be only tangentially affected by the availability of mass media. Insofar as we can regard leisure and sport as an institution in modern society this should perhaps be added to politics and education as the most directly interrelated with the mass media. . . .

. . . The challenge to politics from media institutions has taken several forms, but has been particularly strong just because the press was already involved in political processes and because the introduction of broadcasting was a political act. The diversion of time from political activity was less important than the diversion of attention from partisan sources of information and ideology to sources which were more accessible and efficient, often more attractive as well as authoritative, and which embodied the rather novel political values of objectivity and independent 'expert' adjudication. As we have seen, it has increasingly seemed as if it is the mass media which set the 'agenda' and define the problems on a continuous, day to day, basis while political parties and politicians increasingly respond to a consensus view of what should be done. The communication network controlled by the modern mass party cannot easily compete with the mass media network. . . .

Changes of Culture and Society

If we follow a similar line of analysis for other institutions, it is not difficult to appreciate that we can arrive at one or more versions of ways in which culture and social structure can be influenced by the path of development of media institutions. If the content of what we know, our way of doing things and spending time and the organization of central activities for the society are in part dependent on the media, then the fact of interdependence is evident. Again, the problem is to prove connections and quantify the links. The 'facts' are so scarce, open to dispute and often puny in stature that the question is often answered by reference to alternative theories. For some, the answer may still be provided by a theory of mass society of the kind advanced by Mills (1956) or Kornhauser (1959) and criticized by Shills (1975).

Such a theory suggests that the mass media encourage and make viable a rootless, alienated, form of social organization in which we are increasingly within the control of powerful and distant institutions. For others, a Marxist account of the mass media as a powerful ideological weapon for holding the mass of people in voluntary submission to capitalism (Marcuse, 1964; Miliband, 1969) provides the answer to the most important effects of the rise of the mass media.

A more complex answer is offered by Carey (1969), in his suggestion that the mass media are both a force for integration and for dispersion and individuation in society. Gerbner [and Gross (1976) see] the key to the effects of mass media in their capacity to take over the 'cultivation' of images, ideas and consciousness in an industrial society. [Gerbner] refers to the main process of mass media as that of 'publication' in the literal sense of making public: 'The truly revolutionary significance of modern mass communication is . . . the ability to form historically new bases for collective thought and action quickly, continuously and pervasively across the previous boundaries of time, space and status.' The ideas of McLuhan (1962 and 1964), despite a loss of vogue, remain plausible for some (e.g. Noble, 1975), especially in their particular reference to the establishment of a 'global village' which will be established through direct and common experience from television. The various theories are not all so far apart. A common theme is the observation that experience, or what we take for experience, is increasingly indirect and 'mediated' and that, whether by chance or design, more people receive a similar 'version' of the world. The consequences for culture and society depend, however, on factors about which the theories are not agreed, especially on the character and likely tendency of this version of reality. Similarly, the available theories are not agreed on the basis of the extraordinary appeal of the mass media taken in general. Do they meet some underlying human needs? If so, what is the nature of these needs? Alternatively, is the apparent 'necessity' of the media merely the result of some imposed and artificial want? Certainly, the question of what most wide-ranging consequences follow from the media must also raise the question of motivation and use.

The Social Power of Mass Media— A Concluding Note

It has been the intention of this whole discussion to make very clear that the mass media do have important consequences for individuals, for institutions and for society and culture. That we cannot trace very precise causal connections or make reliable predictions about the future does not nullify this conclusion. The question of the power of the mass media is a different one. In essence, it involves asking how effectively the mass media can and do achieve objectives over others at the will of those who direct, own or control them or who use them as channels for messages. The history of mass media shows clearly enough that such control is regarded as a valued form of property for those seeking political or economic power. The basis for such a view has already been made clear in the evidence which has been discussed. Control over the mass media offers several important possibilities. First, the media can attract and direct attention to problems, solutions or people in ways which can favour those with power and correlatively divert attention from rival individuals or groups. Second, the mass media can confer status and confirm legitimacy. Third, in some circumstances, the media can be a channel for persuasion and mobilization. Fourth, the mass media can help to bring certain kinds of publics into being and maintain them. Fifth, the media are a vehicle for offering psychic rewards and gratifications. They can divert and amuse and they can flatter. In general, mass media are very cost-effective as a means of communication in society; they are also fast, flexible and relatively easy to plan and control. . . .

The general case which can be made out along these lines for treating the mass media as an instrument of social power is sufficiently strong for many commentators to regard it as settled. In this view, all that remains is to discover not *whether* the media have power and how it works, but *who* has access to the use of this power. Generally this means asking questions about ownership and other forms of control, whether political, legal or economic. It is arguable, however, that we need to take the case somewhat further and to probe rather more carefully the initial general assumption. That is, we cannot assume that ownership and control of the means of mass communication does necessarily confer power over others in any straightforward or predictable way. . . .

. . . [M]ore attention should be given to the various structures of legitimation which attract and retain audiences and which also govern their attitudes to different media sources. There are critical differences between alternative forms of control from above and between alternative types of orientation to the media, both within and between societies. This is, as yet, a relatively unexplored area but meanwhile we should be as wary of trying to answer questions of power solely in terms of ownership as we should be of doing so in terms of 'effects.'

References

Baker, R. K. and Ball, S. J., 1969: *Mass Media and Violence*. Report to the National Commission on the Causes and Prevention of Violence.

Belson, W., 1967: *The Impact of Television*. Crosby Lockwood.

Berelson, B. Lazarsfeld, P. F. and McPhee, W., 1954: *Voting*. University of Chicago Press.

Berkowitz, Leonard, 1964: 'The effects of observing violence.' *Scientific American*, vol. 210.

Blumler, H., 1933: *Movies and Conduct*. Macmillan.

Blumler, J. G., 1964: 'British Television: the Outlines of a Research Strategy.' *British Journal of Sociology* 15 (3).

Blumler, J. G. and McQuail, D., 1968: *Television in Politics: its uses and influence.* Faber.

Blumler, J. G., Nossiter, T. and McQuail, D., 1975: *Political Communication and Young Voters.* Report to SSRC.

Butler, D. and Stokes, D., 1969: *Political Change in Britain.* Macmillan.

Cantril, H., Gaudet, H. and Herzog, H., 1940: *The Invasion from Mars.* Princeton University Press.

Carey, J. W., 1969: 'The Communications Revolution and the Professional Communicator.' In Halmos, P., (ed.), *The Sociology of Mass Media Communicators.* Sociological Review Monograph 13. University of Keele.

Cooper, E. and Jahoda, M., 1947: 'The evasion of propaganda.' *Journal of Psychology* 15, pp. 15–25.

Feshbach, S. and Singer, R., 1971: *Television Aggression.* Jossey-Bass.

Frey, F. W., 1973: 'Communication and Development.' In de Sola Pool, I. and Schramm, W. (eds.), *Handbook of Communication,* Rand McNally.

Gerbner, G. and Gross, L., 1976: 'The scary world of TV's heavy viewer.' *Psychology Today,* April.

Golding, P., 1974: 'Mass communication and theories of development.' *Journal of Communication,* Summer.

Greenberg, B. and Parker, E. B. (eds.), 1965: *The Kennedy Assassination and the American Public.* Stanford University Press.

Halloran, J. D., 1964: *The Effects of Mass Communication.* Leicester University Press.

Halloran, J. D. (ed.), 1970: *The Effects of Television.* Paladin.

Hopkins, M. W., 1970: *Mass Media in the Soviet Union.* Pegasus.

Hovland, C. I., Lumsdaine, A. and Sheffield, F., 1950: *Experiments in Mass Communication.* Princeton University Press.

Inkeles, A. and Bauer, R. A., 1959: *The Soviet Citizen: Daily Life in a Totalitarian Society.* Harvard University Press.

Katz, E. and Lazarsfeld, P. F., 1956: *Personal Influence.* Free Press.

Key, V. O., 1961: *Public Opinion and American Democracy.* Knopf.

Klapper, Joseph T., 1960: *The Effects of Mass Communication.* Free Press.

Kornhauser, F. W., 1959: *The Politics of Mass Society.* Routledge.

Lang, K. and Lang, G., 1959: 'The Mass Media and Voting.' In Burdick, E. J. and Brodbeck, A. J. (eds.), *American Voting Behaviour,* Free Press.

Lazarsfeld, P. F., Berelson, B. and Gaudet, H., 1944: *The People's Choice.* Columbia University Press.

Lerner, D., 1958: *The Passing of Traditional Society.* Free Press.

McCombs, M. and Shaw, D. L., 1972: 'The agenda-setting function of mass media.' *Public Opinion Quarterly* 36.

McLuhan, M., 1962: *The Gutenberg Galaxy.* Routledge.

McLuhan, M., 1964: *Understanding Media.* Routledge.

Marcuse, H., 1964: *One-Dimensional Man.* Routledge.

Miliband, R., 1969: *The State in Capitalist Society.* Weidenfeld and Nicolson.

Mills, C. W., 1956: *The Power Elite.* Free Press.

Noble, G., 1975: *Children in Front of the Small Screen.* Constable.

Noelle-Neumann, E., 1974: 'The spiral of silence.' *Journal of Communication,* Spring.

Paletz, D. L. and Dunn, R., 1967: 'Press coverage of civil disorders.' *Public Opinion Quarterly* 33, pp. 328–45.

Pye, Lucian (ed.), 1963. *Communication and Political Development.* Princeton University Press.

Rogers, E. and Shoemaker, F., 1971: *Communication of Innovations.* Free Press.

Rosengren, K. E., 1976: *The Baxby Incident.* Lund University.

Roshier, B., 1973: 'The selection of crime news by the press.' In Cohen, S. and Young, J. (eds.), *The Manufacture of News,* Constable.

Shibutani, T., 1966: *Improvised News.* Bobbs-Merrill.

Shills, E., 1975: 'The Theory of Mass Society.' In *Centre and Periphery,* Chicago University Press.

Trenaman, J. and McQuail, D., 1961: *Television and the Political Image.* Methuen.

Young, J., 1973: 'The amplification of drug use.' In Cohen, S. and Young, J. (eds.), *The Manufacture of News,* Constable.

3

WHY DEMOCRACIES NEED AN UNLOVABLE PRESS

Michael Schudson

Editor's Note

Criticism of the press abounds in this volume. The press, its critics say, relies too much on official sources; it abides by outdated, constraining norms; it keeps its nose too close to daily events and conventional wisdom and revels in conflicts and cynicism. All true, concedes sociologist Michael Schudson. But, in a surprising twist, he shows that these vices may actually be virtues. To understand why unlovable features of the press are vital for democracy, imagine a press without these flaws, a press that avoided official sources and conflicts, abandoned the restraints of journalistic norms, and shied away from reporting the day's events in favor of erudite analyses that never hint at politicians' ulterior motives. Would that be a lovely dream or an awful nightmare?

Michael Schudson is professor of communication and adjunct professor of sociology at the University of California. He is the author or editor of eight books, including *The Sociology of News* (2003) and *The Good Citizen: A History of American Civic Life* (1998). Schudson is one of the foremost students of the history and sociology of the American news media. He also studies advertising and popular culture.

Alexis de Tocqueville, widely cited for his view that the American press is a necessary and vital institution for American democracy, did not actually have much affection for it. He objected to its violence and vulgarity. He saw it as a virtue of the American system that newspapers were widely dispersed around the country rather than concentrated in a capital city—they could do less harm this way. He confessed, "I admit that I do not feel toward freedom of the press that complete and instantaneous love which one accords to things by their nature supremely good. I love it more from considering the evils it prevents than on account of the good it does."[1]

It may well be, taking a leaf from Tocqueville, that today's efforts to make journalism more serious, more responsible, and, generally speaking, nicer, are misplaced. I want to propose that most critics of journalism, in and outside journalism itself, have attacked just those features of the press that, for all their defects, best protect robust public discussion and promote democracy. The focus of the news media on events, rather than trends and structures; the fixation of the press on conflict whenever and wherever it erupts; the cynicism of journalists with respect to politics and politicians; and the alienation of journalists from the communities they cover make the media hard for people to love but hard for democracies to do without. These are the features that most regularly enable the press to maintain a capacity for subverting established power.

This is not to suggest that there is anything wrong with in-depth reporting of the sort that Pulitzer juries and media critics applaud and I greatly admire. Nor do I mean to suggest that the dialogue of democracy should jettison editorial writers, op-ed columnists, investigative reporters, and expert analysts who can produce gems of explanatory journalism. That would be absurd. But I do mean to suggest that the power of the press to afflict the comfortable derives more often than not from the journalistic equivalent of ambulance chasing. Just as the ambulance-chasing trial lawyer sees another person's tragedy as a million-dollar opportunity, the newshound reporter sees it as an attention-grabbing, career-advancing, front-page sensation. I want to explore here the ways the most narrow and unlovable features of news may make the most vital of contributions to democracy.

The Press as an Establishment Institution

The press is presumably the bastion of free expression in a democracy, but too often it has been one of the institutions that limits the range of expression, especially expression that is critical of leading centers of power in society. Almost all social scientific studies of the news reveal that journalists themselves, of their own volition, limit the range of opinion present in the news. There are at least three significant ways this happens. First, there is source-dependence. Reporters rely on and reproduce the views of their primary sources, and these tend to be high government officials. Second, reporters and editors operate according to a set of professional norms that are themselves constraints on expression. Third, journalists operate within conventional bounds of opinion, opinions common among a largely secular, college-educated, upper middle class. All of this has been abundantly documented, . . . I will quickly review this literature, but only as a preface to arguing that this account of the compliant press has been overdrawn.

Dependence on Official Sources

Media scholars have consistently found that official sources dominate the news. This is invariably presented as a criticism of the media. If the media were to fulfill their democratic role, they would offer a wide variety of opinions and perspectives and would encourage citizens to choose among them in considering public policies. If the media allow politicians to set the public agenda, they may unduly narrow public discussion and so diminish democracy. This is the argument made, for instance, by W. Lance Bennett in his account of the "indexing" function of the press. For Bennett, the media "tend to 'index' the range of voices and viewpoints in both news and editorials according to the range of views expressed in mainstream government debate about a given topic." Bennett argues that this helps perpetuate a "world in which governments are able to define their own publics and where 'democracy' becomes whatever the government ends up doing."[2]

Sociologist Herbert Gans makes an argument about official sources related to Bennett's. For him, the routines of daily journalism undermine democracy. If supporting democracy means encouraging citizens to be active, informed, and critical, then the standard operating procedures of mainstream journalism subvert their own best intentions. Since most news is "top down," relaying the views of high government officials over lower government officials, all government officials over unofficial groups and oppositional groups, and groups of any sort over unorganized citizens, it diminishes the standing and efficacy of individual citizens.[3]

Whether the normative implications of journalism's favoring high government officials are as dire as Gans fears may be doubted, but it is indisputable that news media coverage emphasizes the views and actions of leading politicians and other top government officials. It is likewise indisputable that this limits the range of opinion to which the general public is exposed.

The Constraints of Professional Culture

Journalists favor high government officials—but why? The answer is that they work within a professional culture or a set of professional values that holds that a journalist's obligation is to report government affairs to serve the informational functions that make democracy work. . . . That is, in the work of political reporting, journalists emphasize "players, policies, and predictions of what will happen next."[4] So even when the press goes to outside experts rather than inside government officials, they seek people with experience in government, access to and knowledge of the chief players in government, and a ready willingness to speak in the terms of government officials, interpreting and predicting unfolding events. . . .

The Constraints of Conventional Wisdom

Journalists swim in conventional wisdom. They are wrapped up in daily events, and it would be disconcerting for them and for their readers if they took a long view. It might also be disconcerting for them to take a comparative (non-American) view. It would certainly be disconcerting for them to spend too much time with academics or others removed from the daily fray of political life. It is in relation to the conventional wisdom that journalists know how to identify "a story." Individual journalists may take issue with convention. Some journalists who work for publications with nonconventional audiences may write with unconventional assumptions and unusual points of departure. But the mainstream journalist writing for a standard news institution is likely to be ignorant of, or, if informed, dismissive of opinions outside the fold.

In Washington, in state capitals, and even more in smaller countries, journalists pick up conventional wisdom through lives intertwined with the lives of politicians. In France, for instance, Thomas Ferenczi, associate editor of *Le Monde,* complains that journalists and politicians—and it does not matter if they are left-wing or right-wing—belong to the same "microcosm": "when they are young they go to the same schools, later they live in the same areas, go to the same holiday resorts, and so on." Ferenczi warns, "There is real danger for democracy here: namely, that, journalists and politicians, because they are so closely linked, have their own, narrow, idea of what the media should cover . . . and ignore the interests of the people."[5] This is less of a problem in the more pluralistic United States than it is in France. In the United States, there is a more widely dispersed journalistic elite—at least across two cities, New York and Washington, and with important pockets of opinion shapers in Los Angeles, Chicago, and Cambridge-Boston, rather than concentrated in one—and it is much more diverse in social and educational background. However, the same general phenomenon occurs.

Other factors also limit the range of opinion in the American media, vitally important factors, although they lie outside the news media as such. For instance, the American political system generally offers a narrower political spectrum, and one less accommodating of minorities, than most other democratic systems. Ralph Nader complained bitterly after the 2000 election that he had not been well covered in the press. Why, he asked, when he was raising real issues, did he get no coverage while Al Gore and George W. Bush, the Tweedle-dum and Tweedle-dee of American politics, were covered every time they blew their noses?[6] The answer seemed pretty straightforward: Ralph Nader was not going to be elected president of the United States in 2000. Either Al Gore or George W. Bush would. The press—as part of its conventional wisdom—believed its job was to follow what the American political system had tossed up for it. It was not the job of the press to offer the public a wide range of issues but to cover, analyze, and discuss the issues the two viable candidates were presenting. Imagine, however, if Ralph Nader had been running for president in Germany. Would the German press have shown greater interest in his ideas? Yes, but not because the German press is better or more democratic, but because Germany has a parliamentary political system. It is because if Ralph Nader received 5 percent of the vote in Germany, his party would receive 5 percent of the seats in Parliament and would be a force, potentially a decisive force, in forming a government. If Ralph Nader received 5 percent of the vote in the United States, he would get no seats in Congress.

So there are many reasons why media discourse in the United States fails to approximate an ideal of robust and wide-open discussion. Even so, journalism as it functions today is still a practice that offends powerful groups, speaks truth to power, and provides access for a diversity of opinion. How and why does this happen despite all that constrains it? The standard sociological analysis of news places it in so airless a box that exceptional journalistic forays are not readily explained. They are the exceptions that prove the rule. They are the ones that got away from the powers of constraint and cooptation and routine. But these "exceptions" happen every year, every week, at some level every day. How can we explain that?

Strategic Opportunities for Free Expression

Eventfulness

There is a fundamental truth about journalism that all journalists recognize but almost all social scientists do not: things happen. Not only do things happen, but, as the bumper sticker says, shit happens. That is what provides a supply of occurrences for journalists to work with. Shit even happens to the rich and powerful, and it makes for a great story when it does.

Because shit happens, journalists gain some freedom from official opinion, professional routines, and conventional wisdom. Journalism is an event-centered discourse, more responsive to accidents and explosions in the external world than to fashions in ideas among cultural elites. The journalists' sense of themselves as street-smart, nose-to-the-ground adventurers in places where people do not want them has an element of truth to it, and it is very much linked to event-centeredness.

News, like bread or sausage, is something people make. Scholars emphasize the manufacturing process. Journalists emphasize the raw material their work brings them to; they insist that their jobs recurrently place them before novel, unprecedented, and unanticipated events. While sociologists observe how this world of surprises is tamed, journalists typically emphasize that the effort at domestication falls short.[7]

The journalists have a point. Sometimes something happens that is not accounted for in any sociology or media studies. Take President Bill Clinton's efforts to create a system of national service. This was part of his 1992 campaign, and he mentioned it as one of the priorities of his administration the day after his election. He appointed a friend, Eli Segal, to run a new Office of National Service, and Segal set to work to get appropriate legislation through Congress. The administration's efforts led to passage of the National and Community Service Trust Act, which Clinton signed into law in September 1993. One year later, AmeriCorps would be officially launched. Segal took charge of orchestrating a major public relations event that would feature President Clinton swearing in nine thousand AmeriCorps volunteers at sixteen sites around the country by satellite hook-up. Every detail was checked, every contingency plan was rehearsed. Segal looked forward to a triumphant day on the South Lawn of the White House followed by extensive, favorable news coverage. At 4:30 A.M. on the morning of the ceremony, Segal's phone rang. The event as planned would have to be scrapped. Why? Because at that hour a deranged pilot crashed his Cessna aircraft into the back of the White House precisely on the spot where the ceremony was to be staged. The news media predictably went gaga over this bizarre and unprecedented event and could scarcely be bothered by the launching of AmeriCorps—no doubt more important than the plane crash, but infinitely more routine.[8]

Social scientists insist that most news is produced by Eli Segals, not deranged pilots. Quantitatively, they are right; the vast majority of daily news items on television or in print come from planned, intentional events, press releases, press conferences, and scheduled interviews. Even so, journalists find their joy and their identity in the adrenaline rush that comes only from deranged pilots, hurricanes, upset victories in baseball or politics, triumphs against all odds, tragedy or scandal in the lap of luxury, and other unplanned and unanticipated scandals, accidents, mishaps, gaffes, embarrassments, and wonders. The scholars delight in revealing how much of news is produced by the best laid plans of government officials who maneuver news to their own purposes; the journalists enjoy being first to the scene when the best laid plans go awry.

On September 13, 1994, the *New York Times'* lead story, and two related stories, covered the plane crash at the White House. Other news was swamped. The story on AmeriCorps ran on page seventeen. Even there it seemed to be folded into the big story of the day. The third paragraph read: "Some 850 were inducted as more than 2,000 dignitaries and supporters took part in the ceremony on the North Lawn of the White House. They were kept sweltering there for more than two hours, and an elaborately synchronized satellite television transmission was thrown awry because of the crash of a light plane early this morning on the South Lawn where the event was supposed to have taken place."

Journalists make their own stories, but not from materials they have personally selected. Materials are thrust upon them. It can even be argued, as Regina Lawrence has contended, that in recent years news has become more event-driven and less institution-driven. Moreover, the news media take events not as ends in themselves but as "jumping-off points for thematic exploration of social issues." Content analysis of news over the past one hundred years indicates that journalists pay increasing attention to context, to reporting events in detail especially when they serve as "invitations for the news media to grapple, however gracefully or clumsily, with political and social issues."[9] This preoccupation with unpredictable events keeps something uncontrollable at the forefront of journalism. The archetypal news story, the kind that makes a career, the sort every reporter longs for, is one that is unroutinized and unrehearsed. It gives journalism its recurrent anarchic potential. And it is built into the very bloodstream of news organizations, it is the circulatory system that keeps the enterprise oxygenated.

Conflict

Almost all journalists relish conflict. Almost all media criticism attacks journalists for emphasizing conflict. But conflict, like events, provides a recurrent resource for embarrassing the powerful.

Consider a story by Randal C. Archibold that appeared in the *New York Times* on January 11, 2003, with the headline "Nuclear Plant Disaster Plan Is Inadequate, Report Says." To summarize, New York governor George Pataki had commissioned a report on safety at the Indian Point nuclear power plant just thirty-five miles away from midtown Manhattan. The report was produced by a consulting group the governor hired, Witt Associates. James Lee Witt, its chief executive, was formerly the director of the Federal Emergency Management Agency. So journalists knew the report was being written, knew its chief author was a high-ranking former federal official, and knew roughly when it would appear. This sounds like the kind of government-centered "official" news story critics complain about.

But was it? Why did Governor Pataki commission the report? Clearly, he commissioned it after the September 11 terrorist attack made more urgent the concerns that citizens and citizens' groups had already expressed about the safety of the Indian Point nuclear reactor. . . . The Witt report, whose conclusion could not have been fully anticipated by the governor or anyone else if it was to have legitimacy, declared that the disaster preparedness plan was inadequate for protecting people from unacceptable levels of radiation in case of a release at the plant. The elected executive of Westchester County, Andrew J. Spano, commented, "the bottom line is the plant shouldn't be here." The reporter made it clear that Witt Associates did not remark on whether the plant should be shut down but, at the same time, noted that the report's view of the emergency plans for the plant "largely reflected complaints voiced for years by opponents of Indian Point."

The Witt report became news not because the governor's office generated it, but because the governor acted in the face of raging controversy. The continuing controversy made the story news and made the news story interesting. In the end, the report obviously gave support to the environmentalists and others who have urged that Indian Point be shut down. The news story helped keep opponents of government policy alert, encouraged, and legitimated.

Cynicism

Political reporters in the past generation have increasingly made it a point not only to report the statements and actions of leading public officials but to report on the motives behind the actions as best as they can. They report not only the show and the dazzle that the politician wants foregrounded, but the efforts that go into the show and the calculations behind them. They may not intend to undercut the politicians, but they do intend not to be manipulated. The result is a portrait of politicians as self-interested, cynically manipulative, and contemptuous of the general public.

Take, for instance, the *New York Times*' April 16, 2003, front-page story on the proposed Bush tax cut, "In a Concession, Bush Lowers Goal of Tax Cut Plan." The story began by curtly observing that President Bush lowered his target for a tax cut in a tacit admission that his original package was "dead." Then reporter Elisabeth Bumiller cited White House advisers who said "that they were now on a war footing with Capitol Hill" to pass the biggest tax cut they could. They, along with other Republican strategists, said "it was imperative for Mr. Bush to be seen as fighting hard for the economy to avoid the fate of his father, who lost the White House after his victory in the 1991 Persian Gulf war in large part because voters viewed him as disengaged from domestic concerns." The orientation of the story was to the timing and style of the president's speech on the economy, not to its substance. The background—strategy and image—is the foreground. This kind of a story, once exceptional, has become standard.[10]

At the end of September 2003, Laura Bush went to Paris as part of the ceremonies signaling the American reentry to UNESCO after a boycott of nearly two decades. The First Lady's trip was, of course, a well-planned public relations gesture. Would anyone have suspected otherwise? But Elaine Sciolino, the *Times*' veteran foreign correspondent and chief Paris correspondent, made a point of it, noting that Mrs. Bush did not face the American flag as the American national anthem was sung. "Instead, she stood perpendicular to it, enabling photographers to capture her in profile, with the flag and the Eiffel Tower behind. The scene was carefully planned for days by a White House advance team, much to the amusement of longtime UNESCO employees."[11]

... This kind of reporting may not be a sign of a press that motivates or mobilizes or turns people into good citizens. It may do more to reinforce political apathy than to refurbish political will. But it may be just what democracy requires of the press.

Outsider News

Why is Trent Lott no longer majority leader of the U.S. Senate? The answer is that on December 5, 2002, he made remarks at Senator Strom Thurmond's one hundredth birthday party that suggested we would all be better off if Senator Thurmond, running on a segregationist platform for the presidency in 1948, had won the election. The room apparently was full of politicians and journalists, none of whom immediately caught the significance of the remark. . . .

But if no one at the party recognized Lott's remarks as a story, how did it become news and force Lott's resignation from his leadership post? The first part of the answer is that several practitioners of the still novel "blogs," or personal Web sites of a kind of highly individualized public diary, took note of Lott's remarks, including several prominent and widely read bloggers. . . . Although mainstream press outlets, both print and broadcast, noted the remarks (and C-SPAN had aired them), the bloggers pressed the fact that Thurmond ran as a segregationist and that Lott had taken many conservative stands through the years, including speaking before white supremacist groups and voting against the Civil Rights Act of 1990. Matt Drudge, in his online report, even found that Senator Lott had made an almost identical statement in praise of Thurmond in 1980.

Thanks to the "blogosphere," the party that Senator Lott and nearly everyone else present regarded as an insider event was available for outsider news. Moreover, as Heather Gorgura argues, the bloggers succeeded in getting the "dump Lott" bandwagon moving not simply by pointing out an indiscreet remark, but, in documenting Senator Lott's long and consistent history of association with organizations and policies offensive to African Americans, by persuading mainstream journalists that Lott's remarks were not casual and thoughtless but representative of a racism Lott had repeatedly expressed and acted upon.[12]

... The cyber-pamphleteers today can attract broad attention, including the attention of the old media. They do so, I might point out, by name-calling sensationalism. The most prominent and most consequential cases are that of Matt Drudge breaking the Monica Lewinsky story—"The president is an adulterer"—and the bloggers who cried, "The senator is a racist." An unlovable press, indeed, but perhaps just what democracy requires.

Outsiders are always troublemakers. The news media are supposed to be institutionalized outsiders even though they have in fact become institutionalized insiders. There is much more that might be done to keep journalists at arm's length from their sources. This is something that journalism education could orient itself to more conscientiously—for instance, insisting that journalism students take a course in comparative politics or a course on the politics and culture of some society besides the United States. A serious U.S. history course would also help. The idea would be to disorient rather than orient the prospective journalist. Disorientation—and ultimately alienation of journalists—helps the press to be free.

Social scientists regularly observe how much reporters have become insiders, socializing with their sources, flattered by their intimacy with the rich and powerful, dependent on intimacy for the leaks and leads officialdom can provide. All of this is true, but it is all the more reason to observe carefully and nurture those ways in which journalists remain outsiders. Bloggers in the Trent Lott case, although journalists, took up outposts on journalism's frontier. But even standard issue journalists are outsiders to the conventional opinions of government officials in several respects. For one, they advance the journalistic agenda of finding something novel that will set tongues a-flutter across a million living rooms, breakfast tables, bars, lunchrooms, and lines at Starbucks. Second, journalists have access to and professional interest in nonofficial sources of news. Most important of these nonofficial sources is public opinion as measured by polls or by informal journalistic "taking of the pulse" of public opinion. The American press in particular has a populist streak that inclines it toward a sampling of civilian views. A front-page story in the April 24, 2003, *Chicago Tribune*, for instance, by Jill Zuckman, the *Tribune*'s chief congressional correspondent, and datelined Northfield, Wisconsin, was based on both national opinion polls and local interviewing of people who objected to the USA Patriot Act.

. . . [People] had a surprising amount to say about their fears for domestic civil liberties. So the topic Zuckman wrote about was not what she intended to cover, but her populist instinct made it possible to report on a phenomenon that elites did not anticipate and that the administration could not have found comforting.[13]

Conclusion

Journalists are not free agents. They are constrained by a set of complex institutional relations that lead them to reproduce day after day the opinions and views of establishment figures, especially high government officials. They are constrained by broad conventional wisdom that they are not particularly well located nor well enough educated to buck and they are powerfully constrained by the conventions and routines of their own professionalism. At the same time, they are not without some resources for expanding the range of expression in the news. What structures do or could preserve their capacity to speak freely and to expand the range of voices and views they represent in their reporting? What journalistic predispositions do or could enable them to take advantage of their limited but real autonomy to fulfill the potential of a free press for vigorous, robust discussion of public issues? I am defending, somewhat to my surprise, what is usually attacked as the worst features of the American press—a preoccupation with events, a morbid sports-minded fascination with gladiatorial combat, a deep, anti-political cynicism, and a strong alienation of journalists from the communities they cover.

I hasten to add that the journalists I most admire get behind and beneath events, illuminate trends and structures and moods and not just conflicts, believe in the virtues and values of political life and the hopes it inspires, and feel connected and committed to their communities—global, national, or local. The journalists of greatest imagination discover the nonevents that conceal their drama so well. They recognize the story in conflicts that never arose because of strong leadership or a stroke of luck, or the conflict that was resolved peacefully over a painstakingly long time without sparking a front-page "event." But I propose, nonetheless, that some of the greatest service the media provide for democracy lies in characteristics that few people regard as very nice or ennobling about the press. These features of journalism—and perhaps these features more than others—make news a valuable force in a democratic society, and this means that—if all goes well—we are saddled with a necessary institution we are not likely ever to love.

Notes

1. Alexis de Tocqueville, *Democracy in America,* edited by J. P. Mayer (Garden City, N.Y.: Doubleday, 1969), 180.
2. W. Lance Bennett, "Toward a Theory of Press-State Relations in the United States." *Journal of Communication* 40 (spring 1990): 103–25, quotes at 106, 125.
3. Herbert Gans, *Democracy and the News* (New York: Oxford Univ. Press, 2003). Gans and Bennett, like many other contemporary theorists, both presume that the press at its best should not only report the doings of government but that it should do so in a way to encourage and provide for the participation of ordinary citizens, informing them in advance of governmental decisions so that they can make their voices heard. This is by no means an undisputed assumption. As John Zaller has argued, the job of the press in a mass democracy may be to help people evaluate leaders, not policies. The press should try to make it possible for the public to evaluate leaders after they have acted, not policies before they have been put in place. See John Zaller, "Elite Leadership of Mass Opinion: New Evidence from the Gulf War," in *Taken by Storm: The Media, Public Opinion, and U.S. Foreign Policy in the Gulf War,* edited by W. Lance Bennett and David L. Paletz (Chicago: Univ. of Chicago Press, 1994), 201–2.

4. Janet Steele, "Experts and the Operational Bias of Television News: The Case of the Persian Gulf War," *Journalism and Mass Communication Quarterly* 72 (1995): 799–812, quote at 799.

5. Thomas Ferenczi, "The Media and Democracy," *CSD Bulletin,* 8 no. 1 (winter 2000–2001): 1–2.

6. Ralph Nader, "My Untold Story," *Brill's Content* (February 2001), 100–3, 153–4.

7. Scholars . . . have provided important explanations for this autonomy. Daniel Hallin sees autonomy provided structurally by divisions among elites. See Daniel C. Hallin, *"The Uncensored War": The Media and Vietnam* (New York: Oxford Univ. Press, 1986). Laws that make it tough to sue for libel also enhance autonomy. These explanations direct attention to structural opportunities for aggressive reporting, but they do not provide journalists with a motive to pursue challenge and critique.

8. Steven Waldman, *The Bill* (New York: Viking, 1995), 240.

9. Regina Lawrence, *The Politics of Force* (Berkeley: Univ. of California Press, 2000), 188.

10. This is not to mention background stories that are exclusively focused on stagecraft. See, for instance, Elisabeth Bumiller, "Keepers of Bush Image Lift Stagecraft to New Heights," *New York Times,* May 16, 2003, p. 1.

11. *New York Times,* September 30, 2003, A4.

12. Heather E. Gorgura, "Lott Gets a Blogging: Did the Amateur Journalists of the Blogosphere Bring Down Trent Lott?" (unpublished paper, University of Washington, March 2003). This student paper is extremely thoughtful and well documented.

13. Email to the author from Jill Zuckman, September 20, 2003.

4

NEWSPAPERS

Walter Lippmann

Editor's Note

In this classic study Walter Lippmann shows how journalists point a flashlight rather than a mirror at the world. Accordingly, the audience does not receive a complete image of the political scene; it gets a highly selective series of glimpses instead. Reality is tainted. Lippmann explains why the media cannot possibly perform the functions of public enlightenment that democratic theory requires. They cannot tell the truth objectively because the truth is subjective and entails more probing and explanation than the hectic pace of news production allows. Lippmann's analysis raises profound questions about the purity and adequacy of mass media sources of information. Can there be democracy when information is invariably tainted? Are there any antidotes? The answers remain elusive.

Lippmann, who died in 1974, was a renowned American journalist and political analyst whose carefully reasoned, lucid writings influenced American politics for more than half a century. He won two Pulitzer Prizes, the Medal of Freedom, and three Overseas Press Club awards. In addition to books, he wrote articles for the *New Republic,* the *New York World,* and the *New York Herald Tribune.*

The Nature of News

. . . In the first instance . . . the news is not a mirror of social conditions, but the report of an aspect that has obtruded itself. The news does not tell you how the seed is germinating in the ground, but it may tell you when the first sprout breaks through the surface. It may even tell you what somebody says is happening to the seed under ground. It may tell you that the sprout

---

Source: This selection reprinted with the permission of Scribner, an imprint of Simon & Schuster Adult Publishing Group, from *Public Opinion* by Walter Lippmann. Copyright © 1922, 1950 by Walter Lippmann.

did not come up at the time it was expected. The more points, then, at which any happening can be fixed, objectified, measured, named, the more points there are at which news can occur. . . .

Wherever there is a good machinery of record, the modern news service works with great precision. There is one on the stock exchange, and the news of price movements is flashed over tickers with dependable accuracy. There is a machinery for election returns, and when the counting and tabulating are well done, the result of a national election is usually known on the night of the election. In civilized communities deaths, births, marriages and divorces are recorded, and are known accurately except where there is concealment or neglect. The machinery exists for some, and only some, aspects of industry and government, in varying degrees of precision for securities, money and staples, bank clearances, realty transactions, wage scales. It exists for imports and exports because they pass through a custom house and can be directly recorded. It exists in nothing like the same degree for internal trade, and especially for trade over the counter.

It will be found, I think, that there is a very direct relation between the certainty of news and the system of record. If you call to mind the topics which form the principal indictment by reformers against the press, you find they are subjects in which the newspaper occupies the position of the umpire in the unscored baseball game. All news about states of mind is of this character: so are all descriptions of personalities, of sincerity, aspiration, motive, intention, of mass feeling, of national feeling, of public opinion, the policies of foreign governments. So is much news about what is going to happen. So are questions turning on private profit, private income, wages, working conditions, the efficiency of labor, educational opportunity, unemployment,[1] monotony, health, discrimination, unfairness, restraint of trade, waste, "backward peoples," conservatism, imperialism, radicalism, liberty, honor, righteousness. All involve data that are at best spasmodically recorded. The data may be hidden because of a censorship or a tradition of privacy, they may not exist because nobody thinks record important, because he thinks it red tape, or because nobody has yet invented an objective system of measurement. Then the news on these subjects is bound to be debatable, when it is not wholly neglected. The events which are not scored are reported either as personal and conventional opinions, or they are not news. They do not take shape until somebody protests, or somebody investigates, or somebody publicly, in the etymological meaning of the word, makes an *issue* of them. . . .

Let us suppose the conditions leading up to a strike are bad. What is the measure of evil? A certain conception of a proper standard of living, hygiene, economic security, and human dignity. The industry may be far below the theoretical standard of the community, and the workers may be too wretched to protest. Conditions may be above the standard, and the workers may protest violently. The standard is at best a vague measure. However, we shall assume that the conditions are below par, as par is understood by the editor. Occasionally without waiting for the workers to threaten, but prompted say by a social worker, he will send reporters to investigate, and will call attention to bad conditions. Necessarily he cannot do that often. For these investigations cost time, money, special talent, and a lot of space. To make plausible a report that conditions are bad, you need a good many columns of print. In order to tell the truth about the steel worker in the Pittsburgh district, there was needed a staff of investigators, a great deal of time, and several fat volumes of print. It is impossible to suppose that any daily newspaper could normally regard the making of Pittsburgh Surveys, or even Interchurch Steel Reports, as one of its tasks. News which requires so much trouble as that to obtain is beyond the resources of a daily press. . . .

If you study the way many a strike is reported in the press, you will find, very often, that the issues are rarely in the headlines, barely in the leading paragraphs, and sometimes not even mentioned anywhere. A labor dispute in another city has to be very important before the news account contains any definite information as to what is in dispute. The routine of the news works that way, with modifications it works that way in regard to political issues and international news as well. The news is an account of the overt phases that are interesting, and the pressure on the newspaper to adhere to this routine comes from many sides. It comes from the economy of noting only the stereotyped phase of a situation. It comes from the difficulty of finding journalists who can see what they have not learned to see. It comes from the almost unavoidable difficulty of finding sufficient space in which even the best journalist can make plausible an unconventional view. It comes from the economic necessity of interesting the reader quickly, and the economic risk involved in not interesting him at all, or of offending him by unexpected news insufficiently or clumsily described. All these difficulties combined make for uncertainty in the editor when there are dangerous issues at stake, and cause him naturally to prefer the indisputable fact and a treatment more readily adapted to the reader's interest. The indisputable fact and the easy interest, are the strike itself and the reader's inconvenience.

All the subtler and deeper truths are in the present organization of industry very unreliable truths. They involve judgments about standards of living, productivity, human rights that are endlessly debatable in the absence of exact record and quantitative analysis. And as long as these do not exist in industry, the run of news about it will tend, as Emerson said, quoting from Isocrates, "to make of moles mountains, and of mountains moles." [2] Where there is no constitutional procedure in industry, and no expert sifting of evidence and the claims, the fact that is sensational to the reader is the fact that almost every journalist will seek. Given the industrial relations that so largely prevail, even where there is conference or arbitration, but no independent filtering of the facts for decision, the issue for the newspaper public will tend not to be the issue for the industry. And so to try disputes by an appeal through the newspapers puts a burden upon newspapers and readers which they cannot and ought not to carry. As long as real law and order do not exist, the bulk of the news will, unless consciously and courageously corrected, work against those who have no lawful and orderly method of asserting themselves. The bulletins from the scene of action will note the trouble that arose from the assertion, rather than the reasons which led to it. The reasons are intangible. . . .

Every newspaper when it reaches the reader is the result of a whole series of selections as to what items shall be printed, in what position they shall be printed, how much space each shall occupy, what emphasis each shall have. There are no objective standards here. There are conventions. Take two newspapers published in the same city on the same morning. The headline of one reads: "Britain pledges aid to Berlin against French aggression; France openly backs Poles." The headline of the second is "Mrs. Stillman's Other Love." Which you prefer is a matter of taste, but not entirely a matter of the editor's taste. It is a matter of his judgment as to what will absorb the half hour's attention a certain set of readers will give to his newspaper. Now the problem of securing attention is by no means equivalent to displaying the news in the perspective laid down by religious teaching or by some form of ethical culture. It is a problem of provoking feeling in the reader, of inducing him to feel a sense of personal identification with the stories he is reading. . . . In order that he shall enter he must find a familiar foothold in the story, and this is supplied to him by the use of stereotypes. They tell him that if an association of plumbers is called a "combine" it is appropriate to develop his hostility; if it is called a "group of leading businessmen" the cue is for a favorable reaction.

It is in a combination of these elements that the power to create opinion resides. . . . This is the plight of the reader of the general news. If he is to read it at all he must be interested, that is to say, he must enter into the situation and care about the outcome. But if he does that he cannot rest in a negative, and unless independent means of checking the lead given him by his newspaper exists, the very fact that he is interested may make it difficult to arrive at that balance of opinions which may most nearly approximate the truth. The more passionately involved he becomes, the more he will tend to resent not only a different view, but a disturbing bit of news. That is why many a newspaper finds that, having honestly evoked the partisanship of its readers, it can not easily, supposing the editor believes the facts warrant it, change position. If a change is necessary, the transition has to be managed with the utmost skill and delicacy. Usually a newspaper will not attempt so hazardous a performance. It is easier and safer to have the news of that subject taper off and disappear, thus putting out the fire by starving it.

News, Truth, and a Conclusion

The hypothesis, which seems to be the most fertile, is that news and truth are not the same thing, and must be clearly distinguished.[3] The function of news is to signalize an event, the function of truth is to bring to light the hidden facts, to set them into relation with each other, and make a picture of reality on which men can act. Only at these points, where social conditions take recognizable and measurable shape, do the body of truth and the body of news coincide. That is a comparatively small part of the whole field of human interest. In this sector, and only in this sector, the tests of the news are sufficiently exact to make the charges of perversion or suppression more than a partisan judgment. There is no defense, no extenuation, no excuse whatever, for stating six times that Lenin is dead, when the only information the paper possesses is a report that he is dead from a source repeatedly shown to be unreliable. The news, in that instance, is not "Lenin Dead" but "Helsingfors Says Lenin is Dead." And a newspaper can be asked to take the responsibility of not making Lenin more dead than the source of the news is reliable; if there is one subject on which editors are most responsible it is in their judgment of the reliability of the source. But when it comes to dealing, for example, with stories of what the Russian people want, no such test exists.

The absence of these exact tests accounts, I think, for the character of the profession, as no other explanation does. There is a very small body of exact knowledge, which it requires no outstanding ability or training to deal with. The rest is in the journalist's own discretion. Once he departs from the region where it is definitely recorded at the County Clerk's office that John Smith has gone into bankruptcy, all fixed standards disappear. The story of why John Smith failed, his human frailties, the analysis of the economic conditions on which he was shipwrecked, all of this can be told in a hundred different ways. There is no discipline in applied psychology, as there is a discipline in medicine, engineering, or even law, which has authority to direct the journalist's mind when he passes from the news to the vague realm of truth. There are no canons to direct his own mind, and no canons that coerce the reader's judgment or the publisher's. His version of the truth is only his version. How can he demonstrate the truth as he sees it? He cannot demonstrate it, any more than Mr. Sinclair Lewis can demonstrate that he has told the whole truth about Main Street. And the more he understands his own weaknesses, the more ready he is to admit that where there is no objective test, his own opinion is in some vital measure constructed out of his own stereotypes, according to his own code, and by the urgency of his own interest. He knows that he is seeing the world through subjective lenses. He cannot deny that he too is, as Shelley remarked, a dome of many-colored glass which stains the white radiance of eternity.

And by this knowledge his assurance is tempered. He may have all kinds of moral courage, and sometimes has, but he lacks that sustaining conviction of a certain technic which finally freed the physical sciences from theological control. It was the gradual development of an irrefragable method that gave the physicist his intellectual freedom as against all the powers of the world. His proofs were so clear, his evidence so sharply superior to tradition, that he broke away finally from all control. But the journalist has no such support in his own conscience or in fact. The control exercised over him by the opinions of his employers and his readers, is not the control of truth by prejudice, but of one opinion by another opinion that is not demonstrably less true. . . .

. . . It is possible and necessary for journalists to bring home to people the uncertain character of the truth on which their opinions are rounded, and by criticism and agitation to prod social science into making more usable formulations of social facts, and to prod statesmen into establishing more visible institutions. The press, in other words, can fight for the extension of reportable truth. But as social truth is organized today, the press is not constituted to furnish from one edition to the next the amount of knowledge which the democratic theory of public opinion demands. This is not due to the Brass Check, as the quality of news in radical newspapers shows, but to the fact that the press deals with a society in which the governing forces are so imperfectly recorded. The theory that the press can itself record those forces is false. It can normally record only what has been recorded for it by the working of institutions. Everything else is argument and opinion, and fluctuates with the vicissitudes, the self-consciousness, and the courage of the human mind.

If the press is not so universally wicked, nor so deeply conspiring . . . it is very much more frail than the democratic theory has as yet admitted. It is too frail to carry the whole burden of popular sovereignty, to supply spontaneously the truth which democrats hoped was inborn. And when we expect it to supply such a body of truth we employ a misleading standard of judgment. We misunderstand the limited nature of news, the illimitable complexity of society; we overestimate our own endurance, public spirit, and all-round competence. We suppose an appetite for uninteresting truths which is not discovered by any honest analysis of our own tastes.

If the newspapers, then, are to be charged with the duty of translating the whole public life of mankind, so that every adult can arrive at an opinion on every moot topic, they fail, they are bound to fail, in any future one can conceive they will continue to fail. It is not possible to assume that a world, carried on by division of labor and distribution of authority, can be governed by universal opinions in the whole population. Unconsciously the theory sets up the single reader as theoretically omnicompetent, and puts upon the press the burden of accomplishing whatever representative government, industrial organization, and diplomacy have failed to accomplish. Acting upon everybody for thirty minutes in twenty-four hours, the press is asked to create a mystical force called Public Opinion that will take up the slack in public institutions. The press has often mistakenly pretended that it could do just that. It has at great moral cost to itself, encouraged a democracy, still bound to its original premises, to expect newspapers to supply spontaneously for every organ of government, for every social problem, the machinery of information which these do not normally supply themselves. Institutions, having failed to furnish themselves with instruments of knowledge, have become a bundle of "problems," which the population as a whole, reading the press as a whole, is supposed to solve.

The press, in other words, has come to be regarded as an organ of direct democracy, charged on a much wider scale, and from day to day, with the function often attributed to the initiative, referendum, and recall. The Court of Public Opinion, open day and night, is to lay down the law for everything all the time. It is not workable. And when you consider the nature of news, it is not even thinkable. For the news, as we have seen, is precise in proportion to the precision with which the event is recorded. Unless the event is capable of being named, measured, given shape, made specific, it either fails to take on the character of news, or it is subject to the accidents and prejudices of observation.

Therefore, on the whole, the quality of the news about modern society is an index of its social organization. The better the institutions, the more all interests concerned are formally represented, the more issues are disentangled, the more objective criteria are introduced, the more perfectly an affair can be presented as news. At its best the press is a servant and guardian of institutions; at its worst it is a means by which a few exploit social disorganization to their own ends. In the degree to which institutions fail to function, the unscrupulous journalist can fish in troubled waters, and the conscientious one must gamble with uncertainties.

The press is no substitute for institutions. It is like the beam of a searchlight that moves restlessly about, bringing one episode and then another out of darkness into vision. Men cannot do the work of the world by this light alone. They cannot govern society by episodes, incidents, and eruptions. It is only when they work by a steady light of their own, that the press, when it is turned upon them, reveals a situation intelligible enough for a popular decision. The trouble lies deeper than the press, and so does the remedy. It lies in social organization based on a system of analysis and record, and in all the corollaries of that principle; in the abandonment of the theory of the omnicompetent citizen, in the decentralization of decision, in the coordination of decision by comparable record and analysis. If at the centers of management there is a running audit, which makes work intelligible to those who do it, and those who superintend it, issues when they arise are not the mere collisions of the blind. Then, too, the news is uncovered for the press by a system of intelligence that is also a check upon the press.

That is the radical way. For the troubles of the press, like the troubles of representative government, be it territorial or functional, like the troubles of industry, be it capitalist, cooperative, or communist, go back to a common source: to the failure of self-governing people to transcend their casual experience and their prejudice, by inventing, creating, and organizing a machinery of knowledge. It is because they are compelled to act without a reliable picture of the world, that governments, schools, newspapers and churches make such small headway against the more obvious failings of democracy, against violent prejudice, apathy, preference for the curious trivial as against the dull important, and the hunger for sideshows and three legged calves. This is the primary defect of popular government, a defect inherent in its traditions, and all its other defects can, I believe, be traced to this one.

Notes

1. Think of what guess work went into the Reports of Unemployment in 1921.
2. From his essay entitled *Art and Criticism.* The quotation occurs in a passage cited on page 87 of Professor R. W. Brown's *The Writer's Art.*
3. When I wrote *Liberty and the News,* I did not understand this distinction clearly enough to state it, but *cf.* p. 89 ff.

5

THE REAL WAR WILL NEVER GET ON TELEVISION: AN ANALYSIS OF CASUALTY IMAGERY

Sean Aday

Editor's Note

The ideal of a free press that reports reality as journalists experience it is most difficult to achieve in times of war. Journalists must wrestle with patriotic desires to show their country at its best, with the difficulty of gaining access to war zones, and with the pressure to publicize their government's propaganda messages. If they gain access to the fields of battle, the gruesome situations that they witness may seem unsuitable for exposure to audiences unaccustomed to such carnage. Yet, if journalists sanitize the truth, do they serve the public well when the nation's future may hang in the balance? Sean Aday documents the dilemmas of wartime coverage that troubles journalists everywhere.

Sean Aday is assistant professor of media and public affairs at The George Washington University. His keen insights into the problems facing journalists spring from professional experiences as a journalist. He has reported for the *Kansas City Star,* the *Milwaukee Journal,* and the *Greenville News.* His academic research focuses on the mass media and public opinion. He has written numerous articles and book chapters for political science and communication journals.

In 1862, photographer Alexander Gardner visited the battlefield at Antietam and shot several dozen pictures for the New York gallery run by his employer, Mathew Brady. Most of the images he captured were landscapes and group portraits, reflecting the tastes of the limited but enthusiastic contemporary market for photographs, which had only begun to be in mass circulation for about two decades. About a third of his exposures, however, were of dead Confederate soldiers who had not yet been removed from the field.[1] At the time, Gardner had no reason to think these shots would be of any

Source: Sean Aday, "The Real War Will Never Get on Television: An Analysis of Casualty Imagery in American Television Coverage of the Iraq War," in *Media and Conflict in the Twenty-First Century,* ed. Philip Seib, New York: Palgrave Macmillan, 2005, 141–155. Copyright © 2005 by Palgrave Macmillan. Reproduced with permission of Palgrave Macmillan.

commercial interest; they were, after all, the first images of battlefield death scenes circulated in America. As it turned out, the pictures were a sensation, stimulating a highly profitable frenzy of interest in similar scenes from other battles. When Gardner went to Gettysburg a year later, having set off on his own business, three-quarters of his pictures were graphic depictions of the dead, albeit often rearranged into romanticized poses.[2]

Today, our historical memory of the gruesomeness (and romanticism) of the Civil War is illustrated by the pictures of dead soldiers taken by Gardner, Brady, and others. Several factors made it possible to capture these images, notably the wet plate processing method that made outdoor photography easier, and the proximity of many important battles like Antietam and Gettysburg to population centers and roads, especially in the north. Despite these factors, though, the rapid mobility of the armies and the still cumbersome technical requirements of the medium meant that only six battles yielded pictures of dead soldiers. In all, probably no more than 100 such photographs were taken during the entire war.

Yet the history of war photography in the Civil War offers several interesting points of departure for understanding the images transmitted through television coverage of the recent Iraq war. First, as in the 1860s, important technological advances in the visual medium, most notably mobile satellite video, allowed reporters to get closer to the fighting and, if they chose to, show the gory reality of modern warfare to their audiences back home. Second, changes in military policy allowed journalists to be embedded with military units and have even better battlefield access than their Civil War counterparts. Indeed, journalists covering the last several American military engagements before Iraq were intentionally kept from the front by the military. The question is whether American journalists chose to take advantage of these technological advances and increased battlefield access to show audiences not only the exciting whiz bang nature of American military power, but also the grim ramifications of its use.

This chapter begins to answer this question through a detailed and comprehensive content analysis of battle and casualty coverage of the Iraq war on CNN, Fox News Channel (FNC), and ABC.[3] At its most basic level, this study asks: given that broadcast news had the ability to generate a complete portrait of the war, did it do so? Or did it instead reduce the war to a video game and shield viewers from the dead and wounded? . . .

Visualizing War

For millennia, war has been depicted through imagery, be it on a canvas, a plate, or a broadcast signal. Before photography, these images were invariably captured after the fact (often years later) by artists who were nowhere near the action being depicted, and were heavily romanticized even when they were quite graphic.[4] . . . Importantly, the recording of these events has historically been done in a way that glorifies the protagonists (typically the victors, but more generally the countrymen of the artists or culturally similar participants). Hence, these images are more artful in every sense of the word than they are literal. One might even refer to them as propagandistic. At the least, they have often been driven by and reflected marketplace demands, be it from sponsors in the case of pre–twentieth-century painters or collectors and readers of illustrated weeklies in the case of Civil War era photography and woodcuts.[5]

In other words, the imagery of war and battle has historically been intended to do two things: rally the public consciousness around the righteousness of the conflict (even, and perhaps especially, as the event itself drifts back in time and memory), and please a commercial audience.

Critiques of contemporary war coverage in the American press, particularly in broadcast news, often make the same case against the media, with coverage of the 1991 Persian Gulf War being a prime example. In that conflict, the Pentagon enforced strict censorship of the press and instituted a system of pool reporting that virtually eliminated the potential for independent journalistic observers and allowed the military to exercise near total control of the portrait of the war fed to American audiences. Although media organizations and reporters complained about the restrictions, at the same time they dutifully saturated their coverage with Pentagon press briefings that included dramatic visuals of bombs mounted with cameras striking targets in Iraq, and effusive claims of technical wizardry and precision, many of which turned out to be gross exaggerations at best and outright falsehoods at worst.

The result was imagery that made the war look, to use a popular metaphor, like a video game.[6] Daniel Hallin wrote that coverage defined the Persian Gulf conflict as "patriotic celebration and technological triumph."[7] He also showed how coverage mirrored that during the early years of the Vietnam War in many ways, with the war seen as: (1) a national endeavor, complete with use of the first person plural, such as "our troops," a trait of some Iraq war coverage, too;[8] (2) an American tradition, signified by references to World War II and other iconic moments and images in American history; and (3) necessitating a win at all costs commitment.[9] Others showed how these tendencies were particularly pronounced at CNN, whose need to fill a 24-hour news cycle led them to be less analytical and more focused on event-driven, flashy imagery than the network newscast.[10]

In addition to a focus on the alleged technical perfection of the American war effort and the Pentagon-produced images purporting to demonstrate it, a key component of the media's sanitization (and indeed romanticization) of the Persian Gulf War was their near total lack of casualty visuals. Hallin's analysis showed that American audiences were shown an essentially "clean" war,[11] despite the loss of an estimated 100,000 Iraqi soldiers and perhaps the same number of civilians (not to mention more than 100 American troops)." Although much of the explanation for the lack of casualty visuals can be explained by the fact that reporters were kept from the front lines and Baghdad where casualties would occur, others have pointed out that press norms and even ideology were also at play. . . .

That the press largely followed the lead of official Washington in the Persian Gulf War is in many ways to be expected. Between Vietnam and the recent Iraq war, the main finding of scholars looking at war and foreign policy coverage is that the news tends to privilege official sources, especially those from the White House. Most notably, Bennett has shown that news coverage of war and foreign policy is indexed to the limited range of elite opinions, at least in the short run.[12] Dickson, for example, found that government sources defined the range of debate in *New York Times* coverage of the U.S. invasion of Panama.[13] Entman and Page found similar results in coverage leading up to the beginning of the Persian Gulf War, showing that dissenters received less coverage than did officials who exercised some control over war policy, and that even when the press did air criticisms of the administration's policy, those critiques were procedural rather than fundamental in nature.[14]

Although Althaus[15] has recently questioned these assumptions by showing various ways in which dissenting opinions appeared in the press during the Persian Gulf War period, the prevailing finding of scholars to date is that officials exercise a great deal of control over the content and framing of international news, even in the contemporary era of technological advances in news gathering that might theoretically allow for more media independence.[16]

The tendency of modern war reportage, especially on television, to reflect establishment sentiment could be seen as extending to the hesitancy to show images of casualties. As mentioned above, broadcast coverage of the Persian Gulf War fit well with the administration's view that it was waging a moral and relatively painless war. . . .

At the same time, coverage of the Persian Gulf War in other countries, especially Arab ones, showed the gory results of American "smart" bombs, further suggesting that American coverage reflected the biases of its indigenous culture and official point of view in the same way foreign coverage did.[17] Although this chapter reports the results of the first thorough examination of the scale and nature of casualty imagery in American broadcast coverage of the Iraq war, an earlier study looking just at the nightly news across five U.S. networks and two Arabian-based news channels (Al Jazeera and Egypt's Esc-1) also found cultural differences in the overall tone of coverage and in the depiction of casualties.[18] In addition, an exhaustive analysis of British Broadcasting Company coverage of the Iraq war by Cardiff University found casualty coverage largely absent.[19] In that case, researchers noted that British

laws forbidding the airing of graphic imagery prevented the press from showing them, but they expressed apprehension that the resulting bloodless war
shown on television might inure citizens from the grave consequences of military action.

The Iraq War

American broadcast reporters often candidly admit that the norms of their
medium prevent them from showing the same shots of bodily carnage aired
in other parts of the world. Discussing his time covering the recent Iraq war
as a reporter embedded with the Second Light Armored Recognizance Bat-
talion, CBS's John Roberts said bluntly, "In terms of what kind of images we
could air, there are certain pictures that you just can't show on television. *We
saw plenty of those*, so you had to sanitize your coverage to some degree."[20]

Other reporters embedded in Iraq pointed out that most of the casualties
were inflicted at long range, limiting their ability to capture them on film. But
they also implied that even if they did shoot the gore, their superiors at the
network back in America often edited the images out of the final story. . . .

Yet especially since the terrorist attacks on September 11, many, including
several prominent journalists, have argued that to show casualties, especially
civilians, is unpatriotic. Indeed, everything from whether anchors should
wear patriotic lapel pins to how much a network should show civilian casualties has been at issue,[21] with some suggesting that there is no place for de-
tachment in wartime.[22] As FNC lead anchor Brit Hume said in defending his
network's reluctance to show images of civilian casualties during the U.S.–
Afghanistan war in 2001–02: "Look, neutrality as a general principle is an
appropriate concept for journalists who are covering institutions of some
comparable quality. This is a conflict between the United States and murder-
ing barbarians."[23]

This raises the question of what effect showing, or ignoring, casualty imagery might have on shaping public opinion about a given war. Several scholars have explored the role of media coverage in general on generating support
or opposition to war. But while these studies might reference trends in casualty coverage as an explanation for their findings, they do not parse its specific
effects or can only infer them imprecisely from time series analyses.[24] . . .

If the central critique of recent war coverage has been that it sanitized conflicts and reduced them visually and emotionally to the level of a video game,
the war in Iraq offered the press an opportunity to provide a more comprehensive portrait of battle. The Pentagon's policy of embedding reporters with
military units gave the media access to the front lines they hadn't had during
an American war since Vietnam. Granted, the killing still occurred at long
range, but the human aftereffects of that combat were seen in the hours and
days that followed as forces moved past the remnants of vanquished Iraqi

units and toward Baghdad. First-person accounts of embedded reporters after the war describing the carnage they saw make this clear. Second, unlike in the Persian Gulf War, all American networks had correspondents based in Baghdad, where much of the civilian casualties were inflicted. Finally, advances in technology theoretically made it possible for reporters to show viewers exactly what they saw, even live. If a legitimate defense of the press coverage of the first Gulf War was that they were preventing from seeing, much less airing images of casualties, the war in Iraq rendered that excuse moot.

Conclusions

Following the Persian Gulf War, the press came under considerable attack both from outside and inside its ranks for presenting a sanitized version of events to American audiences. Many, again outside and inside the media, blamed the Pentagon for its heavy-handed policy of precensorship, the implication being that freed from their kennels the press would be aggressive and reliable watchdogs.

In 2003, the Pentagon loosened censorship restrictions and embedded reporters with coalition units at the front lines of the Iraq war. Yet the resulting imagery broadcast by American networks did not differ discernibly from those 12 years earlier. Television transformed a war with hundreds of coalition and tens of thousands of Iraqi civilian and military casualties into something closer to a defense contractor's training video: a lot of action, but no consequences, as if shells simply disappeared into the air and an invisible enemy magically ceased to exist.

That those shells end up tearing apart people is clear to anyone who gives it some thought, and certainly to the soldiers embroiled in the fighting. But more to the point, it is obvious to the reporters covering the war because they see it right in front of them. As CBS's John Roberts described of his experience embedded in Iraq:

> It was pretty horrible to see all those guys lying around. There was this one guy whose feet were facing me; he's lying out of the back, his feet were facing me, he was sort of spread-eagled on the ground. As I walked up, his body was in perfect shape, but when I got right up on top of him, his head was missing, like it had been removed. Then there was another guy whose head was blown into three pieces and part of his body had been ripped off by a shell.[25]

Reading the accounts of reporters in Iraq, this was not an uncommon sight. And yet, as this study shows, they rarely turned on their camera and showed even a relatively less gruesome angle to their audiences. The proportion of firefight to casualty images was overwhelmingly in favor of the former, and the dead were rarely shown at all, even by reporters embedded on the front lines who saw hundreds if not thousands of corpses. As Walt Whitman wrote of the Civil War, "The real war will never get in the books."

Indeed, a great irony can be found in comparing the defining images from the Persian Gulf and Iraq wars—the smart bomb hitting its target in the former and artillery firing in the latter: the dominant image of war actually became *more* distanced in Iraq as reporters got closer to the front.

Critics of past war coverage, especially in the Gulf War, worry that such a sanitized portrait dehumanizes an enemy and its citizenry, helps perpetuate (or, if one is so inclined, manufacture) consent for war and any policies an administration might try and link to it, and risks numbing the moral revulsion that leads societies to see war as a last resort. When Roberts saw the broken bodies of the Iraqi soldiers described above, his reaction was compassion: "I said to myself, 'Gosh, this is tragic. These poor people,' regardless of the fact that they're enemy soldiers. You have to have some sort of human pity for them."[26] Pity does not, of course, have to lead journalists to stop doing their job objectively, or even to change their personal opinion on the validity of the war. As Savidge commented:

> You have to realize that people die in war. I'm not saying all wars are bad. I am saying all wars are awful. There is no such thing as a pleasant war. I've been in enough of them to know that. War can be justified. There could be reasons why, as a last resort, you go to war. You must know that once it starts, it's a horrible, terrible thing. People die gruesome, terrible deaths. But in America we'll edit that down. Especially anything that deals with U.S. service personnel.[27]

What is remarkable given the data presented in this study is that war correspondents think this way precisely *because* they have seen the gruesome reality of war, and yet they, or at least their network superiors (themselves often veteran reporters), insist on shielding audiences from that same knowledge.

Reporters—and policymakers—have typically justified this self-censorship by arguing that viewers would be repelled by a more accurate portrait of war. Presumably, the fear here is at one level a commercial one: they might lose their audience to a network presenting a more upbeat story. And indeed, there is research suggesting that they may be right.[28] There is also the perception that such imagery might damage public support for a just war, that Americans don't have the stomach for casualties. Although these are considered part of conventional wisdom, in fact they are testable hypotheses that scholars should spend more time exploring.

Also worth investigating further is the role of new technologies in press–government relations. Livingston and Bennett have shown that contrary to what one might expect, the dominance of news norms privileging official sources overwhelms the potential of these new technologies to create a more independent press in international coverage.[29] Cameras may be mobile, but the news it seems is still tethered to bureaucrats and policymakers.

Finally, it is interesting to note that in the time since the birth of realistic visual media in the form of photography, American popular images of war have become less, not more, authentic. For all the posing and aesthetic manipulations of the dead in photographs of the Civil War, the fact remains that people were able to see contemporary pictures of the true cost of war. Historian John Keegan makes the point that the paradox of modern warfare is that as Western society has become more humane—mostly banning the death penalty, making remarkable advances in medicine and healing, and expressing great concern for the sick and dying—it has simultaneously become increasingly innovative in devising weaponry that destroys human beings in progressively more creative ways.[30] He might have added that this societal cognitive dissonance—or hypocrisy, in his words—is amplified through the images of war we see on television.

Notes

1. Granted, the audiences for their work were northerners and all the dead pictured were Confederates. But this was due to the requisite delays in reaching the battlefield and setting up the camera. By the time that had happened, Union soldiers had already buried their own dead (always the priority) and the only bodies left on the field were those of the enemy.
2. Earl Hess, "A Terrible Fascination: The Portrayal of Combat in the Civil War Media" in P. A. Cimbala and R. M. Miller, eds., *An Uncommon Time: The Civil War and the Northern Home Front* (New York: Fordham, 2002), pp. 1–26.
3. Only network news on ABC was analyzed, not news on its local affiliate. "Network" news included Good Morning America, World News Tonight, and, when it occurred, national break-ins and extended coverage at other times of day that fell during our sample period.
4. H. Bruce Franklin, "From Realism to Virtual Reality: Images of America's Wars," in L. Rabinovitz and S. Jeffords, eds., *Seeing Through the Media: The Persian Gulf War* (New Brunswick, NJ: Rutgers, 1991), pp. 25–44; Francis Haskell, *History and Its Images: Art and the Interpretation of the Past* (New Haven: Yale, 1993).
5. Haskell, *History and Its Images*; Hess, "A Terrible Fascination."
6. Franklin, "From Realism to Virtual Reality"; G. Cheney, "We're Talking War: Symbols, Strategies, and Images," in Bradley S. Greenberg and Walter Gantz, eds., *Desert Storm and the Mass Media* (Cresskill, NJ: Hampton Press, 1993), pp. 61–73.
7. Daniel C. Hallin, "Images of the Vietnam and the Persian Gulf Wars in U.S. Television," in L. Rabinovitz and S. Jeffords, eds., *Seeing Through the Media: The Persian Gulf War* (New Brunswick, NJ: Rutgers, 1991).

8. Sean Aday, Steve Livingston, and Maeve Hebert, "Embedding the Truth: A Cross-Cultural Analysis of Objectivity and Television Coverage of the Iraq War." Paper presented at the annual meeting of the International Communication Association in New Orleans (May 29, 2004).

9. Hallin, "Images," pp. 53–54.

10. R. H. Wicks and D. C. Walker, "Differences Between CNN and the Broadcast Networks in Live War Coverage," in Bradley S. Greenberg and Walter Gantz, eds., *Desert Storm and the Mass Media* (Cresskill, NJ: Hampton Press, 1993), pp. 99–112.

11. Hallin, "Images," p. 55.

12. W. Lance Bennett, "The News About Foreign Policy," in W. L. Bennett and D. L. Paletz, eds., *Taken by Storm: The Media, Public Opinion, and U.S. Foreign Policy in the Gulf War* (Chicago: The University of Chicago Press, 1994), pp. 12–42.

13. Sandra H. Dickson, "Understanding Media Bias: The Press and the U.S. Invasion of Panama," *Journalism Quarterly*, Vol. 71, No. 4 (1995), pp. 809–819.

14. Robert M. Entman and Benjamin I. Page, "The News Before the Storm: The Iraq War Debate and the Limits to Media Independence," in W. L. Bennett and D. L. Paletz, eds., *Taken by Storm: The Media, Public Opinion, and U.S. Foreign Policy in the Gulf War* (Chicago: The University of Chicago Press, 1994), pp. 82–104.

15. Scott L. Althaus, "When News Norms Collide, Follow the Lead: New Evidence for Press Independence," *Political Communication*, Vol. 20, No. 4 (2003), pp. 381–414.

16. Steven Livingston and W. Lance Bennett, "Gatekeeping, Indexing, and Live-Event News: Is Technology Altering the Construction of News?" *Political Communication* (October–December, 2003), pp. 363–380.

17. David L. Swanson and Larry D. Smith, "War in the Global Village: A Seven-Country Comparison of Television News Coverage of the Beginning of the Gulf War," in R. E. Denton, Jr., ed., *The Media and the Persian Gulf War* (Westport, CT: Praeger, 1993).

18. Aday, Livingston, and Hebert, "Embedding the Truth."

19. Cardiff School of Journalism, Media and Cultural Studies, "The Role of Embedded Reporting During the 2003 Iraq War." Report commissioned by the British Broadcasting Company (2003).

20. Bill Katovsky and Timothy Carlson, *Embedded: The Media at War in Iraq* (Guilford, CT: The Lyons Press, 2003), p. 173 (emphasis added).

21. Bill Carter and Felicity Barringer, "At U.S. Request, Networks Agree to Edit Future bin Laden Tapes," *New York Times*, October 11, 2001; Paul Farhi, "For Broadcast Media, Patriotism Pays," *Washington Post* (March 28, 2003, p. C1); Howard Kurtz, "CNN Chief Orders 'Balance' in War News," *Washington Post* (October 31, 2001, p. C1).

22. Tim Graham, "No Honest Eyewitnesses: There's Little Truth Coming Out of Baghdad," *National Review Online* (April 4, 2003); Morton Kondracke, "Memo to U.S. Media: Stop Spreading Negativism Over War," *Roll Call* (November 8, 2001); Dorothy Rabinowitz, "Neutral in the Newsroom," *Opinionjournal.com* (November 6, 2001).

23. Jim Rutenberg and Bill Carter, "Network Coverage a Target of Fire from Conservatives," *New York Times* (November 7, 2001), p. B2.

24. John Mueller, *War, Presidents, and Public Opinion* (New York: John Wiley and Sons, 1973); M. B. Oliver, M. Mares, and J. Cantor, "New Viewing, Authoritarianism, and Attitudes Toward the Gulf War," in R. E. Denton, Jr., ed., *The Media and the Persian Gulf War* (Westport, CT: Praeger, 1993); Scott S. Gartner and Gary M. Segura, "War, Casualties, and Public Opinion," *Journal of Conflict Resolution,* Vol. 42, No. 3 (1998), pp. 278–300.
25. Katovsky and Carlson, *Embedded,* p. 173.
26. Ibid., p. 174.
27. Ibid., p. 277.
28. Oliver et al., *The Media and the Persian Gulf War.*
29. Livingston and Bennett, "Gatekeeping, Indexing, and Live-Event-News," pp. 363–380.
30. John Keegan, *The Face of Battle* (New York: Penguin Books, 1976).

6

NEWS COVERAGE OF ENVIRONMENTAL ISSUES

Linda L. Putnam

Editor's Note

News stories have a significant impact on the course of domestic and international conflicts. By focusing on specific aspects of the conflict, interpreting their overall political significance and projecting their likely consequences, the news media affect the flow of discussions among interested parties. Framing of conflicts reflects journalists' own initiative or the designs of various parties to the conflict whom the media serve as a willing or unintentional tool. Linda L. Putnam illustrates conflict framing with a brief report of her own investigation of a complex environmental dispute.* In the process, she outlines the various steps that systematic research into media effects requires and provides leads to important data resources.

Putnam is professor of speech communication at Texas A&M University and director of the Program on Conflict and Dispute Resolution in the Institute for Science, Technology, and Public Policy in the Bush School of Government and Public Service. She is coeditor of *The Handbook of Organizational Discourse* (2004), *The New Handbook of Organizational Communication* (2001) with Fredric M. Jablin, and *Communication and Negotiation* (1992) with Michael Roloff.

Mass media is a powerful institution in society. It is not simply a reflector or communication channel that plays back what it sees and hears. Rather the media makes the production of news its business. News production consists

---

*This study was supported by the Hewlett Foundation, The Interdisciplinary Research Initiatives Program—TAMU Office of the Vice President for Research, and the Institute for Science, Technology, and Public Policy in the Bush School of Government and Public Service.

of reporters and editors who gather and assemble the process, stockholders and financial investors who contribute funds to the business, the marketplace that generates competition in news industry, and readers who consume the news. All are part of the production process (Douglas, 1992). Various models of media production cast different roles for the media in the coverage of social conflict (Arno & Dissanayake, 1984; Bantz, 1985; Cohen, Adoni & Bantz, 1990; Davison, 1974; Douglas, 1992; Gilboa, 1998; Neuzil & Kovarik, 1996; Wolfsfeld, 1997). Several roles that emerge from the literature include: the media (1) as a powerful entity that tries to control the conflict; (2) as a biased participant who either defends or attacks the status quo; (3) as a third party "watchdog" who provides feedback to the public on local problems; (4) as a gatekeeper who sets agendas, filters issues, and accentuates other positions to maintain a balance of views; (5) as a mediator that builds consensus and manages community tensions; (6) as a corporate entity who celebrates conflicts and benefits through increased sales in covering conflicts. Thus, in its coverage of social conflict, the mass media serves a variety of roles, including, "interested bystander, advocate, legitimator, mediator, arbitrator, . . . truth-seeker, agenda-setter, watchdog, and guard dog" (Douglas, 1992). Although these roles differ depending on the type of dispute, nature and history of coverage, and audience/community of media coverage, what surfaces from this research is that the media is an active agent involved in the social construction of the public image of a conflict. The media frames the conflict, aids in identifying stakeholders and issues in a dispute, and shows how a conflict affects the status quo (Reese, Gandy & Grant, 2001).

Media framing has become a prominent area of mass media research in the past decade (Durham, 1998; Edelman, 1993; Entman, 1993; Iyengar & Simon, 1993; Norris, 1995; Pan & Kosicki, 1993; Price, Tewksbury & Powers, 1997; Scheufele, 1999; Semetko & Valkenburg, 2000; Valkenburg, Semetko & de Vreese, 1999). Although connected to agenda-setting research, framing analysis examines how people talk and think about issues in the news (Pan & Kosicki, 1993). Media framing is selecting aspects of perceived reality to highlight or promote particular definitions and interpretations of situations (Entman, 1993). Thus, frames help convey, interpret, and evaluate information. Considerable work has been done on framing effects, particularly their risk perceptions, opinions of political institutions, and attributions of responsibility (Semetko & Valkenburg, 2000).

Work on types of media frames is growing and considers conflict a generic category of media framing (Cappella & Jamieson, 1997; Patterson, 1993). This work has shown that complex political issues are often reduced to "overly simplistic conflicts" and that news of presidential campaigns are often framed in terms of conflict. Also, the more serious the newspaper, the more the media employs a conflict frame (Semetko & Valkenburg, 2000).

However, most of the work on media use of conflict frames centers on the frequency of this frame type or on its effects. Few studies focus on how the conflict framing occurs in the media and how media framing can be merged with conflict framing to understand how social conflicts are presented in the media. In particular, research is needed to uncover the role of media framing in addressing environmental conflicts.

In the environmental arena, the media has played a strong agenda-setting role through heightening the public's awareness of environmental issues such as waste and pollution (Ader, 1995); through serving as a guard dog of society's dominant institutions (Corbett, 1992); through highlighting the dangers and consequences of global warming (McComas & Shanahan, 1999); and through framing environmental issues for the public (Davis, 1995). Research reveals that the media uses a utilitarian frame to report environmental issues in rural areas and employs a stewardship frame to present stories in urban newspapers (Corbett, 1992). Since media coverage of environmental issues is more likely to be controlled by technical experts, the official coverage in some communities minimizes the consequences of conflict and relegates disputes to a small number of powerful elites. Newspaper coverage of toxic waste is more likely in communities with only a moderate level of economic reliance on manufacturing than in locales with high or low economic dependence on this industry, suggesting that information about health risks from contaminators is filtered and framed for local readers (Griffin & Dunwoody, 1995).

. . . [N]ews coverage of environmental issues differs depending on the economic base in communities—one that is closely tied with status quo institutions. Media framing of environmental issues, then, aims to enhance the legitimacy of status quo organizations through acknowledging problems, justifying them, and recognizing the institutional factors that contribute to them. It also accentuates the conflict through creating binary frames that depict oppositional tensions in a complex, multiparty dispute. The research questions that stem from this literature review include: How is the media likely to frame identity and characterization frames in this controversy? How will media cast or label the dispute? What role will news media play in this controversy?

The Edwards Aquifer Dispute

The environmental dispute selected for this study is the conflict over ground-water allocation in the Edwards Aquifer, located in the Texas Hill Country. The Edwards Aquifer is a unique underground limestone formation that stretches over 160 miles from south of Austin to west of San Antonio. The Aquifer is the sole source of drinking water for San Antonio; it provides irrigation for farming in six counties; it is the main water source for industry and recreational activities in three counties, and it is linked to five endangered species that live at its base—two types of salamanders, three types of fish. Since, in Texas, surface water belongs to the state and underground water is the property of landowners, the dispute about the Edwards Aquifer has been evolving for years, reaching its first big crescendo in 1990 with the dismantling of the Edwards Underground Water District and the ultimate rejection of the Regional Water Management Plan. This dispute evolved into multiple sanctions by state and federal agencies, four major court suits by the Sierra Club, and continued debates among stakeholders about private and public ownership as well as local and state rights (Foss, 1996; Wolff, 1997a, 1997b).

. . . [T]he primary issues in this dispute are fourfold: (1) the management of a scarce environmental resource limited by physical structure and used by many interdependent stakeholders; (2) the regulation of water allocation; (3) the effects of water shortage from excessive pumping on endangered species that live in the Aquifer and its associated springs; and (4) who should control this water resource and how should allocation and distribution be handled (Texas Water, 1993).

. . . This chapter explores the newspaper coverage of this dispute as it relates to conflict and media framing of stakeholders, labeling of the conflict, and depictions of the intractability of the dispute.

Data Collection and Analysis

Newspaper articles on the Edwards Aquifer conflict were located using the NEWSBANK database; press clippings provided through the Texas Natural Resource Conservation Commission (TNRCC); and contributions from stakeholders interviewed in this study. NEWSBANK is a commercial service that indexes newspaper articles in 150 newspapers from all 50 states. Articles were identified through an electronic data search from 1975–1999 using key words, such as "Edwards Aquifer" and "Texas and Aquifer." NEWS-BANK indexes only news articles and thus excludes letters to the editor, editorials, daily features, and other non-news items. Texas newspapers included in the NEWSBANK database were Houston Chronicle, the Dallas Morning News, Austin-American Statesman, the San Antonio Express News, and presses in local communities in the state. This search resulted in 122 articles, covering the period from 1988–1996. The second method of locating newspaper coverage was through the database of TNRCC. TNRCC maintained a comprehensive file of newspaper coverage of articles related to their mission, e.g., reports of natural resources such as air, water, and soil. TNRCC staff scan all major Texas newspapers on a daily basis and has access to local newspaper coverage. This database produced 58 articles, primarily published in 1996–1997.

In addition to this source of newspaper articles, the researchers have interviewed 70 stakeholders in this dispute, including environmentalists; farmers and ranchers; city and state officials; local, regional, and state agencies; media personnel; spokespersons from business and industry; and mediators in this dispute. These people have provided us with copies of news stories, editorials, and letters to the editor that their agencies have collected. An additional 385 articles were collected from local, county, and regional newspapers. Of these articles 149 were editorials and letters to the editor.

For this particular mini-study, only the articles that covered the events surrounding the demise of the Edwards Underground Water District [EUWD] were included in the sample. Most of these 35 articles were published between 1988 and 1991, and 23 of these articles were news clippings that included aspects of framing. Editorials were not included in this analysis. The next stage was to examine each article and extract sentences and/or paragraphs that referred to individuals or stakeholder groups, that is, references that one group made about other stakeholders, references that the media made about any regions or groups, and any sentences that revealed ways the controversy was named, claimed, and/or blamed in the coverage. This data analysis drew from research on language analysis. . . . In addition, the researchers examined statements that reflected the characteristics of intractable disputes through use of words that refer to: (1) non-acceptable agreements such as "non-negotiable demands," "stalemates," "talks have ceased;" (2) use of polarized language such as "versus," "we-them," "rivals," "pitted," (3) references to escalation, "feud," "fighting," "storm," "legal battle;" and (4) comments on the length of the controversy, "months of talks," "long-term efforts." . . . [D]ata analysis is qualitative and exploratory.

Identity and Characterization Frames

In 1987–88 prior to the withdrawal of the western counties from the EUWD, newspapers cast *identity frames* through the lens of *prevailing interests of constituent groups*. For example, "the irrigation farmers in Uvalde, Medina, and Bexar counties are opposed to giving up their traditional 'right of capture' under Texas law and all of the groundwater they can pump" (Krausse, 1988). For the farmers, identity was not occupation, or place, but one of holding to a belief in the sacred principle of "private property rights." San Antonio was cast as advocating pumping limitations as a strategy to gain leverage with voters for "an expensive and politically unpopular" reservoir construction program, and the major interests of Comal and Hays populations were the preservation of the springs and the recreational water parks that supported their growing tourism business (Krausse, 1988). Although these stakeholders were clearly linked to place or region in their identity, the media represented their involvement in this controversy as fundamentally interest-based. Interspersed with the interests of these stakeholders were the concerns of regional and state water agencies for impending droughts, dwindling water in the Aquifer, and the necessity to limit the pumping to a safe yield of 75 percent of the average annual recharge (Jensen, 1988).

These identity frames, however shifted as the controversy ensued. Newspaper articles began to cast the stakeholders into both *place and institutional identity* frames. Stakeholders were no longer referred to by names of counties or occupations, but by locations of western rural and eastern urban counties. Identity frames based on *place* reflected both the polarization of the conflict and the transformation of interests to location. "Efforts to control future aquifer use have split South-Central Texas users along urban and rural lines" (Gillman, 1989). One article, citing the Southwest Property Rights Association in Medina claimed that the Regional Water Management Plan favored the more populated eastern counties over the interests of rural users in the west (Collier, 1988). Or in another article, Senator Bill Sims of San Angelo asserted, "Urban areas have a greater need for the drought management plan than do rural communities" (Michaels & Lewis, 1989). Even though the farmers and irrigators took the lead in labeling their identities as rural, newspaper articles projected the conflict in these terms, "A regional committee of the EUWD rejected a proposed compromise between warring urban and rural factions on future use of the Edwards Aquifer" (Wood, 1988).

Another form of identity began to surface immediately following the withdrawal of the western counties from the EUWD. Identity became linked to institutions, particular ones that could develop and implement rules for managing the Aquifer. The media depicted stakeholders as aligning with institutional allies, for example, the Guadalupe-Blanco River Authority who filed a lawsuit to declare the Edwards Aquifer an underground river subject to state regulation (Krausse, 1989), the federal government who threatened to intervene (Crimmins, 1990d), and the Sierra Club who threatened to file an endangered species suit (Sierra Club, 1990). New splits developed among old allies in which EUWD members challenged San Antonio for "downplaying the problem" to preserve tourism and attract corporations (Crimmins, 1990a). U.S. Fish and Wildlife Services announced that they might take control of the Aquifer if Comal Springs dried up. San Antonio declared that "they are not willing to restrict themselves if everyone else is pumping like crazy" (Gillman, 1990).

Thus, the media's casting of identity frames shifted again as the naming of the dispute evolved from a "fragile consensus" (Krausse, 1988), to a battle between rural and urban interests (Wood & Fuentes, 1990), and to a struggle for exerting control (Crimmins, 1990b). The media cast both sides as blaming each other for the stalemate while they simultaneously depicted the conflict with descriptors of words, like "a revolt" (Wood, 1988), "a fight" (Crimmins, 1990b), and eventually "a takeover" (Bower, 1991; Wood & Fuentes, 1990). The rural communities blamed the urbanites for poor planning and the urban constituents chided the rural counties for being demanding, unrealistic, and refusing to compromise (Gillman, 1990).

Intractability

Descriptors of intractability surfaced early in this controversy. Language patterns that depicted polarized conflict were evident in the way the media framed the identity of constituents as rural versus urban (Wood & Fuentes, 1990). Phrases such as, "warring urban and rural factions," "us against them," and "pitting" appeared in articles that discussed the pull out from the EUWD (Gillman, 1990). Conflict escalation was portrayed through phrases like, "fighting for water" (Michaels & Lewis, 1989; Wood & Fuentes, 1990), "storm brewing in the west" (Wood, 1988), "battle to regulate" (Bower, 1991), "Edwards comes under assault" (Bower, 1991), "latest shots in the regional water battle" (Wood & Fuentes, 1990), "feuding interests" (Crimmins, 1990c), "scuttled by intense fighting" (Michaels & Lewis, 1989), "face off," "raucous five hour hearing" (Bower, 1991), and "surrendering water rights" (Gillman, 1989).

Although these terms depicted a level of escalation that moved from "talking about compromise," to treating the controversy as a "battle" with "nuclear options" (Gillman, 1990) and "political bombshells" (Wood & Fuentes, 1990), the conflict escalation seemed secondary to the ways that the articles framed intractability. Particularly their focus on ultimatums issued by both sides and continual reports of "failed plans," "hitting dead ends" (Crimmins, 1990a), "another impasse," "stymied efforts" (Collier, 1990), . . . and "talks that cease" (Crimmins, 1990a), cast an image of the controversy as stalemated and hopeless. Quoting ultimatums such as Maurice Rimkus from Uvalde, "If you aren't going to fight for your water, then there ain't nothing worth fighting for" (Wood, 1988), "If it is a choice between our rights and the springs going down the tubes, let them go down the tubes" (Krause, 1988), "We'll [the Uvalde delegation] fight them all the way, even if we have to mortgage the family milk cow (Wood, 1988), "A lot of them [farmers] see it [the aquifer] the way they see gun control—you can have my water when you peel my cold, dead hand off my pump. It's that level of emotion," said Mr. Stagner, a San Antonio consultant (Gillman, 1990).

Moreover, although this particular event had ensued for only several years, newspaper articles depicted the conflict as "enduring" with such phrases as, "the last episode of a long-running dispute between rural and urban users" (Wood & Fuentes, 1990), "threats to sue are cries of blackmail in this long-running dispute" (Bower, 1991), and "months of talk" (Crimmins, 1990b). Thus, even before the Edwards dispute reached volatile levels, the controversy was framed as stalled and hopeless. These depictions of intractability appeared immediately after the EUWD vote on the Regional Water Management Plan and became descriptors of the conflict during the polarization stage. In the aftermath of the pull out, these descriptors set the stage for mediation and for the legal battles that followed from this event.

Media Roles in the Controversy

By relying exclusively on the content of the newspaper articles, it is difficult to determine what role the media plays in this controversy. However, an examination of the balance of coverage in these articles, partisanship of papers, and stance on issues in the articles suggests that the media did not function as a biased participant, nor a gatekeeper, consensus builder, or mediator. Overall, the media seems to assume the role of *tertius gaudens,* referring to the third party, outsider, who rejoices (Douglas, 1992). . . . The third party possesses autonomy and can, as a free agent, pursue its own narrow interests. The media needs societal conflict to function; and it profits from the continuation of conflict. To the extent that it acts in its own self-interest, and profits from it, it rejoices (Douglas, 1992). In this exploratory study, the media seems to function as a storyteller that cast the scene, characters, and motives of an evolving melodrama. Its story is a tale of intractability, one that may or may not characterize the incidents as they occurred in 1988. However, the tale itself has become legend, one that contemporary players often recite.

. . . In this particular event, the environmental issues in the conflict were the shortage and rationing of water, the drying up of the springs, the potential threat to endangered species, a plan to register and permit wells, and a goal of pumping to a safe yield of 75 percent of the annual recharge. These issues, however, while presented early in the framing of the controversy, became lost as the media focused on the conflict itself. Thus, one concern for environmental reporters and media coverage of conflict is how to frame a dispute as it evolves from one stage to the next. By centering on a play-by-play analysis of the controversy, media coverage may inadvertently contribute to escalating a conflict through casting the issues as intractable. What is important . . . is to see the media as a critical player in a complex, multifaceted dispute. Since the parties in this conflict are separated geographically and organizationally, media framing plays a very important role in documenting events, representing environmental concerns to the public, and forming images of the nature of a dispute.

References

Ader, C. (1995). A longitudinal study of agenda setting for the issue of environmental pollution. *Journalism & Mass Communication Quarterly, 72(2)*, 300–311.

Arno, A. & Dissanayke, W. (1984). *The news media in national and international conflict.* Boulder: Westview Publishers.

Bantz, C. R. (1985). News organizations: Conflict as a crafted cultural norm. *Communication, 8,* 225–244.

Bower, T. (1991, May 6). Aquifer 'river' ruling comes under assault; Lawmaker vows to thwart panel. *San Antonio Express-News*, pp. 1A, 4A.

Cappella, J. & Jamieson, K. (1997). *Spiral of cynicism*. New York: Oxford University Press.

Cohen, A. A., Adoni, H. & Bantz, C. R. (1990). *Social conflict and television news*. Newbury Park: Sage Publications.

Collier, B. (1988, November 2). Troubles for the Edwards regional management plan. *Houston Chronicle*, pp. C7–C8.

Collier, B. (1990, February 25). Edwards in for a dry spell. *Austin American-Statesman*, p. B7.

Corbett, J. B. (1992). Rural and urban newspaper coverage of wildlife: Conflict, community and bureaucracy. *Journalism Quarterly, 69(4)*, 929–937.

Crimmins, P. (1990a, June 23). Regional plan for aquifer at dead end. *The San Antonio Light*, p. A3.

Crimmins, P. (1990b, June 28). Federal officials to look into aquifer situation. *The San Antonio Light*, p. A4.

Crimmins, P. (1990c, July 7). Agreement surfacing on aquifer plan. *The San Antonio Light*, p. A6.

Crimmins, P. (1990d, July 10). Limitation plan for aquifer doesn't hold water with U.S. *The San Antonio Light*, p. A3.

Davis, J. J. (1995). The effects of message framing on response to environmental communications. *Journalism & Mass Communication Quarterly, 72(2)*, 285–299.

Davison, W. P. (1974). *Mass media and conflict resolution*. New York: Praeger.

Douglas, S. U. (1992). Negotiation audiences: The role of mass media. In L. L. Putnam & M. E. Roloff (Eds.). *Communication and negotiation* (pp. 250–272). Newbury Park, CA: Sage Publications.

Durham, F. D. (1998). News frames as social narratives: TWA Flight 800. *Journal of Communication, 48(4)*, 100–117.

Edelman, M. (1993). Contestable categories and public opinion. *Political Communication, 10*, 231–242.

Entman, R. (1993). Framing: Toward clarification of a fractured paradigm. *Journal of Communication, 43(4)*, 51–58.

Foss, M. G. (1996). "Whiskey is for drinking, water is for fighting over!" A case study analysis of the dispute concerning the Edwards Aquifer water supply. Unpublished manuscript, Texas A&M University.

Gilboa, E. (1998). Media diplomacy: Conceptual divergence and applications. *The Harvard International Journal of Press/Politics, 3*, 56–75.

Gillman, T. J. (1989, May 18). Compromise efforts for aquifer fail. *Dallas Morning News*, pp. A10, A11.

Gillman, T. J. (1990, August 19). Rural, urban interests collide over precious underground resource. *The Dallas Morning News*, p. B8.

Griffin, R. J. & Dunwoody, S. (1995). Impacts of information subsidies and community structure on local press coverage of environmental contamination. *Journalism & Mass Communication Quarterly, 72(2)*, 271–284.

Iyengar, S. & Simon, A. (1993). News coverage of the Gulf crisis and public opinion: A study of agenda-setting, priming, and framing. *Communication Research, 20*, 365–383.

Jensen, R. (1988). A new approach to regional water management; Two plans are developed to manage and protect the Edwards Aquifer. *Texas Water Resources, 14,* 1–6.

Krausse, H. (1988, July 24). San Antonio strengthens effort to protect aquifer. *Austin American-Statesman,* p. B3.

Krausse, H. (1989, June 3). Edwards Aquifer water level sinking to near-record low. *Austin American-Statesman,* p. A1.

McComas, K. & Shanahan, J. (1999). Telling stories about global climate change: Measuring the impact of narratives on issue cycles. *Communication Research, 26(1),* 30–57.

Michaels, J. & Lewis, J. (1989, May 28). Mayor fears worst, pushes for aquifer legislation. *The San Antonio Light,* p. A4.

Neuzil, M. & Kovarik, W. (1996). *Mass media and environmental conflict: America's green crusades.* Thousand Oaks: Sage.

Norris, P. (1995). The restless searchlight: Network news framing of the post-cold war world. *Political Communication, 12,* 357–370.

Pan, Z. & Kosicki, G. M. (1993). Framing analysis: An approach to news discourse. *Political Communication, 10,* 59–79.

Patterson, T. (1993). *Out of order.* New York: Knopf.

Price, V., Tewksbury, D. & Powers, E. (1997). Switching trains of thought: The impact of news frames on readers' cognitive responses. *Communication Research, 24,* 481–506.

Reese, S. D., Gandy, O. H. & Grant, A. E. (Eds.), (2001). *Framing public life: Perspectives on media and our understanding of the social world.* Hillsdale, NJ: Lawrence Erlbaum Associates, Inc.

Scheufele, D. A. (1999). Framing as a theory of media effects. *Journal of Communication, 49(1),* 103–122.

Semetko, H. A. & Valkenburg, P. M. (2000). Framing European politics: A content analysis of press and television news. *Journal of Communication, 50(2),* 93–109.

Sierra Club enters water dispute. (1990, April 18). *Houston Chronicle,* p. A4.

Texas Water Resources Institute. (1993). Legislature agrees on compromise to manage Edwards Aquifer. *Texas Water Resources, 19(3),* 1–13.

Valkenburg, P. M., Semetko, H. A. & de Vreese, C. (1999). The effect of news frames on readers' recall and thoughts. *Communication Research, 26,* 550–568.

Wolff, N. (1997a). Water Wars—I. *Mayor; An Inside View of San Antonio Politics, 1981–1995.* (pp. 65–77). San Antonio, TX: San Antonio Express-News.

Wolff. N. (1997b). Water Wars—II. *Mayor; An Inside View of San Antonio Politics.* (pp. 369–395). San Antonio, TX: San Antonio Express-News.

Wolfsfeld, G. (1997). *Media and political conflict: News from the Middle East.* Cambridge: Cambridge University Press.

Wood, J. (1988, November 15). Uvalde farmers to fight proposed legislation, *San Antonio Express-News,* p. A7.

Wood, J. & Fuentes, D. R. (1990, June 30). South Texans ready to fight for aquifer. *San Antonio Express-News,* pp. A3–A8.

Part II

SHAPING THE POLITICAL AGENDA AND PUBLIC OPINION

The pace of media effects research, which was throttled by the minimal effects findings of the 1960s, began to quicken in 1972 with the publication of a seminal article by Maxwell E. McCombs and Donald L. Shaw in *Public Opinion Quarterly*. The article examined agenda-setting—the ability of the media to focus public attention on a set of issues—rather than the ability of the media to generate specific opinions. The study sparked a spate of empirical research that demonstrates the media's power as transmitters of political information that shapes the political agenda and alerts the public to concerns.

Examples of this scholarship are presented in the comprehensive review of agenda-setting research by Everett M. Rogers and James W. Dearing that opens Part II. They report major agenda-setting effects in various political situations, such as elections, and policymaking for domestic and foreign affairs. Compared to issues that receive little media coverage, issues featured by the media are more likely to become important to the public and to the government officials who can take action.

In the second essay, Benjamin I. Page, Robert Y. Shapiro, and Glenn R. Dempsey discuss the important role played by the media in shaping public opinion about a broad array of public policies. They examine changes in policy preferences expressed in public opinion polls covering eighty issues over fifteen years. Their sample of polls demonstrates convincingly that the intervening television news stories affected policy preferences. Like other scholars, the authors point out that contextual factors determine the degree and direction of news impact. The Page-Shapiro-Dempsey study illustrates how a major research venture, simultaneously involving many different issues over an extended time, can bring results when other, less comprehensive studies fail to attain conclusive findings.

The next essay turns the focus to widespread misperceptions about important political situations. The causes are manifold, but often involve dissemination of false, slanted, or inadequate information by news media.

Large publics then judge policies based on flawed premises. Steven Kull, Clay Ramsay, and Evan Lewis used content analysis to track the sources of common misperceptions about the military threat posed by Iraq in 2003 and the reactions of world opinion to a preventive war. They found a direct link between use of particular news sources and the prevalence of inaccurate views concerning the need and support for war. Viewers of FOX News held the most misconceptions about Iraq war issues; listeners and viewers of public radio and television held the least. Would the United States have gone to war if more people had been free of the misconceptions that made war seem unavoidable? We will never know the answer to this haunting question.

Frank D. Gilliam Jr. and Shanto Iyengar also found a strong link between the thrust of news stories and the opinions and policy preferences of news audiences. But, in addition, they were able to demonstrate that the predispositions of audience members mattered a great deal. When the authors used experimental designs that allowed them to expose selected individuals to various versions of crime stories, they found that prior beliefs about demographic characteristics of frequent offenders came to the fore in interpreting and reacting to the seriousness of the crime threat. The research demonstrates that assessing audience predispositions is an essential part of media effects research. The essay is also notable for its step-by-step description of the design and execution of experimental research, which is an important addition to the media research tool kit.

The last two essays in this section raise questions about the sources of information on which average people draw when they construct the opinions that underlie their policy assessments. The conventional view has been that the regular print and electronic news media are the public's main information sources. That view produced a panic reaction among public opinion analysts when it became clear in recent decades that audiences for the conventional news media were in a steady decline. A dangerous lowering of the civic IQ seemed inevitable. That spirit of doom was relieved somewhat by the discovery that "infotainment" programming—also called "soft" news—that combines entertainment and information, and many outright entertainment offerings on television and radio, contained substantial amounts of "hard," serious, factual news.

Matthew A. Baum's painstaking research of what Americans learn about important political issues when the information is embedded in soft news shows that they learn quite a bit. This holds true for unlikely learners—people who lack an interest in politics—and for topics deemed unattractive to average Americans, namely foreign policies. The entertainment format's sugarcoating makes serious news palatable when it would be shunned otherwise.

Michael X. Delli Carpini and Bruce A. Williams's essay provides further support for Baum's findings. The authors liken television viewing to a conversation between each audience member and the message presenters on the screen. Audience members bring their individual packages of information to the encounter, eager to reach some kind of consensus. Their information packages are eclectic mixtures of past news messages, information nuggets gathered from entertainment shows, and wisdom captured during interpersonal conversations. Delli Carpini and Williams used a combination of experiments and focus group techniques to discover how citizens construct their opinions about environmental policies. They found that the essential elements were citizens' own experiences, as well as exchanges with fellow citizens and information drawn from entertainment and news media. Reliance on media information was universally important, even for people who are aware of their dependence on media information and actively try to resist it and form their opinions independently.

7

AGENDA-SETTING RESEARCH: WHERE HAS IT BEEN, WHERE IS IT GOING?

Everett M. Rogers and James W. Dearing

Editor's Note

In this selection, Everett M. Rogers and James W. Dearing explore research on media power in three different yet related realms. First, what have researchers learned about setting the media agenda? Who decides what is important enough for mass media to publish? Second, what influence do published media messages have on the public's agenda of perceptions and attitudes? And third, how does the public's agenda of policy concerns affect the issues public officials choose to address? In short, what can Agenda-setting research tell us about who sets the media agenda, the public agenda, and the policy agenda? The excerpts presented here concentrate on the conceptual schemes used for analyzing agenda-setting issues and on the main findings.

When this essay was written, Dearing was a doctoral student, and Rogers was the Walter H. Annenberg Professor of Communication at the Annenberg School for Communications at the University of Southern California, Los Angeles. A prolific writer on communication topics, such as the diffusion of innovations and organizational communication, Rogers was then collaborating with Dearing on a major study of agenda-setting.

Public sentiment is everything. With public sentiment, nothing can fail. Without it, nothing can succeed. Consequently, he who molds public sentiment goes deeper than he who enacts statutes and pronounces decisions.
U.S. President Abraham Lincoln, quoted in Rivers, 1970, p. 53

Appreciation for the power of public opinion and the influence wielded by the press has continued since Lincoln's comment. Such concerns address the processes of influence by which American democracy functions. As Lincoln's

Source: "Agenda-Setting Research: Where Has It Been, Where Is It Going?" in *Communication Yearbook 11*, ed. James A. Anderson, Newbury Park, Calif.: Sage, 1988, 555–594. Copyright © 1988 by Sage Publications, Inc. Reprinted by permission of Sage Publications, Inc.

comment shows, in the mid-1800s the earlier notion of classical democracy, whereby a government responds directly to the wishes of its public, with the mass media serving as a go-between, was being questioned. Later, political analysts like Key and Lippmann provided a new view of the democratic process: Elected political elites decide upon policies for the public, and the public can make itself heard through political parties, which serve to link policymakers with their constituents.

Many scholars now see omnipotent mass media systems as the mechanism linking the public with political policymakers. The media have usurped the linking function of political parties in the United States, creating what can now be thought of as a "media democracy" (Linsky, 1986). One method for understanding modern democracy is to concentrate upon mass media, public, and policy *agendas,* defined as issues or events that are viewed at a point in time as ranked in a hierarchy of importance. Agenda research, concerned with investigating and explaining societal influence, has two main research traditions that have often been referred to as (1) *agenda-setting,* a process through which the mass media communicate the relative importance of various issues and events to the public (an approach mainly pursued by mass communication researchers), and (2) *agenda-building,* a process through which the policy agendas of political elites are influenced by a variety of factors, including media agendas and public agendas. The agenda-setting tradition is concerned with how the media agenda influences the public agenda, while the agenda-building tradition studies how the public agenda and other factors, and occasionally the media agenda, influence the policy agenda.

An Overview

. . . [W]e prefer to utilize the terminology of *media agenda-setting, public agenda-setting,* and *policy agenda-setting.* We refer to the entire process that includes these three components as the *agenda-setting process* (Figure 7-1). We call the first research tradition *media* agenda-setting because its main dependent variable is the mass media news agenda. We call the second research tradition *public* agenda-setting because its main dependent variable is the content and order of topics in the public agenda. We call the third research tradition *policy* agenda-setting because the distinctive aspect of this tradition is its concern with policy as, in part, a response to both the media agenda and the public agenda. . . .

Media Agenda-Setting

The issue of the homogenization of the news into a set of topics addressed by all members of the news media was raised early by the Hutchins Report (Commission on Freedom of the Press, 1947). This set of topics was

Figure 7-1   Three Main Components of the Agenda-Setting Process:
              Media Agenda, Public Agenda, Policy Agenda

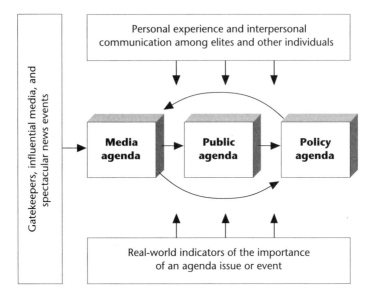

recognized as the media agenda. The question of who sets the media agenda and the implications of that influence for society were initially explored by Lazarsfeld and Merton (1948). Lazarsfeld and Merton conceived of the media issue agenda as a result of the influence that powerful groups, notably organized business, exerted as a subtle form of social control. "Big business finances the production and distribution of mass media. And, all intent aside, he who pays the piper generally calls the tune" (Lazarsfeld & Merton, 1948, reprinted in Schramm, 1975, p. 503). Similarly, Qualter (1985) argued that a commercially sponsored mass media system is operated by those in the ruling class of society; therefore, the media cannot be expected to question the socioeconomic structure of that society seriously. Ball-Rokeach (1985) suggested analyzing the structural dependency organizing the relationship between the political system and the media, which she describes as "cooperation based on mutuality of central dependencies" (pp. 491–492).

The mass media softly but firmly present the perspective of the ruling class to their audiences. The result is consent and support (Schudson, 1986). This result is not a conscious objective of the media. Qualter (1985) stated:

> The media are far from being the sinister manipulators of the popular mind suggested by some conspiracy theories. Their major functions seem to be to

support the system, to uphold conformity, to provide reassurance, and to protect the members of society from excessively disturbing, distracting, or dysfunctional information. (pp. x–xi)

These media functions are perpetuated through recruitment and the socialization of media elites, editors, and journalists. In this way, the traditions, practices, and values of media professionals shape the news agenda.

The Public Agenda

Understanding how public opinion is influenced by the content of the mass media has been an important concern of communication scholars tracing back to the writings of Robert E. Park, founder of the 1915–1935 Chicago School of Sociology (Rogers, 1986, pp. 76–80). Park, who has been termed "the first theorist of mass communication" (Frazier & Gaziano, 1979), expanded upon William James's (1896) notion of how people form an "acquaintance" with information by studying the role of newspapers in forming public opinion. Another seminal thinker on this relationship, and one more commonly credited, was Walter Lippmann, who wrote in response to Wallas's (1914) claim concerning the public's increasing dependence on the mass media. Early empirical research results, however, cast doubt on the mass media's power to bring about audience affects. Lazarsfeld and Stanton, in a series of studies on the effectiveness of radio campaigns, concluded that any effects of the mass media were considerably mediated by interpersonal relationships and by personal experience (Klapper, 1960). Social scientists interpreted Lazarsfeld's results as proof that the mass media had only weak effects.

Scholarly research on the agenda-setting process of the mass media stems most directly from the writings of Bernard Cohen (1963), who observed that the press

> may not be successful much of the time in telling people *what to think,* but it is stunningly successful in telling its readers *what to think about.* . . . The world will look different to different people, depending . . . on the map that is drawn for them by writers, editors, and publishers of the papers they read. (p. 13; emphasis added)

Cohen thus expressed the metaphor that stimulated both traditions of agenda-setting research described later in this chapter.

The Policy Agenda

Of direct importance to assumptions about democratic societies is the relationship of public opinion to policy elites' decisions and actions. Agenda-setting researchers who conceptualize policy information as a dependent variable want to know whether the agenda items that are salient to individuals in the public also become salient to policymakers. Occasionally, policy agenda-setting researchers investigate the extent to which the media agenda influences the policy agenda.

David Hume (1739/1896) was one of the first to propose a theory of government grounded upon, and responsible to, widespread opinion. Hume extended the work of John Locke, who had posited several laws of human nature. The contribution of Hume was his theoretical development of the democratic society, the idea that widespread, supportive opinion alone was the justification by which a government is in power.

Early assessments reflecting on Hume's principle were optimistic (Dewey, 1927). Gradually, however, such optimism was replaced by skepticism, as empirical researchers began looking for evidence of a responsive government. Gabriel Almond (1950) was one of the first scholars of politics to attempt to understand the growing body of survey data and the course of foreign policy. Almond's pioneering emphasis, however, did little to explain how a transfer of opinion from public to policymakers (if indeed there was a transfer) happened. An explanatory mechanism of a policy-to-public transfer suggested by Katz and Lazarsfeld (1955) was a "two-step flow" of communication, whereby opinions in a society are first circulated by the media and then passed on via opinion leaders by interpersonal communication. This concept was expanded to a "four-step flow" by James Rosenau (1961) in his book *Public Opinion and Foreign Policy*. Rosenau played an important role in orienting policy research toward issue salience and agenda-setting: "We know practically nothing about why it is that some situations abroad never become the subject of public discussion, whereas others take hold and soon acquire the status of national issues" (Rosenau, 1961, pp. 4–5). Rosenau served another important function for later policy agenda-setting research by concentrating on the mass media and their relationships with policymakers.

Cohen's reviews (1973/1983) of the evidence supporting the hypothesis that foreign policymakers are responsive to public opinion concluded, "Our knowledge is partial, unsystematic, disconnected and discontinuous" (p. 4). "We are left with the unsatisfactory conclusion that public opinion is important in the policy-making process, although we cannot say with confidence how, why or when" (p. 7). . . .

Why are scholars so fascinated by agenda-setting? The main reason for interest by mass communication scholars is because agenda-setting research appeared to offer an alternative approach to the scholarly search for direct media effects, which had seldom been found in early mass communication research. Many of the agenda-setting publications by mass communication researchers stated or implied their main justification as an attempt to overcome the limited-effects findings of past communication research. . . .

Analysis of the Public Agenda-Setting Literature

"The basic conception of agenda-setting was a theoretical idea without much basis in empirical research until the study by McCombs and Shaw (1972) of the media's role in the 1968 presidential campaign. A sample of 100 undecided voters, as "presumably those most open or susceptible to campaign information," were identified and personally interviewed during a three-week period in September–October 1968. These voters' public agenda of campaign issues was measured by aggregating their responses to a survey question: "What are you *most* concerned about these days? That is, regardless of what politicians say, what are the two or three *main* things that you think the government *should* concentrate on doing something about?" (p. 178n). The number of mentions of each of five main campaign issues was utilized to index the public agenda.

McCombs and Shaw concluded from their analyses that the mass media set the campaign agenda for the public, or in other words, that the media agenda influenced the public agenda. Presumably the public agenda was important in a presidential election because it would determine who one voted for, although McCombs and Shaw did not investigate this consequence of the public agenda. . . .

Distinguishing Issues from Events

What is an *agenda?* It is a list of issues and events that are viewed at a point in time as ranked in a hierarchy of importance. The items on agendas of past study included (1) such *issues* as the war in Vietnam, Watergate, an auto safety law, unemployment, abortion, and drug abuse and (2) such *events* as the Sahel drought, earthquakes, and other natural disasters.

What is an issue? As Lang and Lang (1981) noted: "Without a clear definition, the concept of agenda-setting becomes so all-embracing as to be rendered practically meaningless" (p. 450). A rather wide range of issues have been studied in past agenda-setting research, and little care has been given to defining exactly what an issue is. Most typically, however, public agenda-setting scholars (e.g., McCombs & Shaw, 1972) have investigated general issues like inflation and the war in Vietnam rather than specific news events or media events like a hurricane or a nuclear power plant disaster.

An important step toward pruning the conceptual thicket of what constitutes an agenda item was taken by Shaw (1977), who distinguished between (1) *events,* defined as discrete happenings that are limited by space and time, and (2) *issues,* defined as involving cumulative news coverage of a series of related events that fit together in a broad category. Thus the drug-related deaths of Len Bias and Don Rogers, two young athletes, in 1986 were news events that helped put the issue of drug abuse higher on the national agenda, even though such "real-world" indicators of the drug problem as the total number of drug users in the U.S. population had remained fairly constant for several years. Our perspective is that events are specific components of issues. Both have been investigated in public agenda-setting research (McCombs, 1976), although we conclude that issues have been more often studied than events. The distinction is often difficult to make due to the conceptual confusion in the past regarding just what an issue and an event are. Further, the mass media often fit a news event into a broad category of a larger issue, as they seek to give the event meaning for their audience. For example, a news event like the 1986 *Challenger* explosion was interpreted by the U.S. media into the more general issue of NASA incompetence and the need for higher funding for the U.S. space program (American Association for the Advancement of Science, 1986; Miller, 1987). Similarly, a news event like the 1986 Chernobyl nuclear power plant [explosion] was interpreted by the U.S. media into the issue of the closed nature of Soviet society (and, yet more broadly, into the issue of U.S./Soviet international conflict).

Is it necessary for an issue to involve contention? Political science scholars in the policy agenda-setting tradition generally think so. For example, Eyestone (1974) stated: "An issue arises when a public with a problem seeks or demands governmental action, and there is public disagreement over the best solution to the problem" (p. 3). Similarly, Cobb and Elder (1971) stated: "An issue is a conflict between two or more identifiable groups over procedural or substantive matters relating to the distribution of positions or resources" (p. 82).

Further scholarly effort should be given to classifying the issues and events that are studied in agenda-setting research. Certainly, a rapid-onset news event like the 1986 U.S. bombing of Libya is markedly different from a slow-onset natural disaster issue like the 1984 Ethiopian drought. A high-salience, short-duration issue like the 1985 TWA hijacking is different from such low-salience issues as the ups and downs of U.S. unemployment or from such long-duration issues as Japanese-U.S. trade conflict in that an agenda item (such as in the case of an election issue) may influence the agenda-setting process, as Auh (1977) demonstrated.

Finally, agenda-setting research should recognize more clearly that each agenda item influences other items on the media agenda and on the public agenda. Today's top news story crowds out yesterday's. The salience of an item on the agenda is "not just an absolute but to some extent a relative matter" (Lang & Lang, 1981, p. 453). Issues compete for attention. Unfortunately, agenda-setting researchers have tended to treat each issue on an agenda as if it were *not* dependent on the other items, which is a serious oversimplification. "Some issues . . . very rarely share space on the same agenda, while others quite regularly travel together" (Crenson, 1971, p. 163). One can appreciate the measurement and conceptual difficulties resulting from such interrelationships of agenda items.

Adding the Public Attitudes Link

Several studies raise the possibility that the mass media may be doing more than just setting the public agenda. Weaver, Graber, McCombs, and Eyal (1981), in a study of the 1976 presidential election, concluded that the mass media affected *voter evaluations*, as well as cognitive images of candidates. Davidson and Parker (1972) found a positive correlation between mass media exposure and public support for members of the U.S. Congress. Mazur (1981) found negative correlations between amount of mass media coverage and U.S. public support for fluoridation and for nuclear power:

> Detailed studies of a few technical controversies suggest that there is at least one simple effect of media coverage on attitudes which works in a reliable manner. When media coverage of a controversy increases, public opposition to the technology in question (as measured by opinion polls) increases; when media coverage wanes, public opposition falls off. (p. 109)

Can we then say that the mass media can change public attitudes, as well as public cognitions (like the public agenda)? Becker and McLeod (1976) proposed a model that suggested that public cognitions (the public agenda) could be a direct effect of the mass media agenda, or an indirect effect of mass media semantic content, mediated by public attitudes. Public attitudes, they suggested, could result either directly from mass media semantic content or indirectly from the media agenda, mediated by public cognitions.

A recent analysis of 12 field experiments on television news concluded that public judgments as well as cognitions may result from mass media agenda-setting. Iyengar and Kinder (1987) concluded that television coverage of U.S. presidential performance not only heightened viewer cognizance of the issues, but also set the standards (by highlighting some issues at the expense of others) by which presidential performance was then judged. The concept employed by Iyengar and Kinder (1987) to explain this power of the media is *priming,* defined by Fiske and Taylor (1984, p. 231) as the effects of prior context on the interpretation and retrieval of information. Iyengar and Kinder (1987) use the concept of priming to mean the changes in the standards that underlie the public's political evaluations. Iyengar and Kinder (1987) see priming as "a possibility at once more subtle and consequential than agenda-setting." They found considerable support for both public agenda-setting and priming hypotheses in their field experiments.

Priming, especially in its broader definition by Fiske and Taylor (1984), addresses the importance of both the mass media agenda and mass media semantic content in affecting public attitudes. If the mass media agenda "primes" readers and viewers by giving salience to certain events, these events are not merely made more salient to the audience. The mass media prime focuses on specific issues raised by a news event in the journalistic search for explanation. This selectivity forces these issues, not just the event, to the forefront of mass media coverage and of, perhaps, personal consideration. Moreover, these "event-issues" are prominently publicized by the media, not in an impartial way, but rather with positive or negative valences. Mass communicators may be "telling it like it is," but issues raised by the event retain their media intensity through positive or negative semantic content. An issue will not move through the priming sequence if it has not aroused public interest. As Downs (1972) observed, "A problem must be dramatic and exciting to maintain public interest because news is 'consumed' by much of the American public (and by publics everywhere) largely as a form of entertainment" (p. 42). Thus priming acts upon public attitude formation both through heavy media coverage (media agenda-setting), by showing people that the issue is important, and, in "successful" event-issues, by demonstrating a kind of entertainment value (semantic content).

Other Influences on the Public Agenda

The mass media are not the only influences on the public agenda, which is one reason the correlation of the mass media with the public's agenda of items is less than perfect. "Social processes other than mass communication also affect the public's judgment of an issue or person as important. For one thing, people talk to one another about social issues, and these conversations may play an important part in their judgments" (Wright, 1986, p. 155). In fact, McLeod, Becker, and Byrnes (1974) found that mass media content had a greater effect in forming the news agendas of individuals who participated in conversations about the topics on the media agenda, than for individuals who did not have such interpersonal communication. This finding is entirely consistent with the conclusions from research on the diffusion of innovations, where an individual's exposure to mass media channels often creates awareness of new ideas, but then interpersonal channels are necessary to persuade the individual to adopt the innovation.

Most scholars of agenda-setting seem to take a contingent view of the process: Agenda-setting does not cooperate *everywhere*, on *everyone*, and *always* (McCombs, 1976). Why might an individual's agenda *not* be influenced by the mass media agenda?

Low media credibility. A particular individual may regard the media in general, or the particular medium to which the individual is exposed, as low in *credibility* (defined as the degree to which a communication source or channel is perceived by an individual as trustworthy and competent). For instance, a Wall Street lawyer may regard the *National Enquirer* as less credible regarding international news than the *New York Times;* so when the lawyer reads a headline in the *Enquirer* about a new Soviet disarmament proposal, the medium's salience for this news item likely will not be accepted. The individual is informed about the news item by the media, but is not convinced that the item is important.

Conflicting evidence from personal experience or other communication channels about the salience of the issue or news event. Perhaps an individual hears the president of the United States pronounce in a televised address that America is experiencing a drug crisis, but this individual has recently heard CBS News's Dan Rather state that the number of U.S. drug users has remained constant for several years. Such conflicting statements in the media represent content about the drug issue, but are unlikely to raise that issue on the public agenda.

The individual holds different news values than those reflected by the mass medium or media. The individual's reaction to a newspaper headline might be to think, "How could they regard *that* as important news?"

An important step toward understanding why individuals have different issue agendas was taken by McCombs and Weaver (1973) by introducing the notion of a *need or orientation.* Any individual, when issue relevance is high and uncertainty is high, has a high need for orientation. This need leads to greater media exposure, which in turn leads to greater agenda-setting effects. Nevertheless, as McCombs and Weaver (1985) noted, "Such a limited three-part model is far from the full picture of the mass communication process" (p. 102). Future research should seek to understand more clearly the individual cognitive processes that are involved in the agenda-setting process at the individual level.

Assessing Causality

Agenda-setting research has generally found a positive association between the amount of mass media content devoted to an item and the development of a place on the public agenda for the item. The next step in establishing a causal relationship between the media agenda and the public agenda was to seek evidence for the expected time order; if the public agenda preceded media content, the latter could hardly cause the former. The expected time order of the two conceptual variables has been found in several post hoc studies. Funkhouser (1973a, 1973b) advanced the field of agenda-setting research by investigating a longer time period than in other studies; he utilized years as units of analysis for eight issues that emerged on the public agenda in the United States during the 1960s. The rank-order of these issues on the public agenda corresponded to their degree of mass media coverage. Such media coverage did not correspond to the "real-world" severity of the agenda item; for example, in the case of drug abuse, mass media coverage began its decline well before the social problem began to become less serious, as indicated by "objective" indicators obtained from extramedia sources. When the mass media coverage of the issue and the real-world severity of the agenda item differed, the public agenda followed the degree of media coverage more closely. Overall, Funkhouser's analysis supported the media agenda moving toward public agenda relationship, although this support was limited to the particular era and issues that he studied (MacKuen and Coombs, 1981, p. 24).

Real-world indicators are possible confounders of the media agenda moving toward public agenda relationships. A few studies support this view; for example, MacKuen and Coombs (1981) found a direct influence of real-world indicators on the public agenda, without this relationship going through the media agenda. In contrast, Funkhouser (1973) generally found strong associations between the media agenda and the public agenda, and weaker associations between real-world indicators and either the media agenda or the public agenda. Unfortunately, relatively few agenda-setting scholars have included real-world indicators in their analysis. . . .

In only a few agenda-setting investigations were the researchers able to control the independent variable of the media agenda as it influenced the public agenda (the dependent variable). An example is a field experiment conducted by Iyengar, Peters, and Kinder (1982), in which families were paid to watch only special television news programs created by the investigators. When national defense was stressed in the television news programs constructed by the investigators, this issue became more salient to the families in the field experiment. A similar agenda-setting "effect" was achieved for the topic of pollution in a second field experiment, and for inflation in a third. . . .

. . . [T]here is undoubtedly a two-way, mutually dependent relationship between the public agenda and the media agenda in the agenda-setting process. Media gatekeepers have a general idea of the news interests of their audience, and this perceived priority of news interests is directly reflected in the news values with which media personnel decide the media agenda. A few studies, for example, Erbring, Goldenberg, and Miller (1980), have found a two-way relationship between the media agenda and the public agenda. This influencing of the media agenda by the public agenda is a gradual, long-term process through which generalized news values are created. In contrast, the influence of the media agenda on the public agenda for a specific news item is a more direct, immediate cause-effect relationship, especially when the public lacks alternatives (such as personal experience) that might influence their agenda. However, for general agenda issues like inflation, Watergate, and unemployment, where their priority on the public agenda is built up in a slow, accretionary process over many months or years, the nature of the media agenda moving toward public agenda relationship may be very gradual and indirect. Certainly there must be differences from agenda item to agenda item as to how rapidly they climb the public agenda.

If our present reasoning is correct, it is inappropriate to expect a one-way causal relationship of the media agenda on the public agenda. . . . More realistically, both the media agenda and the public agenda are probably mutual causes of each other. . . . Since there is a great deal of variance in the agenda items studied, some items probably can be expected to demonstrate linear, rather than circular, causality. . . .

The relative influence of the mass media in setting the public agenda for an agenda item depends greatly on whether the event is (1) of major importance or not and (2) a rapid-onset type versus a gradual, slowly developing topic. In a major, quick-onset news event, the importance of the news event is immediately apparent. Almost at once the news event jumps to the top of the media agenda and remains there for some time. The public usually has no other communication channels (such as personal experience) through which to learn of these news events. So the mass media would be expected to place the news event high on the public agenda quickly.

In the case of a relatively slow-onset news issue like a drought, the media often play an important role in "creating" the issue. Typically, the mass media discover the slowly developing news event through a particularly spectacular message about it, which serves as a "triggering device" (Cobb & Elder, 1983, p. 85) in setting the media agenda. In the case of the Ethiopian drought, a film report of a refugee camp at Korem by Mohamed Amin was shown by the BBC and then by NBC in October 1984. Immediately, other U.S. mass media began to feature this disaster as a major news issue, and rather quickly the public considered the Ethiopia drought an important issue. Relief activities by the U.S. government and by rock musicians (who attracted massive financial support from the public) soon followed. In this case, the mass media helped to "create" the news event, set the public agenda, and facilitate amelioration of suffering in Ethiopia through fund raising.

Much public agenda-setting research, especially the studies reported in the 1970s, involved a rather narrow range of political issues. This primary emphasis on political issues is understandable, in the sense that a great many media news events *are* political in nature. But much other news content is not directly political in nature, and these news events should also be included in agenda-setting research, in order to determine the generalizability of public agenda-setting across various types of media content. . . .

For some agenda items, advertising must be very important. For example, the tremendous advertising campaigns for microcomputers in the 1980s by Apple, IBM, and other manufacturers certainly must have raised the American public's consciousness of computers. In recent years, microcomputers represented one of the most advertised products on U.S. television. Despite the obviously important role of advertising as an agenda-setter for certain issues, advertising's role in the agenda-setting process has received very little attention by communication scholars other than that given to political campaign spots. Exceptions are Sutherland and Galloway (1981) and Hauser (1986), who investigated how a consumer's agenda of products is affected by advertising.

In a sense, one of the strongest pieces of evidence of the media's agenda-setting influence may consist of the fact that issues and events that are completely ignored by the mass media do not register on the public agendas. As McCombs (1976) noted: "This basic, primitive notion of agenda-setting is a truism. If the media tell us nothing about a topic or event, then in most cases it simply will not exist on our personal agenda or in our life space" (p. 3). Unfortunately, it is extremely difficult or impossible for scholars to investigate such a "non–agenda-setting" process because of the problem of identifying news events or issues that are not reported by the mass media, which by definition cannot be measured by a content analysis of the media. . . . Perhaps public agenda-setting by the mass media only occurs in the case of transfixing issues and blockbuster events that receive very heavy media attention over an extended period of time. In any event, it is certainly dangerous to extrapolate intuitively from the present findings about agenda-setting for high-salience issues and events to those of much less salience. . . .

Critique of the Policy Agenda Literature

. . . Concomitant with interest in the public opinion–policy relationship has been interest in the influence that the mass media agenda has on U.S. foreign policy. As Cohen (1965) stated:

> The press functions in the political process like the bloodstream in the human body, enabling the [foreign policy] process that we are familiar with today to continue on, by linking up all the widely-scattered parts, putting them in touch with one another, and supplying them with political and intellectual nourishment. (p. 196)

In recent years, scholars often incorporate the media agenda, along with other variables, in research on policy agenda-setting. For example, Lang and Lang (1983, pp. 58–59) found that Watergate was an issue that required months of news coverage before it got onto the public agenda. Then, finally,

Watergate became an agenda issue for action by U.S. governmental officials. In this particular case of policy agenda-setting, public agenda-setting by the mass media led to government action, and then policy formation.

Further exploitation of both the public opinion moving toward policy-maker and mass media moving toward policymaker relationships was advanced by Cohen (1963), who concentrated on the agendas of elites responsible for foreign policy. Yet public opinion as a meaningful determinant of elite agendas was not clearly established in the way that communication scholars were able to replicate the media agenda moving toward public agenda link (e.g., stricter federal laws regulating campaign financing). So there may be various longer-range consequences of the mass media agenda than just forming the public agenda. But the main point of the Lang and Lang analysis of the agenda-building process for Watergate is that the mass media were only one element, along with government and the public, involved in a process through which the elements reciprocally influenced each other. Such multiple agenda-setting for an issue, with complex feedback and two-way interaction of the main components in the agenda-setting process, probably occurs in many cases. The media's influence upon policymakers might be expected to be greater for quick-onset issues when the media have priority access to information; alternatively, when policy elites control the information sources, they might be expected to set the media agenda.

An example of policy agenda-setting research that illustrates the impact of policy elite agendas upon media agendas is Walker's (1977) study of setting the agenda in the U.S. Senate. He commented:

> Once a new problem begins to attract attention and is debated seriously by other senators, it takes on a heightened significance in the mass media, and its sponsors, beyond the satisfaction of advancing the public interest as they see it, also receive important political rewards that come from greatly increased national exposure. (p. 426)

. . . In a recent study of mass media impact upon federal policymaking, Linsky (1986) concluded that the media are far more important than had previously been suggested. Out of 500 former government officials surveyed and 20 federal policymakers interviewed, 96 said that the media had an impact on federal policy. A majority considered the impact to be substantial. Linsky (1986) concluded that the media can speed up the decision-making process by positive issue coverage, as well as slow down the process by negative coverage. . . .

We conclude our review of policy agenda-setting research with three generalizations: (1) The public agenda, once set by, or reflected by, the media agenda, influences the policy agenda of elite decision makers, and, in some cases, policy implementation; (2) the media agenda seems to have direct, sometimes strong, influence upon the policy agenda of elite decision makers, and, in some cases, policy implementation; and (3) for some issues, the policy agenda seems to have a direct, sometimes strong, influence upon the media agenda.

Discussion and Conclusions

. . . What are the main theoretical and methodological lessons learned from the past 15 years of research on the agenda-setting process?

1. The mass media influence the public agenda. This proposition, implied by the Cohen (1963) metaphor, has been generally supported by evidence from most public agenda-setting investigations, which cover a very wide range of agenda items, types of publics, and points in time.
2. An understanding of media agenda-setting is a necessary prerequisite to comprehending how the mass media agenda influences the public agenda.
3. The public agenda, once set by, or reflected by, the media agenda, influences the policy agenda of elite decision makers, and, in some cases, policy implementation.
4. The media agenda seems to have direct, sometimes strong, influence upon the policy agenda of elite decision makers, and, in some cases, policy implementation.
5. For some issues the policy agenda seems to have a direct, sometimes strong, influence upon the media agenda.
6. The methodological progression in agenda-setting research has been from one-shot, cross-sectional studies to more sophisticated research designs that allow more precise exploration of agenda-setting as a process.
7. A general trend in agenda-setting studies across the more than 15 years of their history is toward disaggregation of the units of analysis, so as to allow (1) a wider range of research approaches to be utilized and (2) a more precise understanding of the process of agenda-setting.
8. Scholars in the two main research traditions on the agenda-setting process, especially those studying public agenda-setting, need to become more fully aware of each others' research and theory, so that agenda-setting research can become more of an integrated whole (our analysis of the citations by the two research traditions shows there is little intellectual interchange in this direction). . . .

As pointed out elsewhere in this chapter, initial interest in research on the public agenda-setting process was stimulated by scholars who were questioning the limited direct effects of the mass media, and who thus searched for indirect effects. This expectation now seems to have been fulfilled: The media do indeed have important indirect effects in setting the public agenda. But how could the mass media have relatively few direct effects, and at the same time have strong indirect effects in setting the public's agenda? McQuail and Windahl (1981) stated:

> This hypothesis [agenda-setting] would seem to have escaped the doubts which early empirical research cast on almost any notion of powerful mass media effects, mainly because it deals primarily with learning and not with attitude change or directly with opinion change. (p. 62)

In other words, individuals learn information from the mass media about which agenda items are more important than others; this task is accomplished by the mass media, even though research shows these media are much less capable of directly changing attitudes and opinions. These general research results from agenda-setting research make sense in an intuitive way. Therefore, the theory of McCombs and Shaw (1972) that proposes the media agenda would influence the public agenda, drawn from the Cohen (1963) metaphor, has been largely supported by some 102 studies in the public agenda-setting tradition.

Here we see the main intellectual significance of agenda-setting research. No scholarly issue has been so important to the field of mass communications research as that of the research for media effects. The actual issue driving the mass communication field for the past 30 years or so has been this one: Why can't we find evidence for mass media effects? Agenda-setting research is viewed as important by many mass communication scholars because it has established that the media *do* have an indirect effect, public agenda-setting. This conclusion contains the germ of a lead for future research: Mass communication scholars should investigate indirect media effects on individual knowledge, rather than direct media effects on attitude and behavior change. Obviously, there are many other potential types of indirect media effects on knowledge than just agenda-setting. . . .

References

Almond, G. A. (1950). *The American people and foreign policy.* New York: Harcourt Brace.

American Association for the Advancement of Science. (1986). *Media coverage of the shuttle disaster: A critical look.* Washington, DC.

Auh, T. S. (1977). *Issue conflict and mass media agenda-setting.* Unpublished doctoral dissertation, Indiana University, Bloomington.

Ball-Rokeach, S. J. (1985). The origins of individual media-system dependency: A sociological framework. *Communication Research, 12,* 485–510.

Becker, L. B., & McLeod, J. M. (1976). Political consequences of agenda-setting. *Mass Communication Research, 3,* 8–15.

Cobb, R. W., & Elder, C. D. (1971). The politics of agenda-building: An alternative perspective for modern democratic theory. *Journal of Politics, 33,* 892–915.

Cobb, R. W., & Elder, C. D. (1983). *Participation in American politics: The dynamics of agenda-building* (2nd ed.). Baltimore: Johns Hopkins University Press.

Cohen, B. C. (1963). *The press and foreign policy.* Princeton, NJ: Princeton University Press.

Cohen, B. C. (1965). *Foreign policy in American government.* Boston: Little, Brown.

Cohen, B. C. (1983). *The public's impact on foreign policy.* Lanham, MD: University Press of America. (Original work published 1973).

Commission on Freedom of the Press. (1947). *A free and responsible press.* Chicago: University of Chicago Press.

Crenson, M. A. (1971). *The un-politics of air pollution: A study of non-decision making in two cities.* Baltimore: Johns Hopkins University Press.

Davidson, R., & Parker, G. (1972). Positive support for political institutions: The case of Congress. *Western Politics Quarterly, 25,* 600–612.

Dewey, J. (1927). *The public and its problems.* New York: Henry Holt.

Downs, A. (1972). Up and down with ecology: The issue-attention cycle. *Public Interest, 28,* 38–50.

Erbring, L., Goldenberg, E. N., & Miller, A. H. (1980). Front-page news and real-world cues: A new look at agenda-setting by the media. *American Journal of Political Science, 24,* 16–49.

Eyestone, R. (1974). *From social issues to public policy.* New York: John Wiley.

Fiske, S. T., & Taylor, S. E. (1984). *Social cognition.* Reading, MA: Addison-Wesley.

Frazier, P. J., & Gaziano, C. (1979). *Robert E. Park's theory of news, public opinion and social control.* Lexington, KY: Journalism Monographs.

Funkhouser, G. R. (1973a). The issues of the sixties: An exploratory study in the dynamics of public opinion. *Public Opinion Quarterly, 37,* 62–75.

Funkhouser, G. R. (1973b). Trends in media coverage of the issues of the sixties. *Journalism Quarterly, 50,* 533–538.

Hauser, J. R. (1986). Agendas and consumer choice. *Journal of Marketing Research, 23,* 199–212.

Hume, D. (1896). *A treatise of human nature.* Oxford: Clarendon. (Original work published in 1739).

Iyengar, S., & Kinder, D. R. (1987). *News that matters: Agenda-setting and priming in a television age.* Chicago: University of Chicago Press.

Iyengar, S., Peters, M. D., & Kinder, D. R. (1982). Experimental demonstrations of the "not-so-minimal" consequences of television news programs. *American Political Science Review, 76,* 848–858.

James, W. (1896). *The principles of psychology.* New York: Henry Holt.

Katz, E., & Lazarsfeld, P. F. (1955). *Personal influence.* New York: Free Press.

Klapper, J. T. (1960). *The effects of mass communication.* New York: Free Press.

Lang, G. E., & Lang, K. (1981). Watergate: An exploration of the agenda-building process. In G. C. Wilhoit & H. DeBock (Eds.), *Mass communication review yearbook 2* (pp. 447–468). Newbury Park, CA: Sage.

Lang, G. E., & Lang, K. (1983). *The battle for public opinion: The president, the press, and the polls during Watergate.* New York: Columbia University Press.

Lazarsfeld, P. F., & Merton, R. K. (1948). Mass communication, popular taste, and organized social action [Reprinted in W. Schramm (Ed.), *Mass communication* (2nd ed.)]. Urbana: University of Illinois Press.

Linsky, M. (1986). *Impact: How the press affects federal policymaking.* New York: W. W. Norton.

MacKuen, M. B., & Coombs, S. L. (1981). *More than news: Media power in public affairs.* Newbury Park, CA: Sage.

Mazur, A. (1981). Media coverage and public opinion on scientific controversies. *Journal of Communication, 31,* 106–115.

McCombs, M. E (1976). Agenda-setting research: A bibliographic essay. *Political Communication Review, 1,* 1–7.

McCombs, M. E. & Shaw, D. L. (1972). The agenda-setting function of mass media. *Public Opinion Quarterly, 36,* 176–184.

McCombs, M. E. & Weaver, D. H. (1973, May). *Voters' need for orientation and use of mass communication.* Paper presented at the annual meeting of the International Communication Association, Montreal.

McCombs, M. E., & Weaver, D. H. (1985). Toward a merger of gratifications and agenda-setting research. In K. E. Rosengren, L. A. Wenner, & P. Palmgreen (Eds.), *Media gratification research* (pp. 95–108). Newbury Park, CA: Sage.

McLeod, J. M., Becker, L. B., & Byrnes, J. E. (1974). Another look at the agenda setting function of the press. *Communication Research, 1,* 131–166.

McQuail, D., & Windahl, S. (1981). *Communication models for the study of mass communication.* New York: Longman.

Miller, J. D. (1987). *The impact of the Challenger accident on public attitudes toward the space program* (Report to the National Science Foundation). Northern Illinois University, Public Opinion Laboratory.

Qualter, T. H. (1985). *Opinion control in the democracies.* New York: St. Martin's.

Rivers, W. L. (1970). Appraising press coverage of politics. In R. W. Lee (Ed.), *Politics and the press.* Washington, DC: Acropolis.

Rogers, E. M. (1986). *Communication technology.* New York: Free Press.

Rosenau, J. N. (1961). *Public opinion and foreign policy.* New York: Random House.

Schudson, M. (1986). The menu of media research. In S. J. Ball-Rokeach & M. G. Cantor (Eds.), *Media audience and social structure* (pp. 43–48). Newbury Park, CA: Sage.

Shaw, E. F. (1977). The interpersonal agenda. In D. L. Shaw & M. E. McCombs (Eds.), *The emergence of American public issues: The agenda-setting function of the press* (pp. 69–87). St. Paul, MN: West.

Sutherland, H. & Galloway, J. (1981). Role of advertising: Persuasion or agenda setting. *Journalism Quarterly, 58,* 51–55.

Walker, J. L. (1977). Setting the agenda in the U.S. Senate: A theory of problem selection. *British Journal of Political Science, 7,* 433–445.

Wallas, G. (1914). *The great society.* New York: Macmillan.

Weaver, D., Graber, D. A., McCombs, M. E., & Eyal C. H. (1981). *Media agenda-setting in a presidential election: Issues, images, and interest.* New York: Praeger.

Wright, C. R. (1986). *Mass communication: A sociological perspective* (3rd ed.). New York: Random House.

8

WHAT MOVES PUBLIC OPINION?

Benjamin I. Page, Robert Y. Shapiro, and
Glenn R. Dempsey

Editor's Note

Benjamin I. Page, Robert Y. Shapiro, and Glenn R. Dempsey contend that shortcomings in research design explain why many studies of media impact on
public opinion do not detect substantial agenda-setting effects. The authors
note that most research designs focus on instant opinion formation about single events or classes of events, rather than on opinions produced over longer
periods of time by a multiplicity of media stimuli. Investigators seldom develop
baselines that would allow them to assess opinions prior to news exposure,
and they usually fail to analyze the appeal of stories and the sources who
transmit the news.

Choosing a more realistic design, the authors examine media impact on a
variety of opinions about public policy issues before and after audiences have
been exposed to a wide range of news stories. The findings reported in the
essay demonstrate clearly that television news affects citizens' opinions about
public policy issues. The influence varies, depending on the sources who advocate particular policies.

At the time of this writing Page was the Frank C. Erwin Jr., Centennial Professor
of Political Science at the University of Texas at Austin; he had written about
elections and about the presidency. Shapiro was assistant professor of political
science at Columbia University. His writings had focused on public opinion.
Dempsey was a graduate student in political science at the University of Chicago.

Rational Citizens and the Mass Media

. . . [N]ew information that modifies relevant beliefs can change the expected utility of policies for citizens. This should occur if five conditions are
met: if the information is (1) actually received, (2) understood, (3) clearly rel-

Source: Benjamin I. Page, Robert Y. Shapiro, and Glenn R. Dempsey, "What Moves Public Opinion?" in American Political Science Review, 81:1 (March 1987): 23–43. Reprinted by permission of
Cambridge University Press.

evant to evaluating policies, (4) discrepant with past beliefs, and (5) credible. (For related views of attitude change, see Jaccard 1981; Zaller 1985.)

When these conditions are met to a sufficient extent, new information should alter an individual's preferences and choices among policies. Further, if the conditions are met in the same way for many individuals, there may be a change in collective public opinion that shows up in opinion polls. For example, if many citizens' policy preferences depend critically on the same belief (e.g., "We must spend more on national defense because the Russians are overtaking us") and if highly credible, well publicized new information challenges that belief (e.g., U.S. military spending is reported to rise sharply and a CIA study concludes that Soviet spending has changed little since 1976), then enthusiasm for increased military spending may drop.

Since most people have little reason to invest time or effort learning the ins and outs of alternative policies (Downs 1957), we would not expect new information ordinarily to produce large or quick changes in public opinion. Indeed the evidence indicates that aggregate public opinion about policy is usually quite stable (Page and Shapiro 1982).

By the same token, however, for whatever they do learn about politics, most people must rely heavily upon the cheapest and most accessible sources: newspapers, radio, and television, especially network TV news. When news in the media reaches large audiences and meets our five conditions for many individuals, we would expect public opinion to change.

Television news often meets the exposure condition. Most U.S. families own television sets, and most tune in to network news broadcasts from time to time. Viewers may wander in and out; they may eat or talk or be distracted by children; but every day millions of U.S. citizens catch at least a glimpse of the major stories on TV news. Others see the same stories in newspaper headlines or get the gist of the news from family and friends. Over a period of weeks and months many bits and pieces of information accumulate.

The conditions of comprehension and relevance, too, are often met. The media work hard to ensure that their audiences can understand. They shorten, sharpen, and simplify stories, and present pictures with strong visual impact so that a reasonably alert grade-schooler can get the point. Often stories bear directly upon beliefs central to the evaluation of public policies.

Credibility is a more complicated matter. Rational citizens must sometimes delegate the analysis or evaluation of information to like-minded, trusted agents (Downs 1957, 203–34). The media report the policy-relevant statements and actions of a wide variety of actors, from popular presidents and respected commentators, to discredited politicians or self-serving interest groups. News from such different *sources* is likely to have quite a range of salience and credibility, and therefore quite a range of impact on the public (see Hovland and Weiss 1951–52). The analysis of effects on opinion should allow for such variation.

News may also vary greatly in the extent to which it is or is not discrepant with past beliefs. If it closely resembles what has been communicated for many months or years, if it simply reinforces prevalent beliefs and opinions, we would not expect it to produce change. If, on the other hand, credible new information calls into question key beliefs and opinions held by many people, we would expect changes in public opinion. The extent of discrepancy with past news and past opinions must be taken into account.

We are, of course, aware of the curious notion that the contents of the mass media have only minimal effects (Chaffee 1975; Klapper 1960; Kraus and Davis 1976; McGuire 1985; but cf. Graber 1984; Noelle-Neumann 1973, 1980, 1984; Wagner 1983). This notion seems to have persisted despite findings of agenda-setting effects upon perceptions of what are important problems (Cook, Tyler, Goetz, Gordon, Protess, Leff, and Molotch 1983; Erbring, Goldenberg, and Miller 1980; Funkhauser 1973; Iyengar, Peters, and Kinder 1982; McCombs and Shaw 1972; MacKuen 1981, 1984).

We believe that the minimal effects idea is not correct with respect to policy preferences, either. It has probably escaped refutation because of the failure of researchers to examine collective opinion over substantial periods of time in natural settings and to distinguish among news sources. One-shot quasi-experimental studies (e.g., of presidential debates) understandably fail to find large, quick effects. Cross-sectional studies seek contrasts between media attenders and media "nonattenders" that hardly exist: nearly everyone is exposed either directly or indirectly to what the media broadcast (see Page, Shapiro, and Dempsey 1985a, 2–4). A more appropriate research design yields different results.

Data and Methods

Taking advantage of a unique data set in our possession, we have carried out a quasi-experimental study that overcomes several of the limitations of previous research. The design involved collecting data from many pairs of identically repeated policy preference questions that were asked of national survey samples of U.S. citizens; coding TV news content from broadcasts aired in between (and just before) each pair of surveys; and predicting or explaining variations in the extent and direction of opinion change by variations in media content.

Our design facilitated causal inferences and permitted comparison across types of issues and historical periods. The use of natural settings meant that all real world processes could come into play, including major events and actions, the interpretation of news by commentators and others, and the dissemination of information through two-step or multiple-step flows and social networks (cf. Katz and Lazarsfeld 1965). The examination of moderately long time periods (several weeks or months) allowed enough time for these natural processes to work and for us to observe even slow cumulative opinion changes. In addition, our measurement scheme permitted us to distinguish among different sources of news and to take into account the extent of news story relevance to policy questions, the degree of discrepancy between current and previous media content, and the credibility of news sources.

As part of our ongoing research project on public opinion and democracy, we have assembled a comprehensive collection of survey data on U.S. citizens' policy preferences. It includes the marginal frequencies of responses to thousands of different policy questions asked by various survey organizations since 1935. Among these data we have identified several hundred questions that were asked two or more times with identical (verbatim) wordings, by the same survey organization. (For a partial description, see Page and Shapiro 1982, 1983a.)

For the present research we selected 80 pairs of policy questions from the last 15 years (for which TV news data are readily available) that were repeated within moderate time intervals averaging about three months.

These 80 cases are not, strictly speaking, a sample from the universe of policy issues or poll questions but (with a small number of exceptions) constitute either a random sample of the available eligible survey questions and time points for a given survey organization or *all* the available cases from an organization. They are very diverse, covering many different kinds of foreign and defense ($n = 32$) and domestic ($n = 48$) policies. In nearly half the cases public opinion changed significantly (p < .05; 6 percentage points or more), and in a little more than half, it did not—nearly the same proportion as in our full data set of several hundred repeated items. A list of cases and a more detailed methodological discussion is available in Page, Shapiro, and Dempsey (1985a, b).

The dependent variable for each case is simply the level of public opinion at the time of the second survey (T2), that is, the percentage of the survey sample, excluding "don't know" and "no opinion" responses, that endorsed the most prominent (generally the first) policy alternative mentioned in the survey question. As will be seen, our method of using T2 level of opinion as the dependent variable and including first survey (T1) opinion as a predictor yields nearly identical estimates of media effects as does using a difference score—the magnitude and direction of opinion *change*—as the dependent variable.

For each of the 80 cases, we and our research assistants coded the daily television network news from one randomly selected network (in a few low-salience cases, *all* networks) each day, using the summaries found in the *Television News Index and Abstracts* of the Vanderbilt Television News Archive. These summaries, while rather brief and not intended for such purposes, were generally satisfactory in providing the fairly straightforward information we sought, especially since they were aggregated over several weeks or months. We coded all news stories that were at least minimally relevant to the wording of each opinion item, beginning two months before the T1 survey—in order to allow for lagged effects and for discrepancies or changes in media content—and continuing with every day up to T1 and through to the date of the T2 survey.

Being interested in the effects of particular actors or *sources*—particular providers of information, or Downsian "agents" of analysis and evaluation—whose rhetoric and actions are reported in the media, we distinguished among the original sources found in each news story. We used 10 exhaustive and mutually exclusive categories: the president; fellow partisans and members of his administration; members of the opposing party; interest groups and individuals not fitting clearly into any of the other categories; experts; network commentators or reporters themselves; friendly (or neutral) foreign nations or individuals; unfriendly foreign states or individuals; courts and judges; and objective conditions or events without clearly identifiable human actors (e.g., unemployment statistics, natural disasters, unattributed terrorist acts).

Our independent variables characterize *reported statements or actions by a specified source*. Each such *source story*, or "message," constitutes a unit of analysis in measuring aggregate media content over the time interval of a particular case. For each reported statement or action by a particular source—each source story—we coded the following: 1) its degree of *relevance* to the policy question (indirectly relevant, relevant, or highly relevant); 2) its *salience* in the broadcast (its inclusion in the first story or not, its proximity to the beginning of the broadcast, its duration in seconds); 3) the pro-con *direction* of intended impact of the reported statement or action in relation to the most prominent policy alternative mentioned in the opinion item; 4) the president's popularity (measured by the standard Gallup question) as an indication of his *credibility* as news source at the time of his statement or action; and 5) some judgments—not used in this paper—concerning the quality of the information conveyed, including its logic, factuality, and degree of truth or falsehood.

The most important part of the coding effort concerned the directional thrust of reported statements and actions in relation to each opinion question. Proceeding a little differently from the method of our earlier work on newspapers (Page and Shapiro 1983b, 1984), we measured directional thrust in terms of the intentions or advocated positions of the speakers or actors themselves. We took considerable care in training and supervising coders and in checking the reliability of their work. We prepared detailed written instructions and held frequent group discussions of coding rules and the treatment of problematic cases. All pro-con coding decisions, and those on other variables central to our analysis, were validated by a second coder and also by one of the present authors, who made the final coding decisions.[1] We masked the public opinion data so that coders would not be affected in any way by knowledge of whether or how policy preferences changed; we gave them only the exact wording of each opinion item and the time periods to be examined, not the responses to the questions.

As a result of these efforts we are confident that very high quality data were produced. It proved rather easy to code reported statements and actions on a five-point directional scale with categories "clearly pro," "probably pro," "uncertain or neutral," "probably con," and "clearly con" in relation to the main policy alternative outlined in each opinion question.

For each type of news source in each opinion case, we summed and averaged all the numerical values of pro-con codes (ranging from + 2 to −2, with 0 for neutral) in order to compute measures of total and average directional thrust of the news from each source. The sums and averages of directional codes for television news content prior to T1 and between T1 and T2—for all messages coming from all sources combined and for messages coming separately from each distinct source—constitute our main independent variables. Most of our analysis is based on measures restricted to "relevant" or "highly relevant" source stories because we found that inclusion of less relevant source stories weakened the observed relationships.

Our principal mode of analysis was ordinary least squares regression analysis, in which we estimated the impact of each news source (or all sources taken together) along with opinion levels at T1, upon the level of public opinion at T2. We analyzed all cases together and also each of our two independently selected subsets of 40 cases, as well as subsets of cases involving different kinds of issues (e.g., foreign versus domestic policies), different time periods, and different levels of source credibility (popular versus unpopular presidents).

After testing hypotheses and exploring the aggregate data, we closely examined individual cases of public opinion change, scrutinizing media-reported statements and actions and the precise sequence of events. This served two purposes. First, it helped us with causal inference, shedding light on possibilities of spuriousness or reciprocal influence. Second, it enabled us to generate some new hypotheses about effects on opinion by certain sets of actors not clearly differentiated in our aggregate data.

Findings

. . . News commentary (from the anchorperson, reporters in the field, or special commentators) between the T1 and T2 surveys is estimated to have the most dramatic impact. A single "probably pro" commentary is associated with more than four percentage points of opinion change! This is a startling finding, one that we would hesitate to believe except that something similar has now appeared in three separate sets of cases we have analyzed. It was true of editorial columns in our earlier analysis of 56 two-point opinion series using the *New York Times* as our media source (Page and Shapiro 1983b), in the first 40 TV news cases we collected (Page, Shapiro, and Dempsey 1984), and in the 40 new TV cases, which we analyzed separately before doing all 80 cases together.

We are not convinced that commentators' remarks in and of themselves have such great potency, however. They may serve as indicators of elite or public consensus (Hallin 1984; McClosky and Zaller 1984; Noelle-Neumann 1973, 1980). Or the commentaries may—if in basic agreement with official network sentiment or the attitudes of reporters (perhaps providing cues for reporters . . .)—indicate slants or biases in media coverage that are transmitted to citizens in ways that supplement the statements of the commentators. These could include the selection of news sources and quotes, the choice of visual footage, the questions asked in interviews, camera angles, and so forth.

Certain other estimated effects on opinion are probably important even though some do not reach the .05 level of statistical significance according to a conservative two-tailed test. . . .

Most notably—and clearly significantly—a single "probably pro" story about experts or research studies is estimated to produce about three percentage points of opinion change, a very substantial amount. Presidents are estimated to have a more modest impact of about three-tenths of a percentage point per "probably pro" story, and stories about opposition party statements and actions may also have a positive effect.

There are indications, on the other hand, that interest groups and perhaps the courts (in recent years) actually have negative effects. That is, when their statements and actions push in one direction (e.g., when corporations demand subsidies or a federal court orders school integration through busing) public opinion tends to move in the opposite direction. We are not certain about the negative effect of courts, however, because of the instability of coefficients across data sets.

Certain kinds of news appear on the average to have no direct effect at all upon opinion, or less impact than might be expected. The president's fellow partisans, when acting independently of the president himself, do not appreciably affect opinion. Events may move public opinion indirectly, but they do not speak strongly for themselves. They presumably have their effects mainly through the interpretations and reactions of other news sources. The same applies to statements and actions from foreign countries or individuals, whether friends or foes. U.S. citizens apparently do not listen to foreigners directly but only through interpretations by U.S. opinion leaders.

The marked distinctions among types of news fits well with our idea that information from different sources has different degrees of credibility. It is quite plausible, for example, that the public tends to place considerable trust in the positions taken by network commentators and (ostensibly) nonpartisan experts. Some other sources may be considered irrelevant. Still others, like certain interest groups that presumably pursue narrowly selfish aims, may serve as negative reference points on public issues (see Schattschneider 1960, 52–53). Similarly, the federal courts may have served as negative referents in the 1970s and the early 1980s because of their unpopular actions on such issues as busing and capital punishment. In any case, it is clearly important to distinguish among sources of news. . . .

When presidents are popular, they tend (though the estimate falls short of statistical significance) to have a small positive effect on public opinion. Each "probably pro" statement or action is estimated to produce more than half a percentage point of opinion change. Part of the effect is undoubtedly temporary and part reciprocal. The impact presumably could not be multiplied indefinitely by talkative presidents because of potential saturation and overexposure of the reporters' and editors' desires for fresh topics to cover. Still, this constitutes some evidence that a popular president does indeed stand at a "bully pulpit." On an issue of great importance to him he can hammer away with repeated speeches and statements and can reasonably expect to achieve a 5 or 10 percentage point change in public opinion over the course of several months (see Page and Shapiro 1984).

Unpopular presidents, in contrast, apparently have no positive effect on opinion at all. They may try—like Glendower in *Henry IV*—to call spirits from the vasty deep, but none will come.

There are some indications that the effects of other news sources interact with presidential popularity. . . . [C]ommentaries may have their strongest effects when presidents are unpopular. Perhaps news commentators substitute for a respected leader, challenging the one that is out of favor. In addition, administration officials and the president's fellow partisans in Congress and elsewhere, when acting independently of a popular president, appear to have a slightly negative impact on opinion, whereas they may have positive effects when presidents are unpopular. The opposition party, rather strangely, seems especially potent when presidents are popular. In short, there may be some substantial differences in the dynamics of opinion change depending upon whether the president in office at a particular time is popular or not.

Discussion

Our examination of a number of specific cases of opinion change has bolstered our general confidence in the aggregate findings. . . .

News Commentary

The most dramatic finding . . . is the strong estimated impact of news commentary. Our examination of specific cases provides a number of instances in which the statements of news commentators and reporters clearly parallel opinion change. Examples include Howard K. Smith's praise for Nixon's policies and his criticism of calls for unilateral withdrawal from Vietnam in 1969; various newsmen's support for continued slow withdrawal from Vietnam during 1969–70; commentary favoring conservation and increased production rather than stopping military aid to Israel in order to get cheap oil during 1974–75; Smith's and others' support for more attention to the Arabs during 1974–75 and during 1977–78; Eric Severeid's, David Brinkley's, and Smith's advocacy of campaign contribution limits in 1973; Brinkley's and Smith's backing of stricter wage and price controls during 1972–73; John Chancellor's editorializing on the importance of fighting unemployment (versus inflation) in 1976; Smith's support for federal work projects in 1976; and commentaries in the spring of 1981 that Reagan's proposed tax cuts would benefit the wealthy.

. . . We would not claim that individual news commentators like Howard K. Smith—for all the esteem in which they are held—are, in themselves, the biggest sources of opinion change (but cf. Freeman, Weeks, and Wertheimer 1955). We do not believe that Walter Cronkite single-handedly ended the Vietnam War with his famous soul-searching broadcast in 1968.

Instead, the commentary we have examined may reflect the positions of many journalists or other elites who communicate through additional channels besides TV news or even a widespread elite consensus in the country (see McClosky and Zaller 1984). Or commentators' positions may be indicators of network biases, including subtle influences of reporters and editors upon the selection of news sources and upon the ways in which stories are filmed and reported. Or, again, commentators and other sources with whom they agree may (correctly or not) be perceived by the public as reflecting a climate of opinion or an emerging national consensus on an issue, which may weigh heavily with citizens as they form their own opinions (see Lippmann 1922; Noelle-Neumann 1973). With our present data, we cannot distinguish among these possibilities. But news commentators either constitute or stand for major influences on public opinion.

Experts

. . . [T]hose we have categorized as "experts" have quite a substantial impact on public opinion. Their credibility may be high because of their actual or portrayed experience and expertise and nonpartisan status. It is not unreasonable for members of the public to give great weight to experts' statements and positions, particularly when complex technical questions affect the merits of policy alternatives.

The existence of a reciprocal process, influence by public opinion upon experts, cannot be ruled out (particularly to the extent that the audience-seeking media decide who is an expert based on the popularity of his or her policy views), but it is probably limited in the short run because experts do not face immediate electoral pressures—that is, public attitudes may ultimately influence who are considered experts and what their basic values are, but once established, experts are less likely than presidents or other elected officials to bend quickly with the winds of opinion.

One striking example of the influence of expert opinion as reported in the media concerns the Senate vote on the SALT II arms limitation treaty. Public support for the treaty dropped 5.5% from February to March 1979 and 19% from June to November. During both periods many retired generals and arms experts spoke out or testified against the treaty, citing difficulties of verification and an allegedly unequal balance of forces favoring the Soviets.

Presidents

. . . [N]umerous cases support the inference that popular presidents' actions and statements reported in the media do affect public opinion. These include President Nixon's persistent opposition to accelerating U.S. troop withdrawals from Vietnam during 1969, 1970, and 1971; Reagan's 1981 argument for AWACS airplane sales to Saudi Arabia; Carter's 1977–78 increased attention to Arab countries; Carter's early 1980 movement (during a temporary peak in popularity) toward toughness in the Iranian hostage crisis; Reagan's 1982 bellicose posturing toward the Soviet Union; Ford's 1974–75 defense of military spending; Ford's 1976 and Carter's 1980 advocacies of cuts in domestic spending; and, perhaps, Nixon's 1972–73 support for wage and price controls.

On the other hand, as our regression results showed, unpopular presidents do not have much success at opinion leadership. In a number of cases unpopular presidents made serious efforts to advocate policies but failed to persuade the public. This was true of Ford's attempts to increase military spending in 1976 and his resistance to jobs programs and health and education spending in the same year. Jimmy Carter in early 1979, with his popularity at 43% approval and falling, failed to rally support for SALT II. Carter was also unsuccessful at gaining significant ground on gasoline rationing, the military draft, or the Equal Rights Amendment in 1979 and 1980. Even Ronald Reagan, when near a low point of popularity (44%) in mid-1982, failed to move opinion toward more approval of a school prayer amendment to the Constitution. Because this distinction between popular and unpopular presidents emerged clearly in our previous analysis of newspaper data (Page and Shapiro 1984), we are inclined to believe that it is real (though modest in magnitude) even though the popular president effect does not quite reach statistical significance. . . .

Interest Groups

Our regression analysis indicated that groups and individuals representing various special interests, taken together, tend to have a negative effect on public opinion. Our examination of the cases supports this point but also suggests that certain kinds of groups may have positive effects while others have negative impact.

We found many cases (more than 20) in which public opinion unequivocally moved *away* from positions advocated by groups and individuals representing special interests. In some cases the groups may have belatedly spoken up after public opinion had already started moving against their positions, producing a spurious negative relationship. But in many instances they seem actually to have antagonized the public and created a genuine adverse effect.

Such cases include Vietnam War protesters from 1969 to 1970, protesters against draft registration in 1980, and perhaps the nuclear freeze movement in 1982. U.S. citizens have a long history of opposition to demonstrators and protesters, even peaceful ones, and apparently tend not to accept them as credible or legitimate sources of opinion leadership. . . .

In general, the public apparently tends to be uninfluenced (or negatively influenced) by the positions of groups whose interests are perceived to be selfish or narrow, while it responds more favorably to groups and individuals thought to be concerned with broadly defined public interests. The best examples of the latter in our data are environmental groups and perhaps also general "public interest" groups like Common Cause.

From 1973 to 1974, for example, support for leasing federal land to oil companies declined as TV news reported conservationists challenging the positions of the profit-seeking and presumably less credible oil companies. During the same period, support for a freeze on gasoline, heating, and power prices increased a bit despite opposition by gas station owners and oil companies.

Not only business corporations, but also some mass membership groups representing blacks, women, the poor, Jews, and organized labor seem to have been held in disrepute and to have had null or negative effects on opinion about issues of direct concern to them, including social welfare policies and some Middle East issues. . . .

Conclusion

We believe we have identified the main influences on short-term and medium-term opinion change.

Our analysis does not offer a full account of certain glacial, long-term shifts in public opinion that reflect major social, technological, and demographic changes such as rising educational levels, cohort replacement, racial migration, or alterations in the family or the workplace. The decades-long transformations in public attitudes about civil liberties, civil rights, abortion, and other matters surely rest (at least in an ultimate causal sense) upon such social changes. . . . If news reports play a part in such major opinion shifts, they may do so mainly as transmitters of more fundamental forces.

Within the realm of short- and medium-term effects, however, we have had striking success at finding out what moves public opinion. Our TV news variables, together with opinion at the time of an initial survey, account for well over 90% of the variance in public opinion at the time of a second survey. The news variables alone account for nearly half the variance in opinion change. . . .

The processes of opinion change are not simple. In order to account for changes between two opinion surveys, for example, it is essential to examine media content before the first survey. Discrepancies between current news and prior news (or prior opinion) are important. Part of the media impact is temporary so that there is a tendency for opinion in the T1–T2 period to drift back, to move in a direction opposite to the thrust of the media content prior to T1.

Moreover, it is important to distinguish among news *sources* rather than aggregating all media content together. The effects of news from different sources vary widely.

Among the sources we examined, the estimated impact of news commentary is strongest of all, on a per-story basis, though such messages are aired less frequently than those from other sources. The causal status of this finding, however, is uncertain. Commentary may be an indicator of broader influences, such as media bias in the selection and presentation of other news, of consensus among the U.S. media or elites generally, or of a perceived public consensus.

Experts, those perceived as having experience and technical knowledge and nonpartisan credibility, also have very sizable effects. A policy alternative that experts testify is ineffective or unworkable tends to lose public favor; an alternative hailed as efficient or necessary tends to gain favor.

We found that messages communicated through the media from or about popular presidents tend to have positive effects on opinion. Presidents respond to public desires, but they can also lead public opinion (see Page and Shapiro 1984). Active presidential effort can be expected to yield a 5- or 10-percentage point change in opinion over the course of a few months.

News commentators, experts, and popular presidents have in common a high level of credibility, which we believe is crucial to their influence on the public. Rational citizens accept information and analysis only from those they trust. In contrast, news sources with low credibility, such as unpopular presidents or groups perceived to represent narrow interests, generally have no effect, or even a negative impact, on public opinion.

Some of these findings might be thought to be limited to the recent period we studied, in which the public has relied heavily on TV and is better educated and more attentive to politics than U.S. citizens in the past. Our confidence in the generality of the findings, however, is bolstered by their consistency with our previous analysis (using newspaper stories) of opinion change from 1935 onward (see Page and Shapiro 1983b, 1984). This similarity also reinforces the observation that the national news media in the U.S. are very much of a piece. They all tend to report the same kinds of messages concerning public policy, from the same sources. This can be attributed to the norms and incentives—and the organizational and market structure—of the news industry and especially to the pervasiveness of the wire services (see Epstein 1973; Gans 1980; Roshco 1975). In this respect the contents of one medium is a good indicator of the content of many media.

In terms of our concerns about democratic theory, it is interesting to observe that relatively neutral information providers like experts and news commentators apparently have more positive effects (at least direct effects) than do self-serving interest groups. It is also interesting that popular presidents, who presumably tend to embody the values and goals of the public, are more able than unpopular ones to influence opinions about policy. These findings suggest that objective information may play a significant part in opinion formation and change and that certain of the more blatant efforts to manipulate opinion are not successful.

On the other hand, unobtrusive indirect effects by special interests—through influences on experts and commentators, for example—may be more dangerous than would be a direct clash of interests in full public view. Clearly there is much more to be learned before we can be confident about the fundamental sources of influence on public opinion. The same is true of judging the quality of information received by the public.

In order to judge to what extent the public benefits from constructive political leadership and education and to what extent it suffers from deception and manipulation, we need to examine the truth or falsehood, the logic or illogic, of the statements and actions of those who succeed at gaining the public's trust (see Bennett 1983; Edelman 1964; Miliband 1969; Wise 1973; contrast Braestrup 1983; Robinson 1976; Rothman 1979). This applies to the sources whose messages are conveyed through the media and to the media themselves. There is much to learn about whether various sources lie or mislead or tell the truth; about how accurately or inaccurately the media report what the sources say and do; and about the causes of any systematic distortions or biases in the selection and reporting of policy-related news.

Note

1. . . . Any disagreements about coding were resolved through meetings and discussion. Some reliability analysis was done, with Dempsey and Shapiro coding cases independently. Their intercoder reliability coefficients for the variables coded were

in the .7 and .8 range. For the all-important pro-con codes, the two authors never disagreed by more than one unit on the 5-point scale.

References

Bennett, W. Lance. 1983. *News: The Politics of Illusion.* New York: Longman.

Braestrup, Peter. 1983. *Big Story.* New Haven, Conn.: Yale University Press.

Chaffee, Steven H. 1975. *Political Communication: Enduring Issues for Research.* Beverly Hills: Sage.

Cook, Fay Lomax, Tom R. Tyler, Edward G. Goetz, Margaret T. Gordon, David Protess, Donna R. Leff, and Harvey L. Molotch. 1983. Media and Agenda Setting: Effects on the Public, Interest Group Leaders, Policy Makers, and Policy. *Public Opinion Quarterly* 47:16–35.

Davis, James A. 1975. Communism, Conformity, Cohorts, and Categories: American Tolerance in 1954 and 1972–73. *American Journal of Sociology* 81:491–513.

Downs, Anthony. 1957. *An Economic Theory of Democracy.* New York: Harper.

Edelman, Murray. 1964. *The Symbolic Uses of Politics.* Urbana: University of Illinois Press.

Epstein, Edward J. 1973. *News from Nowhere.* New York: Random House.

Erbring, Lutz, Edie N. Goldenberg, and Arthur H. Miller. 1980. Front Page News and Real World Cues: A New Look at Agenda-Setting by the Media. *American Journal of Political Science* 24:16–49.

Freeman, Howard E., H. Ashley Weeks, and Walter J. Wertheimer. 1955. News Commentator Effect: A Study in Knowledge and Opinion Change. *Public Opinion Quarterly* 19:209–15.

Funkhauser, G. Ray. 1973. The Issues of the Sixties: An Exploratory Study in the Dynamics of Public Opinion. *Public Opinion Quarterly* 37:63–75.

Gans, Herbert J. 1980. *Deciding What's News.* New York: Vintage.

Graber, Doris A. 1984. *Mass Media and American Politics.* 2d ed. Washington, D.C.: Congressional Quarterly.

Hallin, Daniel C. 1984. The Media, the War in Vietnam, and Political Support: A Critique of the Thesis of an Oppositional Media. *Journal of Politics* 46:2–24.

Hovland, Carl I., and Walter Weiss. 1951–52. The Influence of Source Credibility on Communication Effectiveness. *Public Opinion Quarterly* 16:635–50.

Iyengar, Shanto, Mark D. Peters, and Donald R. Kinder. 1982. Experimental Demonstrations of the "Not-So-Minimal" Consequences of Television News Programs. *American Political Science Review* 76:848–58.

Jaccard, James. 1981. Toward Theories of Persuasion and Belief Change. *Journal of Personality and Social Psychology* 40:260–69.

Katz, Elihu, and Paul F. Lazarsfeld. 1965. *Personal Influence: The Part Played by People in the Flow of Communications.* Glencoe, Ill.: Free Press.

Klapper, Joseph T. 1960. *The Effects of Mass Communication.* Glencoe, Ill.: Free Press.

Kraus, Sidney, and Dennis Davis. 1976. *The Effects of Mass Communication on Political Behavior.* University Park: Pennsylvania State University Press.

Lippmann, Walter. 1922. *Public Opinion.* New York: Macmillan.

McClosky, Herbert, and John Zaller. 1984. *The American Ethos: Public Attitudes toward Capitalism and Democracy.* Cambridge, Mass.: Harvard University Press.
McCombs, Maxwell E., and Donald L. Shaw. 1972. The Agenda-Setting Function of the Mass Media. *Public Opinion Quarterly* 36:176–87.
McGuire, William J. 1985. The Myth of Mass Media Effectiveness: Savagings and Salvagings. In *Public Communication and Behavior,* ed. George Comstock.
MacKuen, Michael B. 1981. Social Communications and Mass Policy Agenda. In *More than News: Media Power in Public Affairs,* by Michael B. MacKuen and Steven L. Coombs. Beverly Hills: Sage.
MacKuen, Michael B. 1984. Exposure to Information, Belief Integration, and Individual Responsiveness to Agenda Change. *American Political Science Review* 78:372–91.
Miliband, Ralph. 1969. *The State in Capitalist Society.* London: Quartet.
Noelle-Neumann, Elisabeth. 1973. Return to the Concept of Powerful Mass Media. In *Studies in Broadcasting,* ed. H. Eguchi and K. Sata, 67–112. Tokyo: The Nippon Hoso Kyokai.
Noelle-Neumann, Elisabeth. 1980. Mass Media and Social Change in Developed Societies. In *Mass Communication Review Yearbook.* Vol. 1, ed. G. Cleveland Wilhoit and Harold de Bock. Beverly Hills: Sage.
Noelle-Neumann, Elisabeth. 1984. *The Spiral of Silence.* Chicago: University of Chicago Press.
Page, Benjamin I., and Robert Y. Shapiro. 1982. Changes in Americans' Policy Preferences, 1935–1979. *Public Opinion Quarterly* 46:24–42.
Page, Benjamin I., and Robert Y. Shapiro. 1983a. Effects of Public Opinion on Policy. *American Political Science Review* 77:175–90.
Page, Benjamin I., and Robert Y. Shapiro. 1983b. The Mass Media and Changes in Americans' Policy Preferences: A Preliminary Analysis. Paper presented at the annual meeting of the Midwest Political Science Association, Chicago.
Page, Benjamin I., and Robert Y. Shapiro. 1984. Presidents as Opinion Leaders: Some New Evidence. *Policy Studies Journal* 12:649–61.
Page, Benjamin I., Robert Y. Shapiro, and Glenn R. Dempsey. 1984. Television News and Changes in Americans' Policy Preferences. Paper presented at the annual meeting of the Midwest Political Science Association, Chicago.
Page, Benjamin I., Robert Y. Shapiro, and Glenn R. Dempsey. 1985a. The Mass Media Do Affect Policy Preferences. Paper presented at the annual meeting of the American Association for Public Opinion Research, McAfee, N.J.
Page, Benjamin I., Robert Y. Shapiro, and Glenn R. Dempsey. 1985b. What Moves Public Opinion. Paper presented at the annual meeting of the American Political Science Association, New Orleans.
Robinson, Michael J. 1976. Public Affairs Television and the Growth of Political Malaise: The Case of "The Selling of the Pentagon." *American Political Science Review* 70:409–32.
Roshco, Bernard. 1975. *Newsmaking.* Chicago: University of Chicago Press.
Rothman, Stanley. 1979. The Mass Media in Post-Industrial Society. In *The Third Century: America as a Post-Industrial Society,* ed. Seymour Martin Lipset, 346–88. Stanford: Hoover Institution.

Schattschneider, E. E. 1960. *The Semisovereign People.* New York: Holt.
Wagner, Joseph. 1983. Media Do Make a Difference: The Differential Impact of the Mass Media in the 1976 Presidential Race. *American Journal of Political Science* 27:407–30.
Wise, David. 1973. *The Politics of Lying.* New York: Vintage.
Zaller, John. 1985. *The Diffusion of Political Attitudes.* Princeton University. Photocopy.

9

MISPERCEPTIONS, THE MEDIA, AND THE IRAQ WAR

Steven Kull, Clay Ramsay, and Evan Lewis

Editor's Note

Sound democratic governance requires a public that is correctly informed about the justifications for major political decisions. That tenet was violated when the United States went to war against Iraq in 2003. Many Americans based their support for the war on false beliefs about key aspects of the situation. Steven Kull, Clay Ramsay, and Evan Lewis carefully analyze what happened and lay bare the many factors that played a part in the development of these serious misperceptions. Their detailed analysis shows that media coverage played a major part, with some news venues producing substantially more misconceptions than their competitors. The authors also make it clear that misperceptions of underlying factors distort public opinions and may produce policies contrary to the public's wishes.

At the time of this writing, the three authors were affiliated with the Program on International Policy Attitudes (PIPA). Steven Kull served as director, Clay Ramsay as director of research, and Evan Lewis as research associate. Kull, who is affiliated with the University of Maryland's School of Public Affairs, also directed the Center on Policy Attitudes (COPA), with Ramsay serving as research director. Both are important contributors to the public opinion and foreign policy literature.

The widespread presence of misperceptions [relevant to the rationales for going to war with Iraq] naturally raises the question of whether they are to some extent a function of an individual's source of news. To find out, in three different polls conducted [by the Program on International Policy Attitudes (PIPA) and the polling firm Knowledge Networks (KN)] in June, July, and August-September, an aggregate sample of 3,334 respondents was asked, "Where do you tend to get most of your news?" and offered the options of

Source: Steven Kull, Clay Ramsay, and Evan Lewis, "Misperceptions, the Media, and the Iraq War," in *Political Science Quarterly,* 118 (Winter 2003): 569–598. Reprinted by permission from *Political Science Quarterly.*

"newspapers and magazines" or "TV and radio." Overall, 19 percent said their primary news source was print media, while 80 percent said it was electronic. Respondents were then asked, "If one of the networks below is your primary source of news please select it. If you get news from two or more networks about equally, just go on to the next question." The networks offered were ABC, CBS, NBC, CNN, Fox News, PBS, and NPR. Because the PBS and NPR viewers were such a small percentage, we combined them into one category of public networks. In the case of ABC, CBS, and NBC, we do not know how many people primarily got their news from local affiliates and how many from national news shows. Likewise, we do not know if all of those who said that they got their news from Fox News primarily got their news from the national cable news network and how many from local Fox affiliates.[1]

The same respondents were also asked about their perceptions, with 1,362 respondents receiving all three key perception questions and 3,334 respondents receiving at least one of them—that is, whether evidence of close links between Iraq and al Qaeda has been found, whether [Weapons of Mass Destruction] WMD have been found in Iraq, and whether world public opinion approved of the United States going to war with Iraq. . . .

An analysis of those who were asked all of the key three perception questions does reveal a remarkable level of variation in the presence of misperceptions according to news source. Standing out in the analysis are Fox and NPR/PBS, but for opposite reasons. Fox was the news source whose viewers had the most misperceptions. NPR/PBS are notable because their viewers and listeners consistently held fewer misperceptions than respondents who obtained their information from other news sources. Table 9-1 shows this clearly. Listed are the breakouts of the sample according to the frequency of the three key misperceptions (that is, the beliefs that evidence of links between Iraq and al Qaeda has been found, that WMD have been found in Iraq, and that world public opinion approved of the United States going to

Table 9-1   **Frequency of Misperceptions per Respondent: WMD Found, Evidence of al Qaeda Link, and World Majority Support for War (percentages)**

Number of misperceptions per respondent	Fox	CBS	ABC	CNN	NBC	Print media	NPR/PBS
None of the three	20	30	39	45	45	53	77
One or more misperception	80	71	61	55	55	47	23

Source: Program on International Policy Attitudes/Knowledge Networks.

war with Iraq) and their primary news source. In the audience for NPR/PBS, there was an overwhelming majority who did not have any of the three misperceptions, and hardly any had all three.

. . . The same pattern in the distribution of misperceptions among the news sources was obtained in the cases of each specific misperception. When asked whether the United States has found "clear evidence in Iraq that Saddam Hussein was working closely with the al Qaeda terrorist organization," among the combined sample for the three-month period, 49 percent said that such evidence had been found (Table 9-2). This misperception was substantially higher among those who get their news primarily from Fox, 67 percent. Once again the NPR/PBS audience was the lowest at 16 percent.

Variations were much more modest on the perception that Iraq was directly involved in September 11. As discussed, the view that Iraq was directly involved in September 11 is not a demonstrable misperception, but it is widely regarded as fallacious by the intelligence community. In this case, the highest level of misperceptions was in the CBS audience (33 percent) followed by Fox (24 percent), ABC (23 percent), NBC (22 percent), and CNN (21 percent). Respondents who got their news primarily from print media (14 percent) and NPR or PBS (10 percent) were less likely to choose this description.

Combining the above group with those who had the less egregious but still unproven belief that Iraq gave substantial support to al Qaeda, the pattern was similar. Among CBS viewers, 68 percent had one of these perceptions, as did 66 percent of Fox viewers, 59 percent of NBC viewers, 55 percent of CNN viewers, and 53 percent of ABC viewers. Print readers were nearly as high at 51 percent, while NPR/PBS audiences were significantly lower at 28 percent.

When respondents were asked whether the United States has "found Iraqi weapons of mass destruction" since the war had ended, 22 percent of all respondents over June through September mistakenly thought this had happened. Once again, Fox viewers were the highest with 33 percent having this

Table 9-2   Viewers' Beliefs on Whether the United States Has Found Evidence of an al Qaeda–Iraq Link (percentages)

Clear evidence of al Qaeda link	NBC	CBS	ABC	Fox	CNN	NPR/PBS	Print media
US has found	49	56	45	67	48	16	40
US has not found	45	41	49	29	47	85	58

Source: Program on International Policy Attitudes/Knowledge Networks.

belief. A lower 19 to 23 percent of viewers who watch ABC, NBC, CBS, and CNN had the perception that the United States has found WMD. Seventeen percent of those who primarily get their news from print sources had the misperception, while only 11 percent who watch PBS or listen to NPR had it (Table 9-3).

Respondents were also asked to give their impression of how they think "people in the world feel about the US having gone to war with Iraq." Over the three-month period, 25 percent of all respondents said, incorrectly, "the majority of people favor the US having gone to war" (Table 9-4). Of Fox watchers, 35 percent said this. Only 5 percent of those who watch PBS or listen to NPR misperceived world opinion in this way. As usual, those who primarily get their news from print media were the second lowest, with 17 percent having this misperception.

Numerous respondents also chose the option of saying that in world public opinion, views are evenly balanced between favoring and opposing going to war—a misperception, though less egregious. Combining those who said views were evenly balanced with those who assumed that the majority favored the Iraq war—a more inclusive definition of misperception—the same pattern obtained. Fox viewers had the highest level of misperceiving (69 percent) and NPR/PBS the lowest (26 percent). The others also formed a familiar pattern: CBS viewers at 63 percent, ABC at 58 percent, NBC at 56 percent, CNN at 54 percent, and print media at 45 percent.

The same question was asked about European opinion. Perceptions of European views are more accurate among the U.S. public: only 17 percent thought there had been majority support among Europeans for the war. Over the three months, CBS viewers most frequently misperceived European opinion (24 percent); Fox viewers were second (20 percent). The NPR/PBS audience and those relying on printed media were lowest, both at 13 percent.

If one adds together those who thought there was European majority support with those who thought views in Europe were evenly balanced, 47 percent misperceived European opinion; CBS viewers were highest at 56 percent,

Table 9-3   Perception that the United States Has or Has Not Found Weapons of Mass Destruction (WMD) (percentages)

Weapons of mass destruction	NBC	CBS	ABC	Fox	CNN	NPR/PBS	Print media
US has found	20	23	19	33	20	11	17
US has not found	79	75	79	64	79	89	82

Source: Program on International Policy Attitudes/Knowledge Networks.

Table 9-4   World Public Opinion on the United States Going to War (percentages)

Majority of people in world ...	NBC	CBS	ABC	Fox	CNN	NPR/PBS	Print media
Favor US going to war in Iraq	20	28	27	35	24	5	17

Source: Program on International Policy Attitudes/Knowledge Networks.

NBC and Fox viewers were next at 52 percent and 51 percent respectively, while the NPR/PBS audience was lowest at 29 percent. ABC viewers and those using print sources were tied for second lowest at 41 percent.

The Effect of Variations in Audience Demographics and Attention

The question thus arises of whether the variation in misperceptions is a function of variations in the demographics or political attitudes of the audience. Some audiences varied according to education, party identification, and support for the President. However, . . . when all of these factors are analyzed together, the respondent's primary source of news is still a strong and significant factor; indeed, it was one of the most powerful factors predicting misperceptions.

It would seem reasonable to assume that misperceptions are due to a failure to pay attention to news and that those who have greater exposure to news would have fewer misperceptions. All respondents were asked, "How closely are you following the news about the situation in Iraq now?" For the summer as a whole (June, July, August–September), 13 percent said they were following the news very closely, 43 percent somewhat closely, 29 percent not very closely, and 14 percent not closely at all.

Strikingly, overall, there was no relation between the reported level of attention to news and the frequency of misperceptions. In the case of those who primarily watched Fox, greater attention to news modestly *increased* the likelihood of misperceptions. Only in the case of those who primarily got their news from print did misperceptions decrease with lower levels of attention, though in some cases this occurred for CNN viewers as well.

The most robust effects were found among those who primarily got their news from Fox. Among those who did not follow the news at all, 42 percent had the misperception that evidence of close links to al Qaeda has been found, rising progressively at higher levels of attention to 80 percent among those who followed the news very closely. For the perception that WMD have been found, those who watched very closely had the highest rate of misperception at 44 percent, while the other levels of attention were lower, though they did not form a clear pattern (not at all, 34 percent; not very, 24 percent; somewhat, 32 percent). Among those who did not follow the news at all, 22 percent believed that world public opinion favored the war, jumping to 34 percent and 32 percent among those who followed the news not very and somewhat closely, respectively, and then jumping even higher to 48 percent among those who followed the news very closely.

With increasing attention, those who got their news from print were less likely to have all three misperceptions. Of those not following the news closely, 49 percent had the misperception that evidence of close links has been found, declining to 32 percent among those who followed the news very closely. Those who did not follow the news at all were far more likely to misperceive (35 percent) that WMD had been found than the other levels (not very, 14 percent; somewhat, 18 percent; very, 13 percent). Twenty-five percent of those who did not follow the news at all had the misperception that world public opinion favored the war, dropping to 16 percent for all other categories.

CNN viewers showed slightly, but significantly, lower levels of misperception on finding WMD and world public opinion at higher levels of attention, though not on evidence of links to al Qaeda. . . .

Relative Strength of Various Factors Related to Level of Misperception

To determine which factors had the most power to predict the likelihood of misperceiving, we performed a binary logistic regression analysis, together with eight other factors. Four of the factors were demographic: gender, age, household income, and education. Two other categorical factors were party identification and intention to vote for the President in the next election, as opposed to an unnamed Democratic nominee. In addition, we included the factors of how closely people follow events in Iraq and what their primary news source was. The odds ratio statistic was used to determine the likelihood that respondents would have misperceptions.

In the regression analysis, the most powerful factor was the intention to vote for President Bush. As compared to those who intended to vote for the Democratic nominee or were undecided, those who intended to vote for the President were 2.9 times more likely to believe that close links to al Qaeda have been found, 3.0 times more likely to believe that WMD had been found, and 2.6 times more likely to believe that world public opinion was favorable to the war. Overall, those who intended to vote for the President were 3.7 times more likely to have at least one of these misperceptions.

The second most powerful factor was one's primary source of network news. Analysis shows the factor to be highly significant, but assessing each network is difficult. Though several networks are significant, others are not. To determine the relative importance of each network as a primary source of news, another regression was performed, treating each network as a binary variable and comparing each network's respondents to other respondents. When this analysis is performed, having Fox, CBS, or NPR/PBS as one's primary news source emerges as the most significant predictor of a particular misperception and of misperceptions in general. . . . Overall, Fox viewing has the greatest and most consistent predictive power in the analysis on a variety of . . . statistical measures.

Fox is the most consistently significant predictor of misperceptions. Those who primarily watched Fox were 2.0 times more likely to believe that close links to al Qaeda have been found, 1.6 times more likely to believe that WMD had been found, 1.7 times more likely to believe that world public opinion was favorable to the war, and 2.1 times more likely to have at least one misperception. Interestingly, when asked how the majority of people in the world feel about the war, if the response "views are evenly balanced" is included as a misperception along with "favor," only Fox is a significant predictor of that misperception.

Those who primarily watched CBS were 1.8 times more likely to believe that close links to al Qaeda have been found, 1.9 times more likely to believe that world public opinion was favorable to the war, and 2.3 times more likely to have at least one misperception. However, they were not significantly different on beliefs about the uncovering of WMD.

On the other hand, those who primarily watched PBS or listened to NPR were 3.5 times less likely to believe that close links to al Qaeda have been found, 5.6 times less likely to believe that world public opinion was favorable to the war, and 3.8 times less likely to have at least one misperception. However, they were not significantly different on the issue of WMD.

Level of attention to news was not a significant factor overall, with the exception of those who primarily got their news from Fox. This is consistent with the finding that Fox viewers were more likely to misperceive the more closely they followed events in Iraq. . . .

The third most powerful factor was intention to vote for the Democratic nominee. As compared to those who intended to vote for President Bush or were undecided, those who intended to vote for the Democratic nominee were 2.0 times less likely to believe that close links to al Qaeda have been found and 1.8 times less likely to believe that world public opinion was favorable to the war. Overall, those who intended to vote for the Democratic nominee were 1.8 times less likely to have at least one of these misperceptions, but did not quite achieve significance on the WMD question.

The fourth most powerful factor was education. Those who had no college, as compared to those had at least some college, were 1.3 times more likely to believe that close links to al Qaeda have been found and 1.4 times more likely to have at least one misperception, but did not quite achieve significance on the other misperceptions.

Age was a very weak factor, with older people being very slightly less likely to misperceive. All other factors—gender, party identification (when intention to vote for the President was included), level of attention to news, and income—were not significant. In a separate analysis, region of the country was included and also not found to be significant.

Analysis

These data lead to the question of why so many Americans have misperceptions that appear to be having a significant impact on attitudes about the Iraq war and why these misperceptions vary according to one's source of news and political attitudes. This analysis starts with possible explanations based on exogenous factors and then moves inward.

The first and most obvious reason that the public had so many of these misperceptions is that the Bush administration made numerous statements that could easily be construed as asserting these falsehoods. On numerous occasions the administration made statements strongly implying that it had intelligence substantiating that Iraq was closely involved with al Qaeda and was even directly involved in the September 11 attacks. For example, in his 18 March 2003 Presidential Letter to Congress, President Bush explained that in going to war with Iraq he was taking "the necessary actions against international terrorists and terrorist organizations, including those nations, organizations, or persons who planned, authorized, committed, or aided the terrorist attacks that occurred on September 11, 2001."[2] When Secretary of State Colin Powell addressed the UN Security Council on 5 February 2003, he presented photographs that were identified as al Qaeda training camps inside Iraq, leaving unclear the fact that the camp in question was in the northern part of Iraq, not under the control of the central Iraqi government.[3] . . . [O]n 14 September 2003, Vice President Richard Cheney made the following ambiguous statement: "If we're successful in Iraq . . . so that it's not a safe haven for terrorists, now we will have struck a major blow right at the heart of the base, if you will, the geographic base of the terrorists who have had us under assault now for many years, but most especially on 9/11."[4] . . .

. . . [I]t is quite clear that the public perceived that the administration was asserting a strong link between Iraq and al Qaeda, even to the point of Iraqi direct involvement in September 11. When PIPA/KN asked in June, "Do you think the Bush administration did or did not imply that Iraq under Saddam

Hussein was involved in the September 11th attacks?" 71 percent said that it had. The administration also made statements that came extremely close to asserting that WMD were found in postwar Iraq. On 30 May 2003, President Bush made the statement, ". . . for those who say we haven't found the banned manufacturing devices or banned weapons, they're wrong. We found them."[5]

Another possible explanation for why the public had such misperceptions is the way that the media reported the news. The large variation in the level of misperceptions does suggest that some media sources may have been making greater efforts than others to disabuse their audiences of misperceptions they may have had so as to avoid feeling conflict about going or having gone to war. Of course, the presence or absence of misperceptions in viewers does not necessarily prove that they were caused by the presence or absence of reliable reporting by a news source. Variations in the level of misperceptions according to news source may be related to variations in the political orientations of the audience. However, when political attitudes were controlled for the variations between the networks and the same attitudes still obtained. . . .

There is also evidence that in the run-up to, during, and for a period after the war, many in the media appeared to feel that it was not their role to challenge the administration or that it was even appropriate to take an active pro-war posture. Fox News' programming on the war included a flag in the left-hand corner and assumed the Defense Department's name for the war: "Operation Iraqi Freedom." When criticized in a letter for taking a pro-war stance, Fox News' Neil Cavuto replied, "So am I slanted and biased? You damn well bet I am. . . . You say I wear my biases on my sleeve? Better that than pretend you have none, but show them clearly in your work."[6] Interestingly, even CBS News, which tends to have a more liberal reputation, seemed to think along these lines. CBS anchor Dan Rather commented in a 14 April 2003 interview with Larry King, "Look, I'm an American. I never tried to kid anybody that I'm some internationalist or something. And when my country is at war, I want my country to win. . . . Now, I can't and don't argue that that is coverage without a prejudice. About that I am prejudiced."[7]

A study of the frequencies of pro-war and anti-war commentators on the major networks found that pro-war views were overwhelmingly more frequent.[8] In such an environment, it would not be surprising that the media would downplay the lack of evidence of links between Iraq and al Qaeda, the fact that WMD were not being found, and that world public opinion was critical of the war. Furthermore, the fact shown in the present study that the audiences of the various networks have varied so widely in the prevalence of misperceptions lends credence to the idea that media outlets had the capacity to play a more critical role, but to varying degrees chose not to.

Reluctant to challenge the administration, the media can simply become a means of transmission for the administration, rather than a critical filter. For example, when President Bush made the assertion that WMD had been found, the 31 May 2003 edition of the *Washington Post* ran a front page headline saying, "Bush: 'We Found' Banned Weapons."[9] There is also striking evidence that the readiness to challenge the administration is a variable that corresponds to levels of misperception among viewers. . . . [T]he two networks notably least likely to present critical commentary were Fox and CBS—the same two networks that in the present study had viewers most likely to have misperceptions. . . .

Another contributing factor may also have been a dynamic in reporting that is not unique to the Iraq war: the absence of something does not constitute a compelling story, while even the prospect of the presence of something does. Thus, shortly after the end of the war, numerous headlines trumpeted even faint prospects that evidence of WMD were about to be found. However, when these prospects failed to materialize, this did not constitute a compelling story and, thus, reporting on it was given a far less prominent position. The cumulative effect of repeatedly hearing the expectation that weapons were about to be found, while hearing little or no disconfirmation, could well contribute to the impression that at least one of these leads was indeed fruitful.

Other more subtle dynamics may also have been at work. The fact that world public opinion was so opposed to the United States going to war with Iraq may have been obscured by giving such high visibility to the U.S. conflict with France in the Security Council. The key story became one of French obstructionism, eclipsing the fact that polls from around the world, as well as the distribution of positions in the UN Security Council, showed widespread opposition to U.S. policy.

One could well argue that this plethora of exogenous factors obviates the need for any explanations based on endogenous factors. Indeed, the fact that no particular misperception studied was found in a clear majority of the public and the fact that 40 percent had none of the key misperceptions buttress confidence in the capacity of the public to sort through misleading stimuli. At the same time, a majority had at least one major misperception, raising the question of why so many people have been susceptible.

The seemingly obvious explanation—that the problem is that people just do not pay enough attention to the news—does not hold up. As discussed, higher levels of attention to news did not reduce the likelihood of misperception, and in the case of those who primarily got their news from Fox News, misperceptions increased with greater attention. Furthermore, the presence of misperceptions was not just noise found randomly throughout an inattentive public—the presence of misperceptions formed strong patterns highly related to respondents' primary source of news.

Perhaps the most promising explanation is that the misperceptions have performed an essential psychological function in mitigating doubts about the validity of the war. Polls have shown that Americans are quite resistant to the idea of using military force except in self-defense or as part of a multilateral operation with UN approval. . . . Thus, to legitimate the war without UN approval, the President had to make the case that the war would be an act of self-defense. . . .

Americans had expected that once the United States went into Iraq, they would find evidence that Iraq was linked to al Qaeda and was developing WMD, thus vindicating the decision to go to war as an act of self-defense. Therefore, it is not surprising that many have been receptive when the administration has strongly implied or even asserted that the United States has found evidence that Iraq was working closely with al Qaeda and was developing WMD, and when media outlets—some more than others—have allowed themselves to be passive transmitters of such messages.

Conclusion

From the perspective of democratic process, the findings of this study are cause for concern. They suggest that if the public is opposed to taking military action without UN approval and the President is determined to do so, he has remarkable capacities to move the public to support his decision. This in itself is not worrisome—to the degree it is the product of persuasion, based on the merits of an argument. What is worrisome is that it appears that the President has the capacity to lead members of the public to assume false beliefs in support of his position. In the case of the Iraq war, this dynamic appears to have played a critical role: among those who did not hold the key false beliefs, only a small minority supported the decision to go to war. In a regression analysis, the presence of misperceptions was the most powerful factor predicting support for the war, with intention to vote for the President close behind. This does not prove that the misperceptions alone caused support for the war. It is more likely that it is one key factor that interacted with the desire to rally around the President and the troops. However, it does appear that it would have been significantly more difficult for the President to elicit and maintain support for the decision to go to war if the public had not held such misperceptions.

The President's influence is not limitless. He does not appear to be capable of getting the public to go against their more deeply held value orientations. If he did, then it would not be necessary for the public to develop false beliefs. But he is capable of prompting the public to support him by developing the false beliefs necessary to justify the administration's policies in a way that is consistent with the public's deeper value orientations.

It also appears that the media cannot necessarily be counted on to play the critical role of doggedly challenging the administration. The fact that viewers of some media outlets had far lower levels of misperceptions than did others (even when controlling for political attitudes) suggests that not all were making the maximal effort to counter the potential for misperception.

To some extent, this period may be regarded as unique. We are still living in the aftermath of September 11. With the persisting sense of threat, the public may be more prone to try to accommodate the President, and the media may be more reluctant to challenge the President or to impart news that calls into question the validity of his decisions. And yet, it is also at times of threat that the most critical decisions are likely to be made.

It is likely that with time, public misperceptions will tend to erode. For example, after media coverage of David Kay's interim progress report on the activities of the Iraq Survey Group, the belief that WMD have been found dropped to 15 percent, although the belief that evidence of links to al Qaeda has been found did not drop. At the same time, there was a significant rise in the percentage that said they thought that the President at least stretched the truth when he made the case for war based on Iraq having a WMD program.[10] However, when the mechanisms for informing the public are in some way compromised, the process of the public gradually catching on is a slow one. In the meantime, the administration, by giving incorrect information, can gain support for policies that might not be consistent with the preferences held by the majority of Americans.

Notes

1. Numbers for those naming a network as their primary news source were as follows: Fox, 520; CBS, 258; CNN, 466; ABC, 315; NBC, 420; NPR/PBS, 91. All findings in this section were statistically significant at the $p < 0.05$ level, except where noted.
2. President George W. Bush, "Presidential Letter," 18 March 2003, available at http://www.whitehouse.gov/news/releases/2003/03/20030319-1.html.
3. Secretary Colin L. Powell, "Remarks to the United Nations," New York City, 5 February 2003, available at http://www.state.gov/secretary/rm/2003/17300.htm, 12 October 2003.
4. Vice President Richard Cheney, "Meet the Press," 14 September 2003.
5. Mike Allen, "Bush: 'We Found' Banned Weapons; President Cites Trailers in Iraq as Proof," *Washington Post*, 31 May 2003.
6. David Folkenflik, "Fox News defends its patriotic coverage: Channel's objectivity is questioned," *Baltimore Sun*, 2 April 2003.
7. Dan Rather, during the 14 April 2003 *Larry King Live*. Quoted in Steve Rendell and Tara Broughel, "Amplifying Officials, Squelching Dissent: FAIR study finds

democracy poorly served by war coverage," *Extra!* (May/June 2003), Fairness and Accuracy in Reporting, available at www.fair.org/extra/0305/warstudy.html.

8. Rendell and Broughel, "Amplifying Officials, Squelching Dissent."

9. Allen, "Bush: 'We Found' Banned Weapons," 31 May 2003.

10. See Steven Kull, "Americans Reevaluate Going to War with Iraq," PIPA/Knowledge Networks Poll, 13 November 2003, available at www.pipa.org.

10

NEWS COVERAGE EFFECTS ON PUBLIC OPINION ABOUT CRIME

Frank D. Gilliam Jr. and Shanto Iyengar

Editor's Note

Fear of crime and criminals is a pervasive and powerful force at all levels of political life. It motivates citizens to avoid neighborhoods where crime reputedly thrives and leads them to shun contacts with demographic groups deemed to be prone to criminal acts. Crime and justice system issues, including the appropriateness of penalties, are hotly debated staples in many election campaigns. Yet, despite the prominence of such issues, the factual situation is routinely ignored. Instead, policies and behaviors are governed by the images of crime that pervade the community. To a large extent, these images are spread through the news media. What have the media wrought and what are the consequences? Frank D. Gilliam Jr. and Shanto Iyengar provide answers based on cleverly designed experimental research.

Gilliam is professor and associate vice chancellor at the University of California, Los Angeles, and founder of its Center for Communications and Community. He specializes in racial and ethnic politics, the mass media, and electoral behavior. Iyengar is the Chandler Professor of Communication and professor of political science at Stanford University and director of its Political Communication Laboratory. He has authored numerous pathbreaking books dealing with the effects of television on American politics and is well known for pioneering experimental research and Internet research.

Throughout the early and mid-1990s pundits warned of an impending youth-crime epidemic (DiIulio 1995). To many observers (e.g., Bennett, DiIulio, and Walters 1996), the increasing frequency of juvenile violent

---

Source: Frank D. Gilliam Jr. and Shanto Iyengar, "Super-Predators or Victims of Societal Neglect? Framing Effects in Juvenile Crime Coverage," in *Framing American Politics,* ed. Karen Callaghan and Frauke Schnell, Pittsburgh, Pa.: University of Pittsburgh Press, 2005, chapter 6. © 2005 by the University of Pittsburgh Press. Reprinted by permission of the University of Pittsburgh Press.

crime signified that America was now home to a new breed of so-called super-predators—amoral, radically impulsive, and brutally cold-blooded preadults who murder, assault, rape, burglarize, deal deadly drugs, engage in gang warfare, and generally wreak communal havoc (Bennett, DiIulio, and Walters 1996, 27; Berkman 1995). As proof, analysts noted that teenage homicides and violent-crime arrests doubled between the mid-1980s and the mid-1990s, the number of gun homicides tripled, and juvenile gang murders quadrupled (Bennett, DiLulio, and Walters 1996). Indeed, talk of violent, remorseless teen "super-predators" quickly became part of the public discourse. As criminologist James Fox observed, "Unless we act today, we're going to have a bloodbath when these kids grow up" (quoted in Garrett 1995).

. . . Public alarm over juvenile crime through the mid-1990s was heightened by extensive media coverage. Of course, young people (especially minority youth) who engage in criminal violence are especially newsworthy (see Males 1996; Dorfman et al. 1995); senseless acts of violence by "glassy-eyed, remorseless" teenagers in gang attire (Berry and Manning-Miller 1996) satisfy the media's programming needs. As general trends in American public opinion suggest, the growing reach of local news contributed to increased support for punitive remedies aimed at youth offenders (Dorfman et al. 1995; Gilliam 1998). For instance, the public called for more aggressive law enforcement, and in response policy makers across the country proposed and adopted more severe sanctions on adolescent crime, such as incarceration in adult facilities, trying juveniles as adults, the death penalty, and "three strikes" legislation (Alderman 1994; Jacobius 1996; Tang 1994; Walinsky 1995). Thus the rate of juvenile crime and the increased visibility of juvenile crime to the public through the news media—frequently featuring non-white teenagers engaged in the most violent of acts—were thought to have contributed to the high levels of public concern for crime.

In summary, the reality of violent crime in the mid-1990s was that an individual's age and ethnicity could realistically be considered "threatening" attributes. Our objective in this chapter is to examine the extent to which the public's attitudes toward crime reflect these cues. More specifically, we test the proposition that people become more fearful of crime and more committed advocates of punitive measures for dealing with violent crime when the news media frame the issue in ways that highlight the juvenile and non-white attributes of perpetrators.

The Research Design

We treat the two relevant characteristics of individual perpetrators (race and youth) as orthogonal factors in a fully crossed experimental design. A recently broadcast news story dealing with increased police patrols in the city of Long Beach provided the experimental stimulus. The story described armed police patrols of high-crime areas and the eventual arrest of two males. We manipulated the age of the suspects indirectly by depicting the police activity either as a general effort to reduce crime or, alternatively, as an attempt to curb gang-related crime. Thus, we altered the anchor's introductory lead-in so that the police operation was described as either a "crime sweep" (the words appeared on the television screen during the anchor's introduction) or a "gang sweep" (this label was substituted for "crime sweep" during the lead-in, and later the reporter referred to the suspects as "gang members"). With the exception of these two variations, the gang and non-gang versions of the news report were equivalent.

The race/ethnicity manipulation was more direct. Because the original report included police photographs of the two suspects, we were able to insert different "mug shots" corresponding to different ethnic groups. Depending on the experimental condition, the photos of the two suspects featured African Americans, whites, Hispanics, or Asians. Except for the substitution of the photographs, the news reports were identical in content and appearance.

Experimental participants watched a fifteen-minute videotaped local newscast (including commercials) described as having been selected at random from news programs broadcast during the past week. The objective of the study was said to be "selective perception" of news reports. Depending upon the condition to which they were assigned (at random), participants watched one of the following versions of the news story on the Long Beach police patrols.

1. The "crime-sweep" report that included the close-up photo of the two suspects
2. The "crime-sweep" report, but with all references to particular suspects eliminated
3. The "gang-sweep" report that included the close-up photo of the two suspects
4. The "gang-sweep" report, but devoid of any reference to individual suspects

Control participants watched the same newscast, but without any story on crime. In place of the crime report, they watched a story on a partial solar eclipse.

The design allows us to investigate a variety of questions. First, we can compare viewers' responses to news reports featuring non-white perpetrators (operationally defined as the conditions featuring African Americans and Hispanics) with their responses to coverage in which the suspects were white or Asian or to coverage in which there was no information about specific perpetrators. Second, we can estimate the effects of youth-related crime on public attitudes by comparing reactions to the "gang-sweep" and "crime-sweep" conditions. Third, we can isolate the interactive effects, if any, between the youth and ethnicity factors. Perhaps viewers feel especially threatened when the crime involves juvenile gangs and the gang members are non-white.

In addition to the additive and interactive effects of perpetrator ethnicity and age, we can also assess the relative influence of visual cues (photographs of faces) and semantic cues (the "crime-sweep" versus "gang-sweep" labels) in news coverage of crime. Simple comparison of the difference in viewer responses between the "gang-sweep" and "crime-sweep" conditions that excluded pictures of the suspects with the baseline condition in which there was no reference to crime at all provides an estimate of the effects of crime coverage that lacks visual information about individual perpetrators. A parallel comparison of the gang- and non-gang-related conditions in which photographs of the perpetrator appear reveals the degree to which "pictures speak louder than words."

The report on crime was inserted into the middle position of the newscast, following the first commercial break. Except for the news story on crime, the newscasts were identical. None of the other stories appearing in the newscast concerned crime or matters of race.

The experimental "sample" consisted of residents of West Los Angeles who were recruited through flyers and announcements in newsletters offering fifteen dollars for participation in "media research." The age of the participants ranged from eighteen to sixty-four. Fifty-one percent were white, 30 percent were black, 4 percent were Asian, and 7 percent were Latinos. Fifty-two percent were women. The participants were relatively well educated (40 percent had graduated from college) and, in keeping with the local area, more Democratic than Republican (47 versus 22 percent) in their partisan loyalty.

The experiment was administered during the fall of 1995 at a major shopping mall in West Los Angeles in a two-room suite that was furnished casually with couches, lounge chairs, potted plants, and so on. Participants could browse through magazines and newspapers, snack on cookies and coffee, or (in many cases) chat with fellow participants who were friends or colleagues.

On their arrival, participants were given their instructions and then completed a short pretest questionnaire concerning their social background, party identification and political ideology, level of interest in political affairs, and media habits. They then watched the videotape of the newscast. At the end of the videotape, participants completed a lengthy questionnaire that included questions about their evaluations of various news programs and prominent journalists; their opinions concerning various issues in the news;

their recall of particular news stories; their beliefs about the attributes of particular racial/ethnic groups; and, of course, crime. After completing the questionnaire, subjects were debriefed in full (including a full explanation of the experimental procedures) and paid.

Testing the Super-Predator Hypothesis

Our primary interest lies in examining the effects of news coverage on public opinion toward crime. Two facets of opinion are especially relevant to the "super-predator" hypothesis—fear of violent crime and support for punitive criminal justice policies. . . .

. . . The underlying premise of the hypothesis is that minority offenders are especially threatening to the public. Therefore, we expect that people will become more fearful and punitive when they are exposed to news stories that feature "super-predators." Table 10-1 presents the results of parallel analysis-of-variance tests for the impact of the age (gang sweep versus crime sweep) and ethnicity (non-white versus white/Asian) manipulations on the indices of fear and punitiveness. The top half of the table reveals a robust main effect of the youth-crime manipulation on fear of crime ($p < .05$). As expected, exposure to news coverage of gang-related crime boosted fear by a factor of 10 percent (in relation to news coverage of ordinary crime). Despite their heightened fear, viewers were *not* more likely to mention punitive accounts of crime when they encountered the "gang-sweep" frame. To the contrary, the gang frame made participants significantly ($p < .02$) less punitive in their approach to crime. Thus, these results provide only partial confirmation of the super-predator hypothesis; people are especially threatened by youthful offenders, but youth crime does not prompt them to prescribe harsh treatment of offenders.

The effects of the race/ethnicity manipulation are presented in the second half of Table 10-1. Both measures show the expected pattern—higher levels of fear and punitiveness when the suspects were non-white—but both patterns are weak. If we subject the data to a more pointed test of the hypothesis by comparing the conditions with non-white suspects with those featuring whites or Asians, the results are more telling. The lower level of punitiveness when the suspect is either Asian or white is significant at the .05 level. In the case of fear, the difference is less dramatic ($p < .15$). As compared with their counterparts who encountered Asian or white suspects in news coverage of crime, participants who saw Hispanic or African American suspects were significantly more punitive and somewhat more fearful. These results thus validate the racial component of the super-predator hypothesis.

How is it that people are more fearful of crime but at the same time are less willing to favor punitive measures when presented with youthful offenders? Perhaps the study participants, following the model of criminal

Table 10-1   **Fear of Crime and Punitiveness by Types of Crime and Race of Suspect**

	Type of crime coverage		
	Gang crime	No crime coverage	Ordinary crime
Fear of crime	.58 (132)	.45 (65)	.48 (155)
		F-value: 3.91, p < .05	
Punitiveness	.80 (132)	1.06 (65)	1.18 (155)
		F-value: 3.96, p < .02	

	Race of suspects		
	Asian/white	No crime coverage	Non-white
Fear of crime	.50 (99)	.45 (65)	.57 (95)
		F-value: 2.21, ns	
Punitiveness	.88 (99)	1.06 (65)	1.16 (95)
		F-value: 1.36, ns	

law, reasoned that preadults should not be held individually accountable for their actions. Moreover, gangs are collectivities, making it difficult to pinpoint responsibility. The distinctiveness of the gang label is also suggested by the finding that the significant differences in punitiveness elicited by the race/ethnicity manipulation were conditioned by the distinction between gang crime and ordinary crime. That is, we detected evidence of an interaction between reference to gang crime and the suspects' race. When the news is not framed in gang-related terms, non-white offenders elicit more punitive responses than white or Asian offenders. When the report refers to gangs, on the other hand, the ethnicity cue becomes less informative and participants make no distinction between the white/Asian and black/Hispanic suspects. In effect, the gang frame makes participants noticeably less punitive in their attitudes irrespective of the suspects' race.

Verbal versus Visual Cues

The analysis to this point has ignored qualitative differences in the depiction of crime. Specifically, the differences reported in Table 10-2 were calculated across the conditions that featured both verbal and visual cues (the "gang-sweep" or "crime-sweep" label followed by photos of the two suspects) and conditions that provided only the verbal cue. The effects of the "verbal only" and "verbal plus visual" conditions are presented in Table 10-2.

These results do little to support the maxim that pictures are more persuasive than words. In general, the addition of the photographs of the suspects did not strengthen the manipulation. In the case of gang-related crime, the presence of the visual cues, if anything, tended to reduce viewers' fear and

Table 10-2   Verbal versus Visual Framing of Crime

	Gang crime		No crime coverage	Ordinary crime	
	Pictures	No pictures		No pictures	Pictures
Fear of crime	.58 (88)	.59 (44)	.45 (65)	.48 (155)	.50 (106)
			F-value: 2.25, p < .06		
Punitiveness	.77 (88)	.84 (44)	1.06 (65)	1.10 (49)	1.22 (106)
			F-value: 2.08, p < .08		

punitiveness. On the other side of the manipulation (ordinary crime), the pattern was reversed; participants tended to be more fearful and punitive when the news story included photographs of the suspects. While none of these differences is statistically significant, the pattern suggests that the conceptual distinction between gang-related crime and garden-variety crime takes precedence over the presence or absence of visual cues concerning individual suspects. When viewers are forewarned that the crime in question is gang related, exposure to the pictures of two "gang members" serves to make them slightly less punitive. On the other hand, when viewers are not led to anticipate gang involvement in crime, exposure to the identical pictures elicits slightly higher levels of punitiveness. . . .

Fear of crime was equally affected by exposure to juvenile crime and nonwhite offenders. Among participants who watched the news report on gang-related crime, fear of crime increased by 9 percent; for participants who encountered Hispanic or African American suspects the increase was 8 percent. The interaction of the youth and race factors proved insignificant. That is, the effects of the suspects' race proved uniform in the gang-crime and ordinary-crime versions of the news report.

Turning to the control variables, women and blacks were especially fearful of crime. These individual differences are in keeping with the literature on victimization and fear of crime. In addition to race and gender, people who watch local news on a regular basis are more likely to fear crime, suggesting that the distinctive agenda of local newscasts has been passed on to the audience.

. . . [W]hites, Republicans, and conservatives were in the vanguard of the punitive approach to crime. People who tune in to local news regularly were not only more likely to fear crime; they were also significantly more punitive in their outlook.

In all, our results provide mixed support for the super-predator hypothesis. We found that exposure to news reports featuring juvenile and non-white offenders triggered more responses reflecting concern about crime (as compared with groups who were exposed to crime stories featuring other categories of perpetrators), but there was no outpouring of support for punitive criminal justice policies. Our subjects actually expressed less punitive attitudes when they were exposed to juvenile offenders, no matter what the perpetrators' ethnicity. Apparently, people believed, or at least hoped, that youthful offenders could be reformed with appropriate intervention.

. . . [W]eakness in design and measurement, combined with a significantly changed context, accounts for the incomplete rendering of the super-predator hypothesis. With this in mind, we conducted a second study designed to overcome the liabilities. . . . We paid special attention to securing a more typically episodic news treatment, limiting the analysis to white and black youth, revising dependent measures to reflect views specific to youth crime, and incorporating the role of the violent-crime victim into the youth-crime news narrative. . . . [W]e constructed 3 × 3 design in which we manipulated the crime role and the presence of racial cues in crime news. Subjects were randomly assigned to one of nine conditions (i.e., white perpetrator, no perpetrator, black perpetrator × white victim, no victim, black victim). Depending upon the condition to which they were assigned, subjects watched a news story on crime that included a close-up photo of the suspect and/or victim. . . . [T]he photo depicted either a youthful African American or a white male. The report on crime was inserted into the middle position of the newscast, following the first commercial break. Except for the news story on crime, the newscasts were identical in all other respects. None of the remaining stories on the tape concerned crime or matters of race. . . .

. . . Initial analysis indicated that the critical influence on crime attitudes concerned the pairing of white victim with black perpetrator. There was no statistically significant difference as a function of other configurations of race of perpetrator, race of victim, and crime role. Thus, we conducted parallel analyses for the main effects of exposure to the white victim or black perpetrator (controlling for several common individual differences including education, income, age, gender, marital status, ideology, and party identification) on subjects' crime attitudes.

Table 10-3 presents the results of the second study. The top third of the table provides moderate support for our expectations. For example, exposure to the white-victim condition was associated with a significant increase in fear of random street violence and teen crime and violence. Similarly, exposure to the black-perpetrator condition increased fear of random street violence but did not have an appreciable impact on fear of adolescent crime or punitive crime solutions.

These results are produced, in large part, by the significant difference between white and African American study participants. Thus the second third of the table examines the impact of the dominant frame on whites' crime at-

Table 10-3   Impact of TV News by Crime Role and Race of Subject

	Threat of teen crime	Punitive solutions	Fear of random street violence
All subjects (N = 300)			
White victim	2.36*	2.22**	1.90
Non-white victim	2.23	2.09	1.87
Black perpetrator	2.32*	2.15	1.89
Non-black perpetrator	2.25	2.12	1.88
White subjects (N = 132)			
White victim	2.43**	2.27*	1.96
Non-white victim	2.13	2.11	1.82
Black perpetrator	2.39*	2.29**	1.81
Non-black perpetrator	2.17	2.11	1.90
Black subjects (N = 85)			
White victim	2.41	2.26	1.79
Non-white victim	2.41	2.14	1.84
Black perpetrator	2.45	2.20	1.90
Non-black perpetrator	2.40	2.17	1.80

$* p < .10$ $** p < .05$

titudes. The results of this analysis provide more solid support for the super-predator perspective in four of the six relevant comparisons. In other words, exposure to either a white victim or a black perpetrator was related to heightened fear of youth crime and support for punitive juvenile justice policies. On the other hand, there were no measurable effects on more general fear of crime attitudes. Finally, the last third of the table repeats the analysis for black subjects. The main finding is that the manipulations do not influence African Americans' crime attitudes (see also Gilliam and Iyengar 2000). Presumably this is a result of the fact that African Americans are more likely to have a deeper pool of experiences upon which to base judgments. In other words, they do not rely as heavily on the news media for information about their community.

Discussion

Our results describe a cascade of effects that reveal subtle variations in the applicability of the super-predator hypothesis. Contrary to expectations, our study participants were reluctant to punish juvenile criminals in the context of gang involvement, regardless of the race of the perpetrator. The gang manipulation in our study effectively reduced the proportion of viewers who offered consistently punitive attributions of responsibility. . . . Once the behavior of individuals is placed in the context of gang activity, the public's outlook seems to shift from the failings of individuals to the shortcomings of the broader society. Thematic frames thus lead to societal attributions of responsibility (Iyengar 1991).

. . . Nonetheless, there is still strong support for the super-predator hypothesis as the dominant youth-crime frame available to the American public. Our second study strengthened the mild findings in the first experiment. For example, among white study participants, exposure to the black perpetrator significantly increased the number of people fearful of teen crime and supportive of more punitive juvenile justice policies like placing youth in adult detention facilities. This is all the more interesting given that the black/white juvenile murder-arrest rate is at the lowest it has been in two decades (Snyder 2002).

The addition of the crime role—perpetrator or victim—as an element of the news frame yielded interesting insights. For example, exposure to white teen victims in and of itself raised fear levels and support for punitive crime policies among white participants. In other words, people gain no added leverage by knowing the identity or race of the alleged perpetrator. Simply knowing that the victim was white increased the proportion of harsh crime attitudes.

All told, our evidence suggests the following generalizations. First, both semantic and visual cues condition public attitudes on crime. The word *gang* appears to associate crime with violence and youthful perpetrators. Accordingly, people exposed to the cue become both more fearful of crime and less enthusiastic about punitive remedies. It is worth noting that the effects of the gang cue on support for punitive remedies were "color-blind"—study participants were more lenient with youthful offenders, no matter what their ethnicity. At the same time, our evidence also demonstrated considerable traces of race-based reasoning about crime. Exposure to non-white perpetrators or white victims was sufficient to move the audience in a more punitive direction. In this respect ordinary citizens seem more consistently race oriented than the judicial process. Criminal sentencing, as is well documented, is most extreme when the case involves both a white victim and a non-white perpetrator (Sidanius and Pratto 1999). The court of public opinion, however, is insensitive to perpetrator-victim permutations; the mere presence of a non-white perpetrator or white victim is sufficient to elicit an extreme "sentence."

References

Alderman, J. 1994. Leading the public: The media's focus on crime shaped sentiment, *Public Perspective* 5:26–27.

Bennett, W. Lance, J. J. DiIulio Jr., and J. P. Walters. 1996. *Body count: Moral poverty . . . and how to win America's war against crime and drugs.* New York: Simon and Schuster.

Berkman, H. 1995. A gunshot in Boston sends tremors nationwide. *National Law Journal* 18 (October 9, 1995).

Berry, V., and C. Manning-Miller. 1996. *Mediated messages and African-American culture.* Thousand Oaks, CA: Sage Publications.

DiIulio, J. J., Jr. 1995. The coming of the super-predators. *Weekly Standard* (November 27): 23.

Dorfman, L., K. Woodruff, V. Chavez, and L. Wallack. 1995. Youth and violence on local television news. Unpublished report, Berkeley Media Studies Group.

Garrett, L. 1995. Murder by teens has soared. *New York Newsday* (February 17).

Gilliam, Frank, Jr. 1998. *Reframing childcare: The impact of local television news.* Washington, DC: Charles S. Benton Foundation.

Gilliam, Frank, Jr., and Shanto Iyengar. 2000. Prime suspects: The impact of local television news on attitudes about crime and race. *American Journal of Political Science* 44:560–73.

Iyengar, Shanto. 1991. *Is anyone responsible? How television frames political issues.* Chicago: University of Chicago Press.

Jacobius, A. 1996. Going gangbusters: Prosecutors fight gangs with injunctions banning conduct such as using beepers and applying graffiti. *American Bar Association Journal* 82:24–26.

Males, M. 1996. *The scapegoat generation: America's war on adolescents.* Monroe, ME: Common Courage Press.

Sidanius, Jim, and Felicia Pratto. 1999. *Social dominance: An intergroup theory of social hierarchy and oppression.* Cambridge: Cambridge University Press.

Snyder, H. 2002. *Juvenile arrests 2000.* Washington, DC: Office of Juvenile Justice and Delinquency Prevention.

Tang, B. 1994. INS/VGTF and the NYPD. *Police Chief* 61:33–36.

Walinsky, A. 1995. The crisis of public order. *Atlantic* (July): 39–54.

11

HOW SOFT NEWS BRINGS POLICY ISSUES TO THE INATTENTIVE PUBLIC

Matthew A. Baum

Editor's Note

Ordinary Americans, as well as pundits and scholars, have voiced alarm in recent decades about the sharp decline in the public's consumption of political
news offered by traditional media. They attribute the decline to waning interest in politics, and they fear that many citizens are becoming dropouts who no
longer influence politics. When that happens, government is forced to rely on
unrepresentative public opinions that give the advantage to knowledgeable
elites. Matthew A. Baum is among the small group of public opinion scholars
examining the political content of popular soft news shows as a possible substitute source for citizen enlightenment about vital political issues. His pioneering research provides strong evidence that soft news is, indeed, an important
resource that helps to level the political playing field.

At the time of this writing, Baum was an assistant professor in the Department of Political Science at the University of California, Los Angeles. His research focuses on American foreign policy, mass media, public opinion, and
politics. The article presented here became part of a book-length study published in 2003 by Princeton University Press under the title *Soft News Goes to
War: Public Opinion and American Foreign Policy in the Media Age.*

People who are not interested in politics often get their news from sources
quite different from those of their politically engaged counterparts (Chaffee
and Kanihan 1997). While alternative news sources for the politically unin-
volved have long been available, the last two decades have witnessed a dramatic expansion in the number and diversity of entertainment-oriented,
quasi-news media outlets, sometimes referred to collectively as the soft news
media.

Source: Matthew A. Baum, "Sex, Lies, and War: How Soft News Brings Foreign Policy to the Inattentive Public," *American Political Science Review*, 96:1 (March 2002): 91–109. Reprinted with
the permission of Cambridge University Press.

Political scientists, including public opinion scholars, have mostly ignored the soft news media. And, indeed, most of the time these media eschew discussion of politics and public policy, in favor of more "down-market" topics, such as celebrity gossip, crime dramas, disasters, or other dramatic human-interest stories (Patterson 2000; Kalb 1998). Yet, as I shall demonstrate, on occasion, the soft news media *do* convey substantive information concerning a select few high-profile political issues, prominently among them foreign policy crises. This suggests the proliferation of soft news may have meaningful implications for politics, including foreign policy.

Scholars have long pondered the barriers to information and political participation confronting democratic citizens. The traditional scholarly consensus has held that the mass public is woefully ignorant about politics and foreign affairs (Delli Carpini and Keeter 1996; Converse 1964; Almond 1950), and hence, with rare exceptions, only relatively narrow segments of the public—the so-called "attentive public" or "issue publics"—pay attention to public policy or wield any meaningful influence on policymakers (Graebner 1983; Cohen 1973). By, in effect, broadening access to information about *some* political issues, soft news coverage of politics may challenge this perspective, at least in part. If a substantial portion of the public that would otherwise remain aloof from politics is able to learn about high-profile political issues, such as foreign crises, from the soft news media, this may expand the size of the attentive public, at least in times of crisis. And a great deal of research has shown that intense public scrutiny, when it arises, can influence policymakers, both in Congress and the White House (Baum 2000; Powlick 1995; Bosso 1989).

This possibility raises a number of questions. First, to what extent and in what circumstances do the entertainment-oriented, soft news media convey information about serious political issues? Second, what types of political topics appeal to such media outlets? Third, how might their coverage differ from that found in traditional news sources? Finally, who is likely to consume political news presented in this entertainment-oriented media environment, and why? These are the primary questions motivating the present study.

I argue that for many individuals who are not interested in politics or foreign policy, soft news increasingly serves as an alternative to the traditional news media as a source of information about a select few political issues, including foreign policy crises. This is because the soft news media are in the business of packaging human drama as entertainment. And, like celebrity murder trials and sex scandals—the usual fare of soft news outlets—some political issues, prominently among them foreign crises, are easily framed as compelling human dramas. As a result, the soft news media have increased many politically inattentive individuals' exposure to information about select high-profile political issues, primarily those involving scandal, violence, heroism, or other forms of human drama. Yet public opinion scholars have largely failed to consider how this might influence public views of politics.

This study focuses primarily on foreign policy crises. My argument, however, is general, and so not unique to foreign policy. Indeed, it also applies to a fairly narrow range of domestic political issues. Nonetheless, I focus on foreign crises for three reasons. First, *ceteris paribus*, foreign crises are more likely than most issues to transcend traditional partisan boundaries. Hence, public attention to foreign crises is relatively less likely to be affected by heightened public cynicism regarding partisan politics (Nye, Zelikow, and King 1997; Dionne 1991). Second, beyond celebrity murder trials and sex scandals, few issues are as likely to capture the public's imagination as the prospect of large-scale violence and the potential death of large numbers of Americans at the hands of a clearly identifiable villain. Combined, these two factors make foreign crises an appealing subject matter for the largely apolitical, entertainment-oriented soft news media. Third, Americans know and care less about foreign than domestic affairs (Graber 1984), especially in the post-Cold War era (Moisy 1997; Holsti 1996), and most foreign policy news is typically ignored entirely by the soft news media. Hence, while my argument extends beyond foreign policy, I nonetheless focus on foreign crises as, in effect, a "most difficult" test of the argument.

. . . I argue that by repackaging news about select political issues, including foreign crises, as entertainment, soft news dramatically reduces the cognitive costs of paying attention. As a result, even individuals who are not interested in politics may be willing to pay attention to such information.

Soft News Coverage of Foreign Crises

. . . . [A]ny political relevance of soft news depends on the extent to which such programs actually cover political issues, such as foreign crises. And, indeed, *soft news programs have covered every major U.S. foreign military crisis since 1990.* I searched program transcripts, using Lexis-Nexis, and *TV Guide* listings for a variety of soft news programs to determine whether and to what extent they covered the Persian Gulf War, the ongoing series of post-Gulf War crises with Iraq, and four other high-profile U.S. foreign crises of the past decade—Somalia, Haiti, Bosnia, and Kosovo. Where such transcripts were inaccessible (e.g., *Oprah Winfrey*), I contacted several programs directly. For purposes of comparison, I also searched Lexis-Nexis for soft news coverage of several more traditional and less dramatic political issues. . . . Table 11-1 presents the results of these inquiries. These figures—which represent the number of *separate broadcasts* of each program that addressed a given issue—are extremely conservative, due to limited availability of transcripts, sporadic program listings, and unwillingness of some programs to provide the requested information, as well as recent start-dates or cancellation of several of the programs.

To determine whether these raw figures constitute "significant" coverage, I compared soft news coverage of four foreign crises in the 1990s with coverage of those crises on ABC's *World News Tonight*. The results indicated that, taken together, the number of separate broadcasts of the TV talk shows listed in Table 11-1 mentioning the U.S. interventions in Bosnia and Kosovo, combined, was equivalent to 73% of the total number of separate broadcasts of *World News Tonight* which mentioned those conflicts. The corresponding figure for Somalia and Haiti, combined, was over half (52%) as many broadcasts. Indeed, the number of separate broadcasts mentioning Bosnia presented on one tabloid news program, *Extra*, is equivalent to nearly half (46%) of the total number of *World News Tonight* broadcasts mentioning Bosnia. While soft news programs predictably offered significantly less coverage of these crises than the network news—for instance, network newscasts more frequently present multiple stories on a given topic within a single broadcast and tend to offer greater depth of coverage—these figures nonetheless appear far from trivial.

How Soft News Programs Cover Foreign Crises

While, like traditional news outlets, soft news programs do appear to cover foreign crises regularly, they do not necessarily do so in the same manner. Where traditional news outlets typically cover political stories in manners unappealing—either too complex or too arcane—to individuals who are not intrinsically interested in politics, the soft news media self-consciously frame issues in highly accessible terms—which I call "cheap framing"—emphasizing dramatic and sensational human-interest stories, intended primarily to appeal to an entertainment-seeking audience.

Neuman, Just, and Crigler (1992) identify five common frames readily recognized and understood by most individuals. These include "us vs. them," "human impact," "powerlessness," "economic," and "morality." To this list, Powlick and Katz (1998) add an "injustice" frame. Graber (1984) found that several of these frames—"human impact," "morality," and "injustice"—resonated strongly with her interview subjects.[1] Not surprisingly, these are the prevalent themes found in the soft news media. . . .

A review of the content of soft news coverage of several 1990s foreign crises [shows that in] each case, rather than focus on the more arcane aspects of these crises, such as military tactics or geopolitical ramifications, the soft news media tended to focus on highly accessible themes likely to appeal to viewers who were not necessarily watching to learn about military strategy or international diplomacy. For instance, during the Persian Gulf War, while CNN and the major networks filled the airwaves with graphic images of

Table 11-1   Partial Listings of Soft News Coverage of 1990s U.S. Foreign Crises and Other Political Issues

Program	Gulf War	Somalia	Haiti	Bosnia	Iraq (1992–1999)	Kosovo	1996 primaries	1998 elections	Regulate tobacco	NAFTA	WTO	Lewinsky scandal
							Number of separate broadcasts addressing issue					
Network news magazines												
Dateline NBC	—	4	8	17	52	13	4	4	1	1	0	16
20/20	42	3	4	8	20	10	0	1	0	0	0	4
Primetime Live	36	8	4	11	16	—	3	0	0	1	0	3
48 Hours	2	3	4	3	8	1	2	2	0	0	0	2
60 Minutes	14	4	8	17	51	16	2	1	1	2	2	2
Average	23.5	4.4	5.6	11.2	29.4	29.0	2.2	1.6	0.40	0.80	0.40	5.4
Late-night TV talk shows												
Jay Leno	—	—	39	25	102	14	48	0	0	15	0	45
David Letterman	—	4	20	32	88	21	35	1	0	27	0	37
Conan O'Brien	—	3	22	14	53	4	23	0	0	25	0	30
Politically Incorrect	—	—	—	19	55	15	31	1	5	0	1	34
Average	—	3.5	27.0	22.5	74.5	13.5	34.3	0.50	1.3	16.8	0.25	36.5
Daytime TV talk shows												
Oprah Winfrey	3	6	8	8	4	—	—	—	—	—	—	—

Rosie O'Donnell	—	—	—	3	4	10	—	1	0	0	0	1
Regis and Kathie Lee	—	5	7	10	13	7	0	0	0	4	0	6
Geraldo Rivera	6	3	5	40	13	—	0	0	0	0	0	29
Phil Donahue	—	37	26	59	58	—	5	—	—	0	0	—
Average	*4.5*	*12.8*	*11.5*	*24*	*18.4*	*8.5*	*1.67*	*0.33*	*0.0*	*1.0*	*0.0*	*12.0*
Network TV soft news												
Extra	—	—	16	116	62	8	1	1	0	0	0	24
Entertainment Tonight	—	—	4	16	7	2	0	1	0	0	0	15
Inside Edition	—	—	4	11	24	3	2	1	0	1	1	28
A Current Affair	4	4	1	8	7	—	2	—	—	0	0	—
Average	*4.0*	*4.0*	*6.3*	*37.8*	*25*	*4.3*	*1.3*	*1.0*	*0*	*0.25*	*0.25*	*22.3*
Cable TV soft news												
E! Network	—	3	3	26	6	3	2	0	0	0	0	36
Black Entertainment Television	—	—	23	3	12	6	0	0	0	2	1	8
Comedy Central's Daily Show	—	—	—	3	21	16	—	1	1	3	0	11
MTV News	—	—	7	11	4	7	19	1	0	2	0	5
Average	*3.0*	*11.0*	*10.8*	*10.8*	*8.0*	*7.0*	*0.50*	*0.25*	*1.75*	*0.25*	*15.0*	
Talk radio												
Howard Stern Show	—	—	18	47	32	13	2	1	0	0	28	

Note: "—" indicates either that a given program was not on the air at the time of a given event or that transcripts were unavailable. In several cases, these data exclude "Operation Desert Fox," the December 16–19, 1998, bombing campaign against Iraq.

precision bombs and interviews with military experts, the daytime talk shows hosted by Oprah Winfrey, Geraldo Rivera, and Sally Jesse Raphael, as well as *A Current Affair,* focused on the personal hardships faced by spouses of soldiers serving in the Gulf and on the psychological trauma suffered by families of Americans being held prisoner in Iraq as "human shields."

Similarly, in mid-1995, in covering the escalating U.S. military involvement in Bosnia, a review of the nightly news broadcasts of the three major networks indicates that they addressed a broad range of issues—including international diplomacy, military tactics, the role of NATO, "nation building," and ethnic cleansing, to name only a few. In contrast, the soft news media devoted most of their coverage to a single dramatic story: the travails of U.S. fighter pilot Scott O'Grady, who was shot down over enemy territory on June 2, 1995. Captain O'Grady's heroic story of surviving behind enemy lines for 5 days on a diet of insects and grass, before being rescued by NATO forces, represented an ideal made-for-soft news human drama. To determine the nature and extent of soft news coverage of Bosnia in June 1995, I reviewed Lexis-Nexis transcripts from 12 soft news programs for which the appropriate data were accessible.[2] I found that of 35 total broadcasts on these 12 shows addressing the conflict in Bosnia, 30 (or 86%) featured the O'Grady story. Of course, traditional news programs also covered the story. Yet, in the latter case, this was merely one of *many* storylines. The three major networks, combined, covered the O'Grady story in only 13 of 57 (or 23%) June 1995 national news broadcasts in which Bosnia was addressed. . . .

Incidental Attention

. . . [F]or many Americans, politics, including foreign policy, is of little interest.

Those who consider politics a waste of time are unlikely to pay attention to political information unless the time and effort required to do so (i.e., the expected costs) are extremely small, thereby removing any incentive to ignore it (Salomon 1984). One means of minimizing the costs associated with paying attention to low-benefit political information might be to attach or "piggyback" it to low-cost entertainment-oriented information. This would allow individuals to learn about politics passively (Neuman, Just, and Crigler 1992; Zukin with Snyder 1984), even if they are neither interested in the subject matter nor motivated to learn about it (Zukin with Snyder 1984; Robinson 1974; Wamsley and Pride 1972; Blumler and McQuail 1969; Fitzsimmons and Osburn 1968; Krugman 1965). Political information might thus become a free bonus, or *incidental by-product,* of paying attention to entertainment-oriented information.[3] In effect, piggybacking might, on occasion, render any trade-off between being entertained and learning about politics moot by, in effect, transforming a select few of the major political issues of the day *into* the entertainment that people seek.[4]

This does not imply that transforming news into entertainment will affect all viewers similarly. Indeed, survey evidence . . . indicates that most people who consume traditional news do so primarily (albeit not exclusively) to learn about the issues of the day. This suggests that increasing the entertainment value of news is unlikely to affect significantly these individuals' attentiveness to political news. Indeed, such individuals have already determined that political news is worth their time and effort. Watching soft news programs is unlikely to affect this calculus, even if they occasionally cover political issues. Rather, only individuals who would not otherwise be exposed to politics are likely to be affected by encountering political coverage in the soft news media, or by piggybacking.

Yet, even for the latter, politically uninterested individuals, piggybacking is possible only if information about a political issue can be attached to entertainment-oriented information *without* increasing the costs of paying attention. And this requires framing the information in terms accessible to even politically disengaged individuals (i.e., cheap framing).[5] Paying attention to news that employs highly accessible frames requires less cognitive energy than paying attention to traditional news formats, which might provoke greater cognitive conflict (Krugman and Hartley 1970). Such information is cheap. Indeed, absent cheap framing, piggybacking would almost certainly fail. In fact, for many individuals, if information about a political issue can be piggybacked to low-cost and high benefit, entertainment-oriented information, the associated costs of paying attention are virtually eliminated.

This discussion suggests that by engaging in cheap framing and piggybacking, the soft news media may substantially reduce the expected costs of paying attention to those issues that lend themselves to these practices, such as political sex scandals, celebrity murder trials, and foreign policy crises. This, in turn, might induce individuals who do not normally seek information about politics or foreign affairs to attend to *some* information about such issues, even if their intrinsic interest, per se, remains low.

Summary and Hypotheses

Most of the time, the soft news media avoid politics entirely, in favor of more sensational issues, such as crime dramas, scandals, and celebrity gossip. Many entertainment-seeking television viewers may therefore remain largely uninformed about the day-to-day political issues facing the nation. When, however, an issue crosses over, via piggybacking, from network newscasts to the soft news media, a far broader audience will likely confront it. And unlike the relatively mundane or arcane presentation of political information offered by network newscasts, soft news programs employ cheap framing to appeal to entertainment-seeking audiences. Hence, for many individuals, the expected benefit of learning about politics, per se, is quite small. Yet the cognitive costs of paying attention to information about select political issues, including foreign crises, may, on occasion, be smaller still, due in no small measure to the efforts of soft news programmers to exploit such issues' previously untapped entertainment value and resulting suitability for piggybacking. A number of hypotheses follow from the theory. Four of these, which I test in the next section, are as follows.

H_1: People watch soft news programs to be entertained, not to learn about politics or foreign affairs.

H_2: *Ceteris paribus,* people who are uninterested in foreign affairs and consume soft news should be more attentive to foreign crises (and other similarly accessible issues) than their counterparts who are similarly uninterested in foreign affairs but do not consume soft news.

H_3: *Ceteris paribus,* soft news consumption should be *most* strongly positively related to foreign crisis attentiveness among the *least* politically engaged members of society and *least* strongly positively related to attentiveness among the *most* politically engaged members of the public.

H_4: *Ceteris paribus,* other *less* accessible or dramatic, or *more* partisan, political issues are less likely to be covered by the soft news media, and hence, attentiveness to such issues should *not* be significantly related to consumption of soft news.
[Editor's note: Information about the statistical tests has been sharply abbreviated.]

Why People Watch Soft News

. . . Might some individuals tune in to soft news programs with the explicit intent of learning about foreign crises or other political issues? Such individuals may reason that, when a crisis or other major issue arises, the soft news media will offer more interesting coverage than network newscasts or newspapers. If so, the incidental by-product model would be irrelevant. Hypothesis 1, however, predicts that soft news viewers watch such programs for their entertainment value, *not* to learn about politics. To test this hypothesis, I employ a 1996 survey (Pew Center Media Consumption poll, May 1996), which asked respondents the extent to which they prefer news about entertainment, famous people, crime, national politics, or international affairs (among other topics), as well as to what extent they consume a variety of soft news media.

I created an *entertainment news interest index,* based on the first three items mentioned above and a *soft news consumption index* based upon the latter series of questions. If information about foreign crises, or other political issues, is being piggybacked to entertainment programming, primarily as an incidental by-product, then we should observe a strong positive correlation between interest in entertainment-oriented news and consumption of soft news media, but *not* between interest in news about international affairs or national politics and soft news consumption. In fact, this is just what I find. The entertainment news interest index correlates with the soft news consumption index at an impressive 0.40. The corresponding correlations with interest in international affairs and interest in national politics are nearly zero (-0.01 and -0.03, respectively). This strongly suggests that to the extent that individuals are receiving information about foreign crises, or other national political issues, in the soft news media, they are doing so not by design but, rather, as an incidental by-product of seeking entertainment. Any information about foreign crises or national politics appears in these data to be piggybacked to entertainment-oriented news. This result clearly supports Hypothesis 1.

Soft News Consumption and Following Foreign Crises

For the next investigation, my data are drawn from the aforementioned 1996 Pew Center survey of public media consumption habits. In addition to asking respondents which types of television and radio programming, magazines, and newspapers they watch, listen to, and read, the survey also asked if respondents had followed . . . three foreign crisis-related issues: Bosnia, the Israel-Lebanon conflict, and a congressional debate on terrorism. . . .

. . . As one might anticipate, consumption of hard news is strongly positively associated with attentiveness to each foreign crisis ($p < 0.001$), as is political knowledge in the terrorism and Lebanon models. Interest in international affairs is also positively and significantly related to respondents' attentiveness to the three issues ($p < 0.001$). Most importantly for my purposes, however, exposure to the soft news media is positively and significantly associated with attentiveness to each crisis, thereby, in each instance, supporting Hypothesis 2.

To determine whether exposure to soft news exerts differing effects on respondents with varying levels of overall interest in international affairs, I interact the latter variable with the soft news index. The results strongly support Hypothesis 3. The interaction term is significant, or nearly so, and correctly signed, in all three models ($p < 0.01$, $p < 0.056$, and $p < 0.073$). Because logit coefficients are difficult to interpret, I translate the coefficients on the key variables into probabilities, with all controls held constant at their mean values. The results indicate that, for individuals who report following international affairs "very" or "fairly" closely, exposure to soft news matters little for attentiveness to any of the three foreign crisis issues. Yet individuals who follow international affairs less closely (representing over one-third of the respondents) *do* appear to learn about each issue through the soft news

media. Consistent with Hypothesis 3, the relationships are strongest for respondents who claim to follow international affairs "not at all" closely. . . .
. . . [T]he soft news effect is substantial. As soft news consumption increases, the corresponding probabilities of following the Israel-Lebanon conflict, antiterrorism debate, and Bosnia intervention "fairly closely" increase by 19 (from 0.09 to 0.28), 34 (from 0.08 to 0.42), and 41 (from 0.10 to 0.51) percentage points, respectively. Each of these results clearly supports Hypothesis 3, suggesting that respondents who are uninterested in international affairs are nonetheless exposed to information about all three crisis issues through the soft news media.[6]

The question remains whether, as predicted by Hypothesis 4, the above interaction disappears if the respondents are asked about an issue covered intensely by the traditional news media but *not* by the soft news media. If the interaction persists, this would suggest that the above relationships may be artifacts of some omitted variable(s), such as, perhaps, greater overall media exposure by soft news consumers. One appropriate political issue for addressing this question is a presidential primary election. Primaries are highly partisan events and, hence, less appealing to a politically cynical populace. They ought therefore to be less amenable than foreign crises to cheap framing and piggybacking. . . . In fact, consistent with Hypothesis 4 . . . the soft news media appear in these relationships to contribute to attentiveness to foreign crises but *not* to the 1996 presidential primaries. . . .

Conclusion

Beginning in the 1980s, news broadcasters, facing unprecedented competitive pressures, came to recognize that real-life human drama could attract a large audience and could be produced at a far lower cost than fictional drama. According to Danny Schechter, a former producer for CNN and ABC's news magazine *20/20*, the Persian Gulf War drove home for news executives the huge ratings potential of military conflicts, which could be realized by transforming war reporting into a made-for-television soap opera:

> It started with the Gulf War—the packaging of news, the graphics, the music, the classification of stories. . . . Everybody benefited by saturation coverage. The more channels, the more a sedated public will respond to this. . . . If you can get an audience hooked, breathlessly awaiting every fresh disclosure with a recognizable cast of characters they can either love or hate, with a dramatic arc and a certain coming down to a deadline, you have a winner in terms of building audience. (Scott 1998)

Through cheap framing, the soft news media have successfully piggybacked information about foreign crises (and other highly accessible issues, such as the Lewinsky scandal) to entertainment-oriented information. Soft news consumers thereby gain information about such issues as an incidental by-product of seeking entertainment. My statistical investigations demonstrated that individuals *do* learn about these types of issues—but *not* other, less accessible or dramatic issues—from the soft news media, without necessarily tuning in with the intention of doing so.

Substantial scholarly research has shown that public opinion can, at least sometimes, influence policy outcomes, including in foreign policy (Kernell 1997; Powlick 1995; Bartels 1991; Ostrom and Job 1986; Page and Shapiro 1983). And even *minimal* attention to politics through the mass media disproportionately increases partisan stability in voting (Zukin 1977). This suggests that soft news media coverage of foreign policy may have significant practical consequences for American politics. Indeed, while viewers of many of these programs are not among the most politically engaged Americans (Davis and Owen 1998), low-attention individuals do vote in significant numbers. . . . While determining the precise policy effects of this phenomenon is beyond the scope of this project, in a democratic political system, in which leaders are directly accountable to the public, it seems unlikely that heightened awareness of policy decision making by a previously disengaged segment of the population would be entirely without consequence.

Indeed, I have presented some evidence suggesting that the soft news media may not necessarily cover political issues in the same way that traditional news programs do. And research has shown that the *nature* of the political information people consume can influence the substance of the opinions they express (Iyengar and Kinder 1987). This, in turn, raises the possibility that, at least in some instances, and regarding some issues, the opinions of individuals whose primary source of political information is the soft news media might differ materially from those of their more politically attentive counterparts. . . .

My findings further suggest that some of the barriers to information and political participation confronting democratic citizens may be falling. Where America's foreign policy was once the domain of a fairly small "foreign policy elite," the soft news media appear to have, to some extent, "democratized" foreign policy. This represents both a challenge and an opportunity for America's political leaders. It is a challenge because leaders can no longer count on communicating effectively with the American people solely through traditional news outlets (Baum and Kernell 1999; Hess 1998). To reach those segments of the public who eagerly reach for their remotes any time traditional political news appears on the screen, leaders must reformulate their messages in terms that appeal to programs preferred by these politically uninterested individuals.

The rise of the soft news media also offers an opportunity, because, to the extent that they are able to adapt their messages accordingly, soft news outlets allow leaders to communicate with segments of the population that have traditionally tuned out politics and foreign affairs entirely. This may allow future leaders to expand their support coalitions beyond the traditionally attentive segments of the population. Broader support coalitions, in turn, may translate into more effective leadership, particularly in difficult times.

Finally, from the citizens' perspective, one might be tempted to take heart from the apparent leveling-off of attentiveness to foreign policy across differing groups of Americans. After all, a more broadly attentive public might yield more broad-based participation in the political process. Many democratic theorists would likely consider this a desirable outcome. Yet it is unclear whether more information necessarily makes better citizens, particularly if the quality or diversity of that information is suspect. Indeed, one might also be tempted to wonder about the implications of a citizenry learning about the world through the relatively narrow lens of the entertainment-oriented soft news media.

Notes

1. These findings complement a large literature in social psychology on individual media uses and gratification. This literature (e.g., Katz, Blumler, and Gurevitch 1973–1974; Katzman 1972; Katz and Foulkes 1962) argues that individuals use the media to fulfill various social and psychological needs, including diversion, easing social tension and conflict, establishing substitute personal relationships, reinforcing personal identity and values, gaining comfort through familiarity, learning about social problems, and surveillance. In fact, the frames most frequently employed by typical individuals are directly linked to several of the predominant uses of the media identified by psychologists.

2. The programs I reviewed included *Extra, Dateline, Jay Leno, David Letterman, Conan O'Brien, A Current Affair, Live with Regis and Kathy Lee, Entertainment Tonight, Howard Stern, E! News Daily, The E! Gossip Show,* and *The Geraldo Rivera Show.*

3. Passive learning is possible because individuals are more likely to accept information presented in a nonconflictual manner, which does not arouse excitement (Krugman and Hartley 1970). Individuals learn passively by first *choosing* to expose themselves to a particular type of information (e.g., political news), say by watching the network news, but then surrendering control of the *specific* information to which they are exposed (Zukin and Snyder 1984). For instance, individuals unwilling to *read* about a political issue in the newspaper may be willing to *watch* a news story about the issue, even if they are not particularly interested in the subject matter, simply because watching television requires less effort (Eveland and Scheufele 2000). Incidental learning is merely an extreme form of passive learning, whereby the individual actively seeks one variety of information, say entertainment, and is unwittingly exposed to and accepts information of another sort entirely (e.g., political news).

4. This does not imply that the distinction between traditional and soft news has disappeared or that politically apathetic individuals have come to anticipate heightened benefits from consuming political news. . . . [However,] information attended to by a viewer due to its entertainment value may have the unintended effect of influencing that individual's attitudes toward other things, such as, say, a foreign policy crisis.

5. While there are many potential sources of accessibility, none approach the overwhelming predominance of the mass media in determining which issues command public attention, at least temporarily (Iyengar 1990; Krugman and Hartley 1970). Krugman and Hartley (1970) note that, as an ideal vehicle for passive learning, television has allowed many people to develop opinions on serious issues about which they would previously have replied "don't know" if queried (because they would have avoided learning about such issues).

6. The relationships are strongest for the antiterrorism debate (which is clearly linked by the public to international terrorism). This is most likely due, in large measure, to the national trauma produced by the World Trade Center and Oklahoma City bombings. Millions of Americans perceived themselves as holding a personal stake in the terrorism debate, and so it was a more immediate concern (and thus more accessible) than Bosnia or the Israel-Lebanon conflict.

References

Almond, Gabriel A. 1950. *The American People and Foreign Policy.* New York: Harcourt, Brace.

Bartels, Larry M. 1991. "Constituency Opinion and Congressional Policy Making: The Reagan Defense Buildup." *American Political Science Review* 85 (June): 457–74.

Baum, Matthew A., 2000. *Tabloid Wars: The Mass Media, Public Opinion and the Use of Force Abroad,* Ph.D. dissertation. San Diego: University of California.

Baum, Matthew A., and Sam Kernell. 1999. "Has Cable Ended the Golden Age of Presidential Television?" *American Political Science Review* 93 (March): 99–114.

Blumler, Jay G., and Denis McQuail. 1969. *Television in Politics: Its Uses and Influence.* Chicago: University of Chicago Press.

Bosso, Christopher J. 1989. "Setting the Agenda: Mass Media and the Discovery of Famine in Ethiopia." In *Manipulating Public Opinion: Essays on Public Opinion as a Dependent Variable,* eds. Michael Margolis and Gary A. Mauser. Pacific Grove, CA: Brooks/Cole. Pp. 153–74.

Chaffee, Steven H., and Stacey F. Kanihan. 1997. "Learning About Politics from the Mass Media." *Political Communication* 14 (October–December): 421–30.

Cohen, Bernard C. 1973. *The Public's Impact on Foreign Policy.* Boston: Little, Brown.

Converse, Philip E. 1964. "The Nature of Belief Systems in Mass Publics." In *Ideology and Discontent,* eds. David E. Apter. New York: Free Press. Pp. 206–61.

Davis, Richard, and Diana Owen. 1998. *New Media and American Politics.* New York and Oxford: Oxford University Press.

Delli Carpini, Michael X., and Scott Keeter. 1996. *What Americans Know About Politics and Why It Matters.* New Haven, CT: Yale University Press.

Dionne, E. J. 1991. *Why Americans Hate Politics.* New York: Simon & Schuster.

Eveland, William P., and Dietram A. Scheufele. 2000. "Connecting News Media Use with Gaps in Knowledge and Participation." *Political Communication* 17 (July–September): 215–37.

Fitzsimmons, Stephen J., and Hobart G. Osburn. 1968. "The Impact of Social Issues and Public Affairs Television Documentaries." *Public Opinion Quarterly* 32 (Autumn): 379–97.

Graber, Doris A. 1984. *Processing the News: How People Tame the Information Tide.* New York: Longman.

Graebner, Norman A. 1983. "Public Opinion and Foreign Policy: A Pragmatic View." In *Interaction: Foreign Policy and Public Policy,* eds. E. D. Piper and R. J. Turchik. Washington, DC: American Enterprise Institute. Pp. 11–34.

Hess, Stephen. 1998. "The Once to Future Worlds of Presidents Communicating." *Presidential Studies Quarterly* 28 (Fall): 748.

Holsti, Ole R. 1996. *Public Opinion and American Foreign Policy.* Ann Arbor: University of Michigan Press.

Iyengar, Shanto. 1990. "Shortcuts to Political Knowledge: The Role of Selective Attention and Accessibility." In *Information and Democratic Processes,* eds. John A. Ferejohn and James H. Kuklinski. Urbana and Chicago: University of Illinois Press. Pp. 160–85.

Iyengar, Shanto, and Donald R. Kinder. 1987. *News that Matters.* Chicago: University of Chicago Press.

Kalb, Marvin. 1998. "The Rise of the 'New News': A Case Study of Two Root Causes of the Modern Scandal Coverage." Discussion Paper D-34 (October). Cambridge, MA: Joan Shorenstein Center on the Press, Politics and Public Policy, Harvard University.

Katz, Elihu, and David Foulkes. 1962. "On the Use of the Mass Media as 'Escape': Clarification of a Concept." *Public Opinion Quarterly* 26 (Autumn): 377–88.

Katz, Elihu, Jay G. Blumler, and Michael Gurevitch. 1973–1974. "Uses and Gratifications Research." *Public Opinion Quarterly* 37 (Winter): 509–23.

Katzman, Natan. 1972. "Television Soap Operas: What's Been Going on Anyway?" *Public Opinion Quarterly* 36 (Summer): 200–12.

Kelly, Stanley, Jr., and Thad W. Mirer. 1974. "The Simple Act of Voting." *American Political Science Review* 68 (January): 572–91.

Kernell, Samuel. 1997. *Going Public: New Strategies of Presidential Leadership,* 3rd ed. Washington, DC: CQ Press.

Krugman, Herbert. 1965. "The Impact of Television Advertising: Learning Without Involvement." *Public Opinion Quarterly* 29 (Autumn): 349–56.

Krugman, Herbert E., and Eugene L. Hartley. 1970. "Passive Learning from Television." *Public Opinion Quarterly* 34 (Summer): 184–90.

Moisy, Claude. 1997. "Myths of the Global Information Village." *Foreign Policy* 107 (Summer): 78–87.

Neuman, W. Russell, Marion R. Just, and Ann R. Crigler. 1992. *Common Knowledge: News and the Construction of Political Meaning.* Chicago: University of Chicago Press.

Nye, Joseph S., Philip D. Zelikow, and David C. King, eds. 1997. *Why People Don't Trust Government.* Cambridge, MA: Harvard University Press.

Ostrom, Charles W., Jr., and Brian L. Job. 1986. "The President and the Political Use of Force." *American Political Science Review* 80 (June): 541–66.

Page, Benjamin I., and Robert Y. Shapiro. 1983. "Effects of Public Opinion on Policy." *American Political Science Review* 77 (March): 175–90.

Patterson, Thomas E. 2000. "Doing Well and Doing Good." Faculty Research Working Paper Series, RWP01-001 (December). Cambridge, MA: John F. Kennedy School of Government, Harvard University.

Powlick, Philip J. 1995. "The Sources of Public Opinion for American Foreign Policy Officials." *International Studies Quarterly* 39 (December): 427–52.

Powlick, Philip J., and Andrew Z. Katz. 1998. "Testing a Model of Public Opinion-Foreign Policy Linkage: Public Opinion in Two Carter Foreign Policy Decisions." Presented at the 1998 Meeting of the Midwest Political Science Association, Chicago.

Robinson, Michael. 1974. "The Impact of the Televised Watergate Hearings." *Journal of Communication* 24 (Spring): 17–30.

Salomon, Gavriel. 1984. "Television Is 'Easy' and Print Is 'Tough': The Differential Investment of Mental Effort in Learning as a Function of Perceptions and Attributions." *Journal of Educational Psychology* 76 (December): 647–58.

Scott, Janny. 1998. "The President Under Fire: The Media; A Media Race Enters Waters Still Uncharted." *The New York Times* 1 February, Late Edition-Final, Sect. 1: 1.

Wamsley, Gary, and Richard A. Pride. 1972. "Television Network News: Rethinking the Iceberg Problem." *Western Political Quarterly* 25 (Summer): 434–50.

Zukin, Cliff. 1977. "A Reconsideration of the Effects of Information on Partisan Stability." *Public Opinion Quarterly* 41 (Summer): 244–54.

Zukin, Cliff, and Robin Snyder. 1984. "Passive Learning: When the Media Environment Is the Message." *Public Opinion Quarterly* 48 (Autumn): 629–38.

12

CONSTRUCTING PUBLIC OPINION: THE USES OF FICTIONAL AND NONFICTIONAL TELEVISION IN CONVERSATIONS ABOUT THE ENVIRONMENT

Michael X. Delli Carpini and Bruce A. Williams

Editor's Note

The influence of the news media on the opinions of their audiences is modulated by other opinion-shaping forces in each person's environment. Political scientists Michael X. Delli Carpini and Bruce A. Williams focus on the interplay between television viewers' established memories, their recall of information from factual and fictional television broadcasts, and their interactions with fellow focus group members. Depending on the main thrust of the conversation, these strands are combined in diverse ways into opinion-shaping forces. In the conversations on environmental issues reported here, both fiction and nonfiction mass media information played a major part, demonstrating the permeable boundary between these two informational realms.

Delli Carpini was an associate professor of political science at Barnard College when this essay was written. Williams, his coauthor, was associate professor of urban and regional planning at the University of Illinois at Urbana-Champaign. Delli Carpini's most well-known study, *What Americans Know about Politics and Why It Matters,* written with Scott Keeter, was published in the same year as this essay. Williams's study, written with Albert Matheny and titled *Democracy, Dialogue, and Environmental Disputes: The Contested Languages of Social Regulation,* had appeared a year earlier.

    . . . Envisioning public opinion as a conversation is especially useful in understanding the political relevance of television. As the central source of

Source: Michael X. Delli Carpini and Bruce A. Williams, "Constructing Public Opinion: The Uses of Fictional and Nonfictional Television in Conversations about the Environment," in *Communication Research* 21 (December 1994): 782–812. Copyright © 1994 by Sage Publications, Inc. Reprinted by permission of Sage Publications, Inc.

information in the United States, television provides both the topics and the substance upon which most political conversations are based. In addition, however, our conversational metaphor points to a more active role for television in the shaping of public opinion. Put simply, we argue that the interaction between television and a viewer is similar to a conversation. Of course in an important respect this conversation is one-sided: viewers are seldom seen or heard.[1] And yet the viewer is engaged in a conversation in many important respects. The most obvious example would be when he or she "talks back" to the set or, more indirectly, when two or more viewers comment to each other about a show as it is being watched.

But even when sitting in silence, viewers are interacting with television in ways that are more analogous to conversation than to reading, to writing, or even to contemplation or deliberation. Certainly viewers interact with television in ways that are more similar to conversing than to other commonly used metaphors, such as inputting data or being inoculated. This is so because television consciously mimics the elements of immediate, personal exchange. The information transmitted is ephemeral. Messages are contained in a combination of aural and visual cues, including tone of voice, body language, and so forth. Televised conversants (whether newscasters, celebrities, or fictional characters) are often familiar to the viewer. The illusion of intimacy and dialogue is heightened by techniques such as looking directly into the camera or directly addressing the viewer through asides or stock phrases such as, "We'll be right back" or "I'll see you next time." Television, therefore, serves not only as a source of information for future conversations, but also as both a regular "conversant" in an ongoing discussion and, ultimately, as an important forum for political discourse in the United States. . . .

Focus groups are especially appropriate for exploring the social aspects of public opinion: "The hallmark of focus groups is the explicit use of the group interaction to produce data and insights that would be less accessible without the interaction found in the group" (Morgan 1988, 12). They are also appropriate for examining the relationship between television and politics, especially in light of the conversational metaphor presented earlier. The ubiquitousness of television; the assumption that messages and audiences interact in complex ways that allow for multiple meanings to emerge from the same broadcast; an understanding that television watching is often a social activity in which viewers converse with each other and with the TV: all of this suggests the need to think in terms of *the uses* of television rather than simply its effects. It also suggests that such uses will be subtle, varied, fluid, social, and context dependent. Focus groups, more than most quantitative methods, allow for a systematic reexamination of television and politics that is sensitive to the complexity of this relationship.

Discussing the Environment:
A Case Study in the Construction of Public Opinion

The findings presented [here] are based on nine focus groups conducted in 1990–91.[2] . . . One group consisted of five people, five consisted of four people, and three consisted of three people. Ages varied from eighteen to seventy-two, with a median age of thirty-nine.[3] Occupations ranged from student, to government employee, to full-time homemaker, to both blue- and white-collar worker (one participant was unemployed). Twenty-one of the thirty-four participants were women. Three of the participants were black. Overall our "sample" was slightly less affluent than the larger population from which it was recruited. Based upon responses to a brief telephone survey administered during the initial recruitment, as well as to a self-administered survey completed prior to the start of the focus groups, our participants varied in the strength and direction of their partisan affiliation, their ideological self-placement, and their views concerning issues such as the environment, prayer in schools, government aid to minorities and women, abortion, and defense spending. They also varied in their self-professed interest in politics, their likelihood of talking about politics with friends, and their television-viewing habits. In short, while not a random sample of either the local or the national population, our participants brought a range of backgrounds, beliefs, and opinions to the discussions.

The topic of discussion in each of our nine focus groups was "environmental pollution." Three of the discussions (one from each age group) were preceded by viewing an edited version of the made-for-television docudrama "Incident At Dark River," which dealt with the issue of toxic waste. Another three groups began by viewing an episode of the CBS newsmagazine *48 Hours*, also dealing with the issue of toxic waste.[4] In both cases, the broadcasts were introduced as "a way to get us thinking about the topic." The remaining three groups watched no television and simply began by discussing their views on environmental pollution. The focus groups without television lasted approximately one and a half hours, while those with television averaged an additional forty-five minutes.

The discussion protocol was loosely structured and designed to stimulate discussion rather than to uncover particular pieces of information. . . . The protocol was identical regardless of whether television was present or not, with two exceptions. First, in those groups where television was viewed, discussants were asked what they "thought of the show," prior to turning to a more general discussion of the environment. And second, at the end of sessions that had begun by watching television, discussants were asked a few specific questions about the programs. Other than this, however, the broadcasts were not referred to by the moderator.

Overall, the focus groups were intended to provide three types of "data." First, since at various points in the protocol we directly asked discussants about their reactions to the show they had seen, their views of the media more generally, their television-viewing habits, and so forth, the focus group transcripts provided information concerning people's own perceptions about their relationship with television. Second, by asking people to engage in a public discussion of a timely political issue, we were able to directly observe how citizens converse and the role that television plays in that public conversation. Third, by having people watch television and then requiring them to talk both about the program itself and about issues touched on in the program, we were able to approximate what we argue is the ongoing, silent conversation people are regularly engaged in while watching television.

. . . [W]e have several goals. First, we provide evidence for the extensive role both nonfiction and fiction television play in public discourse. Second, we show that, based on self-reports and our own observations, citizens do interact with television in ways consistent with our "conversation" metaphor. Third, we examine the fluid, often inconsistent nature of public opinion, pointing out how people socially construct rather than retrieve their views on complex issues. Fourth, we explore the role of television in this process of opinion formation, focusing on our discussants' surprising awareness of (and concern for) their dependence on the media. Finally, we provide examples of the real but limited autonomy individuals have in identifying and, where appropriate, resisting television's ideological biases.

The Ubiquitousness of Television in Political Conversation

During coding, we distinguished among three types of media references made by conversants as they discussed environmental issues: references to the specific show watched at the start of the focus group (not applicable to groups where no television was shown); references to television more generally; and references to other mass media (i.e., newspapers, magazines, radio). Included in this last category are general references to "the media." Within each category we distinguished between "direct" and "indirect" references. Direct references refer to comments in which the media were specifically mentioned (e.g., "I picked up a newspaper that had an 'Earth News' section" or "I saw this thing on TV, about how enough pollution could . . . "). When the specific reference was less clear (e.g., "If it's like they showed in Mexico City where the people can't walk down the street" or "You know, when the spotted owl was the big issue . . . they made it the owl against the lumberjacks"), the comment was coded as an indirect reference to the media. In addition, we distinguished between "prompted" and "unprompted" references. The former included any media reference made when we specifically queried about their reactions to the show or about their general views concerning how well the media cover environmental issues. . . . The latter included only unsolicited references to the media.

. . . [M]edia references peppered the conversations: on average, 34 percent of all statements included at least one *unprompted* media reference. . . . The relative number of such references varied depending upon the presence or absence of television. In groups without television . . . the total percentage of unprompted media references was 27 percent, compared to 40 percent . . . in groups that started by viewing a television show. Most of this difference is accounted for by continued reference to the shows after we had turned the discussion to more general issues of the environment. . . .

We have argued elsewhere that understanding the impact of television on the construction of public opinion requires expanding the definition of politically relevant television to include both fictional and nonfictional programming (Delli Carpini and Williams 1994a). Our focus groups support this argument. When participants drew upon media in their conversations, they made few distinctions between fictional and nonfictional television. Unprompted references to the media were as frequent in focus groups viewing fictional as nonfictional programs, and we found little difference in the overall percentage of references to the shows themselves (32 percent in the groups viewing "Incident At Dark River" and 30 percent in those viewing *48 Hours*). Indeed, participants were more likely to make *unprompted* references to the fictional show than the nonfictional show (22 percent of all unprompted comments in the former case, compared to 13 percent in the latter).

Beyond references to these particular shows, discussants were about as likely to invoke fictional as nonfictional programs to make or refute points. For example, where possible we coded direct references to television (other than to the shows viewed during the focus groups) as to whether the programs referred to were fictional or nonfictional. There were 102 references to television that could be coded in this way. Of these, 49 were to fictional media (e.g., *The Day After, The Simpsons*) and 53 were to nonfictional media (e.g., *60 Minutes*, CNN). Groups were about as likely to reference fiction as nonfiction programs regardless of whether they had been shown "Incident At Dark River," *48 Hours*, or no television at all.

The political relevance of fictional media is also revealed by the specific public figures mentioned by our discussants. The following is an inclusive list of the people mentioned at least once in our groups: George Bush, Carl Sagan, Ralph Nader, Ted Turner, Dan Rather, Cher, Captain Planet (a cartoon character), John Ritter, Bill Moyers, Nadia Comaneci, Kitty Kelly, Nancy Reagan, Bette Midler, Ed Begley Jr., Bill Cosby, Jeremy Rifkin, Bob Barker, Phil Donahue, Oprah Winfrey, Sally Struthers, Tom Cruise, Clint

Eastwood, Cindy Lauper, and Al Sharpton. At least two things seem striking to us about this list. First is the frequency with which figures from the
media, especially entertainers associated with environmental issues, were
referenced, often as authoritative sources. Second is the almost complete absence of government representatives: other than a *single* reference to President Bush, there were no mentions of specific elected or appointed public
officials.[5]

The extent to which the mass media in general and television in particular
dominated our conversations about the environment is perhaps best illustrated by comparing the aforementioned numbers to the frequency with
which personal experiences were referenced. Where possible, we coded all
comments that referred to personal experience as a source of information. Included here were statements based on either firsthand experience or experiences of people with whom they were familiar. . . .

How often do people draw upon personal experience in political conversations about the environment? Not very often when compared to mediated
sources. Overall, only 9 percent of the comments referred to personal experience. . . . This percentage varied only slightly between groups shown fictional television (7 percent), nonfictional television (8 percent), and no television (11 percent). Even when citing direct experiences, our discussants
often evaluated them against information drawn from the media. . . .

. . . [A]s we shall discuss in more detail, people are ambiguous about their
dependence on the media for information. Nonetheless, part of the media's
power to shape political discourse comes from an underlying semiconscious
belief that information provided by it is more reliable than other sources, including personal experience.[6]

As final evidence of the general influence of television on political conversation, we compared how often it was addressed, relative to references to
other members of the group. The latter included both direct references to
others (e.g., "I agree with her") and more indirect references in which someone seemed to be taking his or her cue from the comments of another member of the group. Among the groups shown television, we found that the
specific program was addressed almost as much as all the "other" group
members combined. For the groups shown *48 Hours*, 13 percent of all comments contained a direct or indirect, unprompted reference to the show . . .
while 19 percent of all comments contained a direct or indirect reference to
other members of the group. . . . For the groups shown "Incident at Dark
River," the numbers were 22 and 26 percent respectively. . . . And this comparison underestimates the frequency of overall television or media references, since it includes only unprompted references to the specific show.
Clearly, television remained an important "participant" throughout the
conversations.

Conversing with Television

We have argued that citizens often "discover" their political views in the give-and-take of discussions with others. Television plays a central role in this process, in that it is engaged in an ongoing political conversation: when we turn the set on, we dip into this conversation.

Some of the strongest support for our conversational metaphor comes from the discussants' own reports of their viewing habits. Literally all of them said they talked with others about what they saw on television, either while viewing or shortly thereafter, and almost all of them said they did this with great regularity. . . .

Viewers' interaction with television has a conversational quality even when one watches alone. In our focus groups, it was common to see viewers smiling, nodding, groaning, and so forth as they watched television. It was also not unusual for them to gesture at the television during discussions (even though the set was off) much as they gestured at other members of the con-versation. Indeed, many viewers (as we do) talk back to the tube: only three of the thirty-four participants said they never did. Of the three, one woman said that, while she didn't, her husband did all the time. Another one of the three said: "I don't actually verbalize, but I think, boy I'd like to be . . . like on Donahue or something . . . I'd like to be there right then just to say this. . . ." More typical was Catherine's comment: "I scream at the TV, just like I scream at other people when I drive." . . . [S]uch interactions were not limited to news or talk shows. . . .

The Shifting Nature of Public Opinions

One of the most consistent and telling patterns to emerge from the focus groups was the active role conversants took in attempting to make sense of the political and social world. Drawing on their own store of information and beliefs, the views of others in the group, and the views presented by tel-evision, discussants engaged in an ongoing effort to construct their opinions about environmental issues.

Key to understanding the role conversation (with both television and other citizens) plays in the formation and maintenance of public opinion is first un-derstanding the contextual, fluid, and often inconsistent nature of opinions themselves. Freed from the forced restraints of closed-ended surveys, this as-pect of public opinion becomes clear. This inconsistency in part reflects a lack of information, interest, and so forth, but more importantly also reflects the "inherent contestability" of most important public issues. An examination of all the comments made by individual discussants throughout the focus groups demonstrates that even the most thoughtful citizens express views that are contradictory. Indeed, often the most consistent views were expressed by those who were uninterested and unreflective of the issues under discussion. . . .

The Construction of Political Meaning

. . . [People's] "true" opinions do not reside in one or the other of their statements. Rather, their opinions are to be found in the full set of statements they make about a particular issue and can be understood only in the specific context in which they are made. More important, we argue that citizens play an active, if limited, role in the construction of these opinions, and they do so in part through ongoing conversations with other people and, especially, with television.

Examples of our discussants actively using their own experiences, the comments of others, and the "comments" of television abound throughout the transcripts. Many of the examples . . . began with phrases such as "I agree with her," or "It's like on the show we saw." In addition, participants often picked up on themes, topics, and so forth introduced by other members or, in those focus groups with television, by the program they had just watched. For example, the plot of "Incident at Dark River" revolved around a local company's polluting a river with toxic waste. Similarly, one segment of *48 Hours* was devoted to toxic water pollution. In the discussions about the environment following both these shows, people were much more likely to focus specifically on industrial water pollution than were those people in groups who were without television's immediate influence. . . .

Similarly, both programs focused attention on the human costs of pollution by emphasizing its effect on children. In the docudrama, the lead character's daughter dies after playing in a river polluted with toxic waste, while one segment of *48 Hours* centered on parents whose young son had died of leukemia, the possible result of pesticides used in the area. Comments such as the following, found in all the discussions in which television was present, were largely absent from those discussions held without first viewing TV:

> Susan: I think that [pollution] is very serious and that . . . if we don't do something our grandchildren and their children won't have a chance.
>
> Ruby: I don't have any children, but I have nieces and nephews. . . . What kind of world are they going to have? . . .

In one sense these examples simply illustrate the agenda-setting and priming effects demonstrated by mainstream research. Ruby's comment is typical: "I never really think about [environmental issues] too much unless I happen to see something on television." However, allowing people to speak for them-

selves, as in focus groups, also helps expand our understanding of these processes. First, our discussions suggest that the media not only shape what people *think* about, but also what they *talk* about. Second, they provide evidence that people are very much aware of this process. In some important ways, the agenda-setting function of television is not the insidious process often implied in media research.

> Tania: I think people talk about [environmentalism] more now than they did before because it's brought out so much more now. . . . But, I think now you hear so much about it that it's on your mind. Whether you're talking about it or not, you are thinking about it.

> Catherine: I don't think [environmental problems are] something that's a major, major concern. . . . [I]t's like . . . the war in the Persian Gulf. If you asked me about it [when it was going on], I'd say [I talk about it] every day. You know, you talk about it and so people kind of put aside other things.

Often our conversants' understanding of the degree to which they rely on the media was fairly sophisticated. Violet and Catherine, for example, noted the power of television as a visual medium to dramatize environmental issues.

> Violet: I thought [the program] was real interesting. I think lots of times . . . you know, you can have all these ideas in your head then you have this visual representation of a landfill or this visual representation of a child and here's their picture and now they've died. Or, these individuals that are actively campaigning that look like very normal people that you would not normally envision as campaigning on environmental issues. I think that's real important.

> Catherine: [T]hat's what the media is there for, sometimes they don't belong in people's business, but it's a good thing they're being concerned. So we can see what is going on, what needs to be done, they let us know. They're our eyes, kind of. . . . [T]hey let us see. You know, if we didn't get to see what was on TV, well, unless we went to a landfill ourselves, would we really know what it looked like? You know, in our heads, we can visualize what it looked like to have all that.

At the same time that subjects recognized their dependence on the media, they often seemed troubled and ambivalent about the potential such dependence has for selectively shaping their perception of the importance of various political issues. The public's concern over this agenda-setting process, revealed in the following quotes, is often overlooked by researchers:

> Mark: I think I'm concerned, but then on the other hand, I think I spend very little time thinking about it until I see something like this [gestures to

the blank screen] or I see the oil wells burning out of control or something to bring it home . . . I think we need to have more hard facts put before us. I think we need to be bombarded with more things to make us think about it and hopefully therefore to make us act.

Hazel: I think, you know, some of the best people or the most expert people may not have an avenue to get . . . to the public . . . if the media doesn't involve themselves in that, then there's really no way to get the exposure.

Some discussants moved beyond simple ambivalence to an understanding of the reasons for the shifting nature of media coverage. Such sophisticated understandings open up the possibility of maintaining a critical distance between the media's definition of what is important, and other hierarchies of importance. Take this quotation from Paul, for example:

One problem with the media is that . . . if they talk about some issue then two weeks later if it's not changed, they really don't want to do the story again. . . . They don't want to do the same thing over and over, they think the viewers are going to get bored and change to something else. I wonder if the media's attention to environmental concerns is going to be fad like and then they're going to find something else to focus on six months from now. That can be a problem . . . when you involve the media.

The Limited Autonomy of Television Viewers

Elsewhere, after closely analyzing several programs dealing with environmental issues, including the ones we showed to our focus groups, we concluded that these shows adopted a uniform perspective, but one that varied at different levels of politics (Delli Carpini and Williams 1994b). When discussing "the substance of politics" (i.e., issues that are on or becoming part of the political agenda), such shows adopted a liberal perspective, assuming that environmental problems were worse than ever and posed a grave and immediate threat to humans and nature, while denying the need to consider trade-offs between protecting the environment and economic growth. However, when discussing "the institutions and processes of politics" (i.e., the formal channels and institutions of government and the economy), the programs took a conservative populist view. Government was painted as corrupt, incompetent, and completely inadequate to the task of dealing with the problems posed by environmental pollution, while the business sector was represented by either evasive corporate spokespersons or disreputable owners.

Most of our discussants had the ability to critically analyze the slant of these shows and, at a certain level, to resist or accept their messages based upon a comparison with their own ideology. Employing our conversational metaphor, while dependent upon the media for information and the basic structure of political discourse, people continuously integrated and critiqued the media's side of this conversation. The following comments were fairly typical:

> Mark: Well, for the purposes of the movie ["Incident at Dark River"], I guess they wanted them [presented this way] . . . but I saw it as being slanted. I think they really portrayed [the corporate executives] as not having any heart at all and, you know, being guilty. We seem to already draw the conclusion that they were guilty and they didn't care whether they were guilty or not, and if it hadn't been for the little lowly guy at the bottom there which gives us all hope that no matter how big the company, there's always somebody. . . . I thought it was biased.

> Richard: I think it had a pretty liberal slant, which is OK with me because I agree with it, but still you've got to admit it wasn't exactly even-handed. . . .

Discussants also critically evaluated the reliance on sensationalism or emotionalism in both shows. Especially interesting was their ability to see the dramatic elements in *both* fiction and nonfiction. Violet criticizes one segment of *48 Hours* that dealt with a family's grief over their belief that their child had died from exposure to pesticides.

> Yeah, but then like that [show], that was really too sad. . . . I'm sure the parents were really sad and I cannot imagine losing a child, but to show them sending balloons to heaven on a TV show like that, I think that's a bit much.

And Bob makes a similar comment about the emotional appeal of "Incident At Dark River."

> I think it was definitely a bleeding-heart story. The underdog against the whole world. I mean, it brought up quite a few good issues, but I don't know if it was particularly objective.

Similarly, discussants often understood the need to distinguish the dramatic elements from the more factual bases of fictional programming. As Ruby commented, "[W]ith a movie, you find so much of it is factual and so much of it [is included] to make it interesting."

While recognizing the impracticality of only providing facts and figures on television, and the benefits of emotional appeals, our subjects were troubled and divided over the implications of television's use of such dramatic devices. This interrogation of the motives and the methods of the media was fairly subtle and not unsympathetic to the dilemmas of attracting and educating an audience. . . .

However, while these examples suggest the potential for citizens to critically evaluate and resist the media's agenda, other aspects of their use of information were much less accessible to conscious reflection. Consistent with research based on schema theory, we found several examples of the way people unconsciously used preexisting beliefs to interpret information provided by the media. For example, the most widely known environmental group was Greenpeace, which was mentioned several times in all our focus groups (the second-most frequently mentioned group, the Sierra Club, was brought up in fewer than half the groups). When asked to describe what they knew about Greenpeace, most subjects mentioned that the group was "radical," "extremist," or "violent." And in four of our groups, the following story (here told by Marcie) was recounted:

> I mean, you see them with a little rubber dinghy between the Russian trawler and the whales and that type thing which grabs your attention, but I guess they got accused of blowing up a ship once, so . . . they also have a political activist wing.

It appears that, since the schema in which information about Greenpeace is filtered centers on images of "radical activism," the vague recollection of a ship being blown up becomes reconstructed into further evidence for this point of view: Greenpeace blew up a ship. In only one of our focus groups did someone tell the story correctly: that it had been the Greenpeace ship *Rainbow Warrior* that had been blown up.[7]

The inability of discussants to see, and so to actively use or resist, the opinions expressed by television is most apparent once one moves to what we have labeled "the foundations of politics" (i.e., the values and beliefs upon which the very ideas of politics and government are based). At this level the television programs were highly conservative, emphasizing individualism to the exclusion of any form of collective or political action (Delli Carpini and Williams 1994a). In considering such issues, discussants were largely unable to identify or critically resist the media's tendency to present individual actions as the only acceptable form of action. Possible solutions to environmental problems brought up by discussants were limited to individual activities such as recycling or shopping more wisely. . . . A similar ideology is revealed in their attitude toward government: it should do more, but without stepping on individual rights, and in general is too corrupt or incompetent to count on. . . . [C]ollective action is either viewed with suspicion, or else is simply not thought of as a serious alternative. . . .

Once the distinction between levels of politics is made, it becomes less surprising that, despite the critical treatment of government and business, both are essentially absent in discussions about how best to address environmental problems. The closest participants came to identifying this bias in television's treatment of environmental issues was in comments like those of Mark, who saw the potential for a docudrama like "Incident at Dark River" to mobilize political action "if we knew where to go . . . after watching [it]." . . .

Notes

1. It should be noted, however, that the use of "900"-number telephone polls, the reading of viewer mail on the air, experiments with interactive television, and so forth serve to enhance this conversational aspect of television viewing.
2. Participants were residents of Lexington, Kentucky, and were recruited through a public notice placed in the local newspaper. The notice reported that two university professors were engaged in research about public opinion and asked for people interested in participating in small-group discussions about current issues. A twenty-dollar honorarium was offered, and no mention was made of either television or the particular issue to be discussed.
3. Three groups consisted of people in their late teens and twenties; three of people in their thirties and early forties; and three mainly of people in their mid-forties and fifties (though a few were older). This stratification was based on the assumption that people would be more comfortable talking with people roughly their own age.
4. For a detailed description and analysis of the messages contained in these broadcasts, see Delli Carpini and Williams 1994b.
5. In a related point, aside from isolated comments about two government agencies (OSHA and EPA), when participants discussed solutions to environmental problems, they almost always talked about what individuals, not government, could do (i.e., recycling, talking to friends, getting more information, and so forth).
6. This notion was brought home to us in our pilot focus groups conducted with students on the University of Michigan campus. When asked what she thought the Michigan campus was like in the 1960s, one older participant replied apologetically: "It's not really fair to ask me, since I'm from Ann Arbor and lived here during the sixties. . . ."
7. We found other suggestive examples of this kind of information processing regarding political activists: Rebecca's general references to "those kooks" mentioned earlier; the lumping of feminists, other political activists, even Al Sharpton into discussions of environmental activists; and so forth. As one discussant, trying to clarify who he meant by "environmental activists," said, "you know, extremists. . . . People who wear Birkenstocks."

References

Delli Carpini, Michael, and Bruce Williams. 1994a. "Fictional" and "non-fictional" television celebrate earth day (or, politics is comedy plus pretense). *Cultural Studies* 8 (January): 74–98.

___. 1994b. Methods, metaphors, and media research: The uses of television in political conversation. *Communications Research* 21 (December): 782–812.

Part III

INFLUENCING ELECTION OUTCOMES

Practicing politicians are most concerned about media effects when it comes to running for office or campaigning for a pet referendum issue. Ever since the old politics of nominations controlled by strong parties and bosses gave way to candidate-controlled primaries and elections, political campaign organizations have spent much time, effort, and money to influence election outcomes through attracting favorable media attention. When their candidates or causes lose, they frequently blame the tone of media coverage or the lack of adequate media coverage. Because vigorous, information-rich electoral contests are essential to the public life of democracies, scholars regularly put the activities of involved parties, including the mass media, under the microscope.

The readings in Part III scrutinize the major elements of news media coverage of election campaigns. Selections depict the kinds of images that emerge from news stories, advertisements, and the Internet. Authors speculate about the political consequences of this coverage and raise questions about the ability and effectiveness of the press in informing the public about the real issues at stake in each election.

Political advertisements by candidates and their supporters and opponents are among the most important and controversial sources of election information. This section begins, therefore, with a critical look at political advertising during recent presidential election campaigns. Political scientist Darrell M. West discusses the persuasive power of well-crafted advertisements and the interaction between advertiser messages and viewers' predispositions. He confirms that commercials alter the public's knowledge and appraisals of candidates and thereby affect election outcomes.

Much political advertising strikes a negative chord. So do many of the news stories in the printed press and in television, radio, and Internet broadcasts. How do American voters react to this flood of accusations and predictions of doom should opposition candidates and parties come to power? Larry J. Sabato provides answers. His essay explains why negative stories dominate presidential campaigns with unfortunate results. The viciousness of current campaign journalism, which instantly reaches millions of Americans, harms electoral politics. It discourages worthy new entrants, fatally wounds the political careers of many well-qualified contenders, and leaves deep personal and political scars on scores more.

Enter the Internet. It allows candidates and their supporters to tell their stories as they see fit, beyond the reach of hostile reporters. Does that change the political climate, making it more candidate-friendly? Evidence from the 2000 presidential election suggested that the benefits were small because uncommitted or hostile voters rarely visited candidate Web sites. Most visitors were already friends. Matthew Hindman's research of Howard Dean's 2004 presidential campaign, however, points to a different dynamic. The Internet may not be a tool for mass persuasion, but it may well be a tool for fund raising and for training cadres of devoted campaign workers who then reach out to the public. Although the Dean campaign failed in the end, it points to an important new Internet-based approach to campaigning that seems to be especially useful for fund raising.

Whether this new approach will alleviate some of the concerns that Thomas E. Patterson expresses in the next selection remains an open question. In Patterson's view, the quality of American presidential election campaigns has sunk to dangerously low levels. He faults changes in the American electoral system that have made the mass media the chief link between the voters and candidates. Media norms and goals, he argues, make it impossible to set the appropriate tone for elections and to supply the public with the kind of information it needs to make sound political judgments.

The essay by Joseph Hayden that follows Patterson's discussion makes you wonder whether worries about media coverage of election campaigns are much ado about nothing—or about very little at best. Apparently, citizens feel well-served when a campaigning wizard, like presidential candidate Bill Clinton, uses popular new media like talk shows and town meetings to interact directly with them informally and at length. They may not understand the intricacies of the candidate's policy plans, but they get a real feel for whether he is trustworthy, intelligent, diligent, and caring.

The section ends with an analysis of news media coverage of referendum campaigns in a European setting, with a focus on Denmark. The essay by Claes H. de Vreese and Holli A. Semetko illuminates the differences between single-issue referendum campaigns and candidate election contests and demonstrates the impact of political and media structures and cultures on campaigning styles and outcomes. It also shows that, besides their unique features, campaigns have much in common, meaning that experiences on Danish campaign trails provide valuable lessons for people in other countries.

13

LEARNING ABOUT THE CANDIDATES FROM TELEVISION ADVERTISEMENTS

Darrell M. West

Editor's Note

"Air Wars" is the name Darrell M. West uses for television advertising in presidential and senatorial election campaigns. The name is very fitting because commercials are the chief strategic tools that candidates employ in their battles to win the nomination and the final election. Through spot advertisements and longer commercials, a candidate tries to persuade voters that he or she is the most likeable, most qualified, and most electable choice and that opposing candidates are inferior on all scores. The evidence clearly shows that advertisements set the tone of the campaign and are a major source of information for voters and a key factor in their vote. That is why high-level candidates spend a huge share of their campaign budgets on designing, producing, and airing commercials, rather than relying on free publicity provided by news stories. That is also why there is more truth than ever before to the old adage that "money is the mother's milk of politics."

West is the John Hazen White Sr. Professor of Political Science and Public Policy at Brown University and director of its Taubman Center for Public Policy. He has written books and articles on mass media and elections, with a focus on advertising and the corrupting influence of campaign financing. He is also a frequent political commentator for several major national newspapers and television news outlets. His Web site, InsidePolitics.org, features in-depth information on state and national political issues.

Early efforts to study the impact of ads emphasized learning about substantive matters. Do the media provide information that increases voters' knowledge of where candidates stand on the issues? To the pleasant surprise of scholars, research from the 1970s revealed that voters who watched ads got more

Source: Darrell M. West, *Air Wars: Television Advertising in Election Campaigns, 1952–2004,* 4th edition, Washington, D.C.: CQ Press, 2005, chapter 5.

information than did those exposed only to television news.[1] Experimental work also supported claims about the educational virtues of commercials.[2] Ads did not help candidates create new political images based on personality. Rather, political commercials allowed viewers to learn about the issues.

Notwithstanding the undeniable trend of these studies, researchers have persisted in their efforts to examine the effects of advertising. Great changes have taken place in the structure of political campaigns since earlier research was completed. New electoral arenas have arisen that do not have the stabilizing features of past settings. Furthermore, recent campaign experiences run contrary to interpretations that emphasize the educational virtues of commercials. Television is thought to have played a crucial, and not very positive, role in a number of races, a state of affairs that has renewed concern about the power of ads to alter citizens' beliefs.[3]

Indeed, recent studies have found that voters do not often cast ballots based on the issues. Citizens form many impressions during the course of election campaigns, from views about candidates' issue positions and personal characteristics to feelings about the electoral prospects of specific candidates, and those views are decisive. As ads have become more gripping emotionally, *affective models* that describe feelings are crucial to evaluations of candidates' fortunes.[4]

Favorability is an example of an affective dimension that is important to voter choice. Citizens often support the candidates they like and oppose those they dislike. If they dislike all, they vote for the ones they dislike the least. Anything that raises a candidate's favorability also increases the likelihood of selection.[5] Candidates devote much attention to making themselves appear more likable. Values that are widely shared, such as patriotism and pride in national accomplishments, help candidates increase their favorability ratings among voters. Conversely, hard-hitting ads are used to pinpoint the opposition's flaws.

The opening up of the electoral process has brought new factors such as electability and familiarity to the forefront. *Electability* refers to citizens' perceptions of a candidate's prospects for winning the November election. Impressions of electability can increase voters' support of a candidate because citizens do not want to waste their votes. *Familiarity* is important as a threshold requirement. Candidates must become known in order to do well at election time. The development of a campaign structure that encourages less widely known candidates to run makes citizens' assessments of a candidate's prospects a potentially important area of inquiry.

Advertising and the Electoral Context

Past work on television advertising has focused on a particular kind of electoral setting—presidential general elections. For example, Thomas Patterson and Robert McClure's findings were based on the campaign that ended in Richard Nixon's 1972 landslide victory over George McGovern. The ads' apparent lack of effect on voters' assessments of the candidates is not surprising in light of the lopsided race and the fact that by the time of the initial survey in September public perceptions of the two candidates had largely been determined. In that situation, it was appropriate for Patterson and McClure to conclude that people "know too much" to be influenced by ads.[6]

However, as Patterson and McClure have pointed out, other electoral settings display greater opportunities for advertising to have measurable effects. Nominating affairs and Senate races show extensive shifts in voters' assessments of the candidates. Presidential nominations often have unfamiliar contenders vying for the votes of citizens who hold few prior beliefs about the candidates. In these settings, television commercials can play a major role in providing crucial information about the candidates.

Advertising is particularly important when news media time is scarce. In 1980, Ken Bode, then a reporter for NBC, recounted a letter written to him by Sen. Robert Dole, R-Kan., following his unsuccessful nominating campaign: "Dear Ken, I would appreciate knowing how much coverage my campaign received by NBC from the date of my announcement to my final withdrawal. I've been told my total coverage by NBC amounted to fourteen seconds."[7]

Senate races also have become heavily media oriented. Candidates spend a lot of money on television advertising, and Senate contests have taken on the roller-coaster qualities of nominating affairs. Many Senate elections feature volatile races involving unknown challengers. Because some observers have speculated about the effects of advertising, it is important to study advertising in nominating and Senate campaigns to determine whether the impact of advertising varies with the electoral setting.

Citizens' Knowledge and Evaluations of Candidates

Elections in recent decades represent an interesting opportunity to study the impact of political commercials. According to electoral surveys, citizens' assessments of the candidates varied widely depending on electoral setting. Presidential general election candidates were the most well known, with a range of recognition levels from a low in 1992 for Bill Clinton (73 percent) and Ross Perot (67 percent) to a high for Gerald Ford (95 percent) in 1976. The average recognition level in presidential general elections was significantly higher than for nomination candidates or Senate contenders. By the end of the campaign in 2004, 88 percent of respondents recognized John Kerry and 90 percent recognized George W. Bush (see Table 13-1). However, it took Kerry a long time to gain this recognition level. In March, only 57 percent recognized him and in mid-September, 73 percent recognized him. As

Table 13-1   Changes in Voter Perceptions of George W. Bush and John Kerry During the 2004 Campaign

	March 10–14	April 23–27	June 23–27	July 30–Aug. 1	Sept. 12–16	Oct. 1–3	Oct. 9–11	Oct. 14–17	Oct. 28–30
Bush									
Recognition	82%	81%	84%	83%	85%	88%	87%	88%	90%
Favorability	43	38	39	40	47	44	45	43	48
Electability	44	—	—	—	—	—	—	—	49
Caring	63	—	57	59	58	—	46	44	48
Shares your priorities	45	42	41	41	47	47	50	45	49
Conservative	53	56	—	—	—	—	—	66	—
Approve handling of Iraq	49	41	36	38	46	45	42	42	45
Ability to handle crisis	53	44	44	43	51	51	—	46	50
Leadership	67	—	—	58	63	62	62	—	62
Keeps his word	—	—	58	—	—	—	—	—	—
Says what he believes	51	53	58	48	55	59	58	59	60
Kerry									
Recognition	57%	60%	64%	72%	73%	81%	78%	83%	88%
Favorability	28	27	29	39	31	40	38	39	41
Electability	35	—	—	—	—	—	—	—	33
Caring	70	—	64	72	64	—	56	51	53
Shares your priorities	41	37	42	47	44	43	44	44	42
Liberal	39	43	—	—	—	—	—	56	—
Ability to handle crisis	33	39	33	39	32	41	—	42	40
Leadership	61	—	—	58	50	56	54	—	52
Keeps his word	—	—	51	—	—	—	—	—	—
Says what he believes	33	29	34	35	30	35	37	37	37

Source: CBS News/*New York Times* national surveys.

Note: Entries indicate the percentage of voters holding various impressions of the candidates.

discussed later, Kerry's relative lack of recognition gave Republicans an opportunity to use advertising to create unfavorable portraits of the challenger. Citizens' perceptions of candidates' likability and electability have varied extensively. Of recent nominees, Ronald Reagan has been the best liked (66 percent in 1984), and George Bush (23 percent in 1992), Dole (25 percent in 1996), and Perot (18 percent in 1996) the least liked. . . . In regard to electability during the fall, McGovern in 1972 was the candidate seen as least electable (1 percent), whereas George Bush in 1988 was seen as the most electable (85 percent), followed closely by the 83 percent in 1996 who believed Clinton was the most electable. In 2004, more voters (49 percent) saw Bush as electable than Kerry (33 percent).

Voters furthermore have a sense of the policy issues and personal traits associated with each candidate. Foreign policy considerations were prominent in 1972 for McGovern and Nixon because of the Vietnam War, whereas domestic matters dominated thereafter. In terms of personal traits, this period began with candidates' experience being the most cited and ended with leadership being the most cited.

In 2004, George W. Bush was seen as having slightly stronger leadership skills (62 percent) than Kerry (52 percent) and as saying what he believed (60 percent, compared with the 37 percent who felt that way about Kerry). Kerry was seen as slightly more caring (53 percent) than Bush (48 percent). In terms of the issues, Kerry held an advantage over Bush in improving health care, protecting Social Security, and improving schools, whereas Bush was seen as better at bringing fiscal discipline to the government.

Of course, it remains to be seen how political commercials influenced perceptions of the candidates. In general, Senate races showed the strongest advertising effects, with exposure to campaign ads associated with high recognition of political contenders. The average difference in recognition between respondents who scored high on ad viewing and those who scored low was twenty-seven percentage points. Senate campaigners typically are not as well known as presidential contenders, which means that political commercials can be more influential in raising the visibility levels of those who run for senator. . . .

In the nominating process, the magnitude of the difference varied according to how well known the individuals were. Candidates who were not well known used advertising to advance their name recognition. For example, in April 1976, polls from the Pennsylvania primary revealed that Jimmy Carter had a difference of twenty-one points between the high and low ends of his ad exposure scale. . . .

Ads also had effects on citizens' perceptions of favorability; the strongest effects were for Senate and nominating races.[9] In both the 1974 and the 1990 Senate campaigns, ad viewing produced favorability gains for Democratic and Republican candidates. . . .

In 1992, Buchanan displayed the largest improvement in favorability (twelve percentage points) between the low and high ends of his ad exposure scale. He ran the spring's most prominent ad, "Read Our Lips," which painted a negative picture of Bush and questioned the president's character for breaking his promise of no new taxes. Eventually, according to Bush adviser Robert Teeter, the president was able to beat back the Buchanan challenge through attack ads that told voters, "[Our] guy's the goddam president, and the other guy's a goddam typewriter pusher, and the toughest thing he's had to do in his whole life is change the ribbon on his goddam Olivetti."[10]

In terms of electability, ads were associated with significant effects for Nixon in fall 1972, Carter in spring and fall 1976, Dukakis and Bush in spring 1988, Buchanan and Clinton in spring and fall 1992, Clinton in 1996, and George W. Bush and Gore in 2000.[11] Seeing ads for these candidates was related to believing that the candidate was politically strong. . . .

If one looks at ad impact on prominent issues and personal traits, most elections conform to the findings of Patterson and McClure that the effects of advertising on citizens' perceptions of issues were substantially larger than the influence on assessments of personal traits.[12] However, in 1976, Carter ran an image-based campaign that produced stronger advertising effects for evaluations of personal traits than of issue positions.[13] In the 1988 nominating process, Dukakis, Gore, and George Bush had ads that produced strong effects on assessments of both issues and traits.[14]

Clinton was able to use his 1992 and 1996 campaign commercials to help viewers see him as caring and as capable of handling the economy. He used ads in 1992 to tell the story of families having problems affording quality health care. His fall ads helped project an image of hopefulness and of being able to improve the economy, which was important to voters discouraged by the country's dismal economic performance.[15] Bush was the only major candidate in 1992 unable to boost impressions of himself on his positions on either issues or character.[16]

The Impact of the Campaign

When looking at how ads and the campaign affected voter perceptions of the candidates, it is clear there were important effects. . . . [E]xposure to ads influenced people's perceptions of the issue positions of Dukakis (on the military), Gore (on unfair competition from Japan), and George Bush (on deficit reduction). The 1992 race helped viewers understand Buchanan and Clinton on the economy and Paul Tsongas on competition from Japan. Each candidate ran ads that made these subjects a central part of his campaign.[17] During the general election, Clinton worked hard to stake out claims to particular issues, in order to prevent Republicans from trespassing on traditionally Democratic ground, as Bush had done in 1988 when he campaigned on promises to become the environmental and education president. But Clinton's strategy also created problems for himself. One of the criticisms directed against him in spring focus groups was that he was difficult to pin down: "If you asked his favorite color he'd say 'Plaid,'" stated one focus group participant.[18]

Ads had an impact on viewers' assessments of candidates' images, likability, and electability that was at least as strong as the effect on viewers' assessments of issue positions. In terms of perceptions of likability, commercials had a significant impact in many elections. For Gore and Bush in 2000, ad exposure was related to favorability ratings; the same was true for Buchanan and Perot in 1992 and for Senate candidates in 1974 and 1990. There was no ad impact on candidate likability in 2000, although those who saw television news felt Bush was more likable.

In terms of electability, the strongest ad impact came with Dukakis in the 1988 nominating process, but effects were present for Nixon in 1972, Carter in 1976, Buchanan and Clinton in 1992, and Clinton in 1996. Conversely, people who saw Bush's ads in 1992 had a negative sense of the president's electability.

Some campaigners during this period were able to mold public perceptions of personal traits. Those who watched Carter ads saw him as an able leader, and those who saw Gore ads in 1988 felt he was likely to care about people. Those who watched Clinton ads in spring of 1992 believed that he was a caring individual. The ads helped create a positive view of his character, which counterbalanced the negative coverage received after Gennifer Flowers came forward to claim he had an affair with her.[19]

In the 2000 presidential general election, . . . individuals who saw Gore's ads were more likely to report that he was electable. The same was true for Bush to an even greater extent. In 1996, those who said they saw Clinton's ads were much more likely to cite him as electable, whereas those who saw Dole's ads were significantly more likely to say he was not electable. Seeing Perot's ads or the TV news had no impact on his electability.

. . . There also were interesting relationships between viewers seeing TV news and candidates' ads and how those viewers saw candidates' personal qualities and political views. In 2000, those who saw Gore's commercials were more likely to see him as providing fiscal discipline and less likely to believe that Bush would do so. However, those who reported seeing national television news concluded the opposite: that Bush would be fiscally responsible and caring and that Gore would not likely be either.[20]

In 2004, ads were linked to changing perceptions of the candidates. As shown in Table 13-1, voter impressions shifted during the course of the campaign. Using national surveys undertaken by CBS News/*New York Times*, it is apparent that Kerry was far less known (57 percent recognition level in

March 2004) than Bush (82 percent recognition), but became about as well known as the president by the end of October. Throughout most of the campaign, Bush held a higher favorability rating than did Kerry.

. . . Bush used attack ads during the campaign to portray Kerry in unfavorable terms. He characterized the Massachusetts Democrat as a doctrinaire liberal who was also wishy-washy and unprincipled. These two critiques are noteworthy because in some respects, they are inconsistent with one another. It is difficult to be both wishy-washy and a doctrinaire liberal simultaneously. However, by repeating these messages over and over, Bush was able to reinforce these perceptions about Kerry.

Ads and the Vote

Recent campaigns offer interesting opportunities to investigate how ads affect the vote.[21] The 1988 Democratic nominating process was a wide-open, seven-candidate affair with no well-known front-runner until Dukakis began to forge ahead at the time of the March Super Tuesday primaries. . . . How did this sense of momentum develop? An analysis of the Dukakis vote during the critical period of the 1988 Super Tuesday primaries shows how decisive electability was for the Dukakis vote. The more he was seen as being electable, the more likely voters were to support him.

. . . Dukakis's advertising had indirect consequences for the vote by affecting perceptions regarding electability. The strongest predictor of voters' views on electability was exposure to spot commercials. Ads shown prior to Super Tuesday, more than race, gender, or partisanship, influenced voters to see the Massachusetts governor as the most electable Democrat. The same was true when the ads of competing candidates such as Gore were included in the analysis. Seeing ads for the Massachusetts governor was associated with feeling Dukakis was the most electable Democrat. These views about electability had a clear impact on the vote.

In the 1992 Republican primaries, advertising played a different role. At the start of the race, President George Bush was on the defensive over his handling of the economy and his inattention to domestic politics in general. Buchanan ran a series of ads castigating Bush for breaking his famous "no new taxes" pledge. In part because of saturation coverage of the New Hampshire and Massachusetts markets, these commercials achieved a remarkably high level of visibility.

A March survey asked viewers which ad run by a Republican presidential candidate had made the biggest impression. Of the 590 people interviewed, 92 (about 16 percent of the entire sample) were able to name a specific ad. . . . The situation for Democrats was different: Eighty-six people (14 percent) named specific ads, but the ads mentioned were spread among the candidates. . . .

Not only were Bush's commercials unmemorable, but they also had a negative impact on views about the president. A reporter who covered the race said the president's ads about the need for change "weren't connected to reality. People smelled that. They knew he wasn't the candidate of drastic change." In contrast, Buchanan's advertisements "weren't bull. They were real. Bush had broken campaign promises." When people were exposed to ads from both candidates, they were less likely to see the president as electable and also were less likely to vote for Bush.[22] These results are surprising not only because they are negative but also because they contrast so clearly with Bush's ad performance in 1988, when his commercials dominated those of Dukakis.

Part of the problem was that Bush's 1992 spots simply were not as catchy as Buchanan's. The challenger's ads had an air of authenticity surrounding them. Bush's advertising meanwhile did not successfully use visual symbols and narrative to develop his connection with salient issues. . . . [I]t did not address the main issue of concern to voters—getting the economy going again and helping the unemployed with new jobs.

President Bush suffered because media coverage of his 1992 nominating campaign was quite negative. Reporters in New Hampshire questioned Bush's campaigning ability, his concern about human suffering, and his disjointed speaking style (which also was mimicked by comedian Dana Carvey). This pattern of coverage undermined the president's message and made it difficult for him to impress people who saw his ads. Although he ultimately was able to win his party's nomination, Bush's spring commercials did not lay a strong foundation for the fall campaign.

In the 1996 Republican primaries, Dole's early lead produced a political situation in which other candidates, such as Forbes, went on the attack in an effort to undermine the front-runner's support. A late January and early February 1996 national survey conducted before the Iowa caucuses found that Forbes's ads achieved a high level of visibility. Whereas 51 percent indicated they had seen ads for Dole, 40 percent said they had seen Forbes's ads, 24 percent indicated they had seen ads for Buchanan, 20 percent had viewed Phil Gramm's ads, and 10 percent had seen ads for Lamar Alexander.[23]

. . . Dole's ads achieved a high degree of visibility but were not especially memorable to viewers. People remembered seeing the ads but could recall few of their specific details. When asked which specific ad had made the biggest impression on them, the top ads named were Forbes's ad on flat tax (seven mentions), Buchanan's ad on protecting jobs for American workers (two mentions), Alexander's ad showing him in one of his flannel shirts (two mentions), and Alexander's ad proclaiming him to have fresh ideas (two mentions). No Dole ad got more than a single mention.

But Dole's advertising situation improved in the fall. When voters were asked which ad had made the greatest impression on them, more people named ads for Dole (sixty-four mentions) than Clinton (fifty-six mentions) or Perot (forty-eight mentions). . . .

In 2000, a national survey asked people which television ad run by a presidential campaign during the fall had made the biggest impression on them. Overall, 23 percent mentioned some ad, and 77 percent indicated no ad had made an impression on them (about the same as in previous elections). . . .

When looking at the impact of ad exposure on electability and the vote, we find interesting results. George W. Bush was the only candidate for whom there was a negative ad impact on the vote. The more people saw Gore's advertisements, the less likely they were to say they would vote for Bush. In addition, the more liberal, Democratic, and nonwhite respondents were, the less inclined they were to support Bush. These results are consistent with evidence about the memorability of particular commercials. More individuals were likely to cite Gore than Bush advertisements when asked which spot had made the biggest impression on them.

In 2004, voters started the general election showing an eight percentage point lead for President Bush (by a 46 to 38 percent margin). The president's advantage reflected several strengths. At that point, Kerry was not very well known. He had a 57 percent recognition level, compared to 82 percent for Bush. The president was also aided by voter perceptions that he was a strong leader serving in troubled times. His leadership ability and resoluteness created a strong reservoir of support.

By the end of July, right after the Democratic convention, Kerry moved to his first lead in the race. According to the CBS News/*New York Times* national surveys, Kerry was supported by 48 percent of voters, compared to 43 percent for Bush. Kerry's rise reflected a convention acceptance speech that was well received and positive press coverage that accompanied this presentation.

However, August proved to be a very difficult month for Kerry. His campaign was not able to go on the air with commercials during this month because he had exhausted his nomination funds and did not want to use his scarce general election dollars. At the same time, outside groups such as the Swift Boat Veterans for Truth were attacking Kerry's Vietnam record and alleging he was not trustworthy. Under these circumstances, he was not able to sustain his advantage. By September, Bush had regained the lead (50 to 41 percent).

Throughout the remainder of the fall, though, the two candidates were locked in a tight race. Kerry's support rose a little during the three presidential debates. His strong performance in these debates boosted voter backing of his candidacy. But Bush maintained his own support by attacking Kerry's liberal record and inconsistent stances on terrorism. One ad entitled "Wolves" started airing October 22. It showed a pack of wolves running through woods, while a female announcer spoke of the dangers confronting the world and how "Kerry and liberals in Congress" had voted to cut spending on intelligence-gathering in the 1990s. The commercial claimed that weakness invited danger and encouraged those who wanted to harm America.

By the end of the campaign, Bush's post-debate margin had stood up. On a 51 to 48 percent popular vote, Bush beat Kerry and won reelection to the presidency.

Conclusion

To summarize, ads are one of the major ways in which citizens learn about the candidates. From advertisements, voters develop perceptions about personal qualities, values, electability, and issue positions. Not only are these perceptions important for the candidates, they affect the vote. Citizens often support those whom they like, with whom they share values, and who they feel are electable.

Ads do not operate autonomously. People bring prior beliefs such as party attachments, ideological stances, and life experiences relating to their age, gender, education, and race. For this reason, candidates undertake detailed research on voter opinions. Campaign commercials must dovetail with a person's background and political orientation for the ad to be effective. If the spot does not resonate with people, it will not inform viewers in the manner desired by candidates.

Notes

1. Thomas Patterson and Robert McClure, *The Unseeing Eye* (New York: Putnam's, 1976).
2. Ronald Mulder, "The Effects of Televised Political Ads in the 1975 Chicago Mayoral Election," *Journalism Quarterly* 56 (1979): 25–36; Charles Atkin, Lawrence Bowen, Oguz Nayman, and Kenneth Sheinkopf, "Quality versus Quantity in Televised Political Ads," *Public Opinion Quarterly* 37 (1973): 209–224.
3. Kathleen Jamieson, *Packaging the Presidency,* 2d ed. (New York: Oxford University Press, 1992); Edwin Diamond and Stephen Bates, *The Spot* (Cambridge: MIT Press, 1984); L. Patrick Devlin, "Contrasts in Presidential Campaign Commercials of 1988," *American Behavioral Scientist* 32 (1989): 389–414.
4. Larry Bartels, *Presidential Primaries and the Dynamics of Public Choice* (Princeton: Princeton University Press, 1988); Edie Goldenberg and Michael Traugott, *Campaigning for Congress* (Washington, D.C.: CQ Press, 1984), 85–91.
5. See Stanley Kelley Jr. and Thad Mirer, "The Simple Act of Voting," *American Political Science Review* 68 (1974): 572–591.
6. Quoted in Patterson and McClure, *The Unseeing Eye,* 130.
7. On hearing this story at a post-election campaign seminar, John Anderson quipped that Dole's fourteen seconds consisted of a news report about his car breaking down in New Hampshire. Both stories are taken from Jonathan Moore, ed., *Campaign for President: 1980 in Retrospect* (Cambridge, Mass.: Ballinger, 1981), 129–130.

8. For question wording, see Darrell M. West, *Air Wars: Television Advertising in Election Campaigns, 1952–1996*, 2d ed., Washington, D.C.: CQ Press, 1997, chap. 6, note 8.

9. Ibid., note 9.

10. Quoted in "How He Won," *Newsweek*, November/December 1992 (special issue), 64.

11. For question wording, see West, chap. 6, note 11.

12. Ibid., note 12.

13. Ibid., note 13.

14. Ibid., note 14.

15. Michael Kelly, "Clinton, after Raising Hopes, Tries to Lower Expectations," *New York Times*, November 9, 1992, A1.

16. For question wording, see West, chap. 6, note 16.

17. Interview with Elizabeth Kolbert, July 20, 1992.

18. "How He Won," 40.

19. Marion Just, Ann Crigler, Dean Alger, Timothy Cook, Montague Kern, and Darrell M. West, *Cross Talk* (Chicago: University of Chicago Press, 1996).

20. West, chap. 6, note 21.

21. Just et al., *Cross Talk*.

22. The direct effect of electability on the vote in this two-stage analysis was .40 (p .001). People who saw Bush ads were less likely to say they would vote for him ($-.02$; p .05). Exposure to Buchanan ads had no significant impact on the vote. The effect on electability from exposure to Bush ads was $-.02$ (p .10) and from exposure to Buchanan ads was .01 (not significant). The following variables were included in the analysis as control variables: party identification, education, age, gender, race, ideology, political interest, and media exposure.

23. Brown University survey conducted January–February 1996.

14

OPEN SEASON: HOW THE NEWS MEDIA COVER PRESIDENTIAL CAMPAIGNS IN THE AGE OF ATTACK JOURNALISM

Larry J. Sabato

Editor's Note

Modern presidential campaign coverage is often mean-spirited and ugly. It destroys candidates' political careers by magnifying their human foibles and physical infirmities. Larry J. Sabato shows how attack journalism inflicted deep political wounds on Democratic presidential candidate Michael Dukakis and Republican vice presidential candidate Dan Quayle during the 1988 presidential campaign. The consequences of such treatment, Sabato concludes, are candidates who are increasingly secretive because they fear reporters, and reporters who cover less substantive news because they are obsessed with detecting scandals. Deprived of information needed to make sound choices, the public becomes ever more distrustful and filled with disgust for politicians as well as the press.

Sabato was Robert Kent Gooch Professor of Government and Foreign Affairs at the University of Virginia when this essay was written. He is the founder and director of the University of Virginia's Center for Politics and a former Rhodes Scholar and Danforth Fellow. His best known book, *Feeding Frenzy: Attack Journalism & American Politics,* published in 1991, made the phrase "feeding frenzy" part of America's political lexicon. Sabato has been a prolific, highly respected writer and commentator on political campaigns.

. . . The issue of character has always been present in American politics— not for his policy positions was George Washington made our first president— but rarely, if ever, has character been such a pivotal concern in presidential elections, both primary and general, as it has since 1976. . . .

Whatever the precise historical origins of the character trend in reporting, it is undergirded by certain assumptions—some valid, others dubious. First

Source: *Under the Watchful Eye: Managing Presidential Campaigns in the Television Era,* ed. Mathew D. McCubbins, Washington, D.C.: Congressional Quarterly Press, 1992. Reprinted with permission of CQ Press.

and most important of all, *the press correctly perceives that it has mainly re-placed the political parties as the "screening committee" that winnows the field of candidates and filters out the weaker or more unlucky contenders.* Second, many reporters, again correctly, recognize the mistakes made under the rules of lapdog journalism and see the need to tell people about candidate foibles that affect public performance. Third, the press assumes that it is giv-ing the public what it wants and expects, more or less. Television is the pri-mary factor here, having served not only as handmaiden and perhaps mother to the age of personality politics but also conditioning its audience to think about the private lives of "the rich and famous."

Less convincing, however, are a number of other assumptions about elec-tions and the character issue made by the press. Some journalists insist upon their obligation to reveal everything of significance discovered about a can-didate's private habits; to do otherwise, they say, is antidemocratic and elit-ist.[1] Such arguments ignore the press's professional obligation to exercise reasonable judgment about what is fit to be printed or aired as well as what is most important for a busy and inattentive public to absorb. Other re-porters claim that character matters so much because policy matters so little, that the issues change frequently and the pollsters and consultants determine the candidates' policy stands anyway.

Perhaps most troubling is the almost universally accepted belief that pri-vate conduct affects the course of public action. Unquestionably, private be-havior can have public consequences. However, it is far from certain that pri-vate vice inevitably leads to corrupt, immoral leadership or that private virtue produces public good. Indeed, the argument can be made that many lives run on two separate tracks (one public, one private) that should be judged independently. In any event, a focus on character becomes not an at-tempt to construct the mosaic of qualities that make up an individual but rather a strained effort to find a sometimes manufactured pattern of errors or shortcomings that will automatically disqualify a candidate. . . .

Not surprisingly, politicians react rather badly to the treatment they re-ceive from the modern press. Convinced that the media have but one con-spiratorial goal—to hurt or destroy them—the pols respond by restricting journalists' access, except under highly controlled situations. Kept at arm's length and out of the candidate's way, reporters have the sense of being en-closed behind trick mirrors: they can see and hear the candidate, but not vice versa. Their natural, human frustrations grow throughout the grueling months on the road, augmented by many other elements, including a cam-paign's secrecy, deceptions, and selective leaks to rival newsmen, as well as the well-developed egos of candidates and their staffs. Despite being denied access, the press is expected to provide visibility for the candidate, to retail his or her bromides. Broadcast journalists especially seem trapped by their need for good video and punchy soundbites and with regret find themselves falling into the snares set by the campaign consultants—airing verbatim the manufactured message and photoclip of the day. The press's enforced isolation and the programmed nature of its assignments produce boredom as well as disgruntlement, yet the professionalism of the better journalists will not permit them to let their personal discontent show in the reports they file.

These conditions inevitably cause reporters to strike back at the first opportunity. Whether it is emphasizing a candidate gaffe, airing an unconfirmed rumor, or publicizing a revelation about the candidate's personal life, the press uses a frenzy to fight the stage managers, generate some excitement, and seize control of the campaign agenda. Media emotions have been so bottled and compressed that even the smallest deviation from the campaign's prepared script is trumpeted as a major development. . . .

Does press frustration, among other factors, ever result in uneven treatment of presidential candidates, a tilt to one side or the other, further helping to foster attack journalism? In other words, are the news media biased? One of the enduring questions of journalism, its answer is simple and unavoidable: of course they are. Journalists are fallible human beings who inevitably have values, preferences, and attitudes galore—some conscious and others subconscious—all reflected at one time or another in the subjects or slants selected for coverage. To revise and extend the famous comment of Iran-Contra defendant Oliver North's attorney Brendan Sullivan, reporters are not potted plants. . . .

. . . [P]ress bias of all kinds—partisan, agenda setting, and nonideological—has influenced the development of junkyard-dog journalism in covering presidents and presidential candidates. But ideological bias is not the be-all and end-all that critics on both the right and left often insist it is. Press tilt has a marginal effect, no more, no less.

Two Cases of Attack Journalism in the 1988 Presidential Election: Dukakis and Quayle

Michael Dukakis's 1988 mental-health controversy is one of the most despicable episodes in recent American politics. The corrosive rumor that the Democratic presidential nominee had undergone psychiatric treatment for severe depression began to circulate in earnest at the July 1988 national party convention. The agents of the rumormongering were "LaRouchies," adherents of the extremist cult headed by Lyndon LaRouche, who claims, among other loony absurdities, that Queen Elizabeth II is part of the international drug cartel.[2]

Shortly after the Democratic convention, the Bush campaign—with its candidate trailing substantially in the polls—began a covert operation to build on the foundation laid by the LaRouchies. As first reported by columnists

Rowland Evans and Robert Novak,[3] Bush manager Lee Atwater's lieutenants asked outside Republican operatives and political consultants to call
their reporter contacts about the matter. These experienced strategists knew
exactly the right approach in order not to leave fingerprints, explains Steve
Roberts of *U.S. News & World Report:*

> They asked us, "Gee, have you heard anything about Dukakis's treatment?
> Is it true?" They're spreading the rumor, but it sounds innocent enough:
> they're just suggesting that you look into it, and maybe giving you a valu-
> able tip as well.[4]

Many newspapers, including the *Baltimore Sun* and the *Washington Post,* at
first refused to run any mention of the Dukakis rumor since it could not be sub-
stantiated.[5] But on August 3 an incident occurred that made it impossible, in
their view, not to cover the rumor. During a White House press conference a correspondent for *Executive Intelligence Review,* a LaRouche organization magazine, asked Reagan if he thought Dukakis should make his medical records public. A jovial Reagan replied, "Look, I'm not going to pick on an invalid."
Reagan half apologized a few hours later ("I was just trying to be funny and it
didn't work"), but his weak attempt at humor propelled into the headlines a
rumor that had been only simmering on the edge of public consciousness.

   Whether spontaneous or planned, there is little doubt that "Reagan and the
Bush people weren't a bit sorry once it happened," as CNN's Frank Sesno asserts.[6] The Bush camp immediately tried to capitalize on and prolong the controversy by releasing a report from the White House doctor describing their
nominee's health in glowing terms.[7] But this was a sideshow compared with
the rumor itself. The mental-health controversy yanked the Dukakis effort off
track and forced the candidate and then his doctor to hold their own press
conference on the subject, attracting still more public attention to a completely phony allegation. False though it was, the charge nonetheless disturbed
many Americans, raising serious doubts about a candidate who was still relatively unknown to many of them. "It burst our bubble at a critical time and
cost us half our fourteen-point [poll] lead," claims the Dukakis staff's senior
adviser, Kirk O'Donnell. "It was one of the election's turning points; the whole
affair seemed to affect Dukakis profoundly, and he never again had the same
buoyant, enthusiastic approach to the campaign." [8]

   As is usually the case, the candidate unnecessarily complicated his own situation. Until events forced his hand, Dukakis stubbornly refused to release his
medical records or an adequate summary of them despite advance warning that
the mental-health issue might be raised. But the press can by no means be ex-
onerated. While focusing on the relatively innocent casualty, most journalists
gave light treatment to the perpetrators. In retrospect, several news people said

they regretted not devoting more attention to the LaRouche role in spreading the rumor, given his followers' well-deserved reputation as "dirty tricksters." [9]

Overall, one of the most important lessons of the Dukakis mental-health episode is that caution must be exercised in reporting on presidential campaign rumors. "The media are really liable for criticism when we get stampeded by competitive instincts into publishing or airing stories that shouldn't be on the record," says National Public Radio's Nina Totenberg. "We were stampeded on the Dukakis story, and we should never have let it happen." [10]

The perils of vice-presidential candidate Dan Quayle became perhaps the most riveting and certainly the most excessive feature of 1988's general election. For nearly three weeks, coverage of the presidential campaign became mainly coverage of Quayle. Most major newspapers assigned an extraordinary number of reporters to the story (up to two dozen), and the national networks devoted from two-thirds to more than four-fifths of their total evening-news campaign minutes to Quayle. Combined with the juicy material being investigated, this bumper crop of journalists and stories produced, in the words of a top Bush/Quayle campaign official, "the most blatant example of political vivisection that I've ever seen on any individual at any time; it really surpassed a feeding frenzy and became almost a religious experience for many reporters." Balance in coverage, always in short supply, was almost absent. First one controversy and then another about Quayle's early life mesmerized the press, while little effort was made to examine the most relevant parts of his record, such as his congressional career.

It was the big-ticket items about Quayle—his National Guard service, the alleged love affair with Paula Parkinson, and his academic record—that attracted the most attention. At the convention, wild rumors flew, notably the false allegation that Quayle's family had paid fifty thousand dollars to gain him admission to the Guard. It was unquestionably legitimate for the press to raise the National Guard issue, although once the picture became clear— Quayle's family did pull strings, but not to an unconscionable degree—some journalists appeared unwilling to let it go. Far less legitimate was the press's resurrection of a counterfeit, dead-and-buried episode involving lobbyist Paula Parkinson. As soon as Quayle was selected for the vice-presidential nomination, television and print journalists began mentioning the 1980 sex-for-influence "scandal," despite the fact that Quayle had long ago been cleared of any wrongdoing and involvement with Parkinson. "When Quayle's name came up as a vice-presidential possibility, before his selection, the word passed among reporters that Bush couldn't choose Quayle because of his 'Paula problem,' " admitted one television newsman. "It was the loosest kind of sloppy association . . . as if nobody bothered to go back and refresh their memory about the facts of the case."

Some of the rumors about Quayle engulfing the press corps stretched even farther back into his past than did the womanizing gossip. Quayle's academic record was particularly fertile ground for rumormongers. By his own admission, the vice-presidential nominee had been a mediocre student, and the evidence produced during the campaign suggests that mediocre was a charitable description. At the time, however, a rumor swept through Quayle's alma mater, DePauw University, that he had been caught plagiarizing during his senior year. This rumor, which cited a specific teacher and class, was widely accepted as true and became part of the Quayle legend on campus.

Within a day of Quayle's selection as the vice-presidential nominee, the rumor had reached the New Orleans GOP convention hall. Hours after the convention was adjourned, the *Wall Street Journal* published a lengthy article on Quayle's problems, noting unsubstantiated "rumors" of a "cheating incident." [11] This story helped to push the plagiarism rumor high up on the list of must-do Quayle rumors, and soon the press hunt was on—for every DePauw academic who had ever taught Quayle, for fellow students to whom he might have confided his sin, even for a supposedly mysterious extant paper or bluebook in which Quayle's cheating was indelibly recorded for posterity.

As it happens, the plagiarism allegation against Quayle appears to have a logical explanation, and it was apparently first uncovered by the painstaking research of two *Wall Street Journal* reporters, Jill Abramson and James B. Stewart (the latter a graduate of DePauw, which fortuitously gave him a leg up on the competition). Abramson and Stewart managed to locate almost every DePauw student who had been a member of Quayle's fraternity, Delta Kappa Epsilon, during his undergraduate years. Approximately ten did remember a plagiarism incident from 1969 (Quayle's year of graduation), and the guilty student was in fact a golf-playing senior who was a political science major and a member of the fraternity—but not Quayle. The similarities were striking and the mix-up understandable after the passage of nearly twenty years. What was remarkable, however, was the fact that an undistinguished student such as Quayle would be so vividly remembered by the faculty. Abramson and Stewart also uncovered the reason for this, and even two decades after the fact their finding makes a political science professor blanch. Quayle was one of only two 1969 seniors to fail the political science comprehensive exam, a requirement for graduation. (He passed it on the second try.) Abramson's conclusion was reasonable: "Jim Stewart and I believed that people had confused Quayle's failure on the comprehensive exam with his . . . fraternity brother's plagiarism, especially since both events . . . occurred at the same time." [12] Unfortunately for Quayle, however (and also for the public), this explanation did not reach print, even though it might have provided a fair antidote to the earlier rumor-promoting article. Instead, the assumption that Quayle must have cheated his way through college solidified and led to other academically oriented rumors and questions, among them how a student with such a poor undergraduate record could gain admission to law school.

An observer reviewing the academic stories about Quayle is primarily struck by two elements. First, despite the windstorm of rumor that repeatedly swept over the press corps, there was much fine, solid reporting, with appropriate restraint shown about publishing rumors, except for the original *Journal* article mentioning plagiarism and some pieces about Quayle's law-school admission. Of equal note, however, was the overwhelming emphasis on his undergraduate performance. As any longtime teacher knows, students frequently commit youthful errors and indiscretions that do not necessarily indicate their potential or future development. Thus, once again, the question of balance is raised. How much emphasis should have been placed on, and precious resources devoted to, Quayle's life in his early twenties compared with his relatively ignored senatorial career in his thirties?

Consequences

Having examined some of the truths about feeding frenzies, we now turn to their consequences. Attack journalism has major repercussions on the institution that spawns it—the press—including how it operates, what the public thinks of it, and whether it helps or hurts the development of productive public discourse. The candidates and their campaigns are also obviously directly affected by the ways and means of frenzy coverage, in terms of which politicians win and lose and the manner of their running. The voters' view of politics—optimistic or pessimistic, idealistic or cynical—is partly a by-product of what they learn about the subject from the news media. Above all, the dozens of feeding frenzies in recent times have had substantial and cumulative effects on the American political system, not only determining the kinds of issues discussed in campaigns but also influencing the types of people attracted to the electoral arena.

One of the great ironies of contemporary journalism is that the effort to report more about candidates has resulted in the news media often learning less than ever before. Wise politicians today regard their every statement as being on the record, even if not used immediately—perhaps turning up the next time the news person writes a profile. Thus the pols are much more guarded around journalists than they used to be, much more careful to apply polish and project the proper image at all times. The dissolution of trust between the two groups has meant that "journalists are kept at an arm's length by fearful politicians, and to some degree the public's knowledge suffers because reporters have a less well-rounded view of these guys," says Jerry ter-Horst, Gerald Ford's first press secretary and former *Detroit News* reporter.[13] The results are easily seen in the way in which presidential elections are conducted. Ever since Richard Nixon's 1968 presidential campaign, the press's access to most candidates has been tightly controlled, with journalists kept at a distance on and off the trail.[14] And as 1988 demonstrated, the less accessible candidate (Bush) was better able to communicate his message than the more accessible one (Dukakis); the kinder and gentler rewards of victory went to the nominee who was better able to keep the pesky media at bay. . . .

Consequences for the Presidential Candidates

The two cases of attack journalism examined above provide a reliable indication of a frenzy's consequences for a politician. The rumors of Dukakis's mental impairment certainly took his campaign off its stride and probably played at least some role in his defeat. And the attack on Quayle may have permanently damaged his chance of ever being elected to the presidency. Despite somewhat more positive coverage of Quayle during the 1992 campaign, his press secretary, David Beckwith, sees little likelihood that his boss can overcome the frenzy-generated image burdens any time soon: "For the indefinite future there will be lingering questions about Quayle based on what people saw or thought they saw in the [1988] campaign, and it's going to be with him for a number of years." [15] Quayle can be certain that remnants of his past frenzy will resurface and develop in his next campaign. . . .

Consequences for Voters

To voters, what seems most galling about attack journalism in presidential election campaigns is not the indignities and unfairness inflicted on candidates, however bothersome they may be. Rather, people often appear to be irate that candidates are eliminated before the electorate speaks, that irreversible political verdicts are rendered by journalists instead of by the rightful jury of citizens at the polls. The press sometimes seems akin to the Queen of Hearts in *Alice's Adventures in Wonderland,* who declares, "Sentences first—verdicts afterwards."

The denial of electoral choice is an obvious consequence of some frenzies, yet the news media's greatest impact on voters is not in the winnowing of candidates but in the encouragement of cynicism. There is no doubt that the media, particularly television, have the power to influence people's attitudes. With the decline of political parties, news publications and broadcasts have become the dominant means by which citizens learn about public officials; and while news slants cannot change most individuals' basic views and orientation, they can dramatically affect *what* people think about and *how* they approach a given subject.[16] . . .

Consequences for the Political System

The enhanced—some would say inordinate—influence of the contemporary press is pushing the American political system in certain unmistakable directions. On the positive side are the increased openness and accountability visible in government and campaigns during the last two decades. This is balanced by two disturbing consequences of modern press coverage: the trivialization of political discourse and the dissuasion of promising presidential candidacies.

As to the former, the news media have had plenty of company in impoverishing the debate, most notably from politicians and their television consultants. Nonetheless, journalists cannot escape some of the responsibility. First, the press itself has aided and abetted the lowering of the evidentiary standards held necessary to make a charge stick. In addition to the publication of rumor and the insinuation of guilt by means of innuendo, news outlets are willing to target indiscriminately not just real ethical problems, but possible problems and the perception of possible problems. Second, the media often give equal treatment to venial and mortal sins, rushing to make every garden-variety scandal another Watergate. Such behavior not only engenders cynicism, but also cheapens and dulls the collective national sense of moral outrage that ought to be husbanded for the real thing. Third, the press often devotes far more resources to the insignificant gaffe than to issues of profound national and global impact. On many occasions, peccadilloes have supplanted serious debate over policy on the front pages.

The second troubling consequence of media coverage has to do with the recruitment of presidential candidates.[17] Simply put, the price of power has been raised dramatically, too high for some outstanding potential officeholders.[18] An individual contemplating a run for office must now accept the possibility of almost unlimited intrusion into his or her financial and personal life. Every investment made, every affair conducted, every private sin committed from college years on may one day wind up on television or in a headline. For a reasonably sane and moderately sensitive person, this is a daunting realization, with potentially hurtful results not just for the candidate but for his or her immediate family and friends. American society today may well be losing the services of many exceptionally talented individuals who could make outstanding contributions to the commonweal, but who understandably will not subject themselves and their loved ones to abusive, intrusive press coverage. . . .

Fortunately, we have not yet reached the point where only the brazen enter public service, but surely the emotional costs of running for office are rising. Intensified press scrutiny of private lives and the publication of unsubstantiated rumors have become a major part of this problem. After every election cycle, reflective journalists express regret for recent excesses and promise to do better, but sadly the abuses continue. No sooner had the 1992 presidential campaign begun in earnest than Democratic front-runner Bill Clinton was sidetracked for a time by unproven allegations from an Arkansas woman, Gennifer Flowers, about an extramarital affair. The charges were initially published in a supermarket tabloid, the *Star*, and while some news outlets at first downplayed the story because of the questionable source, others ballyhooed it so extravagantly that Clinton was forced to respond, thus legitimizing full coverage by virtually all news organizations.

This classic case of lowest-common-denominator journalism guaranteed the continued preeminence of the character issue for yet another presidential campaign cycle, and in many ways the situation frustrated reporters and voters alike. Both groups can fairly be faulted for this trivialization of campaign coverage: reporters for printing and airing unproven rumors, and voters for watching and subscribing to the news outlets that were the worst offenders. But journalists and their audiences also have it within their power by means of professional judgment and consumer choice to change old habits and bad practice.[19] Hope springs eternal . . . and in the meantime, attack journalism flourishes.

Notes

1. See the journalists quoted by John B. Judis, "The Hart Affair," *Columbia Journalism Review* 25 (July/August, 1987): 21–25.
2. Dennis King, *Lyndon LaRouche and the New American Fascism* (Garden City, N.Y.: Doubleday, 1989). See especially 121–122.
3. Rowland Evans and Robert Novak, "Behind Those Dukakis Rumors," *Washington Post*, August 8, 1988, A13. Reporters from six major news organizations (all three networks, the *Washington Post, U.S. News & World Report*, and the *Los Angeles Times*) told us they had been contacted by Bush operatives about the rumor, and they knew of colleagues at other outlets who had also been called. See also Thomas B. Rosenstiel and Paul Houston, "Rumor Mill: The Media Try to Cope," *Los Angeles Times*, August 5, 1988, 1, 18.
4. Roberts interview.
5. See Edward Walsh, "Dukakis Acts to Kill Rumor," *Washington Post*, August 4, 1988, A1, 6.
6. Frank Sesno, interview with author, Charlottesville, Va., September 27, 1989.
7. Gerald M. Boyd, "Doctor Describes Bush as 'Active and Healthy,' " *New York Times*, August 6, 1988.
8. Kirk O'Donnell, telephone interview with author, June 29, 1990.
9. Dennis King, in *Lyndon LaRouche*, 122, commented upon "the usual [media] reluctance to cover anything relating to LaRouche."
10. Nina Totenberg, telephone interview with author, October 4, 1989.
11. Jill Abramson and James B. Stewart, "Quayle Initially Failed a Major Exam at DePauw, Former School Official Says," *Wall Street Journal*, August 23, 1988, 54.
12. Jill Abramson, interview with author, Washington, D.C., August 4, 1989.
13. Jerald terHorst, interview with author, Washington, D.C., August 4, 1990.
14. See Joseph McGinniss, *The Selling of the President 1968* (New York: Trident, 1969).
15. David Beckwith, telephone interview with author, December 27, 1989. For example, David Broder and Bob Woodward wrote an influential and generally pos-

itive series assessing Quayle's career that ran in the *Washington Post* January 12, 1992. The series helped to take some of the disparaging edge off Quayle's image.

16. Shanto Iyengar and Donald R. Kinder, *News That Matters: Television and American Opinion* (Chicago: University of Chicago Press, 1988); Thomas E. Patterson, *The Mass Media Election* (New York: Praeger, 1980); Charles Press and Kenneth VerBurg, *American Politicians and Journalists* (Glenview, Ill.: Scott, Foresman, 1988), 62–66; Shanto Iyengar, Mark D. Peters, and Donald Kinder, "Experimental Demonstrations of the 'Not So Minimal' Consequences of Television News Programs," *American Political Science Review* 76 (December 1982): 848–858; and Roy L. Behr and Shanto Iyengar, "Television News and Real-World Cues and Changes in the Public Agenda," *Public Opinion Quarterly* 49 (Spring 1985): 38–57.

17. On this general subject, see also Laurence I. Barrett, "Rethinking the Fair Games Rules," *Time* 130 (November 30, 1987): 76, 78; Richard Cohen, "The Vice of Virtue," *Washington Post*, March 10, 1989, A23; Charles Krauthammer, "Political Potshots," *Washington Post*, March 1, 1989; Norman Ornstein, "The *Post's* Campaign to Wreck Congress," May 29, 1989, A25; and "Ethicsgate," *Wall Street Journal* editorial, July 15, 1983, 26.

18. Increasing intrusiveness and scrutiny are also factors in the lessened attractiveness of nonelective governmental service. See Lloyd M. Cutler, "Balancing the Ethics Code," *Washington Post*, March 13, 1989, A15; Ann Devroy, "Current Climate of Caution: Expanded FBI Checks Slow Confirmations," *Washington Post*, March 13, 1989, A1, 4–5.

19. Some remedies from the perspectives of both journalists and news consumers are proposed in Larry J. Sabato, *Feeding Frenzy: Attack Journalism and American Politics* (New York: The Free Press, 1991), Chapter 8.

15

REFLECTIONS ON THE FIRST DIGITAL CAMPAIGN

Matthew Hindman

Editor's Note

In the wake of the 2004 U.S. presidential election, pundits and scholars continued to belittle the Internet's impact on the general public. They argued that the bulk of the audience for political Web sites consists of committed partisan voters, rather than the uncommitted average citizens whom traditional campaigns try to attract. Matthew Hindman contends that these analysts are missing the point. Internet campaigns are, indeed, attracting committed partisans, but this is a strength rather than a weakness. Armed with the inexpensive outreach capabilities of the Web, these youthful partisans become potent political organizers, recruiters, and grassroots-level fund-raisers. While political Web sites do not attract most citizens directly, they spawn the recruiters, networks, and funds needed to mobilize mass publics. Furthermore, reliance on small donors weakens the undue influence of large contributors, who expect policy dividends from their contributions.

When this essay was written, Hindman was an assistant professor of political science at Arizona State University. His writings about new media include his dissertation, completed at Princeton University, which examined the impact of the Internet on American politics. He has also served as a Fellow at Harvard University's National Center for Digital Government.

Howard Dean's presidential bid was notable for many things, including the mixed reaction it drew from political scientists. Many scholars found Dean's ultimate failure predictable. Longstanding political science wisdom suggests several explanations for Dean's defeat: the central issue of electability, which seemed to weigh heavily against his campaign; the fact that pri-

Source: Matthew Hindman, "The Real Lessons of Howard Dean: Reflections on the First Digital Campaign," *Perspectives on Politics,* 3:1 (March 2005): 121–128. Copyright © 2005 by Cambridge University Press. Reprinted with the permission of Cambridge University Press.

mary voters are more moderate than party activists; the well-documented difficulty of regaining lost momentum. Less systematic factors—such as numerous verbal gaffes and one infamous scream—surely contributed as well.

Still, the Dean campaign exposes a curious gap in political science knowledge. If Dean's failure now seems unsurprising, how are scholars to explain his brief but remarkable success? Though he entered the race a relative unknown, he shattered previous fund-raising records, won numerous key endorsements, from Al Gore's to the AFL-CIO's, and had a strong plurality in the polls in the months leading up to the Iowa caucuses.

To understand Dean's early and unexpected rise as the Democratic frontrunner, we should begin by considering one obvious difference between 2004 and previous primary campaigns: the role of the Internet. Dean's use of the Web to organize, invigorate, and finance his campaign has been much celebrated, but it remains too little understood. . . .

The Liberal Medium? Dean and the Political Attitudes of Web Users

In covering the Dean campaign, the popular press consistently emphasized the novelty of its tactics. Howard Dean did something that was smart, brave, and unprecedented—something only a candidate with little to lose would do: he created a genuinely interactive campaign Web site. Previous online campaigns—including those of John McCain and Jesse Ventura, the most celebrated antecedents to Dean's efforts—kept rigid control over their Web presence. Encouraging supporters to generate their own content, join online discussions, create their own Dean sites, and organize their own events necessarily meant that the campaign must give up some control over the messages it wanted to project. In considering what Dean means for the future of digital politics, we should first acknowledge that many campaigns will not follow this lead. Strong candidates have little incentive to take such chances.

Still, Dean's digital innovations are inadequate to explain his successes. To understand what happened during the course of the 2004 primaries, we must look more closely at those who use the Web for political purposes and confront the puzzlingly liberal character of online politics.

From the beginning of the Internet revolution, it was clear that patterns of Web access and usage closely tracked existing social cleavages. The rich and educated used the Internet more than those with less money and education; women lagged behind men; Hispanics and African Americans trailed their white and Asian counterparts. Though most of these usage gaps have narrowed in recent years—particularly gender differences—large inequalities remain. Indeed, as scholars have looked beyond mere "access" to the Internet and focused on essential user skills, these disparities appear to be as profound as ever.

. . . Yet survey data seem to tell a different story. To illustrate this, I turn to the 2000 and 2002 General Social Survey (GSS), the first large-scale surveys to combine measures of Web usage with metrics of users' political and social views. The GSS's political orientation questions show no difference between the political leanings of users and nonusers. Yet although the liberal to conservative ratio among Web users mirrors that of the general population, the two groups have starkly different usage patterns.

Liberals dominate the audience for politics online. Across a wide range of politically relevant activities, from gathering news online to visiting government Web sites, liberals outpace conservatives by a wide margin. . . . [T]he results are particularly dramatic for visits to political Web sites, where more than twice as many liberals as conservatives fall into the highest category of Web use. Among self-identified Democrats, frequent visitors to political Web sites are dramatically more liberal than the party as a whole; they are more highly educated than the general public; and while voters as a group skew older, those who visit political Web sites are disproportionately young.

. . . In the Dean case, . . . the importance of these skewed political demographics is clear. In the early campaign, Dean positioned himself to the left of most competitors, declaring that he represented "the Democratic wing of the Democratic Party" and offering forceful opposition to the Iraq war while other competitors adopted more nuanced positions. If the patterns of political Web usage were reversed—if conservatives visited political sites far more than liberals—the Internet would not have been such an asset for Dean. He would have raised much less money, recruited fewer volunteers, and attracted less positive press coverage.

These findings force us to consider whether Dean's experience might be part of a larger trend in online activism that benefits liberal views. Should we expect this liberal-conservative gap to be temporary or an enduring feature of the online political landscape? At this point, we do not know. There is some reason to expect that conservatives will catch up. The Internet is a young medium, and effective methods of online organizing are still largely experimental. As user sophistication continues to improve, as conservative candidates invest resources in exploiting the Web, and as conservative partisans themselves see online participation as a key part of political activism, online politics may have less of a liberal cast.

Ideological differentials in usage may not fade quickly, though. 2004 is not 1994; the majority of the American public is online and has been for several years. There is no liberal-conservative gap in access more generally, or in time spent online. Moreover, many other mediums of political outreach have had a persistent partisan character. For example, direct mail solicitation has long been a more effective tool for Republicans than Democrats.

The Dean campaign highlights the importance of the liberal-conservative gap in political Web usage, but it does little to show us how this disparity will evolve as online politics matures. Measuring and understanding the ideological divide in political Web usage will be critical to nearly every aspect of online politics.

The Earliest Primary: "Big Mo' " Meets the Internet

Liberal overrepresentation online dovetails with a larger point about the dynamics of the primary process. The concept of momentum enjoys a central place in the scholarship on presidential primaries. The snowball effects of early success (or failure) are substantial: candidates who win the first primaries receive more favorable press coverage, more public interest in the campaign, more volunteers, and more money. The order of these contests is thus critically important. For example, as Larry Bartels shows, it was "pure, unadulterated luck" that states most favorable to Gary Hart—overwhelmingly white states without major urban populations—were first on the 1984 electoral calendar. The Iowa and New Hampshire results greatly magnified the seriousness of Hart's challenge to Walter Mondale.[1]

Dean's candidacy benefited enormously from a digital version of the Gary Hart effect. In June 2003 the leading liberal activist site MoveOn.org sponsored what it termed an "online primary." Dean won, receiving a 44 percent plurality.[2] The symbolism of the win was appropriate: in a larger sense, the entire online campaign came to serve as a sort of virtual primary. Dean's demonstrable successes on the Web generated the sort of coverage, enthusiasm, and compounded success that candidates usually enjoy only after winning an actual electoral contest.

Dean's Internet campaign generated a spiral of positive press coverage. A Lexis-Nexis search finds 1,325 stories in major papers that mentioned Dean's Internet effort during the six months preceding the New Hampshire primary—a priceless publicity boon for a candidate who began as a dark horse. Both the scale of Dean's online organization and his unprecedented success at raising large amounts of money in small donations qualified as newsworthy. Dean's campaign provided other tangible metrics of success: the long list of supportive Weblogs, the number of hits on its home page, the number of Dean house parties, and the number of citizens willing to sign up as supporters on the Dean Web site. Overall, the breadth of Dean's online organization was taken as evidence that Dean had broad grassroots support.

. . . Dean's example shows that it is possible to translate online interest into tangible political resources—money, positive press coverage, and volunteers. It also shows that the Web can grant a partly intangible asset: early momentum. Even if the press proves more skeptical of the next online "groundswell," the financial and organizational advantages to be won online may offer future campaigns a critical early boost.

The Internet and the Infrastructure of Politics

Overall, then, the case of Howard Dean suggests that political behavior in the online world follows unexpected fault lines. There is a second lesson to be drawn from the Dean campaign: the Internet may alter key parts of the nation's political infrastructure. Dean's campaign suggests that the Web's evolution in the business world is being repeated in the political realm. . . . [T]he real success of the Web for commerce has been at the backend. . . . Business-to-business, not business-to-consumer, is where the real transformation has taken place.

Now a similar shift may be taking place with online politics. Initially, most candidates tailored their Web sites to reach swing voters, independents, and the undecided—the elusive median voter. This strategy produced dismal results. Survey data show that most who visit political Web sites are not swing voters, but rather people with strong party affiliations and strong preexisting views on politics.[3] Traffic to most campaign sites has been a trickle, and (at least until the Dean phenomenon) campaign managers commonly saw the Internet as no more than a sideshow of the "real" campaign. Bruce Bimber and Richard Davis thus conclude, in the best study of online campaigning to date, that the Web will have modest effects on mass politics.

Bimber and Davis are right that online campaigning thus far consists of "preaching to the converted." Yet increasingly, Dean and other candidates have turned this fact to their advantage. Instead of online appeals to the median voter, a new breed of campaign Web site seeks to engage and motivate those most likely to become core supporters. If Web sites are not a way to reach the masses, the Dean campaign and others have shown that they can be a powerful tool for fund-raising and energizing the faithful. In short, Dean demonstrates that the Internet can affect what might be termed the supply chain of politics. . . .

Internet Fund-Raising

It is difficult to overstate the importance of Dean's Internet fund-raising. For candidates in presidential primaries, the ability to raise funds is a prerequisite to being taken seriously, and no previous candidate of either party had successfully translated two-digit donations into real money. By the end of January 2004, as the primaries commenced, Dean had raised more than $41 million, much of it online; 318,884 citizens had contributed to the Dean campaign. Overall, 61 percent of Dean's financial resources came from those giving $200 or less. Only 2,851 donors—less than 1 percent of the total— gave $2,000, the maximum under federal law. These large givers provided 11 percent of Dean's total funds.[4]

The distribution of giving for the Dean campaign was almost exactly the reverse of his rivals. . . . By the end of January 2004, . . . large gifts accounted for 68 percent of Bush's total. Donations of less than $200 contributed less than 16 percent of Bush's total funding. And Democratic candidates like John Kerry and John Edwards . . . similarly relied on large donors to get them through the early primaries. At the end of January, those who gave the $2,000 maximum were responsible for 58 percent of Kerry's campaign war chest, and 73 percent of Edward's financial resources.[5]

. . . Verba, Schlozman, and Brady declare that the power of financial contributions is the fact that they are both "loud and clear"—money is key to electoral success and communicates a great deal about the giver's preferred policies.[6] But the sheer number of citizens who donated to the Dean campaign means that the messages were rather soft and indistinct. A hand-delivered $2,000 check carries with it a great deal more information than 40 individual $50 credit card contributions submitted via the campaign Web site. Third, most Internet donations to Dean's campaign were spontaneous. Traditionally, donating money to a political campaign is the type of political participation least likely to be self-generated, and personal social contacts play an important role. Most campaign contributions are solicited, and people that the donor already knows are generally the ones who ask for donations.[7] By contrast, Dean's funding came mostly from individuals who sought out the campaign on their own.

The overall implications are clear. If Dean's success is repeated on a large scale, political scientists will have to reexamine much of what they think they know about the relationship between money and politics: the demographics and political views of contributors, how donations are solicited, the clarity with which money communicates preferred policies, and the extent of the rightward preference distortion that political fund-raising induces in American politics.

Networks of Political Recruitment and the 'Net

Political scientists have often noted that those who participate in politics are those asked to do so. The literature on political participation emphasizes the role that social networks and social pressure play in recruitment. Yet Dean's experience in this regard fails to square with our expectations, for if social networks often serve as gatekeepers in the political process, record numbers of Dean supporters seem to have jumped the fence.

Dean's focus on "meetups"—Web-organized face-to-face meetings of citizens interested in the campaign—seems particularly consequential. Meetups proved to be an elegantly simple organization strategy. At either the official Dean site or at the Meetup.com homepage, citizens could offer their e-mail address and zipcode, and immediately receive e-mail reminders about pro-Dean meetings in their vicinity. The process of signing up for a local Dean meetup could take as little as 30 seconds.

By the time Dean dropped out of the Democratic race, 640,937 people had registered as Dean supporters through the candidate Web site; 188,941 of those had signed up to receive notices about meetings in their area.[8] According to Meetup.com's attendance figures, roughly 40 percent of these supporters—about 75,000 people—actually attended a meeting. Dean meetups were organized in 612 cities nationwide. As one of the founders of a state Dean organization declared, "We always considered the meetups to be our primary recruiting tool."[9] Survey data collected from Dean meetup participants in Massachusetts by Christine Williams, Bruce Weinberg, and Jesse Gordon suggests that these gatherings were indeed an effective tool.[10] More than 96 percent of respondents reported that they wished to become active volunteers after attending a Dean meetup. In both sheer numbers of those who attended early candidate events, and in the wide geographic dispersion of these volunteers, Dean greatly exceeded expectations for an ostensibly minor candidate.

Some popular accounts suggested that Dean's campaign was transforming numerous previously inactive citizens into activists. In their October and January surveys, Williams, Weinberg, and Gordon found that only 39 and 47 percent of their respondents, respectively, had volunteered in previous election cycles, providing some support for that thesis. Most primary volunteers are chronic participators; previous studies have suggested that, for almost every candidate, two-thirds to four-fifths of their primary campaign workers are veterans.[11] . . .

The most surprising fact to emerge from Williams, Weinberg, and Gordon's data, however, is not that Dean's volunteers were relatively inexperienced, but that only 23 and 31 percent of survey respondents first learned about meetups from someone they knew. Almost all of the rest found out about the first gathering they attended through the national Dean Web site, the local pro-Dean site, or the Meetup.com homepage. These figures are a significant departure from the expectations set by previous scholarship. Verba, Schlozman, and Brady, for example, found that more than 80 percent of contacts for campaign recruitment came through personal relationships.[12] According to the civic voluntarism model, ground-level social networks should have been necessary to attract and retain supporters. In Dean's case, these networks were largely absent—yet new technology allowed Dean to create local, decentralized social networks from scratch.

Dean without the Internet:
Considering the Counterfactual

I have so far offered a causal explanation for Howard Dean's initial rise as the Democratic party front-runner. In social science, causal questions are ultimately about counterfactuals. Thus, it is worth putting these observations together to ask: but for the Internet, how should we have expected Dean's campaign to unfold? . . .

In the 2004 primary field, Dean had several potential advantages over his competitors that would have been important with or without the Internet. Many Dean supporters opposed the war in Iraq, and there was no other staunch antiwar candidate. As both governor and medical doctor, Dean presented a compelling personal narrative. His energetic presence on the stump (and the fervor of his attacks against the president) made him stand out. For the dark horse candidate, being ignored is the biggest danger; Dean was consistently quotable.

A completely offline Dean campaign, then, would still have had important strengths. But one thing it would not have done is raise more than a fraction of the $52 million that Dean ultimately received. Dean's campaign defied the example of every previous primary candidate, the Republicans' longstanding advantage in small donations, and every political science model of how much candidates raise and from whom. It is not just the grand sums of money raised that point to the influence of the Internet—though that was important enough—but also the balance between large and small donations. . . .

The second area where Dean's campaign would have unfolded differently concerns his network of volunteers. Comparing Williams, Weinberg and Gordon's data with the profile of volunteers in previous campaigns suggests that, without the meetup phenomenon, Dean's volunteer corps would have been significantly smaller. Moreover, it would have grown far more out of existing interpersonal networks, it would not have been as geographically dispersed, and it would have had proportionally more veterans and fewer previously inactive volunteers.

Finally, the early press coverage that Dean received focused largely on his online success in fund-raising and volunteer recruitment. Without the financial and organizational fruits of the online campaign, much of this coverage would simply not have happened, leaving Dean to struggle with name recognition in a crowded field. And of course, without the extensive press coverage that made his campaign credible, Dean would not have won major endorsements, as he did from previous candidates Al Gore and Bill Bradley, from a parade of congressmen and elected officials, and from key unions initially expected to support opponents like Richard Gephardt.

So where would Howard Dean have been with far less money, with a leaner volunteer organization, and without such ubiquitous (and often glowing) early coverage of his campaign? Not out of the race, probably—with luck, and without the curse of high expectations, strong finishes in Iowa and New Hampshire might have given him a solid base to build on in the later primaries. Nonetheless, without the Internet, it seems impossible that Dean would have become so formidable so early.

Conclusion

. . . In the aftermath of the Dean meltdown, it would be easy for observers to dismiss Dean's candidacy as a failed referendum on the importance of digital politics. Many lessons of the Dean campaign are indeed remedial ones: momentum matters; a candidate's perceived viability and electability matter; candidate gaffes and misstatements matter; and it matters that primary voters have different preferences than party activists. Even the best-funded campaigns are not assured of victory.

But this is not the whole story. In trying to squeeze Dean into established patterns, scholars may miss the important ways in which he simply does not fit. The puzzle for political scientists is not why Dean failed, but how he ever became the front-runner in the first place.

My answer to this question is simple: to paraphrase a previous presidential campaign, it's the Internet, stupid. There is strong evidence the Internet was an indispensable component of Dean's fund-raising success. Dean challenges nearly all of the conventional wisdom on political fund-raising: who gives, to whom, how much, and with what sort of underlying message. With the nomination in hand, Kerry suddenly inherited Dean's fund-raising success, collecting a stunning $40 million just in the first quarter of 2004 ($26 million of that online) and keeping pace with the Bush fund-raising machine. Kerry's online cash influx implies that Dean's campaign was not a fluke, but rather part of an important shift in the American political landscape.

Internet fundraising is not the only Dean legacy. Dean used the Web (and specific sites like Meetup.com) to build a minor candidacy into a national movement. The geographic reach of the campaign, the size of its volunteer corps, and its ability to recruit previously inactive citizens were all a result of Dean's Internet strategy.

Dean's candidacy is thus the best evidence to date that the Web matters for politics. His example makes it doubly important to understand how this resource is distributed, and it highlights important ideological gaps in who uses the Web for politics. The digital divide is not just about access, user skills, or even what Pippa Norris labels a "democracy gap" between the engaged and the politically indifferent.[13] For practical politics, the most crucial divide concerns the attitudes of those who frequent political Web sites. Disproportionate liberal use laid the groundwork for everything Dean accomplished and ensured that the online political audience would be particularly receptive to his message. Much of the future of online politics depends on how persistent this liberal-conservative gap proves to be.

The Dean campaign marks the end of the beginning for the study of the Internet in political science, the moment when the medium dramatically affected traditional concerns like fund-raising and mobilization. There is still a great deal that we do not know about the Internet and its implications for political life. For those who study political campaigns, filling in these gaps is suddenly a lot more important.

Notes

1. Bartels 1988, especially chapter 10; quotation on p. 260.
2. MoveOn.org 2003.
3. Bimber and Davis 2003, chapter 4.
4. Center for Responsive Politics 2004.
5. Ibid.
6. Verba, Schlozman, and Brady 1995.
7. Ibid.
8. Data on number of total supporters from the Dean Web site (http://www. deanforamerica.com). Data on the number of Dean supporters registered for meetups from Meetup.com.
9. Personal communication, Jesse Gordon, cofounder of Mass for Dean, February 19, 2003.
10. Williams, Weinberg, and Gordon 2004; survey data available at http:// Meetupsurvey.com/Study/ReportsData.html.
11. See, for example, Johnson and Gibson 1974.
12. Verba, Schlozman, and Brady 1995, chapter 5.
13. Norris 2001.

References

Bartels, Larry M. 1988. *Presidential primaries and the dynamics of public choice.* Princeton: Princeton University Press.

Bimber, Bruce A., and Richard Davis. 2003. *Campaigning online: The Internet in U.S. elections.* New York: Oxford University Press.

Center for Responsive Politics. 2004. Report on 2004 donor demographics. http:// www.opensecrets.org/presidential/donordems.asp. Accessed February 2004, July 2004, August 2004, and December 2004.

Johnson, Donald Bruce, and James R. Gibson. 1974. The divisive primary revisited: Party activists in Iowa. *American Political Science Review* 68 (1): 67–77.

MoveOn.org. 2003. Report on the 2003 MoveOn.org PAC primary. http://www. moveon.org/pac/primary/report.html.

Norris, Pippa. 2001. *Digital divide: Civic engagement, information poverty and the Internet worldwide.* New York: Cambridge University Press.

Verba, Sidney, Kay L. Schlozman, and Henry E. Brady. 1995. *Voice and equality.* Cambridge: Harvard University Press.

Williams, Christine, Bruce Weinberg, and Jesse Gordon. 2004. When online and off-line politics "meetup." Paper presented at the 2004 APSA conference. http:// Meetupsurvey.com/Study/Components/Reports/APSApaperfinal.doc.

16

THE MISCAST INSTITUTION

Thomas E. Patterson

Editor's Note

There is much "out of order" in presidential election campaigns. The mass media are miscast into filling the political role that political parties ought to play. The norms of journalism and the commercial goals of the press are at odds with the political values that should guide election campaigns in democracies. The candidates are miscast into serving a public relations function designed to snare, rather than enlighten, voters. This forces these candidates to make and keep politically disastrous promises. The voters are equally miscast. They cannot fill the void of political savvy left by ill-functioning parties. Their voting choices, therefore, are poorly grounded in political insights—discernment that the news media are neither inclined nor equipped to supply.

This study, drawn from his book *Out of Order*, was written while Thomas E. Patterson was professor of political science at the Maxwell School of Citizenship and Public Affairs at Syracuse University. The book received the American Political Science Association's Graber Award as the best book of the decade in political communication. The American Association for Public Opinion Research named an earlier Patterson book, *The Unseeing Eye: The Myth of Television Power in National Politics,* published in 1976 with Robert McClure, as one of the fifty most influential books on public opinion in the past half century. Patterson has also published two acclaimed American government texts.

The United States is the only democracy that organizes its national election campaign around the news media. Even if the media did not want the responsibility for organizing the campaign, it is theirs by virtue of an election

Source: Thomas E. Patterson, *Out of Order,* New York: Alfred A. Knopf, 1993, chapter 1. Copyright © 1993 by Thomas E. Patterson. Used by permission of Alfred A. Knopf, a division of Random House, Inc.

system built upon entrepreneurial candidacies, floating voters, freewheeling interest groups, and weak political parties.

It is an unworkable arrangement: the press is not equipped to give order and direction to a presidential campaign. And when we expect it to do so, we set ourselves up for yet another turbulent election.

The campaign is chaotic largely because the press is not a political institution and has no capacity for organizing the election in a coherent manner. . . .

The news is a highly refracted version of reality. . . . The press's restless search for the riveting story works against its intention to provide the voters with a reliable picture of the campaign. It is a formidable job to present society's problems in ways that voters can understand and act upon. The news media cannot do the job consistently well. Walter Lippmann put it plainly when he said that a press-based politics "is not workable. And when you consider the nature of news, it is not even thinkable." [1] . . .

* * *

The press's role in presidential elections is in large part the result of a void that was created when America's political parties surrendered their control over the nominating process. Through 1968, nominations were determined by the parties' elected and organizational leaders. Primary elections were held in several states, but they were not decisive. A candidate could demonstrate through the primaries that he had a chance of winning the fall election, as John Kennedy, the nation's first Catholic president, did with his primary victories in Protestant West Virginia and Wisconsin in 1960.

Nevertheless, real power rested with the party leadership rather than the primary electorate. . . . The nominating system changed fundamentally after the bitter presidential campaign of 1968. . . .

. . . [I]n the Democratic party [it] changed from a mixed system of one-third primary states and two-thirds convention states, controlled by party elites, to a reformed system in which nearly three-fourths of the delegates to the national convention were chosen by the voters in primary elections. Many Democratic state legislatures passed primary-election laws, thereby binding Republicans to the change as well.[2] Serious contenders for nomination would now have to appeal directly to the voters. . . .

Jimmy Carter's efforts in the year preceding his 1976 presidential nomination exemplified the new reality. Instead of making the traditional rounds among party leaders, Carter traveled about the country meeting with journalists. When the *New York Times*'s R. W. Apple wrote a front-page story about Carter's bright prospects one Sunday in October 1975, his outlook indeed brightened. Other journalists followed with their Carter stories and helped to propel the long-shot Georgian to his party's nomination. Carter would not have won under the old rules.

Of course, the news media's influence in presidential selection had not been inconsequential in earlier times, and in a few instances it had even been crucial. Wendell Willkie was an obscure businessman until the publisher Henry Luce decided that he would make a good president. Luce used his magazines *Time, Life,* and *Fortune* to give Willkie the prominence necessary to win the Republican nomination in 1940. . . .

Nevertheless, the media's role today in helping to establish the election agenda is different from what it was in the past. Once upon a time, the press occasionally played an important part in the nomination of presidential candidates. Now its function is always a key one. The news media do not entirely determine who will win the nomination, but no candidate can succeed without the press. The road to nomination now runs through the newsrooms.

Reform Democrats did not take the character of the news media into account when they changed the presidential election process in the early 1970s. Their goal was admirable enough. The system required a change that would give the voters' preferences more weight in the nominating process. But the reformers disregarded the desirability of also creating a process that was deliberative and would allow for the reflective choice of a nominee. In their determination to abolish the old system, they gave almost no thought to the dynamics of the new one. . . .

The modern campaign requires the press to play a constructive role. When the parties established a nominating process that is essentially a free-for-all between self-generated candidacies, the task of bringing the candidates and voters together in a common effort was superimposed on a media system that was built for other purposes. The press was no longer asked only to keep an eye out for wrongdoing and to provide a conduit for candidates to convey their messages to the voters. It was also expected to guide the voters' decisions. It was obliged to inspect the candidates' platforms, judge their fitness for the nation's highest office, and determine their electability—functions the parties had performed in the past. In addition, the press had to carry out these tasks in a way that would enable the voters to exercise *their* discretion effectively in the choice of nominees.

The columnist Russell Baker hinted at these new responsibilities when he described the press as the "Great Mentioner." The nominating campaign of a candidate who is largely ignored by the media is almost certainly futile, while the campaign of one who receives close attention gets an important boost. In this sense, the press performs the party's traditional role of screening potential nominees for the presidency—deciding which ones are worthy of serious consideration by the electorate and which ones can be dismissed as also-rans. The press also helps to establish the significance of the primaries and caucuses, deciding which ones are critical and how well the candidates must perform in them to be taken seriously.

The press's responsibilities, however, go far beyond news decisions that allocate coverage among the contending contests and candidates. The de facto premise of today's nominating system is that the media will direct the voters toward a clear understanding of what is at stake in choosing one candidate rather than another. Whereas the general election acquires stability from the competition between the parties, the nominating stage is relatively undefined. It features self-starting candidates, all of whom clamor for public attention, each claiming to be the proper representative of his party's legacy and future. It is this confusing situation that the press is expected to clarify.[3]

A press-based system seems as if it ought to work. The public gets a nearly firsthand look at the candidates. The alternatives are out in the open for all to see. What could be better?

The belief that the press can substitute for political institutions is widespread. Many journalists, perhaps most of them, assume they can do it effectively.[4] Scholars who study the media also accept the idea that the press can organize elections. Every four years, they suggest that the campaign could be made coherent if the media would only report it differently.[5]

However, the press merely appears to have the capacity to organize the voters' alternatives in a coherent way. The news creates a pseudocommunity: citizens feel that they are part of a functioning whole until they try to act upon their news-created awareness. . . . The press can raise the public's consciousness, but the news itself cannot organize public opinion in any meaningful way. . . .

The proper organization of electoral opinion requires an institution with certain characteristics. It must be capable of seeing the larger picture—of looking at the world as a whole and not in small pieces. It must have incentives that cause it to identify and organize those interests that are making demands for policy representation. And it must be accountable for its choices, so that the public can reward it when satisfied and force amendments when dissatisfied.[6] The press has none of these characteristics. The media has its special strengths, but they do not include these strengths.

The press is a very different kind of organization from the political party, whose role it acquired. A party is driven by the steady force of its traditions and constituent interests. . . . The press, in contrast, is "a restless beacon." [7] Its concern is the new, the unusual, and the sensational. Its agenda shifts abruptly when a new development breaks.[8] The party has the incentive—the possibility of acquiring political power—to give order and voice to society's values. Its raison d'être is to articulate interests and to forge them into a winning coalition. The press has no such incentive and no such purpose. Its objective is the discovery and development of good stories.[9] . . .

The press is also not politically accountable. The political party is made accountable by a formal mechanism—elections. The vote gives officeholders a reason to act in the majority's interest, and it offers citizens an opportunity to boot from office anyone they feel has failed them. Thousands of elected officials have lost their jobs this way. The public has no comparable hold on the press. Journalists are neither chosen by the people nor removable by them. Irate citizens may stop watching a news program or buying a newspaper that angers them, but no major daily newspaper or television station has ever gone out of business as a result.

Other democracies have recognized the inappropriateness of press-based elections. Although national voting in all Western democracies is media-centered in the sense that candidates depend primarily on mass communication to reach the voters, no other democracy has a system in which the press fills the role traditionally played by the political party.[10] Journalists in other democracies actively participate in the campaign process, but their efforts take place within an electoral structure built around political institutions. In the United States, however, national elections are referendums in which the candidates stand alone before the electorate and have no choice but to filter their appeals through the lens of the news media.

. . . [T]he presidential election system has become unpredictable. The nominating phase is especially volatile; with relatively small changes in luck, timing, or circumstance, several nominating races might have turned out differently. There is no purpose behind an electoral system in which the vote is impulsive and the outcome can hinge on random circumstance or minor issues. Stability and consistency are the characteristics of a properly functioning institution. Disorder is a sure sign of a defective system. Although pundits have explained the unpredictability of recent elections in terms of events and personalities peculiar to each campaign, the answer lies deeper—in the electoral system itself. It places responsibilities on its principals—the voters, the candidates, and the journalists—that they cannot meet or that magnify their shortcomings.

*   *   *

The voters' problem is one of overload. The presidential election system places extraordinary demands on voters, particularly during the nominating phase. These races often attract a large field of contenders, most of whom are newcomers to national politics. The voters are expected to grasp quickly what the candidates represent, but the task is daunting. . . . Nor can it be assumed that the campaign itself will inform the electorate. At the time of nomination, half or more of the party's rank-and-file voters had no clear idea of where Carter (1976), Mondale (1984), Bush and Dukakis (1988), and Clinton (1992) stood on various issues.[11] . . . The Republicans' nomination of Ronald Reagan in 1980 is particularly revealing of the public's lack of information. . . . When asked to place Reagan on an ideological scale, 43 percent said they did not know where to place him, 10 percent said he was a liberal, and 6 percent identified him as a moderate.[12]

Nominating campaigns are imposing affairs. They are waged between entrepreneurial candidates whose support is derived from groups and elites joined together solely for that one election. Primary elections are not in the least bit like general elections, which offer a choice between a "Republican" and a "Democrat." If these labels mean less today than in the past, they still represent a voting guideline for many Americans. But a primary election presents to voters little more than a list of names.[13] There is no established label associated with these names, no stable core of supporters, and typically the appeals that dominate one election are unlike those emphasized in others. . . . Voters are not stupid, but they have been saddled with an impossible task. The news media consistently overestimate the voters' knowledge of the candidates and the speed with which they acquire it. . . .

Voters would not necessarily be able to make the optimal choice even if they had perfect information. A poll of New Hampshire voters in 1976 reportedly showed that when each Democratic candidate was paired off successively with each of the others, Jimmy Carter came out near the bottom. . . . Yet he won the primary. New Hampshire's voters divided their support somewhat evenly among the other Democratic contenders, enabling the less favored choice, Carter, to finish first with 28 percent of the vote. The possibility that someone other than the consensual alternative will emerge victorious exists in every multicandidate primary.

There was a time when America's policymakers understood that the voters should not be assigned this type of election decision, even if they were able to make it. Citizens are not Aristotles who fill their time studying politics. People have full lives to lead: children to raise, jobs to perform, skills to acquire, leisure activities to pursue. People have little time for attending to politics in their daily lives, and their appetite for political information is weak. . . . How, then, can we expect primary-election voters to inform themselves about a half-dozen little-known contenders and line them up on the basis of policy and other factors in order to make an informed choice?

Of course, voters *will* choose. Each state has a primary or a caucus, and enough voters participate to make it look as though a reasoned choice has been made. In reality, the voters act on the basis of little information and without the means to select the optimal candidate in a crowded race.

The modern system of picking presidents also places burdens on the candidates that they should not be required to carry. Some of the demands are grotesque. A U.S. presidential campaign requires nearly a two-year stint in the bowels of television studios, motel rooms, and fast-food restaurants. . . .

The system can make it difficult for a person who holds high office to run for nomination. In 1980, Howard Baker's duties as Senate minority leader kept him from campaigning effectively, and he was easily defeated. . . . The strongest candidate for nomination is often someone, like Carter in 1976 and Reagan in 1980, who is out of office. . . .

Advocates of the present system argue that the grueling campaign is an appropriate test of a candidate's ability to withstand the rigors of the presidency. This proposition is a dubious one. It is easy to imagine someone who would make a superb president but who hates a year-long campaign effort or would wilt under its demands. . . .

The current system makes it impossible for the public to choose its president from the full range of legitimate contenders. The demands of a present-day nominating campaign require candidates to decide far in advance of the presidential election day whether they will make the run. If they wait too long to get into the race, they will find their funding and organization to be hopelessly inadequate. Moreover, a candidate who wins the nomination but then loses the general election is likely to acquire a loser's image which may hinder any subsequent run for the presidency. As a consequence, any potential candidate is forced into a strategic decision long before the campaign formally begins. . . .

For those who run, the electoral system is a barrier to true leadership. Candidates are self-starters who organize their own campaigns. . . . As entrepreneurs, they look for support from wherever they can plausibly get it. In the past, the parties buffered the relationship between candidates and groups. Today, it is very difficult for candidates to ignore the demands of interest groups or to confine them to their proper place. Indeed, the modern candidate has every reason for tirelessly courting interest groups—nominating campaigns *are* factional politics. . . .

Contrary to the press's chronic complaint, the central problem of the modern campaign is not that presidential candidates make promises they do not intend to keep; instead, it is that candidates make scores of promises they ought not to make but must try to keep.[14] Politicians with a reputation for breaking promises do not get very far. They attract votes by making commitments and fulfilling them. But it is the nature of the modern campaign to encourage them to overpromise. In this sense, the campaign brings them *too* close to the public they serve. . . .

Politics, like the marketplace, cannot function without ambition. The challenge, as the political scientist James Ceaser notes, is "to discover some way to create a degree of harmony between behavior that satisfies personal ambition and behavior that promotes the public good." [15] All of the nation's great presidents—Washington, Jefferson, Jackson, Lincoln, Franklin D. Roosevelt—were men of towering ambition, but their drive was directed toward constructive leadership.

The electoral reforms of the early 1970s have served to channel ambition in the wrong direction. Today's nominating system is a wide-open process that forces candidates into petty forms of politics. Without partisan differences to separate them, candidates for nomination must find other ways to distinguish themselves from competitors. They often rely on personality appeals of the ingratiating kind. . . .

An electoral system should strengthen the character of the office that it is designed to fill. The modern system of electing presidents undermines the presidential office.[16] The writers of the Constitution believed that unrestrained politicking encouraged demagoguery and special-interest politics,[17] and would degenerate eventually into majority tyranny. If we know now that the Framers were wrong in their belief in the inevitability of a tyrannical majority, we also know that they were right in their belief that an overemphasis on campaigning results in excessive appeals to self-interest and momentary passions.

More than in the candidates or the voters, the problem of the modern presidential campaign lies in the role assigned to the press. Its traditional role is that of a watchdog. In the campaign, this has meant that journalists have assumed responsibility for protecting the public against deceitful, corrupt, or incompetent candidates. The press still plays this watchdog role, and necessarily so. This vital function, however, is different from the role that was thrust on the press when the nominating system was opened wide in the early 1970s.

The new role conflicts with the old one. The critical stance of the watchdog is not to be confused with the constructive task of the coalition-builder. The new role requires the press to act in constructive ways to bring candidates and voters together.

The press has never fully come to grips with the contradictions between its newly acquired and traditional roles. New responsibilities have been imposed on top of older orientations. . . . If the media are capable of organizing presidential choice in a meaningful way, it would be despite the fact that the media were not designed for this purpose. . . . The public schools, for example, have been asked to compensate for the breakup of the traditional American family. The prospects for success are as hopeless as the task is thankless. The same is true of the press in its efforts to fill the role once played by the political party. . . . [T]he press is not a substitute for political institutions. A press-based electoral system is not a suitable basis for that most pivotal of all decisions, the choice of a president.

Notes

1. Walter Lippmann, *Public Opinion* (1922; reprint, New York: Free Press, 1965), p. 229.
2. William Crotty and John S. Jackson III, *Presidential Primaries and Nominations* (Washington, D.C.: American Enterprise Institute, 1977), pp. 44–49.
3. Michael J. Robinson, "Television and American Politics: 1956–1976," in *Reader in Public Opinion and Communication*, 3rd ed., ed. Morris Janowitz and Paul Hirsch (New York: Free Press, 1981), p. 109.
4. See "The Press and the Presidential Campaign, 1988" (Seminar proceedings of the American Press Institute, Reston, Va., December 6, 1988).
5. Ibid.
6. See Everett Carll Ladd, *American Political Parties* (New York: Norton, 1970), p. 2.
7. Lippmann, *Public Opinion*, p. 229.
8. Richard Davis, *The Press and American Politics* (New York: Longman, 1992), pp. 21–27.
9. James David Barber, "Characters in the Campaign: The Literary Problem," in *Race for the Presidency*, ed. James David Barber (Englewood Cliffs, N.J.: Prentice-Hall, 1978), pp. 114–17.
10. Holli Semetko, Jay G. Blumler, Michael Gurevitch, and David H. Weaver, with Steve Barkin and G. Cleveland Wilhoit, *The Formation of Campaign Agendas* (Hillsdale, N.J.: Lawrence Erlbaum, 1991), pp. 3, 4.
11. See, for example, Thomas E. Patterson, *The Mass Media Election* (New York: Praeger, 1980), p. 167, and Paul Taylor, *See How They Run* (New York: Knopf, 1990), pp. 202–03.
12. Scott Keeter and Cliff Zukin, *Uninformed Choice: The Failure of the New Presidential Nominating System* (New York: Praeger, 1983), pp. 110, 136.
13. Austin Ranney, *Channels of Power* (New York: Basic Books, 1983), p. 93.
14. Theodore Lowi, *The Personal President: Power Invested, Promise Unfulfilled* (Ithaca, N.Y.: Cornell University Press, 1985), p. 11.
15. James W. Ceaser, *Presidential Selection: Theory and Development* (Princeton, N.J.: Princeton University Press, 1979), p. 11.
16. Ibid., p. 310.
17. Ibid., pp. 82–83.

17

CANDIDATE BILL CLINTON AND THE PRESS

Joseph Hayden

Editor's Note

In May 1992, the cover of the *New Republic* magazine forecast doom for Bill Clinton's presidential campaign with the headline "Why Clinton Can't Win." But Clinton did win, and in this selection, excerpted from his book, *Covering Clinton: The President and the Press in the 1990s,* Joseph Hayden chronicles why Clinton beat the odds. Hayden gives most of the credit to Clinton's heavy use of talk shows, which allowed him to interact informally with friendly television hosts, answer call-in questions from regular citizens in plain language, and engage in give-and-take discussions with audiences composed of ordinary folks. The format allowed him to create the image of a caring president who empathized with the problems of average Americans and who would be their personal friend in the White House. Deprived of most chances to grill the president and focus on the many skeletons in his political closet, the mainstream media were reduced to commenting on his smooth performances in the new media forums.

Hayden is a freelance writer and a former journalist. Besides analyzing Clinton's 1992 campaign, *Covering Clinton* focuses on issues and events over President Clinton's two terms, emphasizing the press response to Clinton's programs and scandals. More broadly, the book examines the general thrust of president-press relationships in the 1990s, including the roles of consultants, press secretaries, and pollsters.

. . . [P]erhaps the most striking element in the [inauguration 1993] day's exultation was the simple fact that Bill Clinton had beaten the odds, for

Source: Joseph Hayden, *Covering Clinton: The President and the Press in the 1990s,* Westport, Conn.: Praeger, 2002, chapter 1, "The Empathy Candidate and the Living Room Campaign." Copyright © 2002 by Praeger. Reproduced with permission of Greenwood Publishing Group, Inc., Westport, Conn.

many celebrants a deeply satisfying knowledge mixed with the sweet sense of revenge. Here too was a storyteller's dream: the dramatic, even inspiring, comeback story about a down-and-outer who refused to quit and won it all. Clinton, we must remember, was a virtual unknown at the beginning of 1992, and yet the better known he became the more beleaguered he was, because Clinton was not just an underdog but an unlikely candidate with serious liabilities. To be sure, the Arkansas contender sported promising abilities and an encouraging gubernatorial record, but he was also a man with worrisome personal traits and several gaping political vulnerabilities—vulnerabilities so manifest that most pundits were quick to write him off at the outset of the campaign.

Political Baggage

Clinton had evaded the Vietnam War draft in the 1960s. Instead of complying with conscription when his number came up, he sought an exemption and used every contact he could think of to obtain one. Clinton's attempt to avoid the draft was hardly exceptional among college students. . . . Clinton was not exactly honorable in staying out of the draft, however. Upon his release from duty, he returned to Oxford University instead of the Arkansas National Guard, as he had apparently promised and for which he was spared from the army in the first place. Eluding military service during the Vietnam War was, of course, not news then or even two decades later, but Clinton's dishonesty about the details of his past was. He told the press a year before the election that he had always wanted to serve in the armed forces.[1] In 1992, he denied ever having received an induction notice, having had someone pull strings on his behalf, and having even opposed the draft itself. . . .

Clinton was similarly untruthful in answering early questions about his experience using marijuana. At first he said he didn't, then he said he did but didn't inhale, a hilarious excuse which embarrassed even his supporters. By lying, Clinton was doing something that legal writer Alan Dershowitz would later, in the Monica Lewinsky scandal, judge to be among the president's worst faults: attempting to gain some short-term political ground regardless of the long-term consequences.[2] . . .

The third of Clinton's triumvirate of vulnerabilities was his penchant for adulterous affairs and, still more, his lying about them. In 1992, an Arkansas lounge singer named Gennifer Flowers held a press conference to tell the world that for more than a decade she had been the governor's lover. Clinton denied any intimate relationship, even though Flowers played a tape-recorded phone message between the two, which clearly indicated that she, not he, was telling the truth. Clinton could not have incurred any more obvious strikes against his candidacy.

The Clinton Campaign Team

Facing this army of political skeletons was a youthful but surprisingly experienced staff of dedicated political advisors. James Carville headed the campaign team. The forty-seven-year-old strategist, sloganeer, and media ham enjoyed showcasing his quick wit and zestful personality, but he was a chief aide of real substance, someone with limitless energy and reliable political instincts. . . . [A]bove all it was Carville himself who smoothed relations between the media, particularly the more established figures in it, and candidate Clinton. Carville's self-conscious drawl and his relentless sense of humor proved irresistible to journalists, who found him endlessly entertaining and likable, as well as informed, crudely opinionated, and insightful.

Carville's partner was George Stephanopoulos, thirty-one years old, and certainly the youngest-looking member of the Clinton team. Looks were deceiving, however, for the native New Yorker was an unusually bright and resourceful strategist with impressive experience. Stephanopoulos manned what came to be known as "the war room," an operations center responsible for combatting every attack sent their way the second it came out, even, in fact, anticipating likely attacks and squashing them before they did emerge. . . . The war room, in essence, was the campaign's general headquarters for handling the mainstream press, and its military motif was certainly emblematic of Clinton's overall attitude toward older, conventional media, to the Washington press corps, in particular.

The mastermind behind Clinton's appearances on new-media venues was thirty-four-year-old media consultant Mandy Grunwald, daughter of media scion Henry Grunwald, once the editor in chief of *Time* magazine. Mandy Grunwald was a Harvard graduate who had already worked for U.S. senators like Daniel Patrick Moynihan, Wendell Ford, and Patrick Leahy. Despite her eventual preference for alternative media, Grunwald could carry herself, and Bill Clinton, rather well in dealing with established media programs. In January 1992, while responding to questions about Gennifer Flowers, for example, Grunwald acquitted herself so well during a joint appearance with Clinton on the American Broadcasting Company's (ABC's) late-night program *Nightline,* even Ted Koppel was forced to admit on air that she had "done a very effective job of putting me on the defensive."[3]

Clinton and the New Media

Nonetheless, it was precisely those respected programs like *Nightline* that pushed Grunwald to look elsewhere for her boss to make his case to the American people. Mainstream reporters, she felt, were fixated on scandals, crises, and controversies. They seemed more interested in Clinton's reaction to questions about past embarrassments than they were in his ideas for future policies—his perspective on issues concerning the economy, health care, or Social Security. Old-Style reporters wouldn't let him move beyond his less-than-sublime personal history. In fact, journalists were so preoccupied with confronting Clinton about his controversial past that they often failed to observe one of his most impressive qualities on display in the present: a solicitous, reassuring compassion. At one campaign stop, he hugged a woman on the verge of tears because she couldn't afford medical care. "I think he's the smartest guy I've ever met," Clinton's adviser Paul Begala reflected. "But his most compelling attribute is that interpersonal empathy. When he is connecting with someone, the whole world melts away."[4]

Grunwald's challenge, therefore, was to avoid confrontations seeking the governor's apology or defensive reaction, and instead to find forums where he might showcase his gift for more pleasant conversation. The key, she believed, was finding opportunities for Clinton to speak at leisure and at length, so Grunwald sought out television programs with more amicable hosts, more flexible or informal settings, and with younger audiences. By the summer, he was fully immersed in doing so, appearing on the *Arsenio Hall Show,* MTV, *Donahue,* and *Larry King Live.* Clinton, the "empathy candidate," thrived in these arenas. For reasons that can best be summed up in the succinct phrase that he was "good with people," Clinton had obviously found an environment in which to put his interpersonal skills to work. But these environments were uniquely and inherently structured to do that for any candidate, which is why so many other office seekers quickly turned to them as well.

. . . [I]t would be a mistake to conclude that a program like MTV's *Facing the Future with Bill Clinton* was less informative than one like *Meet the Press,* for it was informative in different ways. The point is that candidates rightly viewed the former as friendlier and freer. They could anticipate being able to get across a particular message or set of messages without fierce objection, sarcasm, or incredulity. Such a format provided them with considerable latitude. And for Clinton, who was spending valuable time combatting rearguard scandal-mongers, these programs were a vital and welcoming departure. . . .

From Clinton's perspective, the highlight of the new-media experience in the 1992 campaign was undoubtedly the series of formal debates between the candidates. Not ostensibly new or novel, these forums confirmed the triumph of Clinton's campaign style when he got up out of his chair, strolled toward the audience, and confidently fielded questions. He then proceeded to engage in a bit of give-and-take with the audience, saying the right things, using the right gestures, expressing an appealing and authentic-sounding empathy for the voters in the crowd. "I feel your pain" became the famous mantra associated with Bill Clinton's campaign style. Compared to the more sedentary candidate Ross Perot and the quintessentially self-contained George Bush, Bill Clinton shone as a master of personable political acumen.

When Ross Perot spoke on *Larry King Live* in early 1992, he started what would become the most significant political trend of the year, the gravitation toward unconventional forums for political discussion and imagery. But if Perot launched the new movement, no one better personified it or excelled at it than Bill Clinton. . . .

Clinton is a baby boomer, the nation's first to become president. He had grown up with television; he hadn't looked on warily or dismissively or uncertainly as television grew up. Therefore, he understood in a visceral way the demands of the medium, and the importance of being photogenic. Aides naturally advised him on what to do and say—that's their job—but no one had to tell Clinton, as consultants had to tell George Bush, how crucial it was to impart the right impression to viewers. And that's really the crux of the difference between the two men: Clinton knew that in an electronic age, voters were by definition *viewers*. Bush had to be reminded of that. Furthermore, Clinton's staff did not have to micromanage their boss's appearances. They trusted him to smile and wave, laugh and charm, mug and mingle. Clinton was like Lyndon Johnson without the hard edges. He depended on his attractive, engaging personal manner, his likeability, to win support. . . .

Clinton's affinity for stimulating new forums thus capitalized on his foremost personal strengths. He pushed the boundaries of political television both because he was uniquely capable of it and because he had no other choice if he wanted to win. Clinton personified and best exploited the untapped possibilities of electronic electioneering, proving in the process that staid press conferences and intensely high-pressure tête-à-têtes with journalists were neither the only way to communicate to and through the media, nor necessarily the best way. Bill Clinton rose to power in 1992 on the back of the new media, television talk shows in particular, but his victory was also a story about seemingly new methods. What Clinton realized in 1992 was that soft-news exposure was just as helpful to his campaign as hard-news exposure; that being seen and heard were more important than being written about; and that televised contact with ordinary voters in low-key situations was more profitable than regular meetings with "professional" journalists. Communing with the public was the desired objective, and if some of the people had nonpolitical questions to ask, so much the better.

Clinton's exploitation of the new media had not come serendipitously in 1992. As governor of Arkansas, he had grown wary of conventional news organizations, especially after losing reelection in 1980, and so experimented with alternative media in subsequent races. . . . He also preferred not to share the spotlight, and the correspondents of major media organizations are nothing if not stage-friendly. Even in Arkansas, finding alternatives to the capital press corps proved more reliable than surrendering to the whims of journalists hungry for scoops. At any rate, Clinton thrived in low-key and informal settings. . . .

*   *   *

. . . Clinton, his media consultant, Mandy Grunwald, and other key aides decided that voters were learning too little about the "real" Bill Clinton, so in a strategy dubbed "The Manhatten Project," Clinton would henceforth use direct-access media as much as possible and the mainstream as sparingly as possible or only as necessary.[5] The Fox late-night program offered one such opportunity.

Talk show host Arsenio Hall was, as usual, all giggles for his program on June 3, 1992. On this night, though, the squirming schoolboy routine seemed a little more natural. Governor and presidential candidate Bill Clinton, ac-coutered in zoot suit and sunglasses, was playing saxophone with the band during the show's opening and soloed "Heartbreak Hotel" before a typically animated crowd. Before beginning his monologue, Hall quieted the audience, thanked Clinton for the music, then kidded him: "Okay, just ignore me right now 'cause this is the part of my show that politicians hate." Then, after a few seconds, he added, "Of course, I'll talk about the other guys." It was all part of the chatty mirth show business is famous for, which did not fail to at-tract the notice of wary journalists.

In an editorial for the *Washington Post,* William Raspberry worried that despite the perception that reporters ought to cover "the issues" during the campaign, they were inevitably forced to write about less important matters. "Would you like yours to be the only newspaper whose reporter neglected . . . the gaffes and gossip? Would you like yours to be the only network to feature 'white papers' while your competitors were going with sex, sin and saxophone playing?"[6] Journalists, he said, inevitably wind up dwelling on racehorse (who's ahead, how far) and electability news, which regrettably meant covering Bill Clinton's appearance on *Arsenio Hall,* for example. In other words, Raspberry appears not to assign much journalistic importance to Clinton's appearance on the program. But he seems to change his mind near the end of his column, because after talking about the need for more "serious" information from candidates about "fiscal restraint" and "balanced budgets," he suddenly reconsiders his priorities, conceding that perhaps we do just want to know the basics about political candidates. . . .

Raspberry goes on to challenge the assumption that tough, prosecutorial journalism is the only way to discover a candidate's real character or voice. Or, in other words, cattle-prodding a politician might not be the most effi-cient means to try to understand his views. . . .

Raspberry was right. And intellectual or political vacuity does not at any rate accurately describe the Clinton-Hall encounter. More went on than high-fives and small jokes. After the first several minutes of the program, the two men settled into a discussion of racism and democracy, focusing on the then recent Los Angeles riots and what political leadership might do to resolve the scars evident there and elsewhere. . . .

Many journalists did not remember the program that way, however. They only saw the joking and the saxophone playing and thought, "This is not how a presidential candidate is supposed to act." . . .

. . . The day after Clinton's meeting with Arsenio Hall, Bush press secretary Torie Clarke lambasted both the candidate's performance and his judgment: "I thought it was embarrassing. . . . He looked like a sad John Belushi wannabe. . . . I don't think most Americans want to see their president wearing a goofy tie and sunglasses and blowing on a saxophone, and then talking about smoking pot with a late-night TV host.[7]

"Bullshit," replied Mandy Grunwald, who had promoted the *Arsenio* appearance. "This is how people get information."[8] She had outlined her talk show strategy to Clinton in April and explained that its benefit was to showcase his personal side, "to convey biography and personality," she recalled later to none other than Larry King. "You can't do that on the evening news."[9] Grunwald believed the "undignified" label talk shows earned for conducting programs with political candidates was unfair and untrue. "We were trying to explain that this was a person, not a caricature like the cartoons in your newspaper but a person who has a life . . . I think explaining who you are is not unpresidential." . . .

Raspberry emphasized a corollary: citizens wanted to connect with candidates and hungered for an honest level of conversation missing in most encounters between politicians and journalists. Instead, voters were shuffled into the role of spectator and treated to fish swaps in which candidates traded cold, canned responses for the icy cynicism of journalists. No wonder mainstream media were turning people away. Journalists were hampering dialogue, not opening the way for it. And citizens were tired of the rigamarole that accompanied spectatorship anyway. . . . Some politicians and many more journalists could not see the growing public frustration, and so they failed to understand either the reason for voter apathy or the popularity and importance of alternative forums available to political candidates to contact those disaffected voters. Larry King put the matter succinctly: "The 'Arsenio' controversy was a classic example of dismissive Beltway dwellers laughing—even though the joke was really on them. . . . It was a smart move."[10] . . .

Eventually, even the reluctant Bush campaign team came to appreciate this view, despite the fact that it had first branded the idea "weird," "wacky," and beneath the dignity of the White House. . . . Before the year's end, Bush capitulated and ultimately visited all three network morning programs more than once (and ABC's *Good Morning America* seven times), appeared on *Larry King Live* three times, and even showed up on MTV—four months

after chiding Clinton for doing the same thing.[11] Perot appeared on twice as
many such programs as Bush, and Clinton three times as many as Bush.[12] Yet
Bush's reversal of campaign policy proved that the new media had eclipsed
the old, and that if winning the election depended on courting the former, if
it involved answering call-in questions from viewers on talk shows, candidates would predictably do so. "[W]e are game players," Clinton tactician
James Carville observed. "We are not rule makers."[13]

Bush was the last candidate to get on the bandwagon, but some journalists never did. Again, at any rate, the reckoning for many first came in June,
when Clinton's appearance on *Arsenio Hall* graphically marked the new
manner of political campaigning. William Raspberry's questions mentioned
above capture the powerful need journalists felt to make sense of the new
media. . . . The conformity of coverage among all these sources verifies that
June occasioned the wake-up call for journalists to start paying attention to
the talk shows and similar forums. It also testifies to the unforgettable visual
impact of Bill Clinton's *Arsenio* appearance.

Conclusion

From the summer until the election, Bill Clinton set the standard for talk
show performances. He was still a masterful political candidate in other respects: he was supremely well informed on most major domestic issues—a
real policy wonk, everyone said; he was a productive fundraiser; and he was
an almost inexhaustible campaigner, someone who never seemed to tire of
shaking hands, meeting voters, making friends and contacts. But no one, not
even Ross Perot, demonstrated the flair and ease with which he talked to television hosts, answered callers' questions, or engaged in give-and-take discussion with ordinary citizens. His soothing ability to calm and relate to and
ingratiate himself with voters earned Clinton a reputation as the politician
most in touch with the electorate. Indeed, "his entire candidacy reflected a
willingness to appeal directly to the public."[14] For all his foibles, Americans
perceived him as the candidate who best understood them, and that is why
he won the presidency in 1992. The television talk show, in short, was the
perfect medium for Bill Clinton. . . .

. . . Many candidates and journalists had apparently forgotten that axiom,
the latter perhaps because it was in their interest to do so, to promote their
own role as necessary mediators. The personnel associated with unconventional formats, by contrast, didn't much care; they were happy just to have
booked a hot "talent" or famous celebrity to lift their ratings and boost their
market share. . . . Clinton was the first spectacular beneficiary of the new system, elected to the presidency because many people believed that he appreci-
ated their problems, cared about fixing those things, and knew how to do it.
But within a half-dozen years he would find his prestige challenged by those

same media, as well as others. Indeed, his political success in the 1990s prepared the stage for a whole new era in which the most cutting-edge communications technology in existence was inextricably mixed with politics, and
by the end of the decade Clinton would find his reputation probed, skewered,
and roasted on each of the new media.

Notes

1. Dan Balz, "Clinton, Kerry: A New Set of Questions," *Washington Post* (January
   18, 1992), p. A1.
2. Alan M. Dershowitz, *Sexual McCarthyism: Clinton, Starr, and the Emerging
   Constitutional Crisis* (New York: Basic Books, 1998), p. 146.
3. Quoted by Karen Ball, "Clinton's Media Whiz: Mandy Grunwald," Associated
   Press Wire (September 28, 1992).
4. Paul Begala, quoted in "The Clinton Years," ABC, *Nightline* (January 8, 2001).
5. Larry King, with Mark Stencel, *On the Line: The New Road to the White House*
   (New York: Harcourt Brace & Company, 1993), pp. 31–37.
6. *Washington Post* (June 10, 1992), p. A23.
7. *Washington Post* (June 5, 1992), p. C2.
8. Quoted in Tom Rosenstiel, *Strange Bedfellows: How Television and the Presidential Candidates Changed American Politics, 1992* (New York: Hyperion
   Press, 1993), pp. 174–75; see also Larry King, *On the Line*, p. 37.
9. Larry King, *On the Line*, pp. 32, 37.
10. Larry King, *On the Line*, p. 37.
11. Martha FitzSimon, ed., *The Finish Line: Covering the Campaign's Final Days*
    (New York: Freedom Forum Media Studies Center, January 1993), pp. 124–125.
12. Ibid.
13. *This Week with David Brinkley*, ABC, June 14, 1992.
14. Dale A. Herbeck, "Presidential Debate as Political Ritual: Clinton vs Bush vs
    Perot," in *Bill Clinton on Stump, State and Stage: The Rhetorical Road to the
    White House*, ed. Stephen A. Smith (Fayetteville: University of Arkansas Press
    1994), p. 268.

18

POLITICAL CAMPAIGNING
IN REFERENDUMS

Claes H. de Vreese and Holli A. Semetko

Editor's Note

Referendums are becoming an increasingly important political tool throughout the world for seeking citizens' advice about public policies and laws. In this
essay, Claes H. de Vreese and Holli A. Semetko analyze the Danish euro adoption referendum in 2000 as a prototypical case of campaigning for a referendum. They assess the quantity and quality of print and television coverage of
the issue and the efforts of various stakeholders to control the news agenda.
They also examine the effects of the campaign on voters' opinions about
adopting the euro, their vote in the referendum, and their views about political
leaders. Comparisons with referendum campaigns in other European countries, as well as with other types of elections, reveal some of the variations in
referendum campaigning and the unique features of referendum campaigns
compared to other types of elections.

At the time of this writing, de Vreese was associate professor and Dutch
Science Foundation Fellow in the Amsterdam School of Communication Research
at the University of Amsterdam. Semetko was vice provost for International
Affairs, director of the Claus M. Halle Institute for Global Learning, and professor
of political science at Emory University. Both scholars are prolific authors who
specialize in research on political communication and comparative media.

. . . Referendums on issues of European integration have produced only
sporadic accounts of the media coverage of the campaigns (see Jenssen *et al.*
(1998) for an account of the 1994 referendums in Norway, Finland, and
Sweden on EU membership and Siune and Svensson (1993) and Siune *et al.*
(1994) for descriptive accounts of the previous Danish referendums in the

early 1990s). The lack of systematic knowledge about the media coverage of these key events is an example of the underdeveloped understanding we have of news reporting of European political affairs (Semetko *et al.* 2000). . . .

[The Danish Campaign in the News]

In this chapter we analyze the media coverage of the referendum campaign. We draw on almost 5,000 television news stories and 3,000 newspaper stories during the campaign to analyze the visibility of the referendum issue in the media, the presence and evaluation of key actors in the news, as well as the focus of the media on the electoral content in the form of poll-oriented news coverage. The results show a major increase in the amount of coverage of the referendum in the final four weeks of the campaign, a bias towards strategic and opinion poll-oriented news coverage, and neutral or negative evaluations of key campaign actors. . . .

The news agenda was strongly influenced by the events of the referendum campaign, in particular in the final month leading up to the vote. Our content analysis of television news showed that the share of political and economic news rose by about 15 percent in the final weeks due to a sharp increase in the amount of news about the referendum. In the last four weeks of the campaign, more than 800 newspaper items were devoted to the referendum. The headlines focused on the contradictory predictions of the costs and gains of either a Yes or a No, human interest stories about key campaign leaders, the fall of the euro against the U.S. dollar during the campaign, and the internal disagreement in the Yes camp.

Our content analysis of the coverage also showed a strong presence of polls and reference to public support for the single currency. More than one-third of the stories referred to polls and the Yes and No sides' standing. This emphasis on polls in the news was not in line with the intentions for the coverage as formulated by the journalists and Editors in our interviews. . . .

Turning to our analysis of actors in the news, we saw the importance of key campaign leaders. In the news coverage of the referendum a limited number of key figures from different political parties dominated the coverage. Visibility, however, is only one dimension of media coverage. Evaluations in the news are at least as important. A pattern emerged from our content analysis that showed that the incumbent government, and in particular the Prime Minister, was highly visible in the news, but at the same time was also seen handling the referendum issue poorly, thus the consistently negative evaluations these actors received in the news.

We also identified a number of differences and similarities in the journalistic approach to the campaign. . . . While TV2 was somewhat more reluctant towards pursuing a pro-active role in setting its own agenda, TV1 was, consciously, more assertive and focused on a number of topics based on polls

. . . among their viewers. There was little variation in terms of the application of news selection criteria. Both [national television] programs devoted extra attention to the referendum, i.e. applied a somewhat sacerdotal set of criteria in which "election time is news time." None of the programs, however, implemented a special referendum segment in the news on a daily basis which has been common practice during, for example, national elections. . . .

. . . We found the referendum on the front page of most national newspapers almost daily during the final weeks of the campaign and the referendum took up about 25 percent of national television news in the last month leading up to the referendum which, on average, means about four to five news stories daily. Compared to the 1979 and 1999 European parliamentary election campaign, the 2000 referendum was much more visible in the news (Blumler 1983; de Vreese *et al.* 2004). Danish news spent about 10 percent of the news in the final two weeks leading up to the European elections in 1999 while this was more than 25 percent in the case of the 2000 referendum. This suggests that the referendum was quite visible in the news. . . .

✻ ✻ ✻

How a Referendum Campaign Affects the Media

A referendum forces media organizations to prepare and plan how to report the campaign. Some of this advance planning shares similarities with preparation for other electoral contests, but in a number of ways, media organizations have to respond to characteristics of the referendum contents. Prior to any electoral contest, news organizations typically decide on funding available for the coverage and the allocation of staff and resources. This is no different in a referendum campaign and these measures are basic indicators of the priority given to a campaign. In addition, news organizations typically prepare using background research that results in canned items for television and feature articles in the press. These preparations are made in anticipation of certain issues that are likely to appear in the campaign and when they do, background information for a story as well as potential interviewees and key facts are already on file to make it possible to report in a timely manner. Some news organizations, such as TV1 in our study, may utilize a number of additional tools in the planning, such as commissioning a survey to identify topics of interest to its viewers.

While these elements have more similarities than differences with a national election campaign, there are distinct differences too. The notion of balance is altered in the context of a referendum campaign. While the "typical" interpretation of political balance in television news involves giving access to political parties across the ideological spectrum, often in some ratio of the size of the party (Semetko 2003), a referendum challenges these existing conceptions of balanced news reporting. As the vote in a referendum is neither party nor candidate based, the balance issue becomes a question of hearing the Yes and No camps. This can have the unintended effect of a magnifying glass being placed on smaller parties or individuals on either side of the issue. We found clear evidence of this magnification effect. The interviews with journalists and Editors also revealed that at more occasions news organizations were approached after a program by parties supporting a Yes or a No who both felt that they had been treated disadvantageously in the news. . . .

How a Referendum Campaign Affects Citizens

. . . Broadly speaking, research in political science and political communication takes two perspectives on the contribution of media to the electoral process and the public perception of the political system. One strand of literature contends that the media and political journalism contribute to political alienation, political inefficacy, and a decline in participation in elections (for example, Ansolabehere and Iyengar 1995; Cappella and Jamieson 1997; Patterson 1993). Another strand of literature suggests that the media-public interface is fruitful and contributes to knowledge gains and political participation (for example, Holtz-Bacha 1990; Newton 1999; Norris 2000). Finally, others point out that effects of news coverage on political attitudes and engagement are contingent on various conditions such as political sophistication or expertise (for example, Moy and Pfau 2000; Pinkleton and Austin 2001), watching public broadcasting or commercial news (Aarts and Semetko 2003) or contextual factors (for example, Peter *et al.* 2003).

. . . We expected a national referendum campaign to be distinctively different from a general election in that the broader theme of the campaign is defined a priori. The agenda-setting dynamics was therefore more about subissues emerging within the broader issue. We found limited support of agenda-setting at the aggregate level. That is to say that the composition of the news agenda and the public agenda differed in terms of the ranking of issues.

The referendum, however, increased in salience on the public agenda during the campaign and we found that exposure to news about the referendum contributed to an increase in the salience of the referendum issue. This supports the agenda-setting hypothesis at the individual level. We also explored the meaning of the referendum issue and found evidence that the referendum did not mean the same to the public as it did to the news media. An issue may in other words be important to both the media and the public, but looking beyond this we may find different substantive aspects of that issue being more important to one group than the other.

Our study emphasizes the importance of the battle over a referendum campaign agenda. The No side in a referendum campaign may prevail by campaigning with an agenda that appeals to only a minority of voters. This is particularly important in the context of referendums on European integration. National referendums function as a policy and decision-making instrument and they can have significant domestic political implications. In Denmark, the No side was effective in broadening the scope of the referendum issue to also include themes like national sovereignty and the welfare state. These topics found resonance with the public while the media devoted a lot of attention to the conduct of the campaign itself. In a referendum, winning the battle over the campaign agenda implies not only increasing the salience of the referendum, but also controlling the substantive content and the spin on the issue.

. . . We found a fairly high level of political cynicism about political candidates. During the final month of the campaign the levels of political cynicism and negative campaign evaluations increased. The news media contributed to this increase in cynicism and negativity. Persons who were exposed the most to strategic news about the campaign, even when controlling for a number of other influences, displayed the strongest increases in cynicism and negative evaluations of the campaign.

Despite the cynicism and negativity, we did not find any detrimental influence on turnout or mobilization. The negative consequences of strategic news and political cynicism on political engagement and mobilization have been suggested in previous studies in the United States. While such negative effects may emerge in different political systems, we can conclude that in a context in which most citizens were highly aware of the issues at stake, strategic or negative news while increasing cynicism and negative campaign evaluations played no role in mobilizing electors to go to the polls. We interpret this as an indication that voters can be *cynical* and *engaged*. Voters may be dissatisfied, cynical, and negative, but still mobilized and sufficiently engaged to turn out to vote.

An important yet unanswered question was whether a referendum campaign matters to the public's evaluations of political leaders and the incumbent government. Priming theory suggests that new information can affect the parameters by which we evaluate political leaders. Our study confirmed the basic hypothesis of political priming theory by showing that the overall evaluation of political leaders was strongly dependent upon an issue that was highly salient, readily available, and on the top of citizens' mind.

Drawing on our content analysis of news media we saw that the topic of the referendum became more visible in the media during the campaign. Utilizing our panel data we found that as the importance of the referendum issue increased in the media, its importance for the public for formulating general evaluations of political leaders increased as well. The incumbent government was seen by the public to handle the referendum topic poorly. Subsequently, the government, including its most prominent figures and key campaigners the Prime Minster and the Finance Minister, was evaluated on the basis of their performance on the referendum issue. These findings dovetail with existing priming research and confirms an assumption in previous studies, namely that the phenomena apply to political leaders more generally (Semetko *et al.* 2003a, 2003b). In addition the findings suggest that not only contentious issues such as the Gulf War(s), but also issues of national referendums (such as on the introduction of the euro), can drive general evaluations of political leaders.

Previous research has not been able to assess the effects of *evaluations* of issues and persons in the news media on public evaluations of political leaders. In our study we found that negative news about an issue that was also highly visible in the news bolstered negative evaluations of political leaders. The strongest impact of this negative news was found among politically less involved citizens.

The evaluation of (incumbent) political leaders matters because voting behavior in national referendums can be a function of the popularity of a government. A popular government is more likely to win a referendum and an unpopular government is more likely to loose. We found that a (moderately) popular government can easily take a fall during a referendum campaign. Indeed the (un)popularity of the government (and the decrease in performance rating during the campaign) was a significant predictor of voting No, also in our case study.

. . . Our findings point to the conclusion that information in the final weeks of the campaign mattered to how one voted in the referendum. This was a very close race, with a not insubstantial portion of the electorate still undecided in the final weeks. Mediated sources of information in the final weeks of the campaign exerted a significant influence on crystallizing individual opinion on the vote, even after controlling for all other possible influences. That said, there was no uniform impact of information. Our study found that information effects were dependent upon the characteristics of the news coverage in the various information outlets, and this varied between public and private television news and the Yes and No press. . . .

The Dynamics of a Referendum Campaign: The Contingency of Campaign Effects

We set out to investigate the dynamics of referendum campaigns arguing that the key characteristics of referendums—volatile electorates, uncertainty in elite cues, and issue complexity—mean that these campaigns can really matter. We distinguished between two levels of effects: the individual and the institutional. At the institutional level we analyzed how political parties and the media were affected by the referendum. At the individual level a referendum campaign may affect citizens' awareness of an electoral contest by emerging on the public agenda. Our study demonstrates that the campaign may

1. lead citizens to evaluate the campaign positively or negatively,
2. induce political cynicism, dependent upon the media content to which citizens are exposed and pay attention,
3. affect citizens' evaluations of domestic political leaders,
4. serve to crystallize opinion on the topic of the referendum, and
5. influence some voters on how to vote.

The unpredictability of a referendum should not be exaggerated though. Despite the potential low citizen involvement, the presence of ambiguous elite cues, and the importance of mediated (mass) communication, the campaign is only part of the story about political engagement, electoral mobilization, evaluations of key political leaders, and vote choice. Very importantly, we stress that campaign effects are *conditional*. We neither expected nor found large across-the-board effects of our campaign variables. As Zaller (1992, 2002) has argued, effects of the media in a campaign are not likely to be enormous, but in close electoral races they can be significant. Even in races that appear a foregone conclusion, the campaign can serve to further widen the gap between electoral contesters. We add to these observations that campaign effects driven by the media are contingent upon the context and individual characteristics.

In our study of agenda-setting during a referendum campaign, we found that different groups changed to consider the referendum the most important problem, but that this effect was particularly large for respondents who frequently viewed television news during the campaign. The study of political cynicism and evaluations of the referendum campaign demonstrated that both cynicism and negativity increased at the aggregate level over the course of the campaign, but this increase was strongest for heavy media users. These two examples show that campaign effects are conditional upon the *medium* and the *amount* of news consumed about a referendum.

Our study also demonstrated how negative evaluations of the government handling of a referendum increased over the campaign. This in turn fueled negative overall government evaluations. The media that reported most negatively about political leaders had the largest impact on negative evaluations of key political leaders, in particular for persons with low political involvement. This suggests that the susceptibility to effects of the media in a referendum campaign is moderated by the level of political involvement so that those least involved were more susceptible. Finally, we found evidence that—in addition to other hypotheses about vote choice—the media also mattered. The campaign served to crystallize opinions about the referendum and the government which influenced the vote. In addition exposure to news that reported less negatively about the referendum increased the propensity to vote Yes. This finding emphasizes the importance of considering the *content* of media and even the differential ways of reporting an election when understanding campaign effects.

References

Aarts, K. and Semetko, H. A. (2003). The divided electorate: Effects of media use on political involvement. *The Journal of Politics*, 65 (3): 759–784.

Ansolabeherc, S. and Iyengar, S. (1995). *Going Negative: How Political Advertisements Shrink and Polarize the Electorate*. New York: The Free Press.

Blumler, J. G. (ed.) (1983). *Communicating to Voters: Television in the First European Parliamentary Elections*. London: Sage.

Cappella, J. N. and Jamieson, K. H. (1997). *Spiral of Cynicism: The Press and the Public Good*. New York: Oxford University Press.

Holtz-Bacha, C. (1990). *Ablenkung oder Abkehr von der Politik? Mediennutzung im Geflecht politischer Orientierungen* [Distraction or withdrawal from politics? Media use and political attitudes]. Opladen: Westdeutscher Verlag.

Jenssen, A. T., Pesonen, P., and Gilljam, M. (eds.) (1998). *To Join or Not to Join: Three Nordic Referendums on Membership in the European Union*. Oslo: Scandinavian University Press.

Moy, P. and Pfau, M. (2000). *With Malice Toward All? The Media and Public Confidence in Democratic Institutions*. Westport, CT: Praeger.

Newton, K. (1999). Mass media effects: Mobilisation or media malaise? *British Journal of Political Science*, 29, 577–600.

Norris, P. (2000). *A Virtuous Circle: Political Communications in Postindustrial Societies*. Cambridge: Cambridge University Press.

Patterson, T. (1993). *Out of Order*. New York: Alfred A. Knopf Publishers.

Peter, J., de Vreese, C. H., and Lauf, E. (2003). Healthy disagreement: A cross-national comparative study of the impact of conflict in TV news on satisfaction with EU democracy and engagement in EU politics. Paper presented at the Annual Meetings of The World Association for Public Opinion Research (WAPOR), Prague, Czech Republic.

Pinkleton, B. E. and Austin, E. W. (2001). Individual motivations, perceived media importance and political disaffection. *Political Communication*, 18: 321–334.

Semetko, H. A. (2003). Political bias in the media. In D. H. Johnston (ed.), *Encyclopedia of International Media and Communications*. New York: Academic Press.

Semetko, H. A., van der Brug, W., and Valkenburg, P. (2003a). The influence of political events on attitudes towards the EU. *British Journal of Political Science*, 33: 621–634.

Semetko, H. A., van der Brug, W., and Valkenburg, P. (2003b). Media priming in a multi-party context: Politics in the news and evaluations of political leaders. Manuscript under review.

Semetko, H. A., de Vreese, C. H., and Peter, J. (2000). Europeanised politics–Europeanised media? European integration and political communication. *West European Politics*, 23 (4): 121–142.

Siune, K. and Svensson, P. (1993). The Danes and the Maastricht Treaty: The Danish EC referendum of June 1992. *Electoral Studies*, 12 (2): 99–111.

Siune, K., Svensson, P., and Tonsgaard, O. (1994). The European Union: The Danes said No in 1992 but Yes in 1993: How and why. *Electoral Studies*, 13 (2): 107–116.

de Vreese, C. H., Lauf, E., and Peter, J. (2004). The media and European parliament elections: Second-rate coverage of a second-order event? In C. van der Eijk and W. van der Brug (eds.), *European Elections and Domestic Politics. Lessons from the Past and Scenarios for the Future*. Book manuscript under review.

Zaller, J. (1992). *The Nature and Origin of Mass Opinion*. Cambridge: Cambridge University Press.

Zaller, J. (2002). The statistical power of election studies to detect media exposure effects in political campaigns. *Electoral Studies*, 21: 297–329.

Part IV

CONTROLLING MEDIA POWER: POLITICAL ACTORS VERSUS THE PRESS

Political actors try to control how journalists portray them and their causes in the mass media. The outcome of this perennial struggle is always uncertain because journalists are bombarded with conflicting demands and because they also want to use their own insights. Part IV begins with analyses of the many ways presidents use their power to engage in newsmaking activities to control how media depict their time in office. The opening selections also show how the media often try, and sometimes succeed, in foiling presidential efforts, thereby derailing major policies.

The spotlight then turns to congressional efforts to use media coverage as a policy tool. The contrast between the media strategies pursued by senators and representatives on one hand, and the president on the other, clarifies the distinctions in power and style between these political actors. Congress's ability to command the desired media attention obviously is no match for the president's power to attract, if not control, news coverage. Part IV concludes with two case studies that illustrate how setting the media's agenda, the policymakers' agenda, and the agenda to sway public opinion involves many parties in and out of government whose strategies and tactics interact with largely unpredictable outcomes.

Timothy E. Cook believes that contemporary presidents must control media coverage if they want to pursue their political objectives successfully. In the first essay, he shows how the executive branch has built institutional structures and developed a variety of techniques for interacting with media institutions. But even the best plans fail repeatedly, even when they have been blessed with ample resources and implemented by a vast corps of media-savvy officials and other supporters.

Stephen J. Farnsworth and S. Robert Lichter throw light on the defensive tactics presidents can use when hounded by journalists in hot pursuit of salacious stories. President Clinton, accused in a flood of media stories of lying under oath, multiple adulterous liaisons, and shady real-estate deals, managed to beat back his accusers by generating stories that maligned their motivations and denied the gravity of his alleged offenses. The news media felt compelled to cover his defensive stories because they came from the nation's foremost political leader. The stories convinced the public that Clinton deserved forgiveness and support as a victim of vicious politically motivated assaults. Loath to impeach an embattled president who had retained public support, Congress failed to oust him from office. With the grudging aid of the media, Clinton's well-publicized counterattack succeeded.

Karen M. Kedrowski's essay details efforts to influence the media power equation from the legislative end of Pennsylvania Avenue. She characterizes members of Congress who seek media attention to influence policymaking as "media entrepreneurs," and describes who they are, how they operate, and how successful they are likely to be. Her study takes its place among a growing literature that focuses on the attempts of political leaders, other than the president, to play the media control game. These works make it possible to compare media strategies of different institutions, thereby bringing their unique characteristics into sharper focus.

Stephen Hess speculates about the motivations of members of Congress for seeking media attention. If, as he argues, efforts to attract press coverage have relatively few political payoffs for most legislators, why undertake them? The answer, Hess believes, is vanity—a human quality that politicians nurture because they know that modesty is no asset in their line of work.

From people in formal positions of power, the discussion turns to citizens who band together in organized pressure groups to seek governmental remedies for shared problems or who strive to gain favorable public attention for their chosen causes. Doug McAdam tells how the leaders of the American Civil Rights Movement in the 1960s managed to structure their demonstrations so that they would attract large amounts of favorable media coverage. The secret lay in provoking such vicious and visible repressive actions against the movement that it became a pitiable victim and its enemies despicable assailants. The strategy worked well, and the ultimate outcome was a spate of civil rights legislation designed to protect citizens of color from racial discrimination.

Unfortunately, securing ample media coverage for worthwhile social movements is not a guarantee for success. Itzhak Yanovitzky tracked the publicity given to movements seeking sharp penalties for people who drive automobiles while drunk, endangering their own lives and the lives of many others. He found that news media gave ample coverage to the tragic human toll exacted by intoxicated drivers. Nonetheless, legislation did not follow, unless it fit into the relevant politicians' general strategies. Fierce competition for politicians' attention is the explanation. Politicians deal simultaneously with many important, well-publicized issues. Resource constraints therefore demand selectivity.

19

THE USES OF NEWS: THEORY AND (PRESIDENTIAL) PRACTICE

Timothy E. Cook

Editor's Note

Timothy E. Cook argues that the news media have become a potent political institution, a veritable fourth branch of government. Governing effectively requires synthesizing the political forces generated by all the branches, including the media, to develop and execute policies in tune with the administration's goals. Cook describes how modern American presidents have built a powerful public relations–public information machine in the executive branch to enable them to exercise political control with the help of their media resources. If presidents mishandle their relations with the fourth branch, their control over public policies diminishes. It may even vanish.

Most political practitioners and many scholars share Cook's views about the tremendous importance of maintaining control over an administration's media images. They also concur that a powerful, professionally competent corps of political communicators is now in place. But many balk at the notion of elevating the media to the status of a fourth branch. That designation runs counter to strong cultural norms that bar political interpretations that seemingly contravene the words of the U.S. Constitution.

Cook served as Fairleigh Dickinson Jr. Professor of Political Science at Williams College when this essay was written. He had established a reputation as a serious media scholar with his 1989 book, *Making Laws and Making News: Media Strategies in the U.S. House of Representatives.*

Newsmaking as Policy Making

. . . If government officials need to enlist the news media to help them accomplish their goals, this assistance cannot come without some cost. After

Source: Timothy E. Cook, *Governing with the News: The News Media as a Political Institution,* Chicago: University of Chicago Press, 1998, chapter 6. Copyright © 1998 by the University of Chicago Press. Reprinted with the permission of the University of Chicago Press.

all, the news media have their own concerns and priorities which are never identical with those of the official sources upon whom they rely to help them make the news. This disjuncture was deemed so great by scholars in the 1950s and 1960s that they saw an almost inevitable clash between officials' pursuit of secrecy, in order to preserve maximum leeway, and reporters' devotion to publicity, in order to have enough content to write a story.[1] To be sure, the media can probably do more to derail an initiative through their negative coverage than they can assure its success by favorable coverage.[2] And indeed, insofar as newspersons enter the ongoing negotiation of newsworthiness with important resources of their own and divergent understandings of importance and interest, any political actor who relies on the news media must feel their impact.

Yet for officials seeking strategies to govern, running this risk is often acceptable for several reasons.[3] *First*, making news can be making policy in and of itself, particularly when the deeds of government are directly accomplished by words. *Second*, making news can call attention to one's preferred issues and alternatives (and build one's reputation in the process) and focus the public debate on their importance. *Third*, making news can persuade others to adopt one's stance, whether explicitly (by broadcasting one's inflexibility or amplifying threats) or implicitly (by influencing the context of others' decisions—establishing seemingly indisputable facts or representing public moods that are favorable to one's interests and positions). In a political system where centrifugal forces pulling outward seem to outnumber centripetal forces reinforcing power, both within and across organizations and institutions, the news media's assistance to officials should not be underestimated. Thus, as Martin Linsky's survey of federal officials concluded, "When these policymakers talk about time with the press, they do not see the press as an intrusion into their lives, but as a resource for them in doing their job." [4]

Words as Actions

In the most direct use of the news media in governing, publicity is policy in and of itself. One could easily think of rhetoric as a substitute for or a spur to action, but many governmental pronouncements partake of what the philosopher J. L. Austin dubbed "performative" language, where "the issuing of the utterance is the performing of an action." [5] As contrasted with purely descriptive statements, performatives are actions in and of themselves that could not be accomplished without words. Take the examples of naming a ship or congratulating a graduate. . . .

Performatives are handy for both official and reporter. Reporters habitually use politicians' performatives in their stories because it enables them to produce an account without laborious, time-consuming fact-checking. A defining characteristic of the performative is that it cannot be said to be either true or false; we can doubt whether people who say "I'm sorry" are genuinely sorry or not, for instance, but we cannot doubt that they have apologized.[6] . . . For their part, officials doing something with words have the satisfaction of accomplishing something quickly and directly in a way that otherwise often evades them.[7] . . . Performatives can . . . go awry if misapplied; after President Reagan was shot and wounded in 1981, Secretary of State Alexander Haig probably alarmed his audience and undermined his authority by rushing to the podium in the White House press room to peremptorily announce, "I am in charge in this White House." [8] . . .

Setting the Agenda

When policy requires the assent of others, media strategies are useful for persuading others to act. As face-to-face communication has become more difficult with the growing reach of government, the increasing number of participants and the dispersion and confusion of power and authority, media persuasion is a more attractive and efficient use of resources.[9] By appealing to the media, one can attempt to indicate one's preferences, respond to ongoing events, and attempt to persuade en masse an entire and disparate set of political actors across branches and levels to the correctness of one's stance.

Officials rely on the news for information, which they often receive more quickly than through the bureaucratic channels of their institution, particularly with the rise of all-news stations on cable television and radio which enables new information to be accessible around the clock.[10] Although we usually think of political actors resorting to publicity to communicate across institutional divides or to leak information from the bottom to the top of a political organization, even those in collegial institutions rely upon the news media to reach the colleagues they could easily buttonhole. . . .

It is not far-fetched to suggest that the American news media construct a conception of what any political institution is and does, from which audiences construct their understanding of that institution, even for the individuals who are within it. In thereby saying what an institution should be and what it should do, the news media contribute to the process of institutional leadership.

To use the news, a political actor must initially call attention to one's issues and concerns and place them on the political agenda as problems that demand attention and that could be solved rather than conditions to be endured; issues that are not judged consequential or soluble tend to be bypassed more frequently than those that are.[11] The publicity provided by the news media can offer key assistance to officials here in two ways. First, public opinion tends to see those issues discussed in the news as more important, and citizens are more likely to judge politicians by their stances on those issues, whether or not the news is linked to those officials or not.[12] Second, even if public opinion is not activated, politicians respond differently to more salient issues. . . . [I]ncreasing the visibility of a particular issue also enhances the odds that political actors will do something about it in a way that is responsive to public attention.

Of course, political actors rarely call attention to an issue merely for the sake of doing so; instead, they stress issues that hold together their coalition and fragment the opposition.[13] Moreover, they also strategically define the incipient dispute through terms that, if accepted, would almost automatically guarantee their success. Thus, much of political debate is not merely over what issues should be on the agenda but also what those issues are "really all about" and what "the" two sides of the issue are. Such debate often occurs behind the scenes, but it emerges into the open when an accident breaks the standard routines of officials and reporters alike.[14]

To take an example, how should we have conceptualized the enormous oil spill in Prince William Sound in 1989 caused by the *Exxon Valdez*, and how should we respond with appropriate policy responses? Was it a case of bad navigation by a drunken captain (in which case the courts can take care of it by punishing the infractor, and legislatures can increase penalties for navigating while under the influence)? Or was it the consequence of the use of fragile single-hull vessels (in which case the flow of oil can proceed but with the introduction of double-hull ships)? Or was it simply the inevitable risk of overconsumption of petroleum in the lower forty-eight states (in which case stringent conservation would have to be imposed)? As you can see, even though all sides would presumably see an oil spill of this magnitude as something that must be avoided, the public is led to divergent policies depending on how we understand the spill and its causes. . . .

Thus, merely calling attention to an issue does not ensure that one's preferred alternative will be pursued, let alone enacted.[15] . . . Not least consequentially for officials, calling attention to one's preferred issues and policy options also calls attention to oneself. . . . By being covered as "in a position to know," a reputation can grow that will enhance one's stature, which can be reinvested in further news opportunities, and so on.[16] . . .

Persuasion

Having set the agenda and established oneself as a key participant may well be just the beginning. . . . [N]ews influences the context in which governmental officials bargain and decide. Coverage can influence or even create a public mood that may or may not be favorable to a certain issue or policy proposal, giving a sense of favorability, even inevitability, to some sort of resolution of the newly publicized problem. This may happen by mobilizing public opinion on a newsworthy issue. . . . At other times, the public mood represented in the news may override the more accurate soundings through polls. In 1989, for instance, the media focused on angry elderly citizens confronting their representatives on the catastrophic health care act. The public mood reported in the news pushed members of Congress to quickly repeal the act which had been passed by huge margins the year before—even though polls showed the public at large (including the elderly) favoring its retention.[17]

The news can also publicize particular facts that must be taken into account in the bargaining. The most famous instance is the leak. Information made public may make its way to high officials quicker within an agency or a department and force a decision.[18] But, more generally, success in sending forth a factual definition of a situation, whether by leaks or not, may enhance one's chances of policy success. . . .

In a classic case of what organizational theorists call the "absorption of uncertainty," what starts out in the news as tentative hunches and extemporaneous phrases can become seemingly unquestionable fact upon being repeated from one news story to the next. . . .

. . . [H]ow the news initially frames an issue tends to be long-lived and to constrain later choices.[19] But although it is difficult to change that frame, it is far from impossible, and the advantages thereby gained may well make it worth the effort. Such frames may gain their force by sheer repetition, which may make previously unthinkable possibilities quite imaginable indeed.[20] Insofar as officials can influence the news media's framing so as to favor their preferences, they can boost their likely success in this particular contest and enhance their reputation for future battles.

The Presidential Prototype

To see the uses of news in practice, I begin with sketching the benefits that newsmaking presents for modern presidents. This is, of course, the best-known story of governing with the news, so much so that it is almost a prototype for how to do it. Given the gap between the expectations placed on the office and the actual resources that presidents are able to control, it is no surprise that many scholars have begun to see the presidency as a largely rhetorical office, exercising influence by means of speaking. Given that their abilities to reach people directly seems to be on the wane, presidents must devote ever more time to finding ways to get to an audience indirectly, through the resources of the news media.

This is a familiar story. . . . It sets up . . . a series of expectations that we may use to judge other parts of the federal government that are commonly seen to be less preoccupied with publicity. . . . For presidents, certainly, such preoccupation with the media is a daily task. . . . Interviews reveal a continuing preoccupation with the news media, not merely for how to sell initiatives previously agreed upon behind closed doors but also in the very process of identifying problems, setting agendas, and formulating policy responses. . . .

Nowadays, the typical stories at the White House focus on the individuality of the president, usually seen in Hamiltonian terms of deciding, commanding, and ordering. The irony, of course, of this mass-mediated vision has been that expectations of the president far outstrip the direct powers of the office. As Richard Neustadt brilliantly posited over thirty years ago, every presidential power is less an opportunity for the president to exert his influence than a chance for other actors to get the president to do what *they* want—what Neustadt termed the president's role as clerk.[21] . . .

Activist presidents must grasp at whatever powers they can, and this includes the considerable interest of the news media in the person of the president. So, starting with William McKinley and especially Theodore Roosevelt, presidents finding themselves in the news spotlight have taken full advantage of it, not merely to boost their image but to accomplish policy goals.[22] Lyndon Johnson's press secretary, Bill Moyers, invited Robert Kintner of NBC News to help coordinate the president's communication apparatus by noting, "The President is going to want your creative and sustained thinking about the overall problem of communicating with the American people. Some call it the problem of 'the President's image.' It goes beyond that to the ultimate question of how does the President shape the issues and interpret them to people—how, in fact, does he lead." [23] The central role of the news media in presidential leadership was clear to its aspirants even before Ronald Reagan, as Walter Mondale, then the vice president, revealed in 1980 when he proclaimed that if he had to choose between the power to get on the nightly news and the veto, he would keep the former and jettison the latter.

To be sure, given the potential dispersion and fragmentation within the executive branch, one reason that presidents gravitate toward public speeches and ceremonies is because these are among the few activities that can be entirely accomplished by their own efforts. Yet, while presidents since Truman have increased the number of person-hours devoted to speechmaking,[24] they are most interested in having their speeches reach a larger audience than those assembled to hear them in person. But this is difficult for presidents to manage. Their ability to speak directly to a large audience is limited in several ways—and may be shrinking further yet. Although presidents can ask for time from the major television networks during prime time, the networks can and increasingly do turn them down. . . . With the increased availability of other channels, a presidential prime-time address, even when it is carried on all the networks, reaches a smaller potential audience. . . . And presidents cannot go to the well too frequently, lest they diminish the impact of a nationally broadcast speech; instead, they are strategic speakers.[25] Finally, their ability to go directly to a national audience is limited by the increased tendency of the networks to give the opposition party equal time and journalists' "instant analysis" immediately after the speech—interpretations that help to shape the public response to its content.[26]

In short, to go public, presidents must go through the news media. To be sure, they often attempt an end run around the news outlets they consider more hostile: President Kennedy's decision to hold press conferences that were broadcast live was prompted, at least in part, by his perception of a Republican-controlled press; President Nixon's distrust of the national news media pushed his press operations to reach out to local and presumably more easily impressed journalists; and . . . President Clinton's early preference for televised interview programs and electronic town meetings represented the distrust of what he deemed scandal-preoccupied reporters. But just as often presidents find themselves frustrated by this mediation. For instance, in late 1994, President Clinton mused, "Sometimes I think the president, when I look at it, is least able to communicate with the American people because of the fog that I have to go through to reach them." [27]

Still, presidents face the news media with several advantages. What makes the White House attractive to journalists—its near guarantee of regular exposure in the news—also restricts their creativity. . . . Not only do presidents carry particular political significance and particular political accountability, they are presumably the classic authoritative sources in a position to know. Given the tendency for the news media to craft stories around individuals rather than social forces, the president is the most familiar protagonist around. Whenever presidents act, that is a story; and when other stories occur without their agency, whether a bombing or a blizzard, a president's statement, even when it is banal, is an integral part of the news. Indeed, the problem for contemporary presidents may be the ability to absent themselves from the news in order to be distanced from public problems that might otherwise be laid at their doorstep.

Such forces direct the media toward the chief executive. Instead of having to seek out news opportunities, presidents have the news come to them. While this interest impels presidents to create newsworthy events, they, more than other sources, can dictate the terms of access, given their near-automatic news value. Consequently, reporters, dependent on presidents' cooperation, end up prisoners in the all but hermetically sealed press room, reluctant to roam far from their connection to fame and fortune in the news business. Instead of encouraging innovation and enterprise, the White House breeds concern among reporters about missing out on the story everyone else is chasing.

All of this makes news management easier, so the ultimate sanction of "freezing out" individual reporters is rarely used. Instead, presidents gear their media operations toward serving reporters in ways that will prove beneficial: anticipating reporters' questions in news conferences and preparing accordingly; designing prescheduled events that meet news values of drama, color, and terseness; and providing frequent access to the president albeit in constrained and directed ways. The monopoly over good information and the ability to regulate access to the key newsmaker means that news opportunities can be meted out on a basis decided by the newsmaker himself—*if* that newsmaker is aware of the habits and routines of the press. . . .

[T]hat may be a big "if." The demands of the news media must be taken into account in order to get the kind of boost that presidents seek from publicity. After all, presidents may launch a news item that will go in unpredictable directions thereafter, depending on whether other sources fall in line or offer criticism. With the press corps working in close contact, the ensuing pack mentality of the press, too, can work for or against the president; if something slips, reporters may move against the president with critical questioning, each risk adversely following the next toward the big story. . . . . [P]ress secretaries and communication directors must spend much of their time building bridges and minimizing antagonism between the president and the press. Insofar as press secretaries are ambassadors from the president to the press *and* from the press to the president, this reduces the possibility of one-way manipulation. Finally, presidents must anticipate the news values of journalism to get in on their own terms. Not just anything presidents do is automatically newsworthy, and even the savviest public relations campaign to project certain qualities or certain programs can't be used for just anything. . . .

Nonetheless, these risks are apparently acceptable, given that the power to go public becomes particularly valuable when other avenues are foreclosed. Rhetoric scholar Roderick Hart has shown that presidents tend to give speeches on exactly those topics that are not the subject of legislative initiatives, and when they are in strategic trouble: when the opposition controls Congress, in the second half of the term, when legislative success and/or popularity is low, when economic conditions are bad, and so forth.[28] Presidential communication is thus strategic, but unlike presidents such as Woodrow Wilson or Franklin Roosevelt who went public only when behind-the-scenes maneuvers failed, contemporary presidents often *begin* their initiatives with public appeals.

In order to gain public attention on their own terms, presidents have consequently increased the size of the operations directly connected with the media—beginning with the White House Press Office headed by the press secretary and the White House Office of Communications instituted by President Nixon and resurrected in one form or another by all of his successors. . . .

Although White House records are too vague to indicate who is and who is not working on media-related matters, the best evidence suggests an impressive increase in recent decades.[29] The legendary presidential press secretaries, FDR's Stephen Early and Eisenhower's James Hagerty, ran virtual one-person shops. White House press operations ballooned in the Nixon White House and have stayed at roughly the same level since. . . . After adding on speechwriters, directors of White House projects, schedulers, and the Office of Communications, it is clear that a sizable percentage—perhaps even a majority—of the White House staff is primarily involved with public relations activities.[30]

Presidential press officers, of course, spend much of their day responding to the needs of reporters and acting as emissary from the president to the media and vice versa. Although presidents, of course, employ the press secretary, they may soon learn that it is in their interest not to be adversarial or unresponsive to the White House press corps. . . .

It would be a mistake, however, to see the press secretary as either a cog in the hierarchy on one hand or a simple go-between or an official who reacts more than acts. Although the influence of the press secretary within the White House has varied greatly from one to the next, much of their credibility depends upon being perceived as a well-connected source, and presidents have an incentive to include them in decision making. . . .

It is true that few press secretaries play a role as an advisor on substantive policy, beyond its implications for communication, as part of their job. . . . But, even in such a limited role, by helping presidents to prepare for press conferences (anticipating questions and suggesting answers); by gathering intelligence for the president and the White House staff about reporters' perspectives, opinions, and responses; by searching for initiatives to present proactively to the press; and by advising on when, where, and how to go public, the press secretary helps to set the policy agenda, delineates available options and likely responses among a key constituency (the media), and participates in policy decisions.

Still, for press secretaries, short-term care and feeding tends to overwhelm long-term planning. . . . Proactive media strategies have instead become lodged in the White House Office of Communications, and its activities have further cemented the bond between governing strategies and media strategies. The Office of Communications was launched in the Nixon presidency and was soon institutionalized. Ford and Carter, the two presidents after Nixon, initially sought to avoid such an office so as to exude an image of openness rather than manipulation, only to find late in the term the benefits of an organization that could attempt end runs around the Washington media, such as to local and regional reporters who might be more easily impressed, as well as develop, coordinate, and standardize the policy agenda throughout the executive branch. In particular, by means of the "line of the day" . . . newsmaking and public relations have become an integral and crucial part of daily decision making in the White House.

The "line of the day" originated in Nixon's 1970 campaigns for Republican senatorial candidates. As part of the new public relations orientation that the president demanded, surrogate speakers on the campaign trail would all stress a particular point that, it was hoped, would be picked up by the news—particularly television, which was reluctant to present more than one White House story per day anyhow. . . . The "line of the day," which originated as a means largely to control the mass-mediated image of the president for electoral purposes, has become a way to specify what the presidency is to *be* and to *do*, setting out goals and missions, and coordinating the pursuit thereof throughout the executive branch.

This is not to say that these efforts are always successful. On the contrary, . . . similar media tactics have different successes, depending upon contextual factors such as the state of the economy, the president's popularity, and the place in the term. . . .

Nonetheless, mass-mediated strategies of governing may now be central to chief executives. . . . Public relations are geared toward the news media, and newsmaking becomes of central importance, not merely in calculating how chief executives spend their time but in assessing how they make decisions and seek to make policy.

. . . All political institutions have personnel to deal with and often to guide news media coverage in an optimal direction. The trick here is that the very desire to exploit the news media in pursuit of one's own policy goals may only implicate the needs of news deeper into the process of governing. When we talk about "governing with the news," then, it may be that newsmaking helps political actors in the short run but pushes them toward particular issues, concerns, and events and away from others, to the point that news values become political values, not only within the news media but within government as well.

Notes

1. See, e.g., Douglas Cater, *The Fourth Branch of Government* (Boston: Houghton Mifflin, 1959), p. 17; as well as Bernard C. Cohen, *The Press and Foreign Policy* (Princeton University Press, 1963); and Francis E. Rourke, *Secrecy and Publicity: Dilemmas of Democracy* (Baltimore: Johns Hopkins University Press, 1961).

2. See, e.g., Martin Linsky's survey of federal executive policymakers: 63 percent said positive coverage would make action on an issue in their office or agency easier, versus a slightly larger number (68 percent) who said negative coverage would make action more difficult. Similarly, only 50 percent said positive coverage would galvanize outside support, whereas 66 percent said negative coverage would undermine outside support. That much having been said, however, 79 percent said positive coverage would "increase your chances for successfully attaining your policy goals regarding the issue," compared to 71 percent who said that negative coverage would decrease those chances. Linsky, *Impact: How the Press Affects Federal Policymaking* (New York: W. W. Norton, 1986), appendix C, question 3a, p. 236.

3. These functions, of course, supplement the traditional governmental aims of propaganda and publicity in shaping and mobilizing public opinion. . . .
4. Linsky, *Impact*, p. 82.
5. J. L. Austin, *How to Do Things with Words*, 2d ed., ed. J. O. Urmson and Marina Sbisà (Cambridge, MA: Harvard University Press, 1975), pp. 6–7. . . .
6. Austin suggested several tests for figuring out a performative; the most pertinent are when one cannot say "Does he really?" and when the act could be accomplished without saying anything. *How to Do Things with Words*, pp. 79–80.
7. See, in particular, David R. Mayhew's argument that advertising, credit-claiming and position-taking take precedence over building coalitions and legislating in his *Congress: The Electoral Connection* (New Haven: Yale University Press, 1974).
8. Indeed, given that journalists wish to display their independence from political actors without overtly ideological criticism, they have an interest in pointing out how and when the latter's stage-managed performances have gone awry. . . .
9. . . . Of course, under such circumstances, making such news may be a way of persuading themselves and/or others that they've accomplished something rather than as a means to accomplish something. . . .
10. See, e.g., the questionnaire results in Linsky, *Impact*, appendix C; or the elite interviews in Patrick O'Heffernan, *Mass Media and American Foreign Policy: Insider Perspectives on Global Journalism and the Foreign Policy Process* (Norwood, NJ: Ablex, 1991), passim. One of Linsky's findings, reported in *Impact*, p. 237, indicates, moreover, that policymakers are paying attention to the media as the latter affect their job; in responding to the question, "To what degree did you rely on the mass media for information about your policy area?" 31 percent of the policymakers responded "very much," with another 39 percent saying "somewhat." The survey then asked a similar question about "parts of government outside your policy area"; the response was again 38.8 percent saying "somewhat," but now only 15 percent answering "very much." This tendency to concentrate on news about one's own policy domain or agency is undoubtedly exacerbated by the practice, now common in the White House, agencies, and even some congressional offices, of circulating an internal compendium of news clips that press officers deem to be relevant to their jobs. . . .
11. E. E. Schattschneider, in *The Semi-Sovereign People* (New York: Holt, Rinehart and Winston, 1960), was the first to demonstrate the power of setting the agenda. . . .
12. Shanto Iyengar, Mark D. Peters, and Donald R. Kinder, "Experimental Demonstrations of the 'Not-so-Minimal' Consequences of Television News Programs," *American Political Science Review* 76 (1982): 848–858. . . .
13. Schattschneider, *Semi-Sovereign People*.
14. See Harvey L. Molotch and Marilyn Lester, "Accidental News: The Great Oil Spill," *American Journal of Sociology* 81:235–260.
15. I make this point in some detail with the case study of Representative Don Pease's attempt in the 100th Congress to renew a federal unemployment program. See Timothy E. Cook, *Making Laws and Making News* (Washington, D.C.: The Brookings Institution, 1989), chap. 6.

16. The process is similar to one Bruno Latour and Steve Woolgar noted for scientists who sought credit, not for its own sake but to reinvest it to obtain the monetary resources necessary to allow them to continue playing the scientific game. See Latour and Woolgar, *Laboratory Life* (Princeton: Princeton University Press, 1978), chap. 5. . . .

17. David P. Fan and Lois Norem, "The Media and the Fate of the Medicare Catastrophic Extension Act," *Journal of Health Politics, Policy & Law* 17 (1992): 39–70.

18. See, in general, Stephen Hess, *The Government/Press Connection* (Washington, D.C.: The Brookings Institution, 1984).

19. Linsky, *Impact*, p. 94.

20. This is one reason that we may be better off talking about "agenda-building" rather than "agenda-setting." . . .

21. Richard E. Neustadt, *Presidential Power* (New York: John Wiley, 1960), p. 6.

22. . . . This is not to say that only activist presidents aggressively court the press; the example of Calvin Coolidge's innovation with the media alongside a limited policy agenda proves as much.

23. Memo from Moyers to Kintner, April 8, 1966, quoted in Michael B. Grossman and Martha J. Kumar, *Portraying the President* (Baltimore: Johns Hopkins Press, 1980), p. 82.

24. Lyn Ragsdale, "The Politics of Presidential Speechmaking 1946–1980." *American Political Science Review* 78 (1984): 971–984.

25. On the latter point, see esp. David L. Paletz and Richard Vinegar's experimental study comparing responses to a Nixon speech with and without the journalists' interpretations: "Presidents on Television," *Public Opinion Quarterly* 41 (1977): 488–497.

26. Quoted in Gustav Niebuhr, "Books on Faith Are a Comfort, President Says," *New York Times*, October 4, 1994, p. A17.

27. These results are derived from Roderick P. Hart, *The Sound of Leadership* (Chicago: University of Chicago Press, 1987).

28. Samuel Kernell, *Going Public*, 2d ed. (Washington, D.C.: CQ Press, 1993), chap. 2.

29. See Grossman and Kumar, *Portraying the President*, pp. 83–84, for a variety of estimates in 1976 and 1977.

30. See Douglas Jehl, "After White House Shuffle, Most Old Hands Stand Pat," *New York Times*, September 24, 1994, p. 9; Burt Solomon, "With a Smoothie Behind the Podium . . . The Press Cuts Clinton Some Slack," *National Journal*, June 3, 1995, pp. 1352–1353; and John Aloysius Farrell, "Meet the Press Secretaries," *Boston Globe Magazine*, April 7, 1996, pp. 12–13, 21–28 at 27. . . .

20

THE STRUGGLE OVER SHAPING THE NEWS

Stephen J. Farnsworth and S. Robert Lichter

Editor's Note

What journalists cover and how they cover it can determine winners and los-ers in the political game. The struggle over shaping the news becomes fierce when major political actors—tarred with scandals and under lethal attack from their opponents—and the feuding parties vie for media support. The odds favor the attackers because the media, ever hungry for audience-catching tales, are likely to give full coverage to lurid details about misbehav-ior in high places. There is no better example of such a battle than the saga of President Clinton's political survival, and even resurrection, after flood tides of scandal coverage that culminated in an impeachment trial. Stephen J. Farnsworth and S. Robert Lichter reveal the kinds of tactics that embattled executives have used successfully in the past to counter damaging stories and inflict heavy wounds on their opponents.

When this essay was written, Farnsworth was associate professor of political science at the University of Mary Washington. His writings about television coverage of the presidency benefit from his experiences as a journalist. Lichter was professor of communication at George Mason University and president of the Center for Media and Public Affairs, a nonpartisan, nonprofit media re-search organization in Washington, D.C. Based on his extensive data collec-tions, his many books chronicle highlights in the interactions between the American press and the national government.

While it is clear that scandal coverage has become more pervasive and more negative, scholars disagree about how today's press coverage of personal

Source: Stephen J. Farnsworth and S. Robert Lichter, "Can't We Talk About Something Else? Covering Presidential Scandals," in *The Mediated Presidency: Television News and Presidential Governance,* Lanham, Md.: Rowman and Littlefield, 2005, chapter 5. © 2005 by Rowman and Littlefield Publishers, Lanham, Md. Reprinted with the permission of Rowman and Littlefield Publishers.

matters affects public evaluations of presidents once they are in office (Langman 2002). Clinton's public approval numbers, for example, demonstrate the complexity of the link between scandal coverage and public approval ratings. In December 1997, the month before the [Monica Lewinsky sex] scandal broke, the public's rating of Clinton's performance as president stood at a relatively strong 61 percent approval. By January 1999, the month he was acquitted by the Senate, Clinton's approval rating stood even higher—at 69 percent (Cohen 2002).

It turned out that many people distinguished between Clinton's public and private roles in their evaluations. When asked about his character, or what they thought of him as a person, most expressed disapproval. But they kept these feelings separate from their judgments of his job performance. Scholars who have examined public opinion during this time say that Clinton was able to survive the scandal for two main reasons: (1) the economy's strong performance during 1998, and (2) his success in portraying himself as an ideological moderate—and his opponents as extremists—in the years since the Republican electoral victories of 1994 (cf. Cohen 2002; Newman 2002; Wayne 2000; Zaller 1998). On the first point, it may be risky to banish a president who has been in office during economic good times. On the second, public perceptions of Clinton and his opponents helped the president to portray himself as the victim of fanatical opponents bent on using the scandal to exact revenge. . . .

[The Lewinsky Scandal]

. . . [P]ast allegations [of sexual misconduct] had conditioned the media—and the public—to imagine the worst about the politician opponents had nicknamed "Slick Willie." As a result of the disclosures and the developments throughout the year, the Clinton-Lewinsky saga was by far the leading story of 1998. In all, the network evening news shows devoted one-seventh of their airtime that year to this single story (1,636 broadcast reports in all). The Clinton scandals received more attention than the standoff with Iraq, the bombing of U.S. embassies in Africa, the fighting in the Serbian province of Kosovo, the Israeli-Palestinian conflict, nuclear weapons tests in Pakistan and India, and major financial crises in Asia and in Russia *combined.*

The Clinton-Lewinsky scandal coverage also swamped coverage of the 1998 midterm elections. During the fall campaign season (Labor Day, September 7, through Election Day, November 2) there were six times as many stories on the scandal as on the elections. The Texas governor's race, won by future president George W. Bush, was the subject of only three network news reports.

The subsequent impeachment of the president and its aftermath generated over four hundred more stories in 1999, most of them in the first three months of the year, when the media wrapped up the coverage of the scandal after the Senate's failure to convict the president on charges brought by the House. . . .

The White House fought off the allegations through public denials and efforts to "spin" the story as being a personal vendetta against the president. Foremost among the president's defenders was First Lady Hillary Clinton, who spoke on *The Today Show* on NBC on January 27, 1998, to defend her husband and attack his accusers.

> This is the great story here, for anybody willing to find it and write about it and explain it, is this vast right-wing conspiracy that has been conspiring against my husband since the day he announced for president. . . . Having seen so many of these accusations come and go, having seen people profit, you know, like Jerry Falwell, with videos, accusing my husband of committing murder, of drug running, seeing some of the things that are written and said about him, my attitude is, you know, we've been there before and we have seen this before. (Hillary Clinton, quoted in Blaney and Benoit 2001:109)

. . . The 1992 presidential election was won in part by inducing journalists to train their fire on Clinton's adversaries, short-circuiting further critical coverage of Clinton himself (Ceaser and Busch 1993). A similar pattern occurred in the first weeks of the Clinton-Lewinsky scandal. During the first ten days after the story broke, the president was featured in nearly all (93 percent) of the scandal stories. That figure dropped to 70 percent in the following three weeks, even as the percentage focusing on Monica Lewinsky increased from 47 to 59 percent and the share featuring independent counsel Kenneth Starr also rose from 30 to 41 percent. The growing focus on Lewinsky and Starr in media coverage is a measure of the effectiveness of the Clinton team's approach— increasing the media emphasis on the accusers.

. . . Throughout this period, the only consistent on-air support for Clinton came from the White House and the president's lawyers. Even this group, though, found it necessary to reference the president's admission of improper personal conduct in order to argue that he had done nothing to warrant impeachment, such as lying under oath or encouraging others to do so. As a result, even many sound bites from the Clinton team were negative. In fact, a slight majority (52 percent) of the sound bites from the president himself were positive, as he repeatedly admitted to an inappropriate relationship with Monica Lewinsky. "Indeed, I did have a relationship with Ms. Lewinsky that was not appropriate," Clinton said in a CBS *Evening News* report on September 9. In our age of sophisticated presidential spin, a president has rarely evaluated himself as negatively in his public comments as Clinton did during the second half of 1998.

But the strategy of using offense as the best defense continued to bear fruit. . . . Although the tone of the coverage of Clinton was about two-to-one negative during two periods of peak coverage examined here (the first month of the scandal and the two-month period in the summer of 1998, *Media Monitor*, September–October 1998), coverage of Kenneth Starr, Monica Lewinsky, and other scandal figures were about six-to-one negative. . . .

"Wagging the Dog?"

Presidents facing trouble in Washington—whether from scandal, legislative setbacks, or other unpleasantness—often turn to the international arena. Whether or not they do so to distract the media and the public, presidential performances on the world stage often overshadow other issues, particularly long-running scandals. Even during the Clinton-Lewinsky scandal, an international trip served to drive down the volume of scandal coverage. The three networks broadcast fifty-eight stories on the president's trip to China and his policies toward the Asian superpower from June 24 through July 4, 1998, compared to only nineteen stories on the Clinton-Lewinsky scandal. Coverage of the president likewise was more positive, as four out of five sources quoted on the newscasts evaluated his China policies favorably. Many of the positive assessments came from inside the administration and from the president's Chinese hosts, and the White House reveled in its ability to set the news agenda once again.

The Dynamics of Impeachment Coverage

Two weeks after the 1998 midterm elections, the lame-duck U.S. House Judiciary Committee began holding hearings on whether to impeach President Clinton. During the three weeks of coverage (November 19 through December 12, 1998), the networks aired 108 stories that focused on the hearings. True to form, evaluations of Clinton were mainly (62 percent) negative, while on-air assessments of independent counsel Ken Starr were even more negative (69 percent), and congressional Republicans fared worst of all (77 percent negative).

Context can be decisive for a president's fortunes, as coverage of this scandal illustrates. If Republicans had succeeded in their efforts to frame the Clinton-Lewinsky scandal as a criminal matter of perjury—that is, the felony of lying under oath—they might have been able to drive the president from office. Instead, the media frame was largely that the president's alleged lies were of a more personal nature, the foibles of a philandering husband trying to avoid embarrassing himself and his family. That alternative perspective, presented aggressively by Clinton's defenders through 1998, was adopted by many citizens, making it difficult for the House Republicans to turn public opinion against the president (Bennett 2005; Blaney and Benoit 2001; Klein 2002; Owen 2000; Sabato et al. 2000).

Administration efforts to portray the scandal as a mudslinging contest also worked to the president's advantage. Independent counsel Starr could not defend himself effectively while his investigation was continuing. Holding press conferences to rebut attacks by Hillary Clinton and others would only damage his credibility further. In addition, Starr's GOP allies on Capitol Hill could not win the battle for the airwaves against the White House. The media frames of this story were largely along the lines sketched by the executive branch, as is so often the case. The president may not be able to convince reporters to cover something else, but he retains considerable ability to shape the way the story is discussed, even when the topic is a sex scandal.

Whitewater

The impeachment saga was far from the only major scandal of the Clinton presidency. Near the end of Clinton's first year in office, . . . all three networks reported that former Clinton attorney Vincent Foster's files on the Whitewater Development Corporation had not reached federal investigators for more than five months after his suicide. These reports set off a new round of media inquiries into the ethical practices of the First Family and their associates, a range of questions known collectively as Whitewater.

From those first reports on December 20, 1993, through the first three months of 1994, the network evening news shows aired 193 Whitewater stories with over six hours of airtime. Clinton loyalists frequently attached negative motives to those questioning the First Family. Among the most frequent explanations: partisan politics (including opposition to health care reform, and anti-Hillary Clinton and antiwomen sentiment), self-interest (including jealousy, spite, and financial motivations), and a culture of "negativism" that has made political life and the press more mean-spirited. On ABC on January 7, 1994, David Gergen, a communications staffer for Presidents Clinton, Reagan, Ford, and Nixon, blamed "the cannibalism which is loose in our society in which public figures, such as the Clintons . . . get hammered even though they are trying to do the right thing." Only one source in seven (14 percent) suggested the Clintons' accusers were motivated by genuine concern over possible wrongdoing. . . .

The Clinton media strategies during the Whitewater controversy often involved a combination of offense and defense, as would be employed during the Clinton-Lewinsky scandal several years later. Partisan political sources favorable to the Clintons were aggressive in making the Clintons' case in the media. Supportive comments from administration sources outnumbered negative remarks from congressional Republicans by a margin of nearly three to one. Nevertheless, coverage during this period frequently portrayed the president as politically wounded by the Whitewater affair. . . .

* * *

Conclusion

Twenty years of presidential scandals show how presidents remain the central focus of political news, even—perhaps especially—when things go wrong. But that intense media focus on the executive branch provides a key executive branch power: a president's ability to frame a story more successfully than his competitors and opponents. In scandal after scandal, whether Clinton-Lewinsky or Whitewater, the Abu Ghraib torture photos or the Iran-contra affair, presidents have been able to minimize immediate damage to themselves by working to frame the story in a way less hostile to the White House. The plan for responding to a presidential scandal is simple, and it starts with a direct, consistent message that is echoed by all administration officials (Auletta 2004). . . .

But successful politicians are rarely content to stay on defense. Responding to scandals, especially, requires going on offense as well. Administrations respond to an emerging scandal by attacking their opponents, such as by presenting them as ideological fanatics blinded by their hatred of the president. If the scandal is of a sexual nature, no one can launch a more effective retaliatory strike than the First Lady. Depending on the issue, administration defenders may be able to counterattack by questioning the patriotism of opponents. Reporters love conflict, so countercharges are an effective way to stop playing defense and start playing offense. Sometimes the insults can even muddy the waters, obscuring relevant but—from the point of view of the White House—unhelpful evidence.

For the really big crises, triage is an important part of a president's media defense. During the Clinton-Lewinsky affair, Bill Clinton and his defenders frequently admitted to flaws in the president's character, thereby making the president and his team seem more reasonable to reporters and to viewers of television newscasts. While that approach did not draw investigative bloodhounds like Kenneth Starr and Republican members of the House Judiciary Committee off the scent, the public remained convinced throughout the year-long spectacle that the president should not be removed from office. Though the intensely partisan House impeached the president on a near party-line vote, the less ideologically oriented Senate found it impossible to remove from office a figure receiving such high public approval ratings. The White House also employed triage in the wake of the Iran-contra and Whitewater disclosures. Key administration officials and presidential friends took the fall to protect Clinton and Reagan, a particularly effective strategy for relatively popular presidents.

Making things seem more complicated as a scandal progresses can also strengthen a president's position by depriving opponents of the opportunity to make a clear and simple case. The more justifications a president offers for doing something, the harder it will be for opponents to counter the arguments, particularly given the relatively small amount of television news time provided to voices from outside the executive branch. By moving from "weapons of mass destruction" to "weapons of mass destruction programs" to "weapons of mass destruction activities" to the mass graves found in Iraq, the Bush administration offered a number of after-the-fact justifications for why the United States fought in Iraq. If the question on the lips of reporters is, Does Saddam Hussein deserve to remain in power? then the answer about that brutal tyrant is obvious. The more complicated alternative question offered by the war's opponents—Is Saddam Hussein a greater threat to the United States than, say, al Qaeda or North Korea or Iran?—is a question not likely to be answered effectively on time-pressured television newscasts, which may mean the question will not even be asked by a media-savvy politician.

Lying may seem to be an appealing presidential response to an unfolding scandal, but it is clearly a high-risk strategy. There is the substantial chance that one will be caught in the deceit—all the memos; recalled conversations; and, in the case of Bill Clinton, even DNA samples can undermine the claim that one is telling the whole truth. If that happens, videotape of the damning statements—like Nixon's famous "I am not a crook" response to Watergate and Clinton's finger-wagging denial of a sexual relationship with Monica Lewinsky—are shown over and over again. Although Bill Clinton's presidency survived the scandal, his became a greatly weakened administration, just like the post-Iran-contra Reagan presidency.

Every administration has its dissidents, and their inside views can be very damaging, as a variety of insider books about recent presidents illustrate (Clarke 2004; Reich 1998; Stephanopoulos 1999; Suskind 2004; Woodward 1994). . . . While reporters may hesitate to say plainly that a candidate is lying, today's intensely partisan politics provides a variety of people willing to make such a charge. . . .

The Abu Ghraib scandal is [an] example of how the lack of visual images can influence news media coverage. The mass media were particularly slow to pick up on that story (the most famous incidents happened in November 2003), but reporters made up for lost time with saturation coverage after the pictures were published in April 2004. Once pictures become public, they stay public. Six years after the Clinton-Lewinsky scandal broke—when Bill Clinton started making the rounds of television news programs to peddle his autobiography—news reports illustrating the president's new book returned to the now vintage footage of President Clinton embracing a beret-clad former intern in a White House rope line.

. . . [T]here are limits to how effectively a president can change the subject in midscandal. Indeed, when Clinton sought to engage in foreign policy during scandal periods, some news accounts questioned whether he was doing so to distract the electorate and the press. Bush's efforts in mid-2004 to talk more about a proposed manned space mission to Mars and less about Iraq likewise largely fell flat. . . .

We may be entering an age in which the online news media function as an immense echo chamber, allowing whispered stories to remain alive until mainstream media turn their attention to them. Stories may live longer than ever before, and unsubstantiated allegations may get more attention than ever before as media outlets "race to the bottom" in accuracy in order to be first in this highly competitive industry (cf. Okrent 2004).

References

Auletta, Ken. 2004. "Fortress Bush: How the White House Keeps the Press Under Control." *New Yorker,* February 19.

Bennett, W. Lance. 2005. *News: The Politics of Illusion.* 6th ed. New York: Pearson/ Longman.

Blaney, Joseph R., and William L. Benoit. 2001. *The Clinton Scandals and the Politics of Image Restoration.* Westport, CT: Praeger.

Ceaser, James, and Andrew Busch. 1993. *Upside Down and Inside Out: The 1992 Elections and American Politics.* Lanham, MD: Rowman & Littlefield.

Clarke, Richard A. 2004. *Against All Enemies: Inside America's War on Terror.* New York: Free Press.

Cohen, Jeffrey E. 2002. "The Polls: Policy-Specific Presidential Approval, Part II."

Klein, Joe. 2002. *The Natural: The Misunderstood Presidency of Bill Clinton.* New York: Doubleday.

Langman, Lauren. 2002. "Suppose They Gave a Culture War and No One Came." *American Behavioral Scientist* 46(4):501–34.

Newman, Brian. 2002. "Bill Clinton's Approval Ratings: The More Things Change the More They Stay the Same." *Political Research Quarterly* 55 (4): 781–804.

Okrent, Daniel. 2004. "Weapons of Mass Destruction? Or Mass Distraction?" *New York Times,* May 30.

Owen, Diana. 2000. "Popular Politics and the Clinton/Lewinsky Affair: The Implications of Leadership." *Political Psychology* 21(1): 161–77.

Reich, Robert, 1998. *Locked in the Cabinet.* New York: Vintage.

Sabato, Larry, Mark Stencel, and S. Robert Lichter. 2000. *Peepshow: Media and Politics in an Age of Scandal.* Lanham, MD: Rowman & Littlefield.

Stephanopoulos, George. 1999. *All Too Human: A Political Education.* Boston: Little, Brown.

Suskind, Ron. 2004. *The Price of Loyalty: George W. Bush, the White House, and the Education of Paul O'Neill.* New York: Simon & Schuster.

Wayne, Stephen J. 2000. "Presidential Personality and the Clinton Legacy." In *The Clinton Scandals and the Future of American Government,* ed. Mark J. Rozell and Clyde Wilcox. Washington, DC: Georgetown University Press.

Woodward, Bob. 1994. *The Agenda: Inside the Clinton White House.* New York: Simon & Schuster.

Zaller, John R. 1998. "Monica Lewinsky's Contribution to Political Science." *PS: Political Science & Politics* 31(2): 554–57.

21

HOW MEMBERS OF CONGRESS USE THE MEDIA TO INFLUENCE PUBLIC POLICY

Karen M. Kedrowski

Editor's Note

This essay reports the major findings that emerged from four case studies designed to reveal how members of Congress use the media to influence public policy formation and execution. Karen M. Kedrowski identifies the types of members most likely to become "media entrepreneurs" and delineates the most propitious political circumstances for media initiatives. Other decision makers within the government are the ultimate target audience for media entrepreneurs, but the route to reach them and command their attention is often circuitous. Along the way, as demonstrated repeatedly in other essays, gaining control over the framing of policy issues is paramount for effective use of the media to achieve specific policy objectives.

Kedrowski is a former American Political Science Association congressional fellow. When she wrote this essay based on her dissertation, she was an assistant professor of political science at South Carolina's Winthrop University. The selection has been condensed from the concluding chapter in her study *Media Entrepreneurs and the Media Enterprise in the U.S. Congress*.

The purpose of this book [*Media Entrepreneurs and the Media Enterprise in the U.S. Congress*] is to analyze how members of Congress use the media to influence public policy. The underlying assumption behind this research is that these activities are distinct from members' efforts to use the media to communicate with constituents or to campaign for reelection. The findings from this research verify this assumption. However, a distinct group of members of Congress actively solicits media attention to influence policy: the "media entrepreneurs." They engage the media enterprise by soliciting national media coverage through interviews, op-eds, or committee hearings.

Source: Karen M. Kedrowski, *Media Entrepreneurs and the Media Enterprise in the U.S. Congress.* Copyright © 1996 by Hampton Press, Cresskill, N.J. Reprinted with the permission of Hampton Press.

The purpose of these activities is to influence the outcome of policy. Media entrepreneurs differ from other members in other ways as well. They consistently perceive the media as a more important tool to reach a variety of audiences for the purpose of influencing policy. . . .

Major Research Findings

This research used a survey of congressional offices and case studies to investigate four major research questions: First, who uses the media to influence the development of policy? In other words, who are the media entrepreneurs? Second, when are members most likely to use the media with this goal in mind? Third, who are members trying to reach with these efforts? And fourth, what sources of news are most important in terms of reaching a congressional audience?

Who Are the Media Entrepreneurs?

Media entrepreneurs are those members who believe the media are an effective tool to influence policy. Media entrepreneurs tend to be non-Southern, young, liberal Democrats. There are several possible reasons for these demographic characteristics. At the time of the survey [1991], Democrats were the majority party in Congress. The Democrats controlled the agenda in large part and could create a numerical majority simply by reaching their party colleagues. They rarely had to make the effort to reach many of their Republican colleagues who would be less likely to support their efforts.

Interestingly, media entrepreneurs are not more likely to be Senators than House members. Certainly the Senate enjoys a distinct advantage receiving media coverage, and it always boasts a few "originals", who lead Congress in sheer numbers of television appearances and quotations. Yet, for all these advantages, Senators are not more likely to actively engage the media enterprise than are their counterparts in the House.

Liberals are slightly more likely to become media entrepreneurs than are conservatives. Because Southern Democrats are more conservative than their counterparts in the rest of the country, this fact accounts in part for the regional difference. Also, all of the major national news outlets, save CNN, are headquartered outside the "old South." As a result, Southern members may see less political benefit to using these outlets to influence policy. Furthermore, they may well believe that the "elite press," commonly based in New York or other northern cities, is hostile to Southern moderates and conservatives.

Media entrepreneurs are more likely to be young members. This result is in part due to a generational shift in Congress. Another important variable is having access to a bully pulpit, such as a subcommittee or a full committee chairmanship. The ability to conduct hearings and the credibility that comes from holding a position of political power mean that these members are well situated to launch the media enterprise. The media enterprise is not only an option employed by members who lack access to any other levels of power, it is also most easily used by members who have status within the institution, such as Les Aspin, former Chairman of the House Armed Services Committee.

This situation also helps explain why Democratic media entrepreneurs outnumber Republican media entrepreneurs. At the time the survey was conducted, there was not one committee or subcommittee chaired by a Republican member of the House or Senate. Any leverage Republican members had over committee proceedings, selection of witnesses, or in consideration of legislation was completely at the discretion of the Democratic chairman. Therefore, Republicans had fewer opportunities to influence policy later in the process. Their best bet was to try to shape the agenda. . . .

There are, of course, exceptions to every one of these cases. There are conservative and Republican media entrepreneurs. . . . There are older members who are very proficient at the media enterprise. . . . Many young members . . . do not solicit media attention at all. Southern members are not absent from this process. . . . Yet, for every exception, there are several [others] who fit the profile more exactly.

. . . [W]e are really dealing with a continuum of media activity. At one extreme is a member like [Newt] Gingrich or [Patricia] Schroeder, who have ambitious national media operations and appear frequently in the national press. On the other end falls former Representative Jamie Whitten (D-Mississippi), former chairman of the House Appropriations Committee and indisputably one of the most powerful members of Congress, who shunned the spotlight. Most members fall between these two extremes. By and large they understand that the news media are the principal way in which we as a society communicate. Even Whitten has a press operation, even if it was only to communicate with his district. Media entrepreneurs are a product of a generational shift in Congress. They will become more and more common as the younger generation continues to replace the old.

Demographically speaking, media entrepreneurs differ little from their counterparts, which makes them harder to identify. They do, however, differ dramatically from their colleagues in their attitude toward the media enterprise. Across the board, media entrepreneurs consider the media an effective policy tool. They see it reaching more audiences. They consider the policy process and legislative machinery more permeable to the media's influences than their counterparts, and they themselves consume more news than their colleagues.

The crucial difference between media entrepreneurs and their counterparts is that media entrepreneurs have made a conscious decision to court the media. Media attention rarely "just happens." Instead, it must be solicited. Chairmen call hearings and invite witnesses who will capture the media's

attention. Leaders accept talk show invitations and hold regular press conferences. Rank-and-file members make floor statements or use "1-minute"
speeches and special orders to send a message. And still others choose to do
nothing, preferring a low-profile approach to legislation.

. . . The key to being a successful media entrepreneur is establishing oneself as a credible spokesperson in a policy arena. Clearly, chairing a committee or subcommittee is helpful in this regard. Likewise, party leaders also
carry legitimacy as spokespersons for their partisans. However, some media
entrepreneurs successfully establish credibility in an issue area without these
institutional benefits. Bob Kerrey, for example, was able to use his status as
a veteran and Congressional Medal of Honor recipient as a means to discuss
American policy in the Persian Gulf. . . .

It is important to remember that press coverage itself is not the object of the
media enterprise; influencing policy is. It is possible to receive a lot of press
coverage, but fail to influence the policy process. Paul Wellstone is a good example; he received a lot of attention for his attempts to keep the United States
out of the Persian Gulf War, but he was a stunning failure in terms of leading
any opposition to the authorization of the war. Therefore, credibility is a necessary but not a sufficient condition to achieve success in the media enterprise.
Without establishing him- or herself as a legitimate authority to comment on
public policy, the media entrepreneur may succeed in achieving notoriety, but
he or she will not successfully influence the policy debate.

When Is the Media Enterprise Important?

The Primacy of Agenda Setting and Framing an Issue

The hypothesis behind the second research question is that the agenda-
setting and alternative-selection stages are the best points in the policy process for members of Congress to engage the media enterprise. At this stage,
the potential to influence policy outcome is greatest. Successfully defining an
issue will establish a media entrepreneur as a major player in an issue area
and will enhance his or her efforts to influence the shape of policy as it de-
velops. There is broad consensus among all survey respondents that, indeed,
members are most likely to pursue media attention in order to place an issue
on the national agenda or to frame an issue once it is on the agenda. Media
entrepreneurs share these perceptions. Setting the agenda and defining alternatives allow media entrepreneurs to be proactive; they can work to define
policy solutions. At later stages in the legislative process, media entrepreneurs can only react to proposals developed by others. Their ability to shape
debate is hindered.

Certainly, influencing the agenda is easier for some members than for others. Committee and subcommittee chairmen are best able to shape the policy

debate by conducting hearings. These hearings can be comprised of witnesses who agree with policies favored by the chairman. The discussion can be structured so that the only feasible outcome is legislation that addresses the problems as defined in the hearings. In any case, hearings can be a powerful tool to influence the debate, even if their proceedings cannot be rigidly controlled. . . .

Likewise, the major purposes of the leadership's media enterprise are agenda setting and framing issues as part of their party's message to the country. Leadership press secretaries perceive themselves as foot soldiers in a partisan war to determine and interpret the agenda. Leadership, regardless of party, understands the importance of convincing the American public and the Washington community to accept its interpretation of events and problems as the fundamental basis of winning legislative battles on Capitol Hill.

Another reason for the importance of using the media to set the agenda and frame debate is related to the political realities on Capitol Hill. The minority party does not control the legislative process. Therefore, agenda setting and alternative selection are even more important to them. If minority members waited until a problem is defined through the normal process of drafting and debating legislation, then they are relegated to deciding which majority party proposal they can support most. On the other hand, if they can successfully change the way the debate is framed, then the majority must develop or support legislation that addresses the concerns of members in the minority party.

The case of the unrest in Los Angeles is a good example. The Democrats (the majority party at the time) completely controlled the policy definition process, successfully packaging the events as a result of deep-seated urban economic problems. Republicans were completely unsuccessful in their efforts to characterize the events as a series of individual wanton acts of violence. The Republicans' definition of the problem would have called for a heavy police crackdown on the demonstrators and stiff punishments for those found guilty. Instead, Congress passed an urban aid package that treated Los Angeles less like a riot zone and more like the victim of a natural disaster. In neither case did the debate examine whether the unrest stemmed from a breakdown in the criminal justice system.

When their party controlled the White House, however, congressional Republicans, as the minority party, had a better chance to influence the final outcome of public policy by defining issues early in the process and forcing the Democrats (the majority) into a reactive position. The Civil Rights bill is a fine example. The Republican minority in Congress, starting with Jesse Helms's 1990 reelection campaign, successfully connected civil rights legislation with reverse discrimination and "quotas" that hurt white employees . . . [forcing] Democrats into defending their civil rights bill in terms the Republicans controlled.

. . . Media entrepreneurs . . . do see more potential to influence policy at later stages than do their counterparts. Media entrepreneurs are more likely to see the media as a helpful tool to move legislation through committee, to generate floor support, and to generate support in the other chamber. When this research was conducted, Democrats had numerical majorities in both houses, thus a democratic media entrepreneur stood a better chance of constructing a majority coalition of co-partisans. Likewise, all committees and subcommittees were chaired by Democrats, who were likely to be more receptive to overtures from fellow party members than from Republicans.

[Targeting Key Audiences]

The third research question asked who are the media entrepreneurs trying to reach? The process of using the media enterprise—and its complex structure of audiences—is depicted in Figure 21-1. First and foremost, the media entrepreneur wants to get the media's attention. The media are important for two reasons: They reach out to the other audiences a media entrepreneur wants to eventually reach, and they also talk to each other. In the latter case, the media will take their cues from each other. By covering the same stories as their colleagues, journalists will help amplify the media entrepreneur's message. . . .

Figure 21-1   The Enterprise Process

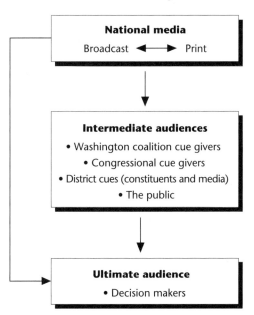

The media entrepreneur

This research found that the single most important medium to reach a Washington audience is the *Washington Post*. Media also take their cues from the Sunday morning talk shows, network news, and the *New York Times* and *Wall Street Journal*. In terms of directly reaching a Capitol Hill audience, the *Washington Post*, CNN, and *Congressional Quarterly Weekly Report* [now *CQ Weekly*] are the single most important sources. The rest of the elite press and national television news are also widely consumed on Capitol Hill. In addition, coverage in *Roll Call*, *National Journal*, and C-SPAN enhance the media entrepreneurs' chances of reaching a Capitol Hill audience.

A media entrepreneur can use the media enterprise to target a partisan audience. Although the *Washington Times* is not widely read in the aggregate, it is a crucial source for Republicans on Capitol Hill. A less remarkable but still important difference is in the audiences of the *New York Times* and National Public Radio, which are preferred by Democrats. An astute media entrepreneur will know that an op-ed in the "Republican's newsletter"—the *Washington Times*—is well placed to reach that specific audience, and an interview on "All Things Considered" is not a bad way to reach Democrats.

If they could design an ideal strategy to reach other members of Congress, media entrepreneurs would opt for op-ed articles and television interviews over news articles and press releases. Op-ed articles provide members with an unfiltered opportunity to present their arguments to a policy-oriented audience. Television interviews also offer an opportunity to put out a message. In fact, the scarcity of congressional coverage in general enhances the networks' prestige on the Hill. However, by consenting to an interview, members do sacrifice some control over the content. Even more control is sacrificed when members stand to get only a 30-second sound bite on a newscast. As a result, some members shy away from national media attention. Yet television interviews and op-ed pages enjoy a wide audience in Washington and outside the beltway. Op-ed pages are read more frequently than the front page of a newspaper, and television coverage reaches a wide audience nationally and in Washington.

The media in turn reach several intermediary audiences, both inside and outside the beltway. First, media entrepreneurs target Washington issue networks. These are comprised of interest groups and the administration. They are important because these actors provide voting cues to other members of Congress. Interest groups provide factual information and solid data to members of Congress. Administration support can help congressional leaders to forge bipartisan coalitions.

Second, media entrepreneurs try to reach a congressional audience. Depending on the purpose of the particular media enterprise, members of Congress may be either the media entrepreneur's ultimate target or they may be an intermediate audience who provide cues to or lobby other members of Congress to support the media entrepreneur's goals. For example, media entrepreneurs may target party leaders. Leadership support is crucial in terms of building legislative coalitions. Leaders not only provide voting cues, but exercise some party discipline through the whip organizations. Therefore, reaching the party leadership is important in terms of being an intermediary audience to other members and in terms of receiving the support of the leaders themselves. Similarly, rank-and-file members can put pressure on recalcitrant committee chairmen to move a piece of legislation. The only exception to this rule is congressional staff, who for obvious reasons can only provide cues to their members.

The third audience is outside the beltway: constituents, district media, and the general public. Political reality indicates that grass-roots pressure and contacts from constituents are possibly the single most important cues that members can receive when making policy decisions, and influencing public opinion and generating letters to members of Congress are the best ways to get other members' support. Because much of the media enterprise takes place in the national media that penetrates outside the Washington area, constituents and the public are apt to overhear the policy conversation in Washington. The most politically efficacious of them will act on this information and contact their members of Congress.

The ultimate audience of the media entrepreneur is other policymakers, most often members of Congress. Depending on the purpose of the media enterprise, the size of the target audience may be as large as one entire chamber—either the House or the Senate—or as small as one committee chairman or a few party leaders. Because most of these efforts are concentrated in agenda setting, the ultimate audience are the members of Congress involved in developing specific legislation in a policy area. However, if there is any administrative law making underway, as in the case of the Centers for Disease Control guidelines regarding health care workers with AIDS, other policy actors may on occasion become the target of the media enterprise.

Because the object of the media enterprise is to influence the outcome of public policy, success may take many forms. Success may not necessarily come in the form of a hard-fought victory on the House floor. In fact, floor debates in both the House and the Senate are usually foregone conclusions. More importantly, the media entrepreneur wants to be considered an important legislator who should be consulted during back-room policy negotiations.

Implications of the Media Enterprise

Media entrepreneurs do not see the media enterprise as a way to replace other, traditional ways of influencing policy. They still engage in insider strategies to influence policy. Personal contacts and getting administration and party leader support for legislative ideas are important to media entrepreneurs just as they are important to their counterparts. The difference lies in the fact that media entrepreneurs see their efforts to attain coverage in the national press as more important relative to these traditional strategies than do their colleagues.

Furthermore, the media entrepreneurs consider using media as a perfectly legitimate means to influence policy. The media enterprise is not pursued only by members who lack any other institutional mechanism to influence policy. Rather, committee and subcommittee chairmen are as likely to solicit national attention as any younger member who lacks any sort of institutional platform. Media entrepreneurs are likely to become more common in Congress as younger members who are comfortable with these efforts move into the institution and gain seniority within it. The principal difference between committee and subcommittee chairmen and other media entrepreneurs is that committee leaders put less stock in the media effectiveness of the media enterprise at later stages of the legislative process.

The importance of using the media has increased in recent years for several reasons. In the last several decades, the Washington community has become larger. Issue networks have replaced the cozy relationships once enjoyed by agency executives, committee chairmen, and interest groups. Now coalitions shift depending on the politics of the policy debate. The numbers of interest groups and PACs, congressional staff, and think tanks have expanded. Using the media to reach this audience has become more and more important and will not wane in the near future. Similarly, the expanding importance of television and the growing realization of the president's power to use it as a political tool have pushed . . . congressional leaders into the media spotlight. They [have] to solicit national media attention in order to counter the agenda-setting efforts and attempts to frame debate emanating from [incumbent] administrations. . . .

[T]here is strong evidence that the members who receive the most media attention are also the most effective members of Congress. . . . Media entrepreneurs want to have an impact on policy, enhance their reputation, or be considered a "player" on an issue. . . . It stands to reason that if they thought media attention would jeopardize their potential effectiveness, media entrepreneurs would look for alternative ways to establish their credibility in the Washington community.

One important implication of these findings is that, for all of the effort spent describing and analyzing the "new Congress," much of the old Congress still remains. Even though media entrepreneurs see the media as an important means to influence policy, they still understand the overriding value of constituent contacts, personal relationships, and the party leadership.

Furthermore, . . . a lot of policy is still made without a lot of media scrutiny. . . . [I]t is still possible to take a low profile in Congress and achieve policy success. . . .

The media entrepreneur operates in a context in which Congress as an institution receives little attention on national or local television and faces declining amounts of coverage in the print media. As a result, understanding that the media enterprise is geared to a Washington audience is even more important. Comprised of thousands of politically oriented professionals, Washington is key to influencing policy by reaching various intermediate audiences to reach other members of Congress. In many ways, the public are irrelevant to this process.

It is also necessary to understand that soliciting media attention is not easy, nor is success guaranteed. . . . [There] is dramatic evidence that interest groups can also successfully engage the media enterprise. Added to this cacophony is the administration, which has its own public relations efforts, and various federal agencies, who wish to advertise their own achievements. A journalist's attention also may be distracted by other news outside Washington, such as natural disasters and international events. As a result, a media entrepreneur's attempts may very well fail to attract the media's attention.

Finally, the media entrepreneur also acts in the context of a member of Congress who has to communicate with his or her own constituents in order to increase support for reelection. As a result, media entrepreneurs do not consider the media enterprise a replacement for their efforts to communicate with their districts. Instead, media entrepreneurs see their constituents and the general public as an additional, important audience for their efforts to receive coverage in the national media, and they engage in the same efforts to reach their constituents as any other members. District newsletters and stories in the local media are just as important to the media entrepreneur as they are to any other member of Congress. Furthermore, there is evidence that media entrepreneurs are more in tune with their districts by their close monitoring of the district press.

Similarly, media entrepreneurs eschew the notion that because they receive a lot of national media attention, the district press is somehow beneath their notice. On the contrary, media entrepreneurs make an even greater attempt to stay in touch with their district, perhaps in order to ward off criticism of "going Washington" if they appear on the network news, but not in the morning paper. Furthermore, there is evidence that receiving favorable national press coverage can have positive benefits at home, as the local press take their cues from the national media. . . .

22

I AM ON TV THEREFORE I AM

Stephen Hess

Editor's Note

In the preceding essay, Karen M. Kedrowski reports that members of Congress believe that media coverage of the House and Senate has significant political consequences. Stephen Hess presents a very different picture. In his study of Congress and the media, which focuses primarily on local media coverage, he contends that members of Congress receive so little publicity, especially on television, that the political consequences are minimal. Nonetheless, senators and representatives crave media attention and make concerted efforts to get it. The main reason for this, Hess thinks, is the pleasure that comes from viewing oneself as a media star. Moreover, most seem to believe that the presence of reporters in their surroundings means that their activities will be publicized. Such wishful thinking is comforting because Congress members cherish the myth that harnessing media power is an essential ingredient for political success.

Hess is a senior fellow in the governmental studies program at the Brookings Institution in Washington, D.C. The book from which this essay was taken is the fourth study in Hess's acclaimed *Newswork* series in which he dissects the relationship between national government institutions and the media.

. . . The press is important to presidents, and hence to the presidency.[1] Even if most Americans—and most news organizations—did not believe that the president is more important than Congress, the oneness of the presidency would give its coverage a unitary character. The nature of White House reporting is to act as a concave reflector, narrowing and maximizing attention. But Congress is 535 individuals with a jumble of interests, and reporting from Capitol Hill has the effect of atomizing the institution, separating par-

Source: Stephen Hess, *Live from Capitol Hill: Studies of Congress and the Media,* Washington, D.C.: Brookings Institution, 1991, 102–109. Reprinted with permission of the Brookings Institution.

ticles of information to fit the diverse needs of legislators and news organizations. One reporter writes of legislation to regulate commodity markets,
another on funding for repaving a highway through Altoona, others on other
subjects.

Congress, of course, demands a fair share of media attention. Borrowing
from a theory of political scientist James Q. Wilson—"organizations come to
resemble the organizations they are in conflict with"—Senator Daniel Patrick
Moynihan invented the Iron Law of Emulation: "Whenever any branch of
the government acquires a new technique which enhances its power in relation to the other branches, that technique will soon be adopted by those
other branches as well." [2] At least since Franklin D. Roosevelt invented the
fireside chat, presidents have attempted to exploit technical advances provided by the news media. Which helps explain why legislators have hired
press secretaries, allowed television cameras into committee rooms, supported the creation of C-SPAN, and expanded House and Senate recording
studios. A great deal of information gets transmitted by means of these innovations. But in the end, partly because of the principle that dissemination
is also dispersion, legislators can rarely concentrate enough video time or
command enough newspaper space to make a difference in promoting a policy or even getting themselves reelected.

Still, not all legislators are equal. From the vantage point of the press, the
House Speaker and the Senate majority leader can be handy institutional
counterweights to the president. During Ronald Reagan's first term, with the
Republicans in control of the Senate, Thomas P. "Tip" O'Neill suddenly became "the most televised Speaker in history." [3] His visibility was further enhanced by his imposing physical stature, by skillful public relations help, and
by Republican attempts to turn him into a campaign issue—a confluence of
circumstances not likely to occur very often. Yet he appeared on less than 7
percent of the network evening news programs—whereas a president almost
always gets at least one story a day (97 percent of the time, by one count)
and usually two or three.[4] And such differences in coverage are not simply
quantitative. Presidents can be certain that everything they want reported
will be reported. This allows them to use the media to semaphore political
friends and foes. Legislators, even the leaders, have no guarantees that the
press will play this game.

Nor, in terms of press coverage, are all issues equal. An investigation of a
Watergate or Iran-contra scandal, a debate on a Panama Canal Treaty or a
resolution to go to war in the Persian Gulf, a confirmation fight over a pivotal Supreme Court appointment—all can galvanize and focus the attentions
of correspondents covering Congress, although the issue is usually framed as
"Will the President Win or Lose?" [5] There are, of course, exceptions. A modest issue such as the members of Congress voting themselves a pay raise can

have "talk radio" resonance. And sometimes there are rare legislators, a Phil Gramm or Newt Gingrich, without seniority or previous celebrity status or even the physical attributes that are supposed to attract television cameras, who have been able to exploit the media to advance themselves and their causes. "No camera, microphone, or notebook could be too inconveniently located for Phil Gramm," recalled National Public Radio's Cokie Roberts of the Texas senator, who was ninety-ninth in seniority when he brought into being the deficit reduction law that bears his name.[6] And Gingrich, then a junior Republican House member in an overwhelmingly Democratic body, is supposed to have said, "We are engaged in reshaping a whole nation through the news media." [7] So far, his campaign has contributed significantly to the unseating of House Speaker Jim Wright and to his own election as minority whip.

That Congress does not get all the television attention it might want partly results from the nature of legislative activity: it represents the quintessential talking-heads story. The president can take the cameras to China as he walks along the Great Wall or to the beaches of Normandy for the fortieth anniversary of D-Day. Even a presidential candidate can make his point from a boat in a polluted harbor. But the best a legislator can usually offer the cameras is a finger pointed at a recalcitrant committee witness. This lack of visual drama has meant that even the regional television bureaus in Washington, once exclusively moored on Capitol Hill, are more and more focusing their attention away from Congress as new technology has given them greater flexibility.[8] But perhaps a deeper reason for the lack of attention is that Congress moves too slowly for the dailiness of American journalism or, for that matter, for the action-now psyches of most reporters. This is the pace I recorded in my Senate diary of October 5, 1984:

> Floor debate on deficit reduction plans continues. . . . Clearly everyone has already said everything, yet it drones on. It is obvious that the reporters have become bored, and, more important, that they do not have front page stories until something passes. So the impression lingers that the Senate isn't doing much. Yet it's a question of time frame. Is several weeks really too much time for cutting the budget by $149 billion over three years?

Since the studies of Joe S. Foote early in the 1980s, it has been confirmed that most legislators are seldom seen on network news. As I showed in *The Ultimate Insiders,* for example, during 1983 one-third of the members of the Senate appeared only one time or not at all on the ABC, CBS, or NBC evening news programs.[9] According to Timothy E. Cook in *Making Laws and Making News,* 53 percent of the members of the House of Representatives were never mentioned on these programs during 1986.[10] But at the same time, virtually every journalist's and scholar's account of Congress-media relations has asserted that the situation is otherwise on local television news, where legislators have been turned into "media stars in [their] home towns." [11] So I looked at who appears on local television news, a strangely ignored area of inquiry, and discovered that most members of Congress also rarely get seen on these programs. Congress remains largely a print story, and as newspapers lose out to television as the news purveyor of choice for Americans, Congress loses out to the president.[12]

The conundrum, then, is why television appears to be so important to the life of Congress. As researchers are finally figuring out how to measure the place of television in the political process, television's importance for Congress is best measured by the degree to which [the] House and Senate are not covered.[13] But members of Congress and congressional reporters do not seem to have noticed. Quite the contrary, in fact: they tend to overestimate the extent of television coverage and hence its importance in the legislative and electoral processes.[14] Partly this stems from the journalist's habit of ignoring the average, the typical, and the routine. When Hedrick Smith in *The Power Game: How Washington Works* made the case for media politics as a staple of the House of Representatives by citing the activities of Stephen Solarz, Les Aspin, Richard Gephardt, and Newt Gingrich, it was as if he had chosen Larry Bird, Patrick Ewing, Michael Jordan, and Magic Johnson as representative players in the National Basketball Association.[15] But a more important explanation is the solipsistic view of the world that permeates Capitol Hill. Reality to reporters is what they can see, to politicians what they can touch. And Capitol Hill is always crammed with cameras, lights, sound equipment, tape recorders, news conferences, handouts, stakeouts. This is their reality. This also contributes to the myth of television's power as they react to its presence rather than to its output.

The output, as I have demonstrated, is often small. Timothy Cook has told the affecting story of Don J. Pease, a staid and hardworking backbench congressman, who wanted to extend a program of unemployment benefits that was about to expire in 1985. His staff convinced him that a visual aid was just what he needed to get himself on television:

When his turn came up [at a rally], Pease vigorously deplored official Washington's callousness toward unemployed workers: "If you want to know the truth, the Reagan administration acts as if you don't exist." Then raising the spatula in his right hand, he shouted, "Do you know what this is? *This* is a burger flipper. *This* is the Reagan administration's answer to unemployment. And *you* can flip burgers all day, and *your spouse* can flip burgers all day, and you *still won't* get above the poverty line!"

The results of this exercise, according to Cook, were that the "network evening news programs ignored the story . . . and the next morning neither the *New York Times* nor the *Washington Post* mentioned it. The staff's one consolation was a color photograph in the *Baltimore Sun,* although the caption neglected to explain why Pease was waving the spatula." The legislation did not get out of committee.[16]

Nevertheless, Congress and its members are spending more each year trying to influence news media coverage.[17] But the interest is not as pervasive as I had expected after reading some accounts of Capitol Hill activities. . . . Electronic news releases, for instance, are far more rare than is suggested by the newspaper and magazine stories that focus on legislators who produce the tapes and ignore those who do not. Press secretaries by my calculations rank a lowly fifth in the pecking order of both House and Senate offices; in the House they also spend a fair amount of time on activities that have nothing to do with the media. And perhaps one House member in five feels virtually no need to seek publicity. Jamie Whitten, chairman of the House Appropriations Committee, in nearly a half-century of being a member of Congress, is said never to have held a press conference: "You do your job best when you do it quietly," he summarized.[18]

Indeed, legislators should know that sound bites on the evening news will not get them reelected. Other avenues of publicity in which they can target the audience and control the message are infinitely more effective and involve less risk of losing voters. The odds of being able to move a policy debate by using television news are very long for the average member of Congress. Why then do they devote such energy to this pursuit?

One answer could be that legislators do not know of television's limited impact because it does not appear limited from their vantage point. It is limited only if the question is framed: How many impressions of me, for how long, how positively, is a voter likely to get from my effort? Rather, staff and friends collect and comment upon their appearances, thus magnifying them. (It is similar to what I witnessed a few years ago when I watched a cabinet officer reading his daily press clippings. His senses told him that an awful lot was being written about him. It was harder for him to recall that he was the only one reading all of it.) Under this closed system, even an obscure cable program at an obscene hour can produce a reenforcing feedback.

Another answer could be that legislators are cockeyed optimists. Is there not some of this quality in everyone who seeks elective office? Senator William S. Cohen believed that the politicians' common denominator is ambition. "Whether it is noble or ignoble," he wrote, "it is an all consuming passion which refuses to acknowledge the folly of its relentless pursuit." [19] In pursuit of the elusive sound bite, surely each member of Congress thinks he is as energetic, articulate, and intelligent as Phil Gramm and Newt Gingrich. Moreover, sound-bite journalism protects legislators from themselves. Although television and newspapers work off the same definition of news, their needs differ—TV needs nine seconds, and thus must edit out redundancy and even the awkward pauses of conversational speech. This will not necessarily make legislators look good, but it keeps them from looking bad.

Add to Senator Cohen's definition of political ambition Joseph A. Schlesinger's theory of progressive ambition: "The politician aspires to attain an office more important than the one he now seeks or is holding." [20] More than a third of the Senate once served in the House. How many senators would rather be president? On December 30, 1971, Jim Wright wrote in his diary, "In two days, a New Year will begin. It is my 50th, will be my 18th in Congress. . . . Maybe just in the past year have I really acknowledged that I won't ever be president." [21] For some legislators, perhaps, being on television has less to do with the next election than with some future election that may only be a dream.

So, as the members of Congress supposedly rush to recording studios to tape instant reactions to the president's State of the Union message, the political pluses outweigh the minuses. Getting on the air is an advantage, even if an exaggerated one. The costs are small, both in time and money, and the money is provided by taxpayers or campaign contributors anyway. Also, because most legislators sincerely wish to be noticed, there is no longer a stigma—the "show horse" label—attached to those who are exceedingly good at getting themselves on television.[22]

Yet there is still something else. It is August 1, 1984, and I am sitting next to Senator Alan Dixon in a screening room in the basement of the Capitol. This is part of the Senate's television complex, a railroad flat of a place carved out of long and narrow space that had once been the path of the [C]apitol subway. There are two television studios with a control room between them, two radio studios with a control room between them, and two TV editing rooms in addition to the room where we are now watching a tape of the town meeting that the senator has recently broadcast from a cable station in Peoria. A question put to him requires a delicate answer. Dixon listens to his response. He smiles, then issues a laugh that comes from deep inside him. "I got out of that pretty good," he says. Watching a man so thoroughly enjoy watching himself is an exquisite experience. Few senators—only Moynihan and Cohen come to mind—get the same satisfaction from the printed word.

For the legislators of Capitol Hill, television is not primarily about politics at all, I realize. Or rather, without elections to be won and legislation to be passed, there would still be the rush to television. For television is about being a celebrity. Television appearances are analogues of the decor of their offices, which are filled with cartoonists' impressions of them and photographs of them taken with famous people at important events. *"The celebrity is a person who is known for his well-knownness,"* said Daniel J. Boorstin. In his brilliant essay, *The Image,* he concluded, "The hero created himself; the celebrity is created by the media." [23] I am on TV therefore I am.

Notes

1. See Elmer E. Cornwell, Jr., *Presidential Leadership of Public Opinion* (Indiana University Press, 1965); Michael Baruch Grossman and Martha Joynt Kumar, *Portraying the President: The White House and the News Media* (Johns Hopkins University Press, 1981); and Richard L. Rubin, *Press, Party, and Presidency* (Norton, 1981).
2. Daniel Patrick Moynihan, *Counting Our Blessings: Reflections on the Future of America* (Little, Brown, 1980), pp. 117–18.
3. Joe S. Foote, *Television Access and Political Power: The Networks, the Presidency, and the "Loyal Opposition"* (Praeger, 1990), p. 129.
4. Speaker O'Neill was seen on the network evening news programs 184 times in 1981, 146 times in 1982, 159 times in 1983, and 168 times in 1984. See Timothy E. Cook, *Making Laws and Making News: Media Strategies in the U.S. House of Representatives* (Brookings, 1989), pp. 196–97. For presidential appearances, see Fred Smoller, "The Six O'Clock Presidency: Patterns of Network News Coverage of the President," *Presidential Studies Quarterly*, vol. 16 (Winter 1986), p. 46. Doris A. Graber, *Mass Media and American Politics*, 3d ed. (Washington: CQ Press, 1989), who charted all network evening news broadcasts from July 1986 to June 1987, found that "the president received roughly seven and one-half hours of television news coverage each month from the networks, compared with slightly over one hour for Congress" (pp. 236–37).
5. See Denis Steven Rutkus, *Newspaper and Television Network News Coverage of Congress during the Summers of 1979 and 1989: A Content Analysis* (Congressional Research Service, 1991), pp. 35–40.
6. Cokie Roberts, "Leadership and the Media in the 101st Congress," in John J. Kornacki, ed., *Leading Congress: New Styles, New Strategies* (Washington: CQ Press, 1990), p. 91.
7. Quoted in John M. Barry, *The Ambition and the Power* (Viking, 1989), p. 166.
8. See Larry Makinson, *Dateline: Capitol Hill* (Washington: Center for Responsive Politics, 1990), p. 62.
9. Stephen Hess, *The Ultimate Insiders: U.S. Senators in the National Media* (Brookings, 1986), p. 16.
10. Cook, *Making Laws and Making News*, p. 60.
11. See Roger H. Davidson and Walter J. Oleszek, *Congress and Its Members*, 3d ed. (Washington: CQ Press, 1990), p. 147.
12. For the case that more coverage does not lead to more power, see Stephanie Greco Larson, "The President and Congress in the Media," *Annals*, vol. 499 (September 1988), pp. 64–74.
13. For some studies that have measured television's political effect, see Thomas E. Patterson, *The Mass Media Election: How Americans Choose Their President* (Praeger, 1980); George Gerbner and others, "Charting the Mainstream: Television's Contributions to Political Orientations," *Journal of Communication*, vol. 32 (Spring 1982), pp. 100–27; Larry M. Bartels, "Expectations and Preferences in Presidential Nominating Campaigns," *American Political Science Review*, vol. 79 (September 1985), pp. 804–15; Benjamin I. Page, Robert Y. Shapiro, and

Glenn R. Dempsey, "What Moves Public Opinion?" *American Political Science Review,* vol. 81 (March 1987), pp. 23–43; and Shanto Iyengar and Donald R. Kinder, *News That Matters* (University of Chicago Press, 1987).

14. See, for example, Michael D. Wormser, ed., *Guide to Congress,* 3d ed. (Washington: CQ Press, 1982), p. 744. Scholars, however, have been less likely to fall into the journalists' trap. A number of studies have noted the modest television coverage of congressional campaigns. See, for example, Mark C. Westlye, *Senate Elections and Campaign Intensity* (Johns Hopkins University Press, 1991), pp. 39, 41. John W. Kingdon, *Agendas, Alternatives, and Public Policies* (Little, Brown, 1984), pp. 61–64, also describes a more limited role for the media in setting congressional agendas.

15. See Hedrick Smith, *The Power Game: How Washington Works* (Random House, 1988), pp. 139–46.

16. See Cook, *Making Laws and Making News,* pp. 132–46. Cook's point, however, is that Pease's media campaign, of which the spatula incident was a part, is what allowed his bill to get within two votes of passage. My interpretation of his case study is that the bill did as well as it did because Pease convinced Speaker O'Neill to support him.

17. See Walter Pincus, "TV Staff for House May Grow," *Washington Post,* April 25, 1990, p. A26, and "House TV Expansion Deferred," *Washington Post,* April 26, 1990, p. A21.

18. Quoted in Peter Osterlund, "Media-Savvy Congress Turns to TV," *Christian Science Monitor,* June 3, 1988, p. 3.

19. William S. Cohen, *Roll Call: One Year in the United States Senate* (Simon and Schuster, 1981), p. 165.

20. Joseph A. Schlesinger, *Ambition and Politics* (Rand McNally, 1966), p. 10. Articles relating ambition theory to Congress include Michael L. Mezey, "Ambition Theory and the Office of Congressman," *Journal of Politics,* vol. 32 (August 1970), pp. 563–79; Jeff Fishel, "Ambition and the Political Vocation: Congressional Challengers in American Politics," *Journal of Politics,* vol. 33 (February 1971), pp. 25–56; David W. Rohde, "Risk-Bearing and Progressive Ambition: The Case of Members of the United States House of Representatives," *American Journal of Political Science,* vol. 23 (February 1979), pp. 126; Paul Brace, "Progressive Ambition in the House: A Probabilistic Approach," *Journal of Politics,* vol. 46 (May 1984), pp. 556–71; and Paul R. Abramson, John H. Aldrich, and David W. Rohde, "Progressive Ambition among United States Senators: 1972–1988," *Journal of Politics,* vol. 49 (February 1987), pp. 3–35.

21. David J. Montgomery, "Jim Wright, The Speaker of the House for the 100th Congress," *Fort Worth Star-Telegram,* December 9, 1986, p. 1.

22. See John R. Hibbing and Sue Thomas, "The Modern United States Senate: What Is Accorded Respect," *Journal of Politics,* vol. 52 (February 1990), pp. 126–45.

23. Daniel J. Boorstin, *The Image: or What Happened to the American Dream* (Atheneum, 1962), pp. 57, 61.

23

STRATEGIES OF THE AMERICAN CIVIL RIGHTS MOVEMENT

Doug McAdam

Editor's Note

Democratic governments lose public support when they appear to act in undemocratic ways. Social movements have learned to exploit these image concerns by deliberately provoking repressive actions through their choice of disruptive forms of protest in locations where they are most hated. When the
authorities respond with force, a David and Goliath scenario emerges that
turns the protesters into abused victims and the authorities into abusing vil-
lains. The greater coercive power of the authorities becomes a liability rather
than an asset. The news media serve as the public stage on which the drama is
played out before rapt public audiences, and media audiences side with the
victims. Doug McAdam illustrates how the strategy works by tracking the activities of the American Civil Rights Movement during the leadership of Martin
Luther King Jr.

McAdam is professor of sociology at Stanford University. He is the coauthor
and coeditor of several books about social movements and American politics.
His research has been instrumental in identifying the important roles played
by news media in the success or failure of social movements.

Political movements face at least six strategic hurdles that typically must
be surmounted if they are to become a force for social change. Specifically,
movement groups must be able to

1. attract new recruits;
2. sustain the morale and commitment of current adherents;

Source: Doug McAdam, "The Case of the American Civil Rights Movement," in *Research on
Democracy and Society,* ed. Frederick D. Weil, Oxford, U.K.: Elsevier, 1997, Vol. 3, 155–176.
Copyright © 1997. Reprinted with permission from Elsevier.

3. generate media coverage, preferably, but not necessarily, of a favorable sort;
4. mobilize the support of various "bystander publics";
5. constrain the social control options of its opponents; and
6. ultimately shape public policy and state action.

. . . [T]he last four of these goals have been the subject of very little empirical research by movement scholars. In what follows, then, I want to make them the principal focus of attention. Together they constitute the broader "environmental challenge" confronting the movement. . . .

In this chapter, I seek to show how the American civil rights movement was able, through the strategic framing efforts of Martin Luther King Jr. and his Southern Christian Leadership Conference (SCLC), largely to accomplish these four goals. . . .

To fully appreciate the daunting challenge that confronted the civil rights movement, one has to understand the depths of black powerlessness on the eve of the struggle. In 1950, fully two-thirds of all blacks continued to live in the southern United States. Yet, through a combination of legal subterfuge and extralegal intimidation, blacks were effectively barred from political participation in the region. . . .

If change were to come, it would have to be imposed from without. This, of course, meant intervention by the federal government. However, with a moderate Republican, Dwight Eisenhower, in the White House and southern Democrats exercising disproportionate power in Congress, the movement faced a kind of strategic stalemate at the national level as well. To break the stalemate, the movement would have to find a way of pressuring a reluctant federal government to intervene more forcefully in the South. This, in turn, meant attracting favorable media attention as a way of mobilizing popular support for the movement.

Attracting Media Coverage

If one were to conduct an ethnographic study of virtually any social movement organization, be it local or national, one would be very likely to uncover a pervasive concern with media coverage among one's subjects. The fact is, most movements spend considerable time and energy in seeking to attract and shape media coverage of their activities. . . .

The simple fact is that most movements lack the conventional political resources possessed by their opponents and thus must seek to offset this power disparity by appeals to other parties. The media come to be seen—logically, in my view—as the key vehicle for such influence attempts. The civil rights movement represents a prime example of this dynamic in action, and no group in the movement mastered this dynamic and exploited its possibilities better than the SCLC and its leader, Martin Luther King Jr.

The media's fascination with King was evident from the very beginning of the Montgomery, Alabama, bus boycott. Launched in December 1955, the boycott inaugurated the modern civil rights movement and catapulted King into public prominence. From then until his death in April 1968, King never strayed far from the front page and the nightly news. What accounts for King's media staying power, and why were he and the SCLC, alone among movement groups, so successful in attracting favorable media attention? In seeking to answer these questions, I will emphasize the role of three factors.

1. *Disruptive actions are newsworthy.* First, the SCLC and King mastered the art of staging newsworthy disruptions of public order. The first requirement of media coverage is that the event be judged newsworthy. Their experiences in Montgomery convinced King and his lieutenants of the close connection between public disruption and media coverage. All of King's subsequent campaigns were efforts to stage the same kind of highly publicized disruptions of public order that had occurred in Montgomery. Sometimes King failed, as in Albany, Georgia, in 1961–1962, when Police Chief Laurie Pritchett responded to King's tactics with mass arrests but without the violence and disruptions of public order so critical to sustained media attention. At other times in other places—most notably in Birmingham, Alabama, in 1963 and Selma, Alabama, in 1965—local authorities took the bait and responded with the kind of savagery that all but guarantees media attention.

Still, his mastery of the politics of disruption explains only how King and the SCLC were able to attract the media but not the overwhelmingly sympathetic tone of that coverage. Given the openly provocative nature of the King/SCLC strategy, the generally favorable coverage accorded King's actions demands explanation. The key to the puzzle would seem to rest with King's consummate ability to frame his actions in highly resonant and sympathetic ways. The final two factors focus on King's framing efforts, first in conventional ideational terms and then in terms of the signifying function of his tactics.

2. *Ideational framing.* As noted previously, all work on framing betrays an exclusive concern with ideas and their formal expression by movement actors. These conscious ideational pronouncements—speeches, writings, and so on are an important component of a movement's overall framing effort; and, in accounting for King's success in attracting sympathetic media coverage, much of the credit must go to the substantive content of his thought. Quite simply, no black leader had ever sounded like King before. In his unique blending of familiar Christian themes, conventional democratic theory, and the philosophy of nonviolence, King brought an unusually compelling yet accessible frame to the struggle. First and foremost, there was a deep "resonance" (Snow et al. 1986) to King's thought. Specifically, in employing Christian themes and conventional democratic theory, King suc-

ceeded in grounding the movement in two of the ideational bedrocks of American culture. Second, the theme of Christian forgiveness that runs throughout King's thought was deeply reassuring to a white America burdened (as it still is) by guilt and a near phobic fear of black anger and violence. King's emphasis on Christian charity and nonviolence promised a redemptive and peaceful healing to America's long-standing racial divide. Third, King's invocation of Gandhian philosophy added an exotic intellectual patina to his thought that many in the northern media (and northern intellectuals in general) found appealing. Finally, while singling out this or that theme in King's thought, it should be noted that the very variety of themes granted those in the media (and the general public) multiple points of ideological contact with the movement. Thus, secular liberals might be unmoved by King's reading of Christian theology but resonate with his application of democratic theory and so on.

3. *The signifying function of SCLC actions.* King and his SCLC lieutenants' genius as "master framers," however, extended beyond the ideational content of their formal pronouncements. In their planning and orchestration of major campaigns, the SCLC brain trust displayed what can only be described as a genius for strategic dramaturgy. That is, in the staging of demonstrations, King and his lieutenants were also engaged in signifying work—mindful of the messages and potent symbols encoded in the actions they took and hoped to induce their opponents to take.

Arguably the best example of SCLC's penchant for staging compelling and resonant dramas is their 1963 campaign in Birmingham. Like virtually all major cities in the Deep South, Birmingham in 1963 remained a wholly segregated city, with blacks and whites confined to their own restaurants, schools, churches, and even public restrooms. In April of that year, the SCLC launched a citywide campaign of civil disobedience aimed at desegregating Birmingham's public facilities; but why, among all southern cities, was Birmingham targeted? The answer bespeaks the SCLC's strategic and dramaturgic genius. As a major chronicler of the events in Birmingham notes, "King's Birmingham innovation was pre-eminently strategic. Its essence was . . . the selection of a target city which had as its Commissioner of Public Safety 'Bull' Connor, a notorious racist and hothead who could be depended on not to respond nonviolently" (Hubbard 1968, 5).

The view that King's choice of Birmingham was a conscious, strategic one is supported by the fact that Connor was a lame-duck official, having been defeated by a moderate in a runoff election in early April 1963. Had the SCLC waited to launch its campaign until after the moderate took office, there likely would have been considerably less violence and less press coverage as well. "The supposition has to be that . . . SCLC, in a shrewd . . . stratagem, knew a good enemy when they saw him . . . one who could be counted on in stupidity and natural viciousness to play into their hands, for full exploitation in the press as archfiend and villain" (Watters 1971, 266).

King and his lieutenants had learned their lessons well. After several days of uncharacteristic restraint, Connor trained fire hoses and unleashed attack dogs on peaceful demonstrators. The resulting scenes of demonstrators being slammed into storefronts by the force of the hoses and attacked by snarling police dogs were picked up and broadcast nationwide on the nightly news. Photographs of the same events appeared in newspapers and magazines throughout the nation and the world. The former Soviet Union used the pictures as anti-American propaganda at home and abroad. Thus, the media's coverage of the events in Birmingham succeeded in generating enormous sympathy for the demonstrators and putting increased pressure on a reluctant federal government to intervene on behalf of the movement.

In short, by successfully courting violence while restraining violence in his followers, King and the SCLC were able to frame the events in Birmingham as highly dramatic confrontations between a "good" movement and an "evil" system. Moreover, the movement's dominant religious ideology granted this interpretation all the more credibility and resonance. These were no longer demonstrators; rather, they were peaceful, Christian petitioners being martyred by an evil, oppressive system. The stark, highly dramatic nature of this ritualized confrontation between good and evil proved irresistible to the media and, in turn, to the American public.

Mobilizing Public Support

While favorable media coverage was the immediate goal of King and his lieutenants, it was never conceived of as an end in itself. Instead, the SCLC courted the media for the role that it might play in mobilizing greater public awareness of and support for the movement. That support, in turn, was seen as the key to breaking the strategic stalemate in which the SCLC and the broader movement found itself. With no chance of defeating the white supremacists in a direct confrontation, the SCLC knew that its prospects for initiating change would turn on its ability to prod a reluctant federal government into more supportive action on behalf of civil rights. Ironically, the election of John F. Kennedy as president in 1960 only intensified the government's long-standing aversion to "meddling" in southern race relations. The specific explanation for Kennedy's reluctance to intervene had to do with his narrow margin of victory in 1960 and the "strange bedfellows" that comprised his electoral coalition. Not only had Kennedy garnered the so-called black vote and the votes of northern liberals and labor, but he was also beholden to the "solid South." In rejecting the Republican Party as the party of Abraham Lincoln, white southerners had voted consistently Democratic since the late nineteenth century. Thus, Kennedy, no less than his party predecessors, counted racist southerners and civil rights advocates among his constituents. The electoral challenge for Kennedy, then, was to preserve his fragile coalition by not unduly antagonizing either white southerners or civil rights forces. More immediately, Kennedy knew that the success of his legislative agenda would depend, to a large extent, on the support of conservative southern congressmen whose long tenure granted them disproportionate power within both the House and the Senate. For both electoral and legislative reasons, then, Kennedy came to office determined to effect a stance of qualified neutrality on civil rights matters.

In this context, the SCLC saw its task as destroying the political calculus on which Kennedy's stance of neutrality rested. It had to make the political, and especially the electoral, benefits of supporting civil rights appear to outweigh the costs of alienating southern white voters and their elected officials. This meant mobilizing the support of the general public, thereby broadening the electoral basis of civil rights advocacy. In concert with the other major civil rights groups, the SCLC was able to do just that. Between 1962 and 1965, the salience of the civil rights issue reached such proportions that it consistently came to be identified in public opinion surveys as the "most important" problem confronting the country. In six of the eleven national polls conducted by Gallup (1972) between January 1961 and January 1966, it was designated as the country's most pressing problem by survey respondents. In three other polls, it ranked second. Only twice did it rank as low as fourth. Moreover, the imprint of the SCLC's dramaturgic genius is clearly reflected in these data. The two highest percentages attached to the issue correspond to the SCLC's highly publicized campaigns in Birmingham (April to May 1963) and Selma (March 1965). Quite simply, the SCLC's ability to lure supremacists into well-publicized outbursts of racist violence kept the issue squarely before the public and ensured the growing support necessary to pressure Kennedy and Congress into more decisive action.

Constraining the Social Control Options of Segregationists

To this point, I have said very little about the effect of the SCLC's tactics on southern segregationists, but, in a very real sense, the success of the SCLC's politics of disruption depended not on the media or the general public but on the movement's opponents in the South. Had segregationists not responded to the SCLC's actions with the kind of violent disruptions of public order seen in Birmingham, the SCLC would have been denied the media coverage so critical to its overall strategy. Indeed, the SCLC's most celebrated failure turned on its inability to provoke precisely this response from segregationists. I am referring to the citywide campaign that the SCLC launched in Albany, Georgia, in November 1961. In all respects, the campaign was comparable to the organization's later efforts in Birmingham and Selma.

However, while the campaigns themselves were similar, the opponents' response to them was anything but. What was absent in Albany were the celebrated atrocities and breakdown in public order characteristic of Birmingham and Selma. This difference owed to Albany Police Chief Laurie Pritchett's clear understanding of the SCLC's strategy and his firm resolve to deny them the villain that they so badly needed. While systematically denying demonstrators their rights, Pritchett nonetheless did so through mass arrests rather than the kind of reactive violence that proved so productive of sympathetic media coverage in Birmingham and Selma. . . .

Shaping Public Policy and State Action

. . . The ultimate goal of King and the SCLC was to prod the government into action and to reshape federal civil rights policy in the process. That they were able to do so is clear. . . . What is also clear is that the extent and pace of their achievements were inextricably linked to their success in orchestrating the politics of disruption described here. In particular, the movement's two most significant legislative victories—the Civil Rights Act of 1964 and the Voting Rights Act of 1965—owed, in large measure, to the Birmingham and Selma campaigns, respectively.

Birmingham, as we have seen, featured the brutality of Bull Connor and, in the waning days of the campaign, a Sunday morning bombing of a black church that claimed the lives of three little girls. As broadcast nightly into the living rooms of America, these atrocities mobilized public opinion like never before and, in turn, put enormous pressure on President Kennedy to act forcefully on behalf of civil rights. The ultimate result was administration sponsorship of the Civil Rights Act, which, even in a much weaker form, had earlier been described as politically too risky by Kennedy himself. Finally, there was Selma. One last time, King and the SCLC orchestrated the by-now familiar politics of disruption to perfection. Initiated in January 1965, the campaign reached its peak in March with a series of widely publicized atrocities by segregationists. . . .

In response to this consistent breakdown in public order and the public outrage that it aroused throughout the nation, the federal government was forced to once again intervene in support of black interests. On March 17, President Lyndon Johnson submitted to Congress a tough voting rights bill containing several provisions that movement leaders had earlier been told were politically too unpopular to be incorporated into legislative proposals. The bill passed by overwhelming margins in both the Senate and the House and was signed into law on August 6 of the same year.

However, Selma was to represent the high-water mark for King, the SCLC, and the movement as a whole. Never again was King able to successfully stage the politics of disruption at which he had become so skilled. The reason for this is simple: As the movement moved out of the American South and sought to confront the much more complicated forms of racism endemic to the North, King was deprived of the willing antagonists he had faced in the South. As King had learned, southern segregationists could be counted on, when sufficiently provoked, to respond with the violence so critical to media attention and the increased public and government support that sympathetic coverage inevitably produced. No such convenient foil was available to the movement outside the South. In fact, more often than not, after 1965 civil rights forces came to resemble a movement in search of an enemy. . . .

Even when the movement was able, as in the 1966 open housing marches in Cicero, Illinois, to provoke southern-style violence in the North, local authorities were unwilling to intervene because they feared the political consequences of doing so. They knew that while the general public was prepared to accept an end to Jim Crow segregation in the South, it was assuredly not ready to acquiesce in the dismantling of de facto segregation in the North. Thus, the absence of supportive public opinion in the North denied the movement the critical source of pressure that had helped compel federal action in the South. The ability to command public and, by extension, state attention and support had been lost. In no public opinion poll since 1965 has the American public ever accorded black civil rights the status of the number one problem confronting the country, nor since then has Congress passed, with the exception of the Civil Rights Act of 1968, any significant civil rights legislation.

References

Hubbard, Howard. 1968. "Five Long Hot Summers and How They Grew." *Public Interest:* 12:3–24.

Snow, David A., Jr., E. Burke Rochford, Steven K. Worden, and Robert D. Benford. 1986. "Frame Alignment Processes, Micromobilization, and Movement Participation." *American Sociological Review* 51 (4):464–481.

Watters, Pat. 1971. *Down to Now: Reflections on the Southern Civil Rights Movement.* New York: Pantheon.

24

THE DYNAMICS OF THE MEDIA-POLICY CONNECTION

Itzhak Yanovitzky

Editor's Note

The perception is widespread that ample media coverage of a public policy issue forces politicians' hands. To placate an aroused public, they must focus on the issue and often act faster and more strongly than they would have otherwise. After examining the connection between media coverage of drunk-driving problems and corresponding legislation over a seventeen-year period, Itzhak Yanovitzky concludes that the perception is wrong. Heavy media coverage does, indeed, increase attention to an issue, but major legislative action follows only when it fits into the plans of political leaders. Prior studies that simply showed an association between the media agenda and policy agenda missed the real dynamics of the interaction.

Yanovitzky wrote this essay, drawn from his doctoral dissertation at the University of Pennsylvania, while he was an assistant professor of communication at Rutgers University. He has published numerous articles and book chapters about media, public policy, and health communication. He is coeditor with Elihu Katz of *Culture, Communication, and Leisure in Israel* (1999).

Communication theory prescribes that media exposure is the primary condition for media effects on individual judgments and behavior (McGuire, 1989). There is little doubt that policy makers meet this requirement. A recent study that explored patterns of media use by members of Congress (Bennett & Yanovitzky, 2000) found that, on average, legislators spend 1.8 hours each day reading a daily newspaper and 1.5 hours a day watching television news programs. An overwhelming majority of them also consider national and local news media to be the single best source of information on

Source: Itzhak Yanovitzky, "Effects of News Coverage on Policy Attention and Actions: A Closer Look Into the Media-Policy Connection," in *Communication Research* 29:4 (August 2002): 422-451. Copyright (c) 2002 by Sage Publications, Inc. Reprinted by permission of Sage Publications, Inc.

national events and events in legislators' states or districts (compared to interpersonal communication channels). . . .

Beyond exposure, however, media effects are contingent on a person's motivation to attend to the message and process the information it contains (McGuire, 1989; Petty & Cacioppo, 1986). Motivation, in turn, is a function of both individual characteristics (e.g., education, interest, and predispositions) and message attributes such as presentation, frames, and quality of persuasive arguments (Kuhn, 1991; Petty & Cacioppo, 1986; Price & Tewksbury, 1997). Policy makers have a strong incentive to process information in the news media (Linsky, 1986). On one hand, given the fluid and competitive nature of the political arena, unresponsiveness of policy makers to issues that climb the media agenda may compromise their current position of power in government (Lemert, 1981; Linsky, 1986). Moreover, allowing the media to construct issues and mobilize public opinion is a politically dangerous position for elected officials and bureaucrats who then risk losing control over how the issue is defined and resolved (Dearing & Rogers, 1996). On the other hand, media construction of a public problem opens a window of opportunity for political gain (Kingdon, 1984). The policy-making process is often opportunistic, and policy makers regularly use the media to accomplish their political goals (Hess, 1984). Favorable media coverage may increase the ability of policy makers to get their policies successfully adopted and implemented (Linsky, 1986) or win them some important political gains with key constituencies (Diani, 1996; Edwards & Wood, 1999).

Policy makers' high stakes in media coverage of public issues motivates them to actively seek, attend, and process related media messages. . . . [A]lthough heightened media attention may attract policy makers' attention to certain issues (Linsky, 1986; Rogers, Dearing, & Chang, 1991), there is a very low likelihood that this coverage will alter their beliefs and attitudes regarding issues they believe to be important, unless they are challenged by cogent contrary information (Kingdon, 1984). Instead, the effect of media coverage of issues on policy making is likely to be manifested in two forms: the timing of intensive issue-related policy making and the type of policy choices pursued by policy makers.

Similar to media organizations, policy makers' work is guided by routines (Edwards & Wood, 1999; Kingdon, 1984). At any given moment, the political system is grappling with a great number of tangible problems that vie for leaders' attention. Because leaders can only attend to a very small number of them at a time, they typically rely on these routines to prioritize their activities (Hilgartner & Bosk, 1988). As a result, policy making tends to be characterized by long periods of relative stability and incrementalism (Baumgartner & Jones, 1993). From time to time, however, this equilibrium is punctured or interrupted by sudden demands for a dramatic change that force leaders to respond quickly to restore equilibrium without fundamentally changing the nature of the system (Baumgartner & Jones, 1993). Because the majority of these sudden demands are communicated through the media (Edwards & Wood, 1999; Kingdon, 1984), policy makers tend to interpret sudden fluctuations in media attention as a cue for action (Linsky, 1986). One would, therefore, expect that the volume of issue-related policy measures would be higher following increased media attention to this issue. Over time, as media attention to this issue wanes, the volume of policy measures should stabilize once again. Furthermore, the degree of policy change in response to increased media attention will depend on the tone set by the media (Baumgartner & Jones, 1993; Zaller, 1992). Enthusiastic, one-sided treatment of the issue will result in a rapid policy change. Debate and criticism are predictive of slower and gradual policy actions.

Besides influencing the timing and intensity of policy making, media attention to issues may also be related to the particular policy choices pursued by policy makers regarding a certain problem. In much the same way that media representations of issues shape lay people's judgments (Gamson, 1992; Iyengar, 1991; Iyengar & Simon, 1993; Price & Tewksbury, 1997), they are likely to influence policy makers' views of public problems (Linsky, 1986). For example, policy makers may use media representations to attribute responsibility to a problem (Iyengar, 1991), learn about some of its solutions (Price & Tewksbury, 1997), or use it as a benchmark against which to evaluate their own performance in dealing with the problem (Iyengar & Kinder, 1987). Nonetheless, as noted above, policy makers are less susceptible to such effects (i.e., priming and framing) because personal knowledge and experience as well as ideological and organizational constraints (e.g., budgetary constraints or the party's stand on issues) effectively inoculate them against media frames (Edwards & Wood, 1999; Kingdon, 1984). . . . Rather, policy makers are likely to follow media prescriptions of responsibility and solutions to problems if they already fit into their own belief structure (Gusfield, 1981; Roessler, 1999) and if they present an opportunity for political gain (Kingdon, 1984). . . .

Hypotheses

. . . Because policy makers have been shown to constitute a fairly homogeneous group of individuals in terms of political motivation, professional concerns, and contact with external sources of influence on their political decisions and behavior (Baumgartner & Jones, 1993; Edwards & Wood, 1999), it seems reasonable to argue that the cognitive process by which each individual policy maker reacts to information in the media is substantively similar to that of other policy makers. If this assumption is correct, three specific predictions regarding the association between media attention to public issues and related policy making may be drawn from the discussion above. The first two pertain to the association between media coverage and policy attention to issues (as a measure of a cognitive response), whereas the last relates to the potential effect of this coverage on policy makers' actual behavior.

Hypothesis 1: Heightened policy attention to a public issue will be prompted by increased media attention to the same issue. Particularly, the volume of issue-related ad hoc activities by policy makers (as a measure of policy attention) will be greater than similar routine activities.

Hypothesis 2: Following a decrease in media attention to this issue, policy attention to the same issue will decrease as well. Specifically, the volume of issue-related ad hoc activities by policy makers will be lower than similar routine activities.

Hypothesis 3: The nature and volume of policy makers' actions will correspond to the solutions advocated in the media regarding this problem and the frequency in which they were mentioned. As media coverage decreases, the volume of policy actions will decrease as well and actions designed to achieve short-term solutions will be replaced with actions designed to achieve long-term solutions.

. . . [U]nlike other formulations of similar hypotheses, a distinction is made here between media effects on policy attention and media effects on policy actions. This, in turn, requires the use of measures that are sensitive to this distinction.

. . . [A]lthough many similar hypotheses argue for an association between changes in media attention to issues and changes in related policy, the language used here implies a causal influence from media coverage to policy making. . . .

Last, and more important, taken together, the study's hypotheses aim at capturing a process of change over time in policy response to media coverage of an issue. . . . [T]his is an attempt to move from a static conceptualization of this association to a more dynamic framework of examining and understanding this association. More specifically, it is an attempt to model the impact of the well-documented media issue-attention cycle on public policy (Dearing & Rogers, 1996; Downs, 1972). For this reason, these hypotheses are tested with longitudinal data on media attention and policy response to the problem of drunk driving (DD) between 1978 and 1995. The choice of DD and this particular time period as the focus of investigation was motivated by findings of previous studies on the DD case (e.g., Borkenstein, 1985; Gusfield, 1981; McCarthy, 1994). These studies showed that although DD was recognized as a major public problem by federal agencies, state and local police, and the research community beginning in the 1970s, this problem received very little media attention until the beginning of the 1980s. The intensity of anti-DD policy actions was low as well during the same period. Then, coinciding with the rise of the grassroots movement against DD (e.g., Mothers Against Drunk Driving), both media and policy attention to the DD problem escalated rapidly throughout the mid-1980s. The use of longitudinal data, therefore, is expected to sort out the nature and direction of the media-policy association in the DD case.

Methodology

Media Attention

Media attention to the DD problem between 1978 and 1995 is the independent variable in this study. Three major national news sources, the *New York Times, Washington Post,* and *Associated Press* (AP) wire service, were selected to represent the national media environment. The *New York Times* and *Washington Post* were chosen for their intermedia agenda-setting power and the strong relationship that exists between these daily national newspapers and other national news sources, including television networks (Dearing & Rogers, 1996; Neuman, 1990; Yanovitzky & Bennett, 1999). In addition, there is evidence that both newspapers are central to elites and policy makers (Bennett & Yanovitzky, 2000; Dearing & Rogers, 1996; Hess, 1984). The AP wire service was included because it feeds many national and local news outlets (both print and electronic) and thus approximates well the national news environment (Fan, 1988). Using a single news story as a coding unit, the Lexis-Nexis on-line database was searched to generate a census of all DD-related news stories that appeared in these national news sources between January 1, 1978 and December 31, 1995. Because a conservative measure of media attention was sought, only news stories whose primary theme was the issue of DD were included in the analysis. The main criterion for exclusion was any mention of DD in passing. For example, a news story in the *Washington Post* that simply compared the success of a citizens' group against child molesters to that of citizen groups against DD (Mathews, 1982) was excluded from the analysis. . . .

All stories were coded for the presence or absence of certain definitions of the DD problem (i.e., crime, alcohol problem, traffic safety problem, public health problem, and a normative problem), references to possible solutions (i.e., tougher laws, stiffer punishments, strict enforcement, treatment, education and prevention, and passive safety measures), and the news story valence (i.e., number of references to opinions that favor or oppose measures aimed at reducing the DD problem). Due to the large number of news stories [1,014 stories] in the analysis, computer-assisted content analysis was used to quantify occurrences and co-occurrences of variables in the text. . . . The results of estimating intercoder agreement using the rigorous Krippendorff's alpha

(Krippendorff, 1980) demonstrated high levels of computer-human coding agreement (.74 > α > .86 for 11 content categories).

Policy Attention and Action

. . . Both policy attention and actions are theoretically important for testing this study's predictions concerning media effects on the process of policy making. Level of policy attention taps into the more immediate response of policy makers to increased level of media attention to a problem. In this respect, one can think of policy attention as a cognitive response to media cues. Policy actions, on the other hand, are measures of policy makers' behavior. As such, they are slower to change in response to increased media attention because they are constrained by external circumstances and organizational routines (e.g., legal and budgetary considerations, committee work, etc.). For this reason, both types of measures are included in this study.

. . . The current study uses two measures of policy attention. The first is the number of congressional hearings on the issue of DD. . . . The second measure of policy attention is all DD-related bills that were introduced to the United States Congress from 1978 to 1995 (see Yanovitzky & Bennett, 1999). . . .

. . . Two measures of DD-related policy actions are used in this study. The first is the annual amount of federal appropriation for curbing DD between 1978 and 1995. . . . The second measure of policy actions is the adoption of anti-DD laws by all 50 states and the District of Columbia between 1978 and 1995. . . .

Results

Media Attention to the DD Issue

Figure 24-1 displays the number of DD-related news stories in each month from 1978 to 1995. Although the monthly number of stories is quite volatile over this time period, the pattern of change in media attention to the DD problem is immediately apparent. There was little media attention to the DD problem between 1978 and 1980 (an average of 7 stories per month). Then, media attention to the problem peaked rapidly between 1981 and 1983 (by about 80%) and from 1984 onward, stayed at about the same level (perhaps even started to decline at the beginning of the 1990s). . . .

The majority of these news stories (81%) can be simply characterized as episodic journalistic reports on actual DD incidents (i.e., accidents, arrests, court proceedings) that took place in communities nationwide. The remaining stories were (although not exclusively) reports on DD-related policy measures such as legislation and appropriation, publicized police sobriety checkpoints and other enforcement efforts (particularly around major holidays),

Figure 24-1   National News Coverage of the Drunk-Driving Issue, United
               States, 1978–1995 (N = 216 months)

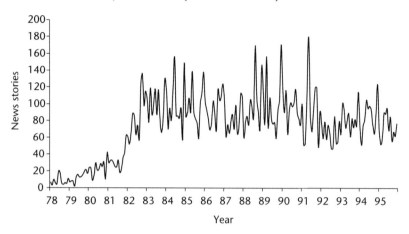

reports about DD-related studies (e.g., evaluations of anti-DD measures such as raising the minimum drinking age and setting lower legal BAC [blood alcohol concentration] levels), and more thematic discussions of the social implications of DD behavior. Ninety-six percent of these stories were coded as favorable toward social measures against DD (i.e., a one-sided issue) suggesting, at least in theory, a greater potential for media effects on policy makers' response to this issue (Baumgartner & Jones, 1993; Zaller, 1992).

DD-Related Policy Attention and Actions

Table 24-1 compares the trend in DD-related news coverage between 1978 and 1995 to the trends in DD-related policy attention and actions. Columns 3 through 6 in this table document changes over time in policy attention to the DD issue. From 1978 to 1980, only 5 DD-related bills were introduced in Congress. The number of bills jumped to 25 in the following period (1981–1984), continued to increase (although not monotonically) from 1985 to 1988 (39 bills), and then gradually declined from 1989 to 1991 (25 bills) and from 1992 to 1995 (24 bills). The number of bills aimed at increasing legal deterrence of drunk drivers was substantially higher than that of other types of bills throughout the entire research period. Overall, deterrence bills occupied about 60% of the DD-related congressional legislative agenda.

A similar pattern characterizes DD-related congressional hearings. Ad hoc DD-related congressional hearings focused on topics such as the legal minimum drinking age, strategies to curb DD, bans on alcohol advertising, alcohol warning labels, and the creation of nationwide information systems for the close monitoring of recidivist drunk drivers. Routine DD-related con-

Table 24-1   Trends in National News Coverage of Drunk Driving (DD) and DD-Related Policy Attention and Actions, United States, 1978–1995

| | | DD-related policy attention | | | | DD-related policy actions | | | |
| | | DD-related congressional bills | | DD-related congressional hearings | | DD-related federal appropriation | | Diffusion of DD-related legislation | |
Period	Average number of news stories per month	All bills	Deterrence bills	Routine hearings	Ad hoc hearings	Deterrence appropriation[a]	Education appropriation[a]	BAC laws[a]	ALR laws[a]
1978 to 1980	14.8	5	5	0	1	.09	.047	.44	0
1981 to 1984	78.5	25	9	5	13	.026	.052	.70	.98
1985 to 1988	93.4	39	23	11	16	.012	.10	.03	.09
1989 to 1991	96.3	25	14	13	4	.0001	.09	.02	.07
1992 to 1995	76.3	24	12	16	7	.005	.065	.01	.065

Note: BAC = blood alcohol concentration; ALR = administrative license revocation.

[a] Entries represent the rate of change between adjacent periods adjusted for each period's length.

gressional hearings, on the other hand, centered on DD-related appropria-tions, reauthorization, and nominations. Recall that according to study hypotheses, media attention to the DD problem is expected to affect ad hoc congressional hearings that, unlike routine hearings, are less likely to be in-fluenced by institutional and organizational routines. As Hypothesis 1 sug-gests, the number of DD-related ad hoc congressional hearings increased rap-idly from 1981 to 1984 (a total of 13 hearings) in comparison to the previous period (a single hearing between 1978 and 1981). Whereas the number of routine congressional hearings increased as well during this time, the ob-served change in the volume of routine hearings (from 0 in the first period to 5 in the second) was not as substantial as the one observed for ad hoc hear-ings. From 1985 to 1988, the number of ad hoc hearings continued to be higher than that of routine hearings (16 compared to 11) but, as proposed by Hypothesis 2, routine hearings were increasingly more common from 1989 to 1995 (29 vs. 11 ad hoc hearings) when media coverage started to wane.

The remaining columns in Table 24-1 examine the proposition of Hy-pothesis 3 that policy actions will decrease as media attention to the DD problem wanes and that, over time, ad hoc solutions to the problem (i.e., de-terrence) will be gradually replaced by more institutional, long-term solu-tions (i.e., investments in education and prevention programs). Before ana-lyzing the information contained in these columns, however, it is worth noting that DD-related policy actions in the beginning of the 1980s centered primarily on deterrence measures. . . . This focus on deterrence is consistent with the findings regarding the nature of policy attention to the DD problem as well as with the Hypothesis 3 expectation that policy actions will corre-spond to the solutions advocated in the media.

Returning to Table 24-1, we note that changes in the volume of policy ac-tions across periods are presented as the rate of change between adjacent pe-riods. The measures of policy actions used in this study are either cumulative (diffusion of DD-related legislation across states) or incremental by nature (DD-related appropriation). This forces the trend in these variables to be lin-ear and incremental over time, thus creating the illusion that the volume of policy actions increased continuously over time. Rate of change, in this re-spect, is a more sensitive measure of fluctuations in the volume of policy actions.

The results demonstrate that the diffusion rate of both ALR and BAC laws increased rapidly between 1981 and 1984 in comparison to the remaining periods (both before and after). Furthermore, from 1985 onward, the rate of diffusion continued to increase but at a more gradual pace than before. A somewhat different pattern characterizes appropriation for enforcement of anti-DD laws. As Table 24-1 shows, appropriation for enforcement increased rapidly between 1978 and 1980, before media attention to the DD problem increased. From 1981 to 1995, rates of change increased at a decreasing rate. A possible explanation for these differential patterns is that different types of policy actions vary in the level of institutional and organizational constraints that are attached to them. Specifically, federal appropriation is the outcome of a lengthy and stable political process that encompasses many governmental units and bureaucratic routines and therefore is less susceptible to rapid change in response to sudden inputs to the political system. Finally, the pattern of change in federal appropriation for prevention and education programs seems to follow the Hypothesis 3 prediction that, over time, policy actions aimed at establishing long-term solutions to the problem will increase at an accelerated rate. Between 1984 and 1995, appropriation for DD-related prevention and public education programs more than tripled (from $33.4 million in 1984 to $83.4 million in 1995), and the rate of change in this measure increased at an accelerated rate (although most of these changes were incremental). . . . [M]ost of these findings are consistent with the study's hypotheses. . . .

Discussion

Overall, the results of the current study support the proposition that intensive periods of media attention to issues are instrumental in attracting policy attention to public problems that are low on policy-makers' agendas while creating a sense of urgency among policy makers to generate immediate, short-term solutions to public problems. The findings also suggest that this impact is likely to be contingent on several key factors. For one, the degree of the media-policy association seems to vary over the life course of the issue on the media agenda. The impact of media attention on policy making is strongest at the beginning of the media issue attention cycle. Once media attention decreases in intensity, related policy outputs decrease as well and gradually shift from ad hoc solutions to long-term solutions for the problem.

Other key factors involve the specific characteristics of the issue at hand and particularly impinge on the likelihood that increased media attention to issues will actually result in policy actions rather than increased policy attention alone. For example, it is clear that in the case of DD, media attention to the issue was overwhelmingly one-sided (i.e., against DD) simply because there was no one who would argue for involvement in DD behavior. Coupled with the media's enthusiastic endorsement of specific solutions to this problem (i.e., increasing deterrence measures), the fact that a significant impact of news coverage on DD-related policy making was present is not surprising but rather expected (cf. Zaller, 1992). It seems reasonable to expect that issues surrounded by social debate and criticism (i.e., gun control and abortion) will be presented as such in the media and would be predictive of slower and gradual change (if any) in policy actions over time.

The other side of this is policy-makers' own stands on the issue prior to its discovery by the media. Previous evidence regarding DD-related policy (McCarthy, 1994; Reinarman, 1988) suggest that policy makers were already supportive of increasing deterrence measures against drunk drivers before media attention to this problem peaked during the early 1980s and therefore had little problem generating policy responses that were similar to the ones advocated in the media. This implies that the impact of media attention on policy is also a function of the extent to which media framing of public problems serves policy-makers' interests or the interests they represent. If media frames of problems put policy makers in an uncomfortable position, they are likely to respond more slowly to the problem by sticking to organizational and institutional routines (e.g., convening a panel or a committee to study the issue). One may also hypothesize, based on the results of the current study, that the ability of news coverage to promote policy changes is contingent on policy options that are available to policy makers and the degree of freedom or flexibility (political, economic, and moral) they have to pursue such options—both of which were fairly high in the DD case. Thus, although the case of DD may be considered unique in several respects, it begins to draw our attention to several dimensions of interest in terms of the expectation for media effects on policy that can then be examined in the context of other public issues.

. . . [P]otential limitations of this study should be noted. . . . One is that the issue of DD was examined in isolation from media and policy attention to other public problems. There is little doubt that the simultaneous competition between issues that seek media and policy attention has an important role in shaping the dynamics of the media-policy connection and that studying several issues at a time may be desirable (Hilgartner & Bosk, 1988). . . . A second potential shortcoming . . . is that the theoretical links examined here are primarily drawn from individual-level processes that were not directly observed with the available data. For this reason, the analysis performed here cannot confirm the presence of these processes but can only speak to their plausibility. Finally, and on a related note, the use of aggregated secondary data in this study did not allow for testing the study's hypotheses as rigorously as possible or testing more elaborated hypotheses about the media-policy connection. . . .

To summarize, the main contribution of this study is in conceptualizing and examining the media-policy connection as a dynamic process. Many studies that examine the media-policy connection simply seek to demonstrate an association between the media agenda and the policy agenda at a given point or over time (Dearing & Rogers, 1996) without testing hypotheses on the dynamic mechanisms that produce this association. At minimum, the findings of the current study point to the importance of separating media effects on policy attention from effects on actual policy outputs as key for studying this dynamic relationship. From this perspective, the question of whether there are effects of news coverage of issues on related policy making may be less important than the question about the particular circumstances under which news coverage is likely to influence policy-makers' decisions and behavior. More specifically, whereas heightened media attention to issues is almost always expected to result in policy-makers' increased attention to this issue, it is the extent to which media attention is capable of moving policy makers from the attention phase to the action phase that seems to be worthy of scholarly attention.

References

Baumgartner, F. R., & Jones, B. D. (1993). *Agendas and instability in American politics*. Chicago: University of Chicago Press.

Bennett, C., & Yanovitzky, I. (2000, September). *Patterns of congressional news media use: The questions of selection bias and third person effect*. Paper presented at the annual meeting of the American Political Science Association, Washington, DC.

Borkenstein, R. F. (1985). Historical perspective: North American traditional and experimental response. *Journal of Studies on Alcohol*, 10, 3–12.

Dearing, J. W., & Rogers, E. M. (1996). *Agenda setting*. Thousand Oaks, CA: Sage.

Diani, M. (1996). Linking mobilization frames and political opportunities: Insights from regional populism in Italy. *American Sociological Review*, 61, 1053–1069.

Downs, A. (1972). Up and down with ecology: The issue-attention cycle. *Public Interest*, 28, 38–50.

Edwards, G. C., & Wood, B. D. (1999). Who influences whom? The president, Congress, and the media. *American Political Science Review*, 93(2), 327–344.

Fan, D. P. (1988). *Prediction of public opinion from the mass media: Computer content analysis and mathematical modeling*. New York: Greenwood.

Gamson, W. A. (1992). *Talking politics*. Cambridge, MA: Cambridge University Press.

Gusfield, J. (1981). *The culture of public problems: Drinking-driving and the symbolic order*. Chicago: University of Chicago Press.

Hess, S. (1984). *The government-press connection: Press officers and their offices*. Washington, DC: Brookings Institution.

Hilgartner, J. R., & Bosk, C. L. (1988). The rise and fall of social problems: A public arenas model. *American Journal of Sociology*, 94(1), 53–78.

Iyengar, S. (1991). *Is anyone responsible? How television frames political issues*. Chicago: University of Chicago Press.

Iyengar, S., & Kinder, D. R. (1987). *News that matters: Television and American opinion*. Chicago: University of Chicago Press.

Iyengar, S., & Simon, A. (1993). News coverage of the Gulf crisis and public opinion: A study of agenda setting, priming, and framing. *Communication Research*, 20, 365–383.

Kingdon, J. W. (1984). *Agendas, alternatives, and public policies.* Boston: Little, Brown.

Krippendorff, K. (1980). *Content analysis.* London: Sage.

Kuhn, D. (1991). *The skills of argument.* New York: Cambridge University Press.

Lemert, J. B. (1981). *Does mass communication change public opinion after all? A new approach to effects analysis.* Chicago: Nelson-Hall.

Linsky, M. (1986). *How the press affects federal policy making.* New York: Norton.

Mathews, J. (1982, May 18). An angry grandmother leads drive against child molesters. *The Washington Post,* pp. A-2.

McCarthy, J. D. (1994). Activists, authorities, and media framing of drunk driving. In E. Larana, H. Johnston, & J. R. Gusfield (Eds.), *New social movements: From ideology to identity* (pp. 133–167). Philadelphia: Temple University Press.

McGuire, W. J. (1989). Theoretical foundations of campaigns. In R. E. Rice & C. K. Atkin (Eds.), *Public communication campaigns* (2nd ed., pp. 43–65). Newbury Park, CA: Sage.

Neuman, W. R. (1990). The threshold of public attention. *Public Opinion Quarterly, 54,* 159–176.

Petty, R. E., & Cacioppo, J. T. (1986). *Communication and persuasion: Central and peripheral routes to attitude change.* New York: Springer-Verlag.

Price, V., & Tewksbury, D. (1997). News values and public opinion: A theoretical account of media priming and framing. In G. A. Barnett & F. J. Boster (Eds.), *Progress in the communication sciences* (pp. 173–212). Greenwich, CT: Ablex.

Reinarman, C. (1988). The social construction of an alcohol problem: The case of Mothers Against Drunk Driving and social control in the 1980s. *Theory and Society, 17,* 91–120.

Roessler, P. (1999). The individual agenda-designing process: How interpersonal communication, egocentric networks, and mass media shape the perception of political issues by individuals. *Communication Research, 26(6),* 666–700.

Rogers, E. M., Dearing, J. W., & Chang, S. (1991). AIDS in the 1980s: The agenda-setting process for a public issue. *Journalism Monographs, 126.*

Yanovitzky, I., & Bennett, C. (1999). Media attention, institutional response, and health behavior change: The case of drunk driving, 1978–1996. *Communication Research, 26(4),* 429–453.

Zaller, J. R. (1992). *The nature and origins of mass opinion.* New York: Cambridge University Press.

Part V

GUIDING PUBLIC POLICIES

The media affect public policies in a variety of ways. Publicity may engender governmental action when none might otherwise have taken place. Or it may narrow, but not foreclose, the policy choices available to public officials. Alternatively, by mobilizing hostile public or interest group opinions, the media may force a halt to ongoing or projected policies. American journalists usually disclaim any motivation to influence public policies through their news stories. Except for the editorial pages, their credo calls for objective, neutral reporting. Investigative stories are the only major exception to this rule; they are designed to probe important social and political problems and engender remedial action. This section contains examples of policy impact studies that involve all of these contingencies in both domestic and foreign policy domains.

The opening selection shows how media coverage may affect the decisions of government officials who deal with foreign policies. From intensive interviews with several hundred public officials, Patrick O'Heffernan concludes that the information base for foreign policy making is heavily influenced by news stories. Media attention to foreign policy issues may force them onto the public policy agenda, often prematurely. Positive comments about projected policies help get them adopted, negative comments hinder adoption. More blatantly, journalists may advocate their own policy preferences or serve as willing conduits for proposals initiated by official partisans of various causes.

Whereas O'Heffernan's essay deals with government officials' beliefs about media impact, Robert M. Entman tracks the actual influence of news media in specific foreign policy situations. His research suggests that influence over policy requires control over the framing of foreign policy issues. Entman acknowledges that it is extraordinarily difficult to assign precise weights to the influence exercised by various stakeholders, but believes that government officials and journalists usually control framing. The influence enjoyed by the public is more problematic because public opinions are articulated by elites, including journalists, who have been active and partisan opinion shapers. Given the elites' firm control over shaping and interpreting public opinions, one must wonder whether media coverage actually impairs the chances for public influence in the realm of foreign policy.

William and Harva Hachten's essay further enhances the concerns over muzzling of the public's voice when it comes to foreign policies. In times of war, when foreign policy stakes often are extraordinarily high, governments usually manage to control the news by barring journalists from gathering news on their own and spoon-feeding them the information that public officials want to disseminate. Government control over the news supply during the 1991 Gulf War is a perfect example. With some notable exceptions, government news manipulations managed to turn the American press into a public relations tool that informed the public about military successes but failed to show the costs of major policy failures.

The Hachtens' essay makes journalists look like docile lapdogs enjoying the news tidbits that government officials drop into their collective mouths. That image is far from the heralded ideal of journalists as watchdogs who alert the public to flawed policies and official misbehaviors. W. Lance Bennett and William Serrin delineate the crucial functions that watchdog journalism, at its best, can serve in keeping government performance in democracies transparent. The authors record a number of brilliant successes. But they also bemoan colossal failures, usually due to inadequate resources for investigative journalism and a waning appetite for the time-consuming, meticulous, and often tedious hunts for information that investigative journalism requires.

The next essay deals with the news media's role in the implementation of public policies that require the public's cooperation on a large scale. Five health communication specialists—May G. Kennedy, Ann O'Leary, Vicki Beck, Katrina Pollard, and Penny Simpson—report on government efforts to enlist media help to publicize information about AIDS prevention and treatment. Their essay confirms that properly designed and attractively packaged health messages, embedded in news or entertainment programs, can stimulate sizeable numbers of readers, viewers, and listeners to act in line with a health policy's goals. Collaboration between the media and public officials works, as do similar efforts undertaken by news organizations on their own initiative.

The section ends with a tale about the significance of the specific frames used in depicting public policy issues—in this case abortion. Nayda Terkildsen, Frauke I. Schnell, and Cristina Ling tracked framing of the issue in news magazines over a twenty-year time span from 1960 onward. They found that arguments about abortion were cast into distinct frames

by parties eager to convince audiences that a particular policy would produce the best results and should therefore be adopted. The authors concluded that individual parties to the debate were unable to dominate media
framing. Rather, the news stories represented the journalists' interpretations
of the key issues that had emerged in the course of the debates among the
opposing parties. No single frame prevailed.

25

MASS MEDIA ROLES IN FOREIGN POLICY

Patrick O'Heffernan

Editor's Note

Do public officials assign an important role to the news media in making U.S. foreign policy? Political scientist Patrick O'Heffernan sought an answer by questioning senior policymakers serving the federal government between November 1977 and March 1988. The data were collected through 25 in-depth interviews conducted by the author, secondary analysis of 8 interview transcripts, and survey data collected from a sample of 483 high-level federal officials. The interview transcripts and survey data were gathered by a team of scholars headed by Martin Linsky for a study described more fully in Part VI, Selection 34. The interview responses, along with three case studies of foreign policy making during the study period, indicate that mass media play a variety of potentially important roles. However, the significance of these roles varies from case to case. Foreign policy officials disagree whether, on balance, mass media influence is a boon or a bane.

At the time of this writing, O'Heffernan taught at the Georgia Institute of Technology in Atlanta. He also held the position of adjunct professor in the Sam Nunn School of International Affairs.

The mass media today play distinct roles in the shaping and reality of American foreign policy. They function as:

- a rapid source of information useful for policy decisions
- an agenda setter which influences the agendas of the U.S. and other nations
- proxy for diplomats

Source: Patrick O'Heffernan, *Mass Media and American Foreign Policy: Insider Perspectives on Global Journalism and the Foreign Policy Process,* Westport, Conn.: Greenwood Publishing Group, Inc., 1991, chapter 5. Copyright © 1991 Allyn & Bacon Publishers. Reproduced with permission of Greenwood Publishing Group, Inc.

- diplomatic signaling system with policy influence
- a tool used by terrorists and nongovernmental organizations.

Television also plays distinct diplomatic roles through space bridges and on-air negotiations, sometimes called "television diplomacy." [1]

A Rapid Information Source

The mass media tell us about wars, disasters, highjackings, and elections around the world, often within hours of the event. In providing this near-instant notification of what is going on globally, the mass media serve four distinct roles as rapid information sources for policy makers: (a) policy officials use the media for immediate useful information, (b) policy makers use the mass media in the early stages of an issue to make decisions, (c) media are often the only source of policy information in crisis situations, and (d) the media's information is often seen as critical for policy making, sometimes more critical than official data. . . .

There was almost no question in the minds of policy makers interviewed that mass media are the fastest source of information on politically important events around the world. There was some divergence of opinion on how useful this information is for substantive decisions. Some policy officials interviewed indicated that the immediate media information's usefulness was limited, while others attested to both the media's speed of information delivery and its importance in their work. . . .

Daniel Kurtzer, Chief of the Middle Eastern Affairs Staff of the Policy and Planning Division of the State Department, argued that the media provided information unavailable from the official sources, even when officials were on the scene:

> . . . The embassy had its people talking to participants. I know, however, that the media's access to the participants was better than ours. So we were watching the media reporting more carefully in some respects than we were watching our own embassy's reporting.[2]

. . . Dennis Harter, Director of Press Operations at the Department of State, differentiated among the types of data delivered by the media and by other sources, and their usefulness:

> I agree [that the media is frequently the fastest source of information] for raw data, but not for analytical information. But raw information is also very important just to get a policy maker started on the right issue.[3]

. . . Eighty-seven percent of the interview respondents could recall cases when the media were the only source of information available for decision making, and 65 percent agreed that the media were frequently the fastest source of information for policy making. A small number of respondents, 8.7 percent, added that the media were the fastest information source only in crisis situations. . . .

A second aspect of the role of media as a rapid information source is the degree to which it is used at the earliest stage of the policy cycle, the Problem Identification Stage. Seventy-four percent of the foreign policy respondents to Linsky's survey indicated that mass media have some impact at this stage, compared to 28 percent who indicated no effect. Forty percent indicated that this effect was "large" or "dominant."

As shown in Table 25-1, 53 percent of the foreign policy officials who responded to Linsky's survey who perceive that the media have a large impact on policy at this stage rely on the media very much and 81 percent rely on it very much or somewhat, compared to 20 percent who perceive the media as having no impact on policy.[4]

Foreign policy personnel often rely on mass media–delivered information during crises. A majority of . . . the policy personnel interviewed indicated that media were frequently the most rapid source of information in crises situations. . . .Virtually all of those interviewed offered an anecdote or observation on the utility of the media in a crisis from their personal involvement. For example, former NSC staffer Robert Pastor pointed out that during a crisis, it is often members of the media who can make contact with key parties when official sources cannot:

> The news media is tremendously effective, more effective than anything else in following a fast-breaking violent crisis because the media can go to places that are under siege that the CIA can't go.[5] . . .

. . . In cases of fast-breaking crisis situations, most foreign policy officials interviewed reported that the media can and often does provide highly cru-

Table 25-1   Media Impact at Earliest Stage of Policy Cycle Compared with Officials' Reliance on Media for Information (percent)

	Reliance on media for information		
Media impact	Very little	Some	Very much
None	52.0	28.0	20.0
Some	21.8	40.6	37.5
Large	18.4	28.9	52.6

χ square = 12.39 @ 6 D.F., Sig = .5, R = .29, N = 95

cial information. Former Assistant Secretary of State Langhorn Motley noted that during highjackings, CNN not only got information out before the other networks, but before official sources could get geared up to let Washington know what was happening and who the players were. Eighty-seven percent of those interviewed agreed . . . and could recall situations wherein the media were the only source of information for policy making in fast-breaking crises or terrorist incidents.

Media Role: Terrorist Tool

Much has been made in the academic and popular press of "terrorvision"—the successful use of the media by terrorists to influence U.S. foreign policy—such as described in the TWA 847 highjacking case. But is terrorvision successful? Do all such media-terrorist relationships lead to changes in U.S. foreign policy? The policy officials interviewed for this research did not think so. They agreed that terrorists were often highly skilled and effective in using the media to provoke government responses to their actions, but they also felt that this did not necessarily result in significant policy changes in any more than a handful of cases. . . .

Eighty-three percent of the foreign policy officials surveyed by Linksy responded that the media magnify the influence of outside organizations, and 64 percent said that the use of media by outside organizations would gain attention from higher levels of government (less than 11 percent saw no effect). However, this increase in influence is not necessarily seen as changing policy outputs. Table 25-2 shows that there is no relation between policy officials' perception of the increase in a group's visibility due to media, and its effect on policy outputs.[6]

Most of those interviewed agreed that terrorists who obtained coverage in the media and used it well were treated differently than those who did not,

Table 25-2   Perception of Media Ability to Magnify Outside Influence and Impact on Foreign Policy Outputs (percent)

	Effect on policy outputs		
Group's influence raised	Low	High	Percentage of total
Yes	66.6	83.5	82.9
No	33.3	16.5	17.1

R = .00867 Sig = .1977
N = 94; χ square = 5.77 @ 4 D.F., Sig = .2168

that is, while overall policy may not necessarily be impacted by terrorist use of the media, tactical response certainly is. Ninety-one percent of the policy makers questioned agreed that the media increase the visibility of terrorists and their power to invoke governmental responses, and 74 percent said the media increase terrorists' power.[7] . . .

The ability of terrorists to use the media to force changes in U.S. foreign policy is as much or more a function of the vulnerability of the administration to publicized terrorists' tactics as to the skill of media use, and is by no means common. Poor use of media by terrorists, such as occurred in the *Achille Lauro* case, has little likelihood of impacting policy; skillful use of media, as in the TWA case, has a higher likelihood of impacting policy, but is not the sole or always the most important determinant of lasting policy change. Other factors include the domestic political situation in the U.S., the skill of the U.S. administration in using the media, the emergence of domestic lobbies and their use of the media, and ongoing relations and discussions with other governments who may be involved in the incident and who are impacted by the policy.

Media's Agenda-Setting Role

. . . The agenda-setting question asked of policy officials in the interviews was: "Does the media set the agenda of U.S. foreign policy officials either by globalizing local and regional events and elevating their salience, or by any other mechanism?" . . .

As noted above, a high percentage of those who responded to the survey perceived that individuals or outside groups who obtained media coverage were able to magnify their influence and gain the attention of higher levels of the foreign policy community. However, the interview transcripts revealed a variance in opinion among the officials on this question. Carter administration National Security Advisor Brzezinski saw the agenda setting going from the White House to the media, not the other way around.

> I think in an administration, if it's activist—and ours was in the area of foreign policy—it tends to determine agenda for the press. Not exclusively, and certainly many events transpire over which you have no control. But by and large we set the agenda.[8]

President Carter saw a definite media role in setting agendas when it globalized regions or countries, and told of an incident when the media's globalization of a regional event that was not even news almost derailed a major policy initiative:

> . . . when reports of Soviet troops in Cuba were broadcast. This was a very disturbing thing to us and interfered with the ratification of the SALT II

treaty, and caused us two–three weeks of research and the ultimate result was that it was not news but some candidate (Frank Church) made it a campaign issue with the help of the media.[9]

. . . The results from survey questions that asked to what degree negative or positive media coverage affected the importance of an issue in the foreign policy bureaucracy, shown in Table 25-3, indicate that a strong majority, 77 percent, of all foreign policy officials who responded to Linsky's survey perceived that positive or negative mass media coverage can increase the importance of an issue to the bureaucracy (the remaining 23 percent perceived no effect).[10]

This result was confirmed in the interview questions: A total of 82 percent of those interviewed for this study perceived that mass media attention to a regional event can put the region or the event on the nation's foreign policy agenda. A majority attributed this capability to media-stimulated domestic political forces, although some qualified this answer by saying this was the case only part of the time.

Additionally, the results of the "action" responses (those survey responses that specify that action was likely as a result of media coverage) provided an important qualification. They indicated that, while the media are perceived to be able to establish the importance of issues and often to move an item to a more senior person, it will rarely lead to a reassessment of a policy position on an issue already on the agenda. . . .

Policy officials often noted that it is . . . "global issues," such as environment, hunger, or amnesty, that are most susceptible to agenda setting by the mass media. They also noted that important events or issues not covered by the mass media can suffer in their ranking on the foreign policy agenda.

Most of those who responded positively to an interview question regarding the agenda-setting influence of the media attributed this influence to mass media's ability to stimulate or maintain domestic political forces. A few noted that the mechanism is one of the media *creating a positive policy environment for policy initiatives to be brought forward*. Often, interviewees said that policies put on the agenda by media were under study but could not be moved for priority or political reasons. Media stories provided the positive

Table 25-3   Perceived Effect of Media Coverage on Foreign Policy Agenda (percent)

Positive coverage affects agenda	15.5
Negative coverage affects agenda	33.0
Positive and negative coverage affects agenda	27.8
Total	77.3

N = 89

environment necessary for them to be moved. Roman Papaduick, Assistant Press Secretary for International Affairs in the Reagan White House, used the drought in Ethiopia as an example of this:

> What television did was bring the image home to the American public, but the policy had always been there. What happens is TV finds the problem, then finds the policy and marries the two. Therefore, [it] makes it look like the policy evolved to meet the problem.[11]

Dennis Harter of the State Department pointed to other areas "discovered" by the mass media after the policy officials had spent some time working on them, such as the international drug trade. But the media's ability to do so is seen by policy officials as circumscribed by three conditions:

1. Media influence varies with the nature of the issue, with global, multilateral issues being more susceptible to media influence then bilateral or military issues.
2. Media influence derives to some extent from the media's ability to stimulate domestic political forces to support or object to a policy initiative.
3. Media influence varies with the prevailing political environment, although it can influence or create that environment.

Media Role: Diplomatic Proxy

The mass media have been often criticized for meddling in foreign policy. But policy makers see media involvement as an infrequent occurrence, although one that can have very serious consequences. The TWA hijacking case provided several examples of media intervention in a negotiation situation, both as an instrument used by all sides, and as an independent entity pursuing its own objectives. The degree of this involvement can be seen from the extreme level of complaints about it during and after the fact: Television was smugly criticized by print media for usurping diplomatic roles;[12] President Reagan criticized the media in general and television in particular for interference in the negotiation process;[13] and television criticized itself for its mostly inadvertent involvement in affairs of state.[14] Even the TWA hostages complained that the television networks were using them to boost ratings and, in doing so, may have complicated efforts to free them.[15]

Whatever the actual involvement in foreign policy was during the TWA hijacking, it signals a basic change in the mass media–foreign policy community relationship. How much of a change can be seen by comparing John Scali's role as a backchannel interlocutor between Kennedy and Soviet officials during the Cuban missile crisis with the activities and criticism of television during the TWA 847 highjacking? Scali's role was kept relatively quiet, and when it did become widely known in the press and policy communities, it was generally seen as a positive, patriotic activity.[16] In the TWA case, television was virtually charged by government, other media, and even by itself with frustrating national policy. . . .

What are the perceptions of foreign policy officials about the involvement of the media in negotiations and diplomacy, either institutionally, or on an individual basis? Do they feel it is a widespread practice and if so, what is the impact on policy outputs? Does it lead to better or worse policies?

I found that policy officials interviewed for this study were generally aware of journalistic involvement in diplomacy: 74 percent of those personally interviewed knew of such cases or had heard of them. However, they rejected the media role as a positive one: 78 percent answered an unqualified "bad" when asked about the effect of this on U.S. policy outputs, and those that did not describe involvement as negative gave a qualified answer indicating that it was justified only under special circumstances.

While the majority of policy officials indicated that they personally knew of such a case, a review of the interview transcripts reveals that most had heard of cases secondhand, rather than firsthand. Most of those interviewed also mentioned the same cases, that is, John Scali in the Cuban missile crisis and Walter Cronkite behind the scenes on the Sadat visit. The interview transcripts show that while policy officials are aware of the incidents, their perception is that journalistic involvement is an infrequent occurrence and not a significant part of the flow of diplomacy. The 78 percent negative response cited above was strongly categorical, that is, journalistic involvement in international relations was seen as bad for policy in all cases, as described by Hodding Carter [a former State Department spokesman], "There is no place in diplomacy for journalists or anyone not authorized by the government." . . .

President Carter's experience gave him a broader point of view when asked about situations involving journalists and diplomacy. While recounting instances of mass media involvement in diplomacy that had very serious negative effects, Carter recognized a valuable role for the mass media in certain circumstances:

> those efforts by journalists can either be very beneficial or damaging. In some cases the journalists have access to terrorists' spokesmen and can receive proposals that might lead to a solution of a kidnapping or a hijacking of a plane when it is almost impossible for government policy to permit contact with criminals of that kind. Obviously, when the news is made known that the terrorists will accept these actions and the hostages will be released or the plane returned, then the government can decide whether it wants to accept terms of that kind without dealing directly with the hostage takers or hijackers.

But he added that the media can damage negotiations and put American lives and policies in danger:

> There are other times when pressures from journalists have resulted in very very serious damage to the well-being of hostages and other citizens of our country. The most notable example of that is when Mike Wallace and other reporters went to Iran and interrogated Ayatollah Khomeni very forcefully and publicly on 60 *Minutes* and news broadcasts, asking "will you release the hostages, will you direct the students to leave the embassy grounds?" and the inevitable response of Khomeni to the world public was "no, not unless the Shah is brought back."
>
> Well, once the news reporters forced Khomeni, possibly against his will, to make a public commitment of that kind, it was impossible for him to meet with or talk to any intermediaries that we would want to send to explore the opportunities at least for the hostages.

. . . Policy officials differed about the emergence of Ted Koppel–style "television diplomacy" in which national representatives are brought together on the air for discussions of the issues that divide them. Paralleling Koppel, networks and independent producers have begun to broadcast "space bridges" which link policy officials and citizens of different countries together by television to discuss issues that divide them.

What are the ramifications of this new use of television medium? Do televised interactions between U.S. and foreign leaders impact foreign policy, and if so, is the influence positive or negative? Television diplomacy was examined extensively in the interviews, both in specific questions and in the unstructured discussions.

Interview respondents were mixed in their view of TV diplomacy's effect on policy, but the weight was toward a negative perception: Only 26 percent said it helped sound policy, 35 percent said it both helped and hindered, 17 percent said it hurt, and 22 percent thought it was irrelevant. . . .

Media Role: Diplomatic Signal

. . . Those interviewed agreed that the most utilized and most effective technique of media use by foreign policy officials is for signaling American preferences to other nations. . . .

President Carter also pointed out the usefulness of the media to a head of state attempting to influence other governments.

> I used international media broadcast in several cases, we had nationwide broadcast to Poland and to Germany, including East Germany, and to Japan, where I would respond to questions from a fairly large audience in a town meeting forum. And with arrangements, even Communist governments [allowed] that the telecasts would be live and nationwide.

Diplomatic aspects of this transformation were frequently mentioned in the interviews, ranging from the use of the media as a communications device to negotiate with governments who cannot be contacted in other ways, to sending influential signals to the people and the agencies of other governments and receiving signals back from them. Examples of this use of the media include Presidential satellite addresses to foreign audiences, exchanging messages with foreign leaders through press conferences and news programs, and satellite conferences with embassy personnel in several countries simultaneously. . . .

Table 25-4 presents the results from analysis of foreign policy officials' response to Linsky's survey regarding government influence on media for policy purposes. The results clearly show a willingness on the part of foreign policy officials who responded to Linsky's questionnaire to obtain press coverage and to use the press for policy purposes: 86 percent of the survey respondents sought to influence media coverage of their agencies, and 72 percent indicated they or their staff were responsible for at least 10 percent of the actual coverage.

Table 25-5 presents results from the interview questions concerning the use of the media to influence foreign governments. These results essentially confirmed the survey findings that the use of the mass media is widespread among the policy officials interviewed: 78 percent reported using the media, many responding that the practice is constant. Table 25-5 also echoes the indications from the transcripts that print is the medium most often used to influence foreign governments (numbers indicate the percentages of respondents who answered positively in each category).

Seventy-eight percent of those interviewed agreed that mass media communication with other nations' peoples is a useful policy tool. Several volunteered that media communication with other nations' peoples has become a fact of life in the foreign policy process. A few also referred to President Reagan's use of WorldNet to broadcast to European audiences, and to the Christmas message broadcast exchange between the U.S. and the Soviet Union, as well as media events and televised speeches by U.S. officials on tour overseas.

Table 25-4   Policy Maker Influence of Media (percent)

Placed 10% or more of stories on agency	72.4
Sought to influence media coverage	85.7
Felt appropriate to leak to media	50.0
Leaks ok to consolidate support	66.7
Leak[s] ok to force action on issue	41.7

$N = 94$

Table 25-5   Policy Maker Perception of Media Use to Influence Other Nations (percent)

	Used to influence other governments	Used to influence other peoples
Print	44	33
TV	22	56
Wires	22	0
All media	33	11
Radio in Third World	11	44
Depends on nation	11	22

Note: Numbers are the percentage of *N. N* = 23. Totals add to more than 100% due to multiple answers.

. . . Print is the . . . medium of choice when using media to influence other government[s'] heads. The wire services and a mix of all media are employed significantly to reach governments, but not significantly in reaching people directly. And finally, radio is seen as . . . important as television in reaching mass audiences in the Third World. . . .

The evidence is also overwhelming that U.S. policy makers perceive that foreign governments try to use American mass media to manipulate American foreign policy. Ninety-two percent of the interview respondents reported that they could recall or had heard of cases of foreign government use of media to influence U.S. policy. The perception was strong in all agencies and in all government rankings. Many of the policy officials interviewed noted that other national leaders have been increasingly turning the media tables on the U.S., using American media to influence American public opinion and policy. Hodding Carter stated it bluntly:

> Certainly foreign governments used the media to influence the U.S. Government. Officials would constantly bring reporters in to get a message across. Sometimes overtly. I know very few sophisticated governments that didn't do it. I have known of reporters that have been used as carriers of messages. The media used the most is print.

. . . Harold Saunders' quote . . . describing the use of mass media as a fact of life in foreign policy sums up mass media's roles in foreign policy:

> International relations today is a continual process of policy making and policy influencing communities on both sides of the relationship, and television is a significant part of that interaction, and so are other forms of communication.

Notes

1. All quotes in this chapter are from my interviews with policy makers unless indicated otherwise.
2. Personal interview, Summer 1987, Department of State.
3. Personal interview, Summer 1987, Department of State.
4. Linsky's survey asked, "In your experience how significant was the impact of the press at this [the identification of the problem] stage of policy making?" and "To what degree did you rely on the [mass media] organizations for information about your policy areas?"
5. Personal interview, Carter Center, Atlanta, GA, Fall 1987.
6. Linsky survey questions cross-tabulated: #II.-10, "Overall, how great do you believe the effect of the media is on [foreign] policy?" and III.-3, "In your experience, did the ability of an individual or outside group to gain attention in the media magnify the group's influence?"
7. Interview questions #1, 2, and #13: N = 23.
8. Unpublished transcripts of Martin Linsky's interviews.
9. Personal interview, Fall 1987, Carter Center.
10. Question II.3a, "When an issue in your office or agency received what you saw as positive or negative coverage in the mass media, did that coverage increase the importance of the issue within the bureaucracy?"
11. Personal interview, Summer 1987, Washington, D.C.
12. *Washington Post,* June 20, 1985.
13. *Washington Post,* June 21, 1985.
14. CBS News, 6/21/85; ABC, CBS specials, 6/26/85; CBS, 6/28/85, with Ken Stein accusing network correspondents of engaging in diplomacy instead of journalism.
15. CBS News, 6/28/85.
16. For more information on Scali and opinions about his role, see *New York Times,* Jan. 13–16, 1989, for stories on meetings between Soviet, Cuban, and American officials involved in the crisis.

26

MEDIATING THE PUBLIC'S INFLUENCE ON FOREIGN POLICY

Robert M. Entman

Editor's Note

Foreign policy results from the interplay of many factors. Robert M. Entman disentangles these factors, using a series of case studies to discover the role played by public opinion. He demonstrates that the interactions produced by the publicity efforts of official and non-official elites, the images held by the public, and the objectives of journalists are so complex, and the actors so interdependent that no firm conclusions are possible about how much weight each factor deserves in a particular decision. However, the evidence clearly shows that the nature of news frames is crucial and that framing is dominated by elites, including journalists. The influence of the citizenry is less clear, partly because public opinion reflects the information disseminated by elites, and partly because using different yardsticks for measuring public opinion yields drastically different conclusions.

Entman is professor of communication and political science at North Carolina State University. He has authored numerous books, articles, and book chapters on media, politics, and public policy. His research has won numerous awards, including prizes sponsored by the American Political Science Association, the National Communication Association, and Harvard University's John F. Kennedy School of Government.

. . . Prior research into the impact of public opinion on public policy offers surprisingly little insight into exactly how elites figure out what the public is thinking. Most treatments simply assume that political motivations lead officials more or less accurately to detect and respond to public opinion. This

Source: Robert M. Entman, *Projections of Power: Framing News, Public Opinion, and U.S. Foreign Policy,* Chicago: University of Chicago Press, 2004, chapter 6, 123–143. Copyright © 2004 by the University of Chicago Press. Reprinted with the permission of the University of Chicago Press.

chapter opens up this critical path of political communication to reveal the complex interplay of news frames with the thinking of elites and citizens. Three insights . . . are especially pertinent here:

1. The public's actual opinions arise from framed information, from selected highlights of events, issues, and problems rather than from direct contact with the realities of foreign affairs.
2. Elites for their part cannot know the full reality of public thinking and feeling, but must rely on selective interpretations that draw heavily on news frames.
3. Policymakers relentlessly contend to influence the very news frames that influence them.

In this process, officials must take account of several facets of public opinion, not just the standard measure of majority preferences. Despite their importance to leaders, these distinct faces of public opinion are rarely tested apart in empirical research. . . .

Framing Is Inescapable

. . . For foreign affairs, few people have direct data, and most information originates in media reports even if it is passed along selectively (or framed) in conversation with informants who themselves saw the news. Answers to questions on how much the United States should spend on defense, for instance (the case discussed below), respond to media threat signals—few citizens have anywhere else to get their information on enemies' military intentions and capabilities.[1] At least for foreign policy, there are few if any cases where a pure, unmediated public opinion emerges directly from reality. That does not mean everyone responds to the media's frames identically, but it does mean that most people's opinions will be influenced by their reactions to the frames. . . .

. . . The real issue, and the important role for media and public opinion in the political process, is determining which problem definition, cause, and policy response gain widespread adherence. These interpretations are rarely automatically deduced from the event itself. . . .

[Public Opinion about] National Defense

. . . That observation brings us to the first case study in this chapter, on defense spending. An important article by Hartley and Russett[2] on the impact of public opinion on defense policy connects normative democratic theory with empirical data to ask "Who governs military spending in the United States?" It serves as a good basis for anchoring the analysis of the inescapability of framing in studying public opinion, and helps to clarify the often-neglected influences of news media on representation. Reflecting a view common in recent political science, the article concludes that "public opinion" significantly helps "govern." However, if much of the public opinion this study identifies is actually polling opinion, and thus has been influenced by media frames, that conclusion demands further scrutiny.

The study finds that between 1965 and 1990, "changes in public opinion consistently exert an effect on changes in military spending."[3] It measures public opinion by responses to a standard survey question: whether government is spending too little, too much, or about the right amount on defense. Employing pooled estimates from six different polling organizations to generate unusually reliable estimates, Hartley and Russett find that changes in the levels of "too little" (or "too much") responses significantly predict alteration in the total defense obligations Congress approved (spending figures in constant 1982 dollars).[4] On this basis the authors argue that, judging by the case of defense spending, Congress responded to public opinion, fulfilling its representative duties according to at least one reasonable version of democracy.

Of particular interest for our purposes here is the period encompassing the Carter and Reagan administrations (1977–89), which saw the widest swings in public sentiment and provided the best opportunity for congressional responsiveness, although similar arguments could be made for the Johnson and Nixon years. Surveys showed a large shift toward favoring more spending during the years 1978–81, and Congress did approve sharp increases in defense spending thereafter.

Yet Congress failed to respond to several other strains of what polls suggest were majority sentiments during the period. Congress did not mandate that Reagan approach nuclear negotiations seriously in his first term,[5] nor did it approve a nuclear freeze, though surveys showed majorities favoring such action, often by upwards of 75 percent. If one used the survey data only on the nuclear freeze while ignoring the data on defense spending, one could well conclude Congress was entirely unresponsive to the public on defense policy. Of course it may be that the public was conflicted on the nuclear freeze or that survey questions on it gave misleading impressions of the actual underlying individual preferences and priorities of citizens. But this only reinforces the point that public opinion is usually a product of selective interpretation or framing.

And the fact that, as Bartels notes, the same polls recording increases in public desires for higher spending on defense simultaneously recorded demands for "social programs, tax reduction, and fiscal responsibility," which "manifestly limited the ability of Congress to respond to each of them separately."[6] In this sense it would appear nearly arbitrary to pick one dimension where opinion and congressional action seemed to coincide while neglecting others where they did not, and then drawing general conclusions on government responsiveness.

Looking more carefully at defense spending data raises additional questions about representation. As Figure 26-1 suggests,[7] there was a noticeable lack of representation from 1982 to 1985, when Congress continued to raise defense spending despite the sharp dovish turn in polling opinion. Those favoring an increase rose from 40 percent in 1979 to 58 percent in 1980 and 60 percent in 1981. But the next year saw this proportion plummet to 35 percent, then to 22 percent in 1983, and even lower after that. Surveyed sentiment shifted even more sharply *away* from defense spending during this time than it had turned *toward* support between 1977 and 1981, so if Congress was responding to altered public sentiment it should have cut defense—or at least slowed the rate of increase—by 1983 or 1984. Yet defense spending began declining in real terms only in *fiscal 1990*. Defense allocations kept growing as public support declined. The *rate* of growth in spending began slowing notably in fiscal 1987, which might signify a response to public opinion.[8] But here we had decisions to raise defense budgets that persisted for eight years (1982–89) against a sharp and persistent dovish trend in opinion, a trend that soon reduced the proportion of citizens favoring those increases to a small minority. Classifying such policies as responsive would seem to mark a striking redefinition of democratic representation.[9]

Now it might be that officials interpreted the 1983 surge in negative media symbols spurred by the KAL incident [Korean Airlines plane shot down by Soviet fighter plane] as signaling that public opinion favored even more spending hikes, despite polls showing it did not. Such a possibility would be

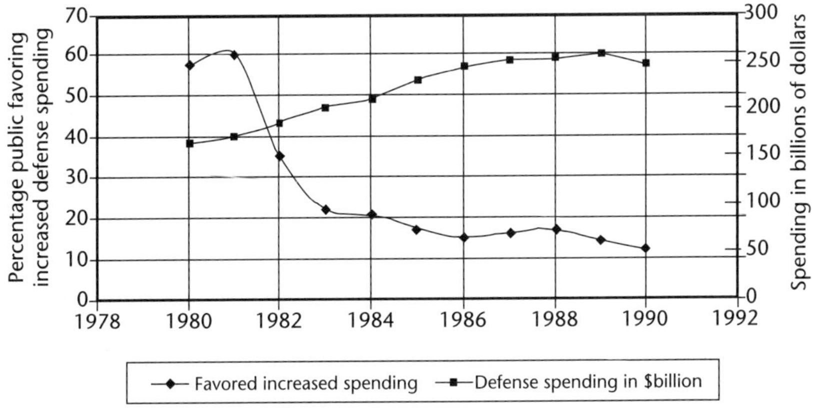

Figure 26-1   Increased Defense Spending Despite Drop in Public Support, 1980–1990

consistent with . . . research . . . indicating that officials infer elements of public opinion—perceived and anticipated majorities, and priorities—from media content. Perhaps elites anticipated that majorities would prefer more defense spending once they digested the heightened threat, and would weigh defense as a high enough priority to punish softness come election time. In addition, public opinion was frequently depicted in the media as highly supportive of the unabashedly hawkish Reagan. Even though Reagan's average approval ratings were actually quite low in his first term, news reports tended to laud his popularity.[10] And indeed, by his second term Reagan's average approval was relatively high. From the perceived majority support in his first term and actual polling opinion in his second, officials might well have inferred a low priority for the public's apparent desires to cut defense spending—and maybe they were correct. This could explain, in part, the lack of congressional responsiveness to the clear turn of surveyed majorities against higher defense budgets starting in 1982.

But another major reason for continued budget growth during this period was that long-term commitments to weapons systems had been made at the outset. Once weapons programs begin they are difficult to stop. Spending momentum is reinforced by electoral incentives in specific congressional districts where military spending is vital to the economy; their representatives often exert disproportionate influence over defense budgets. And an enormous military-industrial complex—very much including the Pentagon itself—has compelling incentives and vast resources to lobby Congress and engage in public relations initiatives to keep the defense contracts coming. These points further underscore the complexity of generalizing about government responsiveness to public opinion. . . .

. . . [T]he survey data on raising or cutting defense spending cannot tell us whether the public ever wanted the *magnitude* of increase approved by Congress during the 1980s. A much smaller increase might have been enough to satisfy most Americans even at their most hawkish. This seems especially likely in view of many other poll findings, some from the very surveys on "more" or "less" government spending that the authors use, of large majorities desiring higher budgets for crime fighting, education, health care, or other domestic priorities.[11] . . .

Furthermore, probing defense spending attitudes during the 1990s, after military budgets were reduced, Kull and Ramsay still found substantial willingness to support further cuts, so long as opinions were probed in detail and in larger context rather than simply asking the one question on spending more or less. Their data also showed elites tending to overestimate public support for high defense spending. . . . [T]o conclude from some poll evidence that the public really preferred to raise defense spending as much as Congress did over alternative uses of the money, scholars and Congress members themselves had to select some polling data and disregard the kinds of polls just cited. Include all the information at once and guidance from public opinion . . . becomes, at the least, murky. . . .

Acknowledging this process suggests limited expectations for democratic responsiveness. Public opinion includes a variety of individual preferences and intensities, contradictions and harmonies, which are imperfectly susceptible to measurement and aggregation whether by public officials or by scholars.[12] As for measuring government response, aside from whatever Congress as a whole decided, the degree to which individual legislators were responding to mass opinion also varied from member to member.

. . . [T]he degree of Soviet threat represented in the mass media corresponds closely to the movement of polling opinion on defense spending. The data in Figure 26-2 were compiled by searching for all *Washington Post* stories since 1977 (the first year the *Post*'s archives were computerized) in which the words "Russia" or "Soviet" occurred within twenty-five words of "aggression," "buildup," or "threat." Each story was checked to ensure the passages containing the terms did refer to the USSR's actions or intentions.[13]

The relationship graphs nicely; Figure 26-2 shows how the two moved in tandem. The number of threat references peaked in 1980, and public backing of higher defense budgets peaked the following year. (The sharp upward movement in mediated threats during 1983 resulted from Reagan's "evil empire" speech in March of that year and, especially, the autumn crisis over the Soviets' destruction of Korean Airlines Flight 007, after which the trend continued downward.) The correlation is quite high for this kind of research (Pearson's $r = .69$, $p < .01$), and the measure is not even very refined. With enough searching and fine-tuning one could probably match up media content with the movement of public opinion even more precisely.

Figure 26-2   Support for More Defense Spending and Media References to Soviet Threat

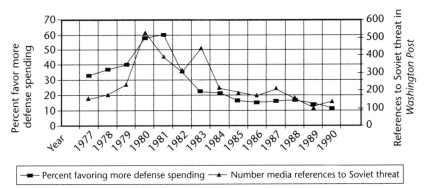

Indeed, if the media measure were entered into the Hartley-Russett calculations while omitting the survey data, one might conclude that Congress responds attentively to *media* rather than to public opinion. That is *not* the argument here. These data do not allow us to infer that alterations in the news caused policy changes; for one thing, again, defense spending did not drop significantly until 1990 despite the decline in mediated threats. Nor can the data prove that the changes in these symbols of threat were significant causes of the shifts in polling opinion. The point is quite different: namely, that it is difficult even conceptually to disentangle these relationships. Entering both the polling and media data together into an equation to explain variation in defense spending would not be appropriate to the complexity of the underlying relationships. Perceived and actual public sentiments influence and are influenced by elites and policy; all of these influence and are influenced by media; and obtainable measures of elite and mass opinion, of policy itself and of media content, are all deeply problematic.

. . . [L]ooking at all these forces at play, it appears the media played a role in shaping outcomes, along with leaders' talk, actions, and perceptions of public opinion, and the public's actual sentiments. In this jumbled spiral, this double helix, of reciprocal influences, movements, and resistances among elites and the public, evidence for the independent influence of public opinion on policy, or for genuinely democratic control of government by the public, is likely to remain incomplete.[14]

The dramatic divergence between surveyed opinion and defense spending during most of the 1980s suggests the need to develop more inclusive models that can explain the many spells of clear unresponsiveness as well as periods that seem to indicate responsiveness, that can distinguish the episodes where polling opinion changes independent of elite information blitzes from those where any shift arises from the White House's management of the news. Public opinion—whether framed as polling opinion, perceived and anticipated majorities, or priorities—appears to be a sporadic constraint,[15] not a controlling force on which government depends to guide its choices. Although media frames do serve as a kind of transmission belt, communicating the public's thinking up to elites as well as moving information in the reverse direction, so many complexities and imperfections mark this process that optimistic conclusions about public control appear unfounded. . . .

The Frozen Out Public

When we turn to public opinion articulated in a more active and precise form than merely answering survey questions, evidence suggests that far from being eager to respond, journalists and elites may in some instances not even favor much public input into foreign policy. Scholars have long recognized that, however accounted and described, public opinion surveys send imprecise signals.[16] Perhaps a more efficient vehicle for the expression of public opinion than surveys are social movements. A paper written jointly with Andrew Rojecki[17] explored the media's unfavorable framing of the "nuclear freeze" movement. This section summarizes its findings and draws lessons for the questions raised in this chapter.

Two factors make the freeze particularly noteworthy as a test of media frames' ability to influence perceptions of public opinion and, . . . perhaps affect government responses. First, poll after poll revealed a stable and large majority in favor of the movement's basic proposal: freezing the nuclear arsenals of the United States and its prime adversary, the Soviet Union, at the levels of overkill prevailing in the early 1980s, and then negotiating strategic arms limitations. If Congress were consistently responsive to public opinion (or in the terms of this chapter, to polling opinion), we would expect to see passage of legislation supporting this stable majority. Second, the freeze was a policy option actively pressed on government by a large, organized, and determinedly mainstream political movement in the best tradition of grassroots activism. Unlike many prior movements, most notably the groups protesting the Vietnam War, freeze advocates and leaders were at pains to portray the movement in ways that would reassure rather than alienate the average, moderate American.[18]

For a movement with national ambitions, grassroots networks can help spread activation, but the media will be crucial for getting the word out to the mass of potential supporters. . . . [U]nfavorable media assessments can seriously weaken a group's recruitment efforts. Apart from this, the news helps determine whether elites feel pressure to support the movement's policy goals. Since elites use news treatment as surrogates for public opinion, positive coverage can convey to them that citizens favor the policy and that the issue merits a high and favorable place on the agenda.[19]

Unfavorable media framing of the movement discouraged involvement by those ordinary citizens who supported the remedy but remained outside the group's activities; these potential recruits may not have been able to tell that they were actually part of a vast majority. The power of the media's framing was to inhibit ordinary Americans—and their leaders—from making mental associations between the freeze and such legitimizing concepts as "democracy" and "public opinion." Instead news frames tended to make delegitimizing associations, at least within media texts, and perhaps influenced audiences' minds. For example, stories frequently alluded to the frivolous hippies or the even more unpopular antiwar dissidents of the 1960s. The dearth of favorable publicity diminished any sense among the movement's inactive supporters that the freeze idea might legitimately demand a place on the agenda and a positive, concrete government response—or that perhaps they should vote against officials who failed to respond. In this way negative media treatment might have lowered the pressure elites felt to act favorably on the proposal— . . . reducing the *priority* of this particular policy preference—thereby providing political cover for an unresponsive government.

Conclusion

Public opinion cannot be divorced from the political discourse and media frames that surround it. The apparent impact of the public on government policy often arises from a circular process in which government officials respond to the polling opinions, anticipated or perceived majorities, and priorities that many of them helped create. Arguably that was the case with defense spending. And when it came to the nuclear freeze proposal, government disregarded and journalists on balance derogated an immense and stable majority of poll respondents. Just as Destler and others have suggested, there is some evidence in this that, rhetorical endorsements of democracy notwithstanding, foreign policy elites (and journalists) would just as soon keep the public out of the loop.[20] In any case, governing elites at best respond to selected interpretations of public opinion, and that almost certainly gives media frames a central role in the process of representation. For these and other reasons discussed above, any match between the majority positions registered by surveys and government decisions supplies imperfect evidence for the extent of democracy in the foreign policymaking process. . . .

Notes

1. This is not to deny that personal ideology plays a major role too. Many Americans, elites and citizens alike, regularly see imminent threats from the communists, terrorists, or other enemies no matter what the media are reporting.
2. Hartley and Russett 1992; also see Wlezien 1996.
3. Hartley and Russett 1992, 905.
4. Ibid., 907.
5. See Talbott 1984, on Reagan's negotiating approach.
6. Bartels 1991, 466.
7. The public opinion figures are the same as those used by Hartley and Russett. The spending figures are actual defense expenditures (not as in Hartley and Russett, defense authorizations), in constant 1982 dollars, taken from the *Budget of the United States Government, Fiscal 1992*, 69–70. . . .
8. Cf. Wlezien 1996, 87.
9. According to Erikson, MacKuen, and Stimson 2002, 359, it takes about eight years for policy (measured as major domestic policy laws passed by Congress) to catch up with and match opinion changes, which they view as appropriate to the Madisonian structure (checks and balances) of the U.S. government. So the findings here do accord with Erikson et al.'s model, since defense spending was finally cut in 1990, about eight years after polls indicated the public wanted reductions. . . . What the finding in this chapter and the findings of the far more complicated and exhaustive study by Erikson et al. reveal, of course, is that there is

no objective basis for concluding a system is doing a good enough job of responding to public desires. . . .

10. This provides another example of the frequent disjunctions between perceived majorities as depicted in the news and actual polling opinion as measured by surveys. See King and Schudson 1991.

11. Page and Shapiro 1992, chaps. 2 and 4.

12. Cf. Herbst 1993, 1998; see Page and Shapiro 1992, 263–74 on the twists and turns in public and elite opinion about foreign policy, and Page 2002 on the many complexities of measuring public opinion and its impacts on policy.

13. Spending opinion data from Hartley and Russett 1992, 909.

14. Page 2002 provides a detailed analysis of these matters. Manza and Cook (2002, 21) write: "Quantitative studies have established a case for . . . policy responsiveness to public opinion. But because these studies tend to include few other covariates they may miss factors that mediate or precede the relationship between opinion and policy." They also note: "[B]ecause foreign and defense policies are often event- and crisis-driven, there are sharp problems of causal inference. When a foreign crisis changes the context within which the public views a question, rapid changes in public attitudes are possible, which may, in turn, appear to be associated with later changes in policy. But in such cases, it appears likely that the same factors that move public opinion also move elites and the overall direction of policy making" (30 n. 7).

15. Cf. Sobel 2001; Jacobs and Shapiro 2000; Powlick and Katz 1998.

16. E.g., cf. Herbst 1993; Verba and Nie 1987.

17. Entman and Rojecki 1993; cf. Rojecki 1999. Also see Meyer 1995.

18. Cf. Gitlin 1980; Rojecki 1999.

19. Cf. Bennett 1993; Lipsky 1968.

20. Destler 2001; Powlick and Katz 1998. Adherents of the realist school (Keohane 1986; cf. Foyle 1999) would defend this elitist position of trying to maintain public quiescence (cf. Edelman 1988; Jacobs and Shapiro 2000) to allow officials maximum freedom of action so they can best pursue the national interest in the anarchic international system.

References

Bartels, Larry M. 1991. Constituency Opinion and Congressional Policymaking: The Reagan Defense Buildup. *American Political Science Review* 85: 457–75.

Bennett, W. Lance. 1993. Constructing Publics and Their Opinions. *Political Communication* 10, no. 2: 101–20.

Destler, I. M. 2001. The Reasonable Public and the Polarized Policy Process. In *The Real and the Ideal: Essays on International Relations in Honor of Richard H. Ullman,* ed. Anthony Lake and David Ochmanek, 75–90. Lanham, Md.: Rowman and Littlefield.

Edelman, Murray. 1988. *Constructing the Political Spectacle.* Chicago: University of Chicago Press.

Entman, Robert M., and Andrew Rojecki. 1993. Freezing out the Public: Elite and Media Framing of the U.S. Anti-Nuclear Movement. *Political Communication* 10, no. 2: 151–67.

Erikson, Robert S., Michael B. MacKuen, and James A. Stimson. 2002. *The Macro-Polity.* New York: Cambridge University Press.

Foyle, Douglas. 1999. *Counting the Public In: Presidents, Public Opinion, and Foreign Policy.* New York: Columbia University Press.

Gitlin, Todd. 1980. *The Whole World Is Watching: News Media in the Making and Unmaking of the New Left.* Berkeley: University of California Press.

Hartley, Thomas, and Bruce Russett. 1992. Public Opinion and the Common Defense. *American Political Science Review* 86: 905–15.

Herbst, Susan. 1993. *Numbered Voices: How Opinion Polling Has Shaped American Politics.* Chicago: University of Chicago Press.

___. 1998. *Reading Public Opinion: How Political Actors View the Democratic Process.* Chicago: University of Chicago Press.

Jacobs, Lawrence, and Robert Y. Shapiro. 2000. *Politicians Don't Pander: Political Manipulation and the Loss of Democratic Responsiveness.* Chicago: University of Chicago Press.

Keohane, Robert. 1986. *Neo-realism and Its Critics.* New York: Columbia University Press.

King, Elliot, and Michael Schudson. 1991. The Myth of the Great Communicator. *Columbia Journalism Review* 26 (November/December): 37–39.

Lipsky, Michael. 1968. Protest as a Political Resource. *American Political Science Review* 62, no. 4: 1144–58.

Manza, Jeff, and Fay Lomax Cook. 2002. The Impact of Public Opinion on Public Policy: The State of the Debate. In *Navigating Public Opinion,* ed. Jeff Manza, Fay Lomax Cook, and Benjamin I. Page, 17–32. New York: Oxford University Press.

Manza, Jeff, Fay Lomax Cook, and Benjamin I. Page, eds. 2002. *Navigating Public Opinion: Polls, Policy, and the Future of American Democracy.* New York: Oxford University Press.

Meyer, D. S. 1995. Framing National Security: Elite Public Discourse on Nuclear Weapons during the Cold War. *Political Communication* 12, no. 2: 173–92.

Page, Benjamin I. 2002. The Semisovereign Public. In *Navigating Public Opinion: Polls, Policy and the Future of American Democracy,* ed. Jeff Manza, Fay Lomax Cook, and Benjamin I. Page, 325–44. New York: Oxford University Press.

Page, Benjamin I., and Robert Y. Shapiro. 1992. *The Rational Public.* Chicago: University of Chicago Press.

Powlick, Philip J., and Andrew Z. Katz. 1998. Defining the American Public Opinion/Foreign Policy Nexus. *International Studies Quarterly* 42, no. 1 (Supp. 1): 29–63.

Rojecki, Andrew. 1999. *Silencing the Opposition: Anti-Nuclear Movements and the Media in the Cold War.* Urbana: University of Illinois Press.

Sobel, Richard. 2001. *The Impact of Public Opinion on U.S. Foreign Policy since Vietnam: Constraining the Colossus.* New York: Oxford University Press.

Talbott, Strobe. 1984. *Deadly Gambits.* New York: Knopf.

Verba, Sidney, and Norman Nie. 1987. *Participation in America: Political Democracy and Social Equality.* Chicago: University of Chicago Press.

Wlezien, Christopher. 1996. Dynamics of representation: The Case of U.S. Spending on Defence. *British Journal of Political Science* 26, no. 1: 81–103.

27

REPORTING THE GULF WAR

William Hachten with the collaboration
of Harva Hachten

Editor's Note

Images of war shown on television screens arouse antiwar sentiment in the
United States; an emotionally stirred public will then stop bellicose leaders
who dare not defy public opinion. This has been the folk wisdom until recently.
But the 1991 Gulf War, pitting Iraq against an alliance of United Nations members, proved that the antiwar scenario does not necessarily occur. War images
can be manipulated by governments to hide the horrors of combat. The military can supply attractive battlefield pictures and stories that journalists find
difficult to refuse. The military also can bar the press from access to potentially
embarrassing scenes and persuade the public that national security requires
such restraints. Reporters' complaints go unheeded until after the war, when it
is too late to undo the effects of controlled coverage. In the Gulf War, the end
result was a picture-book conflict that glorified the battlefield skills of military
leaders and largely concealed the pain and suffering inflicted through air and
ground combat. The public cheered. While the authorities' short-range political
and military aims were well served, questions were raised about the long-term
damage that flows from distortion and concealment of information.

When this essay was written William Hachten, a former newspaper editor
and reporter, was professor emeritus of journalism and mass communication
at the University of Wisconsin. Harva Hachten was a journalist.

> *The first casualty when war comes is truth.*
> Senator Hiram Johnson

The Gulf War—the short but violent conflict between Iraq and the coalition forces led by the United States—lasted only 42 days, but it changed the

Source: William Hachten, with Harva Hachten, *The World News Prism: Changing Media of International Communication,* 3rd ed. Ames: Iowa State University Press, 1992, chapter 9. Copyright ©
1992, Iowa State University Press. Reprinted with the permission of Iowa State University Press.

way that future wars will be reported. Television, and especially Cable News Network, turned much of the world into a global community intently watching as the war unfolded. Because of the involvement of Western powers, particularly the United States and Britain, the Gulf War was the biggest running news story in years, and the telling of it utilized the full resources of the international news system. Eventually, over 1,600 print and broadcast journalists and technicians were in Saudi Arabia alone, with many others in nearby Amman, Baghdad, Tel Aviv, Nicosia, and, of course, Washington and London, two major news hubs.

This avalanche of live global coverage necessarily passed through the prism of deep cultural differences between the West and Islam. Each viewed the war through quite different lenses. When Iraq's Scud missiles fell on Israeli civilians, for example, Westerners were appalled, while Palestinians and Jordanians were elated. To the West and some Arabs, Saddam Hussein was a dangerous, reckless tyrant, to millions of other Arabs and Moslems, he was a hero who stood up to the West—a modern day Saladin.

But for both sides, CNN and other television broadcasters made it a "real-time" war. After hostilities began early on January 17, 1991 (Baghdad time), reporters described antiaircraft tracers in the night sky of Baghdad and flashes of bomb explosions on the horizon. On succeeding nights, viewers were provided with live video reports from Tel Aviv and Riyadh of Scud missiles, some intercepted by Patriot missiles, exploding against the night sky and television reporters donning gas masks on camera.

The press talked of the "CNN effect"—millions anchored hour after hour to their television sets lest they miss the latest dramatic development. Restaurants, movies, hotels, and gaming establishments all suffered business losses. "People are intensely interested in the first real-time war in history and they are just planting themselves in front of their television sets," one expert said. Ratings for CNN soared 5 to 10 times their prewar levels.[1]

The Gulf War was a worldwide media event of astonishing proportions. Global television never had a larger or more interested audience for such a sustained period of time. Television became the first and principal source of news for most people as well as a major source of military and political intelligence for both sides. CNN telecasts, including military briefings, were viewed in Baghdad as they were being received in Riyadh or Washington, D.C.

Because this was a war, the combatants, particularly the governments of Iraq and the United States, tried to control and manipulate the media with subtle and not-so-subtle propaganda and misinformation messages. Western journalists chafed at the restraints on news coverage of the war itself and complained there was much news they were not permitted to report. Most coalition news came from military briefings and from carefully controlled and escorted "pools" of reporters. And some official news given at the briefings was actually disinformation intended to mislead the enemy, not inform the public. For example, viewers were led to believe that Patriot missiles were invariably successful in neutralizing Scud missiles; such was not the case.

Information on the war was tightly controlled on television; one observer called it "the illusion of news." For their own valid security reasons, the military often held back or distorted the news they did release. In the opening days of the war, much was made of the "smart bombs" which hit their targets with about 90 percent accuracy. After the war, the U.S. Air Force admitted that smart bombs made up only 7 percent of all U.S. explosives dropped on Iraq and Kuwait. Television scenes of precision guided bombs going down chimneys or in the doors of targets notwithstanding, the air force said 70 percent of the 88,500 tons of bombs dropped on Kuwait and Iraq missed their targets.[2]

Peter Jennings of ABC News reminded viewers that much of what was revealed in the opening days of war was speculation, mixed with some hard facts and some rumors in the rushing river of information.[3] But whether they were getting hard news or not, many millions of viewers stayed by their television sets if only to find out what would happen next. Public opinion polls showed that the overwhelming majority of Americans supported both the war and the military's efforts to control the news; further, some thought there should be more controls on press reporting. A *Los Angeles Times Mirror* poll found that half of the respondents considered themselves obsessed with war news, but nearly 80 percent felt the military was "telling as much as it can." About the same proportion thought that military censorship may be "a good idea."

But after the war, many in the press felt that the traditional right of the American press to accompany their combat forces and report back news of war had been severely circumscribed. Michael Getler of the *Washington Post* wrote: "The Pentagon and U.S. Army Central Command conducted what is probably the most thorough and consistent wartime control of American reporters in modern times—a set of restrictions that in its totality and mindset seems to go beyond World War II, Korea and Vietnam." [4]

President George Bush and the Pentagon followed a deliberate policy of blocking negative and unflattering news from reaching the U.S. public lest it weaken support for the war. American casualties were reported, but there were few pictures of dead and wounded. Details of tactical failures and mishaps in the bombing campaign were not released. The older generation of military leaders felt strongly, despite evidence to the contrary, that unrestricted and critical press coverage in Vietnam had contributed to the U.S. defeat there. They were determined it would not happen again. Some journalists blamed their own top editors and news executives for agreeing ahead of time to the field censorship and pool arrangements instead of vigorously opposing them.

Coverage Before the War

Every war is different, and the peculiar conditions of the Gulf War affected the ways the war was reported and perceived by the public. Most Americans saw it as a "good war" with a quick, decisive victory with amazingly few U.S. and allied casualties, so press concerns over restrictions on war coverage had little public impact and never became an important issue. Nor did antiwar protests have time to develop.

For over five months, from August 2, 1990, when Iraqi troops first invaded Kuwait, to January 17, 1991, when the bombing of Iraq started, television played a central role in reporting all aspects of the major international crisis involving the United Nations and so many Arab and Western nations. The press covered the rapid buildup of coalition forces in Saudi Arabia with television pictures of armed troops arriving with heavy armor and taking up positions in the desert. This enthusiastic coverage contributed to some Pentagon-inspired misinformation by exaggerating the ability of U.S. troops to repel an invasion. Later, the 101st Airborne troops, first to arrive, admitted that during those first weeks they would have been mere road bumps for invading Iraqi forces.

Television played a clear diplomatic role as well by reporting the fate of the thousands of hostages held by Iraq and the international efforts to obtain their freedom. More importantly, the continuing diplomatic efforts by the United Nations and various foreign governments to resolve the conflict were fully aired and analyzed on television. Such international television reports, instantly available in dozens of world capitals, accelerated the often cumbersome process of diplomacy. . . .

This time, television was better equipped than ever before to report a war. Television crews had the newest technology of small, lightweight cameras and portable up-links that could transmit their video stories home via satellite. Print and radio reporters could call in stories to their news-rooms with suitcase-sized satellite telephones out in the field.

Probably never before have television viewers been exposed to such an endless array of experts—diplomatic, military, political, journalistic—to analyze in excruciating detail each new phase of the unfolding drama. Journalist Elizabeth Drew commented, "Probably in no other prelude to a possible war has the media played such a prominent role as transmission belt—for feelers, for threats, for war scenarios designed to intimidate, and for military information perhaps designed to mislead." [5]

Another impressive facet of network television coverage was its ability to *interconnect* with a variety of news sources thousands of miles apart. When, say, a new peace proposal was announced in Moscow, Peter Jennings on his ABC news program immediately obtained reactions and comments for ABC reporters and their news sources located at the White House, State Department, Pentagon, London, Tel Aviv, Amman, and Paris.

Reporting the War

All this was a prelude to the shooting war, which began just as the evening news programs were beginning at 6:30 p.m. Eastern Standard Time (January 16 in the United States, January 17 in the Middle East). The networks and CNN interrupted their prepared news shows to report that aerial bombing had apparently begun in Baghdad. Then followed one of the most memorable nights in television history: the opening phases of a major conflict reported in "real time" by reporters in Iraq, Saudi Arabia, and Washington.

CNN stole the show that night as three CNN correspondents, John Holliman, Peter Arnett, and Bernard Shaw, gave vivid eyewitness descriptions of the U.S. air attack from the windows of their Baghdad hotel room. As in old-time radio, reporters relied on words, not video, that first night. Other networks reported the fireworks, but CNN with its previously arranged leased lines stayed on the longest after the lines were cut for the other networks. The next day, General Colin Powell jokingly said the Pentagon was relying on CNN for military information.

The second night of the war gave prime-time viewers another long, exciting evening as CNN and NBC reporters in Tel Aviv reported live as Scud missiles landed. Reporters, often with gas masks on, put out raw and unevaluated information. At one point, NBC reported dramatically that nerve gas had been detected in one Scud attack. Tom Brokaw decried the situation for some minutes, but after the report proved false, NBC apologized. For the first three days of the war, people everywhere stayed glued to television and radio sets, including shortwave receivers. Networks expanded to near 24-hour coverage for the first 36 hours, and even the day-time soap operas were preempted briefly for war coverage. There was not that much to report at that point, and the same facts, theories, and speculations were repeated again and again. Nevertheless, the mesmerized public stayed tuned.

During this early bombing phase of the war, the Pentagon held back detailed military information, and the media sought out news elsewhere in Israel, Jordan, and, when it could, Baghdad. Within Saudi Arabia, the U.S. military had tight regulations in place. Information was withheld about the extent of the bombing and destruction within Iraq, and restrictions were placed on interviews with troops and returning pilots. Reporters could cover military activities only in designated "pools," groups of reporters accompanied by an escort officer. (One reporter likened a press pool to a group of senior citizens on a conducted tour.) All interviews with soldiers were on the record, and all reports were subject to censorship before they could be released.

Most information was available in the daily briefings held by the military in both Riyadh and the Pentagon in Washington, but much of this was rather general, vague, and lacking in detail. The military had coherent arguments for its restrictive policies. Destroying Iraq's military command and communications capability was a high priority of the bombing strategy, and it was important not to convey any useful information, via the media, that would reveal troop movements and the intentions of coalition forces. Keeping Iraq's forces off balance and without reliable information was a key part of U.S. strategy. After the ground attack began, it became apparent how important surprise was in General Norman Schwarzkopf's battle plan. . . .

However, some news executives and critics said the press restrictions went well beyond security concerns and appeared aimed at both preventing politically damaging disclosures by soldiers and shielding the American public from seeing the brutal aspects of war. Even before the fighting started, the Defense Department had barred the press from Dover Air Force Base, Delaware, where U.S. war dead are returned. The ban, which was upheld by a U.S. court, was justified by authorities as a protection of the privacy of the troops' families. A suit filed by the press charged the Pentagon's real motive was to prevent television pictures of flag-draped coffins arriving at Dover, as was done in previous wars.

If the war had gone badly, the press would have had difficulty reporting the negative aspects. With over 1,600 reporters in the theater, only about 100 could be accommodated by the pools to report the 500,000 American force. As the ground war neared, the large press corps became increasingly restive and frustrated at this lack of access.

The response of some reporters was to "free-lance"—to avoid the pools and go off on their own. Malcolm Browne reported, "Some reporters were hiding out in American Marine or Army field units, given G.I. uniforms and gear to look inconspicuous, enjoying the affection (and protection of the units) they're trying to cover—concealed by the officers and troops from the handful of press-hating commanders who strive to keep the battlefield free of wandering journalists." [6] Browne noted that nearly all reporters who tried to reach front line U.S. troops were arrested at one time or another and sometimes held in field jails for up to 12 hours, facing the threat of revocation of their press credentials. Reporters for the *New York Times, Washington Post,* Associated Press, and Cox papers were arrested at one time or another. . . .

Psychological Warfare and Propaganda

Intertwined with the flow of war news was the propaganda war between Iraq and the United States, the principal power in the UN-supported coalition. Each side used information and its own, as well as international, news media to seek advantages in world and regional opinion and to undermine enemy morale. Saudi Arabia and Kuwait, both lacking effective media voices, hired prestigious U.S. public relations firms, such as Hill and Knowlton, to get their views across to Western media and publics.

Saddam Hussein's propaganda was considered crude but effective in a region where rumor and fact are often blurred and conspiracies are easily believed. Iraq's most persistent strategy was to blame the gulf crisis on an Israeli-American plot to station foreign forces in the region and seize control of Middle Eastern oil. One disinformation campaign claimed Israeli planes were painted like American planes and that Israeli soldiers had mastered American English.

Saddam's propaganda portrayed the American soldier as a foreign invader who is "drinking alcohol, eating pork and practicing prostitution," according to a broadcast on Holy Mecca Radio, a clandestine station beamed from Iraq into Saudi territory.[7] Iraqi television reported that 40 percent of American servicemen had AIDS. An Indian newspaper with ties to Iraq reported that the Pentagon had sent 5,000 Egyptian women to Saudi Arabia to serve as prostitutes for the American troops. A U.S. Information Agency official commented, "Even though a story can be incredibly preposterous to the Western mind, it can resonate deeply in other parts of the world. The key is the predisposition to believe, not the crudity of the charge."[8] Before the bombing destroyed many of its radio transmitters, Iraq had a greater power than the West to broadcast in the area, including clandestine radio stations for Egyptian and Saudi Arabian listeners. Even though the Voice of America increased its Arabic broadcasts from $7\frac{1}{2}$ to 13 hours a day, Iraq was largely successful in jamming those and BBC Arabic broadcasts during the first weeks of the crisis. . . .

The main U.S. "psychwar" emphasis was on a psychological campaign designed to shake Iraq's confidence and undermine the morale of its armed forces. The campaign included broadcasts of antigovernment propaganda into Iraq and the circulation of audio- and videocassette tapes depicting U.S. forces as militarily strong and Saddam Hussein's government as corrupt. There was also a plan to smuggle thousands of small radios into Iraq to receive American broadcasts. Allied aircraft dropped 1 million leaflets into Kuwait urging the Iraqi infantry to surrender. Many who later did give up came in clutching these air-dropped "safe conduct" leaflets. . . .

The effectiveness of such psychological warfare efforts is always difficult to evaluate. In any case, the propaganda of words always gives way to the propaganda of events, and since Saddam Hussein's forces were so soundly defeated, his propaganda of words was also overwhelmed. . . .

Lessons for the Press

Wars between nations are by definition major international news stories and should be reported by the press as completely and thoroughly as conditions permit. Yet governments at war, even the most democratic, will try to control and manipulate war news to their own strategic and tactical advantage. The Gulf War provided ample reminders of this generalization. Censorship and propaganda, the twin arms of political warfare, are integral components of modern warfare. So, often the press is denied by both sides the opportunity to report objectively what has occurred. In numerous modern wars—Uganda versus Tanzania, the Sudan civil war, Ethiopia's war against Eritrean rebels and Somalia, the Soviet Union's incursion into Afghanistan—both sides either barred foreign correspondents or discouraged any coverage. The long and bloody Iran-Iraq war, precursor of the Gulf War, was severely underreported.

In the Gulf War, over 1,500 journalists were permitted into the war theater but were allowed little freedom to cover the actual fighting. On the Iraqi side, the few foreign reporters in Baghdad were severely restricted.

From all indications, the U.S. military as well as the Bush administration were pleased with the results of their policy and would do the same thing next time. But among the press, especially American and British journalists, there was a general conclusion that the press had been unduly and even illegally denied access to information about the war.

After the war, in July 1991, a report calling military restrictions in the Gulf War "real censorship" that confirmed "the worst fears of reporters in a democracy" was delivered to Defense Secretary Dick Cheney. It was signed by 17 news executives representing the four networks, AP and UPI, and major newspapers and news magazines. The news executives bitterly complained that the restrictions placed on reporters by the Pentagon were intended to promote a sanitized view of the war. The war was called the first in this century to restrict all official coverage to pools. "By controlling what reporters saw and when they saw it, the military exerted great power to shape and manage the news," the report said. Also criticized were the use of military escorts and "unwarranted delays by the military in transmitting copy." [9] The journalists sought a meeting with Cheney in hopes of changing the use of pools in future wars.

Consequently, despite all the wonders of communication technology (and perhaps in part because of them), the Western news media can be severely restricted by their own democratic governments in wartime.

Notes

1. "Tourism Shaken by 'CNN Effect'," *New York Times,* January 28, 1991, p. 8.
2. Tom Wicker, "An Unknown Casualty," *New York Times,* March 20, 1991, p. A15.
3. Alex S. Jones, "Feast of Viewing but Little Nourishment," *New York Times,* January 19, 1991, p. 8.

4. Michael Getler, "The Gulf War, 'Good News' Policy Is a Dangerous Precedent," *Washington Post National Weekly Edition,* March 25–31, 1991, p. 24.

5. Elizabeth Drew, "Letter from Washington," *New Yorker,* December 31, 1990, p. 92.

6. Malcolm W. Browne, "The Military vs. the Press," *New York Times Magazine,* March 3, 1991, p. 45.

7. Elaine Sciolino, "Iraq's Propaganda May Seem Crude but It's Effective," *New York Times,* September 15, 1990, p. E3.

8. Ibid.

9. Jason DeParle, "17 News Executives Criticize U.S. for 'Censorship' of Gulf Coverage," *New York Times,* July 3, 1991, p. A4.

28

THE WATCHDOG ROLE
OF THE PRESS

W. Lance Bennett and William Serrin

Editor's Note

Power corrupts. Keeping a democracy healthy, therefore, requires institutions that check the actions of political elites. The mass media fill that surveillance role in the United States. Yet as W. Lance Bennett and William Serrin point out, their performance record has been, regrettably, quite spotty. The media have scored many important successes, exposing corruption and mismanagement, and corrective action has often followed. But watchdog failures have been more plentiful because most journalists routinely neglect their surveillance role or perform it poorly. The authors suggest remedies for this troubling situation, but the obstacles to effective watchdog journalism currently are so enormous that the chances for success are slim.

Bennett is the Ruddick C. Lawrence Professor of Communication and professor of political science at the University of Washington. He has authored numerous important books covering political communication issues. He is also the founder and director of the Center for Communication and Civic Engagement at the University of Washington, which sponsors communication research and policy initiatives that enhance the quality of citizens' political engagements.

Serrin is associate professor of journalism and mass communication at New York University. He is also an author and a prize-winning journalist who has worked for the *New York Times,* the *Detroit Free Press,* and *Newsweek.* His essays have been published in the *Atlantic Monthly, American Heritage, The Nation, Columbia Journalism Review* and the *Village Voice.*

Source: W. Lance Bennett and William Serrin, "The Watchdog Role," in *The Institutions of American Democracy: The Press,* ed. Geneva Overholser and Kathleen Hall Jamieson, New York: Oxford University Press, 2005, chapter 10. Copyright © 2005 by the Oxford University Press. Reprinted by permission of the Oxford University Press.

To begin with, *watchdog journalism* is defined here as: (1) independent scrutiny by the press of the activities of government, business, and other public institutions, with an aim toward (2) documenting, questioning, and investigating those activities, in order to (3) provide publics and officials with timely information on issues of public concern. Each of these elements—documenting, questioning, and investigating—can be found almost every day in reporting about some matters of importance for the working of American democracy. Yet there are also stunning gaps that, in retrospect, suggest the hesitancy or inability of news organizations to act systematically or routinely as watchdogs in covering other matters of high importance. In this chapter, we explore some of the factors contributing to the fragility of the watchdog role. . . .

. . . [T]he watchdog role of journalism may involve simply documenting the activities of government, business, and other public institutions in ways that expose little-publicized or hidden activities to public scrutiny. Much documentation of this sort does occur, yet journalists also often miss early-warning signs of important activities that later blow up as scandals that prove costly to the public. The energy crises and corporate accounting and fraud scandals of the early millennium come to mind here.

Another defining element of watchdog journalism involves clarifying the significance of documented activities by asking probing questions of public officials and authorities. Again, there are many cases of effective press interrogation of officials, as when high officers of the Catholic Church were challenged in the early 2000s about their knowledge of widespread child abuse at the hands of priests. Yet there are also puzzling lapses of critical questions, as when journalists initially reported administration claims about Iraqi links to the September 11 terror attacks and the presence of weapons of mass destruction in Iraq without giving similar space to the volume of challenging evidence to the contrary. When serious press challenges finally emerged, it was in response to questions raised by congressional leaders and public commissions. But those questions about the war came so late that the administration case for war was by then more a matter for historians to judge.

Also included in the above definition of watchdog journalism are the practices of enterprise or investigative reporting aimed at finding hidden evidence of social ills, official deception, and institutional corruption. Some instances of investigative reporting may point toward constructive reforms, or alert and mobilize publics to take action on pressing problems such as environmental hazards or health care abuses.[1] Other investigative reports may be aimed less at mobilizing broad publics than at finding failures that threaten the integrity of institutions themselves, such as the investigations of David Protess and Robert Warden that reversed the wrongful convictions of four black men accused in the brutal murder of a white couple in Illinois.[2]

Whether it involves merely documenting the behaviors of authorities and asking them challenging questions, or digging up evidence of corruption or deception, the idea of independent journalistic scrutiny of social, economic, and governmental institutions is commonly regarded as fundamental for keeping authorities in line with the values and norms that charter the institutions they manage. The watchdog function may also alert publics to issues that can affect their opinions and their modes of engagement in public life. Despite its prominence among the ideals that have come to define the press and its various professional responsibilities, the watchdog role has been rather weakly institutionalized in the daily routines and responsibilities of the press. In some instances, press performance provides exemplary service to the public interest, such as the disclosure of the My Lai massacre during the Vietnam War, coverage of the Watergate scandal in the 1970s, and the more recent widespread reporting on nursing home abuse and neglect of elderly patients. At the same time, there are examples of equally spectacular failures to challenge the claims of authorities, such as the gross imbalance between the high volume of reports and editorials publicizing Bush administration claims about links between the Iraq invasion and the war on terror, and the low volume of timely reports on available evidence that contradicted those claims.

. . . [New York Times ombudsman Daniel] Okrent's analysis suggests why watchdog journalism is often lost among the other considerations that drive news decisions: the "hunger for scoops" that lead news organizations to tolerate stories based on anonymous and often partisan sources; the "front-page syndrome" that leads reporters and editors to favor more dramatic and less qualified accounts; "hit-and-run journalism" that keeps news organizations from revisiting earlier headlines in light of later contradictory information; "coddling sources" to keep a story going at the price of granting them anonymity that disguises suspect motives and information; and "end-run editing" that leads editors to favor star reporter scoops, while discounting challenges by other reporters in the newsroom who may have different information from other sources.[3] . . .

Why Watchdog Journalism Matters

Journalism is the heart of democracy, the humorist Garrison Keillor once said. What he meant was that hard-edged reporting aimed at making the world a better place is central to democracy. "More crime, immorality and rascality is prevented by the fear of exposure in the newspapers than by all the laws, moral and statute, ever devised," said the publisher Joseph Pulitzer in 1878.[4] Without journalists acting as watchdogs, American democracy—at least in anything close to the form we know it today—would not exist. . . .

Communication scholars generally agree that democracy requires a public sphere where people can communicate about society and government at least somewhat independently of the authorities that convene and govern social institutions. In contemporary societies, the press and, more generally, the media make important contributions to the quality of this public sphere. Yet the mix of professional journalism norms, public tastes, political spin, and business imperatives that construct what we call news makes it difficult to imagine how to keep the public responsibilities of the press in step with a civic life that is also changing in terms of how citizens define their public roles and relations to government. In other words, it is not clear just how the press should facilitate the production of this public sphere. It is not even obvious how much scrutiny of public officials and their activities is the right amount. Too much press intrusion may become annoying and burdensome both to authorities and publics.[5] Too little critical reporting may produce poor-quality public policy debates and weaken the everyday accountability relations between authorities and publics. . . .

Uneven Practice of the Watchdog Role

. . . [I]t is easier to say that journalists should be watchdogs than to find agreement on precisely what this entails or how it might be achieved consistently. Perhaps this is why the mythic status of the watchdog press looms larger than the evidence for its universally accepted practice. . . .

The veteran journalist Murray Marder argues that the problematic standing of watchdog journalism is revealed most clearly in how reporters praise the ideal without having a firm sense of how to put it into practice. In an address on the subject at Harvard's Nieman Center, Marder noted that, all too often, the press appear not as watchdogs, but as a snarling, barking pack, substituting the spectacle or the posture of adversarialism for the sort of journalism that might better serve the public interest. Marder's prescription for restoring the watchdog role involves a simple recommendation to his colleagues:

> Disassociate ourselves wherever we can from crude, discourteous behavior whether by packs of elbowing news people lying in wait for Monica Lewinsky, or by shouting, snarling participants in a television encounter posing as news commentators. . . . That will not come easy. For in my view, watchdog journalism is by no means just occasional selective, hard-hitting investigative reporting. It starts with a state of mind, accepting responsibility as a surrogate for the public, asking penetrating questions at every level, from the town council to the state house to the White House, in corporate offices, in union halls and in professional offices and all points in between.[6]

What Marder implies here is that the press sometimes gets it right and sometimes does not, but that there is great inconsistency in being able to predict when either result might happen. What accounts for this inconsistency and its accompanying lack of institutional grounding? The most obvious and frequently discussed factor is that most news organizations in the United States are driven by business formulas that exert various limits on defining and elevating democratic press functions above other considerations. In the case of public service organizations, news decisions are made in the context of politically sensitive governmental, foundation, or corporate funding constraints. What seems puzzling is that, for all the criticism of the press, there is surprisingly little formal discussion among journalists of just what the watchdog role might look like in practical terms, and how it might be promoted more effectively. . . .

With little elaboration of a clear set of democratic reporting responsibilities, the news that we witness today has evolved as a strange hybrid of deference to authorities, and ritualistic displays of antagonism and feeding frenzy against those same authorities, interspersed with occasional displays of watchdog reporting. . . . [I]t is clear that reporters and news organizations are most drawn to stories that offer the greatest dramatic potential and hold the greatest promise of continuing plot development. Some of those stories end up being manufactured out of little more than spin, staging, and the efforts of the press pack to inject life into the political routine. . . .

When the Watchdog Barks

. . . [T]here are also many times when journalists raise challenges or discover hidden information that changes the thinking of publics or policy makers about important issues. Thomas Patterson has suggested that in its contemporary form, watchdog journalism may work best when in partnership with other institutions that are serving similar watchdog roles—parties and public-interest advocacy groups come to mind. Watchdog journalism may need these institutional partners in order to prosper—partners such as whistle-blowers . . . or political parties that are more concerned about principled opposition than strategic calculations. . . . More probing voices are likely to be introduced into the news for more extended periods when journalists find sources with prominent institutional standing who are already raising critical questions.[7] Hence, the same concerns that existed before the invasion of Iraq (about lack of Bush administration evidence for linking Iraq to the war on terror) were only given sustained voice after the commission investigating September 11 invited witnesses to raise them. By the same explanation, when journalists are the lone voices raising concerns—even documentable concerns—it is far more difficult for them to perform the watchdog function. Ironically, the independent-press watchdog function may work least well when it is most needed.

* * *

Status of the Watchdog Role

What is the institutional status of investigative journalism today? What is the regard for this tradition among journalists and the public? What are the prospects for better integrating investigative and, more generally, watchdog reporting within the constraining matrix of corporate business imperatives, professional standards of the journalism profession, and the needs of citizens? At the opening of the twenty-first century, there was still a good deal of watchdog reporting going on, but it was scattered unevenly across the media. In the case of investigative reporting—defined as enterprise reporting on important public issues involving the discovery and documentation of previously hidden information—far more of it could be said to emerge from the print press than from television news organizations. A five-year study of TV news at the turn of the millennium found investigative reporting on television, particularly at the local level, in continuing decline. By self-report of news directors in 2002, less than 1 percent of all news was station-initiated investigation. By the research team's judgment, the ratio was more on the order of 1 out of 150 stories, down from 1 in 60 in 1998. Most of the reports that qualified as station-initiated and as containing information not already on the public record dealt with government malfeasance, consumer fraud, and health care scandals.[8]

Whether the subject is investigative reporting, or the companion activities of documenting the claims and activities of institutional authorities and raising probing questions about them, most observers agree that the present period is not a time of rich watchdog reporting in any media. Perhaps this reflects the absence of large numbers of citizens mobilized in reform movements eager for a sense of common inclusion and good information about their causes. Perhaps it reflects a time in which political culture—or at least the parties in government and the corporate culture that supports them—is bent away from government regulation and progressive public legislation. History suggests that these conditions may change and kindle more investigative activity. However, as the run of corporate scandals, environmental deterioration, military adventures, and rising levels of inequality in the 1990s and 2000s indicate, there is no lack of material to investigate. Yet reporting on the epidemic of illegal corporate accounting, disclosure, and finance did not hit the front pages until government investigations and whistle-blower reports had already begun. And the timidity with which mainstream journalism handled early evidence of Bush administration distortions in the campaign to go to war against Iraq suggests that news organizations are not eager to reframe heavily spun stories in the absence of voiced outrage from credible political-opposition voices.[9] In light of these patterns, two concerns seem to highlight the watchdog role of the press in the present era:

1. *The watchdog role has become overly stylized or ritualized.* The press has adopted a tone of cynicism and negativity often without offering original documentary material or constructive solutions to accompany that tone.[10] Television news magazines have appropriated a pseudo-investigative style, emphasizing consumer rip-offs and celebrity confessionals of little broad social consequence.

2. *When potentially significant investigative reports do surface, they are often not pursued or even echoed by other organizations cautiously following the collective lead.* . . . Even though such reports were surely read by many journalists, there was little concerted effort to follow them up or to shift general press coverage in a timely fashion—that is, before situations had grown so serious that officials inside government finally began formal investigations.[11]

Perhaps the good news is that neither publics nor journalists seem particularly happy with this state of affairs. Not surprisingly, the public has been less happy with the negative tone of journalism than reporters, who understandably perceive themselves as doing the best they can, often triumphing under challenging organizational conditions. Andrew Kohut summarized polling on the watchdog role by the Pew Research Center for the People and the Press in these terms:

> The biggest gap between the people and the press is over the way news media play their watchdog role. Almost all journalists are sure that media scrutiny of politicians is worth the effort because it prevents wrongdoing. But the percentage of Americans thinking that press criticism impedes political leaders from doing their jobs has increased . . . while the number saying they value the press's watchdog role has fallen. . . . Many Americans see an ill-mannered watchdog that barks too often—one that is driven by its own interests rather than by a desire to protect the public interest.[12] . . .

The good news here is that both journalists and publics seem to recognize that the watchdog role has somehow gone off course, and that it may be time to think more seriously about how to bring it back in line with contemporary public values and concerns. Encouraging poll trends suggest strong public support for the watchdog ideal, if not for the way if is often bent in practice. For example, a review of five national polls from the 1980s through the 1990s showed increases in public support for investigative reporting to a peak of 84 percent in 1997. However, there was also considerable objection to the practices often employed in what passes for investigative journalism today, and the emphasis on pseudo investigation and sensationalism.[13] All of this leads to the question of why watchdog journalism seems to have lost its bearing, and what can be done about it.

The Sleeping Watchdog?

Newsrooms are often organized in an old-fashioned way that dates to the founding of modern journalism in the 1840s. Because of this, many areas that should be important receive little or no watchdog coverage—advertising, the military (except for coverage of war), farming and food policy, taxes, and government regulatory and other so-called alphabet agencies. At the same time, many beats in journalism that should be important essentially are backwaters, among them religion, environment, education, labor, urban affairs, state governments, and road and sewer construction. It is sometimes said that mankind's greatest needs are food, clothing, and shelter: none of these areas are covered well. Beats that came out of the 1960s and 1970s, such as consumer beats, urban affairs beats, and coverage of the environment, had virtually disappeared by 2000.

Generally, rocking boats is not a way to get ahead in newsrooms. Publishers and editors often distrust reporters who they think have a point of view. It is OK to say you want to be a reporter covering sports, politics, or business, say, but if you want to cover the poor or labor or the environment, you are often regarded as a person with an agenda. You often won't be promoted, and you'll be watched with great suspicion.

Journalists have sold their souls for access to public officials. . . . This is not an attitude that makes for good journalism. . . . This is a particular problem in Washington, D.C. Reporters there want to cover the White House or Congress or the Pentagon, but most people do not want to cover the regulatory agencies, where things that affect people happen. Journalistic careers seldom flourish by covering the latter; star journalists are drawn to the glitter of the Georgetown social circuit and the White House. As a result, in the nation's capital, the press is often not the "fourth estate," it is part of government. And the same tendencies apply in the state house, at city hall, and at corporate headquarters.

It is also important to ask the question of who goes into journalism today. As Russell Baker has pointed out, as the news business has become more professionalized, many reporters and editors now come from upper-class and middle-class backgrounds. They are well bred, they have impressive educations, but the average American reporter has little or no knowledge of how people beyond his or her class think or act. "They belong to the culture for which the American political system works exceedingly well," Baker said, adding, "This is not a background likely to produce angry reporters and aggressive editors."[14] . . .

With conglomeration, and Wall Street's definition of what constitutes proper profits, media corporations are often run as if they were nothing more than any other kind of business. Newsrooms are deliberately kept understaffed to save money. Reporters are pressured to do more stories in less time—again, to save money. Expense budgets for travel are cut. . . .

In all this, it must be remembered that watchdog reporting is particularly challenging. In the case of investigative reporting, the journalist is looking for things that people want to keep hidden. It is time-consuming and expensive. Simply documenting the background details of public activities and official claims takes time and work. Rarely can a reporter drop all other responsibilities to concentrate on one investigative story. Moreover, asking challenging questions of sources that must be covered on a regular basis may strain journalists' future relations with those sources. Reporters, beware the watchdog role: You will make enemies doing it.

* * *

Conclusion

In this essay several factors have been identified that affect when the watchdog role of the press is likely to work well, and when it is not. Not surprisingly, watchdog journalism functions best when reporters understand it and news organizations and their audience support it. The business climate of many news organizations today is not fully supportive; nor is the curriculum in most journalism schools; nor are publics who, perhaps rightly, see too much negativity and insider posturing in place of reporters simply asking hard questions about important subjects.

In addition, it may be time to rethink the curious professional norms of the objective or politically neutral press that remains a legacy of the Progressive Era. Such norms often seem to pit the journalistic commitment to balance and objectivity against the values of advocacy or probity. What the public receives as a result are confusing debates that seem impossible to resolve or make much sense of. What, for example, is the point of the construction of a two-sided debate about global warming when one side consists overwhelmingly of scientists who have little scholarly doubt or disagreement, and the other side consists primarily of politicians and business interests who have quite another agenda fueling their skepticism? What was the point of "balancing" the findings of the National Commission on Terrorist Attacks upon the United States (the 9/11 Commission), which stated that there was no evidence of Iraqi involvement, with continued face-value reporting of unsupported claims to the contrary from the president and vice president? How can journalists moderate such debates when their own current practices compel them to report them in ways that may create more confusion than clarity? The flip side of this normative dilemma is the problem of what watchdogs should do when one side of an issue is dominated by spin from a media-savvy source with high social standing, and opponents have failed for whatever reasons to mount an equally effective press relations campaign. All too often, the watchdog retreats, and what is reported as the public record goes unchallenged in the news.

. . . When today's press watchdog serves the public interest, it is generally in a partnership with other public watchdogs such as public interest or consumer advocacy organizations, courts, interest groups, and government itself.

During an era of a conservative turn away from public life and institutions, this somewhat limited watchdog function may be the best that can be hoped for from an embattled press. Yet there is also a prescription here for strengthening the watchdog role in these times:

1. Find new ways to define the democratic responsibilities of the press through journalism education, foundation support, and public discussion.
2. Strike a better balance between currently embattled professional norms and some broad and well-crafted notion of the public interest.
3. Expand beats and sources to give more voice to those who are currently left out of democratic debate, and who might subscribe to papers and watch the news if they saw themselves represented more frequently and more fairly there.
4. Stimulate debate in the profession about steering a clearer course between fear and favor in relations with the powerful sources who continue to dominate the news.
5. Explore new institutional means—including government support and regulation, public commissions, and new business models for news—to create better accountability relations between journalists and other democratic stakeholders.

Mythology aside, perhaps it is the lack of clear democratic standing for the press as expressed in daily reporting practices that best explains why the watchdog sometimes barks when it should, sometimes sleeps when it should bark, and too often barks at nothing.

Notes

1. See David L. Protess et al., *The Journalism of Outrage: Investigative Reporting and Agenda Building in America* (New York: Guilford, 1992).
2. David Protess and Robert Warden, *A Promise of Justice: The 14 Year Fight to Save Four Innocent Men* (New York: Hyperion, 1998).
3. *New York Times*, May 30, 2004.
4. As cited in Judith Serrin and William Serrin, eds., *Muckraking! The Journalism that Changed America* (New York: New Press, 2002).

5. See John Zaller, "A New Standard of News Quality: Burglar Alarms for the Monitorial Citizen," *Political Communication* 20, no. 2 (2003): 109–30.
6. Murray Marder, "This Is Watchdog Journalism" (2 parts), *Nieman Reports* 53, no. 4 (winter 1999), and 54, no. 1 (spring 2000), http://www.nieman.harvard. edu/reports/99-4_00-1NR/Marder_ThisIs.html.
7. W. Lance Bennett, "Toward a Theory of Press-State Relations in the United States," *Journal of Communication* 40 (spring 1990): 103–27.
8. Marion Just, Rosalind Levine, and Kathleen Regan, "Investigative Reporting Despite the Odds: Watchdog Reporting Continues to Decline," Local TV News Project, http://www.journalism.org/resources/research/reports/localTV/2002/ investigative.asp.
9. W. Lance Bennett, "Toward a Theory of Press-State Relations" and "The Perfect Storm? The American Media and Iraq," OpenDemocracy, August 28, 2003, http://www.opendemocracy.net/debates/article-8-92-1457.jsp.
10. Joseph N. Cappella and Kathleen Hall Jamieson, *Spiral of Cynicism: The Press and the Public Good* (New York: Oxford University Press, 1997); Thomas Patterson, "Doing Well and Doing Good: How Soft News and Critical Journalism Are Shrinking the News and Weakening Democracy—And What News Outlets Can Do about It" (working paper, Joan Shorenstein Center on Press, Politics and Public Policy, Kennedy School of Government, Harvard University, Cambridge, Mass., 2000).
11. See Robert M. Entman, *Projections of Power: Framing News, Public Opinion, and U.S. Foreign Policy* (Chicago: University of Chicago Press, 2004).
12. Andrew Kohut, "Public Support for the Watchdog Role Is Fading," *Columbia Journalism Review* (May/June 2001): 46.
13. Lars Willnat and David H. Weaver, "Public Opinion on Investigative Reporting in the 1990s: Has Anything Changed since the 1980s?" *Journalism and Mass Communication Quarterly* 75 (autumn 1998): 449–63.
14. *New York Review of Books,* December 18, 2003, http://www.nybooks.com/ articles/16863.

29

THE SOAP OPERA PATH TO HEALTH POLICY GOALS

May G. Kennedy, Ann O'Leary, Vicki Beck, Katrina Pollard, and Penny Simpson

Editor's Note

Successful implementation of policies often requires the cooperation of millions of citizens. They must learn that the policies exist and what actions they are supposed to take. Mass media are the logical message carriers because of their broad reach and wide appeal. Research indicates that dramatic presentations on entertainment media are uniquely suited to attract the audience's attention to policies dealing with social problems and teach them how citizens can support these policies. This essay demonstrates that people can be encouraged to acquire information about HIV/AIDS policies and to take steps to avoid infections or treat them. Unlike most research on media effects, studies of the impact of health messages provide strong rather than weak evidence that mediated messages can cause major behavioral changes among members of large audiences.

When this essay was written, May G. Kennedy was a communication analyst for the Centers for Disease Control and Prevention (CDC). Her research interests include social marketing, health risk communication strategies, and social and health policy applications of social science. Ann O'Leary was a senior behavioral scientist at the Division of HIV/AIDS at the CDC and author of several books on the subject. Vicki Beck was director of Hollywood, Health & Society at the USC Annenberg's Norman Lear Center. She oversaw outreach and research activity, including studies on the content and effects of health storylines on television. Katrina Pollard was a health communications specialist for CDC's National Center for Environmental Health. Penny Simpson was a research analyst for the American Social Health Association.

Source: May G. Kennedy, Ann O'Leary, Vicki Beck, Katrina Pollard, and Penny Simpson, "Increases in Calls to the CDC National STD and AIDS Hotline Following AIDS-Related Episodes in a Soap Opera," *Journal of Communication* 54:2 (June 2004): 287–301. Reprinted by permission of Blackwell Publishing.

. . . Mass media are efficient and promising communication channels for prevention messages (Jason, 1998), and nationally televised broadcasts reach millions of Americans. Television broadcasts have been shown to increase knowledge of health issues (Brodie et al., 2001; CDC, 1992), promote attitudes and norms that support prevention (Kalichman, 1994; Siska, Jason, Murdoch, Yang, & Donovan, 1992), model prevention behaviors (Basil, 1996), and elicit prevention behaviors (Andrews, McLeese, & Curran, 1995; Brodie et al., 2001; Fan, 1993; Myhre & Flora, 2000).

Compared with other broadcast formats (e.g., free-standing public service announcements [PSAs], news shows, and evening dramas), daytime television dramas or "soap operas" may offer several advantages for the dissemination of HIV prevention messages to high-risk women. The first advantage is that soap operas are relatively efficient in reaching minority women. African American and Hispanic households watch more daytime television than other audiences. . . . Among respondents to the 1999 Healthstyles survey, 31% of African Americans, 25% of Hispanics, and 17% of whites reported that they were regular soap opera viewers (i.e., that they watched at least twice a week; Beck, Pollard, & Greenberg, 2000). The second advantage is that soap operas may be viewed as a more credible source of health information by minority women than by other racial and ethnic groups. Of women who reported regular soap opera viewing, 53% of all women, 56% of Hispanic women, and 69% of African American women said that they had learned something about diseases or how to prevent them from soap operas in the last year (Beck et al., 2000). Finally, regardless of viewer race or ethnicity, the expectation that daytime soap operas would be an unusually effective channel of HIV-relevant communication is consistent with several theories and with the findings of related bodies of research.

Theoretical and Empirical Support

Miguel Sabido pioneered the dissemination of educational messages through broadcasts of serialized novellas, a format analogous to U.S. soap operas but usually less long-running. His approach has come to be known as Entertainment-Education (Singhal & Rogers, 1999). Used predominantly in developing countries to date, Entertainment-Education employs an entertaining format to engage a large audience, eventually weaving in educational messages designed to inform audiences, influence their attitudes about the educational issue, and persuade them to adopt pertinent behaviors (Papa et al., 2000). Some characters perform a recommended behavior and are rewarded with prosperity and happiness, while other characters do not adopt the behavior and meet disastrous ends. A third type of character, constructed to inspire audience identification, observes all of this, strives to overcome various obstacles to performing the behavior, ultimately succeeds, and is rewarded in a manner valued by the target audience.

These elements of Entertainment-Education were intentionally based on Albert Bandura's social cognitive theory (Bandura, 1986, 1994). Social cognitive theory postulates that learning occurs when an individual observes someone else performing a behavior and experiencing the consequences of that behavior. This observational learning influences the learner to perform a behavior by creating a positive outcome expectancy, the expectation that a certain action will result in a positive outcome, and by enhancing self-efficacy, the belief that one is able to perform a behavior. Self-efficacy is thought to be enhanced when the learner identifies with the role model—the individual who performed the behavior and experienced its consequences directly. The learner is considered most likely to engage in repeated attempts to perform the new behavior when two conditions hold. First, the behavioral role model achieves a behavioral goal through effortful mastery, defined as success following persistence in the face of barriers. Second, the reward for succeeding is something the learner values.

Other relevant theoretical models (e.g., McGuire, 1989; Prochaska, DiClemente, & Norcross, 1992) have maintained that individuals who are presented with behavioral recommendations go through a series of information processing and assessment steps before actually performing the behavior. Although an individual can travel recursively through these steps, the route is usually described as a unidirectional linear progression (Papa et al., 2000). Typically, the message recipient (a) becomes aware of and actively attends to a message, (b) comprehends and remembers the message, (c) considers the message, (d) decides to follow the recommendation, and (e) takes prerequisite or preliminary action before (f) actually exhibiting behavior in line with the message.

Taking the first step—becoming aware of the message—is facilitated by sending messages through channels to which a target audience attends; the point that soap operas are efficient channels for reaching high-risk women has already been made. Attention and persuasion are encouraged when messages are delivered dramatically by a character that viewers care about (O'Brien & Albrecht, 1992; Papa et al., 2000); soap operas are very dramatic, and soap opera viewers are often deeply involved with the characters on their favorite shows (Dines & Humez, 1995). In fact, some viewers use soap opera websites to advocate for particular plot developments (see www.cbs.com/daytime/bb for examples). A serialized format presents the opportunity to repeat and develop prevention themes, strategies that have been shown to enhance both comprehension and retention (Waugh & Norman, 1965). Moreover, recall of prevention messages may be enhanced if the messages are presented in the context of a storyline that viewers follow over time (Brinson & Brown, 1997).

. . . Papa and his colleagues (Papa et al., 2000) point out that many media messages are processed in a social context. Conversations and other social interactions stimulated by the media can create new impetus (e.g., collective efficacy) and opportunities for behavior change. Also, Entertainment-Education sparks parasocial interaction (e.g., forming a "relationship" with a fictional character or talking to the television; Papa et al., 2000; Pfau, 1990), which may enhance identification and efficacy. Parasocial interaction fosters active message processing (Papa et al., 2000), a goal-oriented activity that involves a decision to pay attention and the exertion of mental effort to evaluate arguments and seek information (Green, Lightfoot, Bandy, & Buchanan, 1985; Park & Smith, 1989). Active processing improves retention (Larson, 1991) and may lead to more behavior change than does passive processing (Parrott, 1995).

When a health message is easy to follow, self-efficacy and skill modeling are less relevant than they are for complex behaviors. The health belief model (Becker, 1974) has been shown to predict behaviors that require little skill, such as asking for health information (Aiken, West, Woodward, & Reno, 1994; Champion & Miller, 1996; Graham, 2002; Jacobs, 2002). According to the health belief model, health behavior is driven primarily by the perceived seriousness of a disease and one's perceived vulnerability to the disease. Once these factors obtain, an individual is motivated to attempt to reduce the health threat in response to cues to action. Having fewer constructs, this theory may provide a simpler explanation for the influence of serialized dramas on health-relevant behavior than social cognitive theory does. However, predictions based on either the health belief model or social cognitive theory would often be consistent because perceived vulnerability can be construed as an outcome expectancy.

There is not only theoretical support for the Entertainment-Education approach, but also empirical evidence that it can be effective. Relatively weak designs from at least a dozen studies in developing countries suggest that exposure to this kind of serialized novella increases levels of target behaviors (Papa et al., 2000), and there is now confirming evidence from a carefully controlled field experiment. A radio soap opera employed the Entertainment-Education approach to promote HIV risk avoidance in the relatively uncrowded media environment of Tanzania. Compared with respondents in a comparison district in which the soap opera was not broadcast, respondents in the district in which the program was aired reported significant increases in attitudes and behaviors that are consistent with HIV prevention (Rogers et al., 1999). . . .

A Domestic Entertainment-Education Program

There has been much less study of the potential of Entertainment-Education in the United States, where no nationally broadcast soap opera has employed the full approach. However, some Hollywood writers and producers have been willing to collaborate with public health professionals to embed accurate, timely prevention messages and scenarios into major network programming. Several of these collaborations have grown out of a broad entertainment industry outreach program initiated by CDC [the federal Centers for Disease Control and Prevention]. CDC now works in partnership with the Norman Lear Center of the University of Southern California (see www.cdc.gov/communication/entertainment_education.htm) to engage producers and writers by means of regular mailings of health-related resource materials, face-to-face meetings to discuss potential storylines that could address health issues, and an award program called "The Sentinel for Health Award for Daytime Drama." This award is given to the soap opera with the storyline that does the best job of informing viewers and motivating them to make healthy choices.

After collaboration with CDC scientists, a long-running, televised, daytime soap opera, *The Bold and the Beautiful (B&B)*, introduced a subplot about HIV. The Nielson rating for *B&B* during the week of July 30, 2001, through August 3, 2001, was 4.4 (4.4% of the 102.2 million U.S. households with televisions, or 4,496,000 households). The rating indicates that millions of *B&B* viewers saw an attractive young Hispanic man get tested for HIV and learn that his HIV serostatus was positive. He told his doctor he had used condoms consistently with recent sexual partners (all of whom were women), disclosed his positive HIV serostatus to them, and encouraged them to be tested for HIV. He also disclosed his serostatus to the woman that he would eventually marry. He then proceeded to overcome emotional and interpersonal obstacles to living a full, satisfying life. Clearly, the storyline embodied several key elements of the Entertainment-Education approach.

The Present Study

The director of the American Diabetic Association (Graham, 2001) wrote a letter to CDC reporting a large surge in the volume of callers to a helpline after a character from a topically pertinent soap opera episode displayed the helpline number. CDC officials had noted such surges in the past. Documenting this kind of association formally was seen as a feasible way to begin an empirical examination of the impact of disseminating health messages through collaborations between public health agencies and private entertainment media partners.

This study examined data on the number of calls made to the CDC National STD [sexuality transmitted diseases] and AIDS Hotline's English Service (hereinafter referred to as "the Hotline") following *B&B* episodes with powerful AIDS-relevant themes. Calling the Hotline is an important health information-seeking behavior. Based on the theory, empirical findings, and anecdotal evidence reviewed above, we made three directional hypotheses:

H1: Presenting the Hotline number immediately after B&B episodes with an HIV theme would be associated with an increase in the number of calls to the Hotline during that time slot relative to other time slots on that same day.

H2: Presenting the Hotline number immediately after B&B episodes with an HIV theme would be associated with an increase in the number of calls to the Hotline relative to the number of calls during that time slot on other days.

H3: The number of calls made on the 2 days when the Hotline number was presented during B&B episodes with HIV themes would be greater than the number of calls made on days when other kinds of shows were presented.

There was also interest in the kinds of topics callers brought up during calls. A final, qualitative, exploratory research question was this:

RQ1: When Hotline callers say they called because of the B&B episode or a PSA on B&B, what kinds of issues will they bring up?

Method

Participants

During 2001, all calls to the Hotline originating within the United States were tallied by the Federal Technology Service 2000 system and AT&T. These calls were counted whether or not the callers actually reached the Hotline or spoke with Hotline staff. Participants in this study were the individuals who attempted to call the Hotline.

There were 12–15 trained Hotline staff members answering calls during the period that the show aired. When there was high caller volume, some callers heard a taped message asking them to stay on the line until a staff member was available. When the hold queue was full, callers were asked to call back at a later time. It was not possible to distinguish repeat callers from those who called once in the call attempt data presented in this paper.

Design and Procedure

On August 3, 2001, the B&B episode included a male character's diagnosis of HIV. On August 13, 2001, the character disclosed his positive HIV serostatus to his fiancée. During the last 5 minutes of each of these two episodes, a PSA was aired. It displayed the toll-free number of the Hotline (800-342-2437) while the actor who played the HIV-positive character invited viewers to call the Hotline for answers to questions about HIV or AIDS. Hotline staff members were notified of the issues to be addressed in the B&B

HIV storyline and of the days when the PSA would be aired. The episodes were broadcast at 1:30 p.m. Eastern Daylight Time (EDT) and at 12:30 p.m. Central, Mountain, and Pacific time. Calls were tallied by EDT because the Hotline is physically located on the East Coast.

Following the Hotline's standard procedure, both active and passive survey data were collected from a random sample of callers. One in 15 "productive" calls (those that result in service provision) was selected for the sample by a computer program. The staff member asked the selected caller for permission to be interviewed; no data were recorded if the request was not granted. No identifying information was requested or recorded. The standard part of the interview included questions about caller demographics, whether the caller had ever called before, and where the caller had heard about the Hotline. Passive data recorded after these calls included the first question asked or topic discussed during the call, the nature of the service rendered (e.g., referral), and any STD history that the caller mentioned. During August 2001, with approval from the Office of Management and Budget, interviewed callers who said that they heard about the Hotline through a television show were asked which show, how frequently they watched, whether they intended to make any changes or take any action as a result of seeing the show, and what kind of action they intended to take.

Results

Call Attempts

. . . [On] the 2 days on which the PSA was displayed, very large increases, or spikes, in numbers of originating call attempts were observed in the time slot during and immediately after the *B&B* broadcast. Whether or not the number of calls per hour was assumed to be normally distributed, the spikes were found to be significantly higher than call levels at other times of day ($z = 14.63$, $p < .0001$; rank test, $p = .04$). This result constituted support for H1.

On August 3, the Hotline received 1,426 calls originating between 1 p.m. and 2 p.m.; 37% of the calls that day were made in the *B&B* time slot. The day before, there had been only 88 call attempts during that time slot. On August 4, between 1 p.m. and 2 p.m., there were 108 call attempts. There was an even higher spike on August 13; 1,840 calls originated during and shortly after the *B&B* episode. On the previous day, only 94 calls had been made between 1 p.m. and 2 p.m., and on August 14, 234 calls were made during that hour. The number of calls in the spikes were averaged and compared with the average number of calls during that time period on comparison days in a one-tailed statistical test. There were significantly fewer calls in the *B&B* time slot on comparison days . . . so H2 was supported.

There was a possibility that these spikes were a function of time of the month or month of the year, so we examined call attempt patterns on July 2, 3, 4, 12, 13, and 14, 2001, and the same days in August 2000. For the non-*B&B* HIV episode days, numbers of call attempts per daytime time slot fluctuated, but the highest call level during any daytime period was no more than 200 calls higher than the next highest level for that day. . . . In contrast, the call levels for the *B&B* time slots on August 3 and 13, 2001, were more than 1,000 calls higher than the next highest levels for those days. . . . The spike in call attempts during the *B&B* time slot is evident even in the monthly data from 2001. . . .

Active Interviews

On the 2 days that the Hotline number was broadcast, caller volume was so high during and immediately after the *B&B* time slot that the capacity of the Hotline was overwhelmed. Attempted calls were tallied electronically as described above, but only a small fraction of them could be serviced by a health information specialist. Consequently, the number of active interviews with individuals who saw the show is a misleadingly low figure. Of the 1,904 callers who were selected for interviews during August 2001, 1,430 provided active interviews. Of these, only 28 callers indicated that they had heard about the Hotline from a PSA on *B&B* or on the soap opera itself. In all, 194 of the callers surveyed that month said they got the Hotline number from a TV PSA or program. More callers (just under 30%) said they got the number from the telephone book than from any other single source—a typical finding of routine interviews of Hotline callers.

Thirty-six percent of the callers who mentioned *B&B* identified themselves as African American. The majority of the callers reported being first-time callers, female, and prompted to call by the topic of positive HIV serostatus disclosure in the show. Fifty-seven percent said that they intended to make a change or take action after seeing the show; of those, 44% said that they intended to "get tested" and 28% said that they intended to "use condoms." The number of callers was too small to provide a satisfying answer to RQ1.

Discussion

After the Hotline number was displayed at the end of two August 2001 episodes of *B&B* that dealt with AIDS themes, Hotline call volume rose dramatically, as predicted. It is reasonable to conclude that many members of the American public can be motivated to seek health information by a dramatic, televised storyline that addresses health issues.

The increase in calls did not appear to be a regular temporal phenomenon. Similar spikes in call attempts were not observed during the analogous time slots on the same days the previous month, July 2001, or on the same days in August the previous year.

Compared with call spikes associated with other kinds of television broadcasts in 2001 that contained AIDS-relevant information, the *B&B* spikes were higher. Of course, it was not possible to vary comparison shows systematically, and some of the other broadcasts that dealt with HIV/AIDS during 2001 (e.g., *60 Minutes*) did not include the Hotline number. Although most respondents to routine Hotline surveys report getting the number from the telephone book, viewers of broadcasts that did not provide the number may have been unaware of its existence. Even if they knew there was a Hotline, finding its number in a phone book is an extra information-seeking step that would probably depress call numbers. Nonetheless, the demonstrated advantage of the soap opera context is striking, if not definitive.

As a group, these outcomes provide support for the elements of the Entertainment-Education approach in the HIV storyline on *B&B* and are consistent with several information-processing models and social cognitive theory. Moreover, social cognitive theory could be used to explain why the second *B&B* spike was higher than the first. In the second *B&B* episode, the female fiancée character may have sparked deeper identification among the predominantly female audience members than did the male and professional characters depicted in the first episode. She may have prompted more self-efficacy as she vowed to find out all there was to know about HIV and AIDS.

Although this study was a "natural experiment" not designed to test particular theoretical mechanisms of behavior change, the present findings seem to fit the health belief model better than social cognitive theory. A likely effect of exposure to the heterosexual transmission of HIV in the storyline would be to enhance perceptions of personal vulnerability, a key element of the health belief model. Furthermore, the placement of the Hotline number clearly served as a "cue to action." Calling a telephone number does not require a great deal of skill, and it is the more complex behaviors for which notions of skill modeling and self-efficacy enhancement are important. Because the health belief model contains fewer and arguably simpler constructs than social cognitive theory, a storyline guided by the health belief model would consume less air time and require fewer constraints on character and plot development. These efficiencies could be salient to writers of shows in the United States who find the full Entertainment-Education approach too demanding or restrictive either initially or over time.

Another possible limitation of these results is that repeat callers cannot be distinguished in the call attempt data, so there probably were fewer individual callers than the tally indicates. Nonetheless, repeat callers were persistent in health information-seeking, and such persistence is important to encourage.

Unfortunately, during and immediately after the *B&B* episodes, the incoming call volume far exceeded the Hotline's surge capacity. A few survey respondents that month said that they had heard about the Hotline from a soap opera. They were demographically similar to soap opera viewers, and most were making their first call to the Hotline. A substantial percentage of these callers reported either an intention to get an HIV test or to start using condoms, the key HIV risk reduction behaviors for sexually active women. Anecdotal evidence to support the contention that the *B&B* storyline encouraged preventive behavior was presented by the director of *B&B* when the CDC awarded the 2002 Sentinel for Health award to the show. At the ceremony, he described calls and letters stating that viewers had gotten HIV tests because of the storyline. . . .

. . . [B]ecause some of the television programming produced in the United States is broadcast around the world, it is important to understand how health messages in these programs affect international audiences (Blakley, 2001). *B&B* may be the most watched television show in the world, reaching an estimated 300,000,000 viewers in 110 countries daily (Tobin, 2002). The *B&B* HIV storyline emphasized HIV testing and expensive combination drug therapy, and we need to know what viewers in developing countries with limited healthcare resources took away from these broadcasts.

Continued collaboration with entertainment industry partners will be necessary. . . . Such a partnership is important not only to leverage the extensive resources and audience access of the private entertainment industry, but also to benefit from its deep expertise in engaging and communicating with the public.

References

Aiken, L. S., West, S. G., Woodward, C. K., & Reno, R. R. (1994). Health beliefs and compliance with mammography-screening recommendations in asymptomatic women. *Health Psychology, 13*, 122–129.

Andrews, A. B., McLeese, D. G., & Curran, S. (1995). The impact of a media campaign on public action to help maltreated children in addictive families. *Child Abuse & Neglect, 19*, 921–932.

Bandura, A. (1986). *Social foundations of thought and action: A social cognitive theory.* Englewood Cliffs, NJ: Prentice Hall.

Bandura, A. (1994). *Social cognitive theory of mass communication.* In J. Bryant & D. Zillman (Eds.), *Media effects: Advances in theory and research* (pp. 61–90). Hillsdale, NJ: Erlbaum.

Basil, M. D. (1996). Identification as a mediator of celebrity effects. *Journal of the Broadcasting Electronic Media, 40*, 478–495.

Beck, V., Pollard, W., & Greenberg, B. (November 15, 2000). *Tune in for health: Working with television entertainment shows and partners to deliver health information for at-risk audiences.* Paper presented at the annual meeting of the American Public Health Association, Boston, MA. (Data available at www.cdc.gov/communication/healthsoap.htm.)

Becker, M. H. (1974). *The health belief model and personal health behavior.* Thorofare, NJ: Slack.

Blakley, J. (2001). *Entertainment goes global: Mass culture in a transforming world* (Research Reports and Occasional Papers, No. 2). Los Angeles: University of Southern California, Norman Lear Center.

Brinson, S. L., & Brown, M. H. (1997). The AIDS risk narrative in the 1994 CDC campaign. *Journal of Health Communication, 2,* 101–112.

Brodie, M., Foehr, U., Rideout, V., Baer, N., Miller, C., Flournoy, R., & Altman, D. (2001). Communicating health information through the entertainment media. *Health Affairs, 20,* 192–199.

CDC. (1992). Community awareness and use of HIV/AIDS-prevention services among minority populations—Connecticut, 1991. *Mortality and Morbidity Weekly Review, 30*(41), 825–829.

Champion, V. L., & Miller, T. (1996). Predicting mammography utilization through model generation. *Psychology, Health & Medicine, 1,* 273–283.

Dines, G., & Humez, J. (Eds.). (1995). *Gender, race, and class in media: A test reader.* Thousand Oaks, CA: Sage.

Fan, D. P. (1993). Quantitative estimates for the effects of AIDS public education on HIV infections. *International Journal of Biomedical Computation, 33,* 157–177.

Graham, J. (June 13, 2001). Personal letter from the chief executive officer of the American Diabetes Association to Vicki Beck, director of CDC's Entertainment-Education activity.

Graham, M. E. (2002). Health beliefs and self breast examination in black women. *Journal of Cultural Diversity, 9*(2): 49–54.

Green, S. K., Lightfoot, M. A., Bandy, C., & Buchanan, D. R. (1985). A general model of the attribution process. *Basic and Applied Social Psychology, 6,* 159–179.

Jacobs, L. A. (2002). Health beliefs of first-degree relatives of individuals with colorectal cancer and participation in health maintenance visits: a population-based survey. *Cancer Nursing, 25,* 251–265.

Jason, L. A. (1998). Tobacco, drug, and HIV preventive media interventions. *American Journal of Community Psychology, 26,* 151–187.

Kalichman, S. C. (1994). Magic Johnson and public attitudes toward AIDS: A review of empirical findings. *AIDS Education and Prevention, 6,* 542–557.

Larson, M. S. (1991). Health-related messages embedded in prime-time television entertainment. *Health Communication, 3,* 175–184.

McGuire, W. J. (1989). Theoretical foundations of campaigns. In: R. E. Rice & C. K. Atkin (Eds.), *Public communication campaigns* (pp. 43–65). Thousand Oaks, CA: Sage.

Myhre, S. L., & Flora, J. A. (2000). HIV/AIDS communication campaigns: progress and prospects. *Journal of Health Communication, 5* (Supplement), 29–45.

O'Brien, E. J., & Albrecht, J. E. (1992). Comprehension strategies in the development of a mental model. *Journal of Experimental Psychology: Learning, Memory & Cognition, 4,* 777–784.

Papa, M. J., Singhal, A., Law, S., Pant, S., Sood, S., Rogers, E. M., et al. (2000). Entertainment-education and social change: an analysis of parasocial interaction, social learning, collective efficacy, and paradoxical communication. *Journal of Communication, 50,* 31–55.

Park, C. W., & Smith, D. C. (1989). Product-level choice: A top-down or bottom-up process? *Journal of Consumer Research, 16,* 289–299.

Parrott, R. L. (1995). Motivation to attend to health messages. In E. Maibach & R. L. Parrott (Eds.), *Designing health messages: Approaches from communication theory and public health practice* (pp. 7–23). Thousand Oaks, CA: Sage.

Pfau, M. (1990). A channel approach to television influence. *Journal of Broadcasting and Electronic Media, 34,* 195–214.

Prochaska, J. O., DiClemente, C. C., & Norcross, J. C. (1992). In search of how people change: Applications to addictive behaviors. *American Psychologist, 47,* 1102–1114.

Rogers, E. M., Vaughn, P. W., Swalehe, R. M., Rao, N., Svenkernd, P., & Sood, S. (1999). Effects of an entertainment-education radio soap opera on family planning behavior in Tanzania. *Studies in Family Planning, 30,* 193–211.

Singhal, A., & Rogers, E. M. (1999). *Entertainment-education: A communication strategy for social change.* Mahwah, NJ: Erlbaum.

Siska, M., Jason, J., Murdoch, P., Yang, W. S., & Donovan, R. J. (1992). Recall of AIDS public service announcements and their impact on the ranking of AIDS as a national problem. *American Journal of Public Health, 82,* 1029–1032.

Tobin, F. (2002). Report to Frank Tobin Public Relations from Bell-Phillip Television Productions, Los Angeles, CA.

Waugh, N. C., & Norman, D. A. (1965). Primary memory, *Psychological Review, 72,* 92–93.

30

INTEREST GROUPS, THE MEDIA, AND POLICY DEBATE FORMATION: AN ANALYSIS OF MESSAGE STRUCTURE, RHETORIC, AND SOURCE CUES

Nayda Terkildsen, Frauke I. Schnell, and Cristina Ling

Editor's Note

There is a saying that a rose by any other name would smell as sweet. In politics, that is not necessarily true. The names, metaphors, and symbols used by the news media to describe a public policy determine its acceptability for various groups and its ultimate fate. Hence policy advocates go to great lengths to control the symbols associated with their efforts and to persuade the media to publicize them.

This essay describes media coverage of the abortion policy debate during a twenty-year period marked by intense struggles among pressure groups for favorable media attention. In the end, no group was able to dominate the chorus of voices; the news media's own framing carried the day. This outcome supports the authors' contention that the thrust of policy messages and issue rhetoric emerges from battles between journalists and lobbyists over framing choices.

When the three authors, all political scientists, wrote this article Nayda Terkildsen was an assistant professor at the University of California, Davis, Frauke I. Schnell was an associate professor at Pennsylvania's West Chester University, and Cristina Ling was a doctoral student at the State University of New York, Stony Brook.

... Scholars differ on whether the media reflect the political frames and language put forth by others or project their own thematic spins onto the public consciousness. Reporters assert that they report the news, not make it, that is, they act as intermediaries, not catalysts in the policy process. In turn,

Source: This selection was drawn and condensed from "Interest Groups, the Media, and Policy Debate Formation: An Analysis of Message Structure, Rhetoric, and Source Cues," by Nayda Terkildsen, Frauke I. Schnell, and Cristina Ling in *Political Communication* 15:1 (January–March 1998): 45–61. Copyright © Taylor and Francis.

they point to pressure groups and government officials as the originators of issue frames. Other political players point to one another as the real policy fomenters, asserting that it is actually their ideological or political opponents, not themselves, who hold the power. . . . In reality, however, each of these groups has the potential to shape the debate. . . . Therefore, disentangling the influence of any one set of actors and their messages, is akin to solving the riddle of the Sphinx. This is the puzzle that we tackle. In this essay we focus our efforts on specifying one possible relationship among the many links— that of the media and interest groups in shaping public policy debates. We test our hypotheses using a content analysis of print coverage of abortion controversy over a 20-year span.

Specifying the Media–Interest Group Link

. . . Interest groups must rely on the media to have their interpretations of reality inserted into the public debate. . . . Even if the media do pick up an interest group's theme, the position advocated by the group may not be transmitted in its totality, or the message may be placed in an unfavorable context, or, in the worst-case scenario, the interest group's rhetoric may be substantially altered. In other words, once pressure groups put forth an issue spin, the media's subsequent actions are beyond the scope of their control. . . .

Thus, the final communiqué citizens read is not the simple aggregation of interest group activities (e.g., staging of events, press releases, media interviews), but rather the result of a complex interaction between the media and interest groups, which in turn is largely dependent on a series of media decisions about what constitutes news, news space, and reader interests. . . . This mix of elements serves to shape and refine the message citizens ultimately consume.

For example, assume that Planned Parenthood, the largest voluntary family planning organization in the United States, sponsors a rally . . . —a clear attempt to promote their message to the public through the media. The media's response may run the gamut from no news space to a precise replication of the group's message, and everything in between. As the rally unfolds, the media will make a series of choices that are dependent on the actual events occurring at the rally, available news space, other competing issues, the impact of the event, the accessibility of spokespersons, perceptions about public interest, and other editorial judgments about whether the rally will be covered. Planned Parenthood could increase its probability of receiving coverage by packaging its message according to media standards, and perhaps come close to forcing at least a minimal level of media attention. Ultimately, however, the decision to cover the rally and whether or not their particular message reaches the public is up to the media. . . .

Influencing Public Discourse: Message Structure, Message Rhetoric, and Source Cues

Message Structure: Frames and Issue Dualism

One of the central, and best-documented, methods available to political players to structure policy debates is *issue framing*. . . . From a variety of social science research, it is clear that linguistic frames, both in the content (i.e., the specific topical focus) and the format of their representations (i.e., episodic versus thematic story lines), influence citizens' policy support and related political perceptions (Gamson, 1992; Iyengar, 1991; Kinder & Sanders, 1990; Terkildsen & Schnell, 1997).

All players in the public policy realm employ these interpretative structures. Specifically, pressure groups use these boiled-down packages in an attempt to define the gist of the controversy for the public, the media, and other key political agents. The press, in turn, uses policy frames to efficiently convey debate information to its readers. Thus, issue frames involve elements of both cognitive order and political power. In this way the issue frames put forth by the media and other players to structure the public debate may eventually become internalized as cognitive supports. Additionally, whoever controls issue formation delineates the public debate by directly or indirectly setting forth an advocacy position and triggering related value dimensions.

While framing refers to the broader interpretative structures of media coverage that place particular information or events within a context, the structure of a message is also influenced by journalistic norms, values, and routines. Thus, a second element of message structure is issue dualism, or the media's tendency to seek balance in their treatment of controversial issues. In addition to striving for a balanced presentation of issues, the media also emphasize conflict as a means of attracting readership and attention (Neuman et al., 1992). Due to the quest for conflict and the media's desire to be perceived as independent, fair-minded arbitrators of issue debates, issue dualism has come to be viewed as a surrogate for issue fairness both by journalists and by media consumers who have internalized the industry's standards. . . . It is this element of message structure, one that demands the inclusion of conflicting viewpoints, that by default allows the media leeway to create their unique version of reality while maintaining the perception of impartiality.

Message Rhetoric: Symbols and Metasymbols

Symbols. Framing techniques are not the only instruments of impression formation available to the media and policy players. The symbolic use of language can also contribute to opinion formation and may serve either to offset frames or solidify their themes. According to Gamson and Modigliani

(1987, p. 143), "every policy issue is contested in a symbolic arena . . . [where the] weapons are metaphors, catchphrases, and other condensing symbols." . . . Visual cues such as the flag, balloons, children, and enthusiastic crowds, as well as verbal allusions to God, patriotism, and folk heroes are all common examples of political symbols.

Symbols associated with any issue then serve two important functions: to delineate the public debate and to augment voters' policy awareness. Since politics is a symbolic contest about whose views, understandings, and interpretations will prevail, it is essential to analyze which issue emblems are ultimately conveyed to the public. While interest groups are capable of creating symbols to set forth their views, the decision whether or not to incorporate specific language or metaphors is ultimately, once again, up to the mass media. However, groups may be able to maximize their coverage by using dramatic symbols, such as in the abortion controversy, where some pro-life supporters focused on the fetus in a bottle, while some pro-choice groups used the image of wire hangers to galvanize support.

Metasymbols. Metasymbols are the overarching group labels that advocates create to describe their organization and its cause. Over time, metasymbols can become powerful global metaphors that stand as surrogates for an interest group's goals or ideology and become almost impossible to repudiate or modify. Group emblems such as "pro-life," "pro-choice," "black power," "gray panthers," or "jihad" (i.e., holy war) have the potential to capture the media's attention, empower supporters of a cause by evoking a broad set of values, and elevate the debate to a more emotive plane. . . .

Source Cues: Sources Cited and Source Descriptors

The use of select sources at the expense of other potential players and the adjectives journalists use to describe those sources are powerful tools at the disposal of reporters. Although it is up to interest groups to provide the media with memorable and quotable interpretations of their views, the final decision concerning whom to quote and how individuals are characterized is part of the media's domain. The media need spokespersons to fill news holes, meet deadlines, provide drama, and add issue balance. However, not all spokespersons are as able as others. Groups with accessible, coherent, or novel spokespersons are more likely to be quoted and requoted due to media norms. Thus, groups that understand the rules of the game, such as hiring public relations specialists, adding drama or glamour through events or players, and keeping their messages simple and clear, should play a larger role in the media's construction of the conflict.

However, media access does not guarantee favorable coverage. A group may meet the media's criteria for news, yet be depicted in a negative light.

The press' description of a group may either be overwhelmingly negative or subtly so. While journalists' sympathy toward a group's cause may not be a prerequisite for receiving coverage, it is surely a factor that comes into play when portraying a group's beliefs or characterizing its spokespersons. . . . To the extent that journalists add their own value judgments about groups or players to the public discourse, issue cultures become distorted. . . .

Methods

We examine abortion coverage during the 1960s and 1970s. . . . This issue and this time period allow for an ideal test of the media's influence at varying stages of the policy discourse.

In order to test our assumptions, all abortion-related articles published by *Newsweek, Time,* and *U.S. News & World Report* between 1960 and 1979 were assembled for analysis. . . . Assuming reader attentiveness, their combined coverage of the abortion debate had the potential for substantial influence on citizens. In addition, the overall coverage of the three major weeklies reflects trends in the major news dailies such as the *New York Times,* the *Washington Post,* and the *Los Angeles Times* while collectively providing a broader ideological spectrum (Davis, 1992; Hunt & Rubin, 1993). The three major news weeklies published 73 articles on abortion throughout the 1960s and 1970s. Weekly coverage was most active from 1966 to 1972, accounting for 48 percent of all articles. . . .

Articles were coded for issue frames, issue dualism, the use of abortion-related symbols, metasymbols, number of sources, and source descriptors. . . . Inter-coder reliability (Pearson's r) was .82, indicating a substantial level of agreement.

Issue frames were operationally defined by ascertaining how the policy debate was thematically structured, i.e., what arguments were suggested and what policy outcomes were either stated or implied by the articles' topical organization (Gamson, 1992; Gamson & Modigliani, 1987). Coders were trained to identify frames, and their list of frames was later compared with a catalog of possible interest group frames that we assembled from analyzing *amicus curiae* briefs submitted by advocacy groups in the *Roe* decision [*Roe v. Wade,* the 1973 U.S. Supreme Court decision that invalidated all abortion prohibitions at the state level], as well as the scholarly literature on abortion activists (Craig & O'Brien, 1993; Ginsburg, 1989; Luker, 1984). This "blueprint" of frames included eight major frames attributable to interest groups that were later used to determine if frames were media or interest group generated. These frames are (1) legal/constitutional concerns, i.e., privacy and reproductive rights; (2) physician autonomy; (3) family planning; (4) population control; (5) the right to choose; (6) women's safety; (7) regulatory reform of abortion, i.e., licensing, reporting, advertising, fetal viability, consent, notification, public funding; and (8) moral/religious concerns, i.e., rights of the unborn, moral decay.

Issue dualism is defined as the media's tendency to portray conflicting positions and seek even-handed coverage. It is a simple dichotomous measure indicating whether or not groups or spokespersons from both camps were covered in the same article. Symbols, that is, words, phrases, or euphemisms that have evolved to represent abortion (e.g., coat hangers), the fetus (e.g., unborn children), or activists (e.g., baby killers, right-to-life, abortion reformers), were examined verbatim. The source of the symbol was then documented as originating either from the reporter or from a quoted source. The examination of symbolic language utilized in abortion coverage cannot answer the question of the origins of these symbols, but does assess the extent to which the media employed symbolic language to package the abortion debate. Additionally, such an analysis determines the success interest groups had in introducing vocabulary favorable to their cause. While some of the symbols utilized by the press were emblems of their own creation, others were likely to be borrowed from pro-choice and pro-life rhetoric.

This part of the analysis also included measuring the extent to which the media utilized group labels or metasymbols, such as pro-choice and pro-life, put forward by the respective pressure groups. Measures of article sources simply required documenting the names of groups, organizations, and individuals quoted or alluded to in an article. Source descriptors were the traits or adjectives attached directly to individuals or groups by the media.

Results

. . . A content analysis of abortion coverage provides evidence of media involvement in shaping issue frames, symbolic language, metasymbols, issue dualism, and the range of quoted or summarized sources. Source descriptors indicate less media involvement in constructing the issue discourse.

Frames: . . . [T]en unique issue frames were documented between 1960 and 1979. Six of these frames were rooted in terminology or policy positions traceable to a specific interest group or spokesperson. Overall, frames were more likely to be championed by interest groups (68 percent of frames), than the media (32 percent of frames), though the press clearly had an influence in structuring a significant portion of the abortion debate.

"Physician autonomy" and "constitutional rights" were frames promoted by individual physicians, the American Civil Liberties Union, Planned Parenthood, the American Law Institute, and the Association for the Study of Abortion, among others. "Women's safety," "women's right to choose," and "abortion on demand" eventually became feminist rallying cries promoted by the women's movement and some early reformers. The frame highlighting "moral concerns" was championed by the Catholic Church and other anti-abortion coalitions such as Sons of Thunder, Birthright, National Right to Life Committee, Value of Human Life Committee, and multiple statewide Citizens for Life committees. Thus, neither set of antagonists was favored by the media; pro-life frames were used in 38 percent of the total articles, compared to 30 percent for the pro-choice camp.

The remaining four frames—"political division," "legal ebbs in liberalization," "growing strength of the abortion backlash," and "abortion as a medical-moral issue"—represent media compilations of two disparate themes, either as a way to create issue dualism or attempts to repackage a stale debate. For example, while the ethical elements of the "medical-moral" frame would have been pushed by the Catholic Church, the medical portion would have been stressed by abortion reformers. On the other hand, the "abortion backlash" frame was clearly a theme manufactured by the media to reflect the debate's evolution and boost drama.

[There were] three distinct eras of abortion coverage: pre-state liberalization campaigns (1960–1966), pre-*Roe* (1967–January 1973), and post-*Roe* (February 1973–1979). Of the 10 articles published prior to the thrust of the statewide reforms (1960–1966), 50 percent favored anti-abortionists and 40 percent the reformers, while the media framed only one article. Between 1967 and 1973, the height of the state campaigns but prior to the Supreme Court's intervention, the media transmitted pro-choice frames in 39 percent of the articles, pro-life frames in 25 percent of the pieces, and their own thematic interpretations in over one-third of the coverage (36%). In the post-*Roe* era, media-generated frames accounted for almost half of the abortion coverage (47 percent), followed by fetal rights frames (33 percent) and frames championed by reform advocates (20 percent). Unquestionably, media involvement escalated as the debate evolved, suggesting that the media did not actively promote their own issue spins until others had first defined the debate.

An analysis of *metasymbols* and *issue symbols* shows that, particularly during the early stages of the debate, the media were reluctant to adopt the global terminology and the issue placards favored by the pro- and anti-abortion organizations. . . . During the years prior to 1967, the anti-abortionist reformers were described as "people who oppose abortion," or "opponents of liberalized abortion," whereas in later years the media became substantially more likely to employ the pro-life terminology. Seventeen percent of articles published between 1967 and 1973 and more than 50 percent of articles that saw print during the post-*Roe* era called the abortion opponents "pro-lifers." The media were not as hospitable toward the pro-choice coalitions, rarely referring to these groups using their favored metasymbol or group label—"pro-choice." Instead, advocates of liberalized abortion were consistently described as "abortion reformers" or "representatives of abortion reform," "abortion advocates," or "pro-abortionists."

As for *symbols*, such as abortion epidemic, unborn children, back-alley abortions, coat hangers, about one-third (34 percent) were quoted directly from interest groups' messages. The majority of these emblems (66 percent), however, were injected by the media to provide their own version of the abortion debate, without quoting an interest group spokesperson. That does not mean that the symbols the media utilized were emblems of their own cultivation. The media undoubtedly co-opted labels from interest groups' messages. Examples are the [press'] usage of "sleazy back room abortions," "back-alley abortions," or "safe abortions," terms that were apparently borrowed from pro-choice rhetoric, and terms such as "abortion epidemic," which was adopted from pro-life discourse. . . . [M]edia-attributed symbols dominated all 20 years of coverage. Although journalists were more likely to insert pro-abortion symbols during the pre-*Roe* years, the press was equally likely to employ anti-abortion symbols after 1973.

Another indicator of media orchestration is the *range of organizations* that are given news space. . . . [P]ublic discourse during the early years of the conflict (1960–1966) was dominated by physicians and prestigious health research organizations . . . which spoke out in favor of abortion reform. The argument for legalized abortion was also made by groups such as the National Abortion Rights Action League (NARAL) and Planned Parenthood, some liberal church organizations, and politicians, most notably Governor Nelson Rockefeller of New York and other New York State Assembly members who advocated statewide reform. The most striking pattern about the press' portrayal of the pro-choice coalition during the pre- and post-*Roe* years was the absence of feminist organizations. No quotes were included from feminist spokespersons pre-*Roe* and only 9 percent of the quotes after 1973 came from women's coalitions such as the National Organization [for] Women or the National Women's Political Caucus. Arguments against abortion reform were limited to the Catholic Church and a variety of government spokespersons. . . . However, beginning as early as the mid-1960s, the visibility of the Catholic Church was bolstered by the formation of several key pro-life organizations such as the Right to Life Committee, the Coalition for Life, and Birthright.

These results again support the media's crucial role in delineating the public discourse. By repetitively citing certain groups or individuals but omitting others, the weeklies created images of coalitions of interest groups that, at times, only vaguely resembled reality. One clear example is the absence of a feminist link to abortion. Abortion was a centerpiece of the movement's agenda, and the "pro-choice" label was their attempt to linguistically and intellectually connect abortion to women's rights (Conover & Gray, 1983;

Hartmann, 1989; Klein, 1984). By failing to include the feminism-abortion link in their weekly coverage, news magazines created their own version of reality, whether consciously, as a function of the inaccessibility of feminist spokespersons, or due to media judgments about the newsworthiness of events. After *Roe*, pro-choice supporters became defenders of the status quo, a role that is less likely to produce camera-grabbing events and drama. . . .

Finally, an examination of *issue dualism*, operationally defined as coverage that references both pro-choice and pro-life organizations in one article, confirms our speculations about media attempts to create the perception of fairness using balanced coverage. Two-thirds of the articles involved balanced reporting, while 23 percent referred only to pro-choice organizations or spokespersons, and the remaining 11 percent focused exclusively on pro-life activists.

An examination of *source cues* provided only weak evidence of media orchestration. Descriptors were used in only one out of five articles. Cumulatively, there was no difference in the adjectives and traits used to describe the respective movements. However, in the early years, advocates of reform . . . tended to be described in positive terms—prestigious, reputable, prominent—which may have enhanced readers' perceptions about their credibility. Conversely, mildly negative judgments about the emotional state of activists were reserved for pro-lifers, who were depicted as emotional and zealous. However, these descriptors hardly overwhelmed coverage of either pro-choice or anti-abortion groups.

Discussion

An examination of message structure, rhetoric, and source cues suggests that the press was involved in setting much of the overall tone of abortion messages, thus ultimately shaping the public discourse. Framing techniques proved to be a key component in the media's communication arsenal. While the media incorporated the frames championed by interest groups during the earlier years of the debate, reporters and editors began to create their own analytical framework or spin as the conflict matured. Close to 50 percent of post-*Roe* abortion coverage was framed in the media's terms, not those of interest groups. This evidence suggests that the media became active in this debate only after pressure groups initially defined the issue. Thus, once the media stepped in and took an interest in the controversy, they altered the prevailing definition of the conflict (Cobb & Elder, 1983).

Our analysis of symbolic language leads us to a similar conclusion about media autonomy. Reporters did not limit themselves merely to transmitting the symbols associated with interest groups, but instead injected their own symbolic language to delineate the public discourse. The data also reveal that the media's usage of symbols initially favored pro-abortion advocates, par-

ticularly during the pre-state liberalization efforts (1960–1966), yet the symbolic nature of the media-described conflict changed after 1973, when pro-
life symbols became more prevalent.

The argument for relative media autonomy is further supported by pointing toward reporters' and editors' reluctance to use interest group labels or
metasymbols to describe opponents and supporters of legalized abortion.
Whereas the metasymbols employed by the press, such as pro-abortion versus anti-abortion may have been adequate descriptors of the pressure groups
who were active during the early to mid-1960s, these labels certainly did not
capture the public debate after the liberalization of state laws. During the
mid-1960s the abortion conflict was transformed from a medical-legal dispute to a battle over the role of women, privacy, and the sanctity of life. Once
the conflict was expanded, groups on either side of the issue had to appeal to
a much wider audience and changed their labels accordingly (Boles, 1979;
Conover & Gray, 1983). Yet not much of this new terminology was ever
transmitted to the public via the press. . . .

The decision involving which spokespersons to quote is another indicator
of how the media may craft issue debates. By creating group visibility and
linking groups to government actors, the media provide linkages for the public and estimates of coalition strength. For instance, when the media consistently aligned doctors and legal professionals with the pro-abortion side, but
not feminists, they failed to convey an accurate image of pro-choice coalitions to the public. . . . [T]he influence of the Catholic Church was substantially overestimated in the press' version of the controversy. During the early
years of the debate, anti-abortion arguments were synonymous with the
Church's theological canons about the sanctity of life, and the Church appeared to spearhead a grass-roots pro-life movement when none existed. Although we believe that these discrepancies can be attributed largely to the
media's need for issue dualism, the accessibility or inaccessibility of groups'
spokespersons and/or journalists' personal value judgments surely contributed to this pattern of coverage as well.

Although our data thus far portray the media as the real directors of the
public debate, it seems clear that media professionals still allow for individual actors' artistic input, as long as those modifications appeal to audience
members and fit within their proposed paradigm. To achieve maximum coverage, successful political players must work within the known set of media-
imposed constraints. They need to understand the media's news criteria and
tailor their messages accordingly. . . .

. . . [W]e can also assess how well each side met media-imposed criteria. . . . Receiving press attention requires an easily accessible advocate. . . .
Spokesperson accessibility, in turn, seems to facilitate professional contact with reporters. One could argue that the pro-life movement had an

organizational structure that encouraged leadership development a range of strategic repertoires. . . . While early pro-choice organiza\ benefited from a hierarchical structure, the highly decentralized l\(\epsilon\) ...\(\nu\) style of later feminist coalitions likely impeded the media's ability to locate spokespersons. . . . A pre-*Roe* comparison of the coverage of pro-life and feminist groups, indicates that ad hoc and loosely organized anti-abortion organizations were frequently interviewed by the press, while similarly structured women's organizations were not. . . . Our finding . . . seems to indicate that perhaps journalists' personal values and judgments about what is newsworthy came into play as well. However, we should consider the possibility that these ad hoc pro-life organizations were more likely than feminists to create concise group names for themselves. . . .

Women's groups may have further isolated their message from media attention by ignoring the rule of issue simplicity. Instead of following the pro-life strategy of single-mindedness, feminists advocated multiple policy positions about gender equality, of which abortion was but one element.

Drama and event-oriented coverage were two additional media criteria that influenced the effectiveness of these groups. Pro-life organizations were better at staging sensational events, particularly once their followers were galvanized by the shock of *Roe*. Anti-abortion leaders were more likely to engage in provocative or confrontational methods than were their pro-choice counterparts, a typical strategy for groups who want to alter the status quo and redefine and/or expand the conflict (Cobb & Elder, 1983). Their tactics—highly sensational, sometimes violent, and always dramatic—guaranteed media access. After *Roe*, reports on pro-choice groups defending an already-established right no longer fit conventional news narratives. . . . Cumulatively, our data imply that interest groups are not powerless in getting elements of their message through the media gamut of norms, values, news definitions, and editorial decisions. . . .

While it is always dangerous to speculate about the impact of the media on popular attitudes and beliefs without providing causal evidence, we are left to wonder to what extent the media's coverage left an indelible impression on citizens' abortion attitudes. Within the scope of our analysis, we feel confident to say that as coverage of pro-choice groups declined and media attention toward pro-life coalitions surged, readers' perceptions about the various sides' issue commitments, their strength, and the urgency of their appeals were altered. Beyond this contention we leave it up to others to deconstruct the exact influence that media-constructed reality had on public opinion.

In conclusion, our results support the argument that the media are more than a mirror on which public policy players illuminate their messages; rather, the media are the uncredited directors of policy dramas. It is the media who hold the power to interpret the performance of political actors and re-mold the play's structure. However, we caution that final conclusions must remain contingent upon further analyses.

References

Boles, Janet. (1979). *The politics of the Equal Rights Amendment: Conflict and the decision process*. New York: Longman.

Cobb, Roger W., & Elder, Charles D. (1983). *Participation in American politics: The dynamics of agenda building*. Baltimore, MD: Johns Hopkins University Press.

Conover, Pamela J., & Gray, Virginia. (1983). *Feminism and the New Right: Conflict over the American family*. New York: Praeger.

Craig, Barbara H., & O'Brien, David M. (1993). *Abortion and American politics*. Chatham, NJ: Chatham House.

Davis, Richard. (1992). *The press and American politics: The new mediator*. New York: Longman.

Gamson, William A. (1992). *Talking politics*. Boston: Cambridge University Press.

Gamson, William A., & Modigliani, Andre. (1987). The changing culture of affirmative action. In Richard Braungart (Ed.), *Research in political sociology*, vol. 3. Greenwich, CT: JAI Press.

Ginsburg, Faye D. (1989). *Contested lives: The abortion debate in an American community*. Berkeley, CA: University of California Press.

Hartmann, Susan. (1989). *From margin to mainstream: American women and politics since 1960*. New York: Alfred A. Knopf.

Hunt, Todd, & Rubin, Brent. (1993). *Mass communication*. New York: Harper-Collins.

Iyengar, Shanto. (1991). *Is anyone responsible? How television frames political issues*. Chicago: University of Chicago Press.

Kinder, Donald R., & Sanders, Lynn. (1990). Mimicking political debate with survey questions: The case of white opinion and affirmative action. *Social Cognition, 8,* 73–103.

Klein, Ethel. (1984). *Gender politics*. Cambridge, MA: Harvard University Press.

Luker, Kristin. (1984). *Abortion and the politics of motherhood*. Berkeley, CA: University of California Press.

Neuman, W. Russell, Just, Marion, & Crigler, Ann. (1992). *Common knowledge: News and the construction of meaning*. Chicago: University of Chicago Press.

Terkildsen, Nayda, & Schnell, Frauke. (1997). Issue frames, the media and public opinion: An analysis of the women's movement. *Political Research Quarterly, 50,* 877–899.

Part VI

REGULATING AND MANIPULATING MEDIA EFFECTS

Although the scholarly community remains engaged in lively debate about the scope of media power, governments and people everywhere treat the media as extremely powerful political actors. Government officials therefore try to make sure through legislation and less formal means that news stories will not work at cross-purposes with their policies and will not endanger national interests. In fact, most large government units invest sizeable resources in efforts to manipulate the news so that stories favor their causes.

This section begins with an examination of the political forces that come into play in the United States when Congress wrestles with formulating and adopting laws for controlling media power. Since the First Amendment to the U.S. Constitution prohibits Congress from making any "law abridging the freedom of the press," many people wrongly believe that all U.S. media are free from government control. Print media do enjoy ample, although not unlimited, freedom to support or sabotage governmental policies and philosophies and to grant or deny publicity to various interest groups and viewpoints. The situation has been quite different for the broadcast media, although legislators and regulatory commissions explicitly deny any intent to control news content. Still, laws and other government regulations cover many essential aspects of broadcast media operations and shape news content more or less directly.

Who controls the deliberations that produce these laws and regulations? Patricia Aufderheide traces the pressures brought on Congress by various interest groups when a major law, like the Telecommunications Act of 1996, takes shape. In the process, the strident claims of government and industry interests invariably trump the more muted claims made on behalf of the general public. Regulatory policies more often serve the interests of the regulated than those of the presumed beneficiaries of the restraints placed on media.

The growth of the Internet has drastically changed the news media scene. The Web provides a cheap route open to millions of people to send messages worldwide and record their views for anyone willing to read them. Observers have argued that the open architecture of the Internet communications system makes it impossible for anyone, including governments and international organizations, to regulate the circulation of messages on the Web. Daniel W. Drezner throws a wet blanket on this vision—or nightmare—of control-free worldwide communication. He traces the efforts of major governments to keep control over Internet communications and alleges that they have been successful thus far. Many aspects of control have been delegated to nongovernmental organizations or the private sector, but governments still specify and enforce how these controls are exercised.

Obviously, governments have learned that it is often far easier to sport a velvet glove than an iron fist when controlling the behavior of the media and the public. The history of media censorship in times of war or other crises in the United States provides many illustrations. Doris A. Graber's essay traces how the federal government has moved from heavy-handed wartime controls that included everything from imprisonment of government critics to a system of wooing the press through facilitating access to news stories. But the access privileges are limited and the news flow is constrained by swearing most government news sources to secrecy and by equating self-censorship with patriotism. The end result is a controlled press even in the absence of strong censorship laws.

The next essay shows that manipulation of the press is not limited to times of crisis. Martin Linsky details how government officials try to manipulate the media to foster their preferred policies during times of peace and how they dodge the damaging fallout from investigatory journalism. Linsky describes the successful efforts of the U.S. Postal Service to generate news stories in support of postal reforms opposed by powerful interest groups. His research has convinced him that efforts to win favorable publicity are absolutely essential to effective governance. The idea of manipulation may be distasteful, but abandoning the practice would most likely prove disastrous.

If manipulation is inevitable, are there limits that should not be transgressed in democratic societies? Masha Lipman and Michael McFaul suggest where these limits may lie in their criticism of Vladimir Putin's treatment of the Russian press. They accuse Putin of overstepping these limits when he ousts journalists hostile to the government from management of their media and replaces them with those friendlier to the incumbent administration. The authors claim that Putin fabricated false charges to imprison his enemies and that these harsh measures intimidate the remaining journalists. Their conclusions seem to be that rewarding media for supporting the government is permissible, but punishing them severely for attacks smacks of authoritarianism. The carrot passes muster, the stick does not.

In the final selection Jarol B. Manheim focuses on communication strategies used by foreign countries that seek to control their images in the American press. Such efforts to manipulate American media are often successful because astute public relations practitioners know how to attract or discourage media coverage. Their job is particularly easy when news about distant and unfamiliar countries is involved. American journalists are eager to get potentially expensive news cheaply, especially when communication professionals have packaged it attractively for American audiences. Unfortunately, American journalists often lack the expertise to judge these stories critically, making them vulnerable to reporting misinformation.

31

COMMUNICATIONS POLICY AND THE PUBLIC INTEREST

Patricia Aufderheide

Editor's Note

Why should governments regulate telecommunication, and for whose benefit primarily? Patricia Aufderheide sets forth various rationales for a regulatory policy for U.S. telecommunication enterprises. She also delineates the clashing interests of businesspeople, who oppose most restraints, and average citizens, who want government protection from messages they deem socially harmful. The Telecommunications Act of 1996 seeks to juggle these demands in an age characterized by an ever-expanding array of governmental and industry stakeholders in the telecommunications arena. Compared to these experienced and well-financed players in the pressure-group politics game, the civic sector is poorly represented and its interests are short-changed.

At the time of writing Aufderheide was a professor in the School of Communication at American University in Washington, D.C., and director of its Center for Social Media. She is a prolific cultural journalist, policy analyst, and editor on media and society and has received numerous journalism and scholarly awards, including Fulbright and Guggenheim fellowships.

Telecommunications policy is a calculated government intervention in the structures of businesses that offer communications and media services. The public is endlessly invoked in communications policy, but rarely is it consulted or even defined. Policymakers claim that they do what they do in the name of and for the benefit of the people they represent, who may or may not be consumers of the service. Without this connection to the public, policymakers would have no grounds to intervene in these businesses.

Source: Excerpted from Patricia Aufderheide, *Communications Policy and the Public Interest: The Telecommunications Act of 1996,* New York: The Guilford Press, 1999, chapters 1 and 5. Reprinted by permission of The Guilford Press.

Who is the public that U.S. policy represents, and what is its interest? . . . [E]arly communications and antitrust regulators took it to be coterminous with the economic health of a capitalist society, associated with social peace and prosperity. This is a definition that . . . effectively made government regulators the representatives of society's interests as well as of the large, stable businesses the government regulators helped to create and maintain. . . .

Another way to see the public is as an agglomeration of consumers, or potential consumers. . . . While opening the door to much broader (and more politically volatile) participation, this definition can lead to checkbook democracy on a grassroots level, where people participate in society to the extent that they are consumers, and to the extent that they exercise consumer choice. Not only does the definition measure social participation only by purchase, but it also conveniently ignores the social institutional structures within which we all live, and within which consumers make their small choices.

There is also much in communication policy that reaches past traditional economic concerns, whether at the macro- or microlevel, and that reaches into social welfare considerations. Government regulators act as allies of and sometimes protectors of the weak and vulnerable in society. Policies have been made to protect children, the disabled, rural dwellers, the poor; these policies ensure equality of access to a communications technology for everyone, no matter what's in their wallets or on their minds; and these policies further the political promise of free expression. Policies have even attempted to set cultural standards, such as public decency on the airwaves, and have attempted to create cultural spaces, as in the case of public broadcasting.

Each of these social welfare–oriented approaches has a slightly different take on the notion of the public and its relationship to government. Some approaches are blatantly paternalistic, and some respond to the squeaky-wheel version of American politics. But all of them go beyond economic concerns. They indicate, sometimes clumsily, the notion that the public is more than a mass of consumers or the inhabitants of a commercial society, but rather is a social institution important enough to address in nonmarketplace ways. These approaches can easily result in patch-up policies or can be accused of catering to special interests, however vulnerable or worthy those interests may be.

In recent decades, with the rise of deregulation, market liberals who are concerned with policy have basically asserted that the public is roughly the same thing, for the purposes of policymaking, as a vigorous marketplace. They have advocated deregulation, in order to promote an unfettered marketplace. However, in large infrastructure industries, deregulation does not necessarily lead to competition. Even then, these advocates would argue, so long as the sector is vigorous, growing, widely offering more jobs and a greater selection of products and choices, it acts in the public interest.

The equation of public interest with an unregulated marketplace, which has grown to be widely accepted, has resulted in disconnecting social consequences from the cultivation of the marketplace. But the booming electronic media and telecommunications marketplaces inevitably affect cultural habits and have social consequences. Dial-a-porn, Jerry Springer scandal shows, wrong credit rating data spread via the Internet are a few among many of the concerns that have mobilized activists to demand government action. Such concerns are marginalized into a fringe area of policy. A zone of cultural backlash grows, where antipornography, antiviolence, anticensorship, pro-privacy, and anti-hate crimes advocates all sullenly hunker down. Those pioneers of emerging social landscapes find uneasy alliances as often as they carve out new Balkan states of opinion. And inevitably, cultural advocates of all kinds return to policymakers.

This has been a pattern throughout the history of U.S. communications regulation, but it appears ever more boldly as deregulation unleashes new market behaviors and intensifies others. There is a bipolar quality to current communications policies. The passion for regulatory platforms that permit unregulated industries, unbounded by government constraints, vies with the passion for social control over the emerging networks and channels that we plug into each day.

The problem of designing policies appropriate to today's and tomorrow's communications technologies and business environments always comes back to the problem of the public. . . . Communications policy either encourages or discourages public life, whatever its intent. So, of course, do many other social policies, including electoral practices and educational regimes. But communications structures in many ways map our social connections, and our communications practices express our cultural habits and understandings.

Legal scholar Monroe Price (1995) shows that electronic media regulation has long danced around the question of culture. He argues for policies that recognize the importance of electronic media for establishing and maintaining public spaces. Simply endorsing the competitive marketplace, as if to do so were a value-neutral decision, merely displaces problems.

Within this notion of the public, then, policies make the political culture of a democracy a central priority. This argument accords well with those of political philosophers who argue, as does Sandel (1996), that

the formative aspect of republican politics requires public spaces. . . . The global media and markets that shape our lives beckon us to a world beyond boundaries and belonging. But the civic resources we need to master these forces, or at least to contend with them, are still to be found in the places and stories, memories and meanings, incidents and identities, that situate [us] in the world and give our lives their moral particularity. (p. 349)

The revival of what Benjamin Barber (1984) contagiously called "strong democracy"—a more participatory and communitarian political system—requires "constructive civic uses of the new telecommunications technology" (p. 277).

But this approach to the public and the public interest has not been popular within the world of communications regulation. Over the years since the 1927 Radio Act, which was the precursor of the 1934 Communications Act, struggles over the notion of the public interest have inevitably, but often messily and uncomfortably, reflected the relationship between communications and culture. The very principles of economic intervention upon which regulation emerged as a social practice make it hard to see the connection between communication and culture. The First Amendment as it has evolved in the 20th century has also complicated any clear articulation. But tensions and conflicts in policy can often be seen as deriving from the thick and tangled relationship between communications businesses and services, on the one hand, and the expectations and habits of the societies they serve, on the other.

Rewriting the Rules

The creation of the Telecommunications Act of 1996, which President Bill Clinton signed into law on February 8, 1996, raised to public view issues that are often buried in regulatory procedures, and it showcased questions of the social impact of telecommunications policy.

The Act was designed to create a regulatory platform that would permit broad competition among different kinds of telecommunications service providers, encourage innovation, and recognize rapid technological change. The Act attempts to jump-start an era in which communications industries—and especially networked businesses that offer telephony and related network services—can operate as unregulated competitors rather than as monolithic utilities.

To accomplish this, the legislation rewrote the basic law that governs communications policy from top to bottom. That does not mean that the new law abolishes policies of the past or that it is even very foresightful, much less effective. In its amending of the 1934 Communications Act, the new law sketches out some regulatory principles, creates some possibilities, and proposes a controversial premise of interindustry competition. Its sketches may end up being far different from a workable, regulatory regime. But it is without a doubt the first step in a decisively different regulatory universe for communications.

The law lurched and stumbled into existence, driven forward by a combination of ideological and technological changes to the terms of an existing compact between big business and big government. For two decades before its passage, Congress attempted in a variety of ways to comprehend, foster, and get some social benefit from changing communications technologies. The ensuing law contains within it elements of previous regulatory regimes, and elements of a new one as well.

Its inelegance has a long history. The evolution of electronic communications policy has been a complex, and often ad hoc, process. This process has reflected, in part, the separate, independent development of several kinds of businesses. Each of those businesses, ranging from telephony to radio and television to computing, has evolved with its own logic. Government regulation evolved parochially with each industry, and typically with a powerful allegiance to incumbents (Winston, 1986).

But today, the technologies of telephony, mass media, and computing increasingly cross the borders of their traditional business arenas. Would-be entrepreneurs, within and without central industry positions, increasingly chafe at regulatory regimes designed for a former era and oppose opportunities for others than themselves. Those regimes emerge from a welter of places. They include, at the federal level, Congress, the Federal Communications Commission, the Department of Justice, the Federal Trade Commission, and the Department of Commerce. At the state and local level, Public Service Commissions and Public Utility Commissions have powerful sway over telecommunications, while municipalities have plenty to negotiate with any user of their rights of way, such as cable companies.

This state will continue. Under the new law, multiple jurisdictions remain, and industry rivals go on making the most of leverage won by pitting courts, legislators, and regulators against each other. But industry frustration with lack of clarity about the legality and regulatory structure of emerging technology uses was a powerful push toward the rewrite as it finally emerged.

Technological Innovation

Changes in the technical possibilities of telecommunications have been dramatic in the last four decades, building on a hefty investment in communications research during and after World War II. Those innovations have also changed the shapes of the industries involved and have introduced new players (Cairncross, 1997).

Technical innovations have brought new services and also have challenged the value of monopoly. *More*, *bigger*, and *faster* were key words for these changes. These innovations also made increasingly artificial the crafted distinction between common-carriage networks and editor-based mass media. These innovations made it possible to imagine (and even experience) communications networks that had multiple purposes and to imagine spectrum with multiple or shared uses.

Key technical innovations included satellites and digitally based information processing. Satellites permitted, among other things, vastly more efficient, over-the-air, point-to-multipoint transmission of large amounts of information. Satellites turned cable from a small-time, mom-and-pop local business dedicated to improving the television viewer's reception of over-the-air signals into a highly centralized industry featuring local delivery of satellite-delivered signals. Satellites made it economically viable for newspapers to produce regional editions across the nation, using satellite-delivered copy. Satellites generated new mass media services and, indeed, eventually, a new video platform in direct broadcast satellite, or DBS. Satellite access also changed the economics of telephone networks, vastly shrinking the costs of connection and shrinking as well the difference between local and long-distance service.

Digital processing, which is the motor of growth in computing, has been another major disruptive force in the organization of communications industries. The encoding of signals in simple, binary code, allowing computers both to compute and to communicate with great accuracy and speed, has rocked the way we do business in everything from stock trading to shopping for swimsuits and has powerfully affected all telecommunications businesses. It has squeezed and reshaped spectrum, it has multiplied the uses to which we put phones, and it has hosted a new mode of communication, namely, the many-to-many environment of the Internet. It has provided a common electronic language on the spectrum, making the spectrum far more mutable, permitting machines to talk to machines, and blurring the distinction between content and infrastructure on any system.

Perhaps most important, digital processing has changed the very characteristics of communications networks. Rapidly evolving computing that is based on digital processing has made it possible to decentralize networks. Many of the decisions once made in large centralized switches are now made at intermediate stops or even within the consumer's telephone. Along with increased flexibility and the potential to reconfigure the very shape of networks and subnetworks, decentralized digital processing has dramatically increased the amount of intelligence—or the ability to respond to input and take action—in communications networks. This innovation provides a fundamental challenge to the notion of common carriage, or the restriction of network providers to transmission alone, because the clear lines between content and conduit have become muddied. Networks themselves have information, or content, built into them.

Related innovations have greatly, and suddenly, affected the variables of price, speed, and the cost of communication. Fiber optic wires, transmitting digital signals, vastly increased the capacity of wired networks. Compression techniques, ever in refinement, have permitted both increased speed of transmission and also new kinds of transmission. Wireless connections, in combination with wired networks, have permitted cheap, mobile communication in cellular phones as well as in data and even video transmission. Large businesses were the first beneficiaries of these innovations, and the incorporation of these innovations into business practice have driven further development, as well as the appetite for procompetitive policy (Harvey, 1992).

The elements of technological change that pushed toward rewriting the Communications Act were those that made it easy for telecommunications-based services to tap into existing networks and were those that potentially corroded the line between mass media and telecommunications. The first undercut the case for monopoly, and the second blurred regulatory categories. When a broadcaster was able to use part of available spectrum for non-broadcast services such as paging; when a phone company was tempted out of the common carrier box, maybe even to dream of offering cable service; when a cable network was able to offer phone service or Internet service to its customers, many different stakeholders appeared to redraw the rules. And when business—locally, internationally and virtually—had built telecommunications into its own infrastructures, all large users became invested in the prices and terms of provision of service.

The Political Process

The evolution of this rewrite legislation was, however, not primarily understandable as a result of technological innovation that was driving change, although technology transformation was important in it. As described by Robert Horwitz in his pathbreaking analysis *The Irony of Regulatory Reform* (1989), transformations in regulatory approach can best be seen as a political process. Summarizing the historical process of deregulation in infrastructure industries throughout the past three decades, he notes:

> The reasons are, as usual, a complex mosaic of regulatory, political, economic, legal, and ideological factors. In telecommunications and banking they include technological changes as well. But . . . deregulation is at bottom a *political* phenomenon. Deregulation is basically a story of political movement from regulatory activism to regulatory "reform."
>
> Nonetheless, deregulation *could not have occurred* without these supporting, underlying factors. . . . As a result [of the interplay between economic trends, political organizing, and legal actions], by the mid-1970s regulation came to be held responsible for the fall of American economic productivity. That ideological shift was surprisingly important, especially because it underlay the changing terms in which various political elites conceptualized regulation. (p. 198; emphasis in original)

Thus, the very notion of what regulation is and should be was at stake. Progressive Era federal agencies grew up around antitrust concerns generated by the monopolistic behavior of large national corporations. Such regulation safeguarded interests of small producers from large corporations. New Deal era agencies such as the Federal Communications [Commission] were mandated to protect and nurture specific industries. Such agencies ostensibly safeguarded the interests of consumers by providing the context in which dependable, affordable services could grow. The stability of this system "of mutual compromises and benefits to major corporations, organized labor, and even consumers" (Horwitz, 1989, p. 17) was irrevocably undermined in the 1960s and 1970s, with dramatic new technological possibilities. That instability was accompanied and facilitated by ideological ferment, in which the basic notion of what regulation—and even government itself—does came under revision. . . .

The Public Interest Beyond the Act

The Telecommunications Act of 1996 ensures that some kind of competitive telecommunications environment will emerge. But it is still not clear what kind of environment that will be, or what its advantages will be for social equity, democratic relationships, and the civil culture of a pluralist society. The Act ratifies long-developing trends toward a competitive marketplace, vertically integrated corporations, and a minimalist regulatory stance. It does not create a policy framework that resolves conflicts arising from a competitive environment, as the universal service debate demonstrates. It also raises questions about the capacity of government regulators to monitor uncompetitive behavior among the giants who are now unleashed.

If the most basic objectives of the 1996 Act are accomplished, then defining and acting upon the public interest in telecommunications become even more complicated, more contentious, and more public than ever before. FCC chairman Reed Hundt recognized this. As he put it succinctly on the eve of his departure from the Commission,

The primary job of the FCC Chairman historically was to give licenses to the airwaves to a limited group of folk and to rig markets so none would ever do poorly. The good reason was to permit the firms to do well economically; the bad effect was a closed, oligopolized market with little diversity of viewpoint.

The primary job now ought to be the opposite: introduce risk and reward to all sectors of the communications business.

The problem then is how to promote noncommercial purposes—such as conducting civic debate about political issues or educating kids—without simply relying on a cozy partnership between government and a tiny group of media magnates. (Hundt, 1997)

That last problem has no easy answers. The preceding six decades had established no clear precedent about what noncommercial functions or social objectives are appropriate for government attention in communications policy. Instead, that history established that such concerns would be dealt with after the fact, accommodated at the margins, or made the subject of endless and ongoing debate. . . .

The emerging communications landscape is thus, unsurprisingly, impoverished in public sites or even noncommercial arenas of any kind. For instance, in the Act, public TV is simply treated as another broadcaster, potentially benefitting from digital spectrum (but not required to contribute to the quality of public life in any way as a result). Cable access channels that already exist are recognized but not encouraged or given a more general mandate. Schools, libraries, and rural health care facilities are given modest and oblique encouragement to build public relationships through a universal service provision that facilitates their access to advanced communications technologies. That provision sets aside nothing for equipment, teacher training, investment in community education, or civic activities that might make use of such networks.

There are no subsidies here, of course, for programming, production, or content creation associated with civic, community, or democratic behaviors and relationships. And there are no likely sources elsewhere in cultural policy. Such subsidy is being stripped away throughout the society. The National Endowments for the Humanities and Arts are both on the endangered species lists. Even the Department of Commerce's grants for demonstration non-profit-sector projects in distributed networking (the so-called TIIAP, or Telecommunications and Information Infrastructure Assistance Program, grants) are held hostage to congressional whim. To the extent that there are economic benefits to the society from the changing terms of communications businesses, the largesse is thus carefully protected from falling upon the ground of daily political life. The notion of a protected electronic commons has been quashed, by corporations aspiring to be at once the shapers of culture and the delivery systems of it.

The sheer abundance of communications options is unlikely to lead, in itself, to formations of electronic commonses. The promise that burgeoning communications systems will create an abundance of access, making governmentally protected spaces and activities unnecessary, turns out to be hollow as the electronic universe expands. It is not merely that corporations that are developing new services are striving to develop proprietary gates and pathways through that electronic universe. In order to make use of any such common or public spaces, people have to have something to say, someone to talk to, and something that can happen. They need habits, knowledge, history, resources.

A minitest of the opportunities provided by open space was initiated when the FCC addressed the problem of using space set aside for noncommercial purposes on DBS. This was an issue raised in the 1992 Cable Act, then set aside because of legal action for several years. Finally, in 1997, there was, hypothetically, space for noncommercial and public purposes available on direct broadcast satellite services. Who, the FCC basically asked, wanted to use such space, and for what? Viable takers were few. The two entities with ready programming appropriate for the channel—a consortium of universities, and public TV—were long-time recipients of various kinds of public subsidy (Aufderheide, 1998).

At the same time, informational and communications abundance increases in the commercial sphere, often feeding social polarization. Broad discontent and unease does not stop, for lack of ways and places to resolve it. It gets expressed in clumsy policy. The bipolar approach to communications policy sets up a dynamic that pushes for new solutions. The deregulatory era may thus lead to renewed governmental intrusion. It may also create conditions for renewed civic activism around communications, as incoherent discontent is articulated and channeled. The quality of a new wave of regulatory reform will depend on the vitality, diversity, and vision of such civic activism.

Ironically, civic activism may be essential to the success of a much-vaunted competitive business environment. The principle of forbearance, so central to the regulatory logic of the Act, not only assumes the vitality of marketplace forces but implies a vital and active civic sector as a concomitant of functioning markets. And yet that sector is starved of resources.

Government will also continue to be a crucial tool of transition, as Gigi Sohn, executive director of Media Access Project, told an audience at the libertarian Cato Institute:

> Government can play a constructive role in making markets work better, thereby lessening the need for government involvement in the future, and, in particular, obviating intrusive content-based regulation. It can do so by ensuring that all Americans have access to the tools that are becoming more and more central to education, the economy, social interaction, First Amendment values and democracy. And it can do so by making more competitive markets than are currently dominated by entrenched monopolies. (Sohn, 1997, Appendix G)

Predictable cries of outrage at media concentration were common after passage of the Act, especially from journalists (Hickey, 1997; Schechter, 1997) and academics (Barnouw et al., 1997; McChesney, 1997). The Media and Democracy Congresses of 1996 and 1997 featured vigorous denunciations of media fat cats by left-wing journalists, and at Cultural Environment Movement meetings speakers denounced commercialism in media as a kind of pollution.

But far harder for media activists, noted consultant David Bollier, was finding "a coherent, positive *vision* that can help mobilize and unify diverse nonprofit players," in comparison with the "intellectually respectable, highly marketable consumerist and entertainment-oriented vision of the new media" put forward in the corporate world. What was needed was a "sovereign citizen vision" of community and civic life supported crucially by a web of accessible electronic pathways and services. To do that, he argued, there needed to be more, larger, more committed and visible constituencies than civic advocates had been able to mobilize for anything other than consumer price issues (Bollier, 1997). . . .

Advocates of civil society, concerned with communications policy, will have their hands full in coming years. It will be crucial to assess the viability of the association between the public interest and a competitive environment in communications policy. Is competition truly developing? Does it strengthen the economy and workers' and consumers' options within it? Is that competition also fostering or permitting democratic behaviors, public life, and mutual respect? It will also be important to use, even if in demonstration projects, emerging communications to foster habits and relationships of civil society. Systems that have already become the lifeblood of global business surely have applications for vital democratic practices in the global community. Finally, it will be important to promote policies that pay for such experiments in public practice.

The passage and implementation of the legislation revising the platform for U.S. communications policy has demonstrated a continuing and even increased need for social participation on familiar issues of industry structure. It has demonstrated a continuing need for regulators to monitor performance by media corporations of their public obligations. Finally, it has shown the growing importance of the complicated fact that communications systems transmit not merely information but culture.

References

Aufderheide, P. (1998). The public interest in new communications services: The DBS debate. In A. Calabrese & J. C. Burgelman (Eds.), *Communication, citizenship and social policy: Re-thinking the limits of the welfare state*. Lanham, MD: Rowman & Littlefield.

Barber, B. (1984). *Strong democracy*. Berkeley: University of California Press.

Barnouw, E., et al. (1997). *Conglomerates and the media*. New York: New Press.

Bollier, D. (1997). *Reinventing democratic culture in an age of electronic networks*. Chicago: John D. and Catherine T. MacArthur Foundation.

Cairncross, F. (1997). *The death of distance: How the communications revolution will change our lives*. Boston: Harvard Business School Press.

Harvey, D. (1992). *The condition of postmodernity*. Cambridge: Blackwell.

Hickey, N. (1997, January/February). So big: The Telecommunications Act at Year One. *Columbia Journalism Review*, pp. 23–32.

Horwitz, R. B. (1989). *The irony of regulatory reform*. New York: Oxford University Press.

Hundt, R. (1997, September 23). Yale Law School 1997 Dean's Lecture Series. www.fcc.gov.

McChesney, R. (1997). *Corporate media and the threat to democracy*. New York: Seven Stories Press.

Price, M. (1995). *Television, the public sphere, and national identity*. New York: Oxford University Press.

Sandel, M. (1996). *Democracy's discontent: America in search of a public philosophy*. London: Belknap Press of Harvard University Press.

Schechter, D. (1997). *The more you watch the less you know*. New York: Seven Stories Press.

Sohn, G. (1997, September 12). *Why government is the solution, and not the problem* [Speech at Cato Institute]. Washington, DC: Media Access Project.

Winston, B. (1986). *Misunderstanding media*. Cambridge: Harvard University Press.

32

THE GLOBAL GOVERNANCE OF THE INTERNET

Daniel W. Drezner

Editor's Note

Many Internet gurus contend that the Internet is beyond the control of governmental organizations because it cuts across traditional political boundaries and because individuals and organized groups have unrestricted access to it. Daniel W. Drezner presents strong evidence that the gurus are wrong and that states do, indeed, control the Internet. He demonstrates how traditional nation-states, especially the world's strongest powers, shape the global rules for Internet operations. Drezner shows how they often delegate control operations to nongovernmental organizations or the private sector but always in ways that assure that the operations are in tune with what the dominant states want. The outcome is an efficiently managed Internet that does not give monopoly power to any one actor, be it a nation-state, an international body, a nongovernmental organization, or a privately controlled industry.

When this essay was written, Drezner was an assistant professor of political science at the University of Chicago. The essay was adapted from his book manuscript *Who Rules? The Regulation of Globalization*. His writings are concentrated in the fields of foreign policy and global political economy.

. . . Do globalization and the Internet weaken the ability of states to regulate the global economy? This paper argues that . . . states, particularly the great powers, remain the primary actors for handling the social and political externalities created by globalization and the Internet. As the primary actors, the great powers are the most consistently successful in achieving their preferences relative to other actors. Powerful states will use a range of foreign policy substitutes, such as coercion, inducements, delegation, and forum

Source: Daniel W. Drezner, "The Global Governance of the Internet: Bringing the State Back In," *Political Science Quarterly* 119:3 (Fall 2004): 477–498. Reprinted by permission of *Political Science Quarterly.*

shopping across different international institutions to advance their desired preferences into desired outcomes. Nonstate actors can still influence outcomes on the margins, but their interactions with states are more nuanced than the globalization literature suggests.

The substitutability principle is essential to understanding how globalization affects global governance.[1] States can and will substitute different governance structures, and different policy tools to create those structures, depending on the constellation of state interests. Great-power options include delegating regime management to nonstate actors, creating international regimes with strong enforcement capabilities, generating competing regimes to protect material interests, and tolerating the absence of effective cooperation because of divergent state preferences. Because globalization scholars fail to consider the delegation strategy as a conscious state choice, they have misinterpreted the state's role in global governance.

The international regulation of the Internet provides a fertile testing ground for these arguments. Prior analysis on the Internet has been fuzzy, due in part to the assumption that all Internet-related activity can be defined along a single policy dimension. In fact, the Internet has generated multiple areas of governance, including the development of technical protocols, censorship, e-taxation, intellectual property, and privacy rights. For many of these issue areas, states express divergent interests, halt cross-border Internet transactions that contradict their preferences, and use international governmental organizations (IGOs) and treaties to advance their preferences. Even on issues in which there are large zones of agreement, such as the standardization of technical protocols, the great powers will manipulate private forms of authority to achieve their desired ends. . . .

Globalization and the Internet: The Accepted Wisdom

Over the past decade, there has been an energetic debate about how globalization alters governance. From this debate, one can distill two clear hypotheses about the effects of globalization on the management of the global political economy. In the first, globalization undercuts state sovereignty, weakening governments' ability to effectively regulate their domestic affairs. Global market forces are both powerful and uncontrollable, stripping governments of their agency. As Thomas Friedman phrases it, globalization forces states into the "Golden Straitjacket," in which they must choose between "free market vanilla and North Korea."[2] A number of international relations scholars have argued that globalization drastically reduces the state's ability to govern.[3]

The second hypothesis is that as state power has waned, globalization has simultaneously enhanced the power of nonstate actors via the reduction of transaction costs across borders. The characterization of these nonstate actors varies from author to author. Peter Haas argues that when communities of technical experts reach a consensus on a particular policy issue, governments will follow their lead.[4] Paul Wapner posits that the growth of NGOs [nongovernmental organizations] amounts to the creation of a global civic society that is too powerful for states to ignore.[5] Virginia Haufler observes that multinational corporations often create their own governance structures to compensate for the retreating state, leading to new "private authority" structures.[6]

International relations theorists and cyberenthusiasts agree that the Internet greatly enhances both of these effects of globalization. Regarding state power, Frances Cairncross notes, "Government jurisdictions are geographic. The Internet knows few boundaries. The clash between the two will reduce what individual countries can do. Government sovereignty, already eroded by forces such as trade liberalization, will diminish further. . . . One result: no longer will governments be able to set the tax rates or other standards they want."[7] Viktor Mayer-Schüonberger and Deborah Hurley observe, "Governance based on geographic proximity, territorial location and exclusivity of membership to such physical communities will be fundamentally challenged by the advent of numerous non-proximity-based, overlapping virtual communities."[8] Cyberguru John Perry Barlow opined that "By creating a seamless global economic zone, borderless and unregulatable, the Internet calls into question the very idea of the nation-state."[9]

There is also general agreement that the Internet enhances the power of nonstate actors, permitting them to network at an ever-increasing level of sophistication. Stephen Kobrin asserts that because NGOs coordinated their strategies and actions over the Internet, they were able to derail the efforts of the developed countries to fashion a Multilateral Agreement on Investment.[10] Ronald Deibert concurs, arguing: "What the Internet has generated is indeed a new 'species'—a cross-national network of citizen activists linked by electronic mailing lists and World-Wide Web home pages that vibrate with activity, monitoring the global political economy like a virtual watchdog."[11] The increased coordination of protests at venues such as Seattle, Washington, Genoa, and other ports of call speaks to the sophistication of nonstate actors in the Internet age.

Following these arguments to their logical conclusion, the issue area in which the effects of globalization should be at their most concentrated is the regulation of the Internet itself. Internet governance should see states at their most enfeebled and nonstate actors at their most powerful. This is certainly the conclusion of most international relations scholars who study the Internet. Deborah Spar observes, "International organizations lack the power to police cyberspace; national governments lack the authority; and the slow pace of interstate agreement is no match for the rapid-fire rate of technological change."[12] Haufler concurs, noting, "The decentralized, open, global character of . . . the Internet makes it difficult to design and implement effective regulations through top-down, government-by-government approaches.[13] Cyberenthusiasts concur with this assessment. Nicholas Negroponte, the cofounder of MIT's Media Lab, states: "The Internet cannot be regulated. It's not that laws aren't relevant, it's that the nation-state is not relevant.[14] . . .

* * *

When States Disagree about the Internet

. . . Because most goods and services produced for the Internet are created in the advanced industrialized states, [developing] countries have an incentive to enforce IPR [Intellectual Property Rights]. Developing countries prefer lax standards as a way of accelerating the transfer of technology and lowering the cost of acquiring new innovations and ideas.[15]

The emerging international regulatory regime on this issue mirrors great-power preferences. In 1996, the World Intellectual Property Organization . . . negotiated two treaties—one on copyrights and one on performances and phonograms—to cover online [Intellectual Property Rights]. Experts agree that these treaties provide "strong" IPR protection.[16] These efforts came in the wake of American and European efforts to apply economic sanctions against countries with lax IPR regimes.[17] . . . Statistical analyses demonstrate that the threat of WTO sanctions had a significant effect on copyright enforcement. Between 1995 and 2000, software piracy declined by nearly 20 percent in developing countries. . . .

The regulation of data privacy is a good example of the rival-standards outcome. As more commerce is transacted over the Internet, there is increased concern about firms or governments taking advantage of the personal information of online consumers. Opinion polls show that privacy is the biggest concern of Internet users.[18] The European Union and the United States adopted different stances on the issue. The U.S. attitude toward privacy rights is based on freedom from state intervention; in Europe, privacy is considered a fundamental right to be protected by the state. As a result, there was no push in the United States for comprehensive regulation of data privacy. President Clinton's principal advisor for e-commerce, Ira Magaziner, stated his preference that "if the privacy protections by the private sector can be spread internationally, that will become the de facto way privacy is protected."[19]

In contrast, in 1995, the EU passed a sweeping Data Protection Directive that set clear guidance and enforcement mechanisms for European firms. The directive was to take effect in late 1998, and to ensure that firms did not evade the law by carrying out operations beyond the EU jurisdiction, the export of EU citizens' personal data to third countries with inadequate protection was banned.[20] This threat proved sufficiently potent for Australia, Canada, and Eastern European countries to revise their own laws in an attempt to comply with EU preferences.

Several nonstate actors tried to mediate a solution on the issue, with no success. Human rights groups lobbied the U.S. government to accept the EU regulatory position because it represented more-stringent protection of consumers.[21] A transnational business group, the GBDe, attempted to develop a common voluntary framework on data privacy. This effort failed miserably, with both U.S. and EU officials criticizing the final product.[22] Instead, the U.S. response was to encourage American multinationals to establish self-regulatory mechanisms that would meet EU standards. Sets of voluntary principles . . . were developed. At the same time, American and European negotiators agreed to a "safe harbor" compromise. The EU would not impose sanctions against U.S. firms that adhered to a voluntary standard consistent with the Data Protection Directive.

The safe harbor compromise went into effect in November 2000, but the EU (state-directed) and U.S. (self-regulation) approaches remain rival standards. . . . At the same time, U.S. compliance with the EU directive remains uncertain. Few companies registered for the safe harbor in the year after the agreement went into effect. Furthermore, Federal Trade Commission studies show that U.S. firms do not enforce their own privacy principles.[23] "In late 2001, one think tank concluded: "Although Safe Harbor is still in its infancy, its survival is already in doubt."[24] Henry Farrell's assessment of the situation perfectly characterizes the rival-standards outcome: "Both the US and EU sought to preserve and extend their domestic systems of privacy protection. Each sought, in effect, to dictate the terms under which privacy would be protected in the burgeoning sphere of international e-commerce."[25]

The regulation of Internet content—that is, censorship—neatly fits the outcome of sham standards. Governments have wildly divergent preferences regarding the extent to which Internet content should be regulated. Totalitarian governments such as Cuba or Saudi Arabia want absolute control over citizen access to the Internet. Authoritarian governments such as Singapore or China want to exploit the Internet's commercial opportunities while restricting the use of the Internet for political criticism. Liberal democracies also wish to place restrictions on offensive forms of content. These countries' definitions of objectionable content range from child pornography (the United States) to Nazi memorabilia (France). For this issue, there is no bargaining core among nation-states. The predicted outcome would be sham standards and the unilateral use of national regulation to bar undesired content.

Internet enthusiasts have long dismissed the ability of states to take this action. In 1993, John Gilmore, a cofounder of the Electronic Frontier Foundation, famously concluded: "The Net interprets censorship as damage and routes around it." However, the evidence strongly suggests that states can regulate Internet content when they so desire. Such efforts are never 100 percent effective, but that is a goal that few regulatory efforts achieve. As Jack Goldsmith observes: "If governments can raise the cost of Net transactions, they can regulate Net transactions."[26] In particular, governments have discovered that by pressuring Internet service providers, they can exercise significant control over access to content.

The result has been unilateral but successful examples of government regulation of Internet content. For totalitarian states, the modes of regulation have been crude but effective. Cuba simply outlaws the sale of personal computers to individuals; Myanmar outlaws personal ownership of modems.[27] Saudi Arabia censors the Internet by requiring all Web access to be routed through a proxy server that the government edits for content, blocking access to pornographic, religious, and politically sensitive material.[28] A recent assessment of the Saudi filtering system concluded that substantial amounts of Web content are "effectively inaccessible" from Saudi Arabia.[29]

Authoritarian states have succeeded in restricting political content on the Internet without sacrificing its commercial possibilities. Singapore regulates the Internet in the same way that it regulates print or broadcast media, effectively deleting what the government considers to be offensive or subversive material.[30] Singapore's approach has been the model for many East Asian governments, including China.[31] In July 2002, China was able to persuade more than 300 Internet service providers and web portals, including Yahoo!, to sign a voluntary pledge refraining from "producing, posting, or disseminating pernicious information that may jeopardize state security and disrupt social stability."[32]

As for the developed democracies, a French court succeeded in a legal effort to get Yahoo! to drop Nazi paraphernalia from its auction site. Because of the number of "mirror" servers that target Web sites to particular geographic areas, governments have the means to censor the national content of the Web without globally censoring the distribution of information. Unilateral content regulation has succeeded despite the strong normative consensus among Internet enthusiasts against such regulation.[33] The September 11 terrorist attacks and the terrorists' use of the Internet to communicate with each other have only accelerated the pace of content regulation in the developed world. In September 2002, one advocacy group concerned with press freedom noted, "The United States, Britain, France, Germany, Spain, Italy, Denmark, the European Parliament, the Council of Europe and the G8 nations have all challenged cyber-freedoms over the past year."[34]

Human rights NGOs have protested these disparate national efforts to curb Internet content, but this has not led to the creation of any effective system of global governance on the matter. IGOs have been largely hamstrung by the extreme distribution of state preferences over content regulation. This was reflected in the first meeting of the World Summit on the Information Society (WSIS), held in December 2003. One of the key sticking points at this meeting was the language regarding the extent to which any agreement would affect the regulation of speech on the Internet. China, in particular, protested the U.S.-inspired language regarding press freedoms. As a result, although language was inserted into the Declaration of Principles that specifically addressed press freedoms, it was heavily watered down, and language reaffirming state sovereignty was also added.[35] Outside observers agreed that the language papered over irreconcilable differences about content regulation, and that the plan of action provides little guidance for the future.[36]

For each of the issue areas in question, governments have divergent preferences regarding the content of Internet regulation. The resulting global governance structures vary in effectiveness, depending on the distribution of state power. The enforcement of [Intellectual Property Rights] on the Internet has succeeded because the great powers have similar preferences and have been willing to coerce recalcitrant states into compliance. When great powers disagree . . . the outcome is the absence of a stable international regime. When all states have divergent preferences, . . . the result is effective unilateral steps to regulate access to the Internet. Two facts about these issues are particularly salient. First, nonstate actors have been unable to influence government preferences on these issues. Second, when necessary, governments of every stripe have been willing to disrupt or sever Internet traffic in order to ensure that their ends are achieved.

Global Governance of Internet Technical Protocols

. . . For the Internet to be useful for informational and commercial purposes, producers need to agree on the technical protocols that permit users to successfully transmit and access data. Although common protocols create obvious public goods, such standards can also reap disproportionate benefits for actors that either own the standards in a proprietary fashion or have first-mover advantages in exploiting those standards.[37] Because of the huge network externalities that are evident in the Internet, however, we would expect a large bargaining core among states, leading to a harmonized standards outcome.

Popular and scholarly histories of the Internet argue that the technical protocols were created by an epistemic community of computer experts who belonged to the [Internet Engineering Task Force], and that no government could thwart this outcome.[38] A closer look at the origins of these protocols and the regimes for managing them suggests a rather different picture. At two crucial junctures in the growth of the Internet—the acceptance of the Transmission Control Protocol/Internet Protocol (TCP/IP) for exchanging information across disparate computer networks, and the creation of the . . . regime for governing the Internet Domain Name System—governments took active steps to ensure that the outcome serviced their interests and that the management regime remained private but amenable to state interests. In the first episode, governments acted in concert to prevent computer firms from acquiring too much influence over the setting of standards; in the second episode, they acted to prevent particular NGOs and IGOs from acquiring too much influence.

TCP/IP was developed between 1973 and 1978 by members of the Advanced Research Projects Agency Network (ARPANET), the Defense Department's network that connected civilian and military research complexes. The protocols were designed so as to permit interoperability between disparate hardware systems. TCP is responsible for packing and unpacking data such that they can be transferred from one computer to another; IP is responsible for ensuring that data are routed to the appropriate recipients. To use a postal analogy, TCP is the functional equivalent of the envelope, and IP is the functional equivalent of the address/ZIP code on the envelope.

TCP/IP placed minimal code demands on new entrants to the network, which was consistent with the research community's norm of open access.[39] However, this was also consistent with U.S. government preferences as well. . . .

Although Defense Department and ARPANET constituents favored the TCP/IP protocol, other networks did not rely on it. The actors behind these alternative networks had different motivations. Companies with investments in computer networks preferred developing their own proprietary standard, so as to reap the pecuniary rewards of managing their own networks.[40] . . . In other words, TCP/IP was far from the de facto standard when the standards debate of the 1970s started, and it faced strong opposition from corporate actors.

The major economic powers feared the prospect of being held hostage to a firm's ownership of the dominant network protocol. This was particularly true for states with government monopolies of the telecommunications sector. . . .

There were two international responses to this threat. The first was a concerted effort by Canada, Britain, and France to develop a nonproprietary standard, called Recommendation X.25, . . . designed as a public standard freely available to all private firms. The ITU [International Telecommunications Union] approved the standard in 1976; the French, Japanese, and British governments immediately adopted X.25 as the standard for their government networks. Because of the significance of these markets for producers, IBM, Digital, and Honeywell reluctantly agreed to offer X.25-compatible software on their computers in addition to their own proprietary standards. As Janet Abbate concludes: "X.25 was explicitly designed to alter the balance of power . . . and in this it succeeded. Public data networks did not have to depend on proprietary network systems from IBM or any other company."[41]

The . . . initiative was a successful holding action that prevented the emergence of a norm for proprietary standards. The second and more significant initiative was the push by the United States, the UK, France, Canada, and Japan to have the International Organization for Standardization (ISO)—an NGO of technical standard setters—develop compatible network standards for both private and public uses. This push was unusual, in that ordinarily the ISO declared an official standard only after there was a rough consensus among producers. In advocating a role for the ISO at an earlier stage, the major economic powers were clearly trying to accelerate the creation of an international regime consistent with their preferences. This initiative resulted in the 1978 creation of the Open Systems Interconnection (OSI) model. . . . Abbate summarizes OSI's qualities and purpose: "The OSI standards would be publicly specified and nonproprietary, so that anyone would be free to use them; the system would be designed to work with generic components, rather than a specific manufacturer's products; and changes to the standards would be made by a public standards organization, not by a private company."[42]

The creation of OSI had two significant effects on the development of common standards. First, because of the wide ISO membership and the rapid acceptance of its standards, it became prohibitively expensive for any state or firm to create a protocol that was incompatible with OSI. The great powers were particularly enthusiastic about OSI. European governments liked it because it gave their computer producers a chance to compete with IBM, Digital, and other American producers.[43] The U.S. government liked OSI because it was consistent with its preferences for nonproprietary, open source coding.[44]

Second, because OSI stressed openness and accessibility, the TCP/IP code fit more seamlessly with the OSI framework than with other proposed protocols, including X.25. . . . Members of the Internet community often argue that the failure of X.25 or OSI to replace TCP/IP is an example of states being unable to regulate cyberspace.[45] This argument is factually correct but misses the primary motivation of both ventures. . . . If governments had not intervened, the probable outcome would have been a system of proprietary network protocols. The actual outcome reflected the preferences of governments. Furthermore, consistent with the model presented here, states relied on a universal-membership IGO to boost legitimacy and delegated a nonstate actor to manage the actual standards.

The second government intervention over technical protocols came two decades later. As the commercial possibilities of the Internet and World Wide Web emerged in the early nineties, all of the relevant actors recognized the need to create a more robust regime to manage the DNS [Internet Domain Name System] for unique Internet addresses. The DNS is responsible for creating unique identifiers for each individual Internet address. This includes, among others, the valued general Top Level Domains (gTLDs), such as .com, .org, or .edu, as well as the country code Top Level Domains (ccTLDs), such as .de or .uk.

There were three reasons for concern about DNS management. First, Internet commentators agreed that the DNS system represented an excellent focal point through which an actor could control access to the Internet.[46] Second, actors with valued trademarks were concerned about the possibility of "cyber-squatters" acquiring valuable addresses, such as www.burgerking.com or www.nike.com. Third, there were significant commercial opportunities in managing the DNS system. Between 1994 and 1998, the U.S. government contracted the DNS registry to Network Solutions Incorporated (NSI). That monopoly was estimated in 1996 to be worth $1 billion to NSI.[47]

. . . President Clinton . . . [issued] a July 1, 1997 executive order authorizing the commerce secretary to "support efforts to make the governance of the domain name system private and competitive."[48] Presidential advisor Ira Magaziner was put in charge of the initiative, underscoring the high priority the United States gave to settling the issue. U.S. preferences on the issue were clear: to have a nonstate actor . . . manage the DNS regime. Magaziner stated publicly: "As the Internet grows up and becomes more international, these technical management questions should be privatized, and there should be a stakeholder-based, *private international organization* set up for that technical management. In the allocation of domain names, we should, where it is possible, create a competitive marketplace to replace the monopoly that now exists."[49]

Given the ITU's [International Telecommunications Union's] one-nation, one-vote structure, and the secretariat's eagerness to independently manage the issue area, it is not surprising that the United States wanted to switch fora. Historically, the United States has shifted governance of new issue areas away from the ITU in order to lock in its own preferences.[50] Magaziner made the U.S. opposition to an ITU role quite explicit when he stated, "Technical management certainly should not be controlled by an intergovernmental organization or international telecommunications union."[51]

The European Union . . . insisted that the WIPO [World Intellectual Property Association] be involved in any governance structure. This was a hedge against U.S. trademark law being imposed by fiat. The Europeans agreed with the U.S. government that the . . . monopoly of . . . registries had to be broken up. The European motivation for this, however, was preventing total U.S. dominance of the Internet. Finally, there was a desire for a formal governmental channel between any private order and governments. . . . The United States was sensitive to these concerns, and promised that there would be a significant number of Europeans on any Internet governance board.[52]

. . . [T]he resulting governance structure accommodated both U.S. and European concerns. A government advisory committee was created to act as a conduit for government concerns. The . . . monopoly of [registries] was broken, and the ITU was given only a peripheral role in the new regime. A significant fraction of ICANN's [the newly created Internet Consortium for Assigned Names and Numbers] governing board consisted of non-Americans. . . .

. . . [T]he negotiating history of ICANN shows that the key actors were states. It was the U.S. government that . . . ensured the creation of a private order to manage the policy issue.[53] European, Japanese, and Australian governments ensured that the eventual regime would not be dominated by the United States. The key governments vetted the initial roster of ICANN's governing board. In contrast, elements of global civil society were largely shut out of the process. . . .

Had the great powers not intervened, the outcome in this case would have been significantly different. . . . The management of the DNS system would have been housed in the one-country, one-vote ITU, rather than in a private, nonprofit organization. The percentage of Americans running the regime would have been larger. This case demonstrates that nonstate actors have agenda-setting powers. However, once an issue comes to the attention of states, the outcome will reflect great-power preferences.

The great powers repeatedly acted to ensure that the Internet would be governed so as to maximize efficiency without giving monopoly power to any one actor, be it a multinational firm, a nonstate organization, or an IGO secretariat. In the 1970s, governments acted with Internet enthusiasts to ensure that multinational firms would not develop their own proprietary network protocols. In the 1990s, governments acted in concert with multinational firms to prevent NGOs and IGOs from overstepping their policy authority. In both instances, governments delegated regime management to nongovernmental international organizations . . . to ensure efficient outcomes and to retain their influence over future policy shifts.

Notes

1. Benjamin Most and Harvey Starr, "International Relations Theory, Foreign Policy Substitutability, and 'Nice' Laws," *World Politics* 36 (April 1984); 383–406.
2. Thomas Friedman, *The Lexus and the Olive Tree* (New York: Farrar, Strauss, & Giroux, 1999), 86.
3. Susan Strange, *The Retreat of the State: The Diffusion of Power in the World Economy* (Cambridge: Cambridge University Press, 1996); Dani Rodrik, *Has Globalization Gone Too Far?* (Washington, DC: Institute for International Economics, 1997); Ian Clark, *Globalization and International Relations Theory* (Oxford: Oxford University Press, 1999); Richard Rosecrance, *The Rise of the Virtual State* (New York: Basic Books, 1999).

4. Peter Haas, "Introduction: Epistemic Communities and International Policy Coordination," *International Organization* 46 (Spring 1992): 1–35.
5. Paul Wapner, "Politics Beyond the State: Environmental Activism and World Civic Politics," *World Politics* 47 (April 1995): 311–340.
6. Virginia Haufler, *A Public Role for the Private Sector* (Washington, DC: Carnegie Endowment for International Peace, 2001).
7. Frances Cairncross, *The Death of Distance*, 2nd ed. (Cambridge, MA: Harvard Business School Press, 2000), 177.
8. Viktor Mayer-Schüonberger and Deborah Hurley, "Globalization of Communication" in Joseph S. Nye, ed., *Governance in a Globalizing World* (Washington, DC: Brookings Institution, 2000), 23.
9. John Perry Barlow, "Thinking Locally, Acting Globally," *Time*, 15 January 1996, 76.
10. Stephen M. Kobrin, "The MAI and the Clash of Globalizations," *Foreign Policy* 111 (Fall 1998): 97–109.
11. Ronald Deibert, "International Plug 'n Play? Citizen Activism, the Internet, and Global Public Policy," *International Studies Perspectives* 1 (July 2000): 264.
12. Deborah Spar, "Lost in (Cyber)space: The Private Rules of Online Commerce" in Claire Culter, Tony Porter, and Virginia Haufler, eds., *Private Authority and International Affairs* (Albany: SUNY Press, 1999), 47. Spar refined this view in *Ruling the Waves* (New York; Harcourt Brace, 2001).
13. Haufler, *A Public Role for the Private Sector*, 82.
14. Andrew Higgins and Azeem Azhar, "China Begins to Erect Second Great Wall in Cyberspace," *The Guardian*, 5 February 1996.
15. Susan Sell, *Power and Ideas: North-South Politics of Intellectual Property and Antitrust* (Albany, NY: SUNY Press, 1998).
16. Catherine Mann, Sue Eckert, and Sarah Cleeland Knight, *Global Electronic Commerce: A Policy Primer* (Washington, DC: Institute for International Economics, 2000), 118.
17. Sell, *Power and Ideas*, chapter 6.
18. Haufler, *A Public Role for the Private Sector*, 84.
19. Henry Farrell, "Constructing the International Foundations of E-Commerce." *International Organization* 57 (Spring 2003): 277–306.
20. William J. Long and Marc Pang Quek, "Personal Data Privacy Protection in an Age of Globalization: The U.S.-EU Safe Harbor Compromise," Paper presented at the International Studies Association annual meeting, New Orleans, LA, March 2002.
21. Gregory Shaffer, "Globalization and Social Protection: The Impact of EU and International Rules in the Ratcheting Up of U.S. Privacy Standards," *Yale Journal of International Law* 25 (Winter 2000): 1–88.
22. Maria Green Cowles, "Who Writes the Rules of E-Commerce?" AICGS Policy Paper #14, Johns Hopkins University, Baltimore, MD, 2001, 24.
23. Marcus Franda, *Governing the Internet* (Boulder, CO: Lynne Reinner, 2001), 159.
24. Aaron Lukas, "Safe Harbor or Stormy Waters? Living with the EU Data Protection Directive." Trade Policy Analysis No. 16, Cato Institute, Washington, DC, October 2001, 2. . . .

25. Farrell, "Constructing the International Foundations of E-Commerce," 19.
26. Jack Goldsmith, "Regulation of the Internet: Three Persistent Fallacies," *Chicago-Kent Law Review* 73 (December 1998): 1123.
27. Robert Lebowitz, "Cuba Prohibits Computer Sales," Digital Freedom Network, 26 March 2002, accessed at http://dfn.org/news/somalia/sparse-internet.htm, 28 May 2002. Associated Press, "Internet Remains Prohibited in Myanmar," 3 May 2000, accessed at http://www.nua.com/surveys/?f=VS&art_id=905355752rel=true, 28 May 2002.
28. Khalid Al-Tawil, "The Internet in Saudi Arabia," *Telecommunications Policy* 25 (September 2001): 625–632.
29. Jonathan Zittrain and Benjamin Edelman, "Documentation of Internet Filtering in Saudi Arabia," Berkmen Center for Internet and Society, Harvard University, July 2002, accessed at http://cyber.law.harvard.edu/filtering/saudiarabia/, 4 September 2002.
30. Garry Rodan, "The Internet and Political Control in Singapore," *Political Science Quarterly* 113 (Spring 1998): 63–89.
31. Georgette Wang, "Regulating Network Communication in Asia," *Telecommunications Policy* 23 (April 1999): 277–287; Shanthi Kalathil, "China's Dot-Communism," *Foreign Policy* 122 (January/February 2001): 74–75.
32. Christopher Bodeen, "Web Portals Sign China Content Pact," Associated Press, 15 July 2002.
33. Human Rights Watch, "Free Expression on the Internet," accessed at http://www.hrw.org/advocacy/internet/, 25 May 2002.
34. Reporters Without Borders, "The Internet on Probation," September 2002, accessed at http://www.rsf.fr/IMG/doc-1274.pdf, 6 September 2002.
35. World Summit on the Information Society Declaration of Principles, Document WSIS-03/GENEVA/DOC/4-E, 12 December 2003, paragraph 18. The document can be accessed at http://www.itu.int/wsis/; Kieren McCarthy, "Internet Showdown Side-stepped in Geneva," *The Register Newsletter*, 8 December 2003.
36. David Souter, "The View from the Summit: A Report on the Outcomes of the World Summit on the Information Society," *Info* 6 (January/February 2004): 6–11.
37. Carl Shapiro and Hal Varian, *Information Rules* (Cambridge, MA: Harvard Business School Press, 1999), 174.
38. Katie Hafner and Matthew Lyon, *Where Wizards Stay Up Late* (New York; Simon & Schuster, 1996); Mayer-Schüonberger and Hurley, "Globalization of Communication," 135–154.
39. Will Foster, Anthony Rutkowski, and Seymour Goodman, "Who Governs the Internet?" *Communications of the ACM* 40 (August 1997), 17–18.
40. Franda, *Governing the Internet*, 24; David Passmore, "The Networking Standards Collision," *Datamation* 31 (February 1985): 105.
41. Janet Abbate, *Inventing the Internet* (Cambridge, MA: MIT Press, 1999), 153, 172.
42. Janet Abbate, "Government, Business, and the Making of the Internet," *Business History Review* 75 (Spring 2001): 163.
43. Franda, *Governing the Internet*, 39.
44. Hafner and Lyon, *Where Wizards Stay Up Late*, 236–237.

45. Martin Libicki et al., *Scaffolding the New Web: Standards and Standards Policy for the Digital Economy* (Arlington, VA: RAND Corporation, 2000).

46. Lawrence Lessig, *Code and Other Laws of Cyberspace* (New York: Basic Books, 1999).

47. Franda, *Governing the Internet*, 49.

48. Milton Mueller, "ICANN and Internet Governance," *Info* 1 (December 1999): 502.

49. Ira Magaziner, "Creating a Framework for Global Electronic Commerce," July 1999, accessed at http://www.pff.org/ira_magaziner.htm, 10 June 2002 (my italics).

50. Stephen D. Krasner, "Global Communications and National Power: Life on the Pareto Frontier," *World Politics* 43 (April 1991): 336–366.

51. Magaziner, "Creating a Framework," 13.

52. Mueller, "ICANN and Internet Governance," 505.

53. A. Michael Froomkin, "Wrong Turn in Cyberspace: Using ICANN to Route Around the APA and the Constitution," *Duke Law Journal* 50 (2000): 17–184.

33

TERRORISM, CENSORSHIP, AND THE FIRST AMENDMENT

Doris A. Graber

Editor's Note

Although democracies tout the crucial importance of a free press, they routinely try to control the news in times of crisis, such as terrorist assaults and
war. They fear that news, especially if it is negative, will help enemies and harm
efforts to maintain morale and cope with the crisis. Negative news is likely to
undermine support for the government's policies and operations. Accordingly,
governments seek control over news by preventing journalists from covering
potentially sensitive situations, by censoring journalists' news stories, and by
appointing authorized spokespersons who have monopoly control over the
news supply. The public generally supports censorship efforts, especially when
it has been persuaded by the news that the country faces grave dangers that
the government is meeting in the best possible way. The perils of indiscreet
news coverage are real and serious, but so are the dangers of censorship,
which may lead to a poorly informed public and major cover-ups of government failures and misconduct.

Doris A. Graber is professor of political science at the University of Illinois at
Chicago. She has authored numerous books and articles dealing with political
communication, information processing, and management of information in
political organizations. *Media Power in Politics* was originally prepared as a
supplement to her text *Mass Media and American Politics,* which is now in its
seventh edition.

Source: Doris A. Graber, "Terrorism, Censorship and the 1st Amendment," in *Framing Terrorism:
The News Media, the Government, and the Public,* ed. Pippa Norris, Montague Kern, and Marion
Just, New York: Routledge, 2003, chapter 2. Copyright © 2003. Reproduced by permission of
Routledge/Taylor & Francis Group, LLC.

When important values clash in democracies, policy makers and publics face a typical trade-off dilemma. Which should prevail? The dilemma is starkest when the clashing values are national security threatened by terrorism or war, endangering the survival of large numbers of citizens, if not the nation itself, and freedom of the press, which is an indispensable ingredient of democracy. Arguments about whether a free press is actually essential to democracy are beyond the scope of this chapter. Many observers believe that it is and that press freedom is particularly vital in crisis periods because decisions made at that time are apt to produce profound consequences for the nation and its people.

In the post-World War II era, national security risks have appeared in a number of guises. Formal declarations of war have become less common while military confrontations involving terrorism, counter-terrorism, guerilla warfare, peacekeeping operations, and similar so-called 'low intensity conflicts' have increased. Government deliberations, like congressional hearings on the Anti-Terrorism Act of 2001, make it clear that public officials equate the dangers posed by such low-intensity operations with the dangers posed by open warfare.

Many such military missions are comparatively brief with little advance planning and require complete secrecy to succeed. They would be compromised by premature disclosure, especially since reporters are now able to send messages, including pictures, from remote locations at lightening speed. Hence it seems reasonable to consider the history of press restraints during anticipated or actual war as precedent for press freedom policies during periods of anticipated and actual terrorism and subsequent military operations. Periods of ideological onslaught, like the Cold War following World War II, also belong in this category of extreme dangers that generate calls for the suspension or dilution of constitutional guarantees.

The Patterns of Past Solutions

There are basically three approaches to the dilemma of reconciling the conflicting aspects of press freedom and survival security. The *'formal censorship'* approach has been most common. It involves legislation that sets forth what may or may not be published. Such laws vary in the terms and scope of the censorship operations and often stipulate severe penalties for violations. The press may still be allowed to decide what is publishable within the government's guidelines. Alternatively, the decision about what may be published may be in the hands of official censors who use their discretion about the sensitivity of particular information at a specific time. In either case, freedom of the press is in abeyance, as American constitutional lawyers generally interpret it, including the traditional reluctance of American courts to permit prior censorship of potentially harmful news reports (Silverberg 1991).

The opposite *'free press'* approach leaves journalists free to decide what is or is not safe to publish under the circumstances, journalists may choose to follow guidelines provided by the government or respond to specific requests by public officials. But reporters make the ultimate decision free from formal pressure by public officials, although there are always ethical mandates to be risk-averse when national security is at stake.

The third approach, the *'informal censorship'* scheme, is an ingenious combination of the two: There are no censorship laws and the press is left officially free to decide what it does or does not wish to publish. But pronouncements by high-level government leaders constitute informal censorship because they create a coercive climate that forces the press into self-censorship in line with the wishes of public officials. Criticism of government policy is castigated as unpatriotic, flirting with treason. This form of pressure is often enhanced by a barrage of glowing reports about government progress in coping with the crisis. Self-censorship by the press is complemented by self-censorship by government officials who have been admonished by their leaders to keep their lips tightly sealed. Such "voluntary" constraints, as social scientists have documented, can be just as potent as official censorship laws (Aukofer and Lawrence 1995; Carter and Barringer 2001a).

In a 1987 speech at Hebrew University in Jerusalem, Associate U.S. Supreme Court Justice William J. Brennan Jr. reviewed what he called the "shabby treatment" that America's vaunted freedoms have received in times of war and threats to national security (Brennan 1987). He attributed these lapses to the crisis mentality that Americans develop when faced with danger intermittently, rather than living with it constantly. America's decision-makers have been inexperienced in assessing the severity of security threats and in devising measures to cope with them in ways that respect conflicting rights and liberties.

Brennan might also have added that the equally inexperienced American public has traditionally supported restraints on First Amendment rights and civil liberties when it has been polled during crises, especially if it feels militarily or ideologically threatened (Blendon et al. 2002; Kinsley 2002; Pew 2001). For example, 53 percent of the respondents to a Pew poll reported in the press on November 29, 2001, in the aftermath of the September terrorist attack on U.S. sites, agreed that the government should be able to censor news that "it deems a threat to national security" (Pew 2001). The pollsters asked which was more important: the government's ability to censor or the media's ability to report what seemed in the national interest. Four percent of respondents volunteered that both were equally important.

It is important to note that the vote in favor of government censorship hardly constitutes overwhelming agreement. Besides, a bare majority (52 percent) indicated that the media should dig hard for the news rather than accept government refusals to release it, and 54 percent agreed that media's criticism of leaders keeps them from misbehaving. On balance, however, trust in government trumped trust in the media. Sixty-one percent of respondents expressed a fair amount of confidence that the government was giving the public an accurate picture about its response to terrorism, and 70 percent thought that public safety and protection of American military forces were the main reasons for censorship.

The 'Shabby' Record of Protecting Press Freedom

In a nutshell, press freedom has routinely succumbed to national security concerns on the home front as well as on foreign battlefields. Customarily, in the United States and other democracies with strong traditions of press independence from government, this has been accomplished through legislation or orders by the chief executive or administrative agencies. A quick journey through some of the relevant events in U.S. history is instructive. In democracies where the government owns or otherwise controls the press, wartime situations are more amenable to routine press management procedures (Sajó and Price 1996).

On the verge of war with France in 1798, Congress enacted the Alien and Sedition Acts, claiming that home front censorship was essential to forestall enemy espionage and sabotage. The Sedition Act made it unlawful to "write, print, utter or publish . . . any false, scandalous and malicious writing" against government officials intending "to bring them . . . into contempt or disrepute" (1798, 1 Stat. 570). There were 25 arrests, 15 indictments, and 10 convictions under the act, mostly involving newspaper editors and politicians from the party in opposition to the government. Legal challenges to the act were unsuccessful at the time. But when party fortunes changed, the convicted were pardoned, most fines were returned, and it was widely acknowledged that the laws had been an unnecessary aberration. The dangers had been exaggerated.

Still, when the Civil War presented a major test in 1861, the story was quite similar. As soon as armed conflict started, President Lincoln took drastic measures to neutralize disaffected citizens and potential traitors in the name of national security. Through executive orders, he blocked the distribution of dissenting newspapers and, during the latter part of the war, seized control of the telegraph lines that transmitted war news. The most drastic step was the suspension of habeas corpus. Thousands of people were arrested on suspicion of disloyalty and held in military custody, often without charges. Trials were before military tribunals that lacked the procedural safeguards available in civilian courts. Such steps were bound to intimidate reporters. The public, by and large, approved these actions and condemned judges who questioned their constitutionality.

Another example of censorship legislation comes from the First World War. Congress enacted the Espionage Act, making it a crime to utter, print, write, or publish any "disloyal, profane, scurrilous, or abusive language" or any language intended to bring the U.S. form of government or the Constitution or the flag "into contempt, scorn, contumely, or disrepute" (1918, 40 Stat. 553). More than 2000 individuals, including journalists, were prosecuted under the act. Convictions were mostly for criticizing U.S. participation in the war. In *Abrams v. United States* (1919, 250 U.S. 616) the U.S. Supreme Court upheld such convictions. . . .

During the early years of the nation's history, when foreign policies were often highly controversial, the American government considered the media primarily as an obstacle to war that had to be kept under control through strict censorship legislation. That perception had changed by the time World War II started. Impressed by the successful use of propaganda by authoritarian governments, democratic governments had begun to appreciate the power of the press to rally mass publics. They now deemed it a potentially powerful ally in their struggle against the enemies of Western democracies.

The government wanted a policy that would yield ample favorable coverage of the war without risking adverse stories by roaming correspondents. This was to be accomplished by facilitating reporters' access to news about the war, including ongoing battles, but binding them to a gentleman's agreement that they would not reveal anything that might interfere with the military's mission. Instead of the harsh censorship laws of the past, there would be voluntary cooperation. Most reporters knew and complied with the unstated terms of the compact because it gave them broad access to war information; they censored themselves to live within the terms (Thompson 1991; Thrall 2000). This was easy because, unlike the situation in earlier wars, the objectives of World War II were never controversial in the United States.

In addition to these unwritten understandings, there were more formal arrangements as well to provide guidance to reporters about the limits of safe reporting. . . . Compliance with these guidelines was excellent (Aukofer and Lawrence 1995; Thompson 1991). Military authorities in the war zones were authorized to conduct their own censorship operations, which tended to be more restrictive than the civilian censorship at home.

With the Korean War, which began in 1950, the country moved back to the conditions of earlier years when foreign policies had been controversial and civilian and military government leaders feared that hostile reporters might undermine the war effort. The controversial nature of the war made it difficult for the press to keep their stories supportive of the military action while also reflecting the political controversy. Military commanders complained that the system of voluntary self-censorship allowed news sources to publish stories that endangered the war effort. They therefore urged the

Defense Department to provide compulsory guidelines. An official censorship code for war correspondents was issued shortly thereafter, in December 1950. Leaders from the journalism community and the military had agreed, following extensive discussions, that all future reports from Korea should first be cleared with Army headquarters. Stringent screening ensued that caused long delays in the transmission of news from the front and frustrated the press. As is usually the case, many provisions of the code were vague, such as the prohibition of stories that might "injure the morale" of American or Allied forces or stories that might 'embarrass' the United States, its Allies, or neutral countries. That made controversies over the administration of the codes inevitable.

By the time of the Vietnam War, the notion that news stories were likely to harm government efforts had regained full currency. Knowing that its policies in Vietnam would be highly controversial, the American government did not wish to alert the public to the extent of U.S. involvement or to the shortcomings of the South Vietnamese government, which it was supporting. Withholding of news so that it could not be published, exaggerating successes to make policies more palatable, and some outright falsifications of potentially damaging data, became accepted policy tools. News people and their reports would not be formally censored. Instead, correspondents would simply be kept in the dark or government sources would feed them carefully selected, and sometimes doctored, news morsels.

The government instructed the U.S. mission in Saigon to control information related to the war tightly by classifying documents and by keeping reporters away from military operations (Aukofer and Lawrence 1995; Thompson 1991). The U.S. mission also negotiated another code of voluntary restraint between the press and the military. Although the military favored a compulsory code in line with those used in earlier wars, none was instituted because of concerns that it might be unconstitutional absent a formal declaration of war. Overall, the self-censorship worked reasonably well; few serious security breeches occurred (Aukofer and Lawrence 1995; Thompson 1991). Of course, the codes did not prevent correspondents from reporting negative news.

To counterbalance unfavorable media stories, the Johnson administration engaged in large-scale press management. It supplied the press with favorable stories in hopes of gaining ample supportive news coverage. That approach backfired when military reverses presented a sharp contrast to earlier reports and appeared larger than they actually were because of the exaggerated optimism. Negative news provided by war correspondents was contradicted by positive reports from government sources, forcing home-front editors to choose between conflicting visions of the war. Initially, most stuck with the government's optimistic framing, but that changed later on. After the war, the military as well as many civilian analysts blamed negative news coverage for loss of public support for the war and the ultimate failure to accomplish U.S. objectives. That judgment poisoned subsequent relations between the military and the press.

During the mid-century Cold War years, Congress had passed laws to prevent spoken and written communications that might expose the country to the danger of a Communist takeover. These laws included the Smith Act, the Internal Security Act of 1950, and the Communist Control Act of 1954. The Smith Act, for example, made it a crime to advocate in a speech or in print the overthrow of the U.S. government by force (1940, 54 Stat. 671). There were many legal challenges to these laws at the time.

The clearest confrontation between the news media and the government's fight against communism occurred during and following a minor military venture in 1983 when the United States tried to avert a Marxist revolution in Grenada, a tiny Caribbean island nation. During the U.S. military invasion of the island, the media were at first kept out entirely and prevented from filing stories. When journalists were allowed to visit the island, military escorts accompanied them. It became clear after the fighting stopped that the operation had been seriously flawed and that the clumsy censorship had prevented disclosing mishaps to policy makers in the United States and to the American public. To avoid similar fiascoes, the chairman of the Joint Chiefs of Staff established a commission, headed by Major General Winant Sidle to study how relations between the press and the military could be handled better in the future. The commission was composed of experienced journalists as well as military and civilian press relations officers. The panel reported its recommendations in August of 1984. Unfortunately, its most novel recommendation—establishment of press pools for operations, which required limiting the number of reporters who cover the event—failed miserably in Panama in 1989 in a mission designed to oust Panamanian President Manuel Noriega.

Despite revisions, the pool concept did not work smoothly in the 1991 Gulf war. This brief conflict is a textbook example of government control over war news without resorting to formal censorship. The government took almost complete control of the war news supply. It used a handful of top-level military leaders to brief the press on all of the aspects of the war that it cared to disclose. When journalists were allowed to visit the front, military escorts accompanied them. The military also supplied excellent visuals of elegantly executed precision maneuvers for use by television reporters. A few journalists defied the constraints imposed by the military during the war and executives from major American media filed complaints with the Defense Department after the war about the efforts to control what reporters saw and about efforts to sanitize and delay the news. These complaints led to yet another revision of the pool system and new, albeit incomplete, rules designed to make it easier for reporters to cover the battlefronts without being leashed to officials.

The Statement of Principles—News Coverage of Combat—which was adopted in April 1992, failed to settle whose judgment prevails about what is publishable. Journalists and military personnel disagreed, and continue to disagree, about whether the military must have the final say on which stories must be submitted to it for security review and censorship. Multiple efforts to draft new ground rules have continued. But the problem may be insoluble (Department of Defense News 2001). The clashing objectives of the major players prevent permanent resolutions, despite a lot of good will and good faith on both sides.

During the conflict with Afghanistan that began in the winter of 2001, the familiar problems resurfaced. . . . The military initially restricted the media's access to the battle zones, claiming that complete secrecy was required to assure the success of the operation and the safety of the troops. Reporters were actually locked up in a warehouse to prevent coverage of one incident that involved injuries to U.S. troops from a U.S. bombing raid. The outburst of indignation that followed that episode led to a formal apology from the Defense Department and new rules to allow reporters greater access to the battlefronts. Access did improve subsequently, though many sites remained closed for a variety of hotly disputed reasons. As had been true in past wars, the courts sided with the military in censorship disputes brought before them. A federal district court, while agreeing that the First Amendment protects a limited right of access to foreign battle grounds, nonetheless refused to grant an injunction that would force the military to allow correspondents to accompany American troops in Afghanistan *(Flynt v. Rumsfeld,* 2002).

[Embedment Journalism] and Censorship

In anticipation of a second Gulf War, the Pentagon announced in February, 2003 that this would be the best-covered military engagement in American history. The new plan is designed to produce battle front coverage from an American perspective to match coverage by foreign news venues like al Jazeera. Pentagon officials selected and trained a representative pool of approximately 600 print and broadcast war correspondents, including some from foreign countries, to accompany troops from all branches of the military. These 'embedded' journalists received elementary military training so that they would be fit to accompany their assigned units at all times. The journalists were required to sign an agreement on ground rules of coverage that obligated them to submit stories that the military deems sensitive to scrutiny by military censors. However, the Defense Department promised that most stories would remain uncensored. Journalists outside the embedded group were not to be subject to restrictive ground rules. But, in line with past history, freelancers had only very limited access to front-line operations.

It is far too early to assess whether this new plan will, indeed, lead to more extensive and informed coverage or whether it will become merely another form of government news management. It seems questionable whether journalists who are buddies with military folk will be able to retain their objectivity and skepticism when they share the troops' hardships, including combat and casualties on a daily basis. Being 'embedded,' as the term suggests, simply may amount to being 'in bed' with the military.

Post-9-11-01 Home Front Censorship

In the crisis following the September 11, 2001, attack, the main censorship problems on the home front have again involved strenuous government efforts to withhold information from the press, claiming that disclosures would endanger national security. These claims have been coupled with well-publicized appeals for self-censorship as a patriotic duty, adding the pressures springing from publicity to the request. Prominent examples of official secrecy are refusals to discuss war-related matters with reporters, withholding all information about people detained by the government, limiting reports about military activities in Afghanistan to reports by the Secretary of Defense and a few generals, and failure to produce the records of what the government knew prior to the 2001 attack that might have forestalled it (Steinhauer 2002).

The Justice Department has contended, albeit without providing evidence, that press inquiries about the detainees rounded up after September 11 could be denied on national security grounds because "public disclosure would undermine counter-terrorism efforts and put the detainees at risk of attack from angry Americans as well as terrorists" (Sachs 2002). Government lawyers have argued in cases that challenged the refusal to disclose the names of the detainees and the charges against them, that national security interests outweigh any public right to know who was detained for what reasons and for what length of time (Sachs 2002).

To throttle the circulation of war-related information, the government has followed the Gulf War pattern of allowing only a few top-level military and civilian officials to report about ongoing events and plans. Secretary of Defense Donald Rumsfeld, for example, has been very accessible to the media but extraordinarily circumspect in giving facts and making claims (Kilian 2002). Reporters have to accept his messages because most of the military activities are conducted by small groups of special operations forces who can be neither accompanied by journalists nor interviewed.

The Bush administration has also urged all high-level government officials to be extraordinarily, and probably excessively, tight-lipped. For example,

Attorney General John Ashcroft declined to confirm information about the September 2001 terrorists that Prime Minister Tony Blair had given to the British House of Commons in open session. Ashcroft also issued a memorandum urging federal agencies to resist most Freedom of Information Act requests. As has been typical in these most recent examples of censorship, Ashcroft's request was framed as an act to protect cherished rights. Information disclosures, he argued, might endanger institutional, commercial and personal privacy interests. . . .

One effort to suppress information concerned satellite images. It particularly riled the press because it damaged its ability to report the news. The U.S. government had bought exclusive rights to all satellite images of the bombing of Afghanistan available from the civilian satellite Ikonos. That purchase barred the press from seeing and publicizing these privately owned high-resolution images of damage caused by U.S. attacks in Afghanistan. At the time, the Pentagon already had its own, far sharper satellite images. The decision to buy came shortly after reports of heavy civilian casualties near the town of Darunta in Afghanistan. Critics saw it as a stealthy maneuver to hide a disaster.

Government clampdowns on access to video footage were especially damaging for television journalism. News media beyond the borders of the United States were able to feature pictures of the bombing damage in Afghanistan released by the pro-Arab media and framed to reflect anti-American views. There was no matching footage from U.S. sources for friends of the United States, who therefore chose to rely on the interesting footage provided by al Jazeera, the Arab-language satellite television network. . . .

The government's policy of withholding news has been complemented by unusually strong appeals to the press for self-censorship. The debate about the propriety and scope of self-censorship escalated after National Security Advisor Condoleezza Rice phoned the chief executives of the major television networks on October 10, 2001, one month after the terrorist assault, asking them not to broadcast messages from Osama bin Laden, the alleged mastermind behind the terrorist assault on the United States. Rice warned that the taped broadcasts by bin Laden might contain encoded messages for terrorists. They could therefore stir up more violence against Americans and recruit more followers in countries like Malaysia where Muslims are in the majority. She urged broadcasters to edit bin Laden's messages before disseminating them.

. . . [J]ournalists faced strong pressures to comply with White House requests in the wake of the horrific September 11 attacks. . . . Journalists who might be inclined to dissent feared the wrath of their readers and their editors and publishers, possibly leading to loss of their job. Such social pressures transformed White House requests into commands. Predictably, the news executives promised compliance with Condoleezza Rice's request. . . .

It is not unusual for the news media to censor their coverage when they deem it essential for security interests, especially when they agree with the government's objectives and face condemnation and economic penalties for voicing dissent. But self-censorship generally happens quietly behind the scenes to avoid the impression that the media are yielding to compulsion by the government. For example, Leonard Downie, the executive editor of the *Washington Post*, acknowledged that 'a handful of times' in the weeks following the September 11 attacks, the *Post*'s reporting had prompted calls from administration officials who raised concerns that a specific story or more often that certain facts in a certain story, would compromise national security. In response, Downie said, "In some instances we have kept out of certain stories certain facts that we agreed could be detrimental to national security and not instrumental to our readers, such as methods of intelligence collection" (Carter and Barringer 2001b). Similarly, Clark Hoyt, the Washington editor of *Knight Ridder*, said that his organization had held back a report that "some small units of U.S. special operations forces had entered Afghanistan and were trying to locate bin Laden" within two weeks of the 9/11 attacks (Carter and Barringer 2001b). Other examples of self-censorship have been reported that were not directly linked to government requests but were instead produced by an opinion climate that seems hostile to criticism of the government during war. For example, domestic criticism of President Bush abated. . . .

Cloaking Censorship with a 1st Amendment Mantle

A review of recent censorship practices in the United States makes it clear that when push comes to shove in reconciling wartime security and press freedom, the First Amendment is still forced to yield. The review also shows that American public officials, as well as the public, manage to cover censorship laws and admonitions with a cloak of First Amendment covers. The excuses that officials and others gave for censorship in the wake of the September 11, 2001, terrorist attacks, transformed censorship into a defense of First Amendment rights. . . . This is quite typical behavior. America's wars have always been defended as a protection of essential democratic rights. The end—saving democracy—then justifies and hallows the means—self-censorship or censorship by government fiat. For example, a *St. Louis Post Dispatch* editorial on October 11, 2001, noted "Throughout our history, we [Americans] have been willing to trade freedom for safety during wartime."

In an address to the nation delivered on November 8, 2001, . . . President George W. Bush justified censorship measures as necessary to protect the values Americans share. He contrasted Americans with their enemies. . . .

At the same time, people who question whether First Amendment and other civil rights are actually protected by government information policies are condemned as interfering with the war effort. At best, they are accused of lacking in patriotism; at worst they are called traitors willing to help the enemy and harm their fellow citizens. For instance, Attorney General Ashcroft tried to silence critics of censorship policies by suggesting that their pursuit of "phantoms of lost liberty" was unpatriotic, "giving ammunition to America's enemies and pause to Americas friends" (*San Francisco Chronicle* 2001). All the while, Ashcroft continued to proclaim full support for civil liberties, saying that the United States had always met security challenges "in ways that preserved our fundamental freedoms and liberties." . . . Censorship was a weapon to preserve treasured freedoms, not an assault on them. . . .

The recount of past and ongoing current events makes it clear that national security concerns have always trumped first amendment protections in periods of crisis. It also makes it clear that decisions made while the crisis mentality prevailed were later regretted when it became clear that curtailments of first amendment and other civil rights were excessive. Obviously, sound ground-rules for appropriate behavior under crisis conditions are best forged in times of calm. . . .

As for the ultimate trade-off, in situations when national security values and press freedom confront each other directly, history suggests that democracies are best served by balancing the scales in favor of a responsible free press. As the *Baltimore Sun* editorialized on October 15, 2001, about the War on Terrorism:

> The United States is fighting this war in part to preserve democracy and freedom, neither of which can truly be achieved without an informed public. We need to keep the information flowing and work with each other to sort out what's true and what's not. . . . [T]here may be other instances in the next few months in which good judgment should inspire editors to hold back on information that could put the nation's troops or civilians in danger. *But editors, not government, must be the arbiters of what's fit to air or print.* [Italics added.] For a free society that's fighting to retain its freedom and procure it for others around the world, no other alternative is acceptable.

References

Abrams v. U.S., 1919, 250 U.S. 616.

Administration's Draft Anti-Terrorism Act of 2001, *Hearing Before the Committee on the Judiciary, House of Representatives*. September 24, 2001. Serial No. 39. http://www.house.gov/judiciary.

Aukofer, Frank and William P. Lawrence. 1995. *America's Team: The Odd Couple, A Report on the Relationship Between the Media and the Military.* http://www.freedomforum.org/publications/first/media and the military.

Baltimore Sun Editorial. 2001. 'A High-tech Information War.' 10-15-2001.

Blendon, Robert J., Stephen R. Pelletier, and Marcus Rosenbaum, 2002. 'Extra-ordinary Measures: Who Wants Military Tribunals and Who Wants to Listen in when

Suspects Consult their Lawyers?' May 17, 2002. Paper presented at the Annual meeting of the American Association of Public Opinion Research, St. Petersburg, FL.

Brennan, William J., Jr. 1987. 'The Quest to Develop a Jurisprudence of Civil Liberties in Times of Security Crises.' Speech, December 22, 1987, at the Law School of Hebrew University, Jerusalem, Israel.

Carter, Bill and Felicity Barringer. 2001a. 'In Patriotic Time, Dissent Is Muted.' *New York Times,* 9-28-2001.

Carter, Bill and Felicity Barringer. 2001b. 'Networks Agree to U.S. Request to Edit Future bin Laden Tapes.' *New York Times,* 10-11-2001.

Department of Defense. 2001. 'Seminar on Coverage of the War on Terrorism.' http://www.defenselink.mil/news/Nov2001/tll182001-tl108br.html. Statement by the *New York Daily News* reporter Tom DeFrank during the seminar, co-sponsored in November 2001 by the Department of Defense and the Brookings Institution.

Espionage Act, 1918, 40 Stat. 553, 1918.

Flynt v. Rumsfeld. Civ. No. 01=2399, DDC, Jan.8, 2002.

Kilian, Michael. 2002. 'The Pentagon Puzzle.' *Chicago Tribune,* 1-7-02.

Kinsley, Michael. 2002. 'Listening to Our Inner Ashcrofts.' *Washington Post,* 1-4-02.

Office of Censorship, 1941. EO 8985, 12-19-1941, established under First War Powers Act, 55 Stat. 840, 12-18-1941.

Pew Research Center for the People and the Press, 2001. 'Terror Coverage Boosts News Media's Images But Military Censorship Backed.' http://people-press.org/reports/print.php3?PageID=14.

Sachs, Susan. 2002. 'U.S. Defends Withholding Immigrants' Names.' *New York Times,* 5-21-02.

Sajó, András and Monroe Price, eds. 1996. *Rights of Access to the Media.* The Hague: Kluwer Law International.

San Francisco Chronicle Editorial, 2001. 'On Civil Liberties; Under Cloak of Security,' 12-9-2001.

Sedition Act, 1798. 1 Stat. 570, 1798.

Silverberg, Marshall. 1991. 'Constitutional Concerns in Denying the Press Access to Military Operations.' pp. 165–175. In *Defense Beat: The Dilemmas of Defense Coverage,* Loren B. Thompson, Ed. New York: Lexington Books.

Smith Act, 1940, 54 Stat. 671.

St. Louis Post Dispatch, Editorial, 2001. 'The Power of Information.' 10-11-01.

Steinhauer, Jennifer. 2002. 'Records of 9/11 Response not for Public, City Says.' *New York Times,* July 23, 2002.

Thompson, Loren B. 1991. 'The Media Versus the Military: A Brief History of War Coverage in the United States.' pp. 3–56 in *Defense Beat: The Dilemmas of Defense Coverage,* Loren B. Thompson, ed. New York: Lexington Books, 1991.

Thrall, A. Trevor. 2000. *War in the Media Age.* Cresskill, NJ: Hampton Press.

34

HOW POLICY MAKERS DEAL WITH THE PRESS

Martin Linsky

Editor's Note

Based on analyses of six federal policy decisions during the Nixon, Ford, Carter, and Reagan presidencies and interviews with senior policy officials and journalists, Martin Linsky concludes that policymakers must learn how to capture media power to enhance their policy goals. If they do not consider communications aspects of a policy or if they mismanage them, the policy is prone to fail. The case study presented here involved reforms in the U.S. Postal Service. It is an example of highly effective use of the media that brought policy success when failure seemed to be in the cards. As is always true in complex situations, however, it is difficult to pinpoint the precise contribution made by the media campaign. All that can be said with certainty is that the reformers were convinced that their case would not have carried without their efforts to win favorable press coverage and without an advertising blitz.

At the time of writing Linsky was a lecturer in public policy at the John F. Kennedy School of Government at Harvard University. He had experience in government as a three-term member of the Massachusetts House of Representatives and assistant attorney general for the Commonwealth of Massachusetts. His journalism experience includes editorship of Cambridge's *Real Paper* and editorial writing and reporting for the *Boston Globe*.

. . . Postal reform began to emerge as a concern for federal officials in the late 1960s. The volume of mail had just about tripled since World War II, the deficit from operations had increased to $1.1 billion, and systems and equipment were antiquated. If anyone needed tangible evidence of a problem, they got it when the Chicago Post Office nearly shut down in October 1966.

Source: Martin Linsky, *Impact: How the Press Affects Federal Policymaking,* New York: Norton, 1986, 148–168. Copyright © 1986 by the Institute of Politics at Harvard University. Used by permission of W. W. Norton & Company, Inc.

[Larry] O'Brien was postmaster general at the time, and he tried to take advantage of the Chicago crisis by warning that a "catastrophe" was approaching.[1] In April 1967, he told a stunned audience from the Magazine Publishers Association that he favored turning the Post Office Department into a nonprofit (and nonpolitical) government corporation. When O'Brien left the government to work for Robert Kennedy in his campaign for president, whatever momentum there was for postal reorganization went with him.

However dismal the prospects seemed, Nixon had made postal reform a campaign promise and he began to make good on his commitment early into his administration. The first step was a dramatic and unpopular one: Nixon and [Postmaster General Winton] Blount eliminated Post Office political patronage by ending the practice of allowing congressmen to name the postmasters. Republican congressmen, contemplating the fruits of recapturing the White House, were furious, but Nixon and Blount knew that with both the House and Senate controlled by Democrats, there would be no postal reform without Democratic support. If they waited until after filling available postal jobs with friends of Republican congressmen before moving on reform, they knew that the Democrats would never have taken them seriously. The second step, eventually more important but less visible for the time being, was to develop a strategy for convincing the public, and through them the Congress, of the benefits of reorganization. It was really a two-stage process: first the case had to be made that there was a serious and important problem at the Post Office; then, reorganization had to become the solution.

Blount knew that reorganization would not come about without going outside Washington: "Congress owned the Post Office and they liked that old baby just the way it was. We needed the newspaper pressure in the members' districts to shake up things." [2] He decided to set up what POD [Post Office Department] memos referred to as a "front organization" to push for reform. The idea had three enormous advantages: it provided a way to create a lobbying campaign that federal personnel were prohibited from doing directly or allocating funds for; it created a funding channel to allow those who favored reform to offset the efforts of the unions; and, most important, it permitted the public effort on behalf of the Nixon-Blount bill to be bipartisan.

The key to bipartisanship was O'Brien, the former postmaster general and former Democratic Party chairman who was already on record as favoring both reorganization and a grassroots lobbying approach. After some persuading, O'Brien agreed to co-chair the operation, to be called the Citizens Committee for Postal Reform (CCPR). The Republican half of the team was to be Thruston Morton, retired US senator and also a former national party chairman. The final step at the preliminary stage was to hire a marketing expert; Blount settled on William Dunlap, who did marketing for Procter & Gamble.

Dunlap was given an office at the POD, and two weeks to develop a full-scale plan. He remanded his public salary; P&G continued to pay him while he worked on the reorganization during 1969 and 1970. Dunlap wrote a marketing plan, he recalled, "just the way I would at Procter & Gamble. Essentially I took a packaging goods approach that you use to market a product, and applied it to the government sector." His approach was explicit, thorough, and very sophisticated. The purpose was to "stimulate the maximum amount of active support . . . and to utilize this favorable public reaction as a positive force that could be directed toward the members of Congress." [3] In the twenty-eight-page document he prepared, he laid out plans to utilize all the available media, national and local, print and electronic, in all their available slots: letters to the editor, editorials, news stories, feature articles by the postmaster general, and even appearances on entertainment television such as *The Tonight Show* and *The Joey Bishop Show.* The appeal to the media was to be based on their role as opinion makers, their self-interest as mail users, and their commitment to keep their readers and viewers abreast of the news, namely the news about postal reform. It was a saturation strategy in which press support, or at least press cooperation, was crucial.

Kick-off was set for May 27, 1969. During the preceding week, Blount and a handful of his aides gave background briefings to the editorial boards of papers in six major cities to ensure that all the coverage around the announcement was not from the highly political Washington press corps. On May 27, the president sent the reorganization message to the Congress. Nixon read a statement at the White House and Blount followed with a press briefing and a twenty-two–page press packet outlining the legislation. POD designed a special packet for editorial writers. There was a POD headquarters briefing for staff which was wired directly to three hundred top postmasters around the country. A POD publication called *Postal Life,* sent to every postal employee, explained the legislation in great detail. The Mail Users Council sent a "Memo to Mailers" presenting the reorganization proposal to sixty thousand business executives. CCPR, whose formation had been announced on May 26, issued a press release hailing the bill.

Editorial reaction to the reorganization was enthusiastic. Congressional reaction was cool in general, and absolutely frosty among the senior members of the House Post Office Committee (HPOC). Chairman Thaddeus Dulski (D-NY) had his own modest reform bill which stopped far short of establishing a government corporation to replace the Post Office Department. Senior Republicans on the committee were upset because the White House had eliminated congressional patronage in Post Office jobs. The administration had to reach all the way down to the fourth-ranking Republican Edward Derwinski (R-IL) and Democrat Mo Udall (D-AR) to find co-sponsors.

A confidential recap of a June 10 senior POD staff meeting indicated that reaching the postal employees was to be the number one short-run priority of the public relations campaign. Number two was producing favorable editorials in the home districts of congressmen on the Post Office Committee. Specific efforts toward these objectives were to be supported by continuing national coverage. During June and July, Blount appeared on *Meet the Press, Today,* and two nationally distributed radio programs; plus, he gave several dozen interviews to editorial boards, national reporters, and syndicated columnists. O'Brien and Morton testified together before Congress and appeared together before the National Press Club, drawing editorial praise for CCPR and postal reform as being "above politics." Ads soliciting support for CCPR were taken in the *New York Times* and the *Washington Post* in late June. Blount and other top officials at POD began giving background briefings for editorial boards at key papers around the country. POD press kits were mailed to virtually all of the nation's newspapers. Many newspapers used large parts of the press releases and editorials supplied by POD and CCPR. Some prestigious newspapers, such as the *Denver Post* and the *Milwaukee Journal,* were almost in front of the bandwagon, writing editorials urging Blount and CCPR to keep up the good fight against, as the *Journal* said, "the traditionalists in Congress." [4]

The activity produced coverage. As early as June 16, Dunlap counted 194 news stories, 232 editorials, 27 op-ed pieces, and 39 cartoons on the reorganization bill. At the end of June, Blount reported that 88 percent of the editorials favored the bill, now numbered H.R. 11750, with 9 percent undecided and only 3 percent opposed.

The pressure from the coverage was beginning to be felt where it counted—in the Congress. At a[n] HPOC hearing near the end of July, Congressman Robert Tiernan (D-RI), originally opposed but thought to be wavering, referred to the "tidal wave" of local press support generated by CCPR. Testimony to Congress by union officials during the summer reflected their frustration at the success of CCPR in building support for the reorganization; they used words like "brainwashing" to describe what was happening.

By the time HPOC took its first vote in early October, there was as much support on the committee for the administration's bill as for Dulski's. In six months, Blount and his friends had taken a solution that almost no one supported to a problem that few people took seriously and made it politically salient and even compelling.

Soon after the committee vote, postal reform became intertwined with another issue dear to the hearts of postal employees: a pay raise. Udall agreed to support a pay raise bill which was far in excess of what the administration said it would accept, and the Udall pay raise bill was rushed through the House on October 14, despite the threat of a presidential veto. . . .

While the president and the unions were facing each other in this standoff during the fall, CCPR went back to the streets. The press campaign was more or less put on hold; something of a saturation point had been reached and there was no coming event to provide hard news coverage. . . .

CCPR began to gear up the media campaign as the Senate began its hearings on postal reform in November. The unions attacked CCPR: "One of the smoothest and most massive attempts at public brainwashing since the German glory days of Joseph Paul Goebbels," said NALC [National Association of Letter Carriers] President James Rademacher on November 25,[5] while simultaneously taking a page out of the CCPR success story and starting a media campaign of his own.

The objectives of the NALC campaign were to break the connection between reorganization and the pay raise, and to pressure the president into signing the pay raise bill when it reached his desk. It was a three-part initiative. First, ads were run in four hundred newspapers and on three hundred radio stations seeking support for the pay raise bill, and urging people to write to the president. Second, just to make sure the message was received, letter carriers, the ladies' auxiliary, and several unions distributed a total of six million pre-addressed cards with requests that they be filled out and sent to the White House. If Nixon still vetoed the bill, part three of the plan would be implemented: a march on Washington by 15,000 letter carriers, and a television broadcast responding to the veto message. Within a week of the beginning of the NALC marketing blitz the White House received three million pieces of mail in support of the pay raise. . . .

With the assistance of Udall, [Charles "Chuck"] Colson and Rademacher hammered out a compromise in early December, trading substantial collective bargaining provisions and pay raise support, for ending union opposition to the government corporation concept. Rademacher says that he made the deal because he "saw the handwriting on the wall," [6] but he had made a huge tactical error in not involving the rival postal union, the UFPC [United Federation of Postal Clerks], in the White House negotiations. As a result, Rademacher's union was the only one to support the compromise. . . .

Rademacher and Blount met the press and tried to claim that the victory was in everyone's interest, but the New York postal union locals were not convinced. A strike vote was taken on March 17, and on the next day all mail service was halted in New York City as the first postal strike in the nation's history was underway. . . .

Finally, after several weeks of hard bargaining, a package was worked out which provided for an immediate and retroactive pay hike, with a larger hike to take effect when reorganization was signed into law. The reorganization agreed to was in all essential respects the same as the one reported by HPOC. George Meany, who was by then speaking for the unions, hailed it as "a tremendous step forward" because postal employees had won the right to collective bargaining.[7]

The bill passed the House overwhelmingly on June 18. On the Senate side, eight of the twelve members of the Senate Post Office Committee were up for re-election in the fall and didn't want the blood of another postal strike on their hands. David Minton, then counsel to the committee, says that "reform was a high visibility item in the media following the strike and that had a very influential role in pushing reorganization through." [8] The Senate passed the bill in essentially the same form as it had come over from the House. When the House approved the conference committee report on August 6, reorganization was on its way to the White House, where, not surprisingly, the information folks at POD had prepared an elaborate bill-signing ceremony that received enormous and favorable press coverage.

The Impact of the Press

Assessing the impact of the press in the enactment of postal reorganization is complicated. What was produced in the media by the POD and CCPR press strategies went far beyond news coverage, and included commentary, editorials, and advertisements. In addition, there were other elements which played important roles, such as the grassroots organizing and the pressure it generated on members of Congress and the strike. White House support was obviously important. Winton Blount's tenacity was crucial. In the view of Congressman Derwinski, "What got postal reform through was that Blount was an unusually determined, able man who just bulldogged it." [9] Blount himself sees the campaign to win the support of the public and the local media as central to their success, although not solely responsible for it. "There is no key force or event that created postal reform; it was a lot of forces and events working together. . . . The campaign to draw media support was enormously important; that's the way you move the Congress and if we had not had the media support we would have had a bad time. I don't remember specific incidents where a Congressman would cite editorial support in his home district as his reason for changing his position, but you could see that their changes corresponded to periods when public support for reorganization was voiced. . . . If the public had been 'ho-hum,' fifty-fifty, I don't think we would have reorganized the Post Office." [10]

Assessing the impact of the press is further complicated by the understandable tendency to separate news coverage from editorials and both of them from paid advertisements. One of the insights behind the Blount strategy is that all those pieces of the media play a role and have an effect. Advertisements are public relations, not press coverage, but Blount and his allies understood that each element of the media has its own constituency and influence, and that all were important in putting reorganization on the agenda, framing the issue, putting pressure on the Congress, and eventually passing the bill. When it comes to advertising, the press is just a conduit. In the Post Office case, officials were able to get news coverage and editorial support for reorganization that was almost as unfiltered as their ads. It is challenging enough to examine what role in general the press played. The task becomes impossible if it has to include distinguishing impacts among different types of newspaper copy. It also becomes irrelevant, because the point is that the POD and CCPR set out to use the mass media, in all its formats, to help achieve their policy goals and they succeeded. The question is how much credit does the entire media campaign deserve for their success.

When the bill was filed in May 1979, the outlook for its passage was bleak. Postal reform was not a salient issue for the editorial writers, never mind the general public. It was a priority for the Nixon administration, but there was strong opposition from powerful unions, a Democratic Congress, Republicans angered by the patronage shutoff, and those beloved letter carriers who delivered the mail.

Then for a few months, the pro-reorganization forces had the field to themselves. The opposition was there, but asleep. During that period, most of whatever appeared in the newspapers about reform was there at the initiative of CCPR and the POD. When the opposition awoke in September, their advantage had been almost completely dissipated. What looked almost impossible in May now appeared to be about to happen. The unions had wanted a pay raise and wanted to keep their future in the friendly hands of the Congress. By mid-September, it appeared that they might get the worst of both possible worlds, no pay raise and a reorganization bill out of their beloved House Post Office Committee. During the interim, the POD and CCPR had been able to achieve two huge objectives. First, they had taken an issue, postal reform, and put it on the national political agenda. That was no mean feat, and it was aided enormously by the willingness of the president to climb aboard and stay there. Without the press strategy it seems very unlikely that, absent an unforeseen external intervening event such as another Chicago-type crisis, reorganization would have ever gained its momentum in the Congress in general or in HPOC in particular. The second great achievement during that period, besides putting reorganization on the front burner, was to frame the administration's bill in such a way as to give it the best shot at success. The framing had three pieces to it: whatever were the grievances with the Post Office, whether they be late mail or underpaid letter carriers, reorganization was an answer, if not *the* answer; support for the proposal was bipartisan; and the administration bill was the only real reform. While the unions and their supporters in the Congress were talking with each other, these three messages were being systematically trumpeted all over the land in a multimedia spectacular aimed directly at the press and the public, and only indirectly to the legislators themselves. When the music stopped, there was a sense out there that the problems in the POD were real, that the Nixon bill was a positive response to them, and that this was an issue above partisanship.

The unions recognized this and responded with their own press campaign, which stemmed the tide, not by directly countering any of those three messages, but by adding two of their own. The first was the CCPR, which was not what it appeared to be; the second was that the only real issue for the postal employees was pay. The unions appear to have understood that the clear field had given the POD and CCPR the opportunity to put reorganization on the political agenda and to frame it in a way that made the union opposition rhetoric on the merits no longer credible to journalists and editorial writers following the issue. By their own positive campaign, the unions were able to salvage the most they could: reviving the pay raise issue as a high congressional priority, and putting the CCPR and its campaign for reorganization temporarily on the defensive.

There was a third great press campaign in this story: the effort of the White House to try to create a climate during the strike which would help to ensure that whatever happened, reorganization would not be hurt by the walkout. As the strike spread, the White House developed a strategy with four objectives, as recalled by [John D.] Ehrlichman: "Nixon . . . wanted us to paint the strikers as outlaws who were doing something illegal; . . . to convey to the American public how to use the post office during the strike; . . . to use the strike to sell postal reform; and finally, he wanted to make sure that he came out of this looking like a strong leader." [11]

The program was straightforward and well executed. Under the direction of H. R. Haldeman, a game plan was prepared to convey these messages through a variety of means, including saturating television talk and news shows with administration spokespeople and friendly members of Congress. Herb Klein sent fact sheets to three hundred editorial writers and nine hundred radio and television news directors. Handling the combination of messages was tricky; too much strong leadership and strike-baiting might backfire. Letter carriers were generally among the most popular of public employees, and the polls showed that there was substantial sympathy for the postal workers and their specific grievances. The administration did not want to encourage other unions to join the postal workers, or to encourage the most militant among their number to take control.

This campaign, too, was successful, although once again helped significantly by the firm commitment in the White House to sticking with the issue during the hard bargaining which produced the combined pay-and-reform package that eventually was enacted.

The press campaigns played a major role in the outcome of this policy-making. Campaign is not used casually here; these were not one-time efforts, such as a single press conference or individual leak. They were well planned, complicated, continuing, multifaceted, and well executed. Most important, they worked. One moral of the tale is that Ronald Reagan did not invent the concept of press management, but anyone who remembers Franklin Delano Roosevelt's fireside chats knows that anyway.

Notes

1. David Whitman, "Selling the Reorganization of the Post Office (A)," Kennedy School of Government, case C14-84-610, pp. 2–4.
2. Ibid., p. 9.
3. Ibid., pp. 11–12.
4. Ibid., p. 20.
5. Senate Post Office and Civil Service Committee, Postal Modernization, Hearings, 91st Congress, 1st session, 1969, p. 800.
6. Ibid., p. 38.
7. Post Office Department transcript of Winton M. Blount/George Meany press conference, August 5, 1970, pp. 1 and 2.
8. Whitman, Post Office Sequel case, p. 7.
9. Ibid., pp. 7–8.
10. Ibid., pp. 8–9.
11. Ibid., p. 4.

35

MANAGED DEMOCRACY IN RUSSIA: PUTIN AND THE PRESS

Masha Lipman and Michael McFaul

Editor's Note

Masha Lipman and Michael McFaul warn that observers must look beyond democratic structures when determining whether a society's media are truly free, able to choose their targets and story framing. Using the example of Vladimir Putin's Russia, the authors show how a government characterized by authoritarian leanings can take control of democratically organized media institutions and bend them to its will while retaining the democratic organizational shell. After the government forces a few obstreperous independent media out of business, it rids itself not only of troublesome enemies, but it also sends a potent warning message. It demonstrates to the surviving independents that criticizing the political leadership is a potentially fatal error. When a country's free press has been silenced in this manner, democratic governance becomes a sham. That may be Russia's current tragic fate.

Lipman is a political analyst at the Carnegie Moscow Center. She formerly was the deputy editor of *Itogi* magazine, a weekly published in Russia in cooperation with *Newsweek* and absorbed into the Putin-controlled media empire. McFaul is a senior associate at the Carnegie Endowment for International Peace. He is also an associate professor of political science at Stanford University. McFaul is the author and editor of several monographs dealing with democratization in Russia.

... After winning the March 2000 presidential election, [Vladimir] Putin said all the right things about markets and democracy. For anyone who worked to overthrow Soviet communism, the rise to power of an ex-spy in

Source: Masha Lipman and Michael McFaul," 'Managed Democracy' in Russia: Putin and the Press," *The Harvard International Journal of Press/Politics* 6:3 (Summer 2001): 116–127. Copyright 2001 by Sage Publications. Reprinted by permission of Sage Publications Inc.

postcommunist Russia could only be interpreted as alarming. Nonetheless, this new, young, and energetic leader inspired hope with his statements about a new beginning for Russia.

The verdict may still be out regarding Putin's commitment to market reforms, but today, there is no doubt about his antidemocratic proclivities. More than any event in the Putin era so far, the destruction . . . of Media Most, the biggest independent media group in Russia, demonstrates unequivocally that Putin seeks to undermine Russia's fragile and weak democratic institutions. Putin's spin doctors call the project "managed democracy." The system they seek to create will have all the formal institutions of democracy: elections, parties, media, civil society, and so on. But the real autonomy of these institutions and, therefore, their real capacity to influence the actions of the state will be severely limited. The Kremlin's successful campaign to eliminate critical content from the Media Most media outlets without actually eliminating the media outlets themselves represents the latest and perhaps most consequential phase of consolidating managed democracy in Russia.

Public-Private Spheres in Postcommunist Russia

For most of the past century in Russia, there was little space for political, economic, or social life independent of the state. The Soviet system aimed to manage the economy, monopolize political activity, control the media, and destroy all independent associational life, and nearly succeeded in achieving these goals. To the extent that organized social or economic groups did exist outside of the family, they were atomized, apolitical, or illegal. At the same time, the Soviet system crowded private life with a myriad of social, political, and press organizations that mimicked their counterpart organizations in the West in name but actually helped to control society in practice.

In the late 1980s, Mikhail Gorbachev began to liberalize the Soviet political system. In the name of *glasnost*, he allowed several newspapers, literary journals (the so-called *fat journals*), and weekly magazines greater editorial license to criticize the Soviet system, especially its past. Gorbachev's glasnost gave birth to a new generation of independent-minded journalists and commentators. During the peak years of *perestroika*, writers at *Moscow News, Argumenty i Fakty, Ogonyok*, and *Izvestiya* were ahead of the political and civil society in advocating democratic reform. While still enjoying the economic benefits of state subsidization, new independent newspapers . . . appeared for the first time.

The liberalization of television was much slower. Only in the spring of 1991 did the Russian government succeed in compelling the Soviet state to give Russia its own television station, RTR. Yet, the general tendency toward greater pluralism had even begun to penetrate electronic media by the end of the Soviet era. Significantly, however, the state—whether it was the Soviet Union or the Russian Federation—still owned or subsidized every major media outlet in Russia before the collapse of the Soviet Union in December 1991. In other words, a paper such as *Moscow News* could not have survived without state assistance. But because the state's leader, Gorbachev, tolerated a critical press, *Moscow News* and others could publish articles critical of him and his government.

After the collapse of Soviet communism and establishment of an independent Russian state, Boris Yeltsin's reforms created new space for independent political, social, and economic activity. The first postcommunism decade in Russia saw freedom for the press, albeit for various reasons. Yeltsin, at some fundamental level, appeared to value an independent press. At the same time, during most of the early Yeltsin years leading up to the 1996 presidential campaign, Yeltsin and the press were allies against a common threat: a communist comeback. This alliance could have been forged with no normative commitment to loftier principles for democracy. Yeltsin's state was also weak. Fighting many political and economic battles simultaneously, it did not have the capacity to control the media.

Market reforms initially helped to further stimulate the growth of independent media, including, first and foremost, television (Mickiewicz 1997). NTV, the first private television network started by Vladimir Gusinsky in 1993, provided a truly independent source of information that reached beyond Moscow. Defying government threats to revoke its license, NTV earned its credentials as a serious news organization when it provided critical coverage of the first Chechen war. NTV also achieved a new level of post-Soviet professionalism, quality, and style that its rival channels, ORT (Channel 1), and RTR (Channel 2) lacked. News anchor Evgeny Kiselev became a national celebrity by producing and hosting *Itogi*, a Sunday night talk show on politics. Hoping to replicate the success of NTV in other media markets, Gusinsky and his Media Most holding company also bought a stake in a popular radio station, *Ekho Moskvy*, and founded a daily newspaper, *Segodnya*, and a weekly magazine, *Itogi*, published in partnership with *Newsweek*. Other financial and business tycoons followed in Gusinsky's steps, believing that the media, especially television, was an important political tool. . . .

From afar, Russia's oligarchs may have appeared to be buying "private" media outlets and establishing independent media empires. Some were. But even a decade after the collapse of communism, the space for genuinely independent economic or political activity from the state was still limited. The state . . . was still the dominant actor in media, politics, and some profitable sectors of the economy. The Russian federal state was still the majority shareholder in ORT and fully owned RTR, while regional heads of administrations still controlled the major television networks in their regions and subsidized most print media. The electoral success of the progovernmental party, Unity, in the December 1999 elections, and then Putin's own landslide election victory in March 2000, demonstrated the tremendous powers of national television in the state's hands (Colton and McFaul 2000; McFaul 2000).

Gusinsky's Media Most was the most financially independent company. Different from other major media assets, Gusinsky did not privatize a Soviet-era enterprise but started his empire from scratch, meaning that the state did not initially own a share in his companies. But even Gusinsky acquired his initial capital from connections with the Moscow city government (his Most Bank served as the city's banker for years), then obtained additional control over Channel 4, on which NTV broadcast, as a reward for his cooperation with Yeltsin during the 1996 presidential election. He then offered an equity stake to Gazprom, a largely state-owned gas company, to finance his plans for expansion. Gusinsky also secured loans from several sources, including Credit Suisse First Boston. Before the Russian financial crash in August 1998, Gusinsky's business plan and debt-to-equity ratios looked ambitious, but within reason. The crash, however, slashed the advertising market by two-thirds, from approximately $540 million to $190 million (Bohlen, April 29, 2001). The crash also made Gusinsky's dollar-denominated debts significantly more expensive, compelling him eventually (November 2000) to surrender more equity to Gazprom to retire some of these debts. This transfer of shares made Gazprom—or more specifically Gazprom's subsidiary, Gazprom Media—a 46-percent shareholder, left Gusinsky's Media Most as a 49.56-percent shareholder in NTV, with the balance of 4.44 percent owned by an American investment company, Capital Research and Management Group.

Like any other sensible director of an ailing enterprise in Russia, Gusinsky pursued one last strategy to avoid state control: foreign investment. Although the details of the proposed deal are still unclear, Ted Turner and a group of Western investors appeared ready to buy out Gusinsky's stake in NTV (Higgins, January 22, 2001). The only condition Turner wanted was an agreement from the Russian state that it would not interfere in the business or editorial affairs of his new asset. Despite efforts from the State Department to facilitate contact between Turner and Putin's government, Putin never committed to such an agreement. They could not agree, because NTV's problems were never just financial. They were also political.

Gusinsky versus Putin: A Political and Personal Vendetta

NTV's editorial line toward the Russian government has vacillated considerably in recent years. During the first Chechen war (1994–1996), NTV reporters covered the war from within Chechnya, exposing the brutal and ineffective campaign of the Russian military. The coverage had a profound effect on Russian public opinion. By January 1995, only 16 percent of the Russian population supported the use of force in Chechnya, while 71 percent op-posed the war.[1] Opposition to the war translated into opposition to Yeltsin himself. Seventy percent of those polled disapproved of Yeltsin's performance as president in September 1994, growing to 80 percent by January 1995.[2] To secure Yeltsin's reelection in 1996, Yeltsin campaign officials believed that they had to end the war (McFaul 1997). In April 1996, Yeltsin announced a cease-fire.

During the 1996 presidential campaign, NTV reversed course and sup-ported Yeltsin in his reelection bid. NTV's director general, Igor Malashenko, blurred the lines of division between campaign and media when he joined the Yeltsin reelection team without resigning from his television post. In provid-ing unabashedly positive coverage for Yeltsin and very critical reporting of [Gennady] Zyuganov during the campaign, NTV reporters, as well as jour-nalists working for Gusinsky's *Segodnya* newspaper, made a significant con-tribution to the joint effort of keeping the communists out of power. Russian journalists, including those of Gusinsky's media, explained that they were protecting their survival as an independent media. If Zyuganov became pres-ident of Russia, they argued, they would all be closed down. In making this compromise, however, especially when the Yeltsin campaign paid some (al-though not all) reporters large sums of money for pro-Yeltsin pieces, NTV and *Segodnya* tarnished their credentials as independent journalists. Instead, they—like their counterparts working for other oligarchs, as well as for the state, at competitive television networks and newspapers—became increas-ingly viewed as the mouthpieces of their owners.

After the 1996 presidential election, Gusinsky was ready to collect his spoils from good service during the campaign. It was soon after the election that he acquired full control of Channel 4 for NTV. He also hoped to acquire Svyazinvest, a telecommunications company that would dovetail nicely with his business interests in media. In this sale, however, Deputy Prime Minister Anatoly Chubais decided to . . . [offer] Svyazinvest to the highest bidder (Freeland 2000). Gusinsky and his partners lost this bidding contest. Furious after his defeat, he used his media empire to smear government officials re-sponsible for the action, including first and foremost Chubais. The campaign was effective enough to help push him out of office in 1997, an achievement that his supporters never forgave.

After the Svyazinvest scandal, NTV became increasingly critical of Yeltsin and his government, focusing in particular on corruption within the Krem-lin's inner circle. NTV once again provided the only critical coverage of the second Chechen war as it unfolded in the fall of 1999. This second war, how-ever, was much more popular than the first, prompting Kremlin loyalists to call NTV an unpatriotic, profascist (because these loyalists called the Chechen guerrillas fascists), pro-Western organization. The Kremlin claimed that

NTV only reported Russian military atrocities without devoting any coverage to violations of human rights carried out by Chechen guerrillas. Putin, then prime minister, was offended personally by NTV's coverage and made his opinions known both to his colleagues in the government and to Gusinsky.

In the run-up to the December 1999 parliamentary election, NTV did not support the government's candidates but gave much free airtime and positive coverage to opposition political parties, . . . To their credit, especially compared with the other national television networks, NTV news editors allotted huge chunks of prime time to debates between parties and discussions among voters. Yet, NTV did not endorse the Kremlin's party, Unity, in the parliamentary race, nor did it back Putin in the presidential election. Putin noticed that.

After his election landslide, Putin began to articulate a new approach toward the press and democratic institutions in general that differed qualitatively from Boris Yeltsin. Rhetorically, Putin of course endorsed the notion of a free press and the importance of democracy. He . . . repeatedly pledged allegiance to the freedom of the press; he readily [admitted] that it is absolutely necessary in a modern society and that if Russia aspires to become a modern society, it must ensure that the press is free. Yet, his statements and speeches also revealed a poor understanding of these concepts and lack of respect for their importance in the operations of the Russian state, economy, and society. In his first annual address *(poslanie)* to the members of the Russian parliament in June 2000, Putin hinted at his mistrust of the press, claiming, "Sometimes . . . [the media] turn into means of mass disinformation and a tool of struggle against the state." The Doctrine of Information Security issued several months later made it clear that state-owned media must dominate the information market, since only the state can provide the citizens of Russia with objective information about what goes on in the country. The doctrine also pledges to battle disinformation coming from abroad.

When faced with crises that required action, Putin made clear his real attitude toward an independent press. Radio Liberty correspondent Andrei Babitsky was the first journalist to experience Putin's wrath. For his critical coverage of the second Chechen war, Babitsky was secretly arrested in Chechnya by Russian security services and kept incommunicado for several weeks. . . . Putin also vehemently denounced those journalists who criticized the way he and his government handled the crisis caused by the sinking of the Kursk submarine in August 2000. Putin emotionally called these critics traitors. . . .

It is against this background of such statements and actions that the campaign against NTV must be understood. Although NTV's financial woes made the station vulnerable, the state's campaign against the channel is simply another example of what happens to a news organization when it gets in the way of the Kremlin. There was certainly a pragmatic desire in the Kremlin to take the third and only independent national TV channel under control, so that the Kremlin would have uncontested influence over people's minds, but Putin's personal convictions should not be underestimated, either. As Putin saw the interests of the Russian state, Gusinsky was the enemy of the state and the president's personal enemy.

Putin, of course, was too savvy and concerned with his image in the West to simply shut down NTV by force. Instead, those leading the campaign to seize NTV and dismantle Media Most pursued different strategies over several months. One of these strategies was to threaten Gusinsky personally. The idea was to use the prosecutor's office to bring criminal charges against Gusinsky, intimidate him, and thus silence his media. The implementation of this "criminal variant" began with a now-notorious raid on Gusinsky's media office building in May 2000 by masked, gun-toting men who burst in under the pretext of a search. Gusinsky and his people were accused of various crimes, but no convincing evidence was ever presented, and the cases fell apart in a short time. In the months that followed the first raid, affiliate offices of Gusinsky's corporation were raided and searched dozens of times, proceedings were opened and closed, and Gusinsky's employees were interrogated and their apartments searched. . . . Eventually, in June, Gusinsky himself was arrested and then released three days later but was placed under house arrest. A month later, on July 20, 2000, Gusinsky agreed to sign a secret deal to sell his controlling stake in Media Most to Gazprom in return for his freedom. . . .

. . . Realizing that the strategy of intimidation through criminal charges had failed, the Kremlin placed greater attention on the "business variant." In the name of property rights, the state's surrogate, Gazprom, moved to assert its control over NTV. A meticulous litigation campaign—sprinkled with raids, interrogations, and threats of further criminal investigations—ensued. . . . Finally, in April [2001], Gazprom succeeded in changing the management. . . . Alfred Kokh, the executive director of Gazprom-Media, became chairman in place of Gusinsky, and Boris Jordan, a former American investment banker, assumed the role of general director in place of Kiselev.

. . . The assault against independent media did not end with NTV. In the earlier debt negotiations between Gusinsky and Gazprom, Gusinsky relinquished a stake in each of his media assets, including the publishing house Seven Days, which published *Segodnya* and *Itogi*. By the beginning of 2001, Gazprom had enough shares in Seven Days to conspire with the president and shareholder to close *Segodnya* and oust the entire staff of *Itogi*. They did so on April 17. Like NTV, *Itogi* continues to be published, but with an entirely new editorial orientation. . . . The final shoe to fall was Ekho Moskvy, the radio station still owned in part by Media Most. On May 4, a Moscow court affirmed Gazprom's ruling stake in Ekho Moskvy, leaving the editorial future of this important radio station in question.

Putin apologists claim that he played no role in this "merger and acquisition." And that is the point. If he really did care about freedom of the press, he could have stopped this gross violation of democracy with one public statement. But he did not intervene. He broke his silence on this subject only once, during German Chancellor Gerhard Schroeder's visit to Russia a few days after Gazprom changed the NTV management. On this occasion, he once again confirmed his adherence to the freedom of the press but added, "I do not think that I, under these conditions, have the right to interfere in this conflict between different economic players" (*Moscow Times*, April 10, 2001:3).

His inaction reveals his true preferences regarding free and independent media. Journalists can be free and independent just as long as they do not get in the way of the president and his agenda.

Conclusion

The "restructuring" of NTV and *Itogi* and the closing of *Segodnya* does not mean that all independent media have ceased to exist. . . . TV-6 [may become] a genuinely national television network with an editorial line independent of the Kremlin. Smaller cable television networks, although mostly devoid of political content, are still in operation, and regional television networks have begun to sprout. In Moscow, most privately owned newspapers are still in circulation, private radio stations are in business, and a small number of private political Web sites are in operation. Yet, after the dismantling of the Media Most empire, and especially after the takeover of NTV, the balance between state media and private media has become immensely skewed in favor of the state. After all, 90 percent of the citizens report in a poll conducted last year that their main source of political news is television (Colton and McFaul 2001).[3] The Kremlin's success, albeit after a protracted struggle, in shutting down Media Most may embolden regional heads of administration to take the same action against regional media critics, who are already small in number and weak in resources. Another consequence of the campaign against Media Most is self-censorship. Journalists, political commentators, and academics now realize that there are real risks in going too far in criticizing the government.

The blow to Russian democracy more generally cannot be underestimated. Competitive elections cannot occur without a free press. Corruption cannot be fought without a free press. Elected government officials cannot be held accountable to their constituents without a free press. And ultimately, Russia cannot become a normal European country without a free press. Putin continues to believe that these developments at home do not affect his foreign policy mission abroad. He has stated numerous times that he wants to see Russia become a full member of Western institutions, such as the European Union and the G-8. These organizations, however, do not accept applications from nondemocracies.

Is there a future for independent media in Russia? Of course. Most important, a robust economy with a growing middle class will create propitious conditions for the emergence of new, privately owned media companies. Without question, NTV's financial problems, especially after the August 1998 financial crash, made the company more vulnerable. The next NTV-like project will have a greater chance to succeed when profits can be made and sustained in a more vibrant economy.

But a growing economy and better business plan will not be enough. The destruction of Media Most revealed several other conditions necessary for a free and independent press. First, Russia also must develop an independent and uncorrupt judiciary system that can defend not only state interests but also minority shareholders' rights. When push finally came to shove, Gusinsky and his colleagues had no legal means to defend their interests within Russia because no court would stand up to the pressure of the state.

Second, at least in the near future, independent media in Russia can only develop if the leadership in the Kremlin believes in the norms of free press and democracy more generally. For the foreseeable future, the state will continue to have enormous power over private, societal activity. The state, therefore, must be supportive of or at least not hostile toward the development of independent media. In the wake of Putin's latest campaign, Gorbachev's tolerance of and Yeltsin's commitment to independent media is striking.

Third, an independent press in Russia needs popular support. In a poll conducted last year, an overwhelming number of Russian voters—79 percent—said that they considered freedom of the press to be important (Colton and McFaul 2001). Yet, few of these supporters of a free press believed that the destruction of Media Most was a freedom of the press issue (strana.ru, April 27, 2001). Instead, the struggle was understood, following the Kremlin spin, as either a business dispute or a battle between a corrupt oligarch and the state, whose leader, Putin, still enjoys positive approval ratings. Gusinsky, of course, is no Andrey Sakharov. Like all other oligarchs in postcommunist Russia, he most likely bent the rules and relied on rents from the state (the Moscow city government) to amass his fortunes. But Gusinsky's media empire was not destroyed because of past improprieties. Until Russian society values and is willing to defend an independent press as a basic institution of democracy, future media critics of the state will find it difficult to stay in operation. Until then, Putin will continue to consolidate his "managed democracy." Elections will take place, multiple parties will compete for office, and several television channels will broadcast separate news programs, but real societal control over the state will remain minimal.

Notes

1. As quoted in *Segodnya,* January 28, 1995, 3.
2. Vserossiiskii Tsentr Izucheniya Obshchestvennogo Mneniya (VTsIOM) poll, as quoted in *Segodnya,* January 17, 1995:2.
3. The poll was conducted by Timothy Colton and Michael McFaul, in cooperation with DEMISCOPE. A total of 1,919 voters were interviewed between November 13 and December 13, and 1,842 of them were reinterviewed after the Duma election, between December 25 and January 31. A third wave, reinterviewing 1,748 first- and second-wave respondents, was completed in April to May of 2000, soon after the March 2000 presidential election.

References

Bohlen, Celestine. 2001. "Defining a Free Press: The Unique Evolution of Russian TV." *The New York Times,* Apr. 29, sec. 4, p. 4.

Colton, Timothy J., and Michael McFaul. 2000. "Reinventing Russia's Party of Power: Unity and the 1999 Duma Election." *Post-Soviet Affairs* 16(3):201–24.

Colton, Timothy J., and Michael McFaul. 2001. "Are Russians Undemocratic?" (Working paper). Washington, D.C.: Carnegie Endowment for International Peace.

Freeland, Chrystia. 2000. *Sale of the Century: Russia's Wild Ride from Communism to Capitalism.* New York: Crown Business.

Higgins, Andrew. 2001. "Turner Sets Investment in Russia's Media-Most." *Wall Street Journal,* Jan. 22:A16.

McFaul, Michael. 1997. *Russia's 1996 Presidential Election: The End of Polarized Politics.* Stanford, CA: Hoover Institution Press.

McFaul, Michael. 2000. "Russia under Putin: One Step Forward, Two Steps Backward." *Journal of Democracy* 11(3): 19–33.

Mickiewicz, Ellen. 1997. *Changing Channels: Television and the Struggle for Power in Russia.* Oxford, UK: Oxford University Press.

Renaud, Chris. 2001. "NTV Had No 'Financial Crisis'." *Wall Street Journal Europe,* Apr. 30.

Strana.ru. 2001. "Majority of Russians do not feel attack on free speech," Apr. 27.

36

STRATEGIC COMMUNICATION

Jarol B. Manheim

Editor's Note

Journalists' power rests largely in their ability to select news for publication and frame and feature it as they choose. The many people in and outside of government who want media publicity, or a respite from media attention, try to influence these choices. These media clients are increasingly turning to professional public relations experts to help them control media coverage. In recent decades foreign countries have joined the crowds of publicity seekers or avoiders that try to manipulate the media in the United States to their advantage. Jarol B. Manheim explains the motivations behind these efforts, discusses commonly used tactics, and assesses the results. His work is based on systematic comparative analysis of a large sample of nations that contracted for the services of U.S. public relations firms. Manheim's study shows that it is indeed possible for foreign countries to guide their news coverage in the American press. By generating newsworthy events that enhance their image or by making access to news difficult, countries can increase the amount of favorable coverage they receive and reduce the number of potentially harmful stories.

At the time of writing Manheim was professor of political communication and political science at George Washington University. He also directed its political communication program, which later became the National Center for Communication Studies.

The use of strategic communication (and lesser forms of political public relations) by foreign governments—as judged by the number of contracts and client countries—has roughly doubled since the 1970s. The most recent report of the attorney general—listing clients, contractors, and services—numbers

Source: Jarol B. Manheim, *All of the People, All the Time: Strategic Communication and American Politics*, Armonk, N.Y.: M. E. Sharpe, 1991, chapter 6. Copyright © 1991 by Jarol B. Manheim. Reprinted with permission of M. E. Sharpe, Inc.

several hundred pages, and the total value of the contracts each year runs well into eight figures. The client countries over the years have included a veritable Who's Who of folks with an interest in American foreign policy—the Philippines, of course, but also the Shah's Iran, the Soviet Union, South Africa, Israel, South Korea, Canada, Turkey, and many others. And the list of companies serving their needs has been equally distinguished—Hill & Knowlton, Burson-Marsteller, Edelman International, Ruder Finn—in short, all of the biggest names in public relations and many of the lesser lights as well. They are joined by a bevy of Washington law firms, trade consultants, and general lobbyists like Arnold and Porter, a law firm whose list of clients includes corporations and governments from around the world. . . . Many employees of [these] firms are former government officials whose principal asset is a simple one—who they know.[1] . . .

What kinds of services do these companies provide for their clients? One set falls under the general rubric of lobbying. If public affairs firms are hired for who they know—for the access they have to Washington decision makers—then using their access is an important part of what they do. . . .

Perhaps more interesting to us in the present context, however, is a second group of services, those relating to communications with the press and public. Here, a great deal of what is produced—particularly by firms that came to the business from the media rather than the political side—takes the form of the traditional bells and whistles that we commonly associate with the practice of public relations. Truckloads of newsletters, news releases, fact files, glossy photographs, books, pamphlets—multicolored, multifaceted, but totally obvious propaganda—are produced and distributed. The propaganda goes to news organizations, libraries, college professors, and a variety of other target audiences. And when it arrives, most if not all of it finds its way rather quickly—indeed, as if powered by unseen forces—into the nation's sanitary landfills.

When journalists and members of the public think about the public relations activities of foreign governments—if they ever do—this is the stuff they think about, and it is small wonder that they discount its importance or potential influence. As William Safire put it a few years back, "The whole business smacks of rainmaking, and it seems to be about as effective." [2]

What our research suggests, however, is that there is something else going on here—something of far greater significance. For in addition to all the flackery and puffery and pap that they distribute, some of the more sophisticated strategic communication firms also provide their clients with some useful kinds of advice, advice as to how best to package their policies in order to gain approval in the United States, how and when to control access to news and information so that they appear to best advantage in the American press, and how to communicate with and through the American news media. Specifically, these companies teach governments what to say about their policies and activities. They train embassy and other personnel in how to talk to American journalists about such thorny problems as antiregime activity or human rights violations. They help governments to control access to information, potential news makers, and events, and to stage media events. And more generally, they anticipate and employ to their clients' advantage the predictable tendencies of journalistic behavior. In short, they do for their foreign clients very much what they do for their domestic ones.[3]

A case in point was the visit to the United States by Japanese prime minister Yasuhiro Nakasone in early 1985. At the time, as for a long time before and after, the imbalance of trade between the two countries was an issue of some importance. Indeed, anti-Japanese sentiment among Americans was growing, nurtured by resentment over what was perceived as a Japanese pattern of closing markets to American goods, especially agricultural goods for which there was presumed to be considerable demand. In advance of the Nakasone visit, viewers of local newscasts around the country saw reports showing American produce on its way to Japan. Mike Mansfield, United States ambassador to Japan, appeared on the report saying, "Japanese markets aren't as closed as we might think." Timely? You bet. Prominent issues and personalities? You bet. Good film? You bet. News? Well, what the audience was not told was that this report—in whole or in part, depending on the station—had been produced for the Japanese government by Gray and Company [a Washington-based powerful public relations firm].[4] For a professional image-slinger, it was just another notch on the old '45.

Even network news operations can be susceptible to such appealing video packaging. In the same year as the Nakasone visit, for example, Gray and Company scored another coup. CNN ran a feature in which former Washington news anchor Meryl Comer interviewed King Hasan II of Morocco, who advised the United States not to worry about his recently concluded treaty with President Reagan's erstwhile nemesis, Muammar Quaddafi of Libya. "Any harsh reaction from the West," said Comer, "must be tempered with the acknowledgment that Morocco is strategically important to the United States, and that in this part of the world, strong pro-American leaders are hard to find. This is Meryl Comer reporting from the palace in Marrakech." What CNN and local stations that picked up the report did not know was that the piece was prepared and distributed by Gray—which apparently neglected to label it as required by law—and that Comer herself was a vice president of the company.[5]

Added to services like these, those firms that have access to officials of the United States Congress and government—principally the Washington-based lobbying firms—sell it, or, more accurately, rent it out. Advice. Assistance.

Access. It is an altogether enticing package for a government with policy needs in the United States and a little cash to burn.

The results? We see them every day: . . .

- Mark Siegel—former executive director of the Democratic National Committee and later presidential aide in the Carter White House—conducted what he described as a "political campaign" in his orchestration of the 1989 visit to Washington of newly elected Prime Minister Benazir Bhutto of Pakistan. Siegel set out to present the emergence of democracy in Pakistan as a triumph of American political values, and planned a five-day media blitz around this theme. He carefully controlled media access to the prime minister, favoring those he thought most likely to pursue the central theme of cooperation among the world's democracies, and avoiding those he thought might ask other "distracting" questions. In advance of the visit, Bhutto appeared on CBS's "60 Minutes" and PBS's "MacNeil/Lehrer NewsHour," and was interviewed by Connie Chung, then of NBC. During the visit, she was interviewed by Peter Jennings of ABC and appeared on NBC's "Today."

  Siegel saw these interviews as the equivalent of free media in a campaign—seeking to control them indirectly just as a candidate for office might do—while he treated the focal events of the visit as paid media whose scripting could be more directly managed. These included an appearance before a joint session of Congress: "We sacrificed a part of our lives and bore the pain of confronting tyranny to build a just society. We believe in ourselves, in our cause, in our people and in our country. And when you believe, then there is no mountain too high to scale. That is my message to . . . America . . . and to its people." Delivering the commencement address at her alma mater, Harvard University—"Democratic nations should forge a consensus around the most powerful political idea in the world today: the right of people to freely choose their government. Having created a bond through evolving such a consensus, democratic nations should then come together in an association designed to help each other and promote what is a universal value: democracy." And at a state dinner at the White House: "I didn't know until tonight that Yale ever produced a charming man, and I'm glad I've met the only one." [6] The result? An increase in American aid to Pakistan at a time when many foreign assistance programs were being reduced, dropping of the American demand that Pakistan pledge not to enrich uranium above 5 percent, and final approval of a long-pending shipment of sixty F-16 aircraft to Bhutto's country.[7] . . .

We can look at the process from the other side as well—that of the client countries. Some examples:

- Canada. In recent years, the Canadians have taken a comprehensive approach to their image and policy concerns in the United States. In addition to working through Michael Deaver to combat acid rain, which they attribute largely to emissions from utilities in the American Midwest, the Canadians launched a large-scale, and ultimately successful, lobbying effort to extract a free-trade agreement with the United States—an effort which, in the end, proved more difficult to conclude in Ottawa than in Washington. Concerned about tourism as well as trade policy, they commissioned Market Opinion Research—Robert Teeter's Detroit-based firm—to conduct a nationwide poll measuring images of Canada south of the border. What did they discover? That, despite its proximity to the United States—what country, after all, is more proximate?—its cultural affinity, and its status as a major United States trading partner, most Americans did not think about Canada very much, one way or the other.[8]

- South Korea. Korean corporations and industry associations have long been major clients of American public relations and lobbying firms, while the Korean government and a variety of cultural and educational foundations have developed an extensive program of exchange visits similar to the Fulbright Program operated by the United States Information Agency. The Korean approach to protecting its interests in the United States, like that of many foreign countries, is to focus on elite-level contacts. And in selecting consultants, the Koreans tend to favor lobbyists over communicators. One exception to this was the effort to generate maximum favorable publicity in the course of promoting the 1988 Summer Olympics in Seoul, for which Korea selected the public relations firm of Burson-Marsteller. Interesting enough, the Koreans made this selection through elite channels as well—on the advice of former National Security Advisor Richard V. Allen, whose consulting company assists Korean industries on matters of international trade.[9]

- South Africa. The apartheid regime in South Africa has long pursued relations campaigns and lobbying efforts in the United States. In 1979, twenty-two agents represented South African interests; five years later, the number had increased to thirty-one, nine of whom represented the government in one way or another. . . . Altogether, in the decade from 1974 through 1984, South African interests paid some $7 million to American lobbyists and consultants. At one point in the 1970s, a scandal arising from South African efforts to buy influence in the United

States, which included a secret loan to finance the purchase of the *Washington Star* (now no longer published), forced the resignation of Prime Minister John Vorster.[10]

Again, these are but a few of the more prolonged and noteworthy efforts. There are two general strategies available to countries seeking to bolster their images and influence in the United States. One of these—the what-you-see-is-what-you-get style of public relations . . . with its fancy books and mass mailings—focuses on raising the visibility of the client, getting more attention from the news media and the public. One of the more unusual promotional efforts of this type was that undertaken by Saudi Arabia at the time of the 1984 Summer Olympics in Los Angeles. The Saudis spent an estimated $2 million producing and airing on network television a series of commercials designed to enhance their national image in the United States. A more common form of promotional effort—familiar to any reader of such newspapers as the *New York Times,* the *Washington Post,* or the *Wall Street Journal*—is the placing of large advertising supplements, typically four to eight pages in length, in the most influential newspapers of the United States and other countries. Such advertising is usually intended to promote industrial development or tourism, but sometimes it is placed simply for the purpose of bragging. One study found that the most active countries placing such advertisements included (in order of magnitude) France, India, the United Kingdom, Mexico, Japan, Greece, Switzerland, Italy, and Spain, with many others trailing behind. Altogether, during the eleven years studied (1970 through 1980), 114 countries purchased such advertising.[11] Extrapolating from the study, we can estimate that the two United States newspapers that were included, the *Times* and the *Wall Street Journal,* carried more than 10,000 advertisements from foreign governments during this period.

The second approach to political public relations available to these countries is a more subtle, low visibility approach much like the one the Bush campaign employed in the period leading up to the 1988 presidential primary season. It takes the form of news management and information control, and is intended less to persuade than to manipulate perceptions. Such a strategy can be very effective—indeed, more effective when applied in foreign affairs than in domestic. This is the case for several reasons.

First, the issues and participants in foreign affairs are remote. Members of the public—and, importantly, journalists—are unlikely to have any direct experience with them. Most, if not all, of what we know about, say, Namibia, we have learned from the media. . . . Unlike our contacts with the domestic scene, . . . when it comes to foreign affairs, we are entirely dependent on the cameras, microphones, and word processors of the world press. We know only what they tell us. We are vulnerable.

Second, the media themselves are limited in both their ability to cover foreign affairs and their inclination to devote staff and resources to that purpose. . . . As a result, only an elite few—the networks, the prestige press, the wire services—make any serious effort to gather information abroad, and even those efforts they do put forward are limited. Reporters whose responsibilities include two, three, or ten entire countries—think about trying to present an accurate picture of the United States, Canada, and Mexico from a one-person bureau based in Mexico City. Stringers who work part time for news organizations and rush to the scene of an event after the fact to provide us with the news. Journalists who don't speak the language, know the history, or understand the culture of the country they are portraying. They know only what is happening on the surface, and sometimes precious little of that.[12] We are vulnerable.

Third, in foreign affairs, even public officials can have a hard time gathering information, so even they may be dependent on the media for some portion of their understanding of events. . . . At times, even central players can be dependent on the media. In describing early attempts by the Reagan administration to measure the level of political violence in El Salvador, for example—a task required in order to provide Congress with a certification of progress toward ending that country's civil strife—Thomas Enders, at the time the State Department official in charge of the assessment, said in an interview on PBS's "MacNeil/Lehrer NewsHour" that principal among the indicators he used to measure violence was the number of violent incidents reported in the press.[13] And more recently, the likelihood is that most people in our government and others, even at the highest level, received at least as much information about the June 1989 massacre in Beijing's Tiananmen Square from media reports as from diplomatic or intelligence sources. They know little more than we know. We are vulnerable.

Putting all of this together, it is clear that foreign governments—and other foreign interests—have both a motive to influence American opinion and policy, and an opportunity to do so. The question is: How effectively do they do it? Have strategic communications efforts on behalf of these governments improved their standing among the people, the press, and the policy makers of the United States? . . .

With respect to the success of systematic efforts to influence portrayals of foreign countries in the United States press, we do have a growing body of evidence. Let us consider that evidence at some length.[14] . . .

What does a successful effort at influence look like? The initial answer is: It depends on the circumstances. We must begin asking ourselves: What does a given country's news image look like at the time it sets the wheels of strategic communication in motion? In particular, it is useful to differentiate between two aspects of news coverage of the client country—visibility and favorability—and to characterize initial images in these terms. Visibility refers to the amount of coverage a country or government (or anyone else) gets in the press. Favorability is a measure of how positive or negative, on average, its portrayal is. Putting these together yields four different settings, or communication environments, in which countries might be motivated to engage in strategic communication efforts, each of which might lead to a very different communication strategy.

The first setting is that of a country that is very much in the news—and consequently prominent in the public mind—but has a generally negative image. . . .The news image of South Africa over the last several years is typical of a high visibility, high negative country. . . . For countries in this situation, it frankly does not make much sense to engage in a promotional blitz that can do little more than call attention to the country and, perhaps, even heap ridicule upon it. . . .

[Such] governments often conclude that they must restrict the access to news makers and events that they afford to journalists, especially foreign journalists. They cut back on the amount and type of information issued by the government itself. They impose censorship. They create visa problems, satellite transmission problems, staffing problems, and a host of other woes for foreign journalists—moves that play directly to the existing disincentives for news organizations to cover foreign news in the first place. It is the home-court advantage with a vengeance. Sometimes—and South Africa is an extreme case in point—governments outlaw news coverage altogether, or so restrict it as to make the journalists' job all but impossible. They arrest and intimidate journalists, or, more conveniently, their sources; they openly follow them, tap their telephones. They beat—and occasionally murder—perceived media troublemakers, or make clear their intention to do so, as the Chinese army did to photographers in the aftermath of the Tiananmen debacle.[15] No more Mister Nice Guy. It isn't pleasant, or pretty, or smooth. But, bit by bit, they squeeze their way out of the news. Bit by bit, they disappear from public view. We don't hear so much about the troubles now, do we? Indeed, a Canadian government study has found that news coverage of South Africa on American networks declined by two-thirds within a year after December 1986, when very stringent press controls were implemented.[16] Things must be getting better. . . . The news was still substantially negative, but there was a lot less of it.

That, in fact, describes the second of our four communication settings, one in which coverage is generally negative, but visibility is relatively low. . . . Countries with low visibility and negative images—indeed, the lower their visibility, the more this is true—have an opportunity to engineer for themselves a much more favorable portrayal in the press. This is the case because—given their near invisibility in the media—neither journalists nor members of the public are thinking much about them. To put it bluntly, they are just not very important. As a result, the guards of these two groups are lowered, and they will be unlikely to resist positive messages—so long as those messages are subtle and do not directly call attention to the fact that a persuasive effort is underway. The objective of the strategic communicator in this situation, then, is to improve the favorability of the country's portrayal *without calling attention to the effort and without raising its visibility in the news.* . . .

The third and fourth settings in which communication efforts may be undertaken are quite different in that, in each instance, the client country has, not a negative image, but a positive one. There is no need to change people's minds or to distract them. Rather, the objective is to draw their conscious attention to the good thoughts they are already thinking, and to find ways of reinforcing and extending them. . . .

It is in situations like these that promotional efforts . . . and advertising supplements like those placed by so many countries in the *Times* and the *Wall Street Journal* can be expected to pay dividends. Where images are positive but visibility low, the objective is to build recognition. Where visibility is already high, the objective is to firm up support. Social psychologist William McGuire has likened this to inoculating patients to protect them from disease.[17] Here, however, the disease is wrongheaded thinking, and the vaccine is a large dose of positive reinforcement. Promote. Promote. Promote.

For all of its evident national–ego-gratifying appeal, however, promotion is not the only—nor necessarily the most effective—form of inoculation against slippage in a favorable image. Another device is that of encouraging those with favorable views of a country to espouse them publicly—to go on the record with their support. Over the years, for example, Israel has been a particularly effective practitioner of this technique, especially in applying it to members of Congress. The idea is that once a person has made a public proclamation of support, the psychological cost of changing his or her mind—in the form of the public embarrassment that inevitably accompanies the admission of error—is simply too high to bear. The result? A friend for life. To assess the effectiveness of this device, compare the treatment of Israel in the American press and public opinion during the period of the *Intifada*— the uprising of resident Palestinians—with the treatment of the governments of South Korea, China, or the Philippines when confronted with, and responding to, similar antiregime activities. Please pass the vaccine.

All of that, at least, is the theory. . . . Does this actually happen? Do countries with high visibility and high negatives that hire American consultants, in effect, succeed in getting out of the news? Do countries with low visibility and high negatives that hire American consultants actually achieve a more positive image as their visibility bottoms out? And so forth. The answer, in a nutshell, is yes. There are some factors that limit the effectiveness of these efforts to manipulate news images, but by and large, they do succeed.

To arrive at that conclusion, we [Manheim and Albritton] analyzed news coverage of a number of countries in the *New York Times* over a period of years. In each instance, we were able to determine from the Department of Justice records that a contract with an American public relations adviser had been signed, and when it took effect. We then measured the amount and favorability of coverage of each client country for several time points during the year immediately before the contract date and the year immediately after. Comparing these two periods—and adjusting for events, trends, and other factors that might have influenced the results—we ascribed any differences we observed in a given country's news image between the precontract and postcontract years to the efforts of the consultants. What we found was a consistent pattern that resembled very closely the situation-specific objectives of strategic communication set forth above. Our conclusion? Systematic efforts at manipulating news images work. . . .

They work when applied to the *New York Times,* which publishes more foreign news than any other American newspaper, is far less dependent on wire service and other outside sources in gathering that news, and is as well equipped—by virtue of the skill of its journalists—as any American news organization, and better than most, to defend itself against such efforts. If these techniques are effective on the *Times,* they must be even more so when directed at the general run of American news media, which are far more vulnerable. . . .

Notes

1. Phil McCombs, "Inside the Power House," *Washington Post,* 28 June 1984, pp. D1, D9; Phil McCombs, "The Connection Makers," *Washington Post,* 29 June 1984, pp. C1, C6; and Stuart Auerback, "Foreigners Hiring Reagan's Ex-Aides," *Washington Post,* 16 February 1986, pp. A1, A14, A15.
2. William Safire, "An Excess of Access," *Roanoke Times & World News* (VA), 19 February 1986, p. A7.
3. Jarol B. Manheim and Robert B. Albritton, "Changing National Images: International Public Relations and Media Agenda Setting," *American Political Science Review* 78 (1984), pp. 641–57; and Richard S. Tedlow and John A. Quelch, "Communications for the Nation State," *Public Relations Journal* 37 (1981), pp. 22–25.
4. Jeanne Saddler, "Public Relations Firms Offer 'News' to TV," *Wall Street Journal,* 2 April 1985, p. 6.
5. Mary Battiata, "What's News? Well, There's a Gray Area," *Washington Post National Weekly Edition,* 15 April 1985, p. 11.
6. Information about the Bhutto visit is drawn from a personal interview with Mark Siegel, July 1989; the official texts of the prime minister's statements; and Donnie

Radcliffe and Martha Sherrill, "Bhutto, Back at the White House," *Washington Post,* 7 June 1989, pp. C1 and C8.

7. For a more complete discussion of the Bhutto visit see Jarol B. Manheim, "Coming to America: Head of State Visits as Public Diplomacy," paper presented at the Annual Meeting of the International Communication Association, Dublin, Ireland, June 1990.

8. Personal discussion with Norman T. London, Academic Relations Officer, and Harry F. Adams, Counsellor, Embassy of Canada, 1986.

9. Jarol B. Manheim, "Political Culture and Political Communication: Implications for U.S.-Korean Relations," paper presented at the Annual Meeting of the American Political Science Association, Washington, D.C., August 1988; Jarol B. Manheim, "Rights of Passage: Elections, Olympics, and the External Communications of the Republic of Korea," paper presented at the World Congress of the International Political Science Association, Washington, D.C., August 1988; and personal interview with Daryl Plunk, vice president, Richard V. Allen company, 1989.

10. Rick Atkinson, "Law Firm's Split Airs S. African Lobbying," *Washington Post,* 12 March 1984; Greg Goldin, "The Toughest Accounts," *Mother Jones,* January 1985, pp. 28–29; and "Pittsburgh Forces Hand of Pretoria Lobbyists," *Africa News,* 19 March 1984, pp. 6–8.

11. Odekhiren Amaize and Ronald J. Faber, "Advertising by National Governments in Leading United States, Indian and British Newspapers," *Gazette* 32 (1983), pp. 87–101.

12. For some examples see John Weisman, "Ignorants Abroad," *TV Guide,* 28 May 1983, pp. 2–8.

13. The interview was broadcast on January 21, 1983.

14. Portions of the discussion that follows are based on Manheim and Albritton, "Changing National Images," *American Political Science Review.*

15. For other examples, see John Weisman, "Intimidation," *TV Guide,* 23 October 1982, pp. 4–10.

16. Cited in "South Africa's Toughest Censor," *Columbia Journalism Review,* July/August 1988, p. 6.

17. "Inducing Resistance to Persuasion: Some Contemporary Approaches," *Advances in Experimental Social Psychology* 1 (1964), pp. 192–202.

Index

Aarts, K., 223
Abbate, Janet, 383–384, 388n42
ABC, 57, 116, 117, 118, 141, 264
ABC News, 319, 320–321
Abortion, 292–293, 349–360
Abramson, Jill, 186, 190n11, 190n12
Abramson, Paul R., 269n20
Abrams v. United States (1919), 394
Abu Ghraib scandal, 249
Achille Lauro case, 298
ACLU. See American Civil Liberties Union
Acquired immunodeficiency syndrome
  (AIDS). *See* Human immunodeficiency virus
  (HIV)/acquired immunodeficiency syndrome
  (AIDS)
Adams, Harry F., 432n8
Aday, Sean, 6, 56–65, 64n8, 64n18
Ader, C., 68
Administrations. *See* Presidents and
  presidencies; individual presidents
Adoni, H., 67
Advanced Research Projects Agency Network
  (ARPANET), 383
Advertising
  agenda-setting and, 92
  attack and negative commercials, 176
  effects of, 22, 169–170, 173–174, 179,
    408–409
  electoral context and, 170–171, 174–176
  political advertising, 167–168, 169–179
  spot commercials, 176
  strategic communications and, 427, 430
Afghanistan, 60, 324, 397, 398, 399, 400
Agenda-setting and agenda-building. *See also*
  Mass media; News and news media
  campaign agenda, 85
  definitions, 81, 85, 86, 88–89
  issues versus events, 85–89
  mass media and, 28, 31, 77, 81, 82–84, 85,
    87–88, 91, 94–95
  media agenda, 81–83, 85, 86, 87–88,
    89–92, 93–94

media credibility and accuracy, 88–89
policy agenda, 81, 82, 83–84, 92–94
public agenda, 81, 82, 83, 85–95
public opinion and, 100
AIDS (acquired immunodeficiency syndrome).
  See Human immunodeficiency virus (HIV)/
  acquired immunodeficiency syndrome (AIDS)
Aiken, L. S., 340
Albany (GA), 272, 275–276
Albrecht, J. E., 339
Albritton, Robert B., 431, 432n14
Alderman, J., 128
Aldrich, John H., 269n20
Alexander, Lamar, 177
Alger, Dean, 180n19
Alien and Sedition Acts (1798; U.S.), 393
Al Jazeera, 59, 399
Allen, Mike, 19, 125n5, 126n9
Allen, Richard V., 426
Almond, Gabriel A., 84, 139
al Qaeda, 115, 116, 118, 119, 120, 121, 124,
  125. *See also* Iraq War
Al-Tawil, Khalid, 388n28
Althaus, Scott L., 59, 64n15
Amaize, Odekhiren, 432n11
Ambition, 208–209, 266–267, 313
American Association for the Advancement
  of Science, 86
American Broadcasting Company. *See* ABC
American Civil Liberties Union (ACLU), 354
American Civil Rights Movement (1960s).
  See Civil rights movement
American Diabetic Association, 341
American Law Institute, 354
AmeriCorps, 41–42
Amin, Mohamed, 91
Amman (Jordan), 318. *See also* Jordan
Anderson, John, 179n7
Andrews, A. B., 338
Ansolabehere, S., 223
Antietam (VA) battlefield, 56–57
Anti-Terrorism Act of 2001, 391